D1426481

Funds of Hedge Funds

Quantitative Finance Series

Aims and Objectives

- Books based on the work of financial market practitioners and academics
- Presenting cutting-edge research to the professional/practitioner market
- Combining intellectual rigour and practical application
- Covering the interaction between mathematical theory and financial practice
- To improve portfolio performance, risk management and trading book performance
- Covering quantitative techniques

Market

Brokers/Traders; Actuaries; Consultants; Asset Managers; Fund Managers; Regulators; Central Bankers; Treasury Officials; Technical Analysts; and Academics for Masters in Finance and MBA market.

Series Titles

Return Distributions in Finance
Derivative Instruments: theory, valuation, analysis
Managing Downside Risk in Financial Markets: theory, practice & implementation
Economics for Financial Markets
Performance Measurement in Finance: firms, funds and managers
Real R&D Options
Forecasting Volatility in the Financial Markets, Second edition
Advanced Trading Rules, Second edition
Advances in Portfolio Construction and Implementation
Computational Finance
Linear Factor Models in Finance
Initial Public Offerings: an international perspective
Funds of Hedge Funds

Series Editor
Dr Stephen Satchell

Dr Satchell is the Reader in Financial Econometrics at Trinity College, Cambridge; Visiting Professor at Birkbeck College, City University Business School and University of Technology, Sydney. He also works in a consultative capacity to many firms, and edits the journal *Derivatives: use, trading and regulations* and the *Journal of Asset Management*.

Funds of Hedge Funds
Performance, Assessment, Diversification, and Statistical Properties

Edited by

Greg N. Gregoriou

AMSTERDAM • BOSTON • HEIDELBERG • LONDON • NEW YORK • OXFORD
PARIS • SAN DIEGO • SAN FRANCISCO • SINGAPORE • SYDNEY • TOKYO

Butterworth-Heinemann is an imprint of Elsevier
30 Corporate Drive, Suite 400, Burlington, MA 01803, USA
Linacre House, Jordan Hill, Oxford OX2 8DP, UK

Library of Congress Cataloging-in-Publication Data

Funds of hedge funds : performance, assessment, diversification, and statistical
properties / edited by Greg N. Gregoriou.
    p. cm.—(Elsevier professional finance series. Quantitative finance series)
  ISBN 0-7506-7984-0 (hard cover : alk. paper) 1. Hedge funds. 2. Risk management.
3. Hedge funds—Evaluation. 4. Investment analysis—Mathematical models.
I. Gregoriou, Greg N., 1956– II. Title. III. Series.

  HG4530.F836   2006
  332.64′5—dc22   2006002230

British Library Cataloguing-in-Publication Data
A catalogue record for this book is available from the British Library.

ISBN 13: 978-0-7506-7984-8
ISBN 10: 0-7506-7984-0

For information on all Butterworth-Heinemann publications
visit our Web site at www.books.elsevier.com

Typeset by Charon Tec Ltd, Chennai, India
www.charontec.com
Printed in the United States of America

06 07 08 09 10   10 9 8 7 6 5 4 3 2 1

Working together to grow
libraries in developing countries

www.elsevier.com | www.bookaid.org | www.sabre.org

ELSEVIER   BOOK AID International   Sabre Foundation

Contents

Part Three   Construction and Statistical Properties of Funds of Hedge Funds   211

Part Four   Monitoring Risk, Overview of Funds of Funds, Due Diligence, and Special Classes of Funds of Funds   325

Preface

Because of the popularity and growth of funds of hedge funds (FOFs) today, these diversified investments have earned a permanent place in investor portfolios. Not only do FOFs provide added diversification and downside protection, but they allow for institutional investors to have access to the best hedge fund managers. Indeed, since many of these managers have closed their funds to new investors, the only way for new investors to gain access to these funds is through an FOF that has money already placed with the manager. Pension funds, endowment funds, and high-net-worth individuals have now increased the proportion of FOFs in their portfolios. This reader contains 25 exclusive new chapters written by leading academic and practitioners of FOFs investing, dealing with quantitative and qualitative analyses in this hot area. They are intended to introduce readers to some of the latest, cutting-edge research and topics encountered by academics and professionals who study, manage, and invest in FOFs. This book can assist FOF managers, money managers, consulting firms, lawyers, accountants, academics, doctoral graduates, as well as any investor wishing to gain an in-depth knowledge of FOFs. It will enable them to obtain a better view of the performance and assessment of FOFs while providing added insight into this world of privately managed money.

Acknowledgments

I would like to thank Karen Maloney, Dennis McGonagle, and Julie Ochs at Elsevier for guidance throughout the publishing process, as well as Mabel Bilodeau at Maine Proofreading Services. I would also like to thank Geoff Crane for his editorial work as well as Melissa Read, project manager, and Rebecca Rainbow. Finally, I want to thank the handful of anonymous referees that helped in the selection of the papers for this book.

About the editor

Greg N. Gregoriou is an associate professor of finance and coordinator of faculty research in the School of Business and Economics at the State University of New York (Plattsburgh). He obtained his PhD (finance) from the University of Quebec at Montreal and is hedge fund editor for the peer-reviewed scientific journal *Derivatives Use, Trading and Regulation*, published by Henry Stewart publications (United Kingdom). He has authored over 50 articles on hedge funds and managed futures in various U.S. and U.K. peer-reviewed publications, including the *Journal of Portfolio Management, Journal of Futures Markets, European Journal of Finance, Journal of Asset Management, European Journal of Operational Research, Annals of Operations Research*, among others. He has three edited books and one authored book with John Wiley & Sons. This is his third edited book with Elsevier.

List of contributors

Rian Akey is vice president and chief operating officer of Cole Partners based in Chicago, Illinois. Mr. Akey is responsible for overseeing the firm's research and operations. He is a principal of the organization. Mr. Akey was hired in 1999 as the firm's director of research. In that capacity, he has guided the firm's analysis and due diligence of investment managers, industry research, and development of proprietary alternative investment curriculum. In 2003 his role was expanded to include business development and operational oversight responsibilities. Mr. Akey is a registered member of the NASD and the NFA and a member of the Managed Funds Association. He received a BA cum laude from the University of Notre Dame.

Carol Alexander is a professor of risk management and director of research at the ISMA Centre located in Reading, U.K. Among many industry links, she is chair of the Academic Advisory Council of the Professional Risk Managers International Association (PRMIA). Prior to serving at the ISMA Centre, she was a director and head of market risk modeling at Nikko Bank, academic director of algorithmics, and, for many years, lecturer in mathematics at Sussex University. She obtained a PhD (in algebraic number theory) from Sussex, an MSc (in mathematical economics and econometrics) from LSE, and a BSc (in mathematics with experimental psychology) from Sussex. Carol is the author of a best-selling textbook, *Market Models* (Wiley, 2001) and editor of 14 books on mathematics and finance. With Elizabeth Sheedy (of MacQuarie University, Sydney) she has recently edited the three-volume *Professional Risk Managers Handbook*. Carol is now well known for her research in two areas of finance: quantitative strategies for fund management and volatility analysis. Her most recent publications include papers in the *Journal of Portfolio Management,* the *Journal of Banking and Finance,* the *Journal of Applied Econometrics,* and the *Journal of Financial Econometrics.* She consults as an expert witness and designs commercial software for hedge funds, operational risk, and high-frequency pricing.

Dr. Paul U. Ali is an associate professor in the Faculty of Law, University of Melbourne, Australia. Paul was previously a finance lawyer in Sydney. Paul has published several books and journal articles on finance and investment law, including, most recently, *Opportunities in Credit Derivatives and Synthetic Securitisation* (London, 2005) and articles in *Derivatives Use, Trading and Regulation,* the *Journal of Alternative Investments,* the *Journal of Banking Regulation,* and the *Journal of International Banking Law and Regulation.* He is currently coediting a book on corporate governance.

Jean-François Bacmann is a member of the quantitative analysis group of RMF Investment Management, based in Pfäffikon, Switzerland. Within the group he heads the research and implementation of tools team, whose key responsibilities are the development of innovative solutions in the context of alternative investments and the implementation of the quantitative in-house software tools. Prior to joining RMF Investment Management in 2002, he spent five years as a research professional in finance at the Entreprise Institute at the University of Neuchâtel, Switzerland. Mr. Bacmann received his engineering degree in computer science and applied mathematics from the ENSIMAG, France, a master's degree in finance from the University of Grenoble, France, and a PhD in finance from the University of Neuchâtel. He has published several articles in professional and academic financial journals.

Zsolt Berenyi holds an MSc in economics from the University of Economic Sciences in Budapest and a PhD in finance from the University of Munich. His main interest lies in the risk and performance evaluation of alternative investments: hedge funds, CTAs, and credit funds. After working for Deutsche Bank as well as KPMG at various locations for numerous years throughout Europe, Zsolt leads his independent consultancy in Budapest, Hungary.

Keith H. Black is an assistant professor in the Stuart Graduate School of Business at the Illinois Institute of Technology in Chicago. He teaches courses in global market economics, equity valuation, investments, mutual funds, hedge funds, and global investment strategy. Mr. Black's interest in hedge funds inspired him to write the book *Managing a Hedge Fund*, published by McGraw-Hill in 2004. He has earned the designations of Chartered Financial Analyst and Chartered Alternative Investment Analyst, as well as an MBA from Carnegie Mellon University. His professional experience includes commodities derivatives trading at First Chicago Capital Markets, stock options research and CBOE market-making for Hull Trading Company, and building stock selection models for mutual funds and hedge funds for Chicago Investment Analytics. He contributes regularly to the *CFA Digest*, and *Journal of Global Financial Markets* and comments on markets for television and radio financial news shows.

Jean Brunel is the managing principal of Brunel Associates, a firm offering wealth management consulting services to ultra-affluent individuals with head office in Bonita Springs, Florida. He spent the bulk of his career in the investment management group of J.P. Morgan, where he worked in the United States and abroad from 1976 until his retirement in the spring of 1999. In 1990, he assumed the position of chief investment officer of J.P. Morgan's global private bank, where he focused on the issues of special concern to individual investors, such as tax efficiency and downside risk protection. Prior to that, he had served in New York, Tokyo, Hong Kong, Singapore, and Melbourne in various investment and managerial capacities. Upon retiring from J.P. Morgan, he started consulting for wealthy individuals and the institutions that serve them. Thus, he consulted for and then served as chief investment officer of Private Asset Management, at U.S. Bancorp, a position he held until June 2001, when he left to found Brunel Associates. Jean is the editor of the *Journal of Wealth Management*, published by Institutional Investor Journals, is a trustee of the Research Foundation of the CFA Institute, and a director of Culp, Inc., a NYSE-listed textile company. Further, he authored *Integrated Wealth Management: The New Direction for Portfolio Managers* (a book published in 2002 by Institutional Investors and Euromoney Books) and a number of peer-reviewed articles. A graduate of École des Hautes Études Commerciales in France, Jean holds an MBA from the Kellogg Graduate School of Management at Northwestern University and is a chartered financial analyst.

Daniel Capocci, a PhD candidate at the University of Liège in Belgium, has published extensively on hedge funds in various professional and academic journals, such as the *Journal of Empirical Finance*, the *European Journal of Finance*, as well as several hedge funds and CTA readers. He has also published a book on the subject entitled *Introduction aux Hedge Funds* and is Fund of Hedge Funds manager at Kredietbank Luxembourg in Luxembourg.

Ryan J. Davies is an assistant professor and the holder of the Lyle Howland Term Chair in Finance at Babson College, Babson Park, Massachusetts. Prior to joining Babson College, Dr. Davies taught at the ISMA Centre, University of Reading, in England, from 2001 to 2004. He has also taught on the International Capital Market Association's International Fixed Income and Derivatives (IFID) program. His current research interests include European securities market regulation, Canada–U.S. interlisted stocks, stock price manipulation by mutual fund managers, hedge fund portfolio allocation, and portfolio return cross-autocorrelation patterns. His research has been published in the *Journal of Financial Markets*, the *Journal of Futures Markets*, and *Economics Letters*. Dr. Davies received a PhD in economics from Queen's University (Kingston).

Anca Dimitriu is a Visiting Research Fellow at the ISMA Centre in Reading U.K. She holds a PhD in finance from the University of Reading and an MSc in finance from the Doctoral School of Finance and Banking, Bucharest. Her research interests include portfolio optimization, indexing and long-short equity strategies, hedge fund performance, and funds of hedge funds portfolio management. She has published many papers in top international academic journals, and she is an active speaker at conferences in many countries. Ms Dimitriu has been teaching in finance MSc programs for several years and has also been involved in hedge fund consultancy projects.

Eric Dubé is a financial economist with National Bank Financial's economics and strategy group, headed by Clément Gignac. His responsibilities include economic and financial analysis and forecasting of North American and international developments. In this regard he acts as manager of all econometric modeling within the economist team. Among his fields of interest are the application of chaos models to options theory and to the study of psychological factors influencing financial markets, with a particular focus on hedge fund behavior and its modeling.

John E. Dunn III, of Geneva, Switzerland, works with a wide variety of single-manager and multimanager hedge funds worldwide. Previously Dunn was MD of UBS Securities Switzerland, and he currently teaches investment management and hedge funds at Thunderbird, the Garvin School of International Management, Swiss Finance Academy, and the executive training business of Terrapinn Hedge Fund World Conference series. His research focuses on early-stage hedge fund manager selection and tactical asset allocation for hedge fund portfolios. He is an advisory board member of Infiniti Capital, a well-known fund of hedge funds and an alternative asset product provider.

Alain Elkaim is a PhD candidate at HEC — Montreal who coordinates the activities of the HEC — Montreal trading room and gives several courses on financial markets. His area of interest is portfolio management, specializing in the area of stocks and market indices. For many years he was a consultant to institutional portfolio managers.

Laurent Favre holds a BA in economics, an MBA in finance, and a BA in sports (all from the University of Lausanne). He was high school professor of economics, mathematics, and sports during two years in Switzerland. He has published several papers in the *Journal of Alternative Investments*. He is associate researcher at EDHEC School and worked for four years for Investment Solutions, UBS Wealth Management (Zurich, Switzerland), as head of tactical asset allocation. In 2004 he left UBS and founded AlternativeSoft AG (Switzerland). His company develops academic models and programs them in a software dedicated to fund of hedge funds construction, hedge fund rating and hedge fund index returns forecasting. He works in the London office. The company specializes in hedge funds screening, portfolio optimization with hedge funds, and hedge fund index returns forecasting.

Mary Fjelstad has been a senior research analyst with Russell's research and development department since 1996. She conducts academic and empirical research on investment issues and analytical methods and systems, leading to recommendations for consideration by Russell and Russell clients. Ms Fjelstad's areas of expertise are fixed-income systems and analytics and asset allocation. She also participates in the design and testing of proprietary analytical systems developed by research and development and educates and trains other Russell associates in their use. She first joined Russell in 1987 as a senior research analyst in fixed-income manager research, responsible for evaluating quantitative investment strategies and risk control systems. She was promoted to assistant vice president later that year. In 1988, Ms Fjelstad took on a consulting role with the research department at Russell, returning to a permanent position in 1996. In this capacity, she provided research on foreign securities and markets, optimization techniques, asset allocation, option pricing, term structure modeling, and the pricing of nontrading fixed-income securities. She began her career as an applications specialist at Gifford Fong Associates and in 1985 became a bond consultant at BARRA. In both positions, she was responsible for client service and marketing of fixed-income analytical software systems, which included bond valuation, risk analysis, performance attribution, and optimization. She obtained a BA in history from the University of Southern California in 1973, an MA in history from Northwestern University in 1979, and an MBA, with an emphasis in finance, from Pacific Lutheran University in 1983.

Clément Gignac graduated from Laval University with a master's degree in economics. Mr. Gignac began his career with the Quebec Department of Finance. In the summer of 1988 he joined the National Bank of Canada as senior economic advisor, in which capacity he often had occasion to work with the bank's brokerage subsidiary, Lévesque Beaubien Geoffrion. In June 1992 he became chief economist and strategist of Lévesque Beaubien Geoffrion, now National Bank Financial in Montreal, Canada. In April 2002, while retaining his responsibilities at National Bank Financial, he assumed new responsibilities with his appointment as vice president and chief economist of National Bank. In this capacity he acts as spokesperson on economic matters for the National Bank group as a whole. Mr. Gignac is a sought-after speaker and media commentator. The group of economists he leads was ranked by the Brendan Wood survey of funds managers as one of the top two in Canada in every year from 1999 through 2003 — the only team to receive such a consistently high rating.

Clemens H. Glaffig is principal partner of Panathea Capital Partners GmbH & Co KG, an asset management and analytics company, which he founded in January 2000 with offices based in Freiburg, Germany. He is also a member of the board of Arsago-Panathea AG, a hedge fund manager jointly held with the Arsago Group. Prior to this, he was head of structured finance Europe and head of capital markets Central and Northern Europe at CIBC World Markets, London. Before joining CIBC, Mr. Glaffig was executive director at AIG Financial Products/ Banque AIG in London/Paris, responsible for capital markets for the German-speaking region. Prior to his association with AIG, he worked at Commerzbank, Frankfurt, setting up and heading the OTC options operations for equity and fixed-income products. Before joining the finance industry, Mr. Glaffig held academic positions as visiting professor in mathematics at the University of California and research fellow at the University of Bochum, Germany, after obtaining a PhD in mathematical physics from the California Institute of Technology, Pasadena, in 1988.

Niclas Hagelin is a senior analyst at Nordea, the largest banking group in the Nordic and Baltic region located in Stockholm, Sweden. He received his PhD from Stockholm University School of Business, where he also has served as an associate professor. His previous experience also includes senior positions at the Swedish National Debt Office and Danske Securities. Mr. Hagelin has published numerous articles in scholarly journals on various topics, including risk management and portfolio construction.

Georges Hübner (PhD, INSEAD) is the Deloitte Professor of Financial Management at HEC Management School — University of Liège in Belgium and associate professor of finance at Maastricht University. He is senior researcher at the Luxembourg School of Finance, University of Luxembourg, an affiliate professor at EDHEC (Lille/Nice), and an invited professor at the Solvay Business School (Brussels). He has taught at the executive and postgraduate levels in several countries in Europe, North America, Africa, and Asia. Mr. Hübner has published numerous research articles about credit risk, hedge funds, and derivatives in leading scientific journals and books. He was the recipient of the prestigious 2002 Iddo Sarnat Award for the best paper published in the *Journal of Banking and Finance* in 2001. He is also the inventor of the generalized Treynor ratio, a simple performance measure for managed portfolios.

Elaine Hutson holds a PhD in finance from the University of Technology, Sydney, and is now a lecturer at University College Dublin in Ireland. She has published widely in a variety of finance journals, including the *Journal of Empirical Finance*, the *Journal of International Financial Markets, Money and Institutions*, the *International Review of Financial Analysis*, and the *Journal of the Asia Pacific Economy*. Her research interests are broad and include mergers and acquisitions, hedge funds, small business finance, and the performance, regulation, and history of managed funds.

Pierre Jeanneret is a member of the quantitative analysis group of RMF Investment Management, based in Pfäffikon, Switzerland. He is involved in research projects in areas such as factor decomposition, synthetic replication of hedge fund strategies, and performance measurement. Prior to joining RMF Investment Management in 2004, he spent seven years as a research professional in finance at the Entreprise Institute of the University of Neuchâtel, Switzerland. Mr. Jeanneret received his bachelor's degree in business administration from the University of Neuchâtel, a master's degree in finance and economics from the University of Geneva, and a PhD in finance from the University of Neuchâtel. He has published several articles in professional and academic financial journals.

Stephan Joehri holds a masters degree in computer science with specialization in computational science from the Swiss Federal Institute of Technology (ETH), Zurich, Switzerland. During his studies he worked at the Quantitative Investment Solutions Team of UBS Wealth Management, Zurich, developing autonomous stock-picking strategies and alternative portfolio optimization techniques. Currently, Mr. Joehri is writing his PhD thesis at the Swiss Banking Institute of the University of Zurich in the area of quantitative methods for alternative investments. He is also working at AlternativeSoft, Inc. in Zurich and is responsible for the fund of funds construction software HFOptimizer.

Meredith A. Jones is the director of market research at Strategic Financial Solutions, LLC, a software company founded in 1996 with location in Nashville, Tennessee, whose mission is to provide solutions relating to the technological needs of the financial industry. She is responsible for researching, speaking, and writing about alternative and traditional investments as well as developing and implementing marketing initiatives and strategic partnerships for SFS. She has written articles for a number of financial publications, including the *Journal of the Alternative Investment Management Association, Alternative Investment Quarterly*, the *Investment Management Consultants Association's Monitor*, and the *Managed Funds Association Reporter*. Her research has appeared in the *Wall Street Journal, Bloomberg Wealth Manager, Hedge Fund Alert, Infovest 21*, and other publications. Prior to joining SFS, Ms Jones was vice president and director of research for Van Hedge Fund Advisors International, Inc., a global hedge fund consultant with $500 million under management. There she led a staff of 10 research analysts in manager selection, evaluation, and ongoing monitoring. Ms Jones conducted quantitative and qualitative due diligence, onsite visits, and portfolio construction as well as a number of other research functions.

Harry M. Kat is professor of risk management and director of the Alternative Investment Research Centre at the Sir John Cass Business School at City University in London. Before returning to academia, Professor Kat was head of equity derivatives Europe at the Bank of America in London, head of derivatives structuring and marketing at First Chicago in Tokyo, and head of derivatives research at MeesPierson in Amsterdam. He holds MBA and PhD degrees in economics and econometrics from the Tinbergen Graduate School of Business at the University of Amsterdam and is a member of the editorial board of the *Journal of Derivatives* and the *Journal of Alternative Investments*. He has (co-)authored numerous articles in well-known international finance journals, such as the *Journal of Financial and Quantitative Analysis*, the *Journal of Financial Engineering*, the *Journal of Derivatives*, the *Journal of Portfolio Management*, and the *Journal of Alternative Investments*. His latest book, *Structured Equity Derivatives*, was published in July 2001 by John Wiley & Sons.

Aleks Kins is the president and co-chief investment officer of AlphaMetrix Investment Advisors, LLC located in Chicago. He has been actively managing institutional portfolios and investing with commodity-trading advisors and hedge funds for over a decade. Mr. Kins has conducted due diligence on, and allocated to, countless alternative investment-trading advisors. He is frequently cited in industry publications as an authority on alternative investments and is regularly invited to speak on alternative investments at global industry conferences. Previously, Mr. Kins was the president and co-founder of Access Asset Management, which later became known as RQSI/Access, and was responsible for the creation and development of the Emerging CTA Index (ECI). The ECI allocated several hundred million dollars to well over a hundred CTAs and quickly became known as the industry's primary source of seed capital for commodity-trading advisors. Prior to his involvement with RQSI, Mr. Kins was the senior investment manager for Carr Global Advisors (CGA), a subsidiary of Crédit Agricole Indosuez. At CGA, Mr. Kins was in charge of their managed futures allocations, was the head of their research group, and oversaw the development and implementation of their risk-monitoring systems. Prior to working at Crédit Agricole, Mr. Kins worked in the research department at the Chicago Mercantile Exchange. He received a BA in economics from Brown University and is a registered Associated Person with AlphaMetrix.

Maher Kooli is an assistant professor of finance at the School of Business and Management, University of Quebec in Montreal (UQAM). He holds a PhD in finance from Laval University (Quebec) and was a postdoctoral researcher in finance at the Center of Interuniversity Research and Analysis on Organizations. Maher also worked as a senior research advisor for la Caisse de Depot et Placement de Quebec (CDP Capital). His current research interests include alternative investments, initial public offerings, and mergers and acquisitions.

Nicolas Laporte is an investment analyst at Kedge Capital in London, U.K. He was previously an analyst at Citigroup Private Banking and at Morgan Stanley Capital International. He holds a master's degree in banking and finance from H.E.C. Lausanne and has published several articles related to hedge funds and risk management.

David K. C. Lee is managing director and chief investment officer of Ferrell Asset Management in Singapore. He holds a PhD in econometrics from the London School of Economics. He is also a guest lecturer specializing in alternative investments with the Centre for Financial Engineering and Faculty of Business Administration, National University and Faculty of Business, Singapore Management University.

Markus Leippold is an assistant professor of finance at the Swiss Banking Institute of the University of Zurich. Prior to moving back to academia he was working for Sungard, Trading and Risk Management Systems, and the Zurich Cantonal Bank. Mr. Leippold's main research interests are term structure modeling, asset pricing, and risk management. During his PhD studies, he was a research fellow at the Stern School of Business in New York. He obtained his PhD in financial economics from the University of St. Gallen, Switzerland, in 1999. He has published in several journals, such as the *Journal of Financial and Quantitative Analysis*, the *Journal of Economic Dynamics and Control*, the *Journal of Banking and Finance*, the *Review of Derivative Research*, the *Journal of Risk*, and the *Review of Finance*. In 2003 he and his colleagues were awarded by the German Finance Association for their paper on equilibrium impacts of value-at-risk regulation and with an achievement award from RISK for their paper on operational risk. In 2004 their research paper on credit contagion won the STOXX Gold Award at the annual conference of the European Financial Management Association. During 2005, he was a visiting researcher at the Federal Reserve Bank in New York.

François-Serge Lhabitant is responsible for investment research at Kedge Capital. He is a professor of finance at the University of Lausanne and at EDHEC Business School. His specialist skills are in the areas of alternative investment (hedge funds) and emerging markets. Dr. Lhabitant is the author of five books on these two subjects and has published numerous research and scientific popularization articles. He is also a member of the Scientific Council of the Autorité des Marches Financiers, the French regulatory body.

Sa Lu is a PhD student at the ISMA Center, University of Reading, Reading, U.K.

Margaret Lynch was a secondary school mathematics teacher for more than 20 years before completing a masters degree in financial and industrial mathematics. She is currently studying for a PhD at Trinity College Dublin; the topic of her dissertation is skewness in international financial markets.

Andreas Oehler is a full professor of finance at Bamberg University in Germany, where he has held a chair in management, business administration, and finance since 1994. He received his MSc (diploma) and his doctoral degree in economics, business administration, and finance from Mannheim University in 1985 and 1989, respectively and his habilitation (postdoctoral degree) in economics and finance from Hagen University in 1994. During his academic career he worked as a senior and managing consultant at Price Waterhouse and other companies. His major fields of research are empirical, experimental, and behavioral finance, risk management, and banking and financial institutions.

Helder P. Palaro is a PhD student in finance at the Sir John Cass Business School at City University in London, U.K. under the supervision of Professor Harry M. Kat.

Nicolas Papagergiou is an assistant professor in the Department of Finance at the Hautes Études Commerciales (HEC), University of Montreal. His main research interests and publications deal with fixed-income securities, specifically the pricing of structured products and the analysis of fixed-income arbitrage strategies used by hedge fund managers. Dr. Papageorgiou has taught graduate-level courses in Canada and the U.K. and has presented at numerous academic and practitioner conferences in North America, Europe, and North Africa.

Kok Fai Phoon is a senior lecturer and director of postgraduate studies, Department of Accounting and Finance, at Monash University in Australia. He holds a PhD in finance from Northwestern University. He was executive director of Ferrell Asset Management and had also worked with Yamaichi Research Institute and at a multibillion global investment company based in Singapore.

Florent Pochon is a senior analyst for IXIS Corporate and Investment Bank in Paris, where he is involved in quantitative analysis of hedge funds returns and asset allocation problems involving alternative investments. He graduated from ESSEC Business School and holds a master's degree in economics from EHESS

(École des Hautes Études en Sciences Sociales). He previously worked as a quantitative economist for the French Ministry of Finance in charge of studies related to financial markets (fixed-income, equity, and Forex markets).

Bengt Pramborg is a senior analyst at the Swedish National Debt Office and also holds a position as assistant professor at Stockholm University School of Business in Sweden. His area of interest involves issues concerning risk management, capital budgeting methods, and dynamic portfolio allocations. Mr. Pramborg focuses on empirical research and has published his findings in scientific journals such as the *Emerging Markets Review*, and the *Journal of International Financial Management and Accounting*. He has a PhD in finance and an MSc in mathematical statistics from Stockholm University as well as an MBA from Yonsei University, Seoul.

François-Éric Racicot is an associate professor of finance in the Department of Administrative Sciences of the University of Quebec, Outaouais (UQO) located in Hull, Quebec. He holds an MSc in economics with a major in financial econometrics from the University of Montreal and received a PhD in Finance from the University of Quebec, Montreal (UQAM). He is also a permanent member of the Laboratory for Research in Statistics and Probability (LRSP) of Carleton University and the University of Ottawa. His research interest focuses on developing econometric methods applied to financial problems. He has also written several books in quantitative finance and financial econometrics. Dr. Racicot is a consultant in quantitative finance for various banks and investment firms.

Leola Ross joined Russell's investment management and research group in 1998 located in Tacoma, Washington. She is responsible for conducting capital markets research and advising the Australasia-Japan and hedge fund teams on a variety of investment issues. Prior to joining these two teams, Leola conducted research on various regional equity markets. She regularly publishes her research results and is a featured Russell presenter at conferences. In addition, as a member of the Russell publications committee, Leola assists other authors. Leola has authored many research commentaries and reports, practice notes, and other Russell publications for several Russell offices. Additionally, she has published articles on Russell's behalf in the *Journal of Performance Measurement*, the *Journal of Asset Management, Institutional Investor's Investment Guides, Professional Pensions,* and *Investments and Pensions Europe.* She has published on topics ranging from performance fees and measurement to country and sector risk in Europe and Pacific ex Japan; from hedge fund diversification and indexes to the effects of asset growth on fund performance. Before joining Russell, Ms Ross was an assistant professor at Seattle University and East Carolina University, where from 1994 to 1998 she taught and performed research in economics. During her academic years, she presented at academic conferences and published articles in several academic journals, including the

International Journal of the Economics of Business and the *Review of Industrial Organization*. From 1987 to 1990, Ms Ross worked for Austmet, Inc., a commodities trading company. As part of Russell's community support, she tutored at McIlveigh Middle School in Tacoma, Washington, from 1998 to 2003, and she participates in a program to encourage technical education for middle school girls called Expanding Your Horizons. In her spare time, she sings in two choirs, travels, and hikes. She obtained a BA in economics from Drew University in 1987, an MA in economics from Southern Methodist University in 1993, and a PhD in economics from Southern Methodist University in 1994. She is also a CFA Charterholder, CFA Institute, 2001.

Fabrice Rouah is an Institut de Finance Mathématique de Montréal (IFM2) Scholar and a PhD candidate in finance at McGill University, Montreal. Mr. Rouah is a former faculty lecturer and consulting statistician in the Department of Mathematics and Statistics at McGill University. He specializes in the statistical and stochastic modeling of hedge funds, managed futures, and CTAs and is a regular contributor in peer-reviewed academic publications on alternative investments. He obtained his BSc in applied mathematics from Concordia University and his MSc in applied statistics from McGill University.

Stefan Scholz is the head of the quantitative analysis group of RMF Investment Management, based in Pfäffikon, Switzerland. The team focuses on economic and econometric research, asset allocation, portfolio construction and also is involved in investment selection, portfolio management, and risk management. Mr. Scholz is a member of the investment strategy committee and management committee of RMF Investment Management. Prior to joining RMF in 2001 as a quantitative analyst, he spent two years as a research assistant at the Institute of Operations Research at the University of St. Gallen, focusing on the numerical pricing of exotic financial derivatives. From 1994 to 1996 Mr. Scholz worked for Robert Bosch on projects in controlling and strategic planning in Germany and France. Mr. Scholz received his master's degrees in industrial engineering from the University of Karlsruhe, Germany, and from Stanford University and a PhD in finance from the University of St. Gallen, Switzerland.

Oliver A. Schwindler is a doctoral candidate within the Department of Finance at Bamberg University in Germany. He is currently working on his dissertation, "Value Added of Funds of Hedge Funds." His research comprises the risk and performance evaluation of alternative investments, hedge funds, and leveraged and credit funds. He received his Dipl.-Kfm. from the University of Regensburg and is a member of the Hedge Fund Association (HFA) and the International Association of Financial Engineers (IAFE).

Fredrik Stenberg is a PhD student in mathematics at Mälardalen University located in Västerås, Sweden. He has previously worked as a financial consultant in banking and as a software developer for different financial companies, working mostly with VaR-models and asset allocation problems. His research is focused on stochastic regime processes with applications to finance and insurance. He has published his work in scientific journals such as *Communications in Statistics Theory and Methods* and the *Journal of Physics A*.

Max Stevenson holds a PhD in mathematical economics from the University of New South Wales and is currently a senior lecturer in finance at the University of Sydney located in Australia. Mr. Stevenson has a diverse range of research interests, including labor market economics, derivatives and electricity pricing, and market microstructure. He has published in such journals as *Managerial and Decision Economics*, *Studies in Nonlinear Dynamics and Econometrics*, the *Journal of Economic Behavior and Organization*, and *Regional Studies*.

Jérôme Teïletche is a senior analyst for IXIS Corporate Investment Bank in Paris, where he is involved in quantitative analysis of hedge funds returns and asset allocation problems involving alternative investments. He received his PhD in financial economics from the Faculty of Economics, University of Bordeaux, where he is currently a visiting professor. He previously worked for the French Ministry of Finance. He has published research on empirical exchange rate models and portfolio risk analysis with extreme value theory.

Hilary Till is a principal of Premia Risk Consultancy, Inc. located in Chicago, which advises investment firms on derivatives strategies and risk management policy. Ms Till is also the cofounder of Premia Capital Management, LLC. Chicago-based Premia Capital specializes in detecting pockets of predictability in derivatives markets using statistical techniques. The firm's focus is on the natural-resources futures markets. In addition, Ms Till serves as an Advisory Board member of the Tellus Natural Resources Fund and is a member of the Curriculum and Examination Committee of the Chartered Alternative Investment Analyst (CAIA) Association. She is also a member of the Hedge Fund Specialization Exam committee for the Professional Risk Managers' International Association (PRMIA) and is a referee for the *Financial Analysts Journal*. Previously, Ms Till was chief of derivatives strategies at Boston-based Putnam Investments. Her group was responsible for the management of all derivatives investments in domestic and international fixed-income, tax-exempt fixed-income, foreign exchange, and global asset allocation. In 1997, for example, the total notional value of derivatives structured and executed by her group amounted to $93.2 billion. Prior to her association with Putnam Investments, Ms Till was a quantitative analyst at Harvard Management Company (HMC) in Boston, the investment management company for Harvard University's endowment. She has a BA in statistics with general honors from the University of Chicago and an MSc in statistics from the London School of Economics. She studied at LSE under a private fellowship administered by the Fulbright Commission. Ms Till's articles on commodities, risk management, and hedge funds have been published in the *Journal of Alternative Investments*, the *AIMA (Alternative Investment Management Association)*

Journal, Derivatives Quarterly, Quantitative Finance, Risk Magazine, the *Journal of Wealth Management*, and the *Singapore Economic Review*.

Kathryn Wilkens earned a PhD at the University of Massachusetts at Amherst in 1998. She is an associate director of research at the University of Massachusetts' Center for International Securities and Derivatives Markets (CISDM). She was a 2002–2004 Teaching Technology Fellow at Worcester Polytechnic Institute and is now the director of curriculum for the Chartered Alternative Investment Analyst Association based in Boston, Massachusetts. She has published several articles in the *Journal of Alternative Investments, Managerial Finance*, the *Journal of Financial Education*, and other journals and has coauthored several book chapters, including "CTA Performance Evaluation with Data Envelopment Analysis," "Classifying Hedge Funds Using Data Envelopment Analysis," and "Maximum Drawdown Distributions with Volatility Persistence."

Choon Yuan Wong currently works in the risk control department at Deutsche Bank AG in Singapore. He holds an MSc in financial engineering from the National University of Singapore and has a master's degree in applied finance from the Singapore Management University and a bachelor's degree in chemical engineering from the National University. He has passed all three levels of the CFA program.

Part One
Performance

1 Rank alpha funds of hedge funds

Carol Alexander and Anca Dimitriu

Abstract

We examine the performance of portfolios of hedge funds when fund selection is based on the rank of a funds' alpha rather than on the estimated value of the alpha. Different factor models provide very different estimates of a hedge fund's alpha, so when portfolio optimization uses estimated alpha values there is a high degree of model risk. On the other hand, even for the simplest factor models we find that ranking funds according to their alpha estimates is an efficient selection process. In an extensive out-of-sample historical analysis, funds of funds that are selected in this way and then allocated using constrained minimum-variance optimization are shown to outperform an equally weighted index of all funds, minimum-variance portfolios of randomly selected funds, and portfolios that are optimized using estimated alpha values. Of the four factor models considered here the best out-of-sample performance is obtained using the rank alphas from the principal components factor model.

1.1   Introduction

During the bear stock market of the last few years, institutional investors as well as high-net-worth individual investors have found a new source of returns in alternative investment strategies. A rough comparison illustrates the difference in performance between traditional and alternative investments: Over the period January 2000 to December 2003, the MSCI World Index lost on average 5.9% per year, while the CSFB-Tremont hedge fund index gained on average 6.8% per year, with much lower volatility. Despite some high-profile losses, investors are committing more assets to the alternative investment industry. According to TASS Research, 2003 was a record-breaking year for the alternative investment industry, the net flow into hedge funds being estimated at 60 billion USD. According to a special report by *The Economist* (March 2006), the hedge fund industry has now exceeded 1 trillion USD under management.

Portfolio optimization within a large universe of hedge funds has become a key area for academic research. This chapter develops a portfolio construction model that is specifically designed for investors in hedge funds, incorporating specific controls for data reliability issues and operational limitations. In terms of data, the fact that hedge funds report to commercial database providers on a voluntary basis creates a number of sampling issues. First, even if one combines the largest commercial databases available,[1] there is no indication of the size of the population of hedge funds and the degree to which the reporting funds are representative of this population. Beyond the small-sample bias, the databases comprise performance estimates rather than liquid market prices, and this generates both autocorrelation and a significant amount of noise in the data. Regarding the operational limitations, short sales are not possible; there are minimum investment limits, long lockup periods and advance notice, regular subscriptions/redemption as rare as once a year, and sales and early redemption fees.

Given the special features of hedge funds, portfolio management tools that were developed for traditional investments, being heavily reliant on the existence of liquid markets and efficient prices, need refining. High-quality data is an essential ingredient for any portfolio optimization model, but this is unlikely to be achieved for hedge funds in the near future. We use one of the three largest databases, with both dead and alive funds to diminish the impact of survivorship bias. We account for the instant-history bias through the use of dummy variables in factor models and report performance on a relative basis, benchmarked against portfolios that are affected by the same biases. Operational limitations are addressed by imposing constraints on the optimization and by including an estimate of annual turnover as a key diagnostic of the portfolio's performance.

Traditional portfolio optimization models require forecasts of the portfolio expected returns and/or an estimate of their covariance matrix. Often expected returns are estimated via a factor model, but given the highly dynamic and heterogeneous styles used in alternative investments, the nonuniqueness of the factor model representation is one of the most important problems to address when optimizing portfolios of hedge funds. Amenc and Martellini (2003a) show that different factor models can generate very different estimates of a hedge fund's alpha and consequently argue that the hedge fund industry should promote its diversification potential rather than its very uncertain alpha benefits.

In this chapter we show that, though estimates of a fund's alpha do indeed vary widely according to the factor model used, there is still valuable information contained in the alpha estimate. First we use four different factor models to estimate the alpha of individual hedge funds: Our base case model is the simplest representation of the fund returns as a function of the two most important underlying asset classes, equities and bonds; the broad fundamental factor model employs several indices to capture the performance of the main asset classes and other factors representing specific types of nonlinear strategies, such as market timing, volatility trading, and equilibrium trading; the multifactor model is based on hedge fund indices; and finally, the statistical factor model is based on factors extracted from fund returns through principal component analysis. Then, for each of these four factor models, our hedge fund selection

---

[1] Indjic (2003) finds 4,589 funds reporting to at least one of the three most important database providers, TASS, HFR, and CISDM.

process is determined only by the rank of the fund's alpha and not by the actual value of its estimated alpha. We find significant agreement on the ranking of funds based on their estimated alphas from different factor models. Thus there is considerable scope for optimal hedge fund investment models where funds are selected according to their rank alpha.

In contrast to other research on incorporating the uncertainty about parameter estimates into optimal portfolios, we require neither assumptions about investors' preferences nor subjective views on expected returns and/or managerial skill.[2] We deal with the uncertainty in alpha estimates by using classic minimum-variance optimization, which is based solely on the funds' covariance matrix. Having considered several methods of linking allocations to the ordinal rank of the fund's alpha estimate, we find that the best out-of-sample performance is obtained by a simple in–out ranking of the funds, according to whether the alpha estimate is above a predetermined threshold, followed by minimum-variance optimization.

Given the reporting practices of hedge funds, there is a high degree of randomness in the sample covariance matrix, which is likely to distort our minimum-variance optimization. Some authors advocate cleaning the covariance matrix by imposing some factor structure before using it in the portfolio optimization. However, portfolio weight constraints are essential for hedge funds investing, and, because the sampling errors already appear to be significantly reduced through the weights' constraining, we have found no further benefit from imposing a factor structure on the correlation matrix.

1.2 Hedge fund data and biases

Hedge fund data is subject to several measurement biases caused by the data-collection process and by the nature of the industry: survivorship bias, when a database does not include the performance of funds that ceased operating during the sample period; selection or self-reporting bias, when the hedge funds in the database are not representative of the population of hedge funds; instant-history bias, when the funds entering the database are allowed to backfill their results; and multiperiod sampling bias, when the analysis is restricted to funds having a minimum amount of history available. Fung and Hsieh (2000) provide an extensive analysis of biases in the TASS hedge fund database. They estimate a survivorship bias of approximately 3% per annum. Regarding the instant-history bias, they found an average incubation (backfilled) period of one year, with an associated bias of 1.4% per annum, while the multiperiod sampling bias was negligible.

Our fund data comes from the Hedge Fund Research (HFR) dead and alive funds databases, from which we select the period January 1990 to May 2003.

---

[2] See, for example, Black and Litterman (1992), Pastor (2000), Baks, Metrick, and Wachter (2001).

We restrict our analysis to U.S. domiciled funds reporting net of all fees in USD, having funds under management above 10 million USD and not using leverage. Additionally, to minimize the sample bias of alpha estimates, we require that each fund have at least five years of reporting history. After imposing these selection criteria, our database comprises 282 funds.[3]

To determine the impact of the instant-history bias in our database, for each fund we examine the difference between the monthly average of the excess return (over SP500) in the first year and the monthly average of the excess return in the first five years. The difference is equivalent to 3.97%, and the standard deviation of the difference is 1.01% per annum, so there is a clear first-year bias in the reported fund performance. In order to eliminate the instant-history bias on alpha, we use dummy variables for the first year of reporting in all factor models. The estimated multiperiod bias is negligible, at -0.33% per annum. Selection and survivorship biases are addressed by including dead funds that have sufficiently long reporting history. But this is still insufficient to ensure that the portfolio performance is identical to the experience of an investor in these funds, because there is no information on the performance of individual funds after reporting has ceased. Statistics show that some funds stopped reporting to HFR because of extraordinary good performance but some also because of negative performance. If some funds were liquidated, their investors probably recovered only part of the net asset value last reported. To deal with all these potential biases, we present all performance results on a relative basis, benchmarked against the equally weighted index of all funds in our sample. The relative performance can be interpreted as bias-free since both the portfolios and their benchmark are affected by the same biases.

1.3 Factor models for hedge funds

Assuming that investors are only willing to reward managers for superior performance that cannot be easily replicated, a fund's return may be decomposed into the part explained by a factor model, which can be replicated by standard asset baskets and common trading strategies, and the factor model alpha and residual behavior, which are attributed to the fund manager's skill. Various fundamental and statistical multifactor models for hedge funds have been analyzed by Agarwal and Naik (2000), Edwards and Caglayan (2001), Fung and Hsieh (1997), Lhabitant (2001), Liang (2001), and Schneeweis and Spurgin (1998), among others. The wide range of models developed and the fact that no single

---

[3] The strategy representation in our database is the following: convertible arbitrage (10 funds), distressed securities (17 funds), emerging markets (12 funds), equity hedge (53 funds), equity market neutral (26 funds), equity nonhedge (19 funds), event-driven (20 funds), fixed income (17 funds), funds of funds (52 funds), market timing (15 funds), managed futures (18 funds), merger arbitrage (4 funds), sectors (19 funds).

model dominates the others is explained by the large diversity of the strategies employed by hedge funds and their highly dynamic nature.

The general factor model representation is

$$r_{it} = \alpha_i + \sum_{k=1}^{K} \beta_{ik} F_{kt} + \varepsilon_{it}$$

where r_{it} is the net of fees excess return on fund i during month t; α_i is the risk-adjusted performance, for example, the alpha of fund i over the estimation sample; F_{kt} is the excess return on the kth risk factor over the month t;[4] β_{ik} is the loading of the fund i on the kth factor, for example, the sensitivity of the fund i to the factor k over the estimation sample; and ε_{it} is the error term.

Since there is no consensus on the best model, we estimate four factor models: the base case model, a broad fundamental model, the HFR model, and the PCA factor model.

The *base case model* has only two factors, U.S. equities (Wilshire 5000 index) and bonds (Lehman Government/Credit Intermediate index). Asness, Krail, and Liew (2001) show that hedge funds may have more market exposure than one expects, due to stale prices or illiquidity of the securities they trade. So, following Dimson's (1979) arguments, we also include the lagged equity index excess returns as a factor.

The *broad fundamental model* includes the following as factors: equity indices (Wilshire 5000, SP500 growth and value, SP mid-cap and small-cap to capture differences in equity investment styles, MSCI world index excluding U.S. to account for the investment opportunities outside the U.S., and MSCI emerging markets index to capture the emerging markets investment opportunities as a separate asset class); bond indices (Lehman Government, Lehman Credit Bond, Lehman High Yield and Lehman Mortgage-Backed Securities); the FED trade weighted foreign exchange rate index as a proxy for foreign exchange risk; the GS Commodity index to capture commodity-related investment risk factors. It is common practice to go beyond static asset class mixes and analyze the performance of funds using simple trading strategies. As suggested by Treynor and Mazuy (1966), squared market returns can proxy for market timing abilities. Additionally, we include two factors capturing specific nonlinear trading strategies: the prices' dispersion as a leading indicator of equilibrium trading strategies (Alexander and Dimitriu, 2005) and the change in the equity implied volatility index (VIX) to account for volatility trades (Schneeweis and Spurgin, 1998).

The *HFR model* has the HFR indices as factors. Since they represent portfolios with nonlinear exposures to traditional asset classes, this model should

---

[4] With a few exceptions, when the risk factors are not investable indices or portfolios (for example, for volatility and price dispersion risk factors).

explain the returns on individual funds better than the preceding two-factor models (Lhabitant, 2001). We do not reconstruct the indices from the funds in our subsample; the HFR indices are a better choice as factors since they are more representative of the entire population of funds and are also investable.

The *PCA factor model* uses as factors investable portfolios replicating the first four orthogonal components from principal component analysis (PCA) of the system of all funds' returns. The intuition behind statistical factor analysis is that if a group of funds use similar strategies in the same markets, their returns should be correlated. Through PCA, the major common styles can be extracted from fund returns. We use four principal component factors, and the portfolios replicating these are denoted PC1 to PC4.[5] The PC1 portfolio is well diversified across all strategies (with particular emphasis on funds of funds and equity funds because most funds are of these types), and, capturing the common trend in fund returns, PC1 has very similar behavior to an equally weighted index of all funds, to which it is also highly correlated. The PC2 portfolio is clearly dominated by managed futures, which stand out as an investment style with returns uncorrelated to the common trend but still representative of a significant part of the hedge fund population. PC3 comprises mainly equity market neutral and funds of funds, while in PC4 there are technology funds and again equity market neutral funds. Fung and Hsieh (1997) show that the first principal component is explained to a large extent by a linear representation of the traditional asset classes, but this is not the case for the other principal components. Indeed, we find that the first principal component has strong linear relationships with our broad fundamental factors ($R^2 = 0.79$) and hedge fund indices ($R^2 = 0.89$), while the other three principal components have no obvious significant linear relationship with fundamental factors (maximum $R^2 = 0.20$) and a rather weak one with the hedge fund indices (maximum $R^2 = 0.35$). This provides clear evidence that the portfolios replicating the higher principal components are in fact capturing dynamic trading strategies and derivatives as well as style switching.[6]

---

[5] Principal component analysis relies on the quality of the correlation matrix, so we must separate true correlation from noise or measurement errors. Especially for hedge fund returns, where the correlation matrix is typically computed on relatively small samples, the measurement risk is large and separating real information from noise becomes essential. To this end, we use random matrix theory to compare the properties of the correlation matrix of all the funds in our sample — the empirical correlation matrix — with the properties of a correlation matrix of an identical number of mutually uncorrelated returns series, following a method proposed by Plerou, Gopikrishnan, Rosenow, Amaral, Guhr, and Stanley (2002). Deviations of the empirical matrix from the properties of the random matrix reveal information about true correlation between hedge fund returns. We find that only the four largest empirical eigenvalues significantly exceed the range of the random ones, and this result is robust to changes in sample periods. This suggests that the true correlation pattern can be captured with just the first four principal components and that the variation in fund returns relating to the higher eigenvalues is uncorrelated noise.

[6] Results available from the authors on request.

1.4   Model estimation

Each of the four models was estimated by least squares regressions over the period January 1990 to May 2003 on each of the 282 fund returns in excess of the 3-month U.S. T-bill rate. For each fund we used the entire data sample available; some funds entered the database after January 1990 or ceased reporting before May 2003. To select the significant factors for each fund, a backward stepwise regression method was applied; starting with the most complete model that passed a multicollinearity filter,[7] one by one the nonsignificant factors were removed until a parsimonious model was obtained. The results of estimating the four factor models in this way are grouped for presentation, combining results for all funds within the same HFR strategy type. The cells in Tables 1.1 to 1.4 report two figures: the average coefficient estimate over all funds in that strategy (above) and the percentage of these funds for which the coefficient was statistically significant at 10% (below). The coefficient standard errors were computed using the Newey–West (1987) heteroscedasticity- and autocorrelation-consistent covariance matrix.

On average, the base case model explains only 27% of the total variance of fund excess returns (Table 1.1). This is mainly due to the diverse dynamic strategies employed in the alternative investment industry, which induce nonlinear exposures to traditional asset classes. Still, 80% of funds are significantly correlated with the Wilshire 5000 excess returns (average beta = 0.3). Illiquidity is also important, since for 38% of funds the lagged Wilshire excess returns are significant determinants. However, bond index returns are significant for only 20% of funds. The average alpha is insignificant for approximately half the funds, being positive and significant for 48% of funds and negative and significant for only three out of 282 funds.

The broad fundamental model (Table 1.2) includes a total of 17 factors, but the average number of significant factors for an individual fund was only 2.5. Nevertheless, the average R^2 across all funds was 36%, a considerable increase from the base case model. The broad fundamental model better explained the returns of funds in the following classes: emerging markets, equity hedge and nonhedge, event-driven, convertible bonds, financial and technology sectors. However, the returns for some fixed-income, macro, and relative value funds were not well modeled by this approach. The most significant factor, determining the excess returns of 38% of the funds, is the small-cap SP index, which influences funds trading on distressed securities, equity hedge and nonhedge, event-driven, funds of funds, and technology. Additionally, the squared returns of the small-cap SP index are significant in 40% of models, indicating use of leverage and market timing abilities. The other equity-style indices are only significant in

---

[7] Potential multicollinearity problems were addressed by identifying any pairs of factors that were highly correlated over the sample and dropping the factor having lower correlation with the returns of the fund.

Table 1.1 Base case model

	All funds	Convertible arbitrage	Distressed securities	Emerging markets	Equity hedge	Equity market neutral	Equity nonhedge	Event-driven	Fixed income	Funds of funds	Market timing	Managed futures	Merger arbitrage	Sectors
Alpha	0.62 / *60%*	0.64 / *100%*	0.44 / *47%*	1.11 / *17%*	0.75 / *62%*	0.38 / *46%*	0.65 / *53%*	0.6 / *65%*	0.32 / *35%*	0.48 / *77%*	0.7 / *73%*	0.93 / *56%*	0.35 / *75%*	0.8 / *53%*
W5000	0.38 / *80%*	0.04 / *50%*	0.22 / *76%*	0.78 / *100%*	0.61 / *83%*	0.21 / *65%*	0.76 / *95%*	0.39 / *95%*	0.23 / *65%*	0.19 / *81%*	0.07 / *80%*	−0.23 / *61%*	0.1 / *50%*	0.6 / *100%*
W5000 (lagged)	0.12 / *38%*	0.05 / *40%*	0.15 / *76%*	0.44 / *50%*	0.17 / *30%*	0 / *15%*	0.28 / *42%*	0.1 / *45%*	0.07 / *35%*	0.06 / *62%*	NA / *0%*	−0.15 / *28%*	0.06 / *75%*	0.35 / *5%*
LEH Bond Index	−0.25 / *20%*	0.13 / *60%*	−0.4 / *12%*	NA / *0%*	−0.68 / *25%*	−0.15 / *19%*	0.45 / *5%*	−0.2 / *5%*	0.09 / *18%*	−0.46 / *29%*	−0.52 / *20%*	1.15 / *17%*	−0.17 / *25%*	0.14 / *16%*
Dummy (1st yr)	0.32 / *24%*	1.42 / *60%*	−0.16 / *12%*	−3.68 / *8%*	−0.18 / *25%*	2.25 / *19%*	−1.39 / *11%*	−0.53 / *40%*	0.79 / *35%*	−0.1 / *29%*	1.61 / *20%*	2.36 / *28%*	NA / *0%*	−2.15 / *11%*
R^2	0.27	0.2	0.16	0.23	0.32	0.19	0.39	0.32	0.3	0.28	0.24	0.13	0.11	0.29

Table 1.2 Broad fundamental model

	All funds	Convertible arbitrage	Distressed securities	Emerging markets	Equity hedge	Equity market neutral	Equity nonhedge	Event-driven	Fixed income	Funds of funds	Market timing	Managed futures	Merger arbitrage	Sectors
Alpha	0.55 / 60%	0.81 / 100%	0.63 / 59%	1.35 / 50%	0.58 / 47%	0.4 / 54%	0.4 / 47%	0.57 / 65%	0.36 / 47%	0.51 / 79%	0.62 / 67%	0.34 / 39%	0.47 / 100%	0.57 / 63%
W5000	0.62 / 18%	0.04 / 10%	0.18 / 6%	1.14 / 50%	0.82 / 21%	NA / 0%	0.84 / 42%	0.64 / 5%	0.26 / 29%	0.28 / 21%	0.36 / 20%	0.69 / 6%	NA / 0%	0.63 / 21%
SP500g	0.23 / 7%	0.12 / 20%	NA / 0%	NA / 0%	0.29 / 2%	0.29 / 31%	NA / 0%	NA / 0%	-0.08 / 6%	0.01 / 2%	0.23 / 33%	NA / 0%	NA / 0%	0.52 / 5%
SP500v	0.22 / 7%	-0.01 / 20%	0.29 / 12%	0.21 / 8%	0.32 / 2%	0.26 / 15%	0.47 / 5%	0.09 / 5%	0.08 / 6%	-0.31 / 4%	NA / 0%	NA / 0%	NA / 0%	0.45 / 26%
MD400	0.4 / 10%	NA / 0%	0.4 / 6%	0.24 / 25%	0.46 / 21%	0.1 / 4%	0.58 / 11%	0.31 / 15%	NA / 0%	0.15 / 6%	0.15 / 7%	NA / 0%	0.04 / 25%	1.01 / 11%
SC600	0.39 / 38%	0.09 / 10%	0.15 / 47%	0.45 / 8%	0.55 / 47%	0.34 / 15%	0.81 / 37%	0.37 / 70%	0.29 / 24%	0.22 / 62%	0.33 / 7%	NA / 0%	0.07 / 75%	0.76 / 37%
MSCIW (EXUS)	0 / 9%	0.09 / 10%	-0.08 / 6%	0.13 / 8%	0.19 / 6%	-0.01 / 8%	0.41 / 16%	NaN / 0%	0.04 / 6%	0.05 / 4%	NaN / 0%	-0.25 / 50%	NaN / 0%	0.16 / 5%
MSCI (EMF)	0.18 / 20%	0.07 / 20%	0.17 / 24%	0.56 / 67%	0.18 / 21%	0.04 / 12%	0.21 / 16%	0.15 / 5%	0.14 / 12%	0.09 / 31%	0.06 / 20%	-0.22 / 6%	NaN / 0%	0.1 / 11%
LEH (GOV)	0.25 / 6%	0.88 / 10%	NaN / 0%	NaN / 0%	0.3 / 4%	0.41 / 12%	0.66 / 5%	NaN / 0%	0.11 / 6%	-0.22 / 4%	-0.69 / 13%	1.12 / 6%	NaN / 0%	0.41 / 16%
LEH (CREDIT)	-0.21 / 6%	0.09 / 20%	-0.23 / 24%	NaN / 0%	-0.33 / 6%	NaN / 0%	NaN / 0%	-0.47 / 10%	0.03 / 6%	-0.22 / 6%	NaN / 0%	NaN / 0%	-0.1 / 25%	NaN / 0%
LEH (HY)	0.09 / 24%	0.2 / 30%	0.27 / 65%	-0.46 / 8%	-0.11 / 23%	-0.06 / 12%	0.1 / 21%	0.26 / 30%	0.17 / 6%	0.08 / 17%	0.12 / 27%	0.4 / 22%	0.03 / 50%	-0.02 / 37%

(continued)

Table 1.2 (*continued*)

	All funds	Convertible arbitrage	Distressed securities	Emerging markets	Equity hedge	Equity market neutral	Equity nonhedge	Event-driven	Fixed income	Funds of funds	Market timing	Managed futures	Merger arbitrage	Sectors
LEH (MB)	-0.2 / 5%	NA / 0%	-0.65 / 6%	NA / 0%	NA / 0%	NA / 0%	NA / 0%	0.19 / 5%	0.27 / 18%	-0.39 / 10%	NA / 0%	0.05 / 11%	NA / 0%	-1.11 / 5%
FX	-0.45 / 11%	0.08 / 10%	NA / 0%	NA / 0%	-0.48 / 8%	-0.18 / 8%	-0.77 / 16%	-0.51 / 5%	-0.23 / 12%	0.02 / 8%	NA / 0%	-0.65 / 67%	NA / 0%	-0.41 / 16%
GSCI	0.02 / 19%	-0.03 / 10%	-0.13 / 12%	0.17 / 42%	-0.01 / 8%	-0.06 / 12%	-0.03 / 26%	0.08 / 15%	-0.01 / 12%	0.05 / 23%	0.08 / 20%	-0.18 / 39%	-0.07 / 25%	0.27 / 26%
W5000 (Lagged)	0.13 / 18%	0.03 / 10%	0.11 / 18%	0.19 / 8%	0.14 / 28%	0.14 / 4%	0.25 / 26%	0.09 / 25%	0.08 / 18%	0.07 / 17%	-0.27 / 7%	0.38 / 6%	0.05 / 50%	0.21 / 21%
SC600²	0 / 39%	-0.01 / 60%	-0.01 / 53%	-0.02 / 33%	0.01 / 36%	0 / 50%	0 / 42%	-0.01 / 25%	0 / 41%	0 / 35%	0.01 / 33%	0.01 / 50%	0 / 25%	0.01 / 26%
LEH (HY)²	0.01 / 28%	-0.04 / 40%	0.02 / 47%	0 / 33%	-0.02 / 26%	0.02 / 19%	0.13 / 37%	0 / 5%	0.01 / 35%	-0.02 / 19%	-0.01 / 40%	0.04 / 33%	-0.01 / 50%	0.01 / 37%
VIX	0 / 27%	0 / 20%	0 / 18%	-0.01 / 25%	0 / 30%	0 / 38%	0 / 11%	0 / 15%	0 / 6%	0 / 27%	0 / 27%	0 / 61%	0 / 25%	0 / 32%
DISP	0.56 / 29%	NA / 0%	0.63 / 18%	-0.95 / 25%	1.97 / 45%	-1.09 / 23%	1.59 / 26%	-0.88 / 20%	0.4 / 12%	0.44 / 33%	-6.18 / 13%	-2.95 / 17%	-1.37 / 25%	1.41 / 58%
Dummy (1st yr)	0.43 / 25%	0.92 / 50%	0.23 / 24%	-1.39 / 17%	0.05 / 28%	1.55 / 23%	-1.33 / 11%	0.48 / 40%	0.75 / 35%	0.15 / 29%	1.41 / 20%	3.52 / 11%	NA / 0%	-0.44 / 16%
R^2	0.36	0.27	0.29	0.36	0.42	0.24	0.49	0.43	0.38	0.39	0.26	0.22	0.23	0.42

6–10% of the funds. Another important factor is the Lehman high-yield index (for convertible arbitrage, distressed securities, event-driven, managed futures, merger arbitrage, and funds of funds, as well as equity hedge and nonhedge funds, the latter two having a negative average beta) and its squared excess returns (highly significant and positive for funds in distressed securities, equity nonhedge, and managed futures and significant but negative for convertible arbitrage, equity hedge, funds of funds, market timing, and technology funds). The MSCI emerging markets index was significant for 20% of the funds; in addition to the funds primarily trading in emerging markets and funds of funds investing in these, distressed securities, equity hedge and nonhedge, event-driven, and technology funds all have significant exposure to emerging markets. The GS commodity index is a significant factor for emerging markets, event-driven, funds of funds, equity hedge and nonhedge, and, as expected, managed futures. Although the broad equity market indices and the FED trade–weighted forex index are generally less significant than other factors, the change in SP500 implied volatility and the Dow Jones price dispersion index are among the most significant factors. Each of these factors has positive coefficients and is significant for almost 30% of funds. The first-year reporting dummy confirmed a significant positive bias for most strategies. Alpha was most significant for emerging markets and financial sector funds and also for convertible arbitrage, relative value, and short-selling, but for these a high alpha could result just from the lower explanatory power of the model.

The results of estimating the HFR factor model are presented in Table 1.3. The model explains an overall average of 46% of the variance in fund excess returns (ranging from 37% for equity market neutral funds to over 60% for equity nonhedge funds, event-driven, funds of funds, and technology funds). Clearly there are systematic factors, beyond the ones included in the fundamental factor model, that are captured by these HFR-style indices. Each fund's excess returns tend to be determined by the relevant index for their self-stated strategy, indicating no large errors in the HFR classification. At an individual fund level, 17% of funds (equity nonhedge and event-driven, mainly) have negative and significant alphas, while only 11% of funds have positive and significant alpha (mostly from emerging markets, fixed income, market timing, and managed futures).

The estimation results for the PCA factor model are presented in Table 1.4. The only strategies with positive and significant alphas are convertible arbitrage and merger arbitrage, but they also have a low average R^2, so the abnormal return could be due to omitted risk factors. The average R^2 across all strategies is 39%, greater than for the fundamental factor model but less than the HFR model. The strategies with the highest R^2 are the equity hedge and nonhedge, funds of funds, and technology funds, as expected since the database is dominated by these types of funds. The PC1 portfolio is a significant factor for 79% of funds, PC2 portfolio for 39% funds, PC3 for 44% funds, and PC4 for 29% of funds. All strategies, except for managed futures, have positive average betas on the PC1 portfolio. Also, most strategies have positive betas on the PC2 portfolio and negative betas on PC3 portfolio.

Table 1.3 Multifactor HFRI model

	All funds	Convertible arbitrage	Distressed securities	Emerging markets	Equity hedge	Equity market neutral	Equity nonhedge	Event-driven	Fixed income	Funds of funds	Market timing	Managed futures	Merger arbitrage	Sectors
Alpha	-0.12 48%	0.18 60%	-0.34 71%	0.34 42%	-0.24 36%	-0.12 38%	-0.58 47%	-0.56 70%	0.02 47%	-0.01 46%	0.02 40%	0.56 50%	-0.07 100%	-0.31 53%
Convertible arbitrage	0.27 25%	0.89 50%	-0.25 6%	1.84 33%	0.3 25%	0.12 12%	-0.32 11%	0.39 25%	0.42 47%	0.11 29%	0.07 33%	-0.27 28%	-0.06 75%	-0.74 11%
Regulation D	-0.03 27%	-0.01 50%	0 29%	-0.42 42%	0.18 25%	-0.08 12%	-0.32 26%	-0.04 15%	-0.06 53%	0.1 27%	0.02 40%	-0.69 11%	0.06 25%	0.05 26%
Relative value	-0.34 28%	NA 0%	-1.48 6%	-1.64 50%	-0.6 23%	-0.24 35%	-0.39 21%	-0.04 35%	0.09 41%	-0.42 27%	0.5 33%	-0.76 33%	-0.86 25%	0.59 37%
Distressed securities	0.39 30%	0.23 30%	1.3 100%	3.39 17%	-0.4 26%	-0.12 15%	0.12 26%	1.01 60%	-0.65 18%	0.17 33%	0.83 7%	-0.61 28%	0.11 25%	-0.95 11%
Emerging market	0.33 22%	-0.03 30%	-0.2 18%	1.44 100%	-0.02 8%	0.19 15%	0.15 21%	0.29 35%	0.04 29%	0.21 17%	-0.1 33%	-0.26 11%	-0.13 25%	-0.1 16%
Equity hedge	0.68 21%	-0.25 20%	-0.12 12%	NA 0%	1.19 40%	0.98 12%	1.1 11%	0.46 10%	NA 0%	0.47 31%	0.39 13%	-0.58 22%	-0.13 25%	1.03 21%
Equity market neutral	0.29 24%	-0.36 20%	-0.43 18%	1.56 8%	0.05 30%	1.08 58%	0.81 21%	0.06 10%	-0.27 18%	0.18 21%	-0.25 27%	NA 0%	NA 0%	-0.06 37%
Equity nonhedge	0.75 16%	-0.2 10%	0 12%	-0.25 8%	1.13 19%	0.51 15%	1.14 68%	0.42 15%	0.37 12%	0.19 4%	0.34 13%	0.71 6%	0.08 25%	0.78 11%
Event-driven	-0.13 23%	NA 0%	-0.65 18%	-1.65 42%	0.34 11%	-0.04 15%	0.18 16%	0.56 50%	-0.02 12%	0.17 27%	-0.69 20%	-1.31 33%	0 75%	0.23 26%
Fixed income (total)	-0.18 34%	0.61 40%	-0.54 47%	NA 0%	0.49 34%	-1.68 19%	-0.15 32%	-0.08 35%	-0.45 53%	-0.63 38%	0.08 33%	-2.44 17%	0.15 50%	0.95 47%
Fixed income (convertible arbitrage)	-0.01 20%	-0.19 20%	0.2 35%	0.86 8%	-0.2 17%	0.59 4%	-0.2 26%	0.13 20%	0.19 35%	0.13 23%	0.08 7%	-0.43 33%	NA 0%	-0.3 11%
Fixed income (high yield)	0.03 26%	NA 0%	0.07 35%	-0.26 42%	-0.13 19%	0.24 15%	0.96 16%	-0.75 30%	0.78 47%	-0.05 23%	-0.27 40%	0.05 28%	0.02 50%	0.09 26%
Fixed income (arbitrage)	-0.09 25%	0.26 10%	-0.22 41%	-0.57 25%	0.13 25%	-0.3 19%	-0.49 26%	-0.41 35%	0.35 35%	0.16 19%	0.41 33%	-1.02 11%	0.53 25%	-0.37 32%

Fixed income (diversified)	0.27 34%	−0.4 30%	0.66 35%	0.76 25%	−0.59 23%	0.37 19%	0.78 16%	0.3 15%	0.46 41%	0.17 48%	−0.8 33%	1.55 83%	−0.19 50%	−0.48 37%
Fixed income (mortgage backed)	−0.09 28%	−0.51 20%	0.02 29%	−0.42 33%	−0.25 34%	0.37 19%	0.14 11%	0.08 20%	0.19 47%	0.19 29%	−0.36 33%	−0.22 28%	−0.2 50%	−0.67 26%
Funds of funds	0.22 30%	0.07 20%	0.04 18%	−1.34 8%	−0.21 23%	−0.55 8%	−0.66 26%	−0.49 20%	0.33 18%	0.63 65%	0.08 13%	1 50%	NA 0%	−0.36 42%
Market timing	0.08 34%	−0.05 40%	−0.14 41%	0.24 17%	0.14 38%	0.05 31%	−0.08 42%	0.12 25%	0.07 29%	0.05 37%	0.41 67%	−0.87 17%	NA 0%	0.46 26%
Macro	0.31 28%	NA 0%	0.12 18%	−0.6 25%	0.19 26%	0.23 27%	0.34 21%	0.32 25%	0 24%	0.12 23%	0.47 33%	1 72%	0.04 25%	0.23 37%
Short selling	0.04 31%	0.22 10%	−0.04 35%	−0.69 8%	−0.03 36%	0.09 15%	0.08 37%	0.03 35%	−0.12 18%	0.11 37%	0.24 47%	0.23 39%	NA 0%	−0.23 32%
Merger arbitrage	0.6 30%	0.25 10%	0.51 18%	2.24 42%	0.89 32%	0.57 23%	1.29 32%	0.24 50%	−0.33 29%	−0.06 31%	0.89 20%	0.52 6%	0.8 100%	0.66 37%
Sector (total)	−0.02 13%	0.1 30%	−0.05 35%	−0.55 25%	0.3 13%	−0.13 8%	−0.03 11%	0.24 15%	−0.21 12%	−0.05 8%	NA 0%	0.76 6%	NA 0%	−0.54 16%
Sector energy	0.05 30%	0 40%	0.06 6%	0.12 8%	0.04 32%	−0.07 35%	0.07 32%	0.02 45%	−0.02 35%	0.01 23%	0.02 13%	0.27 44%	NA 0%	0.11 58%
Sector financial	−0.03 31%	−0.04 10%	−0.14 24%	−0.13 25%	0.02 36%	0.1 15%	−0.16 47%	0.06 35%	NA 0%	−0.03 37%	−0.07 33%	−0.2 50%	−0.06 25%	0.2 32%
Sector HC/Bio	−0.02 24%	0.01 30%	−0.11 12%	−0.04 25%	0.02 13%	−0.1 54%	−0.1 21%	0.01 30%	0.07 12%	0.03 23%	−0.19 13%	−0.32 28%	0.02 50%	0.39 32%
Sector real estate	0.1 20%	−0.01 40%	−0.51 12%	0.44 17%	−0.16 17%	0.41 12%	0.33 32%	0.13 5%	0.11 29%	0.07 21%	0.56 27%	−0.61 6%	−0.11 50%	0.15 32%
Sector technical	0.37 7%	NA 0%	0.17 12%	NA 0%	0.41 9%	−0.05 8%	0.53 5%	NA 0%	−0.03 6%	0.07 2%	0.38 13%	NA 0%	NA 0%	0.67 26%
Sector miscellaneous	0.06 22%	0.01 30%	−0.1 12%	0.81 8%	0.16 23%	−0.11 15%	0 16%	−0.06 30%	NA 0%	−0.03 23%	−0.16 13%	0.32 39%	0.09 50%	0.01 42%
Dummy (1st yr)	0.46 28%	0.9 40%	0.42 35%	NA 0%	0.52 34%	0.81 27%	−1.15 21%	0.3 30%	1.71 12%	−0.02 27%	1.14 27%	1.99 39%	NA 0%	−0.69 32%
R^2	0.58	0.42	0.56	0.58	0.6	0.37	0.62	0.66	0.59	0.67	0.51	0.47	0.54	0.68

Table 1.4 PCA model

	All funds	Convertible arbitrage	Distressed securities	Emerging markets	Equity hedge	Equity market neutral	Equity nonhedge	Event-driven	Fixed income	Funds of funds	Market timing	Managed futures	Merger arbitrage	Sectors
Alpha	-0.21 *50%*	0.56 *80%*	0.36 *47%*	0.34 *33%*	-0.57 *36%*	0.01 *31%*	-1.09 *58%*	-0.15 *50%*	0.3 *24%*	-0.07 *56%*	0.27 *73%*	-0.92 *78%*	0.31 *75%*	-0.65 *58%*
PC1	0.6 *79%*	0.08 *50%*	0.51 *88%*	1.8 *100%*	0.93 *85%*	0.16 *46%*	1.17 *95%*	0.8 *100%*	0.3 *65%*	0.39 *92%*	0.06 *87%*	-0.18 *28%*	0.13 *75%*	1.12 *89%*
PC2	0.19 *39%*	0.03 *20%*	0.06 *18%*	0.27 *33%*	-0.07 *34%*	0.15 *46%*	0.05 *42%*	0.15 *30%*	0.02 *35%*	0.17 *44%*	0.09 *33%*	1.86 *94%*	0 *0%*	0.04 *37%*
PC3	-0.02 *44%*	-0.07 *20%*	-0.34 *47%*	-1.37 *58%*	0.28 *45%*	0.03 *42%*	0.06 *37%*	-0.24 *65%*	-0.19 *35%*	0.06 *50%*	-0.06 *33%*	0.18 *33%*	-0.04 *25%*	0.16 *37%*
PC4	0.16 *29%*	0.02 *10%*	-0.17 *18%*	0.21 *17%*	0.24 *36%*	0.16 *38%*	0.59 *53%*	0.14 *35%*	-0.07 *18%*	0.02 *25%*	0.37 *20%*	0.24 *22%*	0.04 *25%*	0.23 *37%*
Dummy (1st yr)	0.21 *23%*	0.85 *60%*	0.49 *12%*	0.39 *8%*	0.33 *30%*	0.29 *31%*	0.27 *16%*	-0.16 *25%*	0.24 *35%*	0 *21%*	0.51 *13%*	0.51 *11%*	-0.15 *0%*	-0.45 *16%*
R^2	0.39	0.17	0.23	0.33	0.47	0.22	0.49	0.46	0.32	0.46	0.33	0.52	0.12	0.46

1.5   Rank alpha

Substantial differences in alphas estimated from the four factors models have been identified in Tables 1.1 to 1.4. For the average fund,[8] the two-index model estimated an alpha of 0.69% per month (highly significant and is equivalent to 8.5% per annum). The average fund has an alpha of 5.1% in annual terms according to the broad fundamental model but a negative alpha (though not statistically significant) according to the HFR model and significantly negative according to the PCA model. Despite this, we find significant agreement on the sign of alpha from different models and on the rank of a funds' alpha. Of the funds having at least one positive alpha estimate, in 30% of cases there is perfect agreement between all models in terms of alpha's sign. The largest difference in ranks of alpha estimates arose between the base case and the PCA models (rank correlation = 0.19), the most similar rank alphas were from the base case, and the broad fundamental models (rank correlation = 0.68) and the other rank correlations were all between 0.31 and 0.45. Hence the factor models tend to agree on the sign of alpha and on the alpha ranking of funds, despite the fact that the range of alpha estimates produced by them is wide. Interestingly, this feature has also been found in the TASS hedge fund database by Amenc and Martellini (2003a).

In summary, there is a significant disagreement between the factor models on the average fund alpha, ranging from −2.5% to 8.5% per annum, and the dispersion of alpha estimates is even higher at the level of individual funds. This leads us to conclude that funds of hedge funds that rely on the accuracy of alpha estimates cannot be implemented without significant model risk. However, some agreement can be achieved on the sign and the ranking of alpha for individual funds, and there is considerable scope for more flexible models based precisely on ranking alpha.

1.6   Optimizing funds of hedge funds

Optimizers are well known to be error enhancers (Michaud, 1989), so the quality of the data is essential. Since this is not likely to be achieved with hedge funds in the near future, one can only aim for a better solution than naive diversification. Therefore we begin by testing the benefits of naive diversification through simulation, randomly drawing without replacement 5, 10, and up to 80 funds in multiples of 5 from our database and independently forming equally weighted portfolios having no style consideration. For each size of portfolio we repeat

---

[8] The alphas on individual funds are not independent, so single-sample mean t-tests are not appropriate to assess the significance of an average alpha over all the funds in a particular strategy type. Following Amenc and Martellini (2003a) we estimated the factor models on an "average fund" returns series for each strategy type. We then used the least squares standard error of the intercept to determine the statistical significance of the average alpha.

the experiment 1,000 times, and we estimate the first four moments of the fund of funds portfolio returns distributions for each portfolio size. Our results indicate that diversification across all strategies works well, with most of the diversification benefits obtained at around 30 funds in the portfolio. Practitioner standards also appear to favor portfolios of at least 20–30 funds, so in the following our portfolios will include a number of funds in this range.

Assuming investors have quadratic preferences, the classical portfolio theory of Markowitz (1952) requires knowledge of the first two moments of the returns distribution. Estimating expected returns has been shown to be a difficult task even for traditional asset classes (Merton, 1980; Jorion, 1985), and this can be a main reason why mean-variance efficient portfolios perform poorly out of sample (Frost and Savarino, 1986, 1988; Jorion, 1986; Michaud, 1989; Best and Grauer, 1991). Accurate estimates of expected returns are even more difficult to obtain for alternative investments, as shown in the previous section. On the mean-variance efficient frontier, the only portfolio that does not require estimates of expected returns is the minimum-variance portfolio, so in the hedge funds world this is a natural choice.

1.7 Cleaning the covariance matrix

When no restrictions are imposed, the minimum-variance portfolio weights are given by

$$\mathbf{W}_{MV} = \frac{\Sigma^{-1} \underline{1}}{\underline{1}' \Sigma^{-1} \underline{1}}$$

where Σ is the covariance matrix of the fund returns and $\underline{1}$ is a vector of ones. If restrictions are imposed on weights, the solution can be obtained numerically. Since the covariance matrix of fund returns is the only input required in the model, the results will strongly depend on its accuracy. Given that the number of funds in our sample is much larger than the number of data points, we are concerned with the estimation risk in the sample covariance matrix. Indeed, a large part of the information content of the empirical correlation matrix is driven by randomness. We found that the true correlation structure is captured by the first four eigenvalues, while the rest can be ascribed to noise and measurement errors. Since the presence of such noise is likely to perturb the minimum-variance optimization, its reduction is essential. Several other solutions have been offered, including imposing a factor structure (Sharpe, 1963; Chan, Karceski, and Lakonishok, 1999), the use of an optimal shrinkage toward the mean or the single-factor model (Jorion, 1985, 1986; Ledoit and Wolf, 2003), and the introduction of portfolio constraints (Jagannathan and Ma, 2003). Following Plerou, Gopikrishnan, Rosenow, Amaral, Guhr, and Stanley (2002) for traditional assets and Amenc and Martellini (2002, 2003b) for alternative investments, we reconstruct the empirical correlation matrix using only the eigenvalues that deviate from those of a random correlation matrix. We therefore construct the "cleaned" correlation matrix as

$$C = W\Lambda_c W'$$

where Λ_c is the diagonal matrix of the ordered eigenvalues of the correlation matrix of fund returns with all but the first four eigenvalues replaced by zeros, and W is the matrix of eigenvectors. The diagonal elements of C are set equal to 1, and then the "cleaned" covariance matrix is $V = DCD$, where D is the diagonal matrix of standard deviations of each fund returns.

In order to test the efficiency of the noise-cleaning process, we compared, out of sample, the variances of minimum-variance portfolios constructed from (a) the empirical covariance matrix and (b) the cleaned covariance matrix. We constructed 1,000 portfolios, each with 25 randomly selected funds, and optimized them based on both the cleaned and the sample covariance matrices to achieve minimum variance. For estimating the covariance matrices we used a rolling sample of 60 months. The first portfolios were constructed in January 1998 and rebalanced every six months until January 2003. Between two rebalancing moments, the portfolios are left unmanaged and their out-of-sample performance monitored in order to determine the out-of-sample variance. Table 1.5 summarizes these results: When no constraints are imposed on the portfolio weights, the out-of-sample variance of the portfolio constructed on the cleaned covariance matrix is smaller than that based on the sample covariance matrix, indicating the effectiveness of the noise-cleaning process. However, no short sales are allowed in a hedge funds portfolio, and upper bounds are also normally imposed to reduce concentration risk. We therefore introduce a nonnegativity constraint and an upper bound on individual fund weights at 20%, following standard practice in this respect. When we repeated the previous analysis with the constraints in place, the out-of-sample results were in favor of the sample covariance matrix. Interestingly, this feature has also been observed by Jagannathan and Ma (2003). Hence in the following we use the ordinary sample covariance matrix instead of the "cleaned" one for constrained optimization purposes.

Table 1.5 Out-of-sample performance of randomly selected portfolios

	Unbounded		Bounded	
	Sample matrix	Cleaned matrix	Sample matrix	Cleaned matrix
Annual volatility	2.32	2.3	1.97	2.54
Annual returns	7.49	7.2	7.92	7.69
Skewness	0.03	−0.26	−0.15	−0.4
Excess kurtosis	5.47	5.73	4.14	5.28
Information ratio	3.22	3.12	4.01	3.02

1.8   Performance analysis of rank alpha portfolios

The simulation results can give only a rough idea of the average performance expected from minimum-variance portfolios of hedge funds. Next we enhance the minimum-variance portfolios by introducing a fund selection criterion based on the funds' alpha from each of the four factor models presented in the previous section. For a given factor model, we first select all the funds having positive alphas that are significant at 10%. We also examine a more restrictive selection criterion, which requires that all models rank the fund with positive alpha and that in at least three models the fund's alpha is significant at the 10% significance level. In each case, the portfolio weights are allocated so that the fund of funds has minimum variance.

In order to test the out-of-sample performance of these models we use the period January 1990 to December 1997 to calibrate the factor models and select the first set of funds. We keep the nonnegativity and 20% upper bound constraints in place. The first minimum-variance portfolios are set up in January 1998 and left unmanaged for the next six months. The portfolios are then rebalanced every six months, reselecting funds based on the sign and significance of the alphas estimated over the entire data sample available at the portfolio construction moment and the covariance matrices estimated over the previous 60 months. For reference, we compare these results with an equally weighted (EW) portfolio of all funds in our database.

The portfolios of hedge funds that employ the alpha selection criterion have a significantly improved out-of-sample performance.[9] The portfolio statistics are reported in the columns labeled RAMV (rank alpha minimum variance) in Table 1.6. All portfolios have average annual returns in the range of 8% to 9.5%, with an annual volatility of only 1.3% to 1.7%. Their evolution is very constant, with no more than three months (out of 66) having negative returns in any of the models. The lowest volatility is displayed by the PCA portfolio, and this also has the highest average annual information ratio (6.91). The highest returns are produced by the HFR factor model portfolio, but, given the higher volatility, the information ratio of this portfolio was the lowest (5.56). The null hypothesis of normally distributed out-of-sample returns cannot be rejected for any of these portfolios. We have also examined the out-of-sample performance of portfolios excluding funds of funds, because some institutional investors would prefer to invest solely in hedge funds in order to avoid paying two layers of fees.

---

[9] We have also investigated the out-of-sample performance of portfolios based on the same alpha selection criterion but with allocations determined by the ordinal rank of the alpha. That is, the higher the alpha estimate, the greater the weight in the portfolio. Several ad hoc rank alpha allocation methods were considered. Such portfolios again outperformed the equally weighted portfolios, with information ratios typically between 2 and 4, depending on the factor model and the allocation rule. Also, given the stability in alpha ranks over time, turnover costs were often quite low. But in general their performance was inferior to that of portfolios where a simple in–out rank was used for fund selection and allocations were based on minimum variance. More detailed results are available from the authors on request.

Table 1.6 Out-of-sample performance of rank alpha minimum-variance (RAMV) portfolios, maximum information ratio (MIR) portfolios, and the equally weighted (EW) portfolio of all funds

	Base case		Broad fundamental		HFR		PCA		Overall	
	RAMV	MIR	RAMV	MIR	RAMV	MIR	RAMV	MIR	RAMV	EW
Annual returns	8.28	9.24	8.15	8.55	9.44	10.39	8.94	8.98	9.06	10.44
Annual volatility	1.35	1.86	1.34	1.81	1.7	1.97	1.29	1.44	1.51	6.89
Skewness	0.3	0.71	0.06	0.01	0.1	0.57	0.22	0.5	0.49	-0.07
Excess kurtosis	-0.08	0.57	-0.03	1.92	0.24	0.46	-0.34	0.1	0.35	1.91
Information ratio	6.15	4.97	6.06	4.73	5.56	5.28	6.91	6.22	5.99	1.51
Turnover	6.3	8.99	7.13	9.77	7.66	7.05	4.94	7.59	7.02	4.92

The information ratios of these portfolios were 5.11 for the base case model, 5.26 for the fundamental model, 5.58 for the HFR index model, and 5.69 for the PCA model. The skewness and excess kurtosis stay in the same range as for the portfolios including funds of funds. By contrast, the equally weighted portfolio has comparable returns to the rank alpha portfolios but much higher volatility (resulting in an information ratio of only 1.5 if funds of funds are included and even lower than this if funds of funds are excluded), and its returns display significant excess kurtosis.

For comparison, we also implement a maximum information ratio (MIR) optimization based on the alpha estimates from all four models and the sample covariance matrix, the fund selection being as before. The results are presented in the columns labeled MIR in Table 1.6. Interestingly, the lack of accuracy of individual alpha estimates results in lower information ratios out of sample for these portfolios, compared with minimum-variance portfolios, even though the objective of the optimization was to achieve the maximum in-sample information ratio. Additionally, the MIR portfolios are less stable, so turnover costs are usually higher. Therefore, rather than optimizing on alpha estimates, which we know have a high degree of model risk, we are better off just selecting funds based on alpha estimates and then optimizing solely on the covariance matrix.

Given the significant trading limitations for hedge funds portfolios, we investigate the structural stability of these portfolios. The portfolio turnover is computed as the absolute difference in fund weights from one rebalancing period to the next. With 10 rebalancing points in our out-of-sample test, the maximum turnover is 20 (10 × 200%). The estimated turnover ranges from 4.9 (equivalent to 24% restructuring per annum) for the PCA portfolio and the EW portfolio to 7.6 (equivalent to 38% restructuring) for the HFR portfolio. We note that even the base case portfolio produces good results, and the more conservative overall approach, based on ranking alpha over all four models, generates average results. In summary, compared with the randomly selected funds portfolio results and the EW portfolio of all funds in the database, the factor models have provided valuable information for hedge fund selection.

1.9 Conclusion

Despite the modeling complexity caused by data biases, noisy correlation, inaccurate alphas, and institutional limitations to trading, there is no doubt that alternative investments continue to present attractive opportunities. Their popularity among institutional investors is increasing, and the industry requires more academic studies on optimization of funds of hedge funds. This chapter represents one such study. Aiming to develop a fund selection and optimal allocation process for funds of hedge funds, we have analyzed the out-of-sample performance of portfolio construction models that target alpha through fund selection based on ranking alpha from factor models. To deal with data biases, our database contains both dead and alive funds, we controlled for the instant-history bias, and, to neutralize the effect of any selection, survivorship and multiperiod biases on our results, we reported performance on a relative basis, benchmarked against portfolios affected by the same biases.

Since most traditional portfolio construction models require an estimate of expected returns, we have used a number of factor models to estimate the funds' alphas. Despite significant disagreement on individual alpha estimates, the factor models largely agreed on the ranking of funds' alphas. Thus, though the uncertainty in alpha estimates impairs the efficiency of mean-variance optimal portfolios, we have found that the best model for portfolio optimization is based solely on the covariance matrix. The sample covariance matrix had a high element of randomness, but we found no benefit from imposing a factor structure on the correlation matrix, for the sampling errors are already significantly reduced through the constraining weights, which is operationally necessary for funds of hedge funds.

When funds are selected by the rank of their alphas from any factor model and the portfolios are optimized to have minimum variance, the performance is superior to that of an equally weighted portfolio of all funds and to that of randomly selected minimum-variance optimal portfolios. Of the four factor models considered, all out-of-sample performance measures favor the fund of hedge funds selected using alphas from the PCA factor model. Between January 1998 and May 2003 this had the highest average annual information ratio (6.91) and the lowest turnover (24% per annum), and its returns were also close to normally distributed. Also, for each of the four factor models considered here, the rank alpha minimum-variance optimization produced better results than maximum information ratio optimization. We attribute this to the high degree of model risk arising from the factor model dependency of alpha estimates. To conclude, we have shown that, with some refinements, the traditional tools of portfolio management can still be applied to portfolios of hedge funds to achieve excellent results.

Acknowledgments

The authors would like to thank Michiel Timmerman, Lionel Martellini, and Drago Indjic for very helpful comments on the full version of this chapter, "The Art of Investing in Hedge Funds: Fund Selection and Optimal Allocations," available from www.ismacentre.rdg.ac.uk/dp. Also the financial support from the Foundation of Managed Derivatives Research is gratefully acknowledged. All errors remain our responsibility.

References

Agarwal, V. and Naik, N. (2000). On taking the Alternative Route: Risks, Rewards and Performance Persistence of Hedge Funds. *Journal of Alternative Investments*, 2(4):6–23.

Alexander, C. and Dimitriu, A. (2005). Indexing, Cointegration and Equity Market Regimes. *International Journal of Finance and Economics*, 10(3):1–19.

Amenc, N. and Martellini, L. (2002). Portfolio Optimization and Hedge-Fund-Style Allocation Decisions. *Journal of Alternative Investments*, 5(2):7–20.

Amenc, N. and Martellini, L. (2003a). The Alpha and Omega of Hedge Fund Performance Measurement. Discussion Paper, EDHEC Business School, www.edhec-risk.com.

Amenc, N. and Martellini, L. (2003b). Optimal Mixing of Hedge Funds with Traditional Investment Vehicles. Discussion Paper, EDHEC Business School, www.edhec-risk.com.

Asness, C., Krail, R., and Liew, J. (2001). Do Hedge Funds Hedge? *Journal of Portfolio Management*, 28(1):6–19.

Baks, K., Metrick, A., and Wachter, J. (2001). Should Investors Avoid All Actively Managed Mutual Funds? A Study in Bayesian Performance Evaluation. *Journal of Finance*, 56(1):45–85.

Best, M. and Grauer, R. (1991). On the Sensitivity of Mean-Variance-Efficient Portfolios to Changes in Asset Means: Some Analytical and Computational Results. *Review of Financial Studies*, 4(2):315–342.

Black, F. and Litterman, R. (1992). Global Portfolio Optimization. *Financial Analysts Journal*, 48(5):28–43.

Chan, L. K. C., Karceski, J., and Lakonishok, J. (1999). On Portfolio Optimization: Forecasting Covariances and Choosing the Risk Model. *Review of Financial Studies*, 12(5):937–974.

Dimson, E. (1979). Risk Measurement When Shares Are Subject to Infrequent Trading. *Journal of Financial Economics*, 72(3):197–226.

Edwards, F. R. and Caglayan, M. O. (2001). Hedge Fund Performance and Manager Skill. *Journal of Futures Markets*, 21(11):1003–1028.

Frost, P. and Savarino, J. (1986). An Empirical Bayes Approach to Efficient Portfolio Selection. *Journal of Financial and Quantitative Analysis*, 21(3): 293–305.

Frost, P. and Savarino, J. (1988). For Better Performance: Constrain Portfolio Weights. *Journal of Portfolio Management*, 15(1):29–34.

Fung, W. and Hsieh, D. (1997). Empirical Characteristics of Hedge Fund Strategies. *Review of Financial Studies*, 10(2):425–461.

Fung, W. and Hsieh, D. (2000). Performance Characteristics of Hedge Funds and Commodity Funds: Natural vs. Spurious Biases. *Journal of Financial and Quantitative Analysis*, 35(3):291–307.

Growing pains. *The Economist* (March 2, 2006), pp. 77–79, http://www.economist.com/business/displaystory.cfm?story_id=5572597.

Indjic, D. (2003). Hedge Fund Strategy Classification: AIMA Survey and Analysis of Commercial Classifications. *AIMA Research Day* (October), Paris, www.aima.org.

Jagannathan, R. and Ma, T. (2003). Risk Reduction in Large Portfolios: Why Imposing the Wrong Constraints Helps. *Journal of Finance*, 58(4):1651–1683.

Jorion, P. (1985). International Portfolio Diversification with Estimation Risk. *Journal of Business*, 58(3):259–278.

Jorion, P. (1986). Bayes–Stein Estimation for Portfolio Analysis. *Journal of Financial and Quantitative Analysis*, 21(3):279–292.

Lhabitant, F. (2001). Hedge Funds Investing: A Quantitative Look Inside the Black Box. *Journal of Financial Transformation*, 1(1):82–90.

Ledoit, O. and Wolf, M. (2003). Improved Estimation of the Covariance Matrix of Stock Returns with an Application to Portfolio Selection. *Journal of Empirical Finance*, 10(5):603–621.

Liang, B. (2001). Hedge Fund Performance: 1990–1999. *Financial Analysts Journal*, 57(1):11–18.

Markowitz, H. (1952). Portfolio Selection. *Journal of Finance*, 7(1):77–91.

Merton, R. (1980). On Estimating the Expected Return on the Market: An Exploratory Investigation. *Journal of Financial Economics*, 8(4):323–361.

Michaud, R. (1989). The Markowitz Optimization Enigma: Is "Optimized" Optimal? *Financial Analysts Journal*, 45(1):31–42.

Newey, W. and West, K. (1987). A Simple, Positive Semidefinite, Heteroskedasticity and Autocorrelation Consistent Covariance Matrix. *Econometrica*, 55(3):703–708.

Pastor, L. (2000). Portfolio Selection and Asset Pricing Models. *Journal of Finance*, 55(1):179–223.

Plerou, V., Gopikrishnan, P., Rosenow, B., Amaral, N., Guhr, T., and Stanley E. (2002). Random Matrix Approach to Cross-Correlations in Financial Data. *Physical Review E*, 65(6):1–18.

Schneeweis, T. and Spurgin, R. (1998). Multifactor Analysis of Hedge Fund, Managed Futures, and Mutual Fund Return and Risk Characteristics. *Journal of Alternative Investments*, 1(2):1–24.

Sharpe, W. (1963). A Simplified Model for Portfolio Analysis. *Management Science*, 9(2):277–293.

Treynor, J. and Mazuy, K. (1966). Can Mutual Funds Outguess the Market? *Harvard Business Review*, 44(4):131–136.

2 Funds of hedge funds: bias and persistence in returns

Daniel Capocci and Georges Hübner

Abstract

Persistence in hedge fund returns has been studied for many years. Recently, several authors suggested that funds of hedge funds should be separated from individual hedge funds in empirical studies. In the current chapter, we focus on the persistence in funds of hedge funds returns using a large database including 907 funds of hedge funds (with 254 dissolved). The methodology is adapted from Capocci and Hübner (2005). The measures of persistence include three performance measures (total return, Sharpe ratio, and alpha) and three risk measures (volatility, skewness, and kurtosis). Measures that incorporate volatility show very strong abilities to help investors creating alpha and consistently and significantly outperform classical indices. Some tests of robustness over various market cycles as well as on using various dates for classifying funds confirm the strength of the results.

2.1 Introduction

Since 1997, hedge funds as an industry have been studied by several authors (Fung and Hsieh 1997; Liang 1999). The persistence of their returns has attracted the interest of many (Agarwal and Naik, 2000; Capocci, Corhay, and Hübner, 2005). Various studies lead to different results depending on the period covered, the data considered, and the methodology used, but none of them dissociate individual hedge funds from funds of hedge funds. Our study aims at filling this gap in the literature.

In one of the first persistence studies in this area, Brown, Goetzmann, and Ibbotson (1999) conclude that there is hardly any evidence of the existence of differential manager skills, but persistence is rather due to style effects. Concerning funds of funds, whose returns are mostly attributable to the individual fund selection abilities of the fund managers, we would therefore not expect to observe any persistence based on traditional approaches. Therefore, we choose to apply a methodology adapted from Capocci and Hübner (2005) and Capocci, Corhay, and Hübner (2005), with the identification of a bullish and a bearish market period during which persistence is measured independently.

Furthermore, because we expect funds of funds to exhibit low persistence abilities when their past performance is measured with total returns, we test a series of alternative classification schemes. The measures of persistence used include three performance measures (total return, Sharpe ratio, and alpha) and three risk measures (volatility, skewness, and kurtosis).

This chapter is organized as follows. Section 2.2 presents the database used. In section 2.3 we present the methodology used to measure the funds of funds' required return. Section 2.4 provides the descriptive statistics of the sample, while section 2.5 analyzes the biases of the funds of funds sample. Section 2.6 runs the persistence analysis. Section 2.7 concludes the chapter.

2.2 Database

Three main databases have been extensively used for empirical research on hedge funds: the Managed Account Reports, Inc./Center for International Securities Derivatives Markets, Hedge Fund Research, Inc., and TASS Management. In recent studies, the Barclay database has gained some additional attention because it appears to be complementary to the classical ones (Coën, Desfleurs, Hübner, and Racicot, 2005). In each database, the data provider collects various information on the funds included. For a majority of funds, they record other useful information, such as company name, start and ending dates, strategy followed, assets under management, management and incentive fees, manager's name, and manager's address. There is no consensus on the definition of the strategy followed, but there are similarities. MAR/CISDM defines nine strategies, with a total of 16 substrategies. HFR defines 16 different strategies in two categories, 11 nondirectional and five directional strategies, plus the funds of funds and the sector categories. TASS defines 15 strategies. Finally, Barclay define 20 individual strategies.

We use funds of hedge funds data from MAR/CISDM combined with Barclay's hedge fund data from 1994 to 2002. The MAR database features 647 funds of funds, including 436 funds that were still alive at the end of 2002 and 211 funds that had been dissolved. The Barclay database includes 469 funds of funds, including 384 funds of funds that were still in existence at the end of 2002 and 85 dissolved funds of funds. The treatment of funds in the databases is summarized in Table 2.1.

In each database, we removed funds that appear twice in the same database[1] and funds with quarterly returns. When there were differences in the start and/or end dates between the two databases, we chose the database presenting more data. We obtained 319 funds of funds from the Barclay database and a total of 903 funds of funds. These funds include 653 (72%) surviving funds of hedge funds and 254 (28%) dissolved funds of funds.

In the past, MAR/CISDM has been used in several studies (Fung and Hsieh, 1997; Schneeweis and Spurgin, 1998; Capocci, Corhay, and Hübner, 2005).

---

[1] This happened in three cases: when the same fund (same name, company, and returns) appeared twice in the database; when the same fund (same name and returns) appeared twice in the database with two different company names; and when the same fund (same company and returns) appeared twice in the database with two different fund names.

Table 2.1 Number of funds of hedge funds

	MAR/CISDM	Barclay	Total (gross)	Double counts	Total (net)
Total	647	469	1,116	(209)	907
Alive	436	384	820	(167)	653
Dissolved	211	85	296	(42)	254

The Barclay database has been mainly used in studies focusing on CTAs. To date, the Barclay hedge fund database had not yet been used extensively in empirical studies. The database gives monthly net-of-fee individual returns and other information on individual funds and groups them in indices.

2.3 Methodology

This chapter focuses on the analysis of hedge fund return persistence in performance. The starting point of our study of hedge funds performance is the original Sharpe–Lintner CAPM. As the basic multifactor specification, we use the Carhart (1997) model, because it is widely used in practice and is not dominated by any other unconditional model in the mutual funds performance literature. Finally, we use and adapt the Capocci and Hübner (2005) multifactor model that extends the Carhart (1997) specification by combining it with factors proposed in Agarwal and Naik (2004) and by adding an additional factor of interest. For a further discussion, see Capocci and Hübner (2005) for a full description of their model and the previous ones. We will focus on the particularities of the one we are using.

In order to take into account the complex characteristics of the hedge fund industry, we implement a combination and an extension of Carhart's (1997) four-factor model, the model used by Agarwal and Naik (2004), and the one used by Capocci and Hübner (2005).

This model contains the market risk premium, the Fama and French (1993) size and value factors, Carhart's (1997) momentum factor, five factors introduced by Agarwal and Naik (2004): a factor for non-U.S. equities investing funds (MSCI World excluding U.S.), two factors to account for the fact that hedge funds invest in U.S. and foreign bond indices (Lehman High Yield Bond Index and Salomon World Government Bond Index), one factor that Capocci and Hübner (2005) proved to be highly significant, the JP Morgan Emerging Market Bond Index, and a commodity factor (GSCI Commodity Index), as suggested by Fung and Hsieh (1997). Furthermore, we add an additional bond index factor used in Capocci, Corhay, and Hübner (2005), the Lehman High-Yield Credit Bond, which helps explain the persistence in performance in bull and bear market periods. We do not use the Lehman Mortgage-Backed Securities, as suggested by Capocci, Corhay, and Hübner (2005), because this factor has a low explanatory power. Finally, we add a currency factor to take into account the exposure of some strategies (particularly macro funds) to this market (Fung and Hsieh, 1997; Agarwal and Naik, 2004).

We also include the return strategies of artificial at-the-money (ATM) and out-of-the-money (OTM) index call and put options, in a similar way as in Agarwal and Naik (2004). These risk premiums aim at capturing the optional strategies followed by hedge fund managers.

The market proxy used is the value-weighted portfolio of all NYSE, Amex, and Nasdaq stocks market proxy, which is usually used in mutual funds and hedge funds performance studies.

Several additional factors, such as the MSCI Emerging Markets Index, the Lehman BAA Corporate Bond Index, and the Salomon Brothers Government and Corporate Bond Index proposed by Agarwal and Naik (2004) and Capocci and Hübner (2005) and the Gold index used by Fung and Hsieh (1997),[2] were not included in our extended model because of their high collinearity with our set of indices.

$$
\begin{aligned}
R_{Pt} - R_{Ft} = {} & \alpha_P + \beta_{P1}(R_{Mt} - R_{Ft}) + \beta_{P2}\mathrm{SMB}_t + \beta_{P3}\mathrm{HML}_t + \beta_{P4}\mathrm{PR1YR}_t \\
& + \beta_{P5}(\mathrm{MSWXUS}_t - R_{Ft}) + \beta_{P6}(\mathrm{SWGBI}_t - R_{Ft}) \\
& + \beta_{P7}(\mathrm{JPMEMBI}_t - R_{Ft}) + \beta_{P8}(\mathrm{HY}_t - R_{Ft}) \\
& + \beta_{P9}(\mathrm{GSCI}_t - R_{Ft}) + \beta_{P10}(\mathrm{CUR}_t - R_{Ft}) \\
& + \beta_{P11}\mathrm{ATMC}_t + \beta_{P12}\mathrm{OTMC}_t + \beta_{P13}\mathrm{ATMP}_t + \beta_{P14}\mathrm{OTMP}_t \\
& + \varepsilon_{Pt}
\end{aligned} \tag{2.1}
$$

where R_{Pt} = return of fund P in month t; R_{Ft} = risk-free return in month t; R_{Mt} = return of the market portfolio in month t. SMB_t = the factor-mimicking portfolio for size (small minus big), HML_t = the factor-mimicking portfolio for book-to-market equity (high minus low),[3] and $\mathrm{PR1YR}_t$ = the factor-mimicking portfolio for the momentum effect.[4] These factors aim at isolating the firm-specific components of returns. MSWXUS_t = return of the MSCI World Index excluding the United States; SWGBI_t = return of the Salomon World Government Bond Index; $\mathrm{JPMEMBI}_t$ = return of the JP Morgan Emerging Market Bond Index; HY_t = return of the Lehman High-Yield Credit Bond Index, GSCI_t = return of the Goldman Sachs Commodity Index, CUR_t = return of the Federal Reserve Bank Trade Weighted Dollar Index, and ATMC_t, OTMC_t, ATMP_t, and OTMP_t =, respectively, the Agarwal and Naik (2004) at-the-money (ATMC), out-of-the-money (OTMC) European call option factors, and at-the-money (ATMP) and out-of-the-money (OTMP) European put option factors. ε_{Pt} = error term; α_P and β_P are the intercept and the slope of the regression, respectively. The intercept of this equation, α_p, commonly called Jensen's alpha, is usually interpreted as a measure of out- or underperformance relative to the market proxy used.

---

[2] Agarwal and Naik (2003) suggest that the Goldman Sachs Commodity Index is a better approximation of the commodity market than the Gold index regarding hedge funds.

[3] See Fama and French (1993) for a precise description of the construction of SMB_t and HML_t.

[4] For a description of the construction of PR1YR, see Carhart (1997).

From this model, we use an original way of constructing the deciles that are the heart of the persistence analysis. In all previous persistence studies based on returns (Carhart, 1997; Agarwal and Naik, 2000; Capocci and Hübner, 2005), the deciles were constructed on the basis of past returns only. In our study, following Capocci (2005), we perform the same analysis but also use the Sharpe ratio,[5] the standard deviation, the alpha, the skewness, and the kurtosis. These analyses should help us understand the results and discover the trends in the persistence analyses of performance risk.

2.4 Descriptive statistics

Table 2.2 reports the descriptive statistics of the independent and dependent variable used in our study. The average excess returns of funds of funds appear to be approximately half that of market returns, but with a significantly lower standard deviation. The returns on optional strategies exhibit very high standard deviations, and the average return is negative for three of the four strategies. This result is hardly surprising because the high leverage of these strategies indicate that the point estimate for the expected return is likely to be highly volatile.

2.5 Bias analysis

Performance figures are subject to various biases. The two most important ones are the survivorship bias and the instant-return-history bias. They appear when only the surviving funds are taken into account in a performance analysis study.

2.5.1 Survivorship bias

The common practice among suppliers of hedge funds databases is to provide information on investable funds that are currently in operation. When only living funds are considered, there is a survivorship bias in the figures because dissolved funds tend to have worse performance than surviving funds. In this study, we use data from living and dissolved funds, which means that our database should be free of survivorship bias.

Survivorship bias is particularly important in the case of hedge funds (Fung and Hsieh, 2001; Ackermann, McEnally, and Ravenscraft, 1999). Usually this bias is studied on a global basis for full databases, including a variety of different strategies. In this study, we restrict our analysis of the presence of survivorship bias to the sole category of funds of hedge funds.

---

[5] The Sharpe ratio is defined as the ratio between excess return over the risk-free rate and the standard deviation of the return. We perform the same analysis with the Sharpe score, which is the ratio of the return over the standard deviation, but the results were close.

Table 2.2 Descriptive statistics

	Mean	Standard deviation	Median	Skewness	Kurtosis	Minimum	Maximum	Sharpe ratio
Funds of funds	0.43	1.9	0.81	-0.16	3.08	-7.32	6.93	0.23
Stock market factors								
Market	0.78	4.77	1.58	-0.72	0.37	-15.69	8.33	0.16
MSCI excluding U.S.	0.09	4.36	0.47	-0.45	0.26	-12.89	10.27	0.02
SMB	0.02	4.45	-0.36	0.87	5.56	-16.26	21.38	0.00
HML	0.6	4.16	0.68	0.48	1.14	-8.91	13.67	0.14
PR1YR	1.14	5.74	1.27	-0.73	4.6	-25.13	18.21	0.20
Bond market factors								
Lehman Aggregate	-0.01	1.13	0.19	-0.13	0.61	-2.73	3.87	-0.01
Salomon WGBI	0.5	1.83	0.24	0.45	0.47	-3.44	5.94	0.27
JPM EMBI	0.82	4.67	1.16	-1.64	7.18	-24.2	10.87	0.18
Lehman High-Yield	0.4	2.11	0.66	-0.7	3.58	-7.37	7.49	0.19
Commodity factor								
GSCI	0.59	5.35	0.61	0.27	0.26	-12.28	15.79	0.11
Currency factors								
Broad Dollar Index	0.34	1.11	0.29	0.33	1.29	-2.79	3.93	NA
Option factors								
ATM Call	0.82	84.51	-20.34	0.58	-0.78	-99.04	216.91	NA
OTM Call	-2.97	89.57	-30.35	0.79	-0.41	-99.1	246.85	NA
ATM Put	-11.88	95.02	-56.76	1.62	2.66	-95.29	386.02	NA
OTM Put	-15.73	95.55	-59.39	1.81	3.64	-96.21	400.33	NA

Survivorship bias can be defined in two ways: the performance difference between surviving and dissolved funds (Ackermann, McEnally, and Ravenscraft, 1999) and the performance difference between living and all funds (Fung and Hsieh, 2000). We report the bias via only the second approach, which is the more common one (Table 2.3).

Panel A of Table 2.3 shows that the pattern of funds of funds returns clearly exhibits two periods: (1) prior to 2000; for example, in the bullish period, the living and dissolved funds experienced yearly returns that were close to each other. (2) During the last three years of the sample period, one observes a strong difference between the two series of returns, with an average yearly return of survivors that exceeds the one of dead funds by more than 8%. This finding confirms that of Capocci, Corhay, and Hübner (2005), obtained on a wider sample of hedge funds.

In Panel B of Table 2.3, we obtain a yearly bias of less than 1%. This indicates that survivorship is less likely to vitiate our sample of funds of funds than in most hedge fund studies, for it compares favorably with the levels, ranging from 1.2% to 3.6%, obtained by Fung and Hsieh (2000), Liang (2001), Capocci and Hübner (2005), and Capocci, Corhay, and Hübner (2005). It is also much lower than the industry consensus of 3% reported by Amin and Kat (2003).

2.5.2   Instant-return-history bias

Fung and Hsieh (2000) document a special bias that is related to the fact that hedge fund managers, who are not allowed to advertise, consider inclusion in a database primarily as a marketing tool. The upward instant-history bias occurs because a fund's performance history, which is typically positive because those with a good track record are the most likely to apply, is backfilled after inclusion.

To detect this bias, we first estimate the average monthly return of the observable portfolio that invests in all funds from our database each month. Then we estimate the average monthly return of the adjusted observable portfolio obtained from investing in all these funds after deleting the first 12, 24, 36, 48, and 60 months of returns. Results are reported in Table 2.4.

The average return of funds of funds over the whole period is lower than that of hedge funds reported by Capocci, Corhay, and Hübner (2005) for the same period. However, the observed bias is significantly lower for our sample than the one found in comparative studies. We even obtain a negative value of the bias for a lag of one or two years, indicating that the backfilling of funds of funds is not likely to overweight good performers for a short history. Only for a longer period do we obtain a positive bias, but this is hardly significant.

Overall, we can conclude that the survivorship and instant-history biases are not likely to significantly alter the empirical validity of the analyses performed with our sample.

Table 2.3 Survivorship bias

Panel A: Annual performance (funds of funds)

Year	All funds			Surviving funds			Dissolved funds		
	Return	Standard deviation	Observations	Return	Standard deviation	Observations	Return	Standard deviation	Observations
1994	−2.08	1.42	2,360	−1.11	1.37	1,411	−3.53	−3.53	949
1995	11.95	1.04	3,129	12.66	1.06	1,923	10.80	10.80	1,206
1996	17.61	1.33	3,764	19.24	1.36	2,443	14.59	14.59	1,321
1997	17.25	1.91	4,657	17.88	1.85	3,093	16.05	16.05	1,564
1998	0.83	2.82	5,360	1.47	2.63	3,680	−0.78	−0.78	1,680
1999	26.53	2.23	6,107	26.31	2.07	4,498	27.29	27.29	1,609
2000	7.99	2.47	6,811	10.11	2.24	5,286	0.41	0.41	1,525
2001	5.01	1.14	7,398	6.12	0.96	6,314	−0.51	−0.51	1,084
2002	0.90	0.93	7,979	1.52	0.92	7,533	−7.30	−7.30	446
Mean 1994–2002	9.6	1.70	5,285	10.5	1.60	4,020	6.3	6.30	1,265

Panel B: Living — all funds

Year	Return	
1994	1.0	
1995	0.7	
1996	1.6	
1997	0.6	
1998	0.6	
1999	−0.2	
2000	2.1	
2001	1.1	
2002	0.6	
Bias January 1994–December 2002	0.08	Monthly
	0.96	Yearly

Table 2.4 Instant-history bias

	Mean monthly return	Difference	Annual difference	Number of observations per year
All	0.80%	NA	NA	5,284
Without 12 months	0.87%	−0.07%	−0.90%	4,635
Without 24 months	0.83%	−0.04%	−0.44%	4,035
Without 36 months	0.72%	0.08%	0.91%	3,501
Without 48 months	0.65%	0.15%	1.75%	3,007
Without 60 months	0.77%	0.03%	0.30%	2,573

2.6 Persistence in performance

Following Capocci (2005) and Agarwal and Naik (2004), we use two series of factors while studying hedge fund persistence in performance. First, we adapt and use the model developed by Capocci and Hübner (2005). Second, we add the option factors of Agarwal and Naik (2004).

To study the performance of funds of funds, we will use a set of alternative classification schemes. These schemes belong to two dimensions: performance and risk. For the measure of performance, we use the total return, the alpha, and the Sharpe ratio of the funds during the portfolio formation period. To consider the ranking of funds of funds based on risk measures, we simply use the standard deviation, skewness, and kurtosis of the returns distributions.

To analyze persistence in performance, we follow the methodology of Carhart (1997) using our combined model. Many investors require funds to exist for at least three years before investing. To take this constraint into account, all funds are ranked based on performance or risk measured during a period of three years. Then, we put all funds into 10 equally weighted portfolios, ordered from highest to lowest past performance or risk. Portfolios 1 (low) and 10 (high) are then further subdivided on the same measure. The portfolios are held till the following January and then rebalanced. Funds that disappear during the course of the year are included in the equally weighted average until their death, and then portfolio weights are readjusted appropriately. We carry out the analysis for the remaining sample period (1997–2002) and then for two nonoverlapping periods: a bullish period going from January 1997 to March 2000 and a bearish period from April 2000 to December 2002. This yields a time series of 72 monthly returns on each decile portfolio, to be split in a series of 39 monthly observations (bullish period) and 33 months (bearish period). The objective of classifying funds into deciles is to try to explain the differences in returns between good and bad funds using these factors. A fund may simply have been better than another one because it has been exposed to the equity market during a market rally.

2.6.1   Persistence in performance based on past performance

The results for the total test period are reported in Table 2.5a; the results for the
bullish and bearish subperiods are presented in Tables 2.5b and 2.5c, respectively.

Persistence based on past total returns

The analysis is totally similar to the one performed by Carhart (1997). The
results are reported in the first columns of Table 2.5a, 2.5b, and 2.5c. Similar
to previous findings for hedge funds overall (Capocci and Hübner, 2005;
Capocci, Corhay, and Hübner, 2005), there seems to be persistence in the performance of funds of funds in the middle deciles (3–5), indicating that past
extreme performers are not likely to display significantly better abnormal performance, while many of those who had an average performance manage to get
good values of alpha in the subsequent period. The evidence is rather weak,
unfortunately, because the R^2 of the regressions for these deciles are the lowest,
indicating a poor fit. Furthermore, the analysis by subperiods (Tables 2.5a and
2.5b) does not support the sustainability of persistence at times of extreme market conditions. This result confirms the one reported by Capocci, Corhay, and
Hübner (2005), who only find superior persistence for market neutral funds in
bearish periods.

Table 2.5a Rankings on performance measures — global period

FOF	Total return		Sharpe ratio		Alpha	
	Alpha	R^2	Alpha	R^2	Alpha	R^2
D1	0.37	0.61	0.39	0.60	0.30	0.76
D2	0.29	0.63	0.03	0.67	0.21	0.69
D3	0.34***	0.60	0.03	0.74	0.29	0.71
D4	0.29***	0.69	0.17	0.75	0.27**	0.81
D5	0.40***	0.74	0.20	0.84	0.28**	0.77
D6	0.26	0.78	0.15	0.82	0.29*	0.77
D7	0.26	0.78	0.29**	0.82	0.30***	0.81
D8	0.13	0.82	0.27*	0.78	0.35***	0.79
D9	0.14	0.84	0.36***	0.74	0.32***	0.72
D10	0.25	0.78	0.49***	0.73	−0.12	0.70
D1a	0.34	0.44	0.36	0.36	0.70	0.48
D1b	0.68*	0.43	0.55	0.56	−0.16	0.75
D1c	0.19	0.58	0.07	0.58	0.33	0.82
D10a	0.39*	0.81	0.57***	0.67	0.15	0.62
D10b	0.26	0.78	0.44***	0.72	−0.05	0.52
D10c	0.04	0.69	0.58***	0.60	−0.38	0.61

* − .10 Significance level
** − .05 Significance level
*** − .01 Significance level

Table 2.5b Rankings on performance measures — bullish subperiod

FOF	Total return		Sharpe ratio		Alpha	
	Alpha	R^2	Alpha	R^2	Alpha	R^2
D1	−0.20	0.75	−0.09	0.63	−0.17	0.80
D2	0.06	0.80	−0.36	0.75	0.10	0.75
D3	0.22	0.66	−0.29	0.82	0.07	0.82
D4	0.25	0.79	0.02	0.82	0.17	0.86
D5	0.34**	0.85	0.40**	0.88	0.13	0.82
D6	0.24	0.85	0.17	0.91	0.22	0.83
D7	0.16	0.86	0.36**	0.89	0.40***	0.90
D8	0.23	0.89	0.35**	0.89	0.58***	0.92
D9	0.33*	0.86	0.44***	0.86	0.47***	0.82
D10	0.25	0.86	0.58***	0.83	−0.24	0.83
D1a	0.13	0.49	−0.28	0.40	−0.89	0.60
D1b	−0.13	0.57	0.17	0.58	−0.76**	0.83
D1c	−0.38	0.79	−0.61	0.71	0.59	0.79
D10a	0.75***	0.88	0.66***	0.79	−0.12	0.84
D10b	0.41	0.85	0.57***	0.83	0.25	0.56
D10c	−0.54	0.81	0.61***	0.71	−0.65	0.76

* − .10 Significance level
** − .05 Significance level
*** − .01 Significance level

Table 2.5c Rankings on performance measures — bearish subperiod

FOF	Total return		Sharpe ratio		Alpha	
	Alpha	R^2	Alpha	R^2	Alpha	R^2
D1	−0.27	0.77	−0.29	0.82	−0.60	0.89
D2	−0.08	0.81	−0.41	0.83	−0.36	0.84
D3	0.02	0.80	−0.28	0.94	−0.16	0.91
D4	0.04	0.86	−0.19	0.90	0.15	0.93
D5	0.12	0.80	−0.14	0.91	0.12	0.87
D6	0.02	0.91	−0.03	0.89	0.00	0.93
D7	−0.01	0.87	−0.09	0.90	−0.04	0.88
D8	−0.30	0.86	0.00	0.87	−0.15	0.80
D9	−0.16	0.90	0.18**	0.83	0.00	0.77
D10	0.02	0.91	0.28***	0.76	0.07	0.89
D1a	−0.86	0.66	−0.18	0.62	−0.19	0.75
D1b	0.17	0.67	−0.12	0.76	−0.74	0.80
D1c	−0.27	0.80	−0.52	0.76	−0.71***	0.95
D10a	−0.23	0.88	0.22	0.71	0.19	0.75
D10b	0.12	0.83	0.26**	0.75	−0.19	0.79
D10c	0.19	0.86	0.33***	0.71	0.20	0.84

* − .10 Significance level
** − .05 Significance level
*** − .01 Significance level

Persistence based on Sharpe ratios

We use this statistic to classify individual funds of funds because all investors look-ing at alternative investments, such as funds of funds, are not only looking at the performance; many of them focus on their risk/return characteristics, especially in light of their ability to diversify risks. The Sharpe score aims at taking the total risk and the returns into account. For this reason it is reasonable to use this measure while analyzing the persistence in funds of funds returns.

The idea underlying the analysis is simple: Will the investor who looks at the previous year's best risk/return trade-off hedge fund be able to create consistent returns over time? Various studies used the Sharpe ratio while analyzing hedge fund returns (Ackermann, McEnally, and Ravenscraft, 1999; Liang, 1999; Amin and Kat, 2003), and most of them stressed the shortcut of this measure for alter-native strategies like those applied by hedge fund managers (Goetzmann, Ingersoll, and Ross, 2003). Nevertheless the use of this measure remains predominant in the industry, so we have to consider it here, despite its weaknesses.

Evidence on persistence based on Sharpe ratios is gathered in the middle columns of Tables 2.5a to 2.5c. The results display some rather significant effects and are coherent across subperiods. The best performers in the portfo-lio formation period appear to be able to sustain abnormal performance. The alphas for funds in deciles 6–10 are statistically and economically significant (in a range of a yearly 4% to 6%). The fit provided by the regression is larger than when using total returns as a classification criterion.

The results are very similar, but stronger for the bullish period. The average abnormal performance for deciles 5 and 7–10 is statistically and economically more important. The effect culminates for subdecile 10a, with an annual alpha of 8%.

Even though the results are much weaker for the bearish period, they are much more remarkable: for deciles 9 and 10, we again find evidence of abnor-mal performance. For these two deciles we thus have evidence of persistence in performance across the most extreme market conditions. The intersection of similar effects indicates that Sharpe ratios tend to be excellent predictors of abnormal performance in the subsequent year.

Persistence based on alphas

Like most individual hedge funds, funds of funds aim at creating absolute return in any market environment. Because of this characteristic, most investors who use them as a diversification tool compare the part of their portfolio allo-cated to these funds to the proportion of their portfolio invested in equities to determine if they are a good diversification tool. This process is equivalent to removing the market impact on their alternative investment portfolio and to analyzing the remaining alpha.

The last columns of Tables 2.5a to 2.5c report the results using alphas as a rank-ing device. Note that this part of the study seems to be the most consistent, for we use the same performance measure for the estimation and for the test period.

Nevertheless, the R^2 of the regressions for the global period (Table 2.5a) is not larger than the ones using Sharpe ratios. The results for this whole sample period lie somewhat between the results for the total returns (persistence in the lower-middle deciles) and the ones for the Sharpe ratios (persistence in upper deciles).

These results are confirmed in the bullish subperiod, but nothing left remains for the bearish period; the positive persistence vanishes in bad times, as for the total returns.

2.6.2   Persistence in performance based on past risk measures

Following Capocci (2005), we use some other way of classifying funds into deciles than just net performance. Absolute performance is the most important point in the hedge fund industry. However, some strategies are highly risky (macro funds, for example), whereas others (like market-neutral funds) try to offer relatively low but stable returns. In order to take this aspect into account, we perform the same analysis using risk measurement tools for classifying the hedge funds in deciles. First we use the standard deviation (for investors looking for low-volatility strategies), the skewness (for investors who look for positively skewed returns), and finally the kurtosis (for investors who want to avoid fat tails).

This analysis is interesting because it aims at determining if there is a proof of good or bad performance in hedge fund return on the basis of the risk profile of their returns only. Stated differently, do more volatile, skewed, or fat-tailed funds of funds consistently and significantly out- or underperform funds with the opposite risk profile?

Similar to the previous subsection, the results for the total test period are reported in Table 2.6a, while the results for the bullish and bearish subperiods are presented in Tables 2.6b and 2.6c, respectively.

The use of standard deviations as a risk measure is intimately related to the choice of the Sharpe ratio as a measure of performance. From the previous subsection, we had found that the evidence of persistence was primarily documented for Sharpe ratios rather than total returns. This suggests that the risk exposure of the fund might be a good predictor of future performance.

The study of standard deviations not only confirms but also magnifies the results obtained with Sharpe ratios. Note that persistence now is located in the lower deciles, which is a logical finding since the standard deviation appears in the denominator of the Sharpe ratio. Performance persistence is more pervasive: from deciles 1 to 6 for the whole period (Table 2.6a) and for the bullish subperiod (Table 2.6b), and from deciles 1 to 3 for the bearish subperiod. However, these extremely interesting results are somehow weakened by the relatively low significance levels of the regressions.

The results using skewness and, to a lower extent, kurtosis are highly interesting as well. The remarkable result with these two risk measures is the very high level of the R^2 achieved by portfolios constructed on their basis. The significance levels are particularly high for the bearish subperiod, with coefficients of determination ranging (with one exception) from 83% to 94%. This is evidence

Table 2.6a Rankings on risk measures — global period

FOF	Standard deviation		Skewness		Kurtosis	
	Alpha	R^2	Alpha	R^2	Alpha	R^2
D1	0.32***	0.65	0.26**	0.72	0.32*	0.74
D2	0.34***	0.63	0.31*	0.76	0.34	0.67
D3	0.38***	0.65	0.26**	0.85	0.29	0.75
D4	0.31***	0.71	0.33*	0.71	0.23	0.78
D5	0.34**	0.75	0.28*	0.80	0.48**	0.79
D6	0.30*	0.76	0.11	0.79	0.09	0.78
D7	0.17	0.83	0.22	0.75	0.29*	0.79
D8	0.15	0.71	0.14	0.78	−0.03	0.80
D9	0.18	0.82	0.35	0.64	0.22	0.75
D10	−0.01	0.79	0.29*	0.79	0.28***	0.78
D1a	0.22***	0.58	0.28**	0.59	0.48*	0.57
D1b	0.35***	0.65	0.19*	0.71	0.19	0.77
D1c	0.35***	0.57	0.38**	0.65	0.31	0.67
D10a	0.29	0.76	0.65*	0.63	0.33*	0.68
D10b	−0.07	0.75	0.14	0.67	0.40***	0.73
D10c	−0.54	0.65	0.20	0.72	0.22	0.65

* − .10 Significance level
** − .05 Significance level
*** − .01 Significance level

Table 2.6b Rankings on risk measures — bullish subperiod

FOF	Standard deviation		Skewness		Kurtosis	
	Alpha	R^2	Alpha	R^2	Alpha	R^2
D1	0.31***	0.76	0.21	0.86	0.32	0.77
D2	0.37***	0.78	0.27	0.83	0.27	0.75
D3	0.47***	0.87	0.41***	0.87	0.15	0.82
D4	0.38***	0.82	0.16	0.82	0.24	0.88
D5	0.30*	0.86	0.23*	0.83	0.50**	0.84
D6	0.37*	0.85	−0.21	0.85	−0.02	0.85
D7	0.20	0.89	0.07	0.81	0.27	0.86
D8	−0.21	0.79	0.11	0.87	−0.05	0.85
D9	0.24	0.87	0.28	0.72	−0.02	0.86
D10	−0.44	0.78	0.44**	0.88	0.28**	0.89
D1a	0.21	0.73	0.18	0.80	0.63	0.67
D1b	0.34***	0.76	0.22	0.81	0.16	0.85
D1c	0.28*	0.73	0.32	0.79	0.19	0.74
D10a	0.42	0.76	0.76***	0.77	0.41*	0.79
D10b	−0.24	0.70	0.36	0.72	0.54***	0.84
D10c	−1.35	0.73	0.37**	0.87	0.05	0.81

* − .10 Significance level
** − .05 Significance level
*** − .01 Significance level

Table 2.6c Rankings on risk measures — bearish subperiod

FOF	Standard deviation		Skewness		Kurtosis	
	Alpha	R^2	Alpha	R^2	Alpha	R^2
D1	0.26***	0.76	0.20**	0.87	−0.02	0.85
D2	0.23***	0.72	0.03	0.91	−0.14**	0.91
D3	0.15*	0.74	−0.18	0.94	−0.18	0.88
D4	0.08	0.82	−0.01	0.83	−0.23	0.89
D5	−0.03	0.86	0.01	0.93	−0.05	0.89
D6	−0.18*	0.89	−0.14	0.91	−0.12	0.93
D7	−0.30*	0.91	−0.15	0.91	−0.10	0.86
D8	−0.14	0.88	−0.23	0.87	−0.15	0.89
D9	−0.40	0.88	−0.09	0.72	0.06	0.88
D10	−0.56	0.92	−0.25	0.86	0.10*	0.88
D1a	0.16***	0.75	0.19	0.61	0.05	0.75
D1b	0.31***	0.75	0.23*	0.88	0.30	0.75
D1c	0.31***	0.69	0.21*	0.84	−0.38	0.73
D10a	−0.60	0.88	−0.26**	0.84	−0.13	0.78
D10b	−0.71*	0.93	−0.28	0.86	0.16	0.82
D10c	0.02	0.80	−0.22	0.63	0.15*	0.78

* − .10 Significance level
** −.05 Significance level
*** −.01 Significance level

of a large degree of homogeneity of the type of persistence of funds of funds returns, not necessarily in terms of abnormal performance, but simply in terms of systematic risk exposures.

Surprisingly, there also seems to be positive persistence of performance for the funds with the highest kurtosis, for example, having obtained the most extreme pattern of returns over the formation period. Thus, as far as the fat-tailedness of the returns distribution is concerned, the most extreme funds seem to obtain positive performance. This particular finding should not be interpreted blindly, for this may simply indicate that funds with a very large span of return may deserve an additional risk premium that is not properly captured by the factors we use in our model.

2.7 Conclusion

This study aimed at extending the scope of persistence studies to a subpopulation of hedge funds, funds of funds.

Our preliminary analysis indicates that the sample of funds of funds is not likely to exhibit the traditional biases affecting hedge fund data with a similar magnitude. Thus, similar to samples of mutual funds, our results are likely to be quite reliable.

The persistence study we propose introduces two novelties. On the one hand, we separate the bullish from the bearish stock market periods, which has only been performed by Capocci, Corhay, and Hübner (2005) in the context of hedge funds. On the other hand, we classify funds on the basis of two sets of measures, performance and risk.

It looks like there exists persistence in funds of funds returns, which is best predicted by Sharpe ratios (with performance metrics) but even more significantly by standard deviations. "It is as simple as that" could be the conclusion of this preliminary study. Of course, these simple but important results require additional investigation, which is part of our research agenda.

Acknowledgments

The authors would like to thank Dee Weber from CISDM for providing access to MAR/CISDM data and to Sol Waksman for providing access to the Barclay hedge fund data. Georges Hübner thanks Deloitte (Luxembourg) and the Luxembourg School of Finance, University of Luxembourg for financial support. All errors are ours.

References

Ackermann, C., McEnally, R., and Ravenscraft, D. (1999). The Performance of Hedge Funds: Risk, Return, and Incentives. *Journal of Finance*, 54(3):833–874.

Agarwal, V. and Naik, N. Y. (2000). Multi-Period Performance Persistence Analysis of Hedge Funds. *Journal of Financial and Quantitative Analysis*, 35(3):327–342.

Agarwal, V. and Naik, N. Y. (2003). Risk and Portfolio Decisions Involving Hedge Funds. Working Paper, London Business School, London, U. K., and Georgia State University, Atlanta, GA.

Agarwal, V. and Naik, N. Y. (2004). Risks and Portfolio Decisions Involving Hedge Funds. *Review of Financial Studies*, 17(1):63–98.

Amin, G. S. and Kat, H. M. (2003). Hedge Fund Performance 1990–2000: Do the "Money Machines" Really Add Value? *Journal of Financial and Quantitative Analysis*, 38(2):251–274.

Brown S. J., Goetzmann, W. N., and Ibbotson, R. G. (1999). Offshore Hedge Funds: Survival and Performance 1989–1995. *Journal of Business*, 72(1):91–118.

Capocci, D. (2005). A Multiple Analysis of Hedge Fund Return Persistence. Working Paper, HEC Management School, University of Liège, Belgium.

Capocci, D., Corhay, A., and Hübner, G. (2005). Hedge Fund Performance in Bull and Bear Markets. *European Journal of Finance*, 11(5):361–392.

Capocci, D. and Hübner, G. (2005). Analysis of Hedge Fund Performance. *Journal of Empirical Finance*, 11(1):55–89.

Carhart, M. M. (1997). On Persistence in Mutual Fund Performance. *Journal of Finance*, 52(1):57–82.

Coën, A., Desfleurs, A., Hübner, G., and Racicot, F.-E. (2005). The Performance of Hedge Funds in the Presence of Errors in Variables. In: *Hedge Funds: Insights in Performance Measurement, Risk Analysis, and Portfolio Allocation* (Gregoriou, G., Hübner, G., Papageorgiou, N., and Rouah, F., eds.). J. Wiley & Sons, New York.

Fama, E. F. and French, K. R. (1993). Common Risk Factors in the Returns on Stocks and Bonds. *Journal of Financial Economics*, 33(1):3–56.

Fung, W. and Hsieh, D. A. (1997). Empirical Characteristics of Dynamic Trading Strategies: The Case of Hedge Funds. *Review of Financial Studies*, 10(2):275–302.

Fung, W. and Hsieh, D. A. (2000). Performance Characteristics of Hedge Funds and Commodity Funds: Natural vs. Spurious Biases. *Journal of Quantitative and Financial Analysis*, 35(3):291–307.

Fung, W. and Hsieh, D. A. (2001). The Risk in Hedge Fund Strategies: Theory and Evidence from Trend Followers. *Review of Financial Studies*, 14(2):313–341.

Goetzmann, W. N., Ingersoll, J. E., and Ross, S. A. (2003). High-Water Marks and Hedge Fund Management Contracts. *Journal of Finance*, 58(4):1685–1718.

Liang, B. (1999). On the Performance of Hedge Funds. *Financial Analysts Journal*, 55(4):72–85.

Liang, B. (2001). Hedge Funds Performance: 1990–1999. *Financial Analysts Journal*, 57(1):11–18.

Schneeweis, T. and Spurgin, R. (1998). Multifactor Analysis of Hedge Funds, Managed Futures and Mutual Fund Return and Risk Characteristics. *Journal of Alternative Investments*, 1(2):1–24.

3 Replication and evaluation of funds of hedge funds returns

Harry M. Kat and Helder P. Palaro

Abstract

We use the hedge fund return replication technique introduced in Kat and Palaro (2005) to evaluate the net-of-fee performance of 485 funds of hedge funds. The results indicate that the majority of funds of funds do not provide their investors with returns that they could not have generated themselves in the futures market. Purely in terms of returns, most funds of funds therefore do not add value.

3.1 Introduction

With the first hedge fund dating back to 1949, hedge funds have been around for quite some time. Academic research into hedge funds, however, only took off toward the end of the 1990s, when sufficient data became available. Since then, and inspired by the strong growth of the hedge fund industry worldwide, a respectable number of research papers have provided insight into many different aspects of hedge funds. One question remains -largely unanswered, though. Do hedge funds provide their investors with superior returns? In other words, do hedge funds provide their investors with returns they could not have obtained otherwise?

According to the hedge fund industry itself, the answer to this question is of course affirmative, although with the recent disappointing performance of hedge funds, this point is put forward less often and less forcefully than it used to be. Nowadays, most emphasis is on the diversification properties of hedge funds.

Various authors have attempted to shed light on the issue of hedge fund return superiority. Most studies apply traditional performance measures, such as the Sharpe ratio and alphas derived from factor models, to hedge fund returns obtained from one or more of the main hedge fund databases. The conclusion is often that hedge fund returns are indeed superior. From other studies, however, it is now well understood that raw hedge fund return data may suffer from various biases that, when not corrected for, will produce artificially high Sharpe ratios and alphas. In addition, hedge fund returns are typically not normally distributed and may derive from exposure to quite unusual risk factors. This makes traditional performance measures unsuitable for hedge funds, for deviations from normality as well as every risk factor that is incorrectly specified or left out altogether will tend to show up as alpha, thereby suggesting superior performance where there actually may be none.

In theory, once the relevant risk factors have been identified, factor model–based performance evaluation of hedge fund returns should work. In practice, however, we do not know enough about hedge fund return generation to be sufficiently certain that the relevant risk factors are correctly specified. As a result, factor models typically explain only 25–30% of the variation in individual hedge fund returns, which compares very unfavorably with the 90–95% typical for mutual funds. Although the procedure works better for portfolios of hedge funds, funds of funds, and hedge fund indices, where most of the idiosyncratic risk is diversified away, the low determination coefficients of these models make it impossible to arrive at a firm conclusion with respect to the superiority of hedge fund returns.

Although by far the most popular, factor models are not the only way to evaluate hedge fund returns. Based on previous work by Amin and Kat (2003), Kat and Palaro (2005) (KP for short) developed a technique that allows the derivation of dynamic trading strategies, trading cash, stocks, bonds, etc., that generate returns with predefined statistical properties. The technique not only is capable of replicating (the statistical properties of) funds of funds returns, but it works equally well for individual hedge fund returns. Since the KP replicating strategies are explicitly constructed to replicate the complete risk and dependence profile of a fund, the average return on these strategies can be used as a performance measure. When the average fund return is significantly higher than the average return on the replication strategy, the fund is the most efficient alternative, and vice versa.

The KP replication technique is similar to that used in Amin and Kat (2003). The important difference, however, is that the latter only replicates the marginal distribution of the fund return, while KP also replicate its dependence structure with an investor's existing portfolio. This is a very significant step forward because most investors nowadays are attracted to hedge funds because of their relatively weak relationship with traditional asset classes, i.e., their diversification potential. Only replicating the marginal distribution without giving any consideration to the dependence structure between the fund and the investor's existing portfolio would therefore be insufficient.

From a performance evaluation perspective, replication of a fund's dependence pattern with other asset classes is a necessity. According to theory as well as casual empirical observation, expected return and systematic covariance, coskewness, and cokurtosis are directly related. In other words, it is not so much the marginal distribution but its dependence structure with other assets that determines an asset's expected return. An asset that is highly correlated with stocks and bonds offers investors very little in terms of diversification potential. As a consequence, there will be little demand for this asset. Its price will be low and its expected return therefore relatively high. On the other hand, an asset that offers substantial diversification potential will be in high demand. Its price will be high and its expected return relatively low. Although hedge funds are not priced by market forces in the same way as primitive assets are, they do operate in the latter markets. It therefore seems plausible that a similar phenomenon is present in hedge fund returns as well.[1]

3.2 The KP efficiency measure

When we apply the KP replication technique to hedge funds, the goal is to create a dynamic trading strategy that generates returns with the same statistical properties as a given hedge fund or fund of funds, i.e., returns that are drawings from the same distribution as the distribution from which the actual fund returns are drawn. The basic idea behind the procedure is straightforward. From the theory of dynamic trading it is well known that in the standard theoretical model with complete markets, any payoff function can be hedged perfectly. This observation is the foundation of arbitrage-based option pricing theory. If it is possible to find a payoff function that, given the distribution of the underlying assets, implies the same distribution as the one from which the fund returns are drawn, then the accompanying dynamic trading strategy will generate (returns that are drawings from) that distribution.

From the KP replication technique and following the same reasoning as in Amin and Kat (2003), we derived the following evaluation procedure, consisting of five distinct steps.

1. Monthly return data is collected on the fund to be evaluated, the representative investor's portfolio, and a so-called reserve asset. The latter is the main source of uncertainty in the replication strategy. Because we want to know whether the returns that investors obtain from hedge funds are superior, fund returns should be net of all fees.
2. From the available return data, the bivariate distribution of the fund return and the representative investor's portfolio return is inferred (the desired distribution). The same is done for the bivariate distribution of the investor's portfolio return and the return on the reserve asset (the building block distribution). In line with KP, we initially allow for 54 different joint distributions, choosing from among them using the Akaike information criterion (AIC).[2]
3. Assuming an initial investment in the fund of 100, we determine the cheapest payoff function that is able to turn the building block distribution into the desired distribution. This payoff function, known as the *desired payoff function*, lies at the basis of the KP replication strategies.
4. The desired payoff function is priced in the standard option pricing model, using Monte Carlo simulation. For the pricing of the payoff function, we estimate the required volatility and correlation inputs over the period covered by the track record of the fund being evaluated. We use the average 1-month interest rate over the same period for the interest rate input. We will refer to the price thus obtained as the *KP efficiency measure*.

---

[1] This is confirmed by the results in Kat and Miffre (2005).
[2] See Akaike (1973) for details.

5. Finally, we compare the KP efficiency measure with the 100 initially invested in the fund. If the efficiency measure is 100 as well, then the replication strategy and the fund are equivalent. If the efficiency measure is less (more) than 100, then the strategy is cheaper (more expensive) than the fund and the fund is therefore inefficient (efficient).

Most performance evaluation studies in finance follow the same general procedure. First, using a fund's track record and possibly some additional data over the same period, the fund return is characterized in some way. With the Sharpe ratio, this is done by calculating the volatility of the fund return. In factor model–based studies, this is done by estimating a fund's exposure to the relevant risk factors. Second, based on this characterization, a normal return is determined and compared with the actual average fund return over its track record. With the Sharpe ratio, the benchmark return is derived from the average index return and the volatility of the index, while in factor models it derives from the average returns on the risk factors.

Our procedure is not different. We just use a different characterization. Where others use factor loadings, we use the desired payoff function. Where others use the average returns on the chosen risk factors, we use the average interest rate, index volatilities, and correlation over a fund's track record to set a benchmark. What is different, however, is that we do not need to make any unrealistically strong assumptions concerning the exact nature of a fund's risk exposure or the behavior of markets in general. As shown by KP, a fairly limited set of returns will often be enough to obtain a sufficiently good estimate of the desired distribution and the efficiency measure. As such, our procedure is quite robust.

In the evaluations, we do not use hedge funds' raw returns. The reason is that, as shown in Brooks and Kat (2002) and Lo, Getmansky, and Makarov (2004), monthly hedge fund returns may exhibit high levels of autocorrelation. This results primarily from the fact that many hedge funds invest in illiquid securities, which are hard to mark to market. When confronted with this problem, hedge fund administrators will either use the last reported transaction price or a conservative estimate of the current market price. This creates artificial lags in the evolution of hedge funds' net asset values, i.e., artificial smoothing of the reported returns. As a result, estimates of volatility, for example, will be biased downward.

One possible method to correct for this bias is found in the real estate finance literature. Due to smoothing in appraisals and infrequent valuations of properties, the returns of direct property investment indices suffer from similar problems as hedge fund returns. The approach employed in this literature has been to unsmooth the observed returns to create a new set of returns that are more volatile and whose characteristics are believed to capture more accurately the characteristics of the underlying property values. Nowadays, several unsmoothing methodologies are available. In this study we use the method originally proposed by Geltner (1991).

Table 3.1 Risk statistics for XYZ fund

	Standard deviation	Skewness	Excess kurtosis	1-month autocorrelation
XYZ smooth	0.0370	−1.726	11.505	0.138
XYZ unsmooth	0.0424	−1.746	11.581	0.008

An Example

To clarify the evaluation method, let's look at a worked-out example. XYZ is a well-known fund of hedge funds that started in 1985. Given XYZ's monthly, net-of-fee returns over the period 1985–2004, the first step is to model the joint distribution of XYZ and the investor's portfolio as well as the joint distribution of the investor's portfolio and the reserve asset. Before we can do so we need to decide exactly what the investor's portfolio and the reserve asset are as well as unsmooth the raw fund data. Let's assume that the representative investor's portfolio consists of 50% S&P 500 and 50% long-dated U.S. Treasury bonds. Instead of investing in the cash market, we assume the investor holds fully collateralized (nearby) futures. We use nearby Eurodollar futures as the reserve asset.

Table 3.1 shows the marginal risk characteristics of the raw and unsmoothed XYZ returns. From the table, we see that XYZ's raw returns exhibit negative skewness and positive autocorrelation. Application of the unsmoothing procedure eliminates the autocorrelation and produces returns with the same degree of skewness but with a substantially higher volatility (annualized 14.7% vs. 12.8% for the raw returns).

We are now ready to infer the desired and the building block distribution. Using the same methodology as KP, we find that the best fit (according to the AIC) is provided by the following set of marginals and copulas:[3]

XYZ: Student t ($\mu = 0.0101$, $\sigma = 0.0406$, $df = 4.0544$)
Portfolio: Normal ($\mu = 0.0101$, $\sigma = 0.0282$)
Reserve: Johnson ($\xi = 0.0031$, $\lambda = 0.0046$, $\gamma = -0.60$, $\delta = 1.599$)
Copula (XYZ, portfolio): Normal ($\rho = 0.754$)
Copula (portfolio, reserve): Gumbel ($a = 1.3349$)

Given these distributions, we can derive the desired payoff function following the methodology developed in KP. Subsequently, we price the resulting payoff function using a bivariate Monte Carlo simulation. This produces a value for the KP efficiency measure of 99.46, meaning that, seen over the whole life of the fund, XYZ's returns are not as miraculous as many investors may have thought. Trading S&P 500, T-bond, and Eurodollar futures, investors could have generated the same risk profile as XYZ and obtained a higher average return at the same time.

[3] Distributions and copulas as defined in Kat and Palaro (2005).

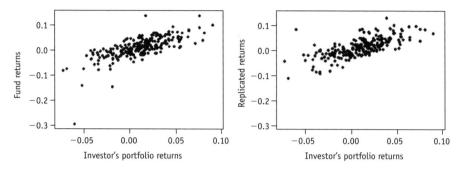

Figure 3.1 Scatter plot of investor's portfolio returns versus XYZ returns (*left*) and replicated returns (*right*)

Table 3.2 Statistics for XYZ fund and replicated returns

	Mean	Standard deviation	Skewness	Skewness (robust)	Excess kurtosis	Excess kurtosis (robust)	Correlation with portfolio	Kendall's tau
XYZ	0.0102	0.0424	−1.7463	−0.1600	11.5812	0.4366	0.714	0.540
Replica	0.0157	0.0388	0.1184	−0.1269	1.2691	0.6889	0.721	0.548

Univariate K-S statistic = 0.054, (approximated) *p*-value = 0.862
Bivariate K-S statistic = 0.056, (approximated) *p*-value 0.924

To see how well the derived payoff function succeeds in replicating the desired distribution, Figure 3.1 shows a scatter plot of the portfolio return versus the XYZ return (left) as well as a plot of the portfolio return versus the replicated return (right). The two plots are very similar, suggesting that the replication has indeed been successful. We see that the replication strategy is unable to replicate the three large losses that XYZ reported during the sample period. This is not too surprising because these are clearly outliers, which simply cannot be captured by a parametric model like ours.

A further indication of the accuracy of the replication strategy comes from comparing the mean, standard deviation, skewness, and kurtosis of XYZ's returns with those of the replicated returns. The latter statistics can be found in Table 3.2, together with the correlation and Kendall's tau with the investor's portfolio. Since the XYZ returns exhibit a few negative outliers, apart from the standard skewness and kurtosis measures, we also report more robust skewness and kurtosis measures.[4] To test whether the marginal distribution of the replicated returns and the joint distribution of the replicated returns and the investor's portfolio are significantly different from the original distributions, we use the univariate and bivariate Kolmogorov–Smirnov (K-S) tests.[5] Comparing the entries

[4] See Hinkley (1975) and Crow and Siddiqui (1967) for details.
[5] See Fasano and Franceschini (1987) for details.

Table 3.3 Funds of funds start and end date details

	Jan 1985	Jan 1988	Jan 1991	Jan 1994	Jan 1997	Jan 2000	Jan 2003	Oct 2004
Start after	479	463	419	329	201	43	0	0
End before	0	0	0	0	12	53	133	209

in Table 3.2, it is clear that the statistical properties of XYZ's returns have been successfully replicated. The replication strategy has replicated not only the marginal distribution of XYZ's returns but also its relationship with the investor's portfolio. The same conclusion follows from both the K-S tests.

3.3 Evaluation results

Having introduced the evaluation procedure, we now present the evaluation results. Our total sample consists of 485 funds of funds with a minimum of four years of history available. All data is obtained from TASS as of November 2004. Funds denominated in a currency other than USD were converted to USD, i.e. the perspective taken is that of a USD-based investor.

Table 3.3 provides some information on the start and end dates of the track records of the funds in our sample. It shows that, reflecting the increasing popularity of hedge funds in the second half of the 1990s, the majority of funds started after 1994. Most hedge fund databases, including TASS, first started collecting data around 1994. As a result, our sample contains no funds that stopped reporting before that date. We also see that out of 485 funds, 209 stopped reporting before October 2004. This confirms that, although lower than for individual hedge funds, the attrition rate in funds of funds is still quite high.

Table 3.4 provides details on the length of the available funds of funds track records. Out of the 485 funds in the sample, only 118 have more than 10 years of history. This reflects the fact that most funds of funds are still relatively young and attrition can be significant.

As in the example in the previous section, in the evaluations we assume that the representative investor's portfolio consists of 50% S&P 500 and 50% long-dated U.S. Treasury bonds while using nearby Eurodollar futures as the reserve asset. For the pricing of the payoff functions, we use 1-month USD Libor as the relevant interest rate while estimating the required volatilities and correlations over the period covered by the track record of the fund that is being evaluated.

To get an idea of the typical accuracy of the replication procedure, Figures 3.2 to 3.4 show scatter plots of the fund standard deviation (Figure 3.2), standard skewness (Figure 3.3), and correlation with the investor's portfolio (Figure 3.4) versus the replicated values for all 485 funds. As is clear from these graphs, on average the replication of these parameters is unbiased and quite accurate. Not

Table 3.4 Length of funds of funds track records

	4–5 years	5–6 years	6–7 years	7–8 years	8–9 years	9–10 years	10–12 years	12–14 years	14+ years
Number of funds	89	81	62	52	43	40	53	31	34

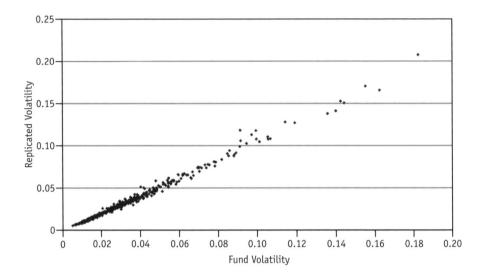

Figure 3.2 Scatter plot of fund vs. replicated standard deviation

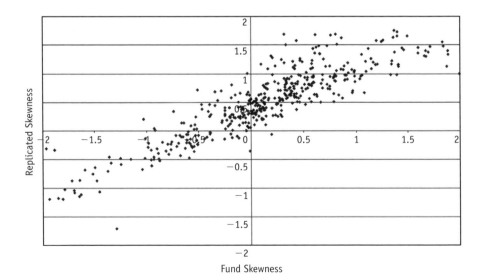

Figure 3.3 Scatter plot of fund vs. replicated skewness

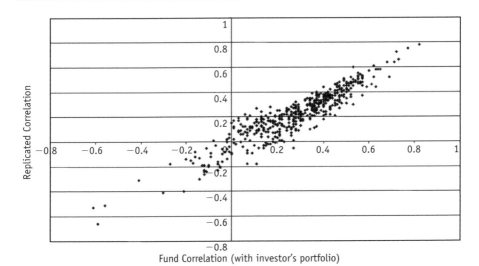

Figure 3.4 Scatter plot of fund vs. replicated correlation with investor's portfolio

surprisingly, the replication of skewness can be difficult at times because fund returns may contain one or more outliers, which will have a major impact on the standard skewness statistic but which cannot be replicated. We encountered this problem earlier in the previous section.

Figure 3.5 shows a histogram of the values of the KP efficiency measure obtained for the 485 funds of funds in our sample. From the graph we see that the majority of funds produce a value for the efficiency measure that is below 100. The average value for the KP efficiency measure over all 485 funds is 99.28. We tested the statistical significance of these efficiency measure results by calculating bootstrapped confidence intervals. We distinguished between the following three cases and obtained the accompanying results:

- The confidence interval is entirely lower than 100: 389 funds
- The confidence interval contains 100: 37 funds
- The confidence interval is entirely higher than 100: 59 funds

This confirms the results in the histogram in Figure 3.5. The majority of funds of hedge funds do not provide their investors with returns they could not have generated themselves in the futures market.

3.4   Distributional analysis

A crucial stage in the evaluation procedure is the proper modeling of the distributional characteristics of the fund, the investor's portfolio, and the reserve asset. This means that, although not explicitly designed to do so, the evaluations provide a wealth of information on the distributional properties of fund of funds returns.

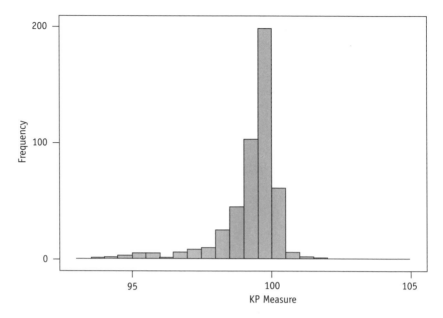

Figure 3.5 Histogram of KP efficiency measure for 485 funds of funds

Table 3.5 Distributional characteristics of fund of funds returns

Marginals	Number	Copulas	Number
Normal	145	Normal	88
Student-*t*	257	Student	49
Johnson	83	Gumbel	36
		SJC	40
		Cook–Johnson	128
		Frank	144

Table 3.5 summarizes how often a given marginal or copula was used in the evaluations for modeling the fund return marginal and the joint distribution of the fund and the investor's portfolio return. It confirms that the majority of fund of funds returns are far from normally distributed, despite an often-substantial degree of diversification. Out of 485 funds, 340 funds' marginal return is better modeled by a Student-*t* or Johnson distribution than a normal distribution. In addition, for only 88 of the 485 funds is the relationship with the investor's portfolio (50% S&P 500, 50% T-bonds) best modeled by the normal copula. This emphasizes once more how important it is to evaluate hedge fund and funds of funds performance using a method that does not rely on the assumption of normally distributed returns.

3.5 Conclusion

In this chapter we have used the hedge fund return replication technique introduced in Kat and Palaro (2005) to evaluate the net-of-fee performance of 485 funds of hedge funds. The results indicate that the majority of funds of funds do not provide their investors with returns they could not have generated themselves in the futures market. Purely in terms of returns, most funds of funds therefore do not add value.

Compared to the many alpha studies that have been performed on hedge funds and funds of funds over the last couple of years, our results are quite unusual. Typically, the conclusion from hedge fund performance studies is that funds of funds generate superior returns, not inferior. This confirms that, although extremely popular, factor model–based performance evaluation is a very tricky business. As long as one can't be sure that all relevant risk factors are accounted for, it will be impossible to know whether unexplained returns are indeed true alpha or just unexplained because one or more risk factors were left out. Basically, a fund's alpha can be put anywhere within a wide range simply by adding or deleting one or more risk factors. Our methodology is a lot more robust, for it relies on only one principle: If it can be replicated, it can't be superior. Of course, we need to make assumptions as well, but these are a lot less crucial for the final outcome of the evaluation than the kind of assumptions required to make factor model–based alphas work.

Finally, it has to be noted that, although in terms of the returns delivered to investors, funds of funds do not seem to add value, this does not mean there is no sound economic reason for funds of funds to exist. Most private and smaller institutional investors lack the skills required to perform the necessary due diligence that comes with hedge fund investment. In addition, given typical minimum investment requirements, small private investors will often lack sufficient funds to build up a well-diversified hedge fund portfolio. They therefore have no choice. If they want hedge funds, they will have to go through a fund of funds.

Large institutions do have a choice. Most of them, however, still prefer to go the fund of funds route. This is quite surprising given the amount of fees that could be saved by skipping the middlemen. Apart from believing that fund of funds managers add enough value to justify their fees (which research suggests is unlikely), part of the reason that many large institutions go for funds of funds lies in the fact that the interests of institutional asset managers are typically not correctly lined up with the interests of those whose money they manage. As a result, job protection becomes an important consideration. By investing in a fund of funds instead of picking hedge funds themselves, institutions avoid having to take responsibility for the bottom-line fund selection. In the end, all they can be held responsible for is the decision to invest in hedge funds and the selection of the fund of funds that they invested in, risks that can easily be hedged by hiring a big-name consultant and a big-name fund manager, as most institutions do.

References

Akaike, H. (1973). Information Theory and an Extension of the Maximum Likelihood Principle. In: Second International Symposium on Information Theory (Petrov, B., and Csaki, F., eds.). Academiae Kiado, Budapest, Hungary.

Amin, G. and Kat, H. (2003). Hedge Fund Performance 1990–2000: Do the Money Machines Really Add Value? *Journal of Financial and Quantitative Analysis*, 38(2):1–24.

Brooks, C. and Kat, H. (2002). The Statistical Properties of Hedge Fund Index Returns and Their Implications for Investors. *Journal of Alternative Investments*, 5(2):26–44.

Crow, E. and Siddiqui, M. (1967). Robust Estimation of Location. *Journal of the American Statistical Association*, 62(318):353–389.

Fasano, G. and Franceschini, A. (1987). A Multidimensional Version of the Kolmogorov-Smirnov Test. *Monthly Notices of the Royal Astronomical Society*, 225:155–170.

Geltner, D. (1991). Smoothing in Appraisal-Based Returns. *Journal of Real Estate Finance and Economics*, 4(3):327–345.

Hinkley, D. (1975). On Power Transformations to Symmetry. *Biometrika*, 62:101–111.

Kat, H. and Miffre, J. (2005). Hedge Fund Performance: The Role of Non-Normality Risks and Conditional Asset Allocation. Working Paper, Alternative Investment Research Centre, Cass Business School, City University London (downloadable from www.cass.city.ac.uk/airc).

Kat, H. and Palaro, H. (2005). Who Needs Hedge Funds? A Copula-Based Approach to Hedge Fund Return Replication. Working Paper, Alternative Investment Research Centre, Cass Business School, City University London (downloadable from www.cass.city.ac.uk/airc).

Lo, A., Getmansky, M., and Makarov, I. (2004). An Econometric Analysis of Serial Correlation and Illiquidity in Hedge Fund Returns. *Journal of Financial Economics*, 74(3):529–609.

4 Performance, size, and new opportunities in the funds of hedge funds industry

Jean-François Bacmann, Pierre Jeanneret, and Stefan Scholz

Abstract

Hedge funds have experienced a tremendous increase in their assets in recent years because of their ability to generate returns in the context of low interest rates and falling stock markets. Hedge fund returns depend on the managers' skills and on their ability to implement complex strategies. Dynamic trading, long/short positions, and option-like payoffs characterize the strategies and make them very different from the long-only universe of traditional investments. Therefore, the estimation of the alpha generated by hedge fund managers must take into consideration these characteristics. In this chapter, we focus on how performance, size and new opportunities impact the life of funds of hedge funds, their action to survive, and the ability of new comers to differentiate from existing ones. We examine funds of hedge funds because they represent the main vehicle to hedge funds for many institutional investors. We use a factor decomposition model and a principal component analysis (PCA) to analyze the variation in risk exposures of funds of hedge funds and to identify new strategies through their unique risk profiles. We also use the factor decomposition model to track the evolution of alpha of fund of hedge funds over time.

4.1 Introduction

Competition is increasing in the funds of hedge funds (FOF) industry, which has seen rapid growth in recent years. A lot of attention has been focused on these investment vehicles, and we often hear negative comments such as "The raw performance of FOFs is decreasing over time" and "Sources of profit have eroded over time and new opportunities are reserved for a small number of FOFs." In this study, we aim to analyze the facts and only the facts in order to explain what has changed in the FOF industry.

In a 2005 paper, Fung, Hsieh, Naik, and Ramadorai (2005) find that FOFs deliver more beta returns than alpha on a time-varying basis. They observe that alpha generated by FOFs tends to decrease over time. They also show that

FOFs generating alpha are more likely to survive than providers of only beta returns. Following their work, we examine the evolution of FOF characteristics over two time periods, January 1995 to December 1999 and May 2000 to April 2005. More specifically, we outline the variables responsible for some FOFs to disappear, for others to survive, and for new ones to penetrate the market. We test the impact of three variables to explain changes in the FOF industry. The first variable related to survival of FOFs is performance. It is decomposed into an alpha term and risk exposures. We analyze the differences between several samples of FOFs (dead, survivor, existing, and new) relating to the two different time periods. Then we introduce size as a discriminating variable. In each sample, FOFs are split into three categories: large, medium, and small. Finally, using principal component analysis, we isolate factors that are unique to newly founded FOFs. We test the statistical links between these unique factors and a large set of hedge fund strategies. If the unique factors represent new opportunities in the FOF industry, they should be related to new and fast-growing hedge fund strategies.

The remainder of the chapter is organized as follows. Section 4.2 describes our experimental framework. The factor model we use to decompose FOF performance is presented in Section 4.3. Section 4.4 is dedicated to the sample formation. Sections 4.5 and 4.6 present our empirical results (performance decomposition and principal component analysis). Section 4.7's summary of the main findings and some ideas for further research conclude the chapter.

4.2   Experimental framework

4.2.1   Synthetic representation of the FOF industry

The FOF industry is alive and well; new funds of funds appear, some existing funds of funds disappear, and others survive. We analyze what differentiates the existing FOFs from the new ones, the survivors from the dead ones. We base our study of funds of funds on data available from the TASS database. To guarantee a sufficient number of FOFs, we restrict ourselves to the period from January 1995 to April 2005. We split the whole period into the *past period* (from January 1995 to December 1999) and the *recent period* (from May 2000 to April 2005). Both subperiods contain 60 months of data. We deliberately drop the first four months of 2000 because a structural breakpoint in the regression models was found around these dates (Fung and Hsieh, 2004; Bacmann and Jeanneret, 2005). The beginning of 2000 also corresponds to the end of the bull market period. The FOFs present in the past period can either survive or disappear. The FOFs in the recent period are either already existing or new. The existing FOFs in the recent period are the ones that survive the past period. Figure 4.1 schematically illustrates our representation of the FOF industry.

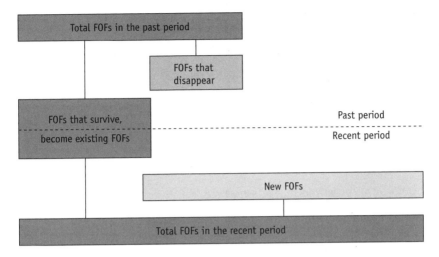

Figure 4.1 Representation of the FOF industry

4.2.2 Important variables to explain disappearance and survivorship of FOFs

Why do some FOFs disappear while others survive? If we exclude FOFs that stop reporting, three main causes are responsible for the disappearance of FOFs: investment risk, business risk, and operational risk; see Kundro and Pfeffer (2003) for an explanation of this typology at the hedge fund level.[1] Kundro and Pfeffer (2003) present size as a direct proxy for business risk. Moreover, size can also be seen as an indirect proxy for operational risk. According to this typology of failure risk, we base our quantitative analysis on the performance of FOFs using size as a discriminating variable. On one side, we rank FOFs in three categories with respect to their assets under management. On the other side, we decompose the performance into alpha and the contribution of systematic risk factors. The estimation of alpha and the systematic contribution depends on the accuracy of the model describing FOF returns. Our model entails a set of explanatory variables combining traditional and alternative factors. The latter type of factors helps achieve high explanatory power, increasing the validity of the alpha from the regression.

---

[1] We assume the same typology applies to funds of funds even if no direct translation can be done between the distribution of failed hedge funds across the three types of risk and that of failed funds of funds. The relation between size and operational risk is less straightforward for funds of funds than for hedge funds. Capacity is less of a constraint for large funds of funds. They could implement programs to secure capacity, or they can get additional capacity by acquiring smaller competitors.

4.2.3   Hypotheses about alpha

FOFs that survive the past period are expected to exhibit better alpha than FOFs that disappear. New FOFs could show more alpha than already existing FOFs if they were able to pick up hedge funds in new, promising strategies. In contrast, already existing FOFs should have more experience in selecting funds in traditional hedge fund strategies. Finally, we test whether alpha has decreased in the recent period in both absolute and risk-adjusted terms. The hypotheses about alpha are set up in order to address the conclusions of Fung, Hsieh, Naik, and Ramadorai (2005).

4.2.4   Hypotheses about risk exposure

FOFs that survive from the past period may have different risk exposures from the FOFs that disappear. These differences should explain the potential underperformance of FOFs that disappear. The risk exposures of FOFs that survive the past period should change in the recent period to adjust for changes in the economic environment. New FOFs should be more exposed to new alternative sources of risk than already existing FOFs. In other words, the number of new FOFs that invest in niche strategies should be larger than that of existing ones.

4.3   Factor model for fund of funds

4.3.1   Traditional risk factors

The traditional risk factors are built to capture three types of passive exposure: the exposure to long-only benchmarks like stock market indices, the exposure to changes in static variables such as interest rates and credit spreads, and the exposure to passive spread trading strategies. These last strategies take into account more complicated exposure to equity risk, like the size effect measured by small minus large firms or momentum spread; see Fama and French (1993) and Carhart (1997) for the justification and the construction of equity spread trading factors. The full list of our traditional factors is presented in the left column of Table 4.1.

Table 4.1 List of risk factors

Traditional risk factors		Alternative risk factors		
S&P 500	S&P 500	Trend-following equity	TF Equity	
Small minus large capitalizations	SMB	Trend-following interest rate	TF STIR	
Momentum spread	MOM	Trend-following currency	TF Curncy	
Change in U.S. 10-year Govt yield	Chg LTIR	Trend-following commodity	TF Comdty	
Change in high-yield spread	Chg HYS			

4.3.2 Alternative risk factors

An alternative source of risk is coming from generic dynamic strategies meant to replicate a broad family of hedge fund specific strategies; see Fung and Hsieh (2002, 2004) for the justification of asset-based factors in explaining hedge fund returns. Our set of alternative risk factors includes trend-following strategies. From our point of view, these strategies are the most appropriate ones to add to the traditional factors in the context of funds of hedge funds. They track risk exposures that are not captured by traditional risk factors.

Our construction of factors replicating trend-following strategies is based on moving averages for a diversified basket of 38 futures markets, including stock indices, short-term interest rates, currencies, and commodities. It generalizes the work of Lequeux and Acar (1998) on the trend-following aspect of currency traders. More specifically, the technical trading rule is given by the position of the current futures price relative to its m-day moving average. Formally, the trading signal at time $t - 1$, B_{t-1}, is given by the following rule:

$$B_{t-1} = 1 \qquad \text{if } P_{t-1} > \frac{1}{m}\sum_{i=1}^{m} P_{t-i} \quad \text{(long position)}$$

$$B_{t-1} = -1 \qquad \text{if } P_{t-1} < \frac{1}{m}\sum_{i=1}^{m} P_{t-i} \quad \text{(short position)}$$

where P_{t-1} is the closing price of the futures at day $t - 1$ and m is the number of days in the moving average. The return of the trading rule, R_t, is given by

$$R_t = B_{t-1}X_t$$

where X_t is the arithmetic return $(P_t/P_{t-1}) - 1$.

The strategy for a given futures market is composed of four moving averages: 224 days, 117 days, 61 days, and 32 days. The strategies are aggregated to form four broad trend-following factors using inverse volatility weights. The trend-following equity factor accounts for nine underlying markets. The trend-following short-term interest rate factor has 11 underlying markets. The trend-following currency factor considers seven underlying markets. The trend-following commodity factor has 11 underlying markets. Table 4.1 summarizes the entire set of traditional (left column) and alternative (right column) risk factors we use in the study.[2]

4.3.3 Factor decomposition model

The general form of the factor model is the following:

$$R_{i,t} = \alpha_i + \sum_k \beta_{i,k}^{\text{traditional}} F_{k,t}^{\text{traditional}} + \sum_m \beta_{i,m}^{\text{alternative}} F_{m,t}^{\text{alternative}} + \varepsilon_{i,t}$$

---

[2] We tested more factors, such as a one-month lagged stock market index, value vs. growth, changes in short-term interest rates, and changes in stock market implied volatility, but they had no significant explanatory power. For the sake of brevity, we have dropped them.

where

$R_{i,t}$ = return on FOF i at time t

α_i = intercept of the regression that proxies the FOF skills to generate excess returns

$\beta_{i,k}^{\text{traditional}}$ = sensitivity of FOF i to traditional factor k

$F_{k,t}^{\text{traditional}}$ = return on the traditional factor k at time t

$\beta_{i,m}^{\text{alternative}}$ = sensitivity of FOF i to alternative factor m

$F_{m,t}^{\text{alternative}}$ = return on the replicating alternative strategy m at time t

$\varepsilon_{i,t}$ = iid error term

4.4   Sample formation

4.4.1   Brief description of the FOF industry

TASS databases report, among other items, the performance of fund of funds products. From now on, when FOF is mentioned, it refers to a fund of funds product and not to the provider of this product. Several products of the same provider may be included in the sample. In order to reduce the survivorship bias, we merge the living TASS database with the graveyard TASS database, which includes all the FOFs that disappear or stop reporting. Table 4.2 presents some descriptive statistics for our merged database.

We show a snapshot of the database for three dates that frame our period of analysis: December 1994, December 1999, and December 2004.[3] The number of FOFs in our sample increases over time from 200 in December 1994 to 654 in December 2004. The overall increase in the number of FOFs is 90% between 1994 and 1999 and 73% between 1999 and 2004. Moreover, the overall assets under management (AUM) tripled between 1999 and 2004, reflecting the growth of the hedge fund industry. In the last part of Table 4.2, we show the repartition of FOFs according to their AUM. Looking at the number of FOFs, we observe that the structure of the FOF industry has changed between December 1999 and December 2004. Growth is limited to the medium- and large-size categories, which, in turn, explains the tremendous growth of AUM.

4.4.2   Sample of FOFs

From the foregoing, our sample includes FOFs with a full track record over one of the two time periods. We find 145 FOFs with a track record during the past period (from January 1995 to December 1999). We consider only one share class

---

[3] We choose end-of-year data to have more consistency.

Table 4.2 Descriptive statistics for the TASS FOF database

	December 1994	December 1999	December 2004
Number of FOFs	200	379	654
Total AUM (million USD)	18,640	33,149	107,512

	Raw variation 1994–1999	Raw variation 1999–2004
Number of FOFs	179	275
Total AUM (million USD)	14,509	74,363

	Relative variation 1995–1999	Relative variation 1999–2004
Number of FOFs	90%	73%
Total AUM	78%	224%

AUM in USD	December 1994		December 1999		December 2004	
	FOFs	%	FOFs	%	FOFs	%
Small FOFs, AUM < 30 million USD	122	61	235	62	239	37
Medium FOFs, AUM between 30 million and 100 million USD	49	25	87	23	203	31
Large FOFs, AUM > 100 million USD	29	15	57	15	212	32

per FOF. These 145 FOFs constitute the total past sample. For the recent period (between May 2000 and April 2005), we have 250 FOFs with a complete track record that are included in the total recent sample.

The formation of the subsamples follows the schematic representation of the FOF industry shown in Figure 4.1. Eighty-two FOFs are common to both, total past and total recent, samples. In the past period they form the survivor subsample, and in the recent period they form the existing subsample. In other words, the survivor and existing subsamples include the same FOFs but in two different time periods. The 63 FOFs that disappear after the past period form the dead subsample. They are the complement to the survivor subsample in the past period. The 168 FOFs that appear in the recent period form the new subsample. They are the complement to the existing subsample in the recent period.

In summary, we have six samples and subsamples, three in the past period (total past, survivor, and dead) and three in the recent period (total recent, existing, and new). The survivor and the existing subsamples include the same FOFs in two different time periods. This feature constitutes a unique way to examine the evolution of the FOF industry.

4.5   Performance decomposition of FOF portfolios

4.5.1   Portfolio definition and descriptive statistics

From the six samples, we form 12 portfolios. The first six portfolios are equally weighted portfolios of the FOFs in each sample. The last six portfolios are value-weighted portfolios. We use the AUM at the beginning of the sample period to determine the weights. For instance, the weights for the total past portfolio are constructed with respect to the AUM in December 1994. Descriptive statistics for the past-period portfolios (January 1995 to December 1999) are shown in Table 4.3a.

Dead FOFs are on average smaller than survivors. Not surprisingly, the performance of the survivors is better than that of the dead, in terms both of returns and of Sharpe and Sortino ratios. The statistics indicate that the better-performing FOFs have a greater probability to survive. Overall, the performance is high, with Sharpe ratios exceeding 1 for the survivor portfolios and about 0.8 for the dead portfolios.

Descriptive statistics for the recent-period portfolios (May 2000 to April 2005) are presented in Table 4.3b. On average, existing FOFs have slightly more AUM than the new FOFs. However, the statistic is biased by few very large FOFs in the existing sample. The distribution across size categories shows that the proportion of large new FOFs is higher than for existing FOFs.

Table 4.3a Descriptive statistics for the past-period portfolios

	Total past		Survivor		Dead	
	Equally weighted	Value weighted	Equally weighted	Value weighted	Equally weighted	Value weighted
Average AUM	USD 125 million		USD 196 million		USD 34 million	
Small FOFs	50%		39%		66%	
Medium FOFs	29%		31%		27%	
Large FOFs	21%		30%		7%	
Compound return	81.85%	96.55%	94.52%	100.05%	66.27%	70.73%
Geometric return annualized	12.70%	14.47%	14.23%	14.88%	10.70%	11.29%
Standard deviation annualized	6.32%	6.45%	6.77%	6.57%	6.26%	6.31%
Downside deviation (libor) annualized	3.31%	3.20%	3.74%	3.27%	3.43%	3.39%
Sharpe (libor) annualized	1.05	1.27	1.19	1.31	0.77	0.85
Sortino (libor) annualized	2.00	2.56	2.15	2.63	1.40	1.58

Examination of the descriptive statistics leads to two main comments. First, the raw average performance of FOFs decreases from the past period to the recent one. However, this reduction in raw performance is not mirrored by the evolution of the risk-adjusted performance (Sharpe and Sortino ratios). For instance, new FOFs manage to generate better risk-adjusted performance than any other category. In contrast, the risk-adjusted performance of existing FOFs has decreased compared with that of the survivor portfolios. Second, size definitely has an impact on the performance of FOFs. In most cases, the value-weighted portfolios show higher Sharpe and Sortino ratios than the equally weighted ones. This result indicates that large FOFs generate higher returns on average than smaller ones. Furthermore, the large proportion of small FOFs in the dead sample (66%) is consistent with the assumption that small FOFs are more subject to business risk and in an indirect manner to operational risk. Size seems to have an impact as well on the likelihood of FOFs to disappear, although it is not independent of the performance.

Table 4.3b Descriptive statistics for the recent-period portfolios

	Total recent		Existing		New	
	Equally weighted	Value weighted	Equally weighted	Value weighted	Equally weighted	Value weighted
Average AUM	USD 259 million		USD 281 million		USD 249 million	
Small FOFs	26%		44%		24%	
Medium FOFs	31%		32%		32%	
Large FOFs	43%		24%		44%	
Compound return	37.63%	39.98%	35.42%	34.73%	38.71%	40.85%
Geometric return annualized	6.60%	6.96%	6.25%	6.14%	6.76%	7.09%
Standard deviation annualized	3.16%	2.88%	3.65%	4.36%	2.96%	2.50%
Downside deviation (libor) annualized	1.59%	1.38%	2.02%	2.34%	1.44%	1.18%
Sharpe (libor) annualized	1.17	1.40	0.93	0.76	1.30	1.67
Sortino (libor) annualized	2.34	2.95	1.70	1.43	2.71	3.53

4.5.2 Alpha and beta exposure of FOFs portfolio

We decompose the risk exposure of the six equally weighted portfolios with respect to our factor model. In addition to the long-only portfolios, we build zero-investment portfolios that are long the survivor (new) FOFs and that are short the dead (existing) FOFs. These zero-investment portfolios allow us to explain the difference in performance between two types of FOFs. A significant alpha would mean that managers of one FOF type are more skilled than managers of the other type. Significant factor coefficients would explain to what extent differences in the risk exposure are responsible for the differences in performance. Results of the factor decomposition of FOF portfolios are presented in Table 4.4a.

All alphas of long-only portfolios are significantly positive, even if portfolios in the recent period have lower alphas than those in the past period.[4] However, on the last row of Table 4.4a, the information ratio (IR annualized) indicates that the reduction in alpha is related to a lower volatility. The information ratio is computed as the alpha divided by the standard deviation of the regression residuals. It is interesting to note that the information ratio of the FOFs present in both time periods (survivor in the past period and existing in the recent period) is stable over time. In contrast, the information ratio of the new FOFs is much higher than that of the dead FOFs. Raw alphas may decrease over time, but the information ratios increase during the recent period. This finding goes a step further than what is done in Fung, Hsieh, Naik, and Ramadorai (2005). It relates the decrease of alphas to a reduction in volatility, showing that the performance by unit of risk is actually increasing.

Table 4.4a Factor decomposition of FOF portfolios

	Total past	Survivor	Dead	Survivor–dead	Total recent	Existing	New	Existing–new
Alpha annualized	$6.91\%^a$	$7.70\%^a$	$5.88\%^a$	1.82%	$5.22\%^a$	$4.67\%^a$	$5.48\%^a$	$-0.81\%^d$
S&P 500	0.190^a	0.227^a	0.141^a	0.085^b	0.130^a	0.159^a	0.116^a	0.044^a
SMB	0.185^a	0.222^a	0.137^b	0.085^c	0.089^a	0.124^a	0.072^b	0.052^a
MOM	0.113^a	0.132^a	0.087^c	0.045^d	0.026^c	0.027^d	0.026^c	0.001
Chg LTIR	-0.418	-0.165	-0.747	0.582	-1.345^a	-1.552^a	-1.245^a	-0.307^c
Chg HYS	-1.709^a	-1.792^a	-1.601^a	-0.191	-0.600^a	-0.536^a	-0.631^a	0.095
TF Equity	0.216^a	0.192^a	0.247^a	-0.055	0.048	0.050	0.046	0.004
TF STIR	0.150^a	0.095^c	0.221^a	-0.126^a	0.050^c	0.064^c	0.044^d	0.021
TF Curncy	0.170^a	0.143^a	0.205^a	-0.062^d	0.087^a	0.086^b	0.087^a	0.000
TF Comdty	0.135^a	0.115^c	0.162^a	-0.047	0.021	0.034	0.014	0.020
Adj. R^2	0.82	0.81	0.78	0.57	0.75	0.77	0.71	0.42
IR annualized	2.76	2.84	2.16	0.85	3.54	2.87	3.72	-0.96

Significance levels:
[a] 0.1%
[b] 1%
[c] 5%
[d] 10%

[4] Using series of excess returns in the regression model shows the same reduction of alpha between the two periods; for example, the decrease in risk-free rate is not responsible for the decrease in alpha.

Table 4.4b Analysis of the exposure to risk factors in a multivariate framework

	Survivor			Dead			Existing			New		
	Short	Not exposed	Long	Short	Not exposed	Long	Short	Not exposed	Long	Short	Not exposed	Long
Alpha annualized	1%	40%	59%	3%	65%	32%	0%	23%	77%	0%	17%	83%
S&P 500	0%	30%	70%	6%	43%	51%	0%	26%	74%	1%	39%	61%
SMB	0%	34%	66%	5%	60%	35%	0%	52%	48%	3%	80%	17%
MOM	0%	45%	55%	2%	56%	43%	4%	57%	39%	1%	68%	31%
Chg LTIR	11%	82%	7%	16%	70%	14%	72%	28%	0%	70%	30%	0%
Chg HYS	39%	61%	0%	29%	71%	0%	45%	55%	0%	64%	35%	1%
TF Equity	1%	45%	54%	3%	49%	48%	7%	82%	11%	4%	82%	14%
TF STIR	0%	83%	17%	2%	70%	29%	0%	71%	29%	1%	67%	32%
TF Curncy	0%	65%	35%	0%	67%	33%	1%	55%	44%	2%	59%	39%
TF Comdty	0%	80%	20%	0%	71%	29%	1%	88%	11%	1%	93%	5%

Boldface figures reflect a significant coefficient in the multivariate regression at the portfolio level

The fact that dead FOFs disappear after the past period is not explained by a lack of alpha. Survivor FOFs do outperform dead FOFs in terms of alpha, but not significantly. The explanatory power of the model is high with most of the adjusted R^2 above 0.70. Because of that, alpha and beta values can be interpreted with a high degree of confidence. The explanatory power of zero-investment portfolios is greater than 0.50 (new–existing equally weighted being an exception), which is a very good score for portfolios of this type.

Returns of the past-period portfolios are explained mainly by equity factors, changes in high-yield spreads, and trend-following factors. It is worth noticing that alternative factors have a strong impact on improving the explanatory power. Although it remains significant, the exposure to equity factors during the recent period is reduced, which is linked to the bear stock market period starting in 2000. At the same time, the exposure to changes in long-term interest rates becomes significantly negative; for example, FOFs adjusted their asset allocation to take advantage of the decrease in interest rates. TF STIR and TF currency are the only alternative factors that are significant in the recent period. None of the portfolios in the recent period is significantly exposed to trends in equities. The transition from the bull stock market in the past period to a bear and then choppy market in the recent period certainly explains this change in exposure. It confirms the fact that FOFs are able to change their risk exposure to adjust to time-varying economic conditions. FOFs that cannot do it may be condemned to disappear.

The difference in performance between survivor and dead FOFs is triggered by significant differences in their risk exposures and not by a significant difference in alpha. As indicated by the results of the survivor–dead zero-investment portfolio, survivor FOFs are more exposed to equity risk and less to trends in short-term interest rates and currencies than dead FOFs. The lower exposure of dead FOFs to equity factors could be due to a greater allocation to arbitrage strategies.

Existing FOFs seem to have inherited their higher exposure to equity risk from their survivor period. In other words, FOFs that gained experience during the bull stock market period maintained a higher exposure to equity risk than new FOFs that were founded after the start of the bear stock market. The adjusted R^2 during the recent period are lower than those observed during the past period. This finding is an indication that new opportunities may have arisen whose risk exposure is not captured by our set of factors.

In summary, dead FOFs do not exhibit less alpha than the ones that survive. However, their risk exposure differs significantly. The conclusion about the difference between existing and new FOFs is different from a statistical point of view. Existing FOFs exhibit less alpha than the new ones and slightly different risk exposures. Given the lower explanatory power, the alpha of the new portfolio could incorporate the benefit of being invested in new alternative strategies.

Table 4.4b shows the proportion of long (positive), short (negative), and not significant (zero) exposures to the risk factors. Individual FOFs are regressed on the set of risk factors.[5] Then individual exposures to risk factors are cross-sectionally aggregated with respect to their sign and significance. Boldface figures mean that the coefficient in the multivariate regression at the portfolio level is significantly different from zero.

Survivor FOFs have a greater proportion of significantly positive alpha than dead FOFs (59% vs. 32%), which shows that even if the difference in alpha is not significant, survivor FOFs are more likely to have better skills than dead ones. The proportion of FOFs that generate significantly positive alpha is greater during the recent period than during the past period. This finding is consistent with the evolution of the information ratio over time and with the fact that FOFs reduce their volatility in the recent period. The 83% of new FOFs with significantly positive alpha mean that more than four out of five FOFs add performance through their skills. FOFs present in both periods are more likely to generate positive alpha during the recent period than during the past period (77% vs. 59%). It is the main difference between Table 4.4a and Table 4.4b. Therefore, the higher alphas observed in the past period are mostly due to a small number of FOFs and may not be representative of the FOF industry. Existing FOFs are not different from the new FOFs. They are as able as the new FOFs in selecting performing hedge funds. Given the fact that they have different risk exposures, both categories have success in selecting hedge funds in different styles.

The proportion of long exposure to equity risk factors is greater for survivor FOFs than for dead FOFs. The same is also true over the recent period between existing and new FOFs (see SMB and MOM). The short exposure to changes in credit spreads during the past period is driven by only a minority of FOFs in both survivor and dead portfolios. Exposures to trend-following factors are also driven by a small number of FOFs in each portfolio, most of the FOFs having no exposure to alternative factors. However, the fact that the exposure is always positive indicates a trend-following behavior. Overall, the absence of significance of one given coefficient is never due to an equal counting of long and short exposure.

During the past period, a large majority of FOFs are not exposed to changes in long-term interest rates. It changes radically during the recent period. About 70% of existing and new FOFs have a significantly negative exposure to the chg LTIR factor. The exposure to the trend-following equity factor also exhibits an important change. During the past period, half of the FOFs are positively exposed and the other half is not exposed. During the recent period, characterized by bear and choppy stock markets, the proportion of not exposed increases to 82%.

4.5.3 Decomposition of the performance with respect to FOF size

The size of an FOF seems to play an important role in its ability to survive or to generate performance. To control for that effect, we split each portfolio into

---

[5] We also examine the exposure to single risk factors by regressing individual FOF on each risk factor separately. The results are consistent with those of the multivariate analysis presented here. They give evidence of the robustness of our findings and are available on request.

three subportfolios (large, with AUM larger than USD 100 million; medium, between USD 30 million and USD 100 million; and small, with AUM smaller than USD 30 million). Results for the survivor and dead portfolios are presented in Table 4.5a.

Significant differences in risk exposures can be found between large survivor and dead FOFs as well as between small survivor and dead FOFs. They are explained mainly by a lower exposure of dead FOFs to equity risk and a higher exposure to trend-following factors.

Table 4.5b shows the results of the size portfolios during the recent period. Large and medium new FOFs are less explained by the factor model, highlighting the possible emergence of new opportunities not captured by the set of risk factors. The exposure of existing FOFs to equity risk increases with their size, whereas it decreases for new FOFs. As a consequence, the difference between large existing and new FOFs is well explained by their exposure to equity risk (adjusted R^2 equals 0.68). In addition, large new FOFs significantly outperform large existing ones in terms of alpha. The difference cannot be related to a lower volatility for large existing FOFs since their information ratio equals half of that of large new FOFs.

The difference between existing and new FOFs for the medium- and small-size categories is not explained by the alpha and only to a small extent by the risk exposures (adjusted R^2 of 0.38 and 0.32, respectively). Our set of factors includes broad systematic sources of risk and may not capture the particular risk profiles of niche strategies. If medium and small new FOFs invest in such niche strategies, our model would not be able to detect it. In order to test for the presence of niche effects, we have to adopt a different methodology.

In summary, differentiating FOFs by their size leads to mixed results. On one side, the differences in risk exposures between survivor and dead FOFs are exacerbated by extreme size (large or small). Large existing FOFs have a smaller alpha than large new FOFs and are much more exposed to equity risk. On the other side, size by itself does not improve significantly our level of understanding about why FOFs disappear or survive and why some of them perform better than others.

4.6   Principal components of FOF returns

One assumption to explain the difference between existing and new FOF performance is that new FOFs are more likely to invest in new alternative strategies. Our factor model would include the marginal performance of new opportunities in alpha. One way to test the new-opportunity assumption is to run a principal component analysis (PCA) and to check whether some principal components explaining the new sample are unique to this sample. The difference in performance between survivor and dead FOFs is driven mainly by differences in risk exposures. A PCA can also be used to identify principal components that are

Table 4.5a Factor decomposition of different-size portfolios (past period)

	Survivor			Dead			Survivor–dead		
	Large	Medium	Small	Large	Medium	Small	Large	Medium	Small
Alpha annualized	7.87%[a]	8.55%[a]	6.60%[a]	8.46%[a]	6.73%[b]	5.27%[b]	−0.59%	1.83%	1.32%
S&P 500	0.257[a]	0.181[a]	0.248[a]	0.084[d]	0.130[b]	0.148[a]	0.173[a]	0.051	0.100[c]
SMB	0.245[a]	0.224[a]	0.202[a]	0.091[d]	0.183[b]	0.116[c]	0.153[a]	0.042	0.086[d]
MOM	0.155[a]	0.151[a]	0.102[c]	0.080[c]	0.144[a]	0.069[d]	0.075[c]	0.006	0.034
Chg LTIR	0.417	−0.208	−0.595	−1.390[d]	−0.718	−0.830	1.807[b]	0.510	0.235
Chg HYS	−1.238[b]	−1.926[a]	−2.116[a]	−1.799[a]	−1.673[b]	−1.549[b]	0.561	−0.253	−0.567
TF Equity	0.180[a]	0.195[a]	0.197[a]	0.229[a]	0.217[a]	0.276[a]	−0.049	−0.022	−0.079[d]
TF STIR	0.063[d]	0.080	0.140[b]	0.120[c]	0.086	0.307[a]	−0.057	−0.006	−0.167[a]
TF Curncy	0.099[b]	0.114[c]	0.205[a]	0.206[a]	0.110[c]	0.256[a]	−0.107[b]	0.004	−0.050
TF Comdty	0.070[d]	0.115[c]	0.151[b]	0.153[b]	0.162[b]	0.168[b]	−0.083[d]	−0.047	−0.017
Adj. R^2	0.86	0.76	0.78	0.66	0.66	0.77	0.61	0.16	0.52
IR annualized	3.33	2.83	2.08	2.68	1.98	1.68	−0.22	0.75	0.48

Significance levels:
[a] 0.1%
[b] 1%
[c] 5%
[d] 10%

Table 4.5b Factor decomposition of different-size portfolios (recent period)

	Existing			New			Existing–new		
	Large	Medium	Small	Large	Medium	Small	Large	Medium	Small
Alpha annualized	3.85%[a]	4.94%[a]	4.86%[a]	5.96%[a]	4.97%[a]	4.53%[a]	−2.11%[b]	−0.03%	0.33%
S&P 500	0.222[a]	0.156[a]	0.134[a]	0.069[a]	0.125[a]	0.179[a]	0.153[a]	0.031[c]	−0.045[c]
SMB	0.145[a]	0.114[a]	0.124[a]	0.050[c]	0.078[b]	0.111[a]	0.095[a]	0.035[c]	0.012
MOM	0.033[c]	0.041[b]	0.012	0.019	0.025[d]	0.039[b]	0.014	0.015[d]	−0.027[c]
Chg LTIR	−1.314[a]	−1.423[a]	−1.819[a]	−1.140[a]	−1.085[a]	−1.279[a]	−0.174	−0.339[d]	−0.540[c]
Chg HYS	−0.576[b]	−0.429[c]	−0.582[b]	−0.700[a]	−0.645[a]	−0.424[c]	0.123	0.217[d]	−0.158
TF Equity	0.073[d]	0.035	0.049	0.025	0.066[c]	0.066[c]	0.048[d]	−0.031	−0.016
TF STIR	0.021	0.056[c]	0.094[b]	0.050[c]	0.023	0.047[d]	−0.029	0.033[c]	0.047[d]
TF Curncy	0.066[c]	0.088[b]	0.097[b]	0.094[a]	0.079[b]	0.076[b]	−0.028	0.010	0.021
TF Comdty	0.027	0.014	0.053[d]	0.020	0.015	0.005	0.007	−0.001	0.049[c]
Adj. R^2	0.79	0.75	0.72	0.66	0.68	0.76	0.68	0.38	0.32
IR Anualized	2.06	3.10	2.56	4.15	3.00	2.86	−1.53	−0.03	0.23

Significance levels:
[a] 0.1%
[b] 1%
[c] 5%
[d] 10%

unique to one of the samples and that could therefore better explain these differences. On a more general level, the PCA should help us describe better how the FOF industry has evolved from one period to the other.

4.6.1 Output of the principal component analysis

Our samples are large (63–250 FOFs) compared with the number of observations (60 months). This characteristic prevents us from using the random matrix theory as a limit of significance for the principal components (PC).[6] Therefore, we set a target level of cumulative explanatory power of 80%, and we consider only the principal components that help reach this limit. The explanatory power of PCs is presented in Table 4.6.

Over the past period, we find seven PCs for the total past sample, six for the dead sample, and five for the survivor ones. Survivor FOFs seem to be concentrated on a smaller number of hedge fund strategies than the dead ones. Over the recent period, 10 PCs represent 80% of the information related to the total recent and new samples, while five PCs suffice for the existing sample. The difference in number of PCs between new and existing FOFs is indirect evidence of the increased number of opportunities in the hedge fund industry. New FOFs seem to be better adapted to take advantage of these new opportunities.

For each specific sample (not considering the total period samples), the cumulative explanatory power of the first two PCs exceeds 60%. The only exception is the new sample, which is another piece of evidence that new FOFs invest more in niche strategies than do existing ones.

4.6.2 Correlation structure of principal components

We examine the correlations of principal components across samples in the same time period. For instance, we compute the correlation matrix between the principal components of survivor and dead (see Table 4.7, upper part). Correlations above 0.75 in absolute value are marked in boldface figures. Correlations between 0.25 and 0.75 in absolute value are marked in italic.

The PCs of the dead samples are cross-correlated with the first four PCs of the survivor sample. The survivor PC5 (last column of the upper part of Table 4.7) is unique to the survivor FOFs. New PC5 (fifth row of the bottom part of Table 4.7), new PC8, and new PC9 are uncorrelated with any of the five PCs of the existing sample. They should represent the new opportunities in the hedge fund industry that our set of risk factors is not able to capture. Therefore, they are worth some deeper examination, namely, of their links to hedge fund strategies.

---

[6] See Marchenko and Pastur (1967) for an explanation of the random matrix theory and Amenc and Martellini (2002) for an empirical example applied to the hedge fund industry. In short, the random matrix theory applies only asymptotically. The ratio between the number of observations and the number of FOFs is too small to lead to pertinent confidence intervals.

Table 4.6 PC explanatory power of FOF samples

PC	Total past		Survivor		Dead	
	Explanatory power	Cumulative	Explanatory power	Cumulative	Explanatory power	Cumulative
1	37.13%	37.13%	52.20%	52.20%	35.43%	35.43%
2	23.93%	61.06%	12.72%	64.92%	25.49%	60.92%
3	5.38%	66.43%	7.68%	72.60%	7.21%	68.13%
4	5.36%	71.79%	5.16%	77.76%	5.33%	73.46%
5	3.95%	75.74%	3.45%	81.20%	4.13%	77.59%
6	2.62%	78.36%			3.16%	80.74%
7	2.20%	80.57%				

PC	Total recent		Existing		New	
	Explanatory power	Cumulative	Explanatory power	Cumulative	Explanatory power	Cumulative
1	29.89%	29.89%	38.41%	38.41%	32.10%	32.10%
2	27.42%	57.31%	29.55%	67.96%	21.55%	53.65%
3	5.34%	62.65%	6.61%	74.57%	5.21%	58.87%
4	3.99%	66.64%	4.05%	78.62%	4.74%	63.61%
5	3.43%	70.08%	3.29%	81.91%	4.00%	67.61%
6	2.77%	72.84%			3.49%	71.10%
7	2.51%	75.36%			2.75%	73.85%
8	2.32%	77.68%			2.70%	76.55%
9	1.95%	79.63%			2.23%	78.78%
10	1.91%	81.53%			1.95%	80.73%

4.6.3 Specific hedge fund strategies offered by survivor and new FOFs

In order to examine the uniqueness of the uncorrelated PCs, we regress them on a broad set of hedge fund strategy indices (HFRI hedge fund strategy indices, Stark indices for managed futures strategies, and Goldman Sachs long-only commodity indices). Each uncorrelated PC is regressed on each index separately to estimate its single risk exposure. Results of the single regressions are presented in Table 4.8.[7]

The survivor PC5 is a combination of Healthcare/Biotech and Merger Arbitrage. The exposure to Healthcare/Biotech could partly explain why survivor FOFs are more exposed to equity risk (S&P 500 and SMB) than are dead FOFs. This exposure is unique to the survivor PC5. None of the dead PCs is statistically linked to this hedge fund strategy.

---

[7] Results for new PC8 and new PC9 are not shown because they were not significant and because of the low explanatory power of these principal components.

Table 4.7 Correlation matrices between PCs of the FOF samples

		Survivor				
		PC1	PC2	PC3	PC4	PC5
Dead	PC1	−0.42	0.75	0.31	−0.04	0.01
	PC2	0.87	0.37	0.10	0.03	0.10
	PC3	0.00	−0.21	−0.13	−0.33	0.16
	PC4	−0.04	0.05	−0.46	0.29	0.19
	PC5	−0.04	0.25	−0.42	−0.16	−0.20
	PC6	0.08	0.15	−0.09	−0.30	−0.02

		Existing				
		PC1	PC2	PC3	PC4	PC5
New	PC1	0.10	−0.91	0.29	−0.12	−0.13
	PC2	0.86	0.16	0.03	−0.24	−0.06
	PC3	−0.01	0.17	0.02	−0.36	−0.38
	PC4	−0.18	0.14	0.40	0.01	−0.18
	PC5	−0.11	0.02	−0.14	−0.09	−0.16
	PC6	0.06	0.06	0.24	−0.15	−0.32
	PC7	−0.26	−0.01	−0.10	−0.22	−0.19
	PC8	−0.08	0.05	0.15	0.05	0.03
	PC9	−0.11	0.02	0.05	0.00	0.19
	PC10	0.01	−0.11	−0.13	0.11	0.25

abs(corr) > 0.75
0.25 < abs(corr) < 0.75

A combination of Equity Market Neutral, Currency, Energy, and Natural Resources characterizes new PC5. The strong link to Equity Market Neutral is consistent with the smaller exposure of new FOFs to equity market risk than of existing FOFs. However, the link to Equity Market Neutral is not unique to new PC5. Three of the five existing PCs have exposure to that hedge fund strategy. Energy and Natural Resources in the commodity space are one of the new opportunities that have appeared in the recent period. The exposure to these sources of risk are not shared with any of the existing and other new PCs. New PC5 represents a new opportunity factor that is specific to new FOFs. The link we find between new FOFs and commodity indices could be even more pronounced if instead of long-only indices we could use factor-mimicking hedge fund strategies on commodities; see Erb and Harvey (2005) for an overview on dynamic strategies involving commodities.

In the previous section, our model had difficulties explaining the difference in performance between medium existing and new FOFs as well as between small existing and new FOFs. One explanation could be that medium and small new FOFs are more likely to invest in niche strategies. To test that, we use new PC5 as a proxy for one type of niche strategies. We regress the zero-investment

Table 4.8 Link between unique PCs and HF strategy indices

Strategy indices	Survivor PC5			New PC5		
	Beta	t-stat	R^2	Beta	t-stat	R^2
HFRI Equity Hedge	0.262	0.99	0.02	−0.192	−0.69	0.01
HFRI Equity Market Neutral	0.930	1.19	0.02	**1.699**	**2.39**	**0.09**
HFRI Short Selling	−0.042	−0.33	0.00	0.071	0.69	0.01
HFRI Sector: Energy	−0.161	−1.49	0.04	−0.160	−1.10	0.02
HFRI Sector: Healthcare/Biotech	**0.245**	**1.96**	**0.06**	0.086	0.74	0.01
HFRI Sector: Technology	0.064	0.54	0.01	−0.063	−0.51	0.00
HFRI Relative Value Arbitrage	−0.942	−1.50	0.04	0.583	0.56	0.01
HFRI Convertible Arbitrage	−1.203	−1.56	0.04	−0.142	−0.24	0.00
HFRI Fixed Income: Arbitrage	0.011	0.02	0.00	−0.747	−0.89	0.01
HFRI Event-Driven	−0.524	−1.44	0.03	−0.520	−1.60	0.04
HFRI Distressed Securities	−0.686	−1.67	0.05	−0.074	−0.18	0.00
HFRI Merger Arbitrage	**−1.321**	**−2.11**	**0.07**	−0.411	−0.60	0.01
HFRI Macro	0.036	0.12	0.00	−0.038	−0.10	0.00
HFRI Emerging Markets	−0.228	−1.67	0.05	−0.170	−0.89	0.01
Stark 300 Trader	−0.084	−0.33	0.00	0.011	0.05	0.00
Stark Agricultural Trader	0.039	0.09	0.00	−0.123	−0.65	0.01
Stark Currency Trader	−0.007	−0.02	0.00	**−0.814**	**−2.21**	**0.08**
Stark Systematic Trader	−0.106	−0.47	0.00	0.015	0.08	0.00
Stark Discretionary Trader	−0.087	−0.18	0.00	0.185	0.44	0.00
Goldman Sachs US Commodity	−0.202	−1.47	0.04	**0.221**	**2.54**	**0.10**
Goldman Sachs Livestocks	−0.109	−0.65	0.01	0.019	0.15	0.00
Goldman Sachs Natural Resources	N/A	N/A	N/A	**−0.203**	**−2.00**	**0.06**
Goldman Sachs Precious Metals	−0.335	−1.65	0.04	0.090	0.58	0.01
GS Energy Commodity	−0.103	−1.30	0.03	**0.147**	**2.48**	**0.10**
GS Industrial Metals Commodity	−0.280	−1.72	0.05	0.038	0.31	0.00

Figures in boldface are significant at the 5% level. Strategy indices in italic have unique exposures to the corresponding PC.

portfolios (overall, large, medium, and small) long existing FOFs and short new FOFs on new PC5. Results of the single regressions are presented in Table 4.9.

Only the medium and small portfolios have an exposure to new PC5 (significant at the 1% level). The explanatory power (R^2) reaches 0.14 for the medium portfolio and 0.18 for the small portfolio. These results help explain in what way medium and small new FOFs are different from medium and small existing ones. They are more exposed to new opportunities than any other type of FOFs. It is also interesting to note that the portfolio that is well explained by our factor model (large) is not exposed to new PC5. In other words, small and medium FOFs seem to be more likely to focus on niche strategies than large FOFs.

Table 4.9 Niche strategies to explain differences between existing and new FOFs

	Existing–new zero-investment portfolios			
	Overall	Large	Medium	Small
New PC5 Coefficient	0.012	−0.012	0.030[a]	0.049[a]
t-stat	1.23	−0.54	2.99	3.53
R^2	0.03	0.00	0.14	0.18

[a] Significant at 1% level.

4.7 Conclusion

In this study, we analyze the changes of the FOF industry during two time periods: the past period (January 1995 to December 1999) and the recent period (May 2000 to April 2005). In the past period, we examine the difference in performance between FOFs that survive and those that disappear afterwards. During the recent time period, we compare FOFs that already exist (the ones that survive the past period) with new FOFs (not present in the past period). The performance of FOFs is decomposed into an alpha term and risk exposures using a factor model. The model we develop includes both traditional and alternative risk factors and has a very satisfying explanatory power (above 65% for all portfolios).

FOFs that survive the past period outperform FOFs that disappear. Although the alpha of surviving FOFs is greater than that of disappearing FOFs, the difference is not statistically significant. More convincing differences are observed in the risk exposures. Surviving FOFs were more exposed to equity risk and less to trends in short-term interest rates and currencies. The disappearing sample is biased toward small FOFs in terms of AUM, while surviving FOFs are equally distributed between small-, medium-, and large-size categories.

Less difference is found between existing and new FOFs in the recent period. The explanatory power is lower for new FOFs than for existing ones, which shows that new opportunities in the hedge fund industry are characterized by new sources of risk. Indeed, the results of PCA indicate that one principal component of the new FOFs is uncorrelated with the PCs of the existing FOFs. The uncorrelated principal component is related to commodity sectors, which represents one of the major new strategies in the industry.

In summary, we show that even if the raw performance of FOFs decreases over time, their risk-adjusted performance increases. FOFs are still able to generate alpha, although the competition has grown strongly. The main difference in performance between FOFs that survive and those that disappear stems from their risk exposures. Surviving FOFs have changed their risk exposure to adjust to changes in the economic environment. New FOFs have invested in new opportunities, while existing FOFs use their experience to generate more performance from traditional hedge fund strategies.

Further research needs to be done in developing asset-based factors to replicate new strategies in the hedge fund industry. The main characteristic of new opportunities is the fact that they give access to new sources of risk. Energy, emissions, volatility, and credit strategies, real estate, emerging markets, and alternative risk transfer are examples of new opportunities hedge fund managers are investing in. From a factor decomposition perspective, their risk exposure cannot be caught by traditional risk factors. Going forward, the proportion of FOF performance that can be attributed to new opportunities will continue to grow. Therefore, the explanatory power of alternative risk factors is expected to increase as well.

References

Amenc, N. and Martellini, L. (2002). Portfolio Optimisation and Hedge-Fund-Style Allocation Decisions. *Journal of Alternative Investment*, 5(2):7–20.

Bacmann, J.-F. and Jeanneret, P. (2005). Funds of Funds Are Still Providing Alpha. *Hedgequest*, 1(1):22–26.

Carhart, M. M. (1997). On Persistence in Mutual Fund Performance. *Journal of Finance*, 52(1):57–82.

Erb, C. B. and Harvey, C. R. (2005). The Tactical and Strategic Value of Commodity Futures. Working Paper, Duke University, Durham, NC.

Fama, E. F. and French, K. R. (1993). Common Risk Factors in the Returns on Stock and Bonds. *Journal of Financial Economics*, 33(1):3–56.

Fung, W. and Hsieh, D. A. (2002). Benchmarks of Hedge Fund Performance: Information Content and Measurement Biases. *Financial Analyst Journal*, 58(5):22–34.

Fung, W. and Hsieh, D. A. (2004). Hedge Fund Benchmarks: A Risk-Based Approach. *Financial Analyst Journal*, 60(5):65–80.

Fung, W., Hsieh, D. A., Naik, N. Y., and Ramadorai, T. (2005). Hedge Funds: Performance, Risk and Capital Formation. Working Paper, London Business School, London.

Kundro, C. and Pfeffer, S. (2003). Understanding and Mitigating Operational Risk in Hedge Fund Investments. Capco White Paper, The Capital Markets Company Ltd.

Lequeux, P. and Acar, E. (1998). A Dynamic Index for Managed Currencies Funds Using CME Currency Contracts. *European Journal of Finance*, 4(4):311–330.

Marchenko, V. and Pastur, L. (1967). Eigenvalue Distribution in Some Ensembles of Random Matrices. *Math. USSR Sbornik*, 72:536–567.

5 Optimal fund of funds asset allocation: hedge funds, CTAs, and REITs

Alain Elkaim and Nicolas Papageorgiou

Abstract

We employ a four-moment polynomial goal programming technique to evaluate the relative importance of three alternative asset classes [commodity trading advisors (CTAs), hedge funds, and real estate income trusts (REITs)] for optimal fund of funds asset allocation. We construct two different types of funds of funds: stand-alone funds and funds that would be added to existing equal-weighted portfolios of stocks and bonds. Our results indicate that the composition of the optimal portfolio is sensitive to the type of fund as well as to the investor's preferences for the different moments. All three asset classes play a significant role in the construction of the optimal fund of funds. For the stand-alone fund of funds, the hedge fund strategies dominate, but the CTA and REIT indices are included when investors increase the weightings for the higher moments. In the funds of funds that are added to a stock and bond portfolio, the number of hedge fund strategies in the optimal portfolios is greatly reduced in favor of trend-following CTA strategies.

5.1 Introduction

Institutional investors, pension funds, and insurance companies are following the lead of high-net-worth investors and endowment funds by allocating a greater proportion of their portfolios to alternative asset classes. According to Greenwich Associates, 32% of European institutional investors put money in hedge funds in 2004, up from 23% in 2003. Morgan Stanley estimates that over 450 billion USD flowed into funds of hedge funds in 2004, a fivefold increase over 2000. The improvement of risk/return characteristics of these portfolios when hedge funds are introduced has been well documented; it results from the low correlation of hedge funds with stocks and bonds and their ability to produce positive returns under a variety of market conditions. Schneeweis and Martin (2001) show that directional hedge funds can be used as return enhancers in portfolios, whereas nondirectional hedge funds can be used as risk reducers. Fung and Hsieh (1997) and Liang (1999) find that little of the variability in hedge fund returns can be attributed to those of financial asset classes, and Agarwal and Naik (2000) extend this analysis to show that incorporating nondirectional hedge fund strategies into portfolios consisting of passive asset classes offers a superior risk–return trade-off than portfolios comprising solely of stocks and bonds.

More recently, however, practitioners and researchers have come to realize that a hidden cost is often associated with investing in alternative investment vehicles. The use of leverage and strategies with optionlike payoffs results in return distributions that are often skewed and fat-tailed. Amin and Kat (2003) show that although the inclusion of hedge funds in a portfolio may significantly improve that portfolio's mean-variance characteristics, it can also be expected to lead to significantly lower skewness and higher kurtosis.

The impact of negative skewness is particularly harmful to long-term returns. Most hedge fund strategies exhibit negative skewness in their return distributions, and this skewness increases when hedge funds are combined into portfolios. Furthermore, when those portfolios are combined with equity and bonds, the overall skewness of the portfolio drops even further. The increase in negative skewness will tend to offset the lower standard deviation that results from the inclusion of hedge funds. In other words, when adding hedge funds, the investor's downside risk might remain unchanged, while at the same time part of his upside potential is diversified away. Obviously this is not what investors are hoping for when opting to include hedge funds in their portfolios.

It is therefore imperative to consider the higher moments of the return distribution and not to limit oneself to strategies that are burdened with a negative skew. One interesting asset class that appears not to suffer from significant drawbacks in its higher moments is CTAs. Although there are two basic types of CTAs, discretionary and trend following, the investment category is dominated by trend followers (also known as *systematic traders*). In this approach, automated programs screen the markets using various technical factors to determine the beginning or end of a trend across different time frames. A successful trend follower will curb losses on losing trades and let the winners ride. That is, false trends are quickly exited and real trends are levered into. In a sense this is the distinguishing feature among trend-following CTAs. The good managers will quickly cut losses and increase their exposure to winning trades. In a sense, the alpha may come from this dynamic leverage. A trend-following strategy aims for a payout profile similar to a long option strategy, because, like a call option, the downside risk is to a certain extent limited and the upside potential rather open. This is in contrast to short option strategies, where one earns steady, small returns but is exposed to infrequent but large drawdowns that many hedge fund arbitrage strategies appear to provide. Kat (2005) finds that adding managed futures to a portfolio of stocks and bonds will reduce that portfolio's standard deviation more than hedge funds will, and without the undesirable side effects on skewness and kurtosis. Overall portfolio standard deviation can be reduced further by combining both hedge funds and managed futures with stocks and bonds.

A third class of assets that offers interesting diversification for stocks and bonds but that has not shared the recent spotlight with hedge funds and CTAs are REITs. The integration of REITs in a global mixed-asset portfolio strategy improves the global performance in the long run (Lee, 2005; Ibbotson, 2002), even when the direct real estate returns are considered in the asset mix (Feldman, 2003; Mueller and Mueller, 2003). Liang and McIntosh (1998) and Chiang and Lee (2002) show that not only are REITs returns difficult to replicate with traditional market factors, but the correlation of REITs returns with other risk factors are not stable over time. Although several studies find a certain level of integration between REITs and the other assets (stock markets, bonds, money market, direct real estate), the relations aren't stable over time. The correlation between REITs and large-cap stocks have tended to decline over time since the 1990s, while the correlation with small-cap stocks has increased (Clayton and MacKinnon, 2001). Mortgage REITs behave more like bonds, whereas equity REITs tend to behave more like value stocks and T-bills (Chiang and Lee, 2002).

The question we attempt to address in this chapter is how institutional portfolios can best profit from the alternative investment vehicles at their disposal. Our analysis goes beyond simply examining the benefits of including a fund of funds in a traditional portfolio; it looks at optimal allocation across a spectrum of alternative investments that offer varying return distribution characteristics.

5.2 Data

The data used in this chapter consists of eight hedge fund indices (seven style indices for hedge funds and a fund of funds index), six CTA indices, and three REIT indices from January 1994 to December 2002. This represents the maximum period for which we have reliable data for the three types of investment vehicles.

The hedge fund style indices are constructed using the funds listed in the HFR database (Hedge Fund Research, 2003). The data set comprises end-of-month returns net of all fees for all funds reporting to HFR. We construct equal-weighted indices for seven different hedge fund classifications (event driven, global macro, short, market neutral, long bias, sector, and global emerging) as well as an equal-weighted index for the fund of hedge funds category. We include live and dead funds during the period to eliminate any survivorship bias. In order for a given fund to be included in an index, it must have reported its results to HFR for a minimum of 12 successive months.

The CTA data is obtained from the Barclay Trading Group. The data set is composed of end-of-month returns for the global CTA Index as well as for six subindices. These subindices are the Barclay Currency Traders Index, the Barclay Financial and Metal Traders Index, the Barclay Systematic Traders Index, the Barclay Diversified Traders Index, the Barclay Discretionary Traders Index, and the Barclay Agriculture Traders Index.

The REIT data, obtained from the national association of real estate income trusts, comprises three total return indices on equity REITs, mortgage REITs, and hybrid REITs. The EREIT index (equity REIT index) aggregates the publicly traded REITs that own, or own an equity interest in, rental real estate. The MREIT index (mortgage REIT) aggregates the publicly traded REITs that make or own loan and other debt securities backed by real estate collateral. The HREIT index (hybrid REIT) aggregates the publicly traded REITs that combine the investment strategies of both equity REITs and mortgage REITs.

Table 5.1 presents the descriptive statistics for the 17 indices. The adjusted R^2 in the last column is the output from the six-factor regression in equation (5.1):

$$R_{i,t} = \alpha_i + \beta_{i,1}\text{Mkt}_t + \beta_{i,2}\text{SMB}_t + \beta_{i,3}\text{HML}_t$$
$$+ \beta_{i,4}\text{CORP}_t + \beta_{i,5}\text{UMD}_t + \beta_{i,6}\text{GOV}_t + \varepsilon_{i,t} \qquad (5.1)$$

where $R_{i,t}$ is the excess return of the ith index return over the 13-week T-Bill rate, Mkt_t is the excess return on the market portfolio, SMB_t is the size factor (small minus big), HML_t is the value premium factor (high minus low book-to-market value of equity), UMD_t is the momentum factor–mimicking portfolio (up minus down), GOV_t is the Salomon World Government Bond Index, and CORP_t is the credit spread between the AAA and BBB corporate bond indices.

The descriptive statistics in Table 5.1 for the 17 indices provide us with an interesting starting point for our analysis. It is quite clear that the return characteristics vary significantly across the different fund types and strategies. Almost all the lowest returns are produced by the CTAs, with the discretionary CTA having the unenviable attribute of being the only strategy to provide negative mean excess returns over the sample period. The CTAs do, however, all offer positively skewed distributions and generally lower standard deviations than do the hedge fund indices or REITS. With the exception of the Discretionary CTA, the other strategies are generally based on quantitative/technical analysis, and hence it is not surprising that the return characteristics are not greatly variable across the different futures markets.

The characteristics of the returns across the hedge fund strategies and REITs are more variable because the strategies and securities employed differ substantially. It is not surprising to see the strategies that generally offer the best returns are also burdened with the highest volatility and, more often than not, a negative skew. The sole exception is the Sector Fund Index, which not only offers the best returns but also has relatively low volatility and exhibits positive skewness. It does, nonetheless, possess relatively fat tails. On the whole, it is not surprising given their investment style, that most of the hedge fund indices suffer from negative skewness. This is a trait that is also shared with two of the three REIT indices. The latter also seem to offer interesting excess returns; however, their volatilities are among the highest of the 17 indices in our sample.

It is important to keep in mind that the inclusion of alternative investments in traditional portfolios not only is in the goal of enhancing returns, but more often than not is a means of diversifying the overall risk. In order to achieve this diversification, it is important to include strategies that are not exposed to the same risk factors as the rest of the portfolio. The adjusted R^2 in the last column

Table 5.1 Descriptive statistics for excess returns

	Mean	Median	Minimum	Maximum	Standard deviation	Skewness	Kurtosis	Adjusted R^2
Systematic Traders Index	0.25	−0.13	−7.07	7.08	2.94	0.28	0.04	0.19
Discretionary Traders Index	−0.18	−0.10	−3.07	3.88	1.33	0.33	0.46	0.06
Fin & Met Traders Index	0.12	−0.02	−4.67	5.90	2.34	0.46	0.11	0.22
Agriculture Traders Index	0.01	−0.11	−6.90	7.20	2.53	0.14	0.72	0.01
Currency Traders Index	0.06	−0.47	−4.05	7.00	2.08	1.12	1.25	0.01
Diversified Traders Index	0.32	−0.23	−6.86	9.73	3.37	0.35	−0.05	0.18
Fund of Funds Index	0.35	0.45	−7.29	6.12	1.76	−0.17	3.56	0.63
Event-Driven Index	0.58	0.84	−8.88	4.59	1.87	−1.11	4.96	0.74
Global Macro Index	0.44	0.20	−4.49	6.62	2.17	0.40	0.54	0.68
Short Fund Index	0.52	0.27	−14.06	12.81	4.51	0.07	0.65	0.79
Market Neutral Fund Index	0.67	0.70	−2.97	3.54	0.95	−0.29	1.36	0.55
Long Bias Fund Index	0.54	1.24	−17.87	12.85	5.81	−0.46	0.20	0.82
Sector Fund Index	1.29	1.76	−13.54	19.47	4.41	0.28	2.79	0.89
Global Emerging Fund Index	0.82	1.48	−22.28	13.91	5.03	−0.68	3.28	0.42
Equity REIT Index	0.45	0.58	−9.87	9.93	3.48	0.20	0.44	0.40
Mortgage REIT Index	0.67	1.61	−21.09	13.63	6.24	−0.84	1.63	0.32
Hybrid REIT Index	0.19	0.57	−16.28	13.97	4.97	−0.40	1.85	0.30

Excess returns are calculated as the difference between the returns on the indices and the return on the 3-month Treasury Bill over the same period. The adjusted R^2 in the last column is the output from the six-factor regression in equation (5.1).

of Table 5.1 provides evidence that the proportion of the excess returns of the different strategies that can be attributed to traditional market factors varies greatly across the different indices. Of the 17 indices, the six CTA indices have the lowest exposure to traditional market factors, reinforcing their position as strong diversifiers. The next three indices with the lowest R^2 are the REIT indices, with values between 0.3 and 0.4. Finally the hedge fund indices, with R^2 ranging from 0.42 for the Global Emerging Fund Index to 0.89 for the Sector Fund Index, seem to offer the least in terms of diversification potential. These results clearly indicate that there is a trade-off to be made between diversification and return enhancement using alternative investments. A fund of funds that seeks to create a stand-alone portfolio that provides competitive returns would be inclined to invest in hedge fund strategies, whereas a fund of funds manager who seeks to create a fund that would be a valuable addition to a traditional portfolio would likely invest a greater amount in CTAs and even REITs.

In order to better appreciate the joint behavior of the different strategies, Tables 5.2 and 5.3 present, respectively, the correlations and the co-skewnesses between the 17 indices. We compute co-skewness via one of the techniques proposed by Harvey and Siddique (2000). Specifically, the co-skewnesses are obtained by estimating the following regression:

$$r_{i,t} = \alpha_i + \text{Co-skew}_{i,j} r^2_{j,t} + \varepsilon_{i,t}$$

where $r_{i,t}$ and $r_{j,t}$ are the monthly returns for indices i and j, respectively.

5.3   Methodology

The methodology employed in order to decide on the asset allocation between the different investment strategies is a polynomial goal programming optimization model. This approach was introduced by Tayi and Leonard (1988), and has been employed by Chunhachinda, Dandapani, Hamid, and Prakash (1997) and Sun and Yan (2003) to incorporate the effect of skewness on portfolio allocation decisions. Davies, Kat, and Lu (2005) have used this approach to incorporate investor preferences for higher models into the construction of funds of funds. They extend the original model in order to account not only for skewness but also for the kurtosis that is prevalent in hedge fund return distributions. This approach allows one to solve for multiple, and often conflicting, objectives and to demonstrate the impact of a change in investor preferences on asset allocation.

In an ideal world, a fund of funds manager would be able to choose the constituents of the portfolio so as to maximize returns and skewness and minimize the volatility and kurtosis of the portfolio. Obviously, the return-maximizing portfolio is not consistent with the skewness-maximizing or kurtosis-minimizing portfolios. As a result, the fund of funds manager must decide on the optimal

Table 5.2 Correlation coefficient matrix across CTA indices, hedge funds indices, and REIT indices

	Syst. Index	Disc. Index	F&M Index	Agri. Index	Curr. Index	Div. Index	FOF Index	ED Index	GM Index	Short Index	MN Index	Long Index	Sect. Index	GE Index	ERT Index	MRT Index	HRT Index
Syst. Index	1.00																
Disc. Index	0.48	1.00															
F&M Index	0.92	0.45	1.00														
Agri. Index	0.06	0.38	0.01	1.00													
Curr. Index	0.65	0.36	0.61	−0.02	1.00												
Div. Index	0.98	0.53	0.87	0.09	0.54	1.00											
FOF Index	0.03	0.08	−0.04	−0.04	0.12	0.00	1.00										
ED Index	−0.15	−0.04	−0.19	0.00	−0.02	−0.19	0.85	1.00									
GM Index	0.17	0.19	0.14	−0.02	0.21	0.14	0.87	0.73	1.00								
Short Index	0.21	−0.04	0.23	−0.07	0.12	0.22	−0.64	−0.7	−0.67	1.00							
MN Index	−0.01	0.01	−0.10	0.01	0.07	−0.06	0.85	0.85	0.73	−0.57	1.00						
Long Index	−0.13	0.09	−0.16	0.03	−0.03	−0.15	0.80	0.83	0.78	−0.82	0.73	1.00					
Sect. Index	−0.11	0.06	−0.16	0.02	−0.02	−0.13	0.82	0.81	0.79	−0.84	0.74	0.87	1.00				
GE Index	−0.16	0.03	−0.20	−0.07	−0.03	−0.17	0.80	0.71	0.62	−0.56	0.65	0.66	0.61	1.00			
ERT Index	−0.05	0.09	−0.01	0.04	0.03	−0.06	0.30	0.42	0.23	−0.19	0.34	0.28	0.25	0.32	1.00		
MRT Index	0.05	0.10	0.07	−0.06	0.09	0.00	0.30	0.40	0.25	−0.21	0.38	0.29	0.19	0.33	0.48	1.00	
HRT Index	−0.12	0.11	−0.09	−0.05	−0.16	−0.10	0.13	0.32	0.06	−0.12	0.23	0.19	0.12	0.18	0.60	0.62	1.00

Table 5.3 Co-skewness coefficient matrix across CTA indices, hedge funds indices, and REIT indices

	Syst. Index	Disc. Index	F&M Index	Agri. Index	Curr. Index	Div. Index	FOF Index	ED Index	GM Index	Short Index	MN Index	Long Index	Sect. Index	GE Index	ERT Index	MRT Index	HRT Index
Syst. Index	9.62	24.32	15.28	0.97	15.65	7.54	9.64	8.28	7.37	0.85	23.98	1.14	0.74	0.83	0.86	0.79	0.60
Disc. Index	2.90	17.86	3.76	1.35	5.29	2.58	2.33	1.61	2.03	-0.09	5.31	0.23	0.05	0.14	0.04	0.30	0.50
F&M Index	7.66	15.00	14.01	-0.57	12.62	5.48	6.73	6.15	4.74	0.18	11.79	0.74	0.21	0.68	0.78	0.74	0.65
Agri. Index	-0.22	11.96	-1.38	6.16	-0.79	1.00	1.72	5.37	0.95	0.87	10.25	0.29	0.31	0.34	0.46	0.08	0.13
Curr. Index	6.59	17.88	9.44	-1.59	17.23	4.11	2.28	-0.74	4.17	-0.15	8.29	-0.33	-0.14	-0.04	-0.80	0.28	0.04
Div. Index	10.85	31.07	16.19	2.03	15.36	9.38	11.40	10.76	7.43	1.21	24.60	1.62	0.91	1.14	1.43	1.00	0.90
FOF Index	-1.16	2.80	-2.51	-1.31	2.47	-1.63	7.03	0.37	10.24	-1.08	46.04	-0.29	1.24	-0.38	-1.27	-0.55	-0.62
ED Index	-3.00	-1.67	-4.78	-1.62	0.73	-3.32	1.94	-0.27	6.72	-1.78	40.77	-0.81	0.63	-0.80	-1.16	-0.59	-0.90
GM Index	0.75	2.25	1.19	-2.89	4.86	-0.20	11.28	4.50	14.79	-1.21	58.50	0.19	1.88	0.04	-0.62	-0.11	-0.16
Short Index	2.16	-3.88	2.94	6.21	-0.17	2.86	-11.1	-4.19	-16.5	3.78	-89.0	-0.01	-3.18	0.75	2.40	0.61	1.04
MN Index	-0.58	1.09	-1.20	-0.19	1.01	-0.99	3.07	0.75	5.09	-0.25	29.78	-0.06	0.67	-0.24	-0.53	-0.30	-0.34
Long Index	-3.58	0.64	-5.35	-11.9	3.29	-5.24	13.92	4.08	22.47	-4.81	129.8	-1.14	3.06	-1.03	-2.79	-0.37	-0.79
Sect. Index	-2.88	4.32	-4.47	-8.25	2.27	-3.83	17.49	4.50	24.50	-2.28	114.2	-0.26	4.25	-0.79	-2.38	-0.56	-0.95
GE Index	-4.51	2.79	-11.1	-3.48	0.89	-4.95	6.38	-7.25	14.60	-4.24	76.96	-2.06	0.75	-0.78	-3.70	-1.88	-1.82
ERT Index	-0.54	8.93	-0.80	0.21	2.96	-1.85	-3.15	-3.85	1.76	-1.76	16.91	-1.46	-0.74	-1.12	6.94	-0.85	-0.58
MRT Index	-0.84	32.50	1.25	1.24	10.71	-4.05	-15.7	-11.5	-5.33	-4.57	30.48	-2.23	-2.14	-1.95	-0.76	-2.58	-0.80
HRT Index	-3.97	22.80	-3.63	4.87	-5.11	-4.27	-20.4	-11.2	-9.66	-3.16	-4.68	-1.85	-2.64	-2.69	3.34	-1.14	-0.80

trade-off between the four moments of the return distribution. The polynomial goal programming technique allows us to optimize the asset allocation for a given investor type by specifying his or her preference for each of the four moments and creating a portfolio that is best suited to the investor's needs.

We will define R as the vector of returns for the different hedge fund, CTA, and REIT indices, X as the vector containing the proportion of the portfolio allocated to each strategy, and V as the variance-covariance matrix. We do not allow for short selling, and we assume there exists a constant risk-free rate r at which investors can borrow and lend. All assets must either be invested in a style index or in the risk-free rate. The inclusion of the risk-free rate is critical because it produces a unique solution for the portfolio allocation that is independent of the variance. We can therefore set the variance to 1 (or any other constant) and run the optimization. For a given set of investor preferences, the portfolio optimization can then be expressed as

$$\text{Minimize} \quad Z = (1 + d_1)^\alpha + (1 + d_3)^\beta + (1 + d_4)^\gamma$$

subject to

$$E[X'R] + x_{rf}r + d_1 = Z_1^*$$
$$E[X'(R - E(R))]^3 + d_3 = Z_3^*$$
$$-E[X'(R - E(R))]^4 + d_4 = -Z_4^*$$
$$d_1, d_2, d_3 \geq 0$$
$$x_{rf} = 1 - I'X$$

where Z_1^* is the mean return for the optimal mean-variance portfolio, Z_3^* is the skewness value for the optimal skewness-variance portfolio, and Z_4^* is the kurtosis value for the optimal kurtosis-variance portfolio. The polynomial goal programming optimization is therefore a two-step procedure. First we must calculate the optimal values of Z_1^*, Z_3^*, and Z_4^* within a unit-variance two-dimensional framework. Then we incorporate these boundaries, as well as the investor preferences represented by α, β, and γ, into the four-moment optimization routine.

The portfolio optimization just described is performed for two types of portfolios. First we investigate the optimal construction for a stand-alone fund of funds for different levels of α, β, and γ. Next we consider optimal fund of funds allocation for an institutional investor that already possesses a diversified bond and stock portfolio. We assume the institutional investor seeks to invest 20% of its assets in alternative strategies. In the latter fund of funds, we must not only account for the co-moments between the alternative investment strategies, but also for the co-moments between the hedge fund, CTA, and REITs indices and the stock and bond returns.

5.4   Results

In this section we discuss the results obtained for the optimal portfolio allocation using the polynomial goal programming approach. In all there are four tables of results, two for the stand-alone portfolio and two for the tailor-made fund of funds that would be added to an already existing stock and bond portfolio.

5.4.1   Stand-alone fund of funds

Tables 5.4 and 5.5 present the optimal allocations across the 17 different strategies for a stand-alone fund of funds. In Table 5.4, the optimization is performed for a variety of investor preferences without imposing any constraints on the proportion invested in each strategy. Table 5.5 presents the results of the same optimizations; however, we impose the constraint that no more than 20% of the portfolio can be allocated to a given strategy, ensuring that the fund of funds is well diversified.

The results in Table 5.4 clearly show that the optimal allocations across the six CTA indices, eight hedge fund indices, and three REIT indices change significantly for different investor preferences. We do, however, note that certain strategies are consistently present in the portfolios, regardless of the weighting of the parameters α, β, and γ. Specifically, the Short and Sector fund indices are important components of the optimal stand-alone fund of funds.

From portfolios II, III, and IV we notice that as we increase the preference for returns (α) while maintaining the other parameters constant, the optimal fund of funds is composed of an increasingly large proportion of hedge fund strategies, specifically Short, Market Neutral, and Sector, with only a small allocation being made to CTA indices and nothing invested in REITs. This is hardly surprising, for, on the whole, the hedge fund strategies have the highest returns over the sample period. It is interesting to note, nonetheless, that the three main holdings have very different market exposures. The Short fund would excel in a bear market, whereas the Sector fund would perform best in a bull market (the correlation coefficient in Table 5.2 between the return series of these two funds is -0.84). Since our sample period from 1994 to 2003 incorporates both the strong bull market of the late 1990s and the ensuing strong correction after the dot-com crash, it is not surprising to find these two conflicting strategies in our fund of funds. A similar optimization on a subsample of the data would surely yield quite different results. The third strategy, the Market Neutral Index, in theory should not be affected by the trend of the overall market. However, we note that the Market Neutral would appear to have a long bias (or at least to perform better in bull markets) because its returns are negatively correlated with the Short fund index and positively correlated with the Sector fund index (see Table 5.2).

The more surprising results were obtained when increasing the weighting for skewness (β) while keeping the other parameters constant (portfolios V, VI, and VII). From the descriptive statistics in Table 5.1, we would have expected to see

Table 5.4 Optimal asset allocation for a stand-alone fund of funds, given investor's preferences over expected returns (α), skewness (β), and kurtosis (γ)

	Portfolio									
	I	II	III	IV	V	VI	VII	VIII	IX	X
α	1.00	0.00	3.00	6.00	1.00	1.00	1.00	1.00	1.00	1.00
β	1.00	1.00	1.00	1.00	0.00	2.00	4.00	1.00	1.00	1.00
γ	1.00	1.00	1.00	1.00	1.00	1.00	1.00	0.00	2.00	4.00
Systematic Index	0.00%	0.00%	0.00%	0.00%	0.00%	0.00%	0.00%	0.00%	0.00%	0.00%
Discretionary Index	14.06%	22.12%	0.00%	0.00%	1.17%	0.00%	0.00%	0.00%	24.30%	29.51%
Fin & Met Index	8.00%	9.02%	2.14%	0.00%	15.68%	3.76%	0.00%	0.00%	9.26%	7.53%
Agriculture Index	0.00%	0.00%	0.00%	0.00%	23.06%	0.00%	0.00%	0.42%	0.00%	0.00%
Currency Index	0.00%	0.00%	0.00%	0.00%	0.00%	0.00%	0.00%	0.00%	0.00%	0.00%
Diversified Index	6.36%	5.28%	8.63%	6.39%	0.00%	7.07%	2.59%	0.00%	6.12%	1.03%
Fund of Funds Index	0.00%	0.00%	0.00%	0.00%	0.00%	0.00%	0.00%	0.00%	0.00%	0.00%
Event-Driven Index	0.00%	5.42%	0.00%	0.00%	0.00%	0.00%	0.00%	0.00%	7.30%	0.00%
Global Macro Index	0.00%	0.00%	0.00%	0.00%	0.00%	0.00%	0.00%	0.00%	0.00%	3.55%
Short Fund Index	24.55%	24.76%	26.68%	29.99%	13.89%	26.28%	30.20%	32.33%	23.95%	25.65%
Market Neutral Index	14.56%	2.10%	31.17%	30.82%	22.30%	31.46%	34.97%	34.45%	0.00%	0.00%
Long Bias Fund Index	4.82%	3.59%	5.96%	1.23%	1.69%	1.01%	0.00%	0.00%	5.23%	5.65%
Sector Fund Index	23.57%	23.24%	23.16%	28.99%	15.20%	27.97%	32.24%	32.80%	19.16%	10.11%
Global Emerging Index	2.77%	3.75%	0.95%	2.58%	0.00%	2.12%	0.00%	0.00%	3.91%	7.09%
Equity REIT Index	0.00%	0.00%	0.00%	0.00%	0.00%	0.00%	0.00%	0.00%	0.00%	9.87%
Mortgage REIT Index	0.00%	0.00%	0.00%	0.00%	7.03%	0.00%	0.00%	0.00%	0.00%	0.00%
Hybrid REIT Index	1.32%	0.72%	1.31%	0.00%	0.00%	0.34%	0.00%	0.00%	0.79%	0.00%
Return	0.95	0.88	1.09	1.15	0.86	1.13	1.18	1.19	0.83	0.74
Skewness	0.31	0.32	0.18	0.23	−0.04	0.28	0.29	0.30	0.31	0.29
Kurtosis	2.08	2.05	2.23	2.48	1.96	2.39	2.71	2.82	2.04	1.93

Table 5.5 Optimal asset allocation for a stand-alone fund of funds, given investor's preferences over expected returns (α), skewness (β), and kurtosis (γ) and maximum allocation of 20% per strategy

					Portfolio					
	I	II	III	IV	V	VI	VII	VIII	IX	X
α	1.00	0.00	3.00	6.00	1.00	1.00	1.00	1.00	1.00	1.00
β	1.00	1.00	1.00	1.00	0.00	2.00	4.00	1.00	1.00	1.00
γ	1.00	1.00	1.00	1.00	1.00	1.00	1.00	0.00	2.00	4.00
Systematic Index	0.00%	0.00%	0.00%	0.00%	0.00%	0.00%	0.00%	0.00%	0.00%	0.00%
Discretionary Index	12.36%	17.61%	0.00%	0.00%	20.00%	0.00%	0.00%	0.00%	20.00%	0.00%
Fin & Met Index	0.00%	0.00%	9.38%	3.73%	2.70%	13.59%	12.67%	10.38%	8.58%	8.76%
Agriculture Index	0.00%	0.00%	4.61%	2.25%	0.00%	1.73%	2.79%	3.17%	0.00%	2.40%
Currency Index	16.43%	13.71%	0.00%	0.00%	8.40%	0.00%	0.00%	0.00%	0.00%	0.00%
Diversified Index	4.85%	5.53%	8.52%	11.89%	4.70%	2.73%	0.00%	0.77%	9.26%	20.00%
Fund of Funds Index	0.00%	0.00%	0.00%	0.00%	0.69%	0.00%	0.00%	0.00%	0.00%	0.00%
Event-Driven Index	0.00%	0.00%	11.87%	20.00%	0.00%	2.45%	1.14%	3.55%	16.07%	0.00%
Global Macro Index	0.00%	0.00%	0.00%	0.00%	0.00%	15.22%	20.00%	19.48%	0.00%	0.00%
Short Fund Index	20.00%	20.00%	20.00%	20.00%	20.00%	20.00%	20.00%	20.00%	20.00%	19.21%
Market Neutral Index	20.00%	15.69%	20.00%	20.00%	14.43%	20.00%	20.00%	20.00%	0.00%	8.26%
Long Bias Fund Index	1.80%	4.04%	3.26%	0.00%	8.44%	0.00%	0.00%	0.00%	5.63%	13.70%
Sector Fund Index	7.40%	6.75%	20.00%	20.00%	2.50%	20.00%	20.00%	20.00%	18.66%	20.00%
Global Emerging Index	4.04%	3.25%	0.00%	0.91%	2.54%	1.39%	0.00%	0.00%	0.00%	0.89%
Equity REIT Index	13.12%	13.43%	0.00%	0.00%	15.61%	1.05%	3.39%	2.64%	0.00%	0.00%
Mortgage REIT Index	0.00%	0.00%	1.28%	1.23%	0.00%	0.00%	0.00%	0.00%	1.56%	4.44%
Hybrid REIT Index	0.00%	0.00%	1.07%	0.00%	0.00%	1.85%	0.00%	0.00%	0.24%	2.34%
Return	0.81	0.77	1.00	1.04	0.73	0.99	0.99	1.00	0.85	0.97
Skewness	0.40	0.38	0.21	0.16	0.26	0.42	0.49	0.46	0.30	0.25
Kurtosis	2.16	2.08	2.18	2.38	1.98	2.36	2.56	2.59	2.05	2.01

a significant allocation to CTA strategies. However, we find that their propor-tion in the portfolio decreases as β increases. As a matter of fact, we once again allocate almost the entirety of our fund of funds to the same three hedge fund strategies that were present in portfolios II, III, and IV — the Sector fund, the Short fund, and the Market Neutral fund. Although these funds do not possess the highest individual skewness coefficients (the Market Neutral fund actually has a negative skewness coefficient), it would appear that they possess co-skewness properties that make them desirable when combined in a portfolio. In Table 5.3, we can note that the co-skewness between the three fund indices is gener-ally negative. This result leads us to believe that skewness shares an important property with volatility. In creating a mean-variance-optimal portfolio, it is imperative to consider the covariance of the assets, because much of the over-all variance can be diversified away. It would appear that the same logic applies when we consider the higher moments of the distribution. It is not sufficient to look at the individual skewness of assets in order to ascertain their potential benefits within a portfolio; it is also vital to account for the co-skewness of the different assets in order to construct an efficient portfolio.

Portfolios VIII, IX, and X present the impact of an increase in the γ coefficient on the allocation across the 17 indices of the optimal portfolio. We clearly observe a shift away from the three strategies that have dominated our portfolios so far (Short, Market Neutral, and Sector indices). We notice in portfolio X that although we continue to favor the Short fund strategy, with over 25% of our portfolio allocated to this index, the investment in Market Neutral drops to zero, and only 10% are invested in the Sector fund. This is a significant drop from the nearly 95% allocated to these three strategies in our high-β portfolio (VII). We find that in a high-γ (low-kurtosis) portfolio, there is an important redis-tribution of assets toward CTA and REIT indices. The discretionary CTA is the most significant beneficiary because 29.51% of assets are invested in the index in portfolio X. Of the six CTA indices, this is the only non-systematic strategy, and its return distribution greatly resembles that of a Global Macro fund. It is therefore not surprising to note that there is a small proportion of the high-γ portfolio that is also allocated to the Global Macro fund index. The systematic CTAs play a smaller but nonnegligible role in the high-γ portfolio, for both the Financials and Metals Index and the Diversified Index are included in the fund of funds. The REIT indices, which were not incorporated in the previous port-folios, seem to offer some value when trying to reduce the overall kurtosis; hence they are allocated a significant proportion (nearly 10%) of the high-γ fund of funds. This result is reinforced by descriptive statistics in Table 5.1, which show that the Equity REIT Index has among the lowest levels of excess kurtosis (0.44) among the 17 indices.

The next step in our analysis is to limit the maximum allocation to any one strat-egy to 20% of the overall fund of funds. This constraint is imposed to ensure suf-ficient diversification across investment styles, a real concern for fund of funds managers. The results for the optimal constrained fund of funds are presented in Table 5.5. Not surprisingly, the return, skewness, and kurtosis obtained in Table 5.5

for the constrained portfolios (last three rows) are lower than the corresponding values in Table 5.4. Style diversification comes at the cost of less attractive performance.

On the whole, the inclusion of the constraint results in an increase in the proportion of CTA and REIT indices in the portfolios. For example, in the low-α and low-β portfolios the majority of the assets are allocated to CTA and REIT indices.

There is also an interesting side effect of imposing this constraint. A priori, we would expect the strategies that had allocations greater than 20% in the unconstrained portfolios to see their allocation reduced to no less than 20%. However, this is not always the case. By limiting the possible allocations to a given style, we need to include other strategies in the portfolio in order to be fully invested. On occasion, the inclusion of these strategies leads to a significant reallocation of funds and even to the exclusion of a previously dominant strategy. For example, in the high-γ portfolio, the allocation to the Discretionary CTA Index drops from 29.5% in Table 5.4 to 0% in Table 5.5. The main beneficiary is the Diversified CTA.

5.4.2 Fund of funds integrated in an existing stock and bond portfolio

Tables 5.6 and 5.7 present the optimal allocations across the 17 different strategies for a fund of funds that would be added to an existing stock and bond portfolio. We assume that the fund of funds will comprise 20% of the overall portfolio, the other 80% being made up of an equal proportion of stocks and bonds. In Table 5.6, the optimization is performed for a variety of investor preferences without imposing any constraints on the proportion invested in each strategy. Table 5.7 presents the results of the same optimizations, however, we impose the constraint that no more than 20% of the fund of funds portfolio can be allocated to a given strategy, ensuring that the fund of funds is well diversified.

The results in Table 5.6 indicate that two strategies are dominant when we construct a fund of funds that would be added to an existing equal-weight portfolio of stocks and bonds. The Short Fund Index and the Diversified CTA Index are the only two funds included in the optimal portfolios, irrespective of the preference for higher moments. The results are not surprising, for the Short Fund will reduce the overall directional exposure of the portfolio to the stock market (the correlation between the two is -0.73), and the trend-following nature of the diversified CTA Index provides an effective risk diversifier. It is also interesting to note that although we invest in only two strategies, the proportion changes significantly as we change the investor's preferences. For example, the high-α portfolio (portfolio IV) is totally invested in the Short Fund Index, whereas the high-γ portfolio (portfolio X) has 68% of its assets invested in the Diversified CTA Index. Also noteworthy is that the Sector Fund, which

Table 5.6 Optimal asset allocation, given investor's preferences over expected returns (α), skewness (β), and kurtosis (γ), for a fund of funds that is being added to an equal-weighted stock and bond portfolio

	Portfolio									
	I	II	III	IV	V	VI	VII	VIII	IX	X
α	1.00	0.00	6.00	12.00	1.00	1.00	1.00	1.00	1.00	1.00
β	1.00	1.00	1.00	1.00	0.00	6.00	12.00	1.00	1.00	1.00
γ	1.00	1.00	1.00	1.00	1.00	1.00	1.00	0.00	6.00	12.00
Systematic Index	0.00%	0.00%	0.00%	0.00%	0.00%	0.00%	0.00%	0.00%	0.00%	0.00%
Discretionary Index	0.00%	0.00%	0.00%	0.00%	0.00%	0.00%	0.00%	0.00%	0.00%	0.00%
Fin & Met Index	0.00%	0.00%	0.00%	0.00%	0.00%	0.00%	0.00%	0.00%	0.00%	0.00%
Agriculture Index	0.00%	0.00%	0.00%	0.00%	0.00%	0.00%	0.00%	0.00%	0.00%	0.00%
Currency Index	0.00%	0.00%	0.00%	0.00%	0.00%	0.00%	0.00%	0.00%	0.00%	0.00%
Diversified Index	45.80%	55.05%	13.85%	0.00%	55.40%	36.30%	34.30%	16.60%	64.90%	67.90%
Fund of Funds Index	0.00%	0.00%	0.00%	0.00%	0.00%	0.00%	0.00%	0.00%	0.00%	0.00%
Event-Driven Index	0.00%	0.00%	0.00%	0.00%	0.00%	0.00%	0.00%	0.00%	0.00%	0.00%
Global Macro Index	0.00%	0.00%	0.00%	0.00%	0.00%	0.00%	0.00%	0.00%	0.00%	0.00%
Short Fund Index	54.20%	44.95%	86.15%	100.00%	44.60%	63.70%	65.70%	83.40%	35.10%	32.10%
Market Neutral Index	0.00%	0.00%	0.00%	0.00%	0.00%	0.00%	0.00%	0.00%	0.00%	0.00%
Long Bias Fund Index	0.00%	0.00%	0.00%	0.00%	0.00%	0.00%	0.00%	0.00%	0.00%	0.00%
Sector Fund Index	0.00%	0.00%	0.00%	0.00%	0.00%	0.00%	0.00%	0.00%	0.00%	0.00%
Global Emerging Index	0.00%	0.00%	0.00%	0.00%	0.00%	0.00%	0.00%	0.00%	0.00%	0.00%
Equity REIT Index	0.00%	0.00%	0.00%	0.00%	0.00%	0.00%	0.00%	0.00%	0.00%	0.00%
Mortgage REIT Index	0.00%	0.00%	0.00%	0.00%	0.00%	0.00%	0.00%	0.00%	0.00%	0.00%
Hybrid REIT Index	0.00%	0.00%	0.00%	0.00%	0.00%	0.00%	0.00%	0.00%	0.00%	0.00%
Return	0.80	0.80	0.85	0.90	0.80	0.80	0.80	0.85	0.75	0.75
Skewness	0.22	0.26	0.12	0.08	0.26	0.19	0.18	0.13	0.29	0.30
Kurtosis	3.55	3.55	3.54	3.55	3.55	3.54	3.54	3.54	3.50	3.47

Note: The fund of funds represents 20% of the total portfolio. The other 80% is an equal-weighted stock and bond portfolio.

Table 5.7 Optimal asset allocation, given investor's preferences over expected returns (α), skewness (β), and kurtosis (γ), for a fund of funds that is being added to an equal-weighted stock and bond portfolio

	Portfolio									
	I	II	III	IV	V	VI	VII	VIII	IX	X
α	1.00	0.00	6.00	12.00	1.00	1.00	1.00	1.00	1.00	1.00
β	1.00	1.00	1.00	1.00	0.00	6.00	12.00	1.00	1.00	1.00
γ	1.00	1.00	1.00	1.00	1.00	1.00	1.00	0.00	6.00	12.00
Systematic Index	20.0%	20.0%	20.0%	0.00%	20.0%	20.0%	20.0%	20.0%	20.0%	20.0%
Discretionary Index	0.00%	0.00%	0.00%	0.00%	0.00%	0.00%	0.00%	0.00%	0.00%	0.00%
Fin & Met Index	20.0%	20.0%	0.00%	0.00%	20.0%	20.0%	20.0%	20.0%	20.0%	20.0%
Agriculture Index	0.00%	0.00%	0.00%	0.00%	0.00%	0.00%	0.00%	0.00%	0.00%	0.00%
Currency Index	0.00%	0.00%	0.00%	0.00%	0.00%	0.00%	0.00%	0.00%	0.00%	0.00%
Diversified Index	20.0%	20.0%	20.0%	20.0%	20.0%	20.0%	20.0%	20.0%	20.0%	20.0%
Fund of Funds Index	0.00%	0.00%	0.00%	0.00%	0.00%	0.00%	0.00%	0.00%	0.00%	0.00%
Event-Driven Index	0.00%	0.00%	0.00%	20.0%	0.00%	0.00%	0.00%	0.00%	0.00%	0.00%
Global Macro Index	0.00%	0.00%	0.00%	0.00%	0.00%	0.00%	0.00%	0.00%	0.00%	0.00%
Short Fund Index	20.0%	20.0%	20.0%	20.0%	20.0%	20.0%	20.0%	20.0%	20.0%	20.0%
Market Neutral Index	20.0%	20.0%	20.0%	20.0%	20.0%	20.0%	20.0%	20.0%	20.0%	20.0%
Long Bias Fund Index	0.00%	0.00%	0.00%	0.00%	0.00%	0.00%	0.00%	0.00%	0.00%	0.00%
Sector Fund Index	0.00%	0.00%	20.0%	0.00%	0.00%	0.00%	0.00%	0.00%	0.00%	0.00%
Global Emerging Index	0.00%	0.00%	0.00%	0.00%	0.00%	0.00%	0.00%	0.00%	0.00%	0.00%
Equity REIT Index	0.00%	0.00%	0.00%	0.00%	0.00%	0.00%	0.00%	0.00%	0.00%	0.00%
Mortgage REIT Index	0.00%	0.00%	0.00%	0.00%	0.00%	0.00%	0.00%	0.00%	0.00%	0.00%
Hybrid REIT Index	0.00%	0.00%	0.00%	0.00%	0.00%	0.00%	0.00%	0.00%	0.00%	0.00%
Return	0.75	0.75	1.00	1.05	0.75	0.75	0.75	0.75	0.75	0.75
Skewness	0.17	0.20	0.01	0.16	0.19	0.17	0.17	0.17	0.17	0.17
Kurtosis	3.11	3.18	2.76	2.44	3.18	3.11	3.11	3.11	3.11	3.11

Note: A maximum allocation of 20% of the fund of funds is permitted per strategy. The fund of funds represents 20% of the total portfolio. The other 80% is an equal-weighted stock and bond portfolio.

previously was a dominant component of the stand-alone fund of funds (Tables 5.4 and 5.5) disappears entirely from the optimal asset allocations in Table 5.6. This can be explained by the common properties of Sector Fund returns and those of the Stock Index. The Market Neutral strategy is also eliminated from the optimal portfolios, for it doesn't seem to be an ideal complement to the existing stock and bond portfolio.

These results confirm our expectation that the optimal asset allocation for a fund of funds being added to an existing portfolio is significantly different from that of a stand-alone fund of funds.

With the constraint of 20% per strategy within the fund of funds, the results are more predictable than for the stand-alone fund. The Diversified CTA Index and the Short Fund Index obtain the maximum allocation for all 10 optimal portfolios. The Market Neutral Fund, which was notably absent in Table 5.6, is once again an important asset in all portfolios. Although not a first-choice addition to a stock and bond portfolio, the Market Neutral Fund nonetheless possesses beneficial return characteristics. The non-discretionary CTA indices also play an important role in the asset allocation. With the exception of the high-α portfolios (portfolios III and IV), in which the Sector Fund provides a strong source of return enhancement, the CTA indices consistently make up 60% of the fund of funds. The null allocation to the REIT indices for the 10 portfolios indicates that for our sample period, there exist better alternative investment strategies for stock and bond portfolios in order to satisfy the investor's objectives.

5.5   Conclusion

In this chapter we employed a four-moment polynomial goal programming technique to evaluate the relative importance of three alternative asset classes in optimal fund of funds allocations. This approach was proposed and applied on a data set of seven different hedge fund styles by Davies, Kat, and Lu (2005). We extended their study to consider CTAs and REITs. We constructed two different types of fund of funds: stand-alone funds and funds that would be added to existing equal-weighted portfolios of stocks and bonds. We calculated the optimal asset allocations, given investor preferences, for the two types of funds of funds, with and without constraints on the maximum allocation to a given strategy.

In accordance with Davies, Kat, and Lu (2005), we noted an important change in the optimal combination of assets conditional on the investor preferences for the different moments. In the stand-alone portfolio, the Short Fund, Market Neutral Fund, and Sector Fund are the most dominant strategies, but a significant investment in both CTA and REIT indices is obtained when the weighting for the higher moments is increased. When we undertake the optimization for a fund of fund that will be added to a stock and bond portfolio, the results are considerably different. We find a greater allocation toward the nondiscretionary CTA indices (generally 60% of the total allocation in the constrained optimization), and we also note that certain hedge fund strategies that were present in the stand-alone fund of funds are not compatible with stocks and bonds. Specifically, the Sector Fund as well as the Discretionary CTA and Macro Funds no longer provide added value.

Acknowledgments

The authors would like to thank Olivier Marquis for his significant contribution to this work.

References

Agarwal, V. and Naik, N. (2000). On Taking the Alternative Route: Risks, Rewards, and Performance Persistence of Hedge Funds. *Journal of Alternative Investments*, 2(4):6–23.

Amin, G. and Kat, H. (2003). Stocks, Bonds and Hedge Funds: Not a Free Lunch! *Journal of Portfolio Management*, 30(2):113–120.

Chiang, K. C. H. and Lee, M.-L. (2002). REITs in the Decentralized Investment Industry. *Journal or Property Investment and Finance*, 20:496–512.

Chunhachinda, P., Dandapani, K., Hamid, S., and Prakash, A. (1997). Portfolio Selection and Skewness: Evidence from International Stock Markets. *Journal of Banking and Finance*, 21(2):143–167.

Clayton, J. and MacKinnon, G. (2001). The Time-Varying Nature of the Link Between REIT, Real Estate and Financial Returns. *Journal of Real Estate Portfolio Management*, 7:43–54.

Davies, R., Kat, H., and Lu, S. (2005). Fund of Hedge Fund Portfolio Selection: A Multiple Objective Approach. Working Paper, Babson College, Babson Park, MA.

Feldman, B. E. (2003). Investment Policy for Securitized and Direct Real Estate. *Journal of Portfolio Management*, 29(5):112–121.

Fung, W. and Hsieh, D. (1997). Empirical Characteristics of Dynamic Trading Strategies: The Case of Hedge Funds. *Review of Financial Studies*, 10(2):275–302.

Harvey, C. and Siddique, A. (2000). Conditional Skewness in Asset Pricing Tests. *Journal of Finance*, 55(3):1263–1295.

Hedge Fund Research, Inc. (2003). Chicago, IL (http://www.hedgefund research.com).

Ibbotson Associates. (2002). Diversification Benefits of REITs, an Analysis. Ibbotson Associates (http://www.nareit.com).

Kat, H. (2005). Integrating Hedge Funds into the Traditional Portfolio. *Journal of Wealth Management*, 7(4):51–58.

Lee, S. (2005). Case for REITs in the Mixed-Asset Portfolio in the Short and the Long Run. *Journal of Real Estate Portfolio Management*, 11(1):55–80.

Liang, B. (1999). On the Performance of Hedge Funds. *Financial Analysts Journal*, 55(4):72–85.

Liang, Y. and McIntosh, W. (1998). REIT Style and Performance. *Journal of Real Estate Portfolio Management*, 4(1):69–78.

Mueller, A. G. and Mueller, G. R. (2003). Public and Private Real Estate in the Mixed Asset Portfolio. *Journal of Real Estate Portfolio Management*, 9(3):193–203.

Schneeweis, T. and Martin, G. (2001). The Benefits of Hedge Funds: Asset Allocation for the Institutional Investor. *Journal of Alternative Investments*, 4(3):7–26.

Sun, Q. and Yan, Y. (2003). Skewness Persistence with Optimal Portfolio Selection. *Journal of Banking and Finance*, 27(6):1111–1121.

Tayi, G. and Leonard, P. (1988). Bank Balance Sheet Management: An Alternative Multiobjective Model. *Journal of Operations Research Society*, 39(4):401–410.

6 The changing performance and risks of funds of funds in the modern period

Keith H. Black

Abstract

How do funds of funds compare to hedge fund investments? We will compare a fund of funds index to a diversified hedge fund index and an index of multistrategy hedge funds. Fees, returns and risk, and the value added by managers of funds of funds will be analyzed. How do the return profiles for each hedge fund index differ in bull vs. bear equity markets? We will also compare each index to underlying factors, such as equity market returns and volatility and fixed-income returns and credit spreads, showing how each index may differ in its underlying factor exposures.

6.1 Characteristics of funds of funds

There are many differences between an investment in a single-manager hedge fund and a fund of funds. Black (2004) and Ineichen (2003) describe the characteristics of funds of hedge funds (FOFs) and how they differ from single-manager hedge funds. The first and most important difference between hedge funds and funds of funds is the diversification of the fund. A single-manager hedge fund has risk concentrated in a single manager and a single trading strategy. If the manager turns out to be dishonest or unskilled, the investor can lose a large portion of the investment or even the entire investment in the fund. Similarly, if the fund specializes in convertible bond arbitrage, the fund will have significant exposures to the risk and returns inherent in that trading strategy. Most funds of funds are highly diversified, investing client assets in over 25 single-manager hedge funds employing at least five different investment styles. The failure of a single fund investment within a fund of funds will typically cause a loss of less than 5% of capital, which significantly reduces the investor's potential loss caused by this type of event. Second, the fund of funds offers the investor the opportunity to make a single investment decision, because the manager of the fund of funds will perform the difficult and expensive search and due diligence process to identify hedge funds for investment. Finally, most investments in funds of funds are available with a minimum investment size of US

$100,000–$250,000, which is much lower than the typical minimum invest-ment of $500,000–$1,000,000 required by a single hedge fund.

Investments in funds of funds are likely most appropriate for either investors with small amounts of capital to invest or those unable or unwilling to select single-manager hedge fund investments. An investor with a net worth of $5 mil-lion may desire to allocate 20% of his or her portfolio to hedge funds, which allows a $1 million investment. This investor can select only one or two single-manager hedge funds to invest with, which leaves a significant risk of the under-performance or failure of a single manager or hedge fund style. The costs to find these single-fund investments likely far exceed the potential fees of investment in a fund of funds. A fund of funds allows this small investor to select a diver-sified hedge fund portfolio while incurring a minimum of manager selection costs.

Ineichen (2003) shows that the most common fee structure of funds of funds is a 1% annual management fee and an incentive fee of 10% of profits (1 and 10), which is in addition to the fees charged by the single-hedge-fund managers. This is an average annual fee of 2.72% of assets, based on the returns to the Hedge Fund Research Fund Weighted Index[1] from 1990 to 2004. Fees on funds of fund products can be as high as 2 and 20, but higher fee structures frequently include a hurdle rate, where the incentive fee is only charged after the fund earns a stated return, such as the risk-free interest rate. The presence of a hurdle rate serves to reduce the average incentive fee paid by the investor. For example, an investor who pays a 10% incentive fee on a 10% return without a hurdle rate pays the same as an investor who is charged a 20% incentive fee with a 5% hurdle rate. These fee calculations can help explain the buy-versus-build decision faced by institutional investors. A pension plan that desires to invest in hedge funds can choose to pay fees to a fund of funds or directly incur the costs of searching for and investing in a portfolio of single-manager hedge funds. This break-even point may be near $10 million in hedge fund investments, where an investor can diversify assets between 10 and 20 single-manager funds. If an investor spends $272,000 per year on one or two hedge fund analysts, their travel costs, and subscriptions to hedge fund databases, this is 2.72% of a $10 million invest-ment. Clearly, the largest investors in hedge funds would incur a lower cost of building their own portfolio of hedge funds than by employing a fund of funds manager.

6.2   Comparing returns: funds of funds vs. hedge funds

Our first order of business is to compare the risk and return profile of a fund of funds investment to that of the average hedge fund. The HFR Fund Weighted Index is an equal weighted index of single-manager hedge funds that currently

---

[1] The returns to the HFR Fund Weighted Index and the HFR Fund of Funds Index are courtesy of Chicago-based Hedge Fund Research, Inc., and are used by permission.

tracks the returns of about 1,700 funds with $320 billion in assets under management. The HFR Fund of Funds Index is an equal-weighted index of 750 funds of hedge funds managing approximately $150 billion. These two indices combine to cover nearly half of the estimated $1 trillion in combined assets managed by hedge funds and funds of funds. Table 6.1 shows the returns to each index as well as a pro-forma computation of an after-fee version of the fund weighted index, to approximate the return to the average hedge fund after the fund of funds manager has earned a 1% annual management fee and an incentive fee of 10% of profits.

As you can see from Table 6.1, the fees charged by fund of funds managers cause fund of funds returns to fall far below those of the average hedge fund as measured by the Fund Weighted Index. For example, the Fund Weighted Index returned an annual average of 14.95% from 1990 to 2004, while the return of the same index after charging typical fund of funds fees falls to 12.23%, showing the average fees paid to a fund of funds manager as 2.72%. When the Fund Weighted Index has higher returns, the fees charged will be higher, such as the 3.25% average fee in the 1990–1997 period, when the Fund Weighted Index returned 19.20% before FOF fees and 15.95% after those fees. From 1999 to 2004, the average fee was 2.21%, the difference between the 11.34% and 9.13% returns.

We can show that fund of funds managers are adding value when their risk-adjusted return exceeds that of the Fund Weighted Index after accounting for FOF fees. Unfortunately, FOF returns since 1990 have been 10.44%, with a Sharpe ratio of 1.11, while the fee-adjusted Fund Weighted Return was 12.23%, with a Sharpe ratio of 1.22. The Sharpe ratio measures the average return to the index in excess of the three-month Treasury bill yield, divided by the annualized standard deviation of monthly returns. While the standard deviation of FOF returns, 5.63%, was below that of the fee-adjusted Fund Weighted Index,

Table 6.1 Returns and risk of hedge fund indices, 1990–2004

	1990–2004	1990–1997	1999–2004
HFR Fund Weighted Index			
Annual return	14.95%	19.20%	11.34%
Standard deviation	6.93%	5.68%	7.28%
Sharpe ratio	1.55	2.5	1.14
HFR Fund of Funds Index			
Annual return	10.44%	13.61%	8.80%
Standard deviation	5.63%	4.82%	5.41%
Sharpe ratio	1.11	1.78	1.07
Fund Weighted Index after median FOF fees			
Annual return	12.23%	15.95%	9.13%
Standard deviation	6.57%	5.28%	6.90%
Sharpe ratio	1.22	2.07	0.88

6.93%, this reduced volatility came at the cost of reduced returns and a lower Sharpe ratio. Funds of funds outperformed the fee-adjusted Fund Weighted Index in only three of the eight years from 1990 to 1997 and in two of the six years from 1999 to 2004.

6.3 Ancient history vs. modern history: LTCM as the defining moment

Lowenstein (2000) describes the demise of Long-Term Capital Management (LTCM), a $5 billion fixed-income arbitrage hedge fund that used enormous amounts of leverage to control positions with a notional value exceeding $125 billion. As a result of defaults in the Russian bond market in the summer of 1998, LTCM was faced with a flight-to-quality market, where they experienced losses in their short positions in U.S. Treasury securities as well as losses in their long positions on many types of risky and illiquid bonds from nearly 30 countries, ranging from Russian government bonds to Danish and U.S. mortgage-backed securities. The scale of this fund failure was so large that the U.S. Federal Reserve Bank eased interest rates and coordinated a bailout of the fund by several large commercial and investment banks. Many investment banks that had similar fixed-income arbitrage positions saw their stock prices decline by over 40% in just a few weeks.

LTCM's story is an important one because it was the first large-scale failure of a hedge fund. Before this time, hedge funds were a little-known investment, and investors who did know about hedge funds may not have fully understood the risks. Investors may have been comfortable choosing investments in a single hedge fund, for they may have discounted the possibility of extreme investment losses in a hedge fund investment. After 1998, funds of funds assets grew dramatically, perhaps in recognition that individual investors decided they needed the assistance of a professional fund of funds manager in order to build a hedge fund portfolio that properly diversified the risks of failure of a single hedge fund manager or trading strategy.

As a result of this heightened sensitivity to hedge fund risks after the 1998 LTCM debacle, we will divide hedge fund history into the ancient period and the modern period. The ancient period will be the time from 1990 to 1997, before hedge funds and single-manager risks were well known to investors. The modern period is 1999–2004, after investors had time to digest the implications of the demise of LTCM.

In the ancient period, funds of funds earned an average annual return of 13.61%, dramatically underperforming the Fund Weighted Index, both before, 19.20%, and after, 15.95%, the implied fees charged by funds of funds managers. The Sharpe ratio of the FOF index, 1.78, trailed that of the fee-adjusted Fund Weighted Index, 2.07. During this time, the FOF index had only a 64% correlation to the Fund Weighted Index, implying that FOF managers were building portfolios of hedge funds that deviated significantly from those of all hedge funds.

Besides the extra layer of fees, there are perhaps four explanations why funds of funds returns may differ from the returns to all hedge funds. First, the FOF manager typically chooses a smaller portfolio, perhaps 15–45 funds, which can differ from the average return of over 1,000 funds in the Fund Weighted Index. Second, the FOF manager may explicitly manage the risk of the fund, for some managers will even implement their own hedges in the futures or currency markets. Next, some FOF managers may implement tactical-style allocations, seeking to aggressively change their portfolio investment mix in anticipation of changing future returns to hedge fund styles. For example, an FOF manager who expects a bear market in equity securities can reduce the weight on long–short equity funds and increase the weight on market-neutral equity funds, thus reducing the beta of the fund to the returns in equity markets. Should the manager's view be accurate, this move will reduce risk and increase returns as a result of this reallocation of assets between different hedge fund styles. Finally, we would hope that FOF managers would be able to add value in their manager selection process, by choosing managers with a lower probability of large drawdowns than would be experienced by the average hedge fund.

6.4 Factor analysis of returns

Factor analysis of hedge fund returns, as discussed by Gehin and Vaissie (2005) and Schneeweis, Kazemi, and Martin (2001), is becoming a common theme in the hedge fund literature. While hedge funds are marketed as absolute-return investments that are insensitive to the moves of stock and bond markets, statistical analysis shows that many hedge funds retain significant exposure to different types of market risk factors. The returns related to these factors can be attributed to taking beta exposures to market risk factors. The manager's skill can be measured by alpha, which is the return in excess of that earned as compensation for incurring market risk in the fund.

Table 6.2 describes the factor exposures of the HFR Fund Weighted Index and the HFR Fund of Funds Index. This analysis uses data from the entire time period 1990–2004 as well as the ancient (1990–1997) and modern (1999–2004) periods. Five factors were statistically significant in explaining the return to the Fund Weighted Index over the 1990–2004 period. Hedge funds tended to have higher returns when the S&P 500 stock index was rising in value and when the Russell 2000 index of small-capitalization stocks beat the return of the large-capitalization stocks included in the S&P 500 index. Funds earned larger returns in times of declining risk, as measured by the CBOE VIX index of stock market volatility and by a decline in credit spreads, as reflected in rising returns of the Merrill Lynch High-Yield index. Finally, hedge funds tended to earn higher returns when the yield on the 10-year U.S. Treasury note was at high levels. R-squared for this regression was 0.786, showing that these market risk factors explained

Table 6.2 Factor exposures of the HFR Fund Weighted Index and the
HFR Fund of Funds Index, 1990–2004

	1990–2004	1990–1997	1999–2004
HFR Index			
R-squared	0.786	0.755	0.805
Intercept	0.709 (0.151)	1.933 (0.005)	−1.560 (0.085)
S&P 500 return	0.311 (0.000)	0.266 (0.000)	0.322 (0.000)
High-yield return	0.110 (0.010)	0.179 (0.006)	0.085 (0.160)
Small–large equities	0.256 (0.000)	0.244 (0.000)	0.248 (0.000)
VIX	−0.033 (0.009)	−0.043 (0.048)	0.007 (0.734)
10-year treasury yield	1.410 (0.039)	−0.449 (0.718)	4.843 (0.008)
FOF Index			
R-squared	0.33	0.113	0.572
Intercept	0.519 (0.463)	1.645 (0.129)	−1.407 (0.156)
S&P 500 return	0.157 (0.000)	0.123 (0.011)	0.171 (0.000)
High-yield return	0.030 (0.625)	0.006 (0.954)	0.052 (0.435)
Small–large equities	0.138 (0.000)	0.023 (0.649)	0.183 (0.000)
VIX	−0.033 (0.070)	0.011 (0.757)	−0.001 (0.950)
10-year treasury yield	1.583 (0.115)	−1.611 (0.423)	4.734 (0.017)

nearly 80% of returns to the average hedge fund. Notice the consistency of
R-squared over time for this regression, because the 0.755 during the ancient
period closely tracked that of the 0.805 of the modern period. The exposure of
hedge funds to large- and small-capitalization stocks was little changed from one
period to the next, but hedge funds in the modern period seem to have more
exposure to government bond yields and less exposure to credit spreads and
equity market volatility than in the ancient period. These beta exposures may
concern some investors, for it would be difficult for the average hedge fund to
post large gains should the large- and small-capitalization U.S. stock markets enter
a large and long-lasting bear market. The intercept, or alpha, shows the risk-
adjusted return to manager skill. Hedge funds, on average, earned a monthly alpha
of 1.933% in the ancient period, which led to an impressive annual average
return of 19.20%. Unfortunately, the modern period return to the Fund Weighted
Index averages only 11.34%, because the funds have moved to a negative alpha
of −1.560% per month. A change in variables in the regression will show that
alpha may not have declined nearly as much as implied in this regression.

Interestingly, the returns to FOFs have been much more difficult to predict
using market risk factors, as shown by the lower 0.33 R-squared over the entire
time period. This FOF regression uses the same factors that were statistically
significant in explaining the return to hedge funds. We find that funds of funds
do not have a significant relationship to either Treasury note yields or high-
yield bond returns over the entire period. The coefficients on the S&P 500 return
and the difference between large- and small-cap stock returns show that funds

of funds, on average, have only about one-half of the beta exposure to these market returns than is experienced by the average hedge fund. The smaller standard deviation of funds of funds returns, then, may be directly attributed to a lower amount of market risk borne by these funds.

More striking, however, is the change in the behavior and risk exposures of funds of funds from the ancient period to the modern period. While funds of funds returns had a 64% correlation to Fund Weighted returns in the ancient period, this correlation rises to 94% in the modern period. While market factors explained only 11.3% of funds of funds returns in the ancient period, R-squared rises to 0.572 in the modern period. Not only are funds of funds more closely tracking the return to the Fund Weighted Index, but the FOF managers seem to be seeking more exposure to the returns to Treasury notes and small- and large-cap stocks than in the previous period.

The modern period has experienced a lower return to all classes of traditional and alternative investment classes, with the possible exceptions of real estate and commodities. The Fund Weighted Index returned 19.2% in the ancient period, which fell to 11.34% in the modern period, while the Sharpe ratio fell from 2.50 to 1.14. The Sharpe ratio fell due to declining returns as well as to an increased standard deviation of fund returns, which moved from 5.68% to 7.28%. A significant portion of the decline in returns to the average hedge fund is directly related to the declining returns of equity and fixed-income investments in the modern time period.

There is, however, some good news for FOF managers in the modern time period. The returns to FOFs eroded at a significantly slower rate than was experienced by the average hedge fund. FOF returns declined from 13.61% to 8.80%, while the standard deviation increased slightly from 4.82% to 5.41%. The Sharpe ratio of FOF returns fell from 1.78 in the ancient period to 1.07 in the modern period. This Sharpe ratio of 1.07 exceeds the 0.88 Sharpe ratio of the fee-adjusted Fund Weighted Index in the modern period. We can conclude, then, that FOF managers earned higher risk-adjusted returns than the average hedge fund, after accounting for the 1 and 10 fees charged by the FOF. In a time of weak returns to traditional investments, the smaller exposure to equity and fixed-income returns is able to reduce the risk of the FOF investment without significantly reducing the FOF returns relative to that of the average hedge fund.

6.5 The future of funds of funds

What, then, is the future of funds of funds? As the industry evolves, we see that these multimanager funds are taking more market risk and are becoming more correlated with the average hedge fund. Funds of funds managers will be forced to explain the value they are adding for the high level of fees that they charge, especially if traditional investments continue to offer lower returns. Historically, funds of funds have been a more attractive investment for individuals than for institutional investors, given their ability to quickly diversify a small investment over a variety of hedge fund managers and trading styles. FOF fees and asset flows will be pressured from two sides. First, the majority of asset flows to hedge funds are from institutional investors, who are likely making their own buy-versus-build decisions. The larger the assets an investor is dedicating to hedge funds and the higher the FOF fees, the more cost effective it becomes for the institution to make its own efforts to allocate assets to individual hedge fund managers. Second, new products are being introduced that will pressure the funds of funds, because each allows investors to place assets with hedge funds at a lower cost than through a fund of funds investment. Morningstar has announced their intentions to market a product that analyzes the returns of single-manager hedge funds. This product has the potential to dramatically reduce the cost of hedge fund analysis and due diligence, which is a key source of value added by funds of funds managers. Standard and Poors quickly raised over $1 billion in assets for their investible hedge fund index product. This index fund allows diversification over many hedge fund managers and strategies for a low minimum investment but at a lower cost than the fees charged by the typical FOF. Should the performance of hedge fund index funds be respectable, then FOFs will be forced to make changes to remain competitive. Managers of funds of funds, then, may need to improve performance, reduce fees, or make their returns more diversifying to traditional investments by reducing their rising exposures to equity and fixed-income returns in order to justify their current market share of the hedge fund industry, which has grown dramatically in recent years.

Acknowledgments

Many thanks to Gerald Laurain, CFA, Director of Alternative Investments at ABN Amro Asset Management. He defined the modern period and ancient period of hedge fund history.

References

Black, K. (2004). *Managing a Hedge Fund: A Complete Guide to Trading, Business Strategies, Risk Management and Regulations.* McGraw-Hill, New York.

Gehin, W. and Vaissie, M. (2005). The Right Place for Alternative Betas in Hedge Fund Performance: An Answer to the Capacity Effect Fantasy. Working Paper, Edhec Risk and Asset Management Research Center, Lille, France.

Ineichen, A. (2003). *Absolute Returns: The Risk and Opportunities of Hedge Fund Investing.* Wiley, Hoboken, NJ.

Lowenstein, R. (2000). *When Genius Failed: The Rise and Fall of Long-Term Capital Management.* Random House, New York.

Schneeweis, T., Kazemi, H., and Martin, G. (2001). *Understanding Hedge Fund Performance: Research Results and Rules of Thumb for the Institutional Investor.* Lehman Brothers, New York.

7 Hedge fund indices: Are they cost-effective alternatives to funds of funds?

Kathryn Wilkens

Abstract

Some consider investable hedge fund indices to be cost-effective alternatives to funds of funds (FOFs) as means to gain access to "hedge fund beta." If this view becomes widespread, it is possible that assets may flow from FOFs to these indices. The indices, however, may underperform FOFs. One argument against hedge fund index investing holds that FOF managers skillfully select enough good managers to outperform indices. This study suggests that if one must choose one or a few funds from among the universe of FOFs, the likelihood of outperforming an index is approximately equal to that of underperforming an index. Yet if a large diversified portfolio of FOFs is attainable, it may slightly outperform an index.

7.1 Introduction

Investable hedge fund indices have evolved from noninvestable benchmark indices to provide low-cost access to returns correlated with the hedge fund industry as a whole. In addition, subindices designed to represent style-specific hedge fund strategies allow investors, including FOFs and structured product providers, to gain access to specific return patterns generated within the hedge fund universe that may be superior to overall average hedge fund returns under certain market conditions. Some of the benefits of investable indices over FOFs are very apparent: Benefits of investable indices relative to FOFs include (generally) lower fees, fuller transparency, and less restrictive redemption notice periods, thereby providing increased liquidity to investors. Investable hedge fund indices also serve as a benchmark for FOFs, and their subindices may serve as benchmarks for individual single-strategy hedge funds.

However, investable hedge fund indices have their share of critics, who are often severe and generally point to the disparity in performance among the indices, primarily attributed to challenges in structuring the products and necessitating trade-offs between, for example, investability and completeness. In particular, two serious and often-cited criticisms are (1) poor performance due to the presence in the broad hedge fund universe of a higher number of average performing funds and (2) the lack of a theoretical basis for indexing actively managed funds. Poor performance is also often attributed to good funds' being closed or not having a need or desire to raise capital from being included in an index.

Relative to traditional stock and bond portfolios, a portfolio of traditional assets including allocations to hedge funds offers two primary advantages: (1) higher alpha, from hedge fund exposure providing returns to active asset management with relatively few restrictions on short and leveraged positions, and (2) lower risk, from a low correlation between hedge fund and traditional asset returns. From the perspective of choosing between FOFs and investable hedge fund indices, if the returns are comparable, then the relative benefits of diversification should also be examined.

Liew (2003) argues against hedge index fund investing by considering the universe of single-strategy funds and the skill required by FOF managers to outperform a passively managed index. He finds that a portfolio of 70% of good managers will outperform an index, and he suggests that FOFs have the ability to select that proportion of good managers. Here we examine instead a universe of FOF managers only, and we compare their performance to that of the indices. We will see that approximately half of the FOFs appear to have such ability to outperform the indices. Thus, if one must choose one or a few funds from among the universe of FOFs, there is an equal likelihood of underperforming the index. However, if a large diversified portfolio of FOFs is attainable, it may slightly outperform an index. Results also indicate that FOFs do not have a clear advantage over investable indices with respect to their ability to reduce risk through lower correlations with traditional asset returns. The approach used in the analyses in this chapter also provides some insight into issues surrounding the theoretical basis or lack thereof for the use of hedge fund indices and, more generally, the use of alphas and betas in the hedge fund space.

7.2   Funds of funds

Forty-eight consecutive months of net-of-fee return data (from January 31, 2001 to December 31, 2004) for diversified funds of funds (FOFs) are obtained from the Center for International Securities and Derivatives Markets (CISDM) database. Returns are reported net of fees. Two of the 397 funds (with maximum and minimum mean excess return) are removed, resulting in a set of 395 FOFs to which the index returns are compared.

7.3   Investable hedge fund indices

Table 7.1 lists the seven investable hedge fund index return series used in this study. All data was gathered from the websites of the index providers and are not adjusted for fees unless otherwise noted. Because these are relatively new products, only three of the indices have four or more years of monthly returns prior to 2005.

Table 7.1 Investable hedge fund indices

Variable name for series used	Start date*	No. of months	Website and source of describing quote
MSCI	8/29/2003	17	http://www.msci.com/hedge

"The MSCI Hedge Invest Index^{SM} is designed both to be investable and to reflect the overall structure and composition of the hedge fund universe. The composite-level MSCI Hedge Invest Index includes funds from a wide range of hedge fund investment strategies available on a third-party platform."

HFRXEW	4/30/2003	21	http://www.hedgefundresearch.com

"The HFRX Equal Weighted Strategies Index is equal-weighted, offering a more balanced diversification and lower volatility. Built on a 'strategy-up' basis from eight single-strategy indices representing the main hedge fund strategies. All indices comprise hedge funds that are open for investment."

SP	10/31/2002	27	http://www.standardandpoors.com

"Standard & Poor's offers a growing family of hedge fund indices. The main S&P Hedge Fund Index (S&P HFI) offers investors an investable benchmark that is designed to be representative of the broad range of major strategies that hedge funds employ. The index currently has 42 constituents from three subindices: S&P Arbitrage Index, S&P Event-Driven Index, and S&P Directional/Tactical Index, which in turn represent a total of nine specific strategies. These strategies include: Equity Market Neutral, Fixed Income Arbitrage, Convertible Arbitrage, Merger Arbitrage, Distressed, Special Situations, Equity Long/Short, Managed Futures, and Macro. The strategies are equally weighted to ensure well-rounded representation of hedge fund investment approaches and to avoid overrepresentation of recently outperforming or widely sold strategies."

DJ	1/31/2002	36	http://www.djhedgefundindexes.com

"Dow Jones Hedge Fund Strategy Benchmarks are intended to be style-pure hedge fund strategy indexes based on the performance of a managed account platform structured to meet the needs of institutional investors.... Benchmark performance is measured by computing changes in the aggregated net-of-fees net asset value of all separate managed accounts within a strategy. Managers within each benchmark are selected based on minimum track record, minimum assets under management, cluster and quantitative analyses, correlation to other related indices, due-diligence review, qualitative analysis, willingness to run a managed account and to adhere to leverage limitations, and Advisory Committee review. As a result, the Dow Jones Hedge Fund Strategy Benchmarks should reflect the performance that an investor with stringent guidelines for liquidity, transparency, manager track record, and style purity would expect from an allocation to hedge funds."

(continued)

Table 7.1 (*continued*)

Variable name for series used	Start date*	No. of months	Website and source of describing quote
FTSE	1/31/01	48	http://www.ftse.com/indices_marketdata/ftsehedge/index_home.jsp

"FTSE Hedge opens the door to the previously complex world of hedge fund investing. It's an investable index that combines complete transparency and accessibility with the proven quality and discipline of FTSE Group's index products and services."

| CFSB | 1/31/01 | 48 | http://www.hedgeindex.com |

"The CSFB/Tremont Investable Hedge Fund Index is designed to provide a transparent, representative, and rules-based benchmark of the investable index universe. The unique features of the Investable Index allow it to serve as the underlying investment in a broad suite of products offered as tailor-made solutions, enabling investors to participate in a liquid and diversified market barometer of the hedge fund universe."

| Van (Van Global Hedge Fund Index) | 1/31/01 | 48 | http://www.hedgefund.com |

"Van Investable Index — The VI2 reflects the 17-year track record of the Van Global Hedge Fund Index, a widely recognized metric for the performance of the overall hedge fund industry. Designed with the institutional investor in mind, products built around the VI2 follow the performance of 45+ hedge funds in a variety of strategies that can be weighted based on the needs and goals of the client. This specialized fund of funds is highly correlated to the full Van Global Hedge Fund Index."

*All dates end on 12/31/04. The starting dates listed above describe the start date for the return series used in this study, not necessarily the inception date for the index. All data series used in this study end on 12/31/04.

While some index providers may have subindices that go further back, this study used only diversified indexes that are comparable to diversified (rather than single-strategy) funds of funds. The Dow Jones index used here was created as an equally weighted average of the subindices available since January 31, 2002. Where results are presented for the indices with shorter histories, they should be interpreted with caution. For some analyses, only the FTSE, CFSB, and Van Hedge indices are used because of the relative statistical accuracy gained from their longer time series.

7.4 Distribution of returns and potential biases

Hedge fund returns are known to exhibit nonnormal returns (notably leptokurtosis) and suffer from many biases. Yet, using the Lilliefors (Kolmogorov–Smirnov) test for normality, we cannot reject the assumption of normality for any of the index return series. In addition, we cannot reject the assumption of normality for the majority (85%) of the FOF return series. Because the funds analyzed in this study are diversified, investing in several underlying hedge funds, their return distributions are normal relative to that of single-strategy hedge funds. This facilitates the use of traditional statistical inferences based on the assumption of normality.

Biases include selection bias (due to the voluntary nature of the decision to enter a hedge fund database, resulting in a sample that is not necessarily representative of the universe of hedge funds), survivorship bias (due to the fact that funds that are no longer operating or reporting to the database and that may have a bad performance are deleted from the database), instant history bias (due to new funds entering a database with back-filled performance data in the case of successful funds but not unsuccessful funds). It has been argued that FOFs are less prone to these biases (Fung and Hsieh, 2000), and to the extent that these biases exist in the CISDM FOF database, they may also exist in the investable indices because it is not always clear how well index providers correct for them. Furthermore, one should keep in mind that many index returns are pro-forma and not actual returns.

While both FOF returns and the underlying funds in the indices are net of fees, not all investable indices report results net of their charges. As a rule of thumb, the monthly returns for the investable indices not reporting net of all fees should be reduced by 12½ basis points (150 basis points per year).

Biases in hedge fund index returns is one of the main reasons cited for the unsuitability of indexes as benchmarks for hedge funds. This is directly related to the concern over a lack of a theoretical basis for indexing actively managed funds and confusion over what constitutes an alpha and what a hedge fund beta really is. In this study, where the interest is in the performance of the indices themselves, it makes even less sense to use an index as a benchmark. Therefore we follow Fung and Hsieh (2004) and use benchmarks based on asset returns rather than hedge fund returns.

7.5　Asset-based style factors

Seven hedge fund risk factors used by Fung and Hsieh (2004) to capture the risk of well-diversified hedge fund portfolios are employed in the present study to calculate alphas and betas for the individual FOFs and investable indices. The hedge fund risk factors or asset-based style factors are as follows:

- Three trend-following risk factors constructed based on the article by Fung and Hsieh (2001), which are available on Hsieh's website: (1) PTFSBD, a bond trend–following factor, (2) PTFSFX, a currency trend–following factor, and (3) PTFSCOM, a commodity trend–following factor
- Two equity-oriented risk factors: (1) an equity market factor (the Standard & Poors 500 index monthly total return, available at http://www.barra.com) and

(2) a size spread factor (Wilshire Small Cap 1750 – Wilshire Large Cap 750 monthly return)

• Two bond-oriented risk factors: (1) the bond market factor [the monthly change in the 10-year Treasury constant maturity yield (month end to month end), available at the Board of Governors of the Federal Reserve System], and (2) the credit spread factor [the monthly change in the Moody's Baa yield less 10-year Treasury constant maturity yield (month end to month end), available at the Board of Governors of the Federal Reserve System]

Table 7.2 presents the results of the Fung and Hsieh model for the FOFs and for three of the investable indices (with the longest performance records).

Table 7.2 Performance statistics for FOFs and indices

		(1) Statistics for average FOF	(2) Average of FOFs statistics	(3) FTSE	(4) CSFB	(5) Van
	Coefficients					
1	Alpha	0.0029	0.0029	0.0025	0.0038	0.0028
2	PTFSBD	−0.0055	−0.0055	−0.0034	−0.0006	0.0005
3	PTFSFX	0.0129	0.0129	0.0099	0.0085	0.0087
4	PTFSCOM	−0.0003	−0.0003	0.0157	−0.0023	0.0053
5	Equity	0.1180	0.1180	0.0827	0.0269	0.2595
6	Bond	−0.0098	−0.0098	−0.0115	−0.0057	−0.0113
7	Size	0.1138	0.1138	0.0828	−0.0426	0.1760
8	Credit	−0.0096	−0.0096	−0.0100	−0.0152	−0.0156
	p-Values					
9	Alpha	0.0003	0.1842	0.0182	0.0008	0.0012
10	PTFSBD	0.2242	0.3999	0.5743	0.9286	0.9199
11	PTFSFX	0.0043	0.2573	0.0929	0.1619	0.0610
12	PTFSCOM	0.9606	0.5744	0.1006	0.8164	0.4795
13	Equity	0.0000	0.1765	0.0082	0.3878	0.0000
14	Bond	0.0056	0.2466	0.0145	0.2291	0.0026
15	Size	0.0002	0.2061	0.0307	0.2735	0.0000
16	Credit	0.1693	0.3712	0.2855	0.1218	0.0384
	Other statistics					
17	R-squared	0.7089	0.4439	0.4157	0.1719	0.8957
18	Mean excess return	0.0043	0.0043	0.0036	0.0040	0.0049
19	StdRaw	0.0083	0.0136	0.0080	0.0069	0.0147
20	Sharpe	0.5213	0.3808	0.4436	0.5784	0.3307
21	Correlation w/60–40	0.5652	0.3093	0.3062	0.2255	0.8318
22	Liquidity	0.4509	0.2846	0.2536	0.0744	0.3539
23	LiqP	0.0013	0.1506	0.0820	0.6152	0.0136
24	IR	0.6530	0.2889	0.4033	0.6091	0.5816

In addition, more traditional performance statistics are reported for comparison purposes (mean excess returns, Sharpe ratios), as well as some other statistics that are discussed at length shortly.

The first row shows that the alphas of the FOFs and the investable indices are very close. Column 1 shows results for an equally weighted portfolio of FOFs. Column 2 shows the average statistic for each individual FOF. While these are identical for the regression coefficients and the mean excess returns, the p-values for the coefficients, R^2, and other statistics are not the same. Notice that the variability in the performance of the individual FOFs is reflected in column 2, where the p-values are higher, the standard deviation is higher, and the R^2 statistic is lower. In general, if one examines performance statistics for only an average, the results will appear less variable than is truly reflected in the population. For example, the average Sharpe ratio for the FOFs is 0.38, not 0.52, as implied by the portfolio of 395 FOFs. For this reason, the entire distribution of statistics for the FOFs is examined later and used as a comparison against the statistics for the index returns. However, the results in Table 7.2 suggest that a broadly diversified portfolio of FOFs (column 1) outperforms two of the three indices examined here. Furthermore, where the indices seem to outperform the average FOF, results should be interpreted in light of the earlier-noted potential biases and problems in measuring the actual performance of the investable indices.

7.6   Mean excess return and Sharpe ratio comparisons

Figure 7.1 illustrates the relative rankings of investable indices and all FOFs in terms of their mean excess returns and Sharpe ratios. Panel A shows that all of the investable indices have mean excess returns that fall within one standard deviation of the mean excess return for the FOF sample. Approximately four (half) are below the mean and approximately three (half) are above the mean. Panel B shows that on a risk-adjusted basis (as measured by the Sharpe ratio), the investable indices appear to do better, with only two falling below the mean FOF Sharpe ratio but not more than one standard deviation below the mean FOF Sharpe ratio. One index is more than one standard deviation above the mean FOF Sharpe ratio (but not more than two standard deviations above).

7.7   Fung and Hsieh model alphas and information ratio comparisons

The information ratio is defined as $\alpha/\sigma_\varepsilon$. Intuitively, it is a reward-to-risk ratio, where the reward, α, is the return above the risk-free rate remaining after subtracting out the total price of systematic risk taken, and here the amount of systematic risk is measured by the seven risk factors, and σ_ε is the nonsystematic

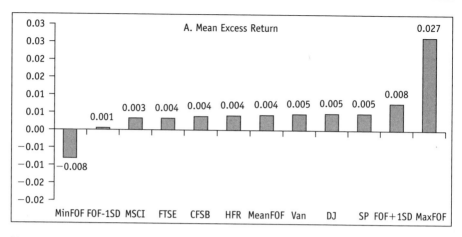

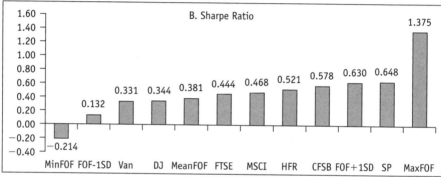

Figure 7.1 Mean excess return and Sharpe ratio statistics

risk, or diversifiable risk. Since R^2 measures the percentage of total variation in the returns ($\sigma_{r,i}^2$) explained by the model, a tautology is

$$\sigma_{\varepsilon,i} = [(1 - R^2)\sigma_{r,i}^2]^{1/2}$$

While the information ratio is generally used relative to a single benchmark, here it provides a statistical summary measure relative to the F&H model.

Figure 7.2 illustrates the relative rankings of investable indices and FOFs along their alphas and associated information ratios, using the F&H model. Most indices have alphas below that for the mean FOF alpha (Panel A) but information ratios above that for the mean information ratio for the FOFs (Panel B).

The Fung and Hsieh model results are strongest for the indices with the longest time series (FTSE, Van, and CFSB), and all three of these indices have statistically significant alphas. However, the F&H model does not describe well

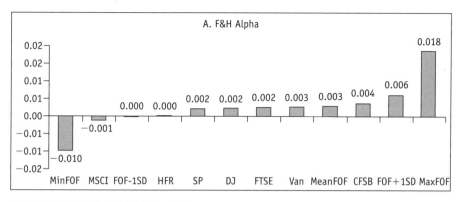

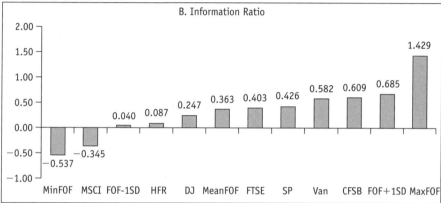

Figure 7.2 Fung and Hsieh model alphas and information ratios (IR)

the returns of the CFSB index, in particular, because none of the beta coefficients are significant. In Table 7.2, we saw that the model describes the FTSE and Van indices fairly well, where most coefficients are significant and the R-squared statistics are 41.6% and 89.6%, respectively. In Table 7.2 (row 14, column 2), we saw that on average 44% of the variation in the FOF returns is explained by the model.

In evaluating the ability of this model to describe hedge fund returns, Fung and Hsieh (2004) note that the significance of the factors vary over time. Here we examine how they vary across funds. Table 7.3 summarizes the results of the 400 regressions for the FOFs, showing the percentage of FOFs that had a significant coefficient at the 5% and 10% levels. Over half of the FOFs had a statistically significant alpha. Very few FOFs' returns were explained by two of the three look-back straddle returns (less than 20% for PTFSB and less than 5% for the PTFSCOM). The average number of statistically significant coefficients is 2.57 and 3.25 at the 10% significance level and for over half of the FOFs at the 5% level, respectively. More than two coefficients were statistically significant for 73% of the FOFs at the 10% significance level.

Table 7.3 Percentage of significant coefficients

Alpha	PTFSBD	PTFSFX	PTFSCOM	Equity	Bond	Size	Credit	Average number	Percentage with more than two
5%	0.516	0.123	0.320	0.038	0.539	0.401	0.463	0.171	2.572	0.537
10%	0.589	0.191	0.463	0.055	0.615	0.509	0.559	0.272	3.254	0.730

7.8   Correlation with traditional asset returns and lagged equity return comparisons

Figure 7.3 illustrates the correlation between the FOF and investable hedge fund index returns with a traditional 60/40 stock/bond portfolio's returns (Panel A) and lagged equity returns (Panel B). Most of the correlations are positive.

On average, FOFs appear to have no clear advantage relative to the investable indices with respect to having lower correlation with traditional asset returns. The Van index, however, appears to be highly correlated with traditional assets, and this was reflected in the Fung and Hsieh regression model results. In addition, three additional indices are more correlated with the traditional asset returns than with the average FOF. However, three other indices have a relatively lower correlation with traditional assets returns, and two of these three have longer time series, with more reliable statistics.

The results for the liquidity measure show that most indices have correlations, with lagged equity returns clustering around the mean statistic for the FOFs. One of the reasons for examining this statistic is to gauge how much potential smoothing exists in reported returns due to illiquidity in the FOFs' and indices' underlying assets, which may bias the performance statistics upward (Getmanksy, Lo, and Makarov, 2004). There appears to be no relationship between the performance rankings previously discussed and the amount of illiquidity indicated by this statistic. The correlation is statistically significant at the 5% level for only one of the indices (HFR), and correlation coefficients for two of the investable indices are significant at the 10% level (S&P and FTSE). The remaining three investable indices lack statistically significant correlations with lagged equity returns. The average benchmark fund of funds' correlation coefficient has a significance level of 15%.

Table 7.4 shows that the moments of the distribution of these statistics indicate that they are not normal (although the Sharpe ratio is closer to a normal distribution than is the mean excess return), so we cannot perform a traditional hypothesis test for the differences between the statistics. Nevertheless, the results do not support the notion that investable indices underperform FOFs, on average. While the distribution of alphas is not normal, the distribution of the information ratios is much closer to being normal. Since correlation statistics are bounded between -1 and $+1$ and most of the coefficients are positive, there is some skewness and kurtosis due to some FOFs' negative correlations.

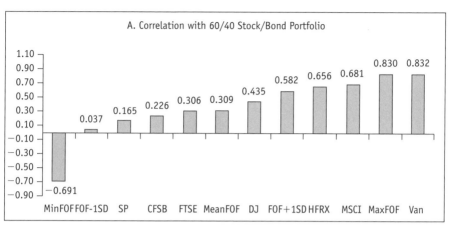

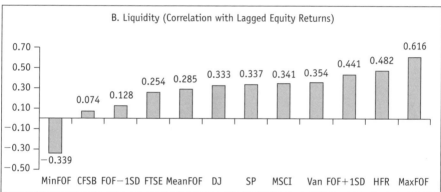

Figure 7.3 Correlations with traditional 60/40 stock/bond portfolio and lagged equity returns (liquidity)

Table 7.4 Moments for the distributions of statistics

	Mean excess return	Sharpe	Alpha	IR	Correlation w/60–40	Liquidity
Standard deviation	0.004	0.248	0.003	0.323	0.274	0.154
Skewness	1.736	0.500	0.575	0.348	−0.504	−0.883
Kurtosis	8.490	0.773	3.671	0.357	0.097	1.263

7.9   Conclusion

This study compared the performance of large set of FOFs to that of several investable hedge fund indices. Performance statistics were calculated using the same methodologies for both types of investment vehicles, thus avoiding the unresolved problem of using an appropriate index as a benchmark. Several potential problems in the comparisons were noted and examined, however. The ranking of the statistics shows that along several dimensions, about half of the FOFs outperform the indices and about half of the FOFs underperform the indices. Therefore, if the primary consideration in choosing between the two types of vehicles is solely performance (and not other differentiating factors, such as liquidity and transparency), then the decision should be based on the investor's ability to diversify across FOFs. The results of this study show that a broadly diversified portfolio of FOFs is likely to outperform an investable index. However, a less diversified portfolio of FOFs has a good chance of underperforming an index.

References

Fung, W. and Hsieh, D. A. (2000). Performance Characteristics of Hedge Funds and Commodity Funds: Natural vs. Spurious Biases. *Journal of Financial and Quantitative Analysis*, 35(1):291–307.

Fung, W. and Hsieh, D. A. (2001). The Risk in Hedge Fund Strategies: Theory and Evidence from Trend Followers. *Review of Financial Studies*, 14(2):313–341.

Fung, W. and Hsieh, D. A. (2004). Hedge Fund Benchmarks: A Risk-Based Approach. *Financial Analysts Journal*, 60(5):65–80.

Getmansky, M., Lo, A. W., and Makarov, I. (2004). An Econometric Model of Serial Correlation and Illiquidity in Hedge Fund Returns. *Journal of Financial Economics*, 74(3):529–609.

Liew, J. (2003). Hedge Fund Indexing Examined. *Journal of Portfolio Management*, 29(2):113–123.

8 Simple hedge fund strategies as an alternative to funds of funds: evidence from large-cap funds

Greg N. Gregoriou, Georges Hübner,
Nicolas Papageorgiou, and Fabrice Rouah

Abstract

We propose a simple alternative to investing in funds of funds. In order to avoid a second layer of management and performance fees, we show that it is easy to construct simple equal-weighted portfolios of large-capitalization hedge funds whose performance characteristics dominate those of the largest funds of funds. We compare the performance of the two investment possibilities using three different measures: alpha, the Sharpe ratio, and the information ratio. We demonstrate that there exists sufficient persistence in returns, especially for nondirectional strategies, so that we can create simple portfolios of hedge funds that outperform the best funds of funds based on all three measures.

8.1   Introduction

The benefits of including hedge funds in traditional portfolios composed solely of equities and bonds is now well documented in the literature. The improvement of risk/return characteristics of these portfolios when hedge funds are introduced is a stylized fact, due mostly to the negative, low, or zero correlation of hedge funds with stock and bond indices and to their ability to produce positive returns under a variety of market conditions. This has been demonstrated, among others, by Amin and Kat (2003), Fung and Hsieh (1999), Agarwal and Naik (2004), and Schneeweis and Martin (2001) over various time periods and using different hedge fund databases. The decision that investors are now faced with is no longer whether to include this asset class to enhance the performance of traditional portfolios, but, rather, what is the most effective manner of incorporating it. Investors wishing to commit themselves to hedge funds are faced with a dilemma. On the one hand, funds of hedge funds (FOFs) are the safest and simplest way to invest in hedge funds, because the FOF manager performs the due diligence, regular monitoring, and performance evaluation of the individual funds on behalf of investors, including collection of monthly return and NAV information. Moreover, FOFs produce returns that are usually less volatile than those of individual hedge funds. On the other hand, investors pay a premium for the safety and benefits of FOFs, in terms of an extra layer of fees charged by the FOF manager, which can be substantial. To further complicate matters, Brown, Goetzmann, and Liang (2005) show that the triggering of incentive fees and of high-water marks of FOFs can vary depending on when investors enter the FOFs.

The alternative to investing in an FOF is to select a small pool of individual funds that will provide characteristics similar to those of large FOFs. Of course, investors adopting this strategy will need to perform the due diligence and regular monitoring of the individual hedge funds. However, for institutional investors willing to commit large amounts of capital to hedge funds, these costs would be small compared to the extra layer of fees charged by FOFs. By limiting our analysis to the largest funds, we are focusing on the funds that have the longest track records and for which due diligence is, on average, easier to perform.

In this chapter we propose a simple strategy to construct portfolios of hedge funds whose risk/return characteristics dominate those of FOFs. Considering that any reasonable contender of funds of funds portfolios would argue that these vehicles offer a trade-off between absolute abnormal performance and risk exposures, one has to be careful in defining the notion of dominance in performance. Should it be a model-free performance measure that is widely accepted by financial practice? In this case, the Sharpe ratio is a relevant benchmark. If one wants an absolute percentage return obtained in addition to the required return on the financial markets, then one would consider the alpha, measured against a properly designed returns-generating model, as the adequate performance metrics. But many practitioners would argue that the real skill of the fund manager should be measured with respect to the additional residual risk that she accepts to bear; the information ratio is then the relevant measure to use. As a matter of fact, one could argue that different classes of hedge funds would exhibit different levels of comparative advantages with respect to each of these performance measures, but none should be able to dominate all the others in an absolute fashion. The purpose of this chapter is to provide a practical answer to this last question.

The portfolios we construct contain a maximum of four hedge funds, equally weighted in the portfolio, making it possible for individual investors to adopt our methodology. The information used for fund selection is restricted to size and past performance. This chapter lies on both sides of two important strands of literature on hedge funds, portfolio construction and performance persistence.

We observe that a strategy that selects the best nondirectional funds is very likely to dominate portfolios of funds of funds on all three performance measures. The portfolios display a significant amount of persistence when performance is measured with the Sharpe ratio or the information ratio. This makes the portfolios attractive alternatives to FOFs, which only show persistence in alphas but without sufficient performance levels to compare favorably to the best hedge funds portfolios. The large risk exposure of directional hedge fund strategies does not make them likely to dominate funds of funds, even in combination with nondirectional hedge funds.

8.2   Data

The data consists of monthly returns, net of all fees, of hedge funds in the HFR database (Hedge Fund Research, Inc., 2003), from January 1995 to December 2003. The HFR database contains performance and managerial information on roughly 2,300 hedge funds worldwide in operation on December 2003. In this chapter, we separate the data into three subcategories: nondirectional funds, directional funds, and funds of funds, following Agarwal and Naik (2000a, 2000b). For purposes of this chapter, however, only the 18 largest hedge funds (in terms of average assets under management over the period 1995–2003) for each of the three classifications are selected.[1] More specifically, we select 18 directional funds (the six largest sector funds, the six largest macro funds, and the six largest long and short funds), 18 nondirectional funds (nine market-neutral funds and the nine largest event-driven funds), and the 18 largest funds of funds. In order for a fund to qualify for the study, the returns had to be available in the HFR database from January 1995 to December 2003. By restricting our study to the largest funds, we limit the effect of survivorship bias on our results, because the mortality rate is much smaller for larger funds.[2]

Descriptive statistics for the selected funds classifications are presented in Tables 8.1a, 8.1b, and 8.1c. Comparing Tables 8.1a and 8.1b, we notice a distinct difference between the returns from the 18 nondirectional and 18 directional funds. Although all 36 hedge funds exhibit positive absolute returns, the directional funds offer higher average returns. An equally weighted portfolio of the 18 nondirectional funds would have provided an average monthly return of 0.995%, whereas a similar portfolio of the directional funds would have resulted in an average monthly return of 1.365%. Not surprisingly, this superior performance in terms of return comes at a cost of substantially greater return variability. Of the 18 directional funds, the one with the lowest standard deviation of monthly returns is long/short 2, which presents a standard deviation of 2.87%. Astonishingly, 16 of the 18 nondirectional funds have a lower standard deviation of returns than does the least risky directional fund. The average assets under management for the directional and nondirectional funds are of similar magnitudes.

The descriptive statistics for the 18 largest funds of funds that reported over the entire sample period seem to indicate that there is perhaps value to be found in creating one's own pool of hedge funds. The average monthly return of these funds of funds was 0.962% (lower than both other classifications), and the standard deviation of monthly returns, though considerably lower than the directional funds, is on average higher than the standard deviation of the nondirectional funds. This observation would lead us to believe that the fund-selection skills

---

[1] The data was obtained without charge from HFR Inc., so we did not have access to the names of the funds — these are coded instead.

[2] Of course, the funds that proved to be the largest of their category during the whole sample period may not have been the largest ones during the first half, but this issue is minor for our comparative perspective.

Table 8.1a Description of the 18 nondirectional hedge funds (sorted by average assets under management)

Fund	Average assets ($ million)	Average monthly return	Standard deviation of returns	Minimum return	Maximum return
Event-driven 1	865.31	0.82	1.55	−3.42	9.80
Event-driven 2	822.13	1.01	2.40	−16.95	7.83
Event-driven 3	557.94	0.94	0.84	−2.75	3.25
Event-driven 4	439.91	0.98	1.29	−4.00	5.50
Event-driven 5	344.04	0.56	5.10	−18.23	18.53
Event-driven 6	337.58	2.54	6.96	−38.79	19.66
Event-driven 7	283.12	1.10	2.27	−15.87	5.81
Event-driven 8	243.17	0.98	1.29	−4.00	5.50
Event-driven 9	213.17	1.21	2.27	−6.70	8.18
Market-neutral 1	2079.77	0.54	1.70	−5.83	4.95
Market-neutral 2	2004.19	0.94	0.69	−0.27	3.36
Market-neutral 3	1130.34	0.50	0.42	−1.32	1.77
Market-neutral 4	725.91	0.54	1.77	−4.02	4.29
Market-neutral 5	651.27	1.38	1.25	−5.54	4.50
Market-neutral 6	632.56	0.90	1.77	−9.96	3.76
Market-neutral 7	609.03	1.05	2.71	−16.20	5.77
Market-neutral 8	584.14	1.41	1.98	−9.12	5.34
Market-neutral 9	564.45	0.52	3.58	−14.70	11.70

Table 8.1b Description of the 18 directional hedge funds (sorted by average assets under management)

Fund	Average assets ($ million)	Average monthly return	Standard deviation of returns	Minimum return	Maximum return
Sector 1	571.9	2.52	13.59	−28.56	75.89
Sector 2	261.4	1.93	5.55	−11.72	22.35
Sector 3	192.7	0.95	4.18	−19.49	8.68
Sector 4	174.9	0.95	4.15	−18.72	8.64
Sector 5	164.1	0.94	3.99	−10.78	11.76
Sector 6	124.4	1.35	3.51	−12.64	11.31
Global/macro 1	585.04	2.08	4.99	−34.55	12.60
Global/macro 2	304.10	0.73	5.11	−8.41	19.21
Global/macro 3	294.99	1.26	7.43	−36.54	22.70
Global/macro 4	209.42	0.76	11.06	−38.47	39.01
Global/macro 5	201.02	1.40	8.36	−52.37	27.50
Global/macro 6	117.11	1.83	4.96	−31.58	14.10
Long/short 1	1895.99	0.98	4.48	−14.95	10.35
Long/short 2	1317.17	1.30	2.87	−5.80	8.10
Long/short 3	947.75	1.45	4.91	−14.60	12.50
Long/short 4	945.4	0.95	2.84	−8.93	10.00
Long/short 5	895	1.64	5.58	−19.90	19.35
Long/short 6	849.28	1.48	4.27	−14.11	9.96

Table 8.1c Description of the 18 funds of funds
(sorted by average assets under management)

Fund	Average assets ($ million)	Average monthly return	Standard deviation of returns	Minimum return	Maximum return
Fund of funds 1	2714.9	0.44	3.91	−9.71	12.64
Fund of funds 2	1340.74	1.03	1.43	−6.69	4.92
Fund of funds 3	1182.41	0.93	3.59	−13.97	8.76
Fund of funds 4	737.96	1.16	2.52	−7.92	10.13
Fund of funds 5	662.65	1.32	1.68	−1.49	7.24
Fund of funds 6	479.72	0.97	2.98	−9.00	9.52
Fund of funds 7	425.27	0.91	3.47	−11.60	9.37
Fund of funds 8	403.01	0.80	1.02	−5.93	2.27
Fund of funds 9	324.22	0.81	4.06	−14.80	10.54
Fund of funds 10	313.77	0.96	2.93	−9.60	10.15
Fund of funds 11	300.56	0.78	2.52	−8.19	7.52
Fund of funds 12	286.58	1.20	1.88	−5.50	7.58
Fund of funds 13	255.73	0.92	0.99	−5.36	2.68
Fund of funds 14	251.17	1.04	1.77	−3.77	6.14
Fund of funds 15	237.91	1.12	1.84	−2.50	10.00
Fund of funds 16	236.67	0.85	0.59	−2.79	1.97
Fund of funds 17	231.69	1.17	3.55	−14.16	15.98
Fund of funds 18	189.33	0.90	2.37	−7.16	9.65

and market-timing ability funds of funds managers do not compensate sufficiently for the second layer of management fees. It is important to note, nonetheless, that even across the 18 funds of funds in our study, there is substantial variability in the risk–reward payoff.

8.3 Methodology

8.3.1 Portfolio construction

The study will comprise two parts. A first examination will compare the performance of portfolios of directional and nondirectional funds without using any past performance measures to select the best possible funds. All possible combinations of equal-weighted portfolios comprising up to four hedge funds will be created and compared to the performance of the 18 largest funds of funds over the entire nine-year period. The performance measures that will be employed for the comparison are the Sharpe ratio, the alpha of a nine-factor model, and the information ratio.

In the second part of study, we break up the nine-year observation period into two subperiods of 4.5 years each: January 1995 through June 1999 (period 1) and

July 1999 through December 2003 (period 2). We assume the perspective of a forward-looking investor at June 1999 with 4.5 years of historical data who is considering what investments to undertake for the next 4.5 years. At this point in time, the investor has witnessed an unambiguous bullish trend on the stock market. Although we know ex post that the subsequent subperiod has been characterized by a further expansion of the technology bubble (until March 2000) followed by a sharp market downturn, we commit not to make use of this hindsight for the portfolio selection strategy. Therefore, we calculate the three performance measures of each fund over the first subperiod and use this information to condition the funds that we incorporate in our portfolios over the second subperiod. We then compare the performance of the portfolios of hedge funds against the funds of funds over the second subperiod using the same three performance measures.

The underlying hypothesis is that there exists some persistence in the performance of large hedge funds over time, although the literature on the performance persistence of hedge funds points to more ambiguous conclusions. Where persistence has been found, it is usually in the short term (yearly or quarterly) or, unfortunately, due to losing hedge funds continuing to lose rather than to winning hedge funds continuing to succeed (Agarwal and Naik, 2000b; Edwards and Caglayan, 2001) and is heavily dependent on the time period and the database employed (Capocci, Corhay, and Hübner, 2005). Brown, Goetzmann, and Ibbotson (1999) find that winning managers repeat their winning performance in only half of the years. Even after accounting for size and fees, no consistent pattern of persistence was found. The results are, however, heavily dependent on the method used, the measure applied to evaluate performance, the time period under consideration, and the database employed.

8.3.2 The performance measures

We evaluate the performance of the different funds via three different measures: the Sharpe ratio, the alpha of a multifactor model, and the information ratio.

The Sharpe ratio is calculated as the ratio of the excess return divided by the standard deviation of returns:

$$SR_i = \frac{r_{i,t}}{\sigma_r} \tag{8.1}$$

The alpha and the information ratio are obtained from the regression of the fund returns against nine market factors. The returns-generating model is a combination and extension of Carhart's (1997) four-factor model, the model used by Agarwal and Naik (2004), and the ones used by Capocci and Hübner (2004).

Specifically we run the following regression:

$$r_{i,t} = \alpha_i + \beta_{i,1}\,\mathrm{Mkt}_t + \beta_{i,2}\,\mathrm{SMB}_t + \beta_{i,3}\,\mathrm{HML}_t \\ + \beta_{i,4}\,\mathrm{UMD}_t + \beta_{i,5}\,\mathrm{WXUS}_t + \beta_{i,6}\,\mathrm{WGB}_t + \beta_{i,7}\,\mathrm{EMB}_t \\ + \beta_{i,8}\,\mathrm{GSC}_t + \beta_{i,9}\,\mathrm{HDMZD}_t + \varepsilon_{i,t} \tag{8.2}$$

where $r_{i,t}$ is the fund return in excess of the 13-week T-bill rate for the ith fund, Mkt_t is the excess return on the portfolio obtained by averaging the returns of the Fama and French (1993) size and book-to-market portfolios, SMB_t is the factor-mimicking portfolio for size (small minus big), HML_t is the factor-mimicking portfolio for the value premium (high minus low book-to-market value of equity), UMD_t is the factor-mimicking portfolio for the momentum effect (up minus down), $WXUS_t$ is the return on the MSCI World excluding US Index, WGB_t is the return on the Salomon World Government Bond Index, EMB_t is the return on the JP Morgan Emerging Market Bond Index, GSC_t is the return on the Goldman Sachs Commodity Index, and $HDMZD_t$ (high dividend minus zero dividend) represents the differential between equally weighted monthly returns of the top 30% quantile stocks ranked by dividend yields and of the zero-dividend yield stocks. Alpha is obtained by taking the intercept of this regression.

The information ratio (IR) is defined as alpha as estimated from the multifactor model presented earlier, divided by the standard deviation of the residual error from the multifactor regression. More formally,

$$IR_i = \frac{\alpha_i}{\sigma_{\varepsilon_i}} \tag{8.3}$$

Our premise for selecting these three performance measures is that we expect them to capture the different characteristics of our three fund types. Specifically, we believe the alphas will vary substantially across the three categories of funds as they will have very different factor loadings. We would expect directional (D) funds to have the most significant loadings of the factors, followed by funds of funds (FOFs), and then nondirectional (ND) funds. We might therefore expect higher alphas from the two latter fund types. The Sharpe ratio, which favors well-diversified funds, should be highest for FOFs, and we would expect the ND funds to outperform D funds using this measure, due to the higher volatility and cyclical nature of the returns of D funds. The IR should be highest for D funds, due to their significant factor loadings, reducing their residual variance, and we would expect the ND funds to be the worst performers using this measure, for the opposite reason.

8.4 Empirical results

8.4.1 Global analysis

Table 8.2 presents the performance measures of all the funds, by category (FOF, ND, and D), over the entire sample period and for the two subperiods. For each subperiod, the multifactor model is independently reestimated, so the results for the second subperiod can be interpreted as out of sample with respect to the first subperiod.

Table 8.2 Performance measures of funds of funds (FOF), nondirectional (ND), and directional (D) hedge funds over the entire sample period and the subperiods

	Global period (January 1995–December 2003)				First subperiod (January 1995–June 1999)				Second subperiod (July 1999–December 2003)			
	All	FOF	ND	D	All	FOF	ND	D	All	FOF	ND	D
Alpha												
Average	0.65	0.50	0.78	0.68	0.78	0.55	1.03	0.77	0.55	0.45	0.58	0.62
Standard deviation	0.42	0.25	0.46	0.47	0.49	0.35	0.50	0.50	0.51	0.31	0.51	0.67
Maximum	2.24	0.78	2.24	1.49	2.55	0.99	2.55	1.63	1.78	0.93	1.60	1.78
Minimum	−0.05	0.05	0.28	−0.05	−0.09	−0.09	0.34	0.02	−0.45	−0.16	−0.45	−0.29
Sharpe ratio												
Average	0.31	0.25	0.39	0.29	0.35	0.25	0.41	0.28	0.30	0.35	0.40	0.17
Standard deviation	0.20	0.14	0.21	0.24	0.21	0.14	0.28	0.15	0.29	0.31	0.31	0.22
Maximum	0.87	0.58	0.87	0.86	1.05	0.58	1.05	0.53	1.03	1.03	0.92	0.79
Minimum	0.02	0.02	0.04	0.05	−0.06	0.02	0.09	−0.01	−0.07	−0.03	−0.02	−0.07
Information ratio												
Average	0.43	0.44	0.60	0.25	0.43	0.45	0.82	0.32	0.45	0.49	0.57	0.29
Standard deviation	0.38	0.42	0.42	0.21	0.38	0.43	0.56	0.22	0.44	0.48	0.47	0.32
Maximum	1.61	1.61	1.50	0.57	1.61	1.64	2.28	0.75	1.68	1.68	1.54	1.09
Minimum	−0.02	0.02	0.10	−0.02	−0.02	−0.03	0.18	0.01	−0.14	−0.14	−0.11	−0.13

Over the entire period, the nondirectional funds provide the highest alphas and information ratios, whereas the directional funds offer the highest Sharpe ratio. The results are somewhat different when we consider the two subperiods. They indicate that highest alphas are obtained among ND funds in period 1, whereas the D funds seem to perform best under this measure in the second subperiod. In both periods, however, ND funds have higher Sharpe ratios and information ratios than D funds. This suggests identifying a strategy that keeps the alphas high while preserving the high values of the Sharpe and information ratios inherent in the ND funds. Note that the standard deviation of each performance measure is high, so an investor cannot expect to beat the FOF strategies by randomly picking among ND and D funds.

8.4.2 Persistence analysis

The challenge facing the investor confronted with a universe of directional and nondirectional funds is to select a portfolio on the basis of relevant past observations, hoping that there is sufficient persistence in performance to sustain abnormal performance for all criteria in the forthcoming subperiod.

Unlike traditional persistence analysis, which focuses on a single measure of performance, the issue to be examined involves a tridimensional performance: The selected portfolio should be able unequivocally to dominate any funds of funds on three distinct performance measures — those that can a fortiori beat any FOF on all measures — during a long period. We are thus interested in long-term persistence for a vector of performance measures.

In order to evaluate the persistence of the performance measures, we must investigate more thoroughly their ability to predict future performance. In order to achieve this, we proceed to rank the 18 FOFs over the first subperiod using the three performance measures. We then investigate the performance over the second period of the best-, top-three-, and top-half-ranked funds from period 1. The results of this exercise are presented in Table 8.3.

Clearly, alpha is the most effective measure for predicting future performance. The first three columns of Table 8.3 show that the FOFs with the highest alphas over the first subperiod perform significantly better over the second subperiod, independent of the performance measure by which we evaluate their period 2 performance. Specifically, the top-half FOFs (H1) in terms of alpha in period 1 have significantly higher alphas, Sharpe ratios, and information ratios (at the 1% level) in period 2 than the FOFs that rank in the lower half in terms of alpha in period 1 (H2). These results point to significant persistence when FOFs are selected on the basis of their alpha. The results using Sharpe ratios and information ratios are less emphatic; nonetheless, there does appear to be a certain amount of persistence in performance when the funds are ranked in period 1 using the information ratio. There is a significant difference in the Sharpe ratios and information ratios (at the 1% level) in period 2 between the best- and worst-ranked funds in period 1 in terms of information ratio. The results in Table 8.3 indicate that a good Sharpe ratio is not necessarily a good indicator of strong future performance for FOFs.

Table 8.3 Performance of portfolios of hedge funds for the subperiod July 1999–December 2003 based on their classification for the period January 1995–June 1999

	Alpha			Sharpe ratio			Information ratio		
	Alpha	SR	IR	Alpha	SR	IR	Alpha	SR	IR
Best	0.58	0.34	0.40	0.68	1.03	1.68	0.68	1.03	1.68
Top 3	0.60	0.54	0.64	0.60	0.65	0.82	0.65	0.88	1.35
H1	0.61	0.58	0.81	0.45	0.47	0.62	0.56	0.57	0.79
H2	0.30	0.11	0.17	0.45	0.22	0.35	0.35	0.12	0.18
H1 − H2	0.31**	0.46***	0.64***	0.01	0.25*	0.28	0.21	0.46***	0.61***

Portfolio rankings are obtained from the alphas, Sharpe ratios, and information ratios, respectively, during the January 1995–June 1999 period. *, **, and *** apply to differences in average performance that are significantly positive at the 10%, 5%, and 1% levels, respectively.

Now that we have established that there exists some persistence in performance of FOFs, we investigate whether a similar persistence in individual fund performance will allow us to use the performance measures over the first subperiod to construct portfolios that outperform the best FOFs over the second period. Table 8.4 compares the performance of these equal-weighted conditional portfolios of directional and nondirectional funds to the FOFs using the three different measures as a basis for fund selection. Panel A presents the results when the portfolios of funds are selected on the basis of alpha over the first period. When we construct the portfolios using both directional and nondirectional funds, the results are very disappointing. Specifically, none of the top 50 portfolios over the first period dominates the best FOF in the second period.[3] When we look at the results by decile, we actually find that the portfolios with a lower alpha in period 1 have a better chance of dominating the best FOF. Although the results are marginally better for portfolios comprising strictly nondirectional funds, using the alpha as a screening tool is clearly ineffective. The results using the other two performance measures will, however, provide much more support.

The Sharpe ratio (Panel B) and the information ratio (Panel C) provide a far superior tool for selecting nondirectional and directional portfolios. More specifically, Panel B indicates that choosing one portfolio of funds from among the 50 on the basis of the Sharpe ratio over the first period will lead to a 68.0% chance of obtaining a portfolio that dominates the best FOF in the second period. This percentage increases to 78.0 when we consider only the nondirectional funds. The alpha, Sharpe ratio, and information ratio of the portfolios in period 2 will be, on average, 0.73, 0.84, and 1.32, respectively, each of which is significantly higher than the average of the top FOFs at the 1% level.

---

[3] By *dominate*, we are referring to outperforming with respect to all three performance measures.

Table 8.4 Performance of selected funds of funds and equally weighted portfolios of hedge funds for the subperiod June 1999–June 2003: **panel A,** classification based on alphas; **panel B,** classification based on Sharpe ratios; **panel C,** classification based on information ratios

	All funds				Nondirectional			
	α	SR	IR	Dominant	α	SR	IR	Dominant
Panel A								
Best	0.67	0.21	0.21		0.97	0.55	0.63	
Top 10	0.70	0.23***	0.22***	0.0%	0.79*	0.51	0.64	20.0%
Top 30	0.72**	0.25***	0.25***	0.0%	0.62	0.43	0.55	10.0%
Top 50	0.65*	0.25***	0.24***	0.0%	0.60	0.43	0.56	10.0%
Top 100	0.66*	0.26***	0.26***	2.0%	0.57	0.43**	0.58	18.0%
D1	0.54***	0.24***	0.28***	0.6%	0.58	0.42	0.54	8.1%
D2	0.52***	0.25***	0.34**	1.1%	0.57	0.48	0.68	30.7%
D3	0.54***	0.28***	0.40**	5.9%	0.53**	0.44	0.61	22.6%
D4	0.51***	0.27***	0.40**	5.0%	0.68**	0.60	0.90	54.8%
D5	0.55***	0.32**	0.49*	10.1%	0.55*	0.49	0.71	30.7%
D6	0.51***	0.30**	0.47*	9.4%	0.62	0.56	0.85	46.8%
D7	0.50***	0.32**	0.49*	10.5%	0.62	0.60	0.91	53.2%
D8	0.51***	0.32**	0.51*	11.0%	0.59	0.59	0.89	43.6%
D9	0.51***	0.34**	0.54	11.4%	0.65	0.62	0.98	53.2%
D10	0.50***	0.34**	0.55	11.4%	0.59	0.60	0.90	50.0%
Mean	0.52***	0.30**	0.45**	7.6%	0.60	0.54	0.80	39.3%
Panel B								
Best	0.78	1.17	1.95		0.78	1.17	1.95	
Top 10	0.75**	0.98***	1.57***	80.0%	0.75**	0.98***	1.57***	80.0%
Top 30	0.76***	0.88***	1.46***	76.7%	0.77***	0.93***	1.47***	87.7%
Top 50	0.73***	0.80**	1.33***	68.0%	0.73***	0.84**	1.32**	78.0%
Top 100	0.71***	0.71	1.19**	44.0%	0.70***	0.75*	1.17**	52.0%
D1	0.60	0.46	0.73	25.9%	0.72***	0.80**	1.25**	71.0%
D2	0.52***	0.32**	0.48*	9.4%	0.64	0.62	0.93	48.4%
D3	0.51***	0.29**	0.44**	7.5%	0.63	0.57	0.87	45.2%
D4	0.47***	0.27***	0.40**	5.9%	0.59	0.55	0.77	35.5%
D5	0.49***	0.28***	0.41**	6.2%	0.59	0.52	0.77	41.9%
D6	0.50***	0.27***	0.39**	4.4%	0.58	0.49	0.71	27.4%
D7	0.49***	0.26***	0.38**	3.8%	0.56	0.48	0.70	35.5%
D8	0.53***	0.27***	0.41**	4.0%	0.58	0.47	0.69	33.9%
D9	0.54***	0.28***	0.40**	4.6%	0.54*	0.45	0.65	25.8%
D10	0.55***	0.28***	0.42**	4.4%	0.56	0.48	0.66	32.3%
Average	0.52***	0.30**	0.45**	7.6%	0.60	0.54	0.80	39.3%

(*continued*)

Table 8.4 (*continued*)

	All funds				Nondirectional			
	α	SR	IR	Dominant	α	SR	IR	Dominant
Panel C								
Best	0.78	1.17	1.95		0.78	1.17	1.95	
Top 10	0.79***	1.03***	1.71***	90.0%	0.78***	1.05***	1.70***	90.0%
Top 30	0.74***	0.78*	1.32**	66.7%	0.70**	0.81**	1.30**	70.0%
Top 50	0.70***	0.67	1.14*	48.0%	0.63	0.68	1.09	56.0%
Top 100	0.66**	0.57	0.97	30.0%	0.61	0.58	0.81	40.0%
D1	0.61	0.45	0.75	22.2%	0.62	0.66	1.06	54.8%
D2	0.57•	0.38•	0.64	13.6%	0.58	0.52	0.80	30.7%
D3	0.58	0.36•	0.60	11.7%	0.53•••	0.46	0.69	22.6%
D4	0.60	0.35•	0.58	11.4%	0.52•••	0.43	0.66	22.6%
D5	0.57•	0.32••	0.50•	6.2%	0.58	0.51	0.75	35.5%
D6	0.53•••	0.26•••	0.39••	3.7%	0.58	0.51	0.78	37.1%
D7	0.50•••	0.25•••	0.33••	3.9%	0.59	0.51	0.75	37.1%
D8	0.48•••	0.23•••	0.28•••	2.0%	0.62	0.54	0.78	41.9%
D9	0.43•••	0.20•••	0.22•••	0.7%	0.67**	0.60	0.85	48.4%
D10	0.33•••	0.17•••	0.15•••	0.7%	0.70**	0.66	0.86	59.7%
Average	0.52•••	0.30••	0.45••	7.6%	0.60	0.54	0.80	39.3%

In panels A, B, and C, portfolios are based on the rankings obtained from the alphas, Sharpe ratios, and information ratios, respectively, during the January 1995–June 1999 period. *,**, and *** apply to average portfolio performances that are significantly higher than the corresponding value of the portfolio "H1" of the best nine funds of funds classified based on alphas for the period January 1995–June 1999 at the 10%, 5%, and 1% levels, respectively. •,••, and ••• apply to coefficients that are significantly lower than the corresponding value of H1 at the 10%, 5%, and 1% levels, respectively are lower than the corresponding values of the H1 portfolio of funds of funds classified based on alphas for the period January 1995–June 1999. For each category of funds, the last column reports the percentage of portfolios that dominate H1 on all three performance measures.

Importantly, as we move down the deciles, the probability of dominating the FOFs decreases monotonically. This lends further support to the notion that the funds (or portfolio of funds) exhibit persistence in their performance. A similar conclusion is reached when the portfolios are selected on the basis of their information ratio (Panel C), but the results are less striking. For example, choosing one portfolio among the top 30 portfolios comprising directional and nondirectional hedge funds would lead to a 66.7% chance of obtaining higher measures than the FOF (Panel C). In this case, the average alpha, Sharpe ratio, and information ratio of this portfolio in period 2 would be 0.74, 0.78, and 1.32, respectively, significantly higher than those of the top FOFs in period 2 at the 5% level. Again, we find that limiting our selection to nondirectional funds increases the probability of beating the best FOFs.

8.5   Conclusion

We have shown that it is possible to construct portfolios of large nondirectional and directional hedge funds that outperform the best large hedge FOFs in the HFR database, in terms of alpha, Sharpe ratio, and information ratio. Furthermore, it is not necessary for investors to enter into a large number of hedge funds to accomplish this. We demonstrate that equal-weighted portfolios of no more than four funds are sufficient to dominate the best of the largest FOFs.

This dominance holds for the total sample period but, more importantly, when the sample is split in two subperiods of equal length. We find the Sharpe ratio to be the best measure by which to evaluate persistence from one period to the next and, to a lesser extent, the information ratio. Importantly, we find that nondirectional funds tend to exhibit greater persistence and that limiting the portfolios to include only nondirectional funds with the best performance over the first period greatly increases the likelihood of dominating the best FOFs. These results seem to imply that the extra layer of fees paid to funds of funds managers are largely unmerited, for we can create portfolios of funds, using simple portfolio-construction rules and readily available market information, that greatly outperform the best FOFs.

Acknowledgments

Georges Hübner thanks Deloitte (Luxembourg) and the Luxembourg School of Finance, University of Luxembourg for financial support. Nicolas Papageorgiou and Fabrice Rouah thank the Centre for Research in E-Finance (CREF) at HEC Montreal for financial support. We are responsible for all errors.

References

Agarwal, V. and Naik, N. Y. (2000a). Multiperiod Performance Analysis of Hedge Funds. *Journal of Financial and Quantitative Analysis*, 35(3): 327–342.

Agarwal, V. and Naik, N. Y. (2000b). On Taking the Alternative Route: Risks, Rewards, and Performance Persistence of Hedge Funds. *Journal of Alternative Investments*, 2(4):6–23.

Agarwal, V. and Naik, N. Y. (2004). Risks and Portfolio Decisions Involving Hedge Funds. *Review of Financial Studies*, 17(1):63–98.

Amin, G. and Kat, H. (2003). Hedge Fund Performance 1990–2000: Do the "Money Machines" Really Add Value? *Journal of Financial and Quantitative Analysis*, 38(2):251–275.

Brown, S. J., Goetzmann, W. N., and Ibbotson, R. J. (1999). Offshore Hedge Funds: Survival and Performance, 1989–95. *Journal of Business*, 72(1):91–117.

Brown, S. J., Goetzmann, W. N., and Liang, B. (2005). Fees on Fees in Funds of Funds. Working Paper, Yale University, New Haven, CT.

Capocci, D., Corhay, A., and Hübner, G. (2005). Hedge Fund Performance in Bull and Bear Markets. *European Journal of Finance*, 11(5):361–392.

Capocci, D. and Hübner, G. (2004). Analysis of Hedge Fund Performance. *Journal of Empirical Finance*, 11(1):55–89.

Carhart, M. M. (1997). On Persistence in Mutual Fund Performance. *Journal of Finance*, 52(1):57–82.

Edwards, F. R. and Caglayan, M. O. (2001). Hedge Fund Performance and Manager Skill. *Journal of Futures Markets*, 21(11):1003–1028.

Fama, E. F. and French, K. R. (1993). Common Risk Factors in the Returns on Stocks and Bonds. *Journal of Financial Economics*, 33(1):3–56.

Fung, W. and Hsieh, D. A. (1999). A Primer on Hedge Funds. *Journal of Empirical Finance*, 6(3):309–331.

Hedge Fund Research, Inc. (2003), http://www.hfr.com.

Schneeweis, T. and Martin, G. (2001). The Benefits of Hedge Funds: Asset Allocation for the Institutional Investor. *Journal of Alternative Investments*, 4(3):7–26.

Part Two
Diversification, Selection, Allocation, and Hedge Fund Indices

9 Funds of funds of hedge funds: welcome to diworsification

François-Serge Lhabitant and Nicolas Laporte*

Abstract

Hedge funds are often thought of as being high-risk investments, and many investors in the past have shied away from them for fear of incurring large losses. However, in recent years, hedge funds have generally substantially outperformed equities, with much lower volatility. As a consequence, they are now in strong demand, particularly when one remembers that any risk associated with hedge fund investing diminishes in importance when the funds are repackaged into fund of funds products. However, once one admits that portfolio diversification reduces manager risk, there is a fundamental issue that needs to be addressed: the optimal number of funds of hedge funds to effectively benefit from diversification. Using the Altvest database, we provide evidence that from a pure market risk perspective, existing funds of hedge funds are sufficiently well diversified. Consequently, mixing them in a portfolio does not result in significant diversification benefits, but adds an extra layer of fees that is harming investors.

9.1 Introduction

Markowitz' (1952) seminal paper on modern portfolio theory contains the foundation of what seems to be a free lunch, namely, the reduction in risk that is obtainable through diversification. Simply stated, an investor who spreads his wealth among many securities can reduce the volatility of his portfolio, provided that the underlying securities are imperfectly correlated. There is no reduction in average return and thus — apparently — no bill for the lunch. Many investors initially thought they could easily benefit from this free lunch. For instance, in the U.S. market of the 1960s, a single randomly selected stock had a volatility that was 35 percentage points higher than a portfolio invested in an equally weighted index of all available stocks. An equally weighted portfolio of 20 randomly selected individual stocks could reduce this excess risk to a modest level of about 5 percentage points. This was the basis for the well-known rule of

---

* The opinions expressed in this chapter are solely the views of the authors and not of any institution they may belong to.

thumb that a 20-stock portfolio was adequately diversified. However, since the mid-1990s, the free lunch seems to have shrunk or at least become more difficult to obtain. Due to the increased globalization and integration of financial markets, correlations were rising, and many more than 20 stocks were needed in a portfolio to achieve effective diversification. This has progressively fueled the growth of collective investment vehicles such as mutual funds and hedge funds, which were able to provide diversification and professional portfolio management in a simple and convenient package.

However, most investors are uncomfortable with the idea of being exposed to a single fund manager. Just as choosing a bad manager may easily wipe out all the benefits of a hedge fund allocation, investing in only one hedge fund is likely to be suboptimal. Thus, most of the time, investors chose a fund of hedge funds as their preferred structure for entering the alternative investment arena. It frees investors from the responsibility of monitoring individual managers and provides instant diversification within the hedge fund universe. This is, in simple terms, appealing — or at least it was when there were only a few funds of funds to select from. More recently, funds that group stakes in various fund of funds — and thereby attempt to reduce the risk of investing in any one fund of funds — have appeared. They are being marketed as an even safer and more diversified version of funds of funds. But is there any value added in these new funds of funds of funds? Do the benefits, if any, cover the additional layer of fees? This is precisely our focus in this chapter.

9.2   The art and science of diversification

Numerous papers have been written on the subject of how many assets are needed to reach an optimally diversified portfolio.[1] More recently, a few papers have also focused on how many hedge funds are needed to achieve an optimally diversified portfolio.[2] The consensus seems to be that approximately 5 to 10 managers is sufficient to significantly reduce the overall risk of a portfolio of hedge funds. Increasing the number of hedge funds beyond that limit has only a marginal impact on further reducing the risk of the portfolio.

All these studies were carried out using a naive diversification approach, often referred to as the "1/N heuristics" method, because it essentially entails evenly dividing the total allocation among the available assets. Naive diversification attributes no importance to the relationship between assets to create a portfolio.

---

[1] See, for instance, Elton and Gruber (1977), Evans and Archer (1968), Latane and Young (1969), Fisher and Lorie (1970), Mokkelbost (1971), Wagner and Lau (1971), Johnson and Shannon (1974), Lorie (1975), Upson, Jessup, and Matsumoto (1975), Lloyd, Hand, and Modani (1981), Tole (1982), Statman (1987), Newbould and Poon (1993), and O'Neal (1997), among others.

[2] See, for instance, Billingsley and Chance (1996) for managed futures, Henker and Martin (1998) for CTAs, and Henker (1998), Lhabitant, and Learned (2002) and Schneeweis, Kazemi, and Karavas (2003).

That is to say, the correlation between the assets is not utilized in the allocation decision. This method of diversification does, indeed, reduce volatility, and it is simple to use when there is a lack of knowledge about the assets and interrelationships. By contrast, optimized diversification follows the work Markowitz set out in his dissertation in 1952. His mathematical approach takes into account the correlation between assets in order to maximize the benefits and minimize the overlap. Hence, assets with high volatilities but negative correlation are good combinations in a portfolio, whereas assets that have high volatilities and high correlation are less optimally diversified.

In practice, most hedge fund investors adopt a naive approach to diversification rather than the Markowitz optimization. There are several reasons for this. First, most optimizers are unable to effectively incorporate the operational constraints demanded by hedge fund investments, such as minimum investments, lockup periods, and redemption notifications. Second, in terms of quantity and quality, the lack of hedge fund information limits the capacity of econometric modeling; optimizers require precise and stable forecasts of risks, returns, and correlations, whereas hedge fund returns and strategies are by definition dynamically evolving. In addition, the difficulties of predicting the future economic environment are ever present. Finally, hedge fund return distributions are not always normal, meaning that they tend to exhibit skewness and fat tails, whereas mean–variance optimizers work on the assumption of a normal distribution.

9.3 Analysis

In this study, our aim was to assess the existence of effective diversification benefits provided by investing simultaneously in several funds of hedge funds rather than just one of them. Our starting data set was made of the 304 funds of hedge funds available in the Investorforce/Altvest database with monthly returns from January 2000 to August 2005.

With this data set, we used Monte Carlo simulation to create series of equally weighted portfolios of increasing size ($N = 1, 2, \ldots, 50$ funds) of funds of hedge funds that were randomly selected. For each portfolio, we built a time series of returns and used it to generate various statistics (average return, volatility, etc.). For each portfolio size, this process was repeated 500 times to obtain 500 observations of each statistic. This is necessary to estimate the typical behavior of a portfolio of size N.

The benefit of diversification using this naive diversification approach (i.e., equal weights across randomly selected funds of funds) is a function of the difference between the average variance of the individual funds of funds in our sample and the average covariance of the funds of funds within the same sample universe. The more homogeneous our sample, the fewer the number of funds of funds required to reduce the volatility of the portfolio to that of the sample from which the funds of funds are drawn.

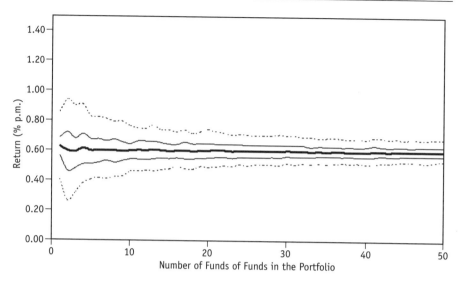

Figure 9.1 Evolution of the mean return of a fund of funds of hedge funds portfolio as a function of the number of underlying funds of hedge funds (The thick line represents the average, the thin lines the 25th and 75th percentiles, and the dotted lines the 5th and 95th percentiles.)

9.4   Diversification results

Not surprisingly, our study finds that a relatively small number of funds of funds is needed to maximize the potential diversification benefits.

Figure 9.1 shows the effect on the portfolio's return as the number of funds of hedge funds in the portfolio changes. The thick line represents the average situation in our 500 simulations, the two thin lines the 25th and 75th percentiles, and the two dotted lines the extreme cases (i.e., 5th and 95th percentiles). Not surprisingly, the return on the portfolio is not significantly affected by the number of funds of funds. This result is due to the linearity of the average operator.[3] It is evident that the mean return varies widely across strategies and over time.

Figure 9.2 shows the effect of the number of funds of funds on the volatility of the portfolio. On average, adding new funds of funds in the portfolio has almost no impact on its volatility. Even when considering the 25th and 75th percentiles, the extra diversification provided is small. It is only in the extreme situations — basically, if the investor starts with a portfolio made of one of the worst funds of funds — that additional funds of funds will deliver significant benefits.

As mentioned earlier, hedge fund returns are generally not normally distributed. Asymmetry and fat tails in the return distribution are a result of the

---

[3] The average operator is linear. In a sense, the figure we obtain for a one-fund portfolio is the average of 500 hedge funds returns, while the figure for a two-fund portfolio will simply be the average of 1,000 hedge funds. The number will, therefore, rapidly converge to the sample average.

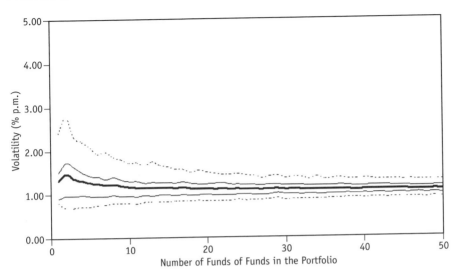

Figure 9.2 Impact of diversification on the volatility of a fund of funds of hedge funds portfolio (The thick line represents the average, the thin lines the 25th and 75th percentiles, and the dotted lines the 5th and 95th percentiles.)

complexity of their trading styles. If a fund's returns are positively skewed, the investor is probably quite happy. If the tails are fat, the investor can expect a more thrilling investment ride. The characteristics of a hedge fund's past performance do not determine its future performance, as all disclosure statements continually remind us. However, a fund that is highly positively skewed most certainly gives the investor a different gut feeling from one that is negatively skewed. For this reason, we have included in this study the effect of the number of funds of hedge funds in a portfolio on skewness and kurtosis (see Figures 9.3 and 9.4).[4] Skewness is known to disappear with diversification, because funds with negative skewness are mixed with positively skewed ones so that, at the aggregate level, these individual effects cancel each other out. For the same reason, we expect excess kurtosis somehow to be reduced by diversification.

Our simulated portfolios seem to exhibit positive skewness and positive kurtosis. Both skewness and kurtosis increase moderately as more funds of hedge funds enter the portfolio and then stabilize. Extreme levels of skewness and kurtosis are observed at the 5th and 95th percentiles, but they are attributable to a few very specific funds of hedge funds.

---

[4] Skewness characterizes the degree of asymmetry of a distribution around its mean. Positive skewness indicates a distribution with an asymmetric tail extending toward more positive values. Negative skewness indicates a distribution with an asymmetric tail extending toward more negative values. Kurtosis characterizes the relative peakedness or flatness of a distribution compared with the normal distribution. Positive kurtosis indicates a relatively peaked distribution. Negative kurtosis indicates a relatively flat distribution.

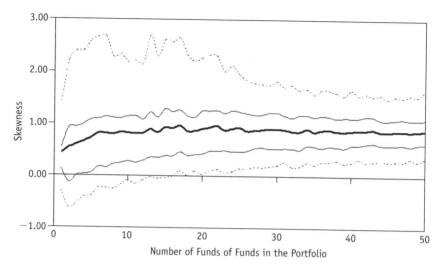

Figure 9.3 Impact of diversification on the skewness of a fund of funds of hedge funds portfolio (The thick line represents the average, the thin lines the 25th and 75th percentiles, and the dotted lines the 5th and 95th percentiles.)

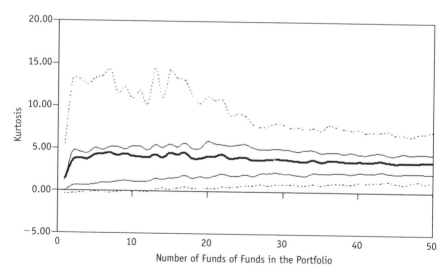

Figure 9.4 Impact of diversification on the kurtosis of a fund of funds of hedge funds portfolio (The thick line represents the average, the thin lines the 25th and 75th percentiles, and the dotted lines the 5th and 95th percentiles.)

We also analyzed the behavior of two generally accepted downside-risk statistics: the worst monthly return and the value at risk (see Figures 9.5 and 9.6). The largest monthly loss is the greatest decline in net asset value for a particular hedge fund for any one-month period during the time span considered. The value at risk (VaR)

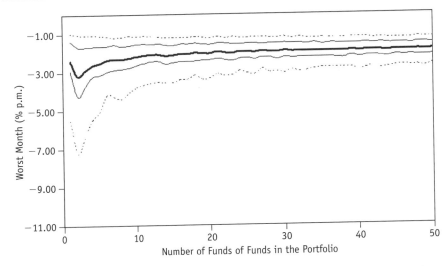

Figure 9.5 Impact of diversification on the worst month of a fund of funds of hedge funds portfolio (The thick line represents the average, the thin lines the 25th and 75th percentiles, and the dotted lines the 5th and 95th percentiles.)

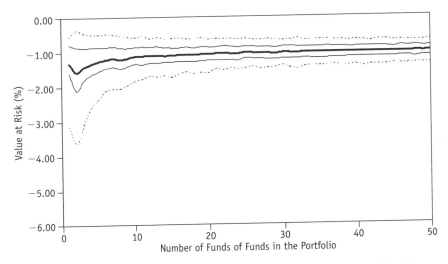

Figure 9.6 Impact of diversification on the value at risk (95%, one-month holding period) of a fund of funds of hedge funds portfolio (The thick line represents the average, the thin lines the 25th and 75th percentiles, and the dotted lines the 5th and 95th percentiles.)

is an estimate of the maximum a particular fund could lose over a one-month period in normal market conditions. In our case, we defined normal market conditions as being 95% of the time, and we calculated VaR by simply taking the 5th percentile of the empirical return distribution over the considered period.

Whatever the risk measure, we arrive at the same conclusion: On average, adding new funds of funds in the portfolio has a very limited impact on its risk. Even when considering the 25th and 75th percentiles, the extra diversification provided is small. Once again, it is only in the extreme situations — basically, if the investor starts with a portfolio made of one of the worst funds of funds — that additional funds of funds will deliver significant benefits.

Recent statistics evidence an increase in the dispersion of returns of funds of funds in the most recent past, particularly on the downside. This trend is primarily attributable to the lack of barriers to entry to the fund of hedge funds industry and to the widening gap between talented and less talented managers. Consequently, investors must select a first quartile fund of hedge funds to unlock the alpha in the hedge fund industry. However, at the same time, it is becoming easier to identify the real top quartile fund of hedge funds, based on their experience, network, ability to manage risk, access to the best hedge funds, track record, integrity, and alignment of interest.

9.5 How about the fees?

If no costs were associated with adding funds of hedge funds to a portfolio, then holding the entire universe of funds of hedge funds would result in the optimum reduction in diversifiable risk. However, the fund of hedge funds reality is by definition costly. Here is an illustration.

- At the individual fund of funds level, there are the costs associated with initial and ongoing due diligence, compliance, and other operational aspects. These costs are often duplicated when two funds of funds analyze simultaneously the same underlying hedge fund.
- The more diversified a fund of hedge funds is, the greater the likelihood that the investor will incur an incentive fee on one or more of the constituent managers, regardless of the overall performance. Creating a fund of funds of hedge funds further magnifies this problem.

In order to illustrate the impact that fees can have in such a pyramidal construction, let us assume that all hedge fund managers charge 2 and 20 (i.e., 2% management fees and 20% performance fees), all funds of hedge fund managers charge 1 and 10, and the fund of funds of hedge funds charges an extra 1%. If all hedge fund managers were able to deliver a gross performance of 15%, the net performance would be 10% at the hedge fund level. Funds of funds would reduce it down to 8%, and the fund of funds of funds would finally shrink it to 7% after fees. Now, if all hedge fund managers were able to deliver a more realistic gross performance of 10%, the final investor would receive only 3.4%. Thus, despite the potential theoretical reduction in risk, the cost of having a manager to select other managers who select hedge fund managers that select securities seems prohibitive.

9.6   Conclusion

The proliferation of hedge funds, the increasing participation of investors in alternative investments, the growing collection of articles analyzing hedge funds, and the omnipresent uncertainty of future market conditions all give rise to a greater need to choose the right hedge funds when allocating to alternative assets. As illustrated by Lhabitant and Learned (2002) and Schneeweis, Kazemi, and Karavas (2003), although some level of diversification proves better than no diversification at all, investors should be cautious and limit the number of hedge funds in their portfolios because the practice of diversifying a portfolio's hedge fund exposure is not as simple as it is in traditional asset classes. Hedge funds themselves are already diversified, so there is only a limited gain to using more than 5–10 hedge funds in a portfolio. Adding more hedge funds still provides benefits, but the gains seem marginal compared to the drawbacks of managing the enlarged portfolio.

When considering the next layer (i.e., a portfolio of funds of hedge funds), our study therefore confirms our initial expectation: There is almost no diversification benefits, except when the selection skills are extremely poor. There are several reasons to explain this result. First, investors pay out more in fees when investing in funds of funds of hedge funds than they earn in returns. Second, investing is not collecting. To an art collector, 20 masterpieces by Picasso are at least 20 times better than one. But 20 funds of hedge funds are not 20 times better than one fund of hedge funds; they are, in all likelihood, far worse. Since the average hedge fund already owns more than 100 stocks, and since most funds of hedge funds and funds of funds of hedge funds are managed by sheep in human clothing, you'll just end up buying and selling the same companies over and over again, and paying anyone involved in the process another fee to select something. That's not diversification, it is "diworsification." Last but not least, portfolios with large numbers of funds of hedge funds end up mimicking the performance of a passive investment in a broad hedge fund index while also incurring excessive management fees.

References

Billingsley, R. S. and Chance, D. M. (1996). Benefits and Limitations of Diversification Among Commodity Trading Advisors. *Journal of Portfolio Management*, 23(1):65–80.

Elton, E. and Gruber, M. (1977). Risk Reduction and Portfolio Size: An Analytical Solution. *Journal of Business*, 50(4):415–437.

Evans, J. L. and Archer, S. H. (1968). Diversification and the Reduction of Dispersion: An Empirical Analysis. *Journal of Finance*, 23(5):761–767.

Fisher, L. and Lorie, J. H. (1970). Some Studies of Variability of Returns on Investments in Common Stocks. *Journal of Business*, 43(2):99–134.

Henker, T. (1998). Naive Diversification for Hedge Funds. *Journal of Alternative Investments*, 1(3):33–38.

Henker, T. and Martin, G. (1998). Naïve and Optimal Diversification for Managed Futures. *Journal of Alternative Investments*, 1(2):25–39.

Johnson, K. H. and Shannon, D. S. (1974). Diversification and the Reduction of Dispersion. *Journal of Financial Economics*, 4:365–372.

Latane, H. A. and Young, W. E. (1969). Test for Portfolio Building Rules. *Journal of Finance*, 24(1):595–612.

Lhabitant, F. and Learned, M. (2002). Hedge Fund Diversification: How Much Is Enough? *Journal of Alternative Investments*, 5(3):23–49.

Lloyd, W. P., Hand, J. H., and Modani, N. K. (1981). The Effect of Portfolio Construction Rules on the Relationship between Portfolio Size and Effective Diversification. *Journal of Financial Research*, 4(3):183–193.

Lorie, J. (1975). Diversification: Old and New. *Journal of Portfolio Management*, 25:25–32.

Markowitz, H. M. (1952). Portfolio Selection. *Journal of Finance*, 7(1):77–91.

Mokkelbost, P. (1971). Unsystematic risk over time. *Journal of Financial and Quantitative Analysis*, 6(2):785–797.

Newbould, G. D. and Poon, P. S. (1993). The Minimum Number of Stocks Needed for Diversification. *Financial Practice and Education*, 3(2):85–87.

O'Neal, E. D. (1997). How Many Mutual Funds Constitute a Diversified Mutual Fund Portfolio? *Financial Analysts Journal*, 53(2):37–46.

Schneeweis, T., Kazemi, H., and Karavas V. (2003). Fund Diversification in Fund of Funds Investment: How Many Hedge Funds Are Enough? Working Paper, CISDM, Amherst, MA.

Statman, M. (1987). How Many Stocks Make a Diversified Portfolio? *Journal of Financial and Quantitative Analysis*, 22(3):353–363.

Tole, T. (1982). You Can't Diversify Without Diversifying. *Journal of Portfolio Management*, 8(2):5–11.

Upson, R., Jessup, P., and Matsumoto, K. (1975). Portfolio Diversification Strategies. *Financial Analysts Journal*, 31(3):86–88.

Wagner, W. and Lau, S. (1971). The Effect of Diversification on Risk. *Financial Analysts Journal*, 27(6):48–53.

10 Style analysis of funds of hedge funds: measurement of asset allocation and style drift

Oliver A. Schwindler and Andreas Oehler

Abstract

Due to the limited information disclosure of funds of hedge funds, their underlying asset allocation is hard to analyze. Therefore, we analyze Sharpe's style analysis technique in the context of hedge funds in order to estimate quantitatively the asset allocation of funds of hedge funds. We analyze the influence of the three parameters of Sharpe's style analysis model, which are defined by the user: the number of indices in the set of investment indices, the length of the rolling time window, and the nature of the return series (smoothed or unsmoothed). We show in our analysis that Sharpe's method can distinguish four hedge fund groups reasonably well from each other and that unsmoothed returns do not enhance the results. We also analyze whether this technique is able to monitor quantitatively and consistently the styles of funds of hedge funds and detect possible style drifts. We find that Sharpe's method combined with the style drift score can reasonably well measure quantitatively the style drift of a fund of hedge funds.

10.1 Introduction

Returns-based style analysis (RBSA), developed by Sharpe (1988, 1992) as a low-cost alternative to portfolio-based style analysis, is widely used in practice. The purpose of RBSA as proposed by Sharpe (1988) is to determine a manager's effective asset mix with respect to a set of asset classes. This analytical tool was originally developed for the style analysis of mutual funds, and it has since been used in various studies (Fung and Hsieh, 1996; Brown and Goetzmann, 1997; DiBartolomeo and Witkowski, 1997; Chan, Chen, and Lakonishok, 2002). As the hedge fund industry has matured, the RBSA has more frequently been used for the analysis of hedge funds (Fung and Hsieh, 1997; Agarwal and Naik, 2000; Dor and Jagannathan, 2002; Brown and Goetzmann, 2003). A look at these studies reveals that Sharpe's method is not consistently applied. This could be due to the close connection between constrained multivariate regression and returns-based style analysis. Becker (2003) shows that dropping the alpha from a constrained multivariate linear regression produces the same results as Sharpe's model.

However, the description "constrained multivariate linear regression with zero alpha" has in the past been misunderstood because many researchers performed a constrained multivariate linear regression with alpha constrained to zero, which does not deliver the same results as Sharpe's method.

The possible field of applications for a style analysis model are performance evaluation, risk management, and classification. The last application ensures that funds are correctly classified, since different investment strategies exhibit different risk and return patterns. Furthermore, a style analysis model should also detect migrations (for example, style drifts) of funds from one class to another. For the performance evaluation of funds of hedge funds, an appropriate benchmark is essential. A style analysis model can be used to construct this necessary benchmark by means of either public available indices or asset-based style factors (Fung and Hsieh, 2002). Lhabitant (2001a, 2001b) suggests an application for the risk management of hedge funds and funds of hedge funds, where the outputs of the style analysis model proposed by Sharpe are used to estimate value-at-risk figures of hedge funds and funds of hedge funds. However, each of the mentioned applications does make different demands on the style analysis model. For a risk management application, the data generated by the style analysis model must be accurate, up-to-date, and fine grained. For the case of performance evaluation or classification of hedge funds, the output of the style analysis model must not be as fine grained as for a risk management application. The timeliness and the accuracy depend on the length of the rolling time window. The accuracy and the level of detail can be directly influenced by the choice of the number of different investment strategies. Due to these outlined factors, we analyze the influence of three different rolling time windows (12 months, 24 months, and 36 months) and the influence of two different sets of indices (16 hedge fund strategy indices and 4 hedge fund group indices) on the up-to-dateness, the accuracy, and the level of detail of the style analysis model.

Confirming the results of Getmansky, Lo, and Makarov (2004) and Brooks and Kat (2002) we find significant autocorrelation of hedge fund index returns. Therefore, we additionally analyze the impact of the unsmoothing technique suggested by Geltner (1991, 1993) on the output and the accuracy of the style analysis model.

Overall we find that Sharpe's method can distinguish four hedge fund groups reasonably well from each other. Building on this, we analyze the capability of the RBSA to quantitatively measure the style drift of a fund of hedge funds.

10.2   Sharpe's model for style analysis

Sharpe's approach is to regress a fund's historical return against the returns of a set of passively constructed reference portfolios, whereas each reference portfolio represents an asset class or investment style. This is done by minimizing the variance of the error term ε_t of

$$R_t = \sum_{i=1}^{I} w_i r_{it} + \varepsilon_t \tag{10.1}$$

where

R_t = historical return of the analyzed fund
i = the asset class or investment strategy
w_i = style weight of asset class or investment strategy i
r_{it} = return of asset class or investment strategy i for period t
ε_t = error term

Sharpe imposed two restrictions. The first restriction is the portfolio restriction, which requires that the estimates for the style weights w_i be interpreted as portfolio holdings. This (equality) restriction is

$$\sum_{i=1}^{I} w_i = 1 \tag{10.2}$$

The second restriction is the short-selling restriction, which requires that all estimated portfolio holdings be long positions expressed by the inequality restrictions

$$0 \le w_i \le 1, \quad i = 1, \ldots, I \tag{10.3}$$

Since a fund's style can change substantially over time, it is also helpful to study how the exposures to various style benchmarks evolve. For that purpose we conduct a series of style analyses, using a fixed number of months (T) for each analysis, rolling the time period used for the analysis through time. Because of the inequality constraints, the style weights cannot be obtained by applying ordinary least squares (OLS) as in a classical multivariate linear regression. Therefore, quadratic programming (QP) algorithms are applied to solve for the style weights. However, as opposed to OLS, confidence regions are not readily obtained when using QP. A solution to this problem is presented by Lobosco and DiBartolomeo (1997), who approximate confidence intervals[1] for each style weight via the following formula for the calculation of the standard error for each weight w_i:

$$\mathrm{SE}_{w_i} = \frac{\sigma_a}{\sigma_{B_i} \times \sqrt{T - k - 1}} \tag{10.4}$$

---

[1] As Lobosco and DiBartolomeo (1997) note, a traditional t-statistic can be used for testing the significance of the weights w_i.

where

 i = index corresponding to the style weight being estimated
 SE_{wi} = standard error of the style weight w_i for index i
 σ_a = active standard deviation of the style analysis (σ_e)
 σ_{B_i} = unexplained Sharpe style index volatility for index i
 T = number of returns used in the style analysis
 k = number of market indices with nonzero style weights

The unexplained Sharpe style index volatility for an index i (σ_{B_i}) is calculated by performing a returns-based style analysis with the remaining $(I - 1)$ indices as explanatory variables without the inequality restrictions (10.3) for the individual weights. This procedure provides the standard deviation of the residuals from the unconstrained style analysis of each index i relative to the remaining $(I - 1)$ indices, which is called *unexplained Sharpe style index volatility*. Sharpe (1992) proposed that the R^2 value is identified as attributable to the mutual funds' style and the remainder $(1 - R^2)$ to selection. Using the traditional definition, R^2 is given by

$$R^2 = 1 - \frac{\text{Var}(\varepsilon_t)}{\text{Var}(R_t)}$$

It is important to recognize that this measure indicates only the extent to which a specific model fits the data at hand. Clearly, minimizing the variance of the error term ε_t, which is what returns-based style analysis does, is equivalent to minimizing, $\text{Var}(\varepsilon_t)/\text{Var}(R_t)$, which in turn is equivalent to maximizing the explained variance $1 - \text{Var}(\varepsilon_t)/\text{Var}(R_t)$.

The solution to a style analysis problem is indeterminate if any of the investment strategy indices used as factors can be formed as a linear combination of other investment strategy indices. Sharpe (1992) stated that "asset class returns should have either low correlations with one another or, in cases in which correlations are high, different standard deviations." This statement is only a qualitative description of selecting the right investment strategy indices. The unexplained Sharpe style index volatility is a quantitative tool that can ease the search for an ideal combination of the different investment strategy indices for the style analysis model. All investment strategy indices should have high unexplained Sharpe style index volatilities to ensure a reliable decomposition of a fund's of hedge funds asset allocation. In this context, returns of hedge fund strategy or hedge fund group indices are used for investment strategy indices.

10.3   Data set

For our empirical analysis we use the hedge fund strategy indices from two different index providers: CSFB/Tremont and Van. Both hedge fund index providers have compared to other index providers a unique feature in the construction of

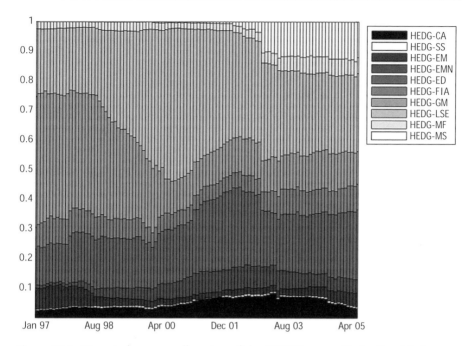

Figure 10.1 Historical strategy allocation of the CSFB/Tremont Hedge Fund Index

their indices.[2] We have chosen Van Global indices because of their large database and the fact that all collected hedge funds are included in the calculation of the hedge fund indices. The second important feature of the Van Global indices is that the 16 different hedge fund strategy indices are aggregated into four broader hedge fund group indices, the Market Neutral Group (VANG-MN), the Long/Short Equity Group (VANG-LSE), Directional Trading Group (VANG-DT), and the Specialty Strategies Group (VANG-SST). The indices from CSFB/Tremont are the only indices that are capital weighted, and they are widely known and followed by industry experts. Because the CSFB/Tremont Hedge Fund Index is capital weighted, it is similar to a real fund of hedge funds. Figure 10.1 shows the historical strategy allocation of the CSFB/Tremont Hedge Fund Index from January 1997 to June 2005.

10.4   Hedge fund classification

10.4.1   Overview

Hedge funds that use various trading strategies, each having different risk and return characteristics, have been labeled and categorized by managers, database

---

[2] For a detailed overview about all hedge fund indices and their calculation, see Amenc, Martellini, and Vaissié (2004).

vendors, and academicians. Because there is no universal style classification, the classifications vary by database vendor. A style classification in a database is often self-assigned. Hedge fund database providers, such as Van and Tremont TASS, classify funds into 16 and 12 investment styles, respectively. There is a vast academic literature on how to classify hedge funds. Kazemi, Gupta, and Daglioglu (2003) provide an overview of various methodologies that can be applied for classifying hedge funds. In contrast to the practical hedge fund classification, studies by Fung and Hsieh (1997) and Brown and Goetzmann (2003) have identified between five and eight investment styles in the hedge fund industry. Bianchi, Drew, Veeraraghavan, and Whelan (2005) find the presence of only three different hedge fund styles. The ongoing discussion about the correct hedge fund classification system and these findings suggest that the four hedge fund group indices from Van could be more suitable for the style analysis of funds of hedge funds than a large set of different hedge fund strategy indices. Therefore, we take a look at the properties of the individual investment strategy indices of these two classification systems and analyze only the interactive effects between the indices in each of the classification systems, which are relevant for Sharpe's style analysis model.

10.4.2   Hedge fund strategies

Table 10.1 gives an overview of the descriptive statistics of the hedge fund strategy indices.[3] The different means and standard deviations reveal divergences between few strategy indices of CSFB/Tremont and Van. The latter reports for the Fixed Income Arbitrage strategy an average monthly return of 0.75%, which is almost twice the return of 0.44% reported by CSFB/Tremont, even with a marginal lower standard deviation. The Van Global Futures Index exhibits a 47% higher return than the corresponding index from CSFB/Tremont, and the Van Global Macro Index has an average monthly return of 0.57%, which is only half the average monthly return documented by CSFB/Tremont. Furthermore, the standard deviations of the Equity Market Neutral and the Multi-Strategy indices of Van are much higher than their representatives from CSFB/Tremont. These differences can be attributed to the larger database of Van Hedge and the construction methodology of their indices. A major difference has to be pointed out between the two short-selling indices, the index from Van exhibits a marginal positive monthly return, whereas the CSFB/Tremont Short Selling Index exhibits a negative monthly return. This suggests that these two indices actually measure a different group of hedge funds. Because the nonnormality of hedge funds is well documented (Brooks and Kat, 2002; Agarwal and Naik, 2004; Bacmann and Pache, 2004), we present the third and fourth moment of the empirical return distributions of the used hedge fund indices. Regarding the skewness and kurtosis of the Convertible Arbitrage Index and the Multi-Strategy Index, it can be reported that these measures are significantly higher for the CSFB/Tremont representatives than for their counterparts from Van. This can be explained by the broader diversification of

---

[3] An explanation of the abbreviations used is provided in the appendix to this chapter.

Table 10.1 Descriptive statistics of hedge fund strategy indices returns

	Mean	Standard deviation	Skewness		Kurtosis		Autocorrelation coefficients					LB-statistic	
							1 month		2 month		3 month		
CSFB/Tremont														
HEDG-CA	0.72	1.46	−1.364	***	6.024	***	0.536	***	0.372	***	0.109		47.20	***
HEDG-SS	−0.14	5.40	0.925	***	4.914	***	0.104		−0.043		0.016		4.31	
HEDG-EM	0.73	4.63	−1.178	***	9.256	***	0.256	***	0.026		0.080		7.64	
HEDG-EMN	0.84	0.83	0.482	**	3.509		0.177	*	0.047		−0.018		5.30	
HEDG-ED	0.87	1.78	−3.708	***	26.400	***	0.331	***	0.138		0.029		14.45	**
HEDG-FIA	0.44	1.16	−3.251	***	18.927	***	0.372	***	0.022		−0.057		16.14	***
HEDG-GM	1.06	2.98	−0.136		6.851	***	0.107		0.058		0.105		5.09	
HEDG-LSE	1.02	3.26	0.291		6.338	***	0.133		0.051		−0.037		8.97	
HEDG-MF	0.63	3.58	0.112		2.957	***	0.070		−0.071		−0.022		6.28	
HEDG-MS	0.76	1.05	−1.513	***	9.592	***	0.202	**	0.014		0.093		5.92	
Van Hedge														
VANG-EMN	0.95	1.29	1.452	***	7.970	***	0.199	**	0.125		0.049		6.11	
VANG-DS	0.98	1.51	0.036		5.330	***	0.300	***	0.071		0.023		10.28	*
VANG-MA	0.71	0.96	−2.005	***	13.194	***	0.302	***	0.273	***	0.228	**	33.77	***
VANG-SSI	0.94	2.18	−0.069		6.604	***	0.261	***	0.084		−0.001		9.09	
VANG-CA	0.85	1.17	−0.605	**	4.061	**	0.554	***	0.268	***	0.159		43.54	***
VANG-FIA	0.75	1.02	−4.710	***	37.900	***	0.316	***	0.103		−0.099		15.53	***
VANG-LSEA	1.10	4.90	0.711	***	4.816	***	0.182	*	0.146		0.004		7.30	
VANG-LSEO	1.21	3.22	1.833	***	11.540	***	0.171	*	0.120		0.007		5.81	
VANG-LSEV	1.25	3.24	−0.219		3.872	**	0.177	*	−0.015		−0.040		6.37	
VANG-SS	0.08	6.69	0.092		5.612	***	0.129		−0.086		−0.027		5.29	
VANG-MF	0.93	3.42	0.219		3.035		0.009	*	−0.120		−0.038		4.32	
VANG-GM	0.57	2.88	0.437	*	6.011	***	−0.038		−0.022		0.009		2.74	
VANG-MT	1.00	2.77	1.028	***	5.636	***	0.145		0.122		−0.063		4.56	
VANG-EM	0.83	5.46	−0.182		5.423	***	0.215	**	0.103		−0.002		6.92	
VANG-GI	0.61	1.27	−2.203	***	15.475	***	0.168	*	0.086		−0.131		8.74	
VANG-MS	0.91	2.48	−0.280		4.310	**	0.187	*	0.017		−0.005		5.13	

See chapter appendix for an explanation of the abbreviations used.
*, **, and *** denote significance at the 10%, 5%, and 1% levels, respectively.

the Van Hedge indices.[4] In order to test for nonnormality of skewness and kurtosis, we use both the test proposed by D'Agostino (1970) for skewness and the test proposed by Anscombe and Glynn (1983) for kurtosis.[5] Table 10.1 reveals that nearly all hedge fund strategy indices exhibit a nonnormal kurtosis, but only a smaller number shows nonnormal skewness. However, these differences do not hamper the analysis.

Table 10.1 presents the mean, standard deviation, skewness, kurtosis, and first three autocorrelation coefficients of the hedge fund strategy index returns from CSFB/Tremont and of the hedge fund strategy index returns from Van during the entire sample period from January 1997 to June 2005 (102 monthly returns). To test the significance of the first three autocorrelation coefficients we use the method suggested by Tsay (2002). For testing jointly whether several autocorrelations are zero, the LB-test proposed by Ljung and Box (1978) is used.

Serial correlation is a well-documented property of hedge fund returns (Getmansky, Lo, and Makarov, 2004; Brooks and Kat, 2002), and this was confirmed for our sample because the LB-tests,[6] documented in Table 10.1, reveal a significant degree of autocorrelation for several hedge fund strategy indices. As discussed in Brooks and Kat (2002), this is most likely caused by marking-to-market problems,[7] which will mislead investors to underestimate the true standard deviation. Therefore, to provide a better picture of the true characteristics of the return series we use Geltner's (1991, 1993) unsmoothing technique. Following Geltner (1991, 1993), the observed (or smoothed) value V_t^* of a hedge fund index at time t could be expressed as the weighted average of the true value at time t, V_t, and the smoothed value at time $t - 1$, V_{t-1}^*:

$$V_t^* = \alpha V_t + (1 - \alpha)V_{t-1}^*$$

Given this equation, it is possible to derive an expression that will yield an unsmoothed return series with zero first-order autocorrelation:

$$r_t = \frac{r_t^* - \alpha r_{t-1}^*}{1 - \alpha} \tag{10.5}$$

where r_t and r_t^* are the true underlying (unobservable) return and the observable return at time t, respectively. The variable α is set equal to the first-order

---

[4] For a detailed analysis of the diversification effects for hedge fund portfolios, see Lhabitant and Learned (2002). However, the very high kurtosis value for the Van Hedge Global Fixed Income Arbitrage Index remains unclear.

[5] A two-sided test is used for skewness because the direction of the deviation from normality can be positive or negative. Kurtosis is tested using a one-tailed test as prior research studies clearly show that hedge funds exhibit a positive excess kurtosis.

[6] Since the power of the LB-test depends on the number of lags (m) used for its calculation, we follow Tsay (2002), who suggests the choice of $m \approx \ln(T)$.

[7] For a detailed discussion of the stale pricing issue in the context of hedge funds, see Gaber, Gregoriou, and Kelting (2005).

autocorrelation coefficient. The newly constructed series, r_t,will have the same mean as r_t^*, but nearly zero first-order autocorrelation. Table 10.2 presents the mean, standard deviation, skewness, kurtosis and the first three autocorrelation coefficients of the unsmoothed hedge fund strategy index returns from CSFB/Tremont and of the unsmoothed hedge fund strategy index returns from Van during the entire sample period from January 1997 to June 2005 (102 monthly returns).

By comparing Tables 10.1 and 10.2, we can see that after unsmoothing the returns, all values of the standard deviations show a significant increase. The higher the first-order autocorrelation coefficient found in the raw data, the higher the rise. The biggest increases are documented for the Convertible Arbitrage and the Fixed Income Arbitrage indices. This can be explained by the fact that these hedge funds usually trade a significant amount of illiquid assets, which can cause valuation problems because of their stale pricing. On the other side, we document for hedge funds that trade in very liquid markets, like Global Macro and Managed Futures funds, only a marginal increase of their standard deviations. For the non-normality of hedge fund returns the picture gets clearer. After unsmoothing, nearly all hedge fund strategies exhibit nonnormal kurtosis, but only half the indices exhibit nonnormal skewness. The unsmoothing process eliminates the autocorrelation for all hedge fund strategy indices, except for Van's Merger Arbitrage Index. However, these differences again do not hamper the analysis.

10.4.3 Hedge fund strategy groups

Because CSFB/Tremont does not publish broader hedge fund group indices like Van does, we construct indices in the manner of Van for a Market Neutral Group (HEDG-MN), a Long/Short Equity Group (HEDG-LSE), a Directional Trading Group (HEDG-DT), and a Speciality Strategies Group (HEDG-SST) for the CSFB/Tremont index family. To get a realistic return series for each of these indices we use the corresponding historical weights of the individual strategy indices in the CSFB/Tremont Hedge Fund Index. Because Brooks and Kat (2002) show that forming portfolios of hedge funds itself tends to create serial correlation, we unsmoothed the returns of the CSFB/Tremont hedge fund group indices after their construction. Table 10.3 shows the descriptive statistics for the raw returns (Panel A) and unsmoothed returns (Panel B) of the four constructed hedge fund group indices for the index family from CSFB/Tremont and the descriptive statistics of the four hedge fund group indices from Van. This table presents the mean, standard deviation, skewness, kurtosis, and first three autocorrelation coefficients of the hedge fund group index returns from CSFB/Tremont and of the hedge fund group index returns from Van during the entire sample period from January 1997 to June 2005 (102 monthly returns).

After building hedge fund group indices, all of the corresponding hedge fund group index pairs exhibit similar monthly returns and standard deviations (Panel A in Table 10.3). However, some indices show extreme differences for skewness

Table 10.2 Descriptive statistics of unsmoothed hedge fund strategy indices returns

	Mean	Standard deviation	Skewness		Kurtosis		Autocorrelation coefficients			LB-statistic
							1 month	2 month	3 month	
CSFB/Tremont										
HEDG-CA	0.70	2.66	−0.864	***	7.211	***	−0.065	0.186 *	−0.160	7.59
HEDG-SS	−0.14	6.00	0.904	***	4.826	***	0.006	−0.057	0.034	3.07
HEDG-EM	0.71	5.97	−1.517	***	9.933	***	0.007	−0.061	0.080	1.10
HEDG-EMN	0.84	0.99	0.314		3.760	*	−0.005	0.031	−0.031	1.97
HEDG-ED	0.86	2.51	−4.001	***	30.317	***	−0.011	0.041	−0.003	0.73
HEDG-FIA	0.43	1.71	−1.716	***	12.281	***	0.051	−0.104	−0.082	2.91
HEDG-GM	1.04	3.29	−0.082		6.300	***	−0.005	0.041	0.112	4.54
HEDG-LSE	1.02	3.72	0.222		5.921	***	−0.004	0.040	−0.030	7.22
HEDG-MF	0.63	3.85	0.013		3.013		0.006	−0.075	−0.006	4.95
HEDG-MS	0.76	1.29	−1.529	***	10.047	***	0.007	−0.048	0.087	1.72
Van Hedge										
VANG-EMN	0.95	1.58	1.269	***	7.715	***	−0.017	0.082	0.028	0.94
VANG-DS	0.98	2.05	0.220		6.092	***	0.006	−0.022	0.001	0.20
VANG-MA	0.71	1.31	−1.950	***	14.766	***	−0.065	0.150	0.133	10.50
VANG-SSI	0.94	2.85	0.180		6.749	***	−0.004	0.023	−0.017	2.21
VANG-CA	0.85	2.18	0.209		4.776	***	0.039	−0.063	−0.008	0.62
VANG-FIA	0.74	1.41	−4.335	***	35.660	***	−0.003	0.049	−0.115	2.78
VANG-LSEA	1.10	5.89	0.720	***	4.486	***	−0.021	0.120	−0.018	4.51
VANG-LSEO	1.21	3.83	1.840	***	11.569	***	−0.016	0.096	−0.016	3.23
VANG-LSEV	1.25	3.87	−0.140		3.601	*	0.008	−0.040	−0.023	4.59
VANG-SS	0.08	7.62	0.037		5.703	***	0.013	−0.103	−0.000	2.05
VANG-MF	0.93	3.46	0.209		3.039		0.001	−0.119	−0.036	4.23
VANG-GM	0.57	2.97	0.447	*	5.927	***	0.000	−0.023	0.014	2.68
VANG-MT	1.00	3.21	0.900	***	5.186	***	−0.015	0.113	−0.019	3.27
VANG-EM	0.83	6.79	−0.318		5.485	***	−0.013	0.065	−0.006	2.16
VANG-GI	0.61	1.51	−2.300	***	16.203	***	−0.009	0.083	−0.135	4.29
VANG-MS	0.91	2.99	−0.223		4.061	***	0.003	−0.017	0.005	1.61

See chapter appendix for an explanation of the abbreviations used.
*, **, and *** denote significance at the 10%, 5%, and 1% levels, respectively.

Table 10.3 Descriptive statistics of the raw and unsmoothed hedge fund group indices returns

	Mean	Standard deviation	Skewness		Kurtosis		Autocorrelation coefficients			LB-statistic	
							1 month	2 month	3 month		
Panel A: Raw data											
CSFB/Tremont											
HEDG-MN	0.75	1.24	−3.040	***	19.852	***	0.401 ***	0.231 **	0.014	23.85	***
HEDG-LSE	1.00	3.12	0.391	*	6.243	***	0.135	0.056	−0.041	9.37	*
HEDG-DT	0.98	2.91	−0.005		5.765	***	0.088	0.032	0.109	4.91	
HEDG-SST	0.61	4.23	−1.203	***	10.721	***	0.256 ***	0.024	0.098	8.08	
Van Hedge											
VANG-MN	0.88	1.19	0.281		5.965	***	0.366 ***	0.151	−0.006	17.19	***
VANG-LSE	1.12	2.95	0.512	**	4.928	***	0.192 *	0.083	−0.006	5.55	
VANG-DT	0.88	2.46	0.228		2.654	***	−0.064	−0.078	−0.073	4.91	
VANG-SST	0.74	3.88	−0.602	**	6.295	***	0.172 *	0.083	−0.031	5.25	
Panel B: Unsmoothed data											
CSFB/Tremont											
HEDG-MN	0.73	1.90	−3.250	***	24.489	***	−0.036	0.121	−0.093	3.55	
HEDG-LSE	1.00	3.60	0.316		5.786	***	−0.005	0.045	−0.035	7.62	
HEDG-DT	1.00	3.21	0.054		5.401	***	−0.004	0.014	0.121	5.00	
HEDG-SST	0.59	5.52	−1.548	***	11.271	***	0.003	−0.068	0.093	1.50	
Van Hedge											
VANG-MN	0.88	1.74	0.355		5.666	***	−0.007	0.045	−0.048	1.49	
VANG-LSE	1.12	3.59	0.538	**	4.590	***	−0.009	0.053	−0.018	2.02	
VANG-DT	0.87	2.10	0.268		2.678	***	−0.005	−0.087	−0.088	5.36	
VANG-SST	0.73	4.62	−0.703	***	6.600	***	−0.030	0.066	−0.011	2.23	

See chapter appendix for an explanation of the abbreviations used.
*, **, and *** denote significance at the 10%, 5%, and 1% levels, respectively.

and kurtosis. The CSFB/Tremont Market Neutral Index has a high negative skewness of -3.040 and a high kurtosis of 19.852, whereas the Van Global Market Neutral has a small positive skewness of 0.281 and a kurtosis of 5.965. A similar picture is documented for the Speciality Strategies group indices. The CSFB/Tremont Index exhibits a high negative skewness of -1.203 and a high kurtosis of 10.721, and Van reports a skewness of -0.602 and a kurtosis of 6.295. Panel B in Table 10.3 shows that the unsmoothing process causes higher standard deviations for all hedge fund strategy group indices and that the effects on skewness and kurtosis are only marginal, except for the kurtosis of the CSFB/Tremont Market Neutral group index, which increases by 23% to 24.489%. The moment tests reveal that almost all hedge fund group indices exhibit a nonnormal kurtosis and that only half the indices have a skewness that can be classified as nonnormal. The LB-tests reveal that the unsmoothing process reduces the autocorrelation coefficients for all hedge group indices.

10.4.4   Differences of hedge fund classifications

As Lobosco and DiBartolomeo (1997) note, the unexplained Sharpe style index volatility (σ_{B_i}) is a measure of independence of an investment strategy index that can be used as a quantitative tool in the search for an ideal combination of the different investment strategy indices. To analyze the interactive effects between the indices in each classification system, we present the unexplained Sharpe index volatilities of the Van Global hedge fund strategy indices with smoothed returns and the Van Global hedge fund group indices with smoothed returns from December 1999 to June 2005 in Figures 10.2a and 10.2b, respectively. For this analysis, a rolling 24-month time window is used.[8] To ensure comparability between the CSFB/Tremont and the Van Global indices, the average unexplained Sharpe style index volatility of the three Van Global Long/Short Equity indices (Aggressive Growth, Opportunistic, and Value) for the Van Global Long/Short Equity strategy index and the average unexplained Sharpe style index volatility of the Distressed Securities Index, the Merger Arbitrage Index, and the Special Situation Index for the Van Global Event Driven Index are used. Figure 10.2a shows a pattern where all hedge fund strategy indices converge to a level below 1%, except the Managed Futures Index, which remains on a high level.

Given that all hedge fund strategy indices exhibit an unexplained Sharpe index volatility below 1% in recent months, it can be concluded that Sharpe's style analysis model will have difficulty providing a fine-grained decomposition of a portfolio of hedge funds when the model uses the large set of different hedge fund strategy indices.

Figure 10.2b reveals that the second index set with the hedge fund group indices produces reasonably stable levels near 1% for all of the group indices.

---

[8] We present the results only for the 24-month rolling time window because the analysis reveals that a 24-month time window gives the best results for the style analysis model.

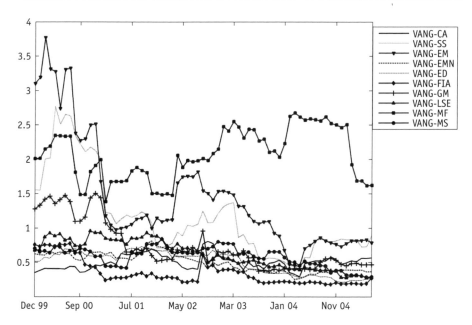

Figure 10.2a Unexplained Sharpe index volatilities of the Van Global hedge fund strategy indices with smoothed returns (rolling 24-month time window)

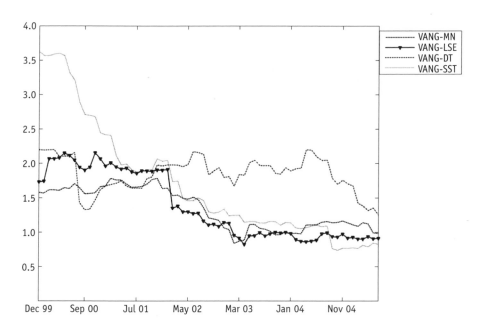

Figure 10.2b Unexplained Sharpe index volatilities of the Van Global hedge fund group indices with smoothed returns (rolling 24-month time window)

Comparing Figures 10.2a and 10.2b, we can deduce that the small set of four hedge fund group indices will produce more accurate results than the large set of the 16 hedge fund strategy indices.

Both the choice of the rolling time window and the unsmoothing process do not change the presented pictures of the unexplained Sharpe index volatilities for the two index sets.[9]

10.5   Accuracy of Sharpe's model

10.5.1   Absolute deviations

One of the basic questions an analyst might ask is how well RBSA evaluates the style exposure of a fund's current portfolio. RBSA, by definition, is a constrained estimate of the portfolio's past and current exposures. However, the output of RBSA frequently serves as a proxy for the fund's current portfolio. The issue then becomes, since RBSA is an estimate, what the error term is. To assess the accuracy, we use the absolute deviation between the estimate, generated by the RBSA, and the true portfolio weight.[10] These absolute deviations of the individual hedge fund strategies or hedge fund groups can combine the aggregated with the J-statistic[11] to one measure. The J-statistic is a coefficient of agreement between the weights derived from the style analysis and the actual weights and is defined as

$$
J_t = 1 - \frac{\sum_{i=1}^{I} \left| (w_{p,i,t} - w_{i,t}) \right|}{2} \tag{10.6}
$$

where $w_{p,i,t}$ is the true weight of hedge fund strategy i in the CSFB/Tremont Hedge Fund Index in period t and $w_{i,t}$ is the estimate of hedge fund strategy i obtained from the style analysis for period t. The J-statistic is calculated for each time period t. The statistic ranges from zero to 1. A value of 1 means that the estimates of the RBSA are 100% identical to the true portfolio weights. However the J-statistic does not reveal where the difference comes from. Therefore, we calculate D-statistics,[12] which designate the proportion of disagreement between the weights of the paired portfolios that is due to a difference in the hedge fund strategies or

---

[9] We do not present the figures for the unexplained Sharpe index volatilities for the unsmoothed returns of the two hedge fund index sets because these results are qualitatively identical to those seen in Figures 10.2a and 10.2b. These figures and the ones for the 12-month and 36-month rolling time windows can be obtained from the author's Website at http://www.oliverschwindler.com.

[10] Because we alter the number of the hedge fund indices from 16 hedge fund strategies to four hedge fund groups, we use the absolute deviation instead of the mean absolute deviation, to ensure comparability of the results.

[11] For a discussion of the J-statistic, see Johnson (1974).

[12] For a discussion of D-statistics, see Lovins, Johnson, and Shannon (1979).

groups contained in the portfolios (D_s) and the proportion of the disagreement due to a difference in weights of the agreeing hedge fund strategies or groups (D_w). These two different statistics are calculated as follows:

$$D_{s,t} = \frac{\sum_{i=1}^{I} \left|(w_{p,i,t} - w_{i,t})\right|}{\sum_{i=1}^{I} \left|(w_{p,i,t} - w_{i,t})\right|} \qquad \text{(when either } w_{p,i,t} \text{ or } w_{i,t} = 0) \atop \text{(for all } i) \qquad (10.7)$$

$$D_{w,t} = \frac{\sum_{i=1}^{I} \left|(w_{p,i,t} - w_{i,t})\right|}{\sum_{i=1}^{I} \left|(w_{p,i,t} - w_{i,t})\right|} \qquad \text{(both } w_{p,i,t}, w_{i,t} > 0) \atop \text{(for all } i) \qquad (10.8)$$

By definition, $D_w = 1 - D_s$. The analysis reveals that the proportion of the differences in the weights that are due to differences in weights of agreeing hedge fund strategies or groups (D_w) is larger than the proportion of the differences in the weights that are due to differences in hedge fund strategies or groups (D_s). Therefore, we present only the values of D_w. Tables 10.4 and 10.5 present the J-statistics and D_w-statistics for 12 different style analyses of the CSFB/Tremont Hedge Fund Index, where three different rolling time windows are used (12-month, 24-month, and 36-month) and two different sets of indices (16 hedge fund strategy indices and 4 hedge fund group indices) are used. Furthermore, we use both smoothed (observed) and unsmoothed returns for the analyses.

Sharpe (1992) notes that the weights w_i obtained via the style analysis can be interpreted as an estimate of the average of the true weights over the rolling time window. Corielli and Meucci (2004) note that Sharpe's model for style analysis fails to yield correct results even in a simple case of a buy-and-hold strategy that only invests in the market indices. To see how large this failure is in the context of this study, we perform an in-sample test with the two index sets from CSFB/Tremont. The results are displayed in Table 10.4. This table presents the averages, standard deviations (in parentheses), maximums, and minimums of the J-statistics and D_w-statistics and the average R^2 values for 12 different style analyses where the CSFB/Tremont hedge fund strategy indices (panel A) or the CSFB/Tremont hedge fund group indices (panel B) are regressed on the CSFB/Tremont Hedge Fund Index. The table shows the results over the period from December 1999 until June 2005. Table 10.4 reveals that this kind of error is even quite high for the most accurate regression model, which has an average J-statistic of 0.94. However, there is currently no solution to reduce this failure.

Table 10.5 presents the results of regressing the smoothed or unsmoothed returns of the Van hedge fund strategy indices or the Van hedge fund group indices on the CSFB/Tremont Hedge Fund Index. The analysis reveals that the style analyses

Table 10.4 J-statistics and $D_{w,t}$-statistics for different style analyses with CSFB/Tremont indices

Panel A: 10 Hedge Fund Strategy Indices

| | Smoothed returns | | | | | | | Unsmoothed returns | | | | | | |
| | J-statistics | | | D_w-statistics | | | | J-statistics | | | D_w-statistics | | | |
	Avg	Max	Min	Avg	Max	Min	R^2	Avg	Max	Min	Avg	Max	Min	R^2
12-month	0.85 (0.07)	0.96	0.66	0.85 (0.14)	1.00	0.55	0.99	0.75 (0.05)	0.87	0.62	0.78 (0.12)	1.00	0.51	0.98
24-month	0.83 (0.08)	0.95	0.60	0.88 (0.12)	1.00	0.59	0.99	0.76 (0.05)	0.87	0.61	0.86 (0.08)	1.00	0.63	0.98
36-month	0.76 (0.09)	0.91	0.56	0.88 (0.13)	1.00	0.50	0.99	0.73 (0.05)	0.82	0.60	0.87 (0.12)	1.00	0.61	0.98

Panel B: 4 Hedge Fund Group Indices

| | Smoothed returns | | | | | | | Unsmoothed returns | | | | | | |
| | J-statistics | | | D_w-statistics | | | | J-statistics | | | D_w-statistics | | | |
	Avg	Max	Min	Avg	Max	Min	R^2	Avg	Max	Min	Avg	Max	Min	R^2
12-month	0.94 (0.03)	0.99	0.86	0.99 (0.03)	1.00	0.77	0.99	0.85 (0.06)	0.96	0.72	0.96 (0.06)	1.00	0.67	0.97
24-month	0.87 (0.06)	0.98	0.72	1.00 (0.00)	1.00	1.00	0.99	0.83 (0.06)	0.93	0.68	0.96 (0.05)	1.00	0.74	0.97
36-month	0.82 (0.04)	0.92	0.70	1.00 (0.00)	1.00	1.00	0.99	0.792 (0.04)	0.89	0.69	0.95 (0.10)	1.00	0.62	0.97

Table 10.5 J-statistics and $D_{u,t}$-statistics for different style analyses with Van Hedge indices

Panel A: 16 Hedge Fund Strategy Indices

| | Smoothed returns | | | | | | | Unsmoothed returns | | | | | | |
| | J-statistics | | | D_w-statistics | | | | J-statistics | | | D_w-statistics | | | |
	Avg	Max	Min	Avg	Max	Min	R^2	Avg	Max	Min	Avg	Max	Min	R^2
12-month	0.30 (0.08)	0.55	0.13	0.72 (0.12)	0.92	0.50	0.96	0.41 (0.18)	0.70	0.06	0.59 (0.21)	0.94	0.14	0.96
24-month	0.31 (0.08)	0.49	0.17	0.78 (0.10)	0.96	0.54	0.92	0.40 (0.15)	0.67	0.11	0.76 (0.19)	0.97	0.30	0.92
36-month	0.37 (0.08)	0.53	0.22	0.84 (0.07)	0.97	0.67	0.89	0.47 (0.08)	0.63	0.33	0.86 (0.06)	0.99	0.70	0.86

Panel B: 4 Hedge Fund Group Indices

| | Smoothed returns | | | | | | | Unsmoothed returns | | | | | | |
| | J-statistics | | | D_w-statistics | | | | J-statistics | | | D_w-statistics | | | |
	Avg	Max	Min	Avg	Max	Min	R^2	Avg	Max	Min	Avg	Max	Min	R^2
12-month	0.66 (0.10)	0.89	0.47	0.86 (0.16)	1.00	0.50	0.85	0.61 (0.10)	0.96	0.41	0.74 (0.20)	1.00	0.50	0.78
24-month	0.69 (0.09)	0.85	0.46	0.93 (0.11)	1.00	0.60	0.84	0.64 (0.06)	0.77	0.47	0.87 (0.16)	1.00	0.56	0.80
36-month	0.72 (0.09)	0.87	0.57	0.96 (0.09)	1.00	0.72	0.81	0.68 (0.06)	0.80	0.57	0.88 (0.16)	1.00	0.58	0.99

with smoothed returns of the Van Global hedge fund group indices produce the highest *J*-statistic and, therefore, provide the most accurate results. The influence of the unsmoothed return series depends on the set of investment strategy indices used. Regressions with unsmoothed return series of hedge fund strategy indices exhibit a higher *J*-statistic, whereas regression with unsmoothed return series of hedge fund group indices have lower *J*-statistics than the regression with smoothed return series. A look at the row with the average R^2 of the style analysis reveals that the style analyses with the Van Global hedge fund strategy indices have higher average R^2 than the style analyses with the Van Global hedge fund group indices. However, the *J*-statistic uncovers that the deviations between the estimated weights by the style analysis and true weights are higher for the style analyses with the Van Global hedge fund strategy indices. Also, the low D_w-statistics of the analyses with the hedge fund strategy indices reveal that these analyses cannot evaluate the true asset allocation correctly, because, as Figure 10.1 shows, the CSFB/ Tremont Hedge Fund Index always consists of all hedge fund strategies. Figure 10.3 shows the *J*-statistic and the deviation for the four Van Global hedge fund group indices from the true portfolio weights for the regression with smoothed returns and a 24-month rolling time window. Figure 10.3 reveals that the style analysis model underestimates the weight for the Long/Short Equity Group and at the same time overestimates the weight for the Market Neutral Group over the entire period.

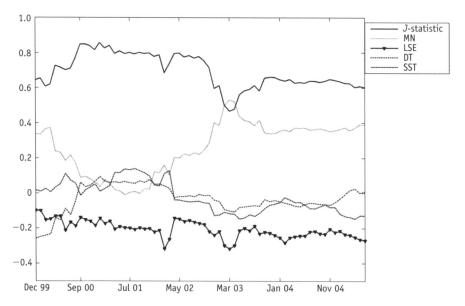

Figure 10.3 *J*-statistic and absolute deviation of the individual hedge fund group indices for the regression with the four Van Global indices (smoothed returns, rolling 24-month time window)

10.5.2 Standard errors

Given the foregoing results it can be concluded that R^2 is not the correct measure to assess the accuracy of the style analysis model. The aforementioned question then becomes, since the true weights are unknown to the analyst, how can the user of the style analysis model evaluate its accuracy? The only available figures for estimating the accuracy are the standard errors of the weights w_i, which are defined by Eq. (10.4). Figures 10.4a and 10.4b display the standard errors for the regression with the Van Global hedge fund strategy indices (10.4a) and the Van Global hedge fund group indices (10.4b). For both figures, smoothed returns and a 24-month rolling time window is used.

To ensure comparability for the regressions with the hedge fund strategy indices, the average standard error of the three Van Global Long/Short Equity indices (Aggressive Growth, Opportunistic, and Value) and the average standard error of the Distressed Securities Index, the Merger Arbitrage Index, and the Special Situation Index for the Van Global Event Driven Index are used. The standard errors of the hedge fund strategy indices in Figure 10.4a do not exhibit a clear trend like the unexplained Sharpe index volatilities in Figure 10.2a. However, Eq. (10.4) would suggest an upside sloping trend for the standard errors, given the downward sloping unexplained Sharpe index volatilities. Furthermore, because the number of nonzero style weights (k) is increasing, Figure 10.4a should exhibit a clear upward-sloping trend. However, this expected upward-sloping trend is absorbed by a decreasing active standard deviation of the style analysis (σ_a), which causes a gradual increase in R^2 over time.

The downward-sloping standard errors of the Market Neutral, Long/Short Equity, and Directional Trading group indices in Figure 10.4b can be attributed solely to the gradual decrease of the active standard deviation of the style analysis (σ_a), because the unexplained Sharpe index volatilities are reasonably stable (see Figure 10.2b) and because there are seldom nonzero style weights.

Unfortunately, we find no relationship between the actual deviations measured by the J-statistics and the standard errors calculated by the methodology proposed by Lobosco and DiBartolomeo (1997).[13] Therefore, the analyst has no opportunity to check the accuracy of his estimation of the true portfolio weights. We leave it to the interested reader to employ other, more complex techniques to build confidence intervals for the estimated weights. For instance, Kim (2005) develops a Bayesian method and Otten and Bams (2000) employ the Kuhn–Tucker algorithm to obtain confidence intervals.

10.6   Measuring the style drift

Traditional econometric techniques for measuring changes or differences in sets of coefficients are usually applied to the residuals resulting from a standard linear

---

[13] Neither a linear regression nor a correlation analysis reveals a meaningful relationship between the J-statistic and the standard errors.

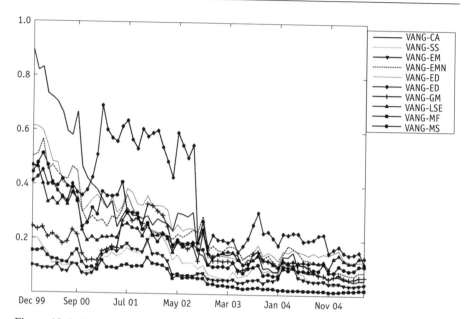

Figure 10.4a Standard errors of the individual hedge fund strategy indices for the regression with the 16 Van Global indices (smoothed returns, rolling 24-month time window)

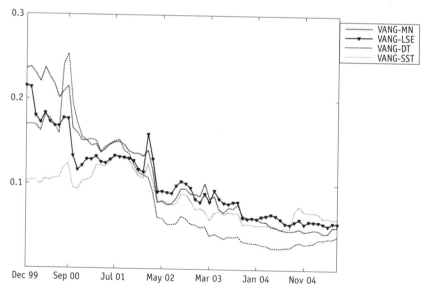

Figure 10.4b Standard errors of the individual hedge fund group indices for the regression with the four Van Global indices (smoothed returns, rolling 24-month time window)

regression, but returns-based style analysis residuals are not the same as the standard linear regression residuals. Therefore, Idzorek and Bertsch (2004) developed the style drift score (SDS), which is the square root of the sum of the variances of the style weights:

$$SDS = \sqrt{\sum_{i=1}^{I} \sigma_{w_i}^2} \qquad (10.9)$$

where $\sigma_{w_i}^2 = \mathrm{Var}\{w_{i,1}, w_{i,2}, \ldots, w_{i,N}\}$ is the variance of the ith style weight over a defined rolling period N. We use 12 months, 24 months, and 36 months as rolling time windows. To see which one of the 12 analyzed models best tracks the style drift of the CSFB/Tremont Hedge Fund Index, the correlation coefficients between the style drift scores generated by the 12 style analysis models and the true style drift score of the CSFB/Tremont Hedge Fund Index are calculated. To ensure comparability, the time horizon for this analysis covers the period from November 2002 to June 2005. Table 10.6 presents the results.

From Table 10.6 it can be concluded that the choice of the rolling time window for the style drift measurement is crucial, for some correlation coefficients turn out to be negative. Moreover, we show that a style analysis based on the hedge group indices produces more accurate results for the style drift measurement.

Table 10.6 Correlation coefficients of style drift scores

	Panel A: Hedge Fund Strategy Indices					
	SDS with smoothed returns			SDS with unsmoothed returns		
	$N = 12$	$N = 24$	$N = 36$	$N = 12$	$N = 24$	$N = 36$
12-month style analysis	0.5154	0.9033	0.9507	0.5108	0.7245	0.8288
24-month style analysis	0.9055	0.9567	0.8428	0.2700	0.7437	0.2898
36-month style analysis	0.3249	0.0134	−0.8566	−0.3224	−0.9353	−0.9353

	Panel B: Hedge Fund Group Indices					
	SDS with smoothed returns			SDS with unsmoothed returns		
	$N = 12$	$N = 24$	$N = 36$	$N = 12$	$N = 24$	$N = 36$
12-month style analysis	0.4856	0.2561	0.8953	0.8130	0.6122	0.8376
24-month style analysis	0.9062	0.6577	0.8791	0.7601	0.5356	0.9643
36-month style analysis	0.6378	0.4810	−0.7809	0.6960	0.5648	0.8121

The best choice for this data set would be a 24-month style analysis model with the four hedge fund group indices combined with a 12-month rolling time window for the calculation of the style drift score. The high correlation coefficient of 0.9062 suggests that the style drift can be measured reasonably well with these two techniques.

10.7   Conclusion

The main purpose of the study is to reveal how accurate Sharpe's style analysis model is in the context of the analysis of funds of hedge funds. Therefore, we analyze the influence of the three parameters of a style analysis model, which are defined by the user: the number of indices in the set of investment indices, the length of the rolling time window, and the nature of the return series (smoothed or unsmoothed). Because we find that the unexplained Sharpe index volatilities for the hedge fund group indices are much higher and more stable than the ones for the hedge fund strategy indices, we can conclude that the former are more suitable for such an accurate style analysis model. This is confirmed by higher J-statistics for the regressions with the hedge fund group indices in Table 10.5. Regarding the choice of the rolling time window, we find that the length of the rolling time window has practically no influence on the accuracy of the model. However, unsmoothing the returns does not enhance the results.

Because we find that in general Sharpe's method can distinguish only four hedge fund groups reasonably well from each other, its usage for the risk management tools is limited. Given that each hedge fund strategy exhibits a different form of risk,[14] such as credit risk or market risk, a fine-grained decomposition is needed to get an accurate evaluation of the fund's of hedge funds risks. For the purpose of performance evaluation and classification of funds of hedge funds, a splitting into four broader hedge fund groups can be satisfactory in some cases.

Acknowledgments

We thank Mr. Hoffmann and Mr. Jupp for providing the data set of the historical strategy allocations of the CSFB/Tremont Hedge Fund Index and Marco Rummer, Dirk Schiefer and Stefan Wendt for helpful comments.

References

Agarwal, V. and Naik, N. Y. (2000). Generalized Style Analysis of Hedge Funds. *Journal of Asset Management*, 1(1):93–109.

---

[14] For a detailed overview of the inherent risks of different hedge fund strategies, see Jaeger (2002).

Agarwal, V. and Naik, N. Y. (2004). Risks and Portfolio Decisions Involving Hedge Funds. *Review of Financial Studies*, 17(1):63–98.

Amenc, N., Martellini, L., and Vaissié, M. (2004). Indexing Hedge Fund Indices. In: *Intelligent Hedge Fund Investing* (Schachter, B., ed.). Risk Books, London.

Anscombe, F. J. and Glynn, W. J. (1983). Distribution of the Kurtosis Statistic b_2 for Normal Samples. *Biometrika*, 70(1):227–234.

Bacmann, J. F. and Pache, S. (2004). Optimal Hedge-Fund-Style Allocation Under Higher Moments. In: *Intelligent Hedge Fund Investing* (Schachter B., ed.). Risk Books, London.

Becker, T. (2003). Exploring the Mathematical Basics of Returns-Based-Style Analysis. In: *The Handbook of Equity-Style Management* (Coggin, T. D. and Fabozzi, F. J., eds.). John Wiley & Sons, Hoboken, NJ.

Bianchi, R. J., Drew, M. E., Veeraraghavan, M., and Whelan, P. (2005). An Analysis of Hedge Fund Styles Using the Gap Statistic. *Proceedings of the Economic Society of Australia*.

Brooks, C. and Kat, H. M. (2002). The Statistical Properties of Hedge Fund Index Returns and Their Implications for Investors. *Journal of Alternative Investments*, 5(2):26–44.

Brown, S. J. and Goetzmann, W. N. (1997). Mutual Fund Styles. *Journal of Financial Economics*, 43(3):373–399.

Brown, S. J. and Goetzmann, W. N. (2003). Hedge Funds with Style. *Journal of Portfolio Management*, 29(2):101–112.

Chan, L. K. C., Chen, H. L., and Lakonishok, J. (2002). On Mutual Fund Investment Styles. *Review of Financial Studies*, 15(5):1407–1437.

Corielli, F. and Meucci, A. (2004). Pitfalls in Linear Models for Style Analysis. *Statistical Methods and Applications*, 13(1):103–127.

D'Agostino, R. B. (1970). Transformation to Normality of the Null Distribution of G1. *Biometrika*, 57:679–681.

DiBartolomeo, D. and Witkowski, E. (1997). Mutual Fund Misclassification: Evidence Based on Style Analysis. *Financial Analysts Journal*, 53(5):32–43.

Dor, A. B. and Jagannathan, R. (2002). Understanding Mutual Fund and Hedge Fund Styles Using Return-Based-Style Analysis. Working Paper, National Bureau of Economic Research (NBER).

Fung, W. and Hsieh, D. A. (1996). Performance Attribution and Style Analysis: From Mutual Funds to Hedge Funds. Working Paper, Duke University, Fuqua School of Business, Durham, NC.

Fung, W. and Hsieh, D. A. (1997). Empirical Characteristics of Dynamic Trading Strategies: The Case of Hedge Funds. *Review of Financial Studies*, 10(2): 275–302.

Fung, W. and Hsieh, D. A. (2002). Asset Based Style Factors for Hedge Funds. *Financial Analysts Journal*, 58(5):16–27.

Gaber, M., Gregoriou, G. N., and Kelting, W. (2005). Hedge Funds and the Stale Pricing Issue. In: *Hedge Funds: Insights in Performance Measurement, Risk Analysis, and Portfolio Allocation* (Gregoriou, G. N., Hübner, G., Papageorgiou, N., and Rouah, F., eds.). John Wiley & Sons, Hoboken, NJ.

Geltner, D. (1991). Smoothing in Appraisal-Based Returns. *Journal of Real Estate Finance and Economics*, 4(3):327–345.

Geltner, D. (1993). Estimating Market Values from Appraised Values Without Assuming an Efficient Market. *Journal of Real Estate Research*, 8(3): 325–345.

Getmansky, M., Lo, A. W., and Makarov, I. (2004). An Econometric Model of Serial Correlation and Illiquidity in Hedge Fund Returns. *Journal of Financial Economics*, 74(3):529–609.

Idzorek, T. M. and Bertsch, F. (2004). The Style Drift Score. *Journal of Portfolio Management*, 31(1):76–83.

Jaeger, L. (2002). *Managing Risk in Alternative Investment Strategies*. Pearson Education, London.

Johnson, K. J. (1974). Efficiency and Restrictions on Portfolios Formed Using Quadratic Programming. Proceedings of the Institute of Management Science, Southeast Region, Atlanta, GA.

Kazemi, H., Gupta, B., and Daglioglu, A. (2003). Alternative Methodologies for Hedge Fund Classification. In: *Hedge Funds: Strategies, Risk Assessment, and Returns* (Gregoriou, G. N., Karavas, V. N., and Rouah, F., eds.). Beard Books, Washington, DC.

Kim, T. H. (2005). Asymptotic and Bayesian Confidence Intervals for Sharpe-Style Weights. *Journal of Financial Econometrics*, 3(3):315–343.

Lhabitant, F. S. (2001a). Assessing Market Risk for Hedge Funds and Hedge Funds Portfolios. Working Paper, International Centre for Financial Asset Management and Engineering (FAME).

Lhabitant, F. S. (2001b). Hedge Funds Investing: A Quantitative Look Inside the Black Box. *Journal of Financial Transformation*, 1:82–90.

Lhabitant, F. S. and Learned, M. (2002). Hedge Fund Diversification: How Much Is Enough? *Journal of Alternative Investments*, 5(3):23–49.

Ljung, G. and Box, G. E. P. (1978). On a Measure of Lack of Fit in Time-Series Models. *Biometrika*, 65(2):297–303.

Lobosco, A. and DiBartolomeo, D. (1997). Approximating the Confidence Intervals for Sharpe-Style Weights. *Financial Analysts Journal*, 53(4):80–85.

Lovins, G. W., Johnson, K. H., and Shannon, D. S. (1979). Effects of Differential Tax Rates on Realized Returns from Portfolios Formed via Markowitz Allocation. *Journal of Economics and Business*, 31(3):208–212.

Otten, R. and Bams, D. (2000). Statistical Tests for Return-Based-Style Analysis. Working Paper, Maastricht University, Department of Finance, Netherlands.

Sharpe, W. (1988). Determining a Fund's Effective Asset Mix. *Investment Management Review*, December:59–69.

Sharpe, W. (1992). Asset Allocation: Management Style and Performance Measurement. *Journal of Portfolio Management*, 18(2):7–19.

Tsay, R. S. (2002). *Analysis of Financial Time Series*. John Wiley & Sons, Hoboken, NJ.

Appendix: Key to abbreviations used in tables and figures

Abbreviation	Van Global hedge fund index name
VANG-MN	VAN Global Market Neutral Group Index
VANG-EMN	VAN Global Equity Market Neutral Index
VANG-ED	VAN Global Event-Driven Index
VANG-DS	VAN Global Distressed Securities Index
VANG-MA	VAN Global Merger Arbitrage Index
VANG-SSI	VAN Global Special Situations Index
VANG-MNA	VAN Global Market Neutral Arbitrage Index
VANG-CA	VAN Global Convertible Arbitrage Index
VANG-FIA	VAN Global Fixed Income Arbitrage Index
VANG-LSE	VAN Global Long/Short Equity Group Index
VANG-LSEA	VAN Global Aggressive Growth Index
VANG-LSEO	VAN Global Opportunistic Index
VANG-LSEV	VAN Global Value Index
VANG-SS	VAN Global Short Selling Index
VANG-DT	VAN Global Directional Trading Group Index
VANG-MF	VAN Global Futures Index
VANG-GM	VAN Global Macro Index
VANG-MT	VAN Global Market Timing Index
VANG-SST	VAN Global Specialty Strategies Group Index
VANG-EM	VAN Global Emerging Markets Index
VANG-GI	VAN Global Income Index
VANG-MS	VAN Global Multi-Strategy Index

Abbreviation	CSFB/Tremont hedge fund index name
HEDG-CA	HEDG Convertible Arbitrage
HEDG-SS	HEDG Dedicated Short Bias
HEDG-EM	HEDG Emerging Markets
HEDG-EMN	HEDG Equity Market Neutral
HEDG-ED	HEDG Event-Driven
HEDG-FIA	HEDG Fixed Income Arbitrage
HEDG-GM	HEDG Global Macro
HEDG-LSE	HEDG Long/Short Equity
HEDG-MF	HEDG Managed Futures
HEDG-MS	HEDG Multi-Strategy

11 Gains from adding funds of hedge funds to portfolios of traditional assets: an international perspective*

Niclas Hagelin, Bengt Pramborg, and Fredrik Stenberg

Abstract

We investigate the certainty-equivalent wealth gain from adding funds of hedge funds to portfolios of traditional assets for investors in the G7 countries. This allows us to incorporate the effect of currency exposure and different proxies of equity performance. We find that for many investors, access to funds of hedge funds is as valuable as access to international equity markets. Differences between investors in different countries are documented. These differences are due to the relative performance of the different equity markets as well as the fact that hedge fund exposure contains currency exposure that vigilant investors should take care in hedging to reduce unnecessary volatility.

11.1 Introduction

The fund of hedge funds industry is experiencing unprecedented growth as investors have become aware of the benefits of combining alternative and traditional assets. Academic studies have shown positive effects of adding hedge fund exposure to generic portfolios of traditional assets. In these portfolios, some U.S. equity index or a dollar-denominated global equity index is typically used to proxy for equity.

In this study, we take a somewhat different perspective and estimate the potential gain from adding hedge fund exposure to portfolios of traditional assets for investors of different nationalities. More specifically, we estimate the possible gain for investors in the G7 countries from having access to funds of hedge funds, which allows us to incorporate the effect of currency exposure and

---

* This chapter presents the opinions of the authors alone and may not be representative of their respective institutions.

different proxies of equity performance. To measure gains from diversification, we estimate the certainty-equivalent wealth gains (CEWGs) from having access to an additional asset or market. Access to an additional asset that is not redundant increases the investor's expected utility level. The CEWGs tell us how much an investor would be willing to sacrifice for access to that particular asset.

In our first setting, we estimate the gain from access to funds of hedge funds for an investor permitted to invest only in its own domestic equity market and the risk-free rate. Overall, the evidence suggests that funds of hedge funds should contribute to investors' utility, independent of their home market. In fact, most investors, with the exception of some relatively risk-willing ones, would be willing to pay more for access to the funds of hedge funds than for access to the other G7 markets. Some interesting effects between investors in different countries do exist, however. As could be expected, investors in countries with historically strong-performing equity markets give less value to the opportunity of adding hedge funds.

In our second setting, we estimate the gain from access to funds of hedge funds for investors that already have access to all equity markets of the G7 countries. Even though the estimated utility increases are smaller than those for the first setting, they could still be regarded as substantial for investors expressing some, but not considerable, aversion toward risk. As expected, access to the same equity markets creates a greater overall similarity in the pattern of utility increases across the seven countries. Despite this greater overall similarity, substantial differences in utility gains for U.S. and Canadian investors and investors of the other five countries do exist, however. Investors in the United States and Canada would, on average, be willing to pay more to access funds of hedge fund investments than would other investors. We contend that funds of hedge fund returns contain currency exposure to European and Japanese investors, making them unwilling to direct as much as U.S. and Canadian investors to funds of hedge funds.

To explore the impact of currency exposure on fund of hedge fund allocation, we construct a third setting, where investors also have access to all equity markets of the G7 countries and are able to hedge their currency exposure due to foreign equities and funds of hedge funds. As could be expected, this opportunity to hedge currency exposure results in portfolios that are much more similar across investors in different countries. The possibility to hedge currency exposure causes investors in Japan and Europe to increase considerably their allocations to funds of hedge funds, with a subsequent utility gain. This evidence highlights that hedge fund exposure contains currency exposure, which vigilant investors should take care in hedging to reduce unwanted and unnecessary volatility. Hence, the home currency of the investor is a concern that needs to be addressed when hedge fund exposure is considered.

This chapter is organized as follows. Section 11.2 describes the data used, while Section 11.3 outlines the methodology. Section 11.4 reports the results, and Section 11.5 provides conclusions from the study.

11.2   Data

We use fund of hedge funds indices from the Hedge Fund Research (HFR) database to represent hedge fund investment opportunities. More specifically, we use the FOF Composite Index to represent a broad portfolio of funds of hedge funds investments and the four FOF subindices to represent more specialized portfolios of funds of funds investments. These four subindices are the FOF Conservative Index, the FOF Diversified Index, the FOF Market Defensive Index, and the FOF Strategic Index.[1]

The use of fund of hedge funds data for analyzing the contribution of hedge funds to portfolios of more traditional assets is beneficial, for numerous reasons. First, it is well known that the data-collecting process of data vendors and the fact that reporting is voluntary give rise to a variety of biases in hedge fund data. These biases include survivorship bias, instant-history bias, and selection bias (Ackermann, McEnally, and Ravenscraft, 1999; Fung and Hsieh, 2000; Liang, 2000). Fung and Hsieh (2000), however, argue that index data on funds of hedge funds is almost free of the many biases contained in databases of individual hedge funds. For this reason, the use of fund of hedge funds indices eliminates this potential problem. Second, through the double fee structure, the use of fund of hedge funds indices also incorporates realistic costs associated with the creation of hedge fund portfolios. These are costs likely to arise from due diligence processes and so forth, independent of whether investors choose to create their own portfolios of hedge funds or rely on existing services from fund of hedge funds managers.

To represent equities, we use country indices from Morgan Stanley Capital International (MSCI) for each G7 country, which we downloaded from the MSCI Website (http://www.msci.com). We use each country's T-bill rate to represent the nominal risk-free rate of interest. These rates were purchased from Global Financial Data Inc. (http://www.globalfindata.com), together with inflation rates. The latter are needed to calculate real returns.

From the historical MSCI monthly return data, we compute basic inflation-adjusted descriptive statistics in terms of both U.S. dollars and the local currency. The results for the equity indices are presented in Table 11.1, panels A and B. The mean annual returns in terms of local currency range from −3.22% to 8.58%. The United States has the highest mean return, and Japan has the lowest. From the table, it can also be seen that the high mean return for the U.S. equities was accompanied by the lowest volatility. The overall picture is not

---

[1] The FOF Conservative Index includes funds dedicated to conservative strategies such as arbitrage strategies and should be characterized by market neutrality and low volatility. The FOF Diversified Index includes a broad variety of strategies and should be close to the FOF Composite Index. The FOF Market Defensive Index includes managed futures funds and short-selling. It should be negatively correlated with equity markets. Finally, the FOF Strategic Index includes funds investing in emerging markets, equity hedged strategies, and specific sectors. This index should deliver high returns accompanied by high volatility.

Table 11.1 Descriptive statistics

Panel A: Stock markets, USD (%)

	US	UK	JAP	ITA	GER	FRA	CAN
Mean	8.58	6.82	−0.40	4.77	5.06	7.70	5.98
Median	13.52	6.61	−5.75	5.69	9.29	13.47	15.34
Standard deviation	14.96	15.51	25.18	24.27	20.81	18.80	17.93
Skewness	−0.45	−0.10	0.35	0.23	−0.39	−0.32	−0.75
Excess kurtosis	0.53	−0.07	0.37	0.34	2.37	0.62	2.04

Panel B: Stock markets, Local Currency (%)

	US	UK	JAP	ITA	GER	FRA	CAN
Mean	8.58	5.90	−3.22	6.19	4.76	7.32	6.51
Median	13.52	9.59	−5.22	−2.21	7.88	12.47	11.88
Standard deviation	14.96	14.94	21.02	23.80	21.01	19.27	15.37
Skewness	−0.45	−0.43	0.00	0.48	−0.54	−0.39	−0.76
Excess kurtosis	0.53	0.28	0.76	0.55	1.95	0.33	2.31
Mean inflation	2.82	3.14	0.61	3.52	2.20	1.86	2.23

Panel C: FOFs, USD (%)

	FOF COMP	FOF CONS	FOF DIV	FOF DEF	FOF STRA
Mean	6.93	5.71	6.25	6.81	10.23
Median	6.25	6.68	5.87	5.49	12.97
Standard deviation	5.71	3.34	6.13	5.98	9.18
Skewness	−0.19	−0.32	−0.03	0.10	−0.37
Excess kurtosis	4.19	3.55	4.15	0.96	3.43

altered by the conversion of all returns to a common currency. In terms of U.S. dollars, the U.S. stock market experienced the highest mean return, while the Japanese market delivered the lowest.

Panel C in Table 11.1 provides the same statistics for the fund of hedge funds index and the four subindices, in U.S. dollars, as Panel A does for equities. From the table, it is evident that there exist substantial differences in terms of mean returns and standard deviations among the four subindices over the sample period. The highest mean return is recorded for the FOF Strategic Index, which experienced a striking annual real return, expressed in U.S. dollars, of 10.23%. This high return, however, was accompanied by the highest volatility among the four fund of hedge funds subindices. While the other three fund of hedge funds subindices as well as the composite index provided investors with relatively similar returns over the sample period, the FOF Conservative Index experienced considerably lower volatility than did the other four indices. In terms of deviations from normality, it can be seen from Table 11.1 that the strategies behind fund of hedge funds returns tend to generate returns with fatter tails than investments in equity.

11.3   Method

11.3.1   Certainty-equivalent wealth gains

To investigate the gains from including funds of hedge funds in the investment opportunity set, we need a methodology for evaluation. For this purpose, we assume investors with power utilities. Thus, the utility function may be written

$$u(R) = \frac{1}{1 - \gamma} R^{1-\gamma}, \qquad \gamma \geq 0, \quad \gamma \neq 1 \tag{11.1}$$

where R is the one-period gross return and γ is a parameter for risk aversion. Higher values of γ imply more risk aversion, while $\gamma = 0$ represents the risk-neutral investor. A special case is when $\gamma \rightarrow 1$, in which case the utility is logarithmic:

$$u(R) = \ln R, \qquad R > 0 \tag{11.2}$$

The logarithmic utility implies, and is implied by, a strategy for maximizing capital growth. Therefore, this utility is often referred to as the *growth-optimal strategy* (for a comprehensive account of capital growth theory, see Hakansson and Ziemba, 1995). The utility functions for investors (with $\gamma > 0$) differ from the standard mean–variance framework in that *all* moments of the return distribution affect the utility of the investor.

With the assumption of power utility investors, we can then investigate the expected gains from including funds of hedge funds in portfolios of investors of different nationalities by using a measure similar to that of Hentschel and Long (2004) and DeMiguel, Garlappi, and Uppal (2005). This measure treats any expected utility gain as a certainty-equivalent wealth gain (CEWG). For a power-utility investor, the utility gain from access to a larger market, e.g., access to international stock markets and/or funds of hedge funds, is the fraction, ψ, of wealth that he/she demands as a *certain* compensation to forgo the higher expected utility for accessing the larger market.[2] With the smaller market (e.g., the local stock market only) nested into the larger market (e.g., all G7 stock

---

[2] The certainty-equivalent wealth gain we use is similar to Sharma's (2004) alternative investments risk-adjusted measure (AIRAP), which is also expressed as a certainty-equivalent compensation for risk for power-utility investors.

markets, including the local market), ψ is set so as to make the following equivalence hold:

$$\max_{\varphi_S} E\left[\frac{1}{1-\gamma}[(1 + \psi)\varphi_S' \mathbf{R}_S]^{1-\gamma}\right] = \max_{\varphi_L} E\left[\frac{1}{1-\gamma}(\varphi_L' \mathbf{R}_L)^{1-\gamma}\right] \qquad (11.3)$$

where φ_S (φ_L) is a vector of weights and $\mathbf{R}_S$ ($\mathbf{R}_L$) is a vector of gross returns for the small market (large market). Thus, the CEWG may be written as

$$\psi = \left[\frac{\max\limits_{\varphi_L} E[(\varphi_L' \mathbf{R}_L)^{1-\gamma}]}{\max\limits_{\varphi_S} E[(\varphi_S' \mathbf{R}_S)^{1-\gamma}]}\right]^{\frac{1}{1-\gamma}} - 1 \qquad (11.4)$$

which is always greater than or equal to zero because the smaller market is nested in the larger market (we use an equivalent form for the logarithmic utility).

11.3.2   *Practical implementation*

Estimation

To implement the model, we need a way of estimating the distribution of future asset returns ($\mathbf{R}_k$). One estimation procedure used by Grauer and Hakansson (2001), among others, is called the *empirical probability assessment approach (EPAA)*. With this approach, estimation is based on looking back at past realized returns. At time t, an estimation window, using the total sample period, is formed. In our case, this results in an estimation window of 218 months ($T = 218$), contemporaneous realized asset returns for each past month, $\mathbf{R}_{t-j}$ ($j = 1, \ldots, 218$), are used, and the set of realized returns for each past month is given the weight $1/T$. Thus, we assume 218 possible future states at the end of the subsequent month, each equally likely and each exactly corresponding to one of the actual past observed sets of monthly asset returns. The estimate of returns for the next month is then $E_{t-1}[\mathbf{R}_t] = 1/218 \sum_{j=1}^{218} \mathbf{R}_{t-j}$. Thus, using EPAA, estimates are obtained in their raw form without adjustments. On the other hand, since the objective function (utility function) requires the entire joint distribution to be specified and used, there is no information loss; all moments and correlations are implicitly taken into account.

Optimization

We model investors in each country as power-utility investors and solve a constrained nonlinear optimization problem. For this purpose, the investor is required to choose a risk-aversion parameter, γ. We model investors with different risk aversion by setting γ to equally distanced values over the range 0–20, indicating risk attitudes ranging from risk neutral ($\gamma = 0$) to substantially risk averse ($\gamma = 20$), where $\gamma = 1$ corresponds to the logarithmic utility.[3]

At the end of our sample period, for example, the end of June 2004, the investor chooses a portfolio, $\varphi_k(k = S,L)$, based on which scenario is chosen (small or large market) and on some γ, subject to the relevant constraints faced by the investor. Then the investor optimizes utility, including the assets allowed (e.g., with or without funds of hedge funds, respectively), which is equivalent to solving the following problem:

$$\max_{\phi_k} E_t \left[\frac{1}{1-\gamma} (\varphi'_{k,t+1} \mathbf{R}_{k,t+1})^{1-\gamma} \right] = \max_{\phi_k} \frac{1}{(1-\gamma)T} (\varphi'_k \mathbf{R}_k \mathbf{1})^{1-\gamma} \qquad (11.5)$$

subject to

$$\phi_{k,i} \geq 0, \qquad \forall i \qquad\qquad\qquad (11.6)$$
$$\phi_{rf} \geq 0$$

$$\sum_{i=1}^{N} \phi_{k,i} + \phi_{rf} = 1 \qquad\qquad\qquad (11.7)$$

where

$\varphi'_k \mathbf{R}_k \mathbf{1}$ = sum of gross returns during the estimation period on the portfolio ($k = S,L$) (the estimation period is from $t - T$ to t, where t is the date of estimation and T is a chosen estimation period)

γ = risk-aversion parameter

$\phi_{k,i}$ = proportion of wealth invested in risky asset i

ϕ_{rf} = proportion of wealth invested in the risk-free asset

φ_k = vector of weights ($\phi_{k,1}, \ldots, \phi_{k,N}, \phi_{rf}$)

$\mathbf{R}_k$ = $T \times (N + 1)$ matrix of total gross return for the N risky assets and the risk-free asset, R_f

$\mathbf{1}$ = $T \times 1$ identity vector

Constraint (11.6) rules out short sales, and constraint (11.7) is the budget constraint.[4] The inputs into the model are based on the estimation method

---

[3] We use a step size of 0.2, resulting in 101 risk-aversion parameters to produce smooth graphs.
[4] The model can be augmented to allow for leveraged portfolios, see, e.g., Grauer and Hakansson (1987), Hagelin and Pramborg (2004), and Hagelin, Pramborg, and Stenberg (2005).

described earlier, and for each investor, System (11.5)–(11.7) is solved by a sequential quadratic programming method, using returns from the estimation period (January 1990–June 2004). Then the CEWG is calculated as the ratio of the expected utility of access to the larger market ($k = L$) and the expected utility of access to the smaller market ($k = S$).[5]

11.4 Results

Here we present the gains from having access to funds of hedge funds as an investment vehicle. To investigate possible utility gains, we estimate numerous portfolios for various investment combinations and the associated expected utility. Access to an additional investment that is not redundant increases the investor's expected utility level. This increase in utility is conveniently stated in terms of certainty-equivalent wealth gains.

In the first setting, the base case is an investor with access to the local stock market and a local risk-free asset, and we estimate the CEWGs from access to any of the following investment opportunity sets: international stock markets (G7), the FOF Composite Index (FOF), or the four fund of hedge funds subindices (FOF4). We also display the CEWGs from access to three subindices (FOF3), excluding the FOF Strategic Index. The latter is displayed because we want to investigate the *general* additional gain from including the subindices, and the FOF Strategic Index's superior performance could render too optimistic conclusions. Figure 11.1 shows the CEWGs for each G7 investor over different risk attitudes, ranging from risk neutral ($\gamma = 0$) to highly risk averse ($\gamma = 20$), where $\gamma = 1$ corresponds to the log-utility investor.

From Figure 11.1, a few points are noteworthy. First, independent of home country and attitude toward risk, investors would be willing to sacrifice some of their wealth for access to the fund of hedge funds universe. In fact, all investors would be willing to sacrifice more for access to the four fund of hedge funds subindices than they would for access to international diversification through the other G7 equity markets. Moreover, with the exception of some relatively risk-willing investors, most investors would be willing to pay more for access to the FOF Composite Index than for access to the other G7 markets. This is remarkable since, from the investors' point of view, the FOF Composite Index is only one asset (there are no possibilities to allocate within funds of hedge funds), while in the G7 case the investor is allowed to allocate optimally between the

---

[5] It should be noted that this type of optimization procedure, and also traditional mean variance optimization, should be used with caution. Because of parameter uncertainty, this type of optimization results in portfolios with superior in-sample performance but typically with poor out-of-sample performance (Jorion, 1985; DeMiguel, Garlappi, and Uppal, 2005; Martellini and Ziemann, 2005). However, the methodology is well suited for our purposes; i.e. understanding the possible contribution of specific assets to portfolios of other assets.

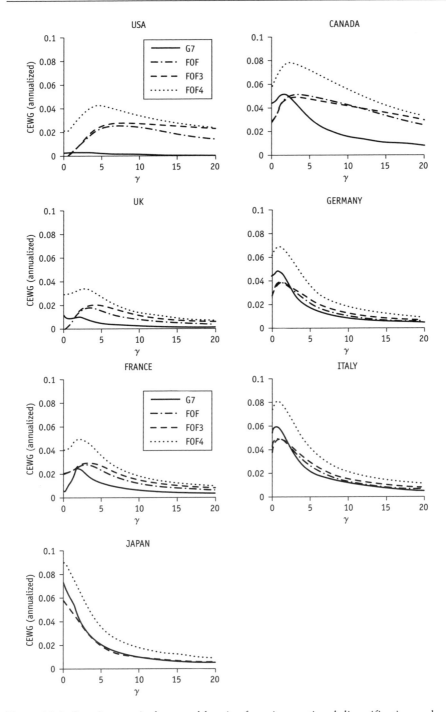

Figure 11.1 Certainty-equivalent wealth gains from international diversification and funds of hedge funds

local market and six different international stock markets. Taken together, this evidence suggests that funds of hedge funds should be able to contribute to investors' utility, independent of their home market and risk attitudes.

Second, some interesting differences with respect to the utility increases for investors with different risk attitudes and home markets do exist. With respect to risk attitudes, there is a general tendency for the utility gain to increase up to some point and then to decrease monotonically with the investor's risk aversion. This hump-shaped curvature is a result of two opposing effects. First, higher risk aversion implies that, in the presence of a risk-free alternative, an investor values access to an additional risky asset less. The second effect derives from the fact that, in the presence of a high-return-performing equity index, highly risk-tolerant investors do not value the opportunity to diversify into hedge funds with lower expected return as much as do more risk-aversive investors. The importance of the performance of the domestic equity index on the utility increase becomes evident when comparing the results for the United States with those for Japan (see also Table 11.1). This result is not unexpected, but it highlights that the choice of setting is of importance when analyzing the contribution of an additional investment opportunity.[6]

In our second setting, the base case is an investor with access to all equity markets of the G7 countries, and we estimate the CEWG from having access to any of the following investments: the FOF Composite Index (FOF), the four fund of hedge funds subindices (FOF4), and the three fund of hedge funds subindices (FOF3). Despite the tendency of investors to overweight their home market, it could be argued that this setting is somewhat more realistic than the previous one. Figure 11.2 gives the estimated CEWGs, for the second setting, over different risk attitudes and G7 investors.

Some interesting points can be made from the estimations. First, even though the estimated utility increases are smaller than those presented in Figure 11.1, they could still be regarded as considerable when the four fund of hedge funds subindices are considered for investors with reasonable attitudes toward risk.[7] Second, as could be expected, when they have access to each other's equity markets, there is greater overall similarity in the pattern of utility increases across the seven countries. Despite this greater overall similarity, substantial differences in utility gains for the U.S. and Canadian investors and investors of the other five countries do exist. Investors in the United States and Canada would, on average, be willing to pay more to access fund of funds investments than would other investors. This difference is most notable for investors with a relatively high risk

---

[6] We note that this is also the case for utility increases from allowing access to other G7 markets. For U.S. investors, independent of risk attitudes, there is basically no utility increase at all from having access to international diversification. For all other markets, utility increases do exist to varying degrees. This result could be understood, considering the historical performance of the U.S. equity index.

[7] Friend and Blume (1975) empirically estimated the average risk aversion of investors and found evidence that it is somewhat above the value of 2.

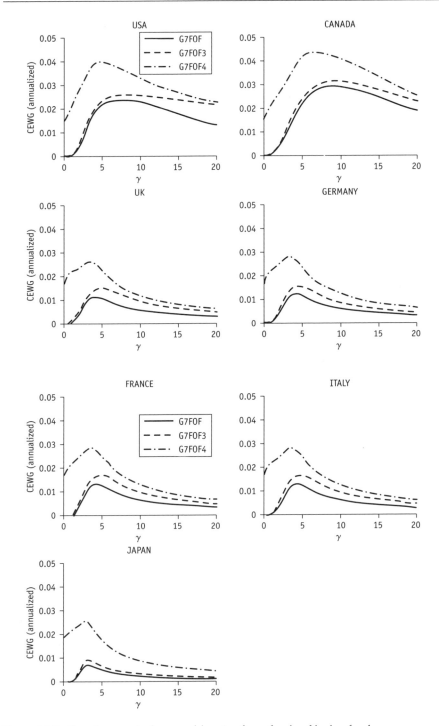

Figure 11.2 Certainty-equivalent wealth gains from funds of hedge funds

aversion. On this basis, we conclude that even though differences in utility gains across investors with different home markets decrease when they are allowed to diversify internationally, significant differences still do exist.

To further investigate the effect of allowing investors to access the fund of hedge funds market and how these effects differ across investors with different home markets, we compute the portfolio weights. Figure 11.3 plots the portfolio weights for the second setting using the FOF Composite Index as the additional investment opportunity. Similarities as well as differences in the figure are of interest. For most risk preferences, U.S. and Canadian investors tend to allocate substantially more to the FOF Composite Index than do investors in the other five countries. Instead, investors in these five countries, which to some degree exhibit risk aversion, elect to allocate a considerably larger amount of resources to the risk-free asset.

Based on the evidence in Figures 11.2 and 11.3, it is tempting to conclude that fund of hedge funds returns contain currency exposure to European and Japanese investors, making them unwilling to allocate as much as U.S. and Canadian investors to the fund of hedge funds indices.[8] Instead, they prefer to allocate resources to the domestic risk-free asset that contains no currency exposure at all. Such a conclusion is in line with the French and Poterba (1991) argument that the home bias is out of choice rather than because of institutional constraints.

To address the issue of currency exposure, we formulate an additional setup, where investors are allowed to hedge their currency exposure due to foreign equities and funds of hedge funds. Hedging positions are created through borrowing in foreign currencies. Formally, we replace Restrictions (11.6) and (11.7) with

$$\phi_{k,i} + \phi_{FX,i} \geq 0, \qquad \forall i \qquad\qquad (11.6')$$

$$\phi_{FX,i} \leq 0 \qquad\qquad (11.7')$$

$$\phi_{rf} \geq 0 \qquad\qquad (11.8')$$

$$\sum_{i=1}^{N} (\phi_{k,i} + \phi_{FX,i}) + \phi_{rf} = 1 \qquad\qquad (11.9')$$

where all variables are as described earlier, except for $\phi_{FX,i}$ which is the proportion of wealth hedged by borrowing in currency i. Restriction (11.6') forces the investor to have (zero or) positive positions in each country. Restriction

---

[8] The hedge fund industry has historically been dominated by funds denominated in U.S. dollars. The proportion of European funds is increasing; in 2005 it constituted approximately 25% of the hedge fund universe in terms of assets under management. We note, however, that the currency exposure is not determined by the choice of denomination or the fund manager's geographical base. To what extent a hedge fund contains currency exposure is determined by its investment strategy.

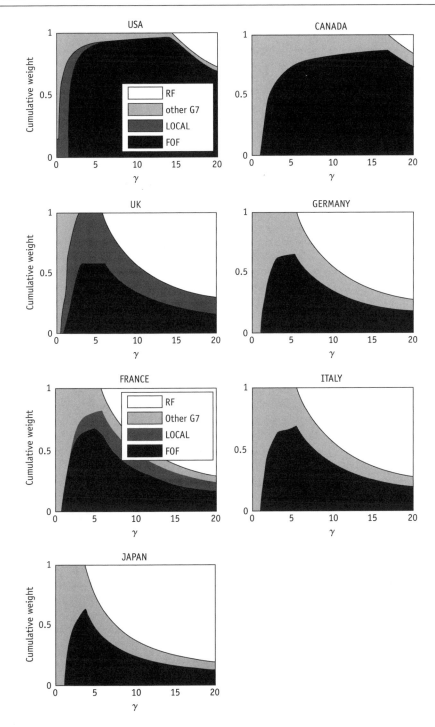

Figure 11.3 Optimal portfolio weights

(11.7′) forces the investor to hold zero or short positions (for example, borrow) in foreign currencies,[9] and Restriction (11.8′) forces the investor to have (zero or) positive positions in the local risk-free asset. Restriction (11.9′) is the usual wealth constraint.

Figure 11.4 depicts the portfolio weights for our third and final setting, which also uses the FOF Composite Index as the additional investment opportunity but allows for hedging of currency exposure as outlined earlier. As could be expected, the opportunity to hedge currency exposure leads to portfolios that are much more similar across investors in different countries. Specifically, the possibility to hedge currency exposure causes investors in Japan and Europe to considerably increase their allocations to the FOF Composite Index and to lessen their net position in the risk-free assets.[10] Overall, the allocations of European and Japanese investors become relatively similar to those of U.S. investors when currency exposure hedging is not allowed (see Figure 11.3). This evidence highlights that hedge fund exposure contains currency exposure that should not be overlooked by investors, at least not by non-U.S. ones.

Table 11.2 displays the increase in CEWGs from allowing currency exposure hedging for investors with risk-aversion coefficients $\gamma = 1, 5, 10, 20$.[11] From the table, it is evident that for a U.S. investor, the possibility to avoid unnecessary currency exposure does not improve the utility to any greater extent. For example, the annualized CEWG for a U.S. investor with a risk aversion of $\gamma = 10$ is a meager 0.02%. However, for other nationalities, the possibility to hedge currency exposure renders considerably higher expected utilities. The increase in utility is particularly striking for risk-averse European and Japanese investors. For example, a Japanese investor with a risk aversion of $\gamma = 10$ gains a substantial 3.24%. This demonstrates that the ability to remove undesirable currency exposure is very valuable for many investors.

11.5 Conclusion

Overall, our evidence suggests that adding funds of hedge funds to portfolios of equities and risk-free assets is, for many investors, as valuable for G7 investors

---

[9] We set the expected real rate of return equal for all currencies. Thus, borrowing in foreign currencies does not affect the expected return, but leads to higher moments of the return distribution. Therefore, these positions will be for hedging purposes only.

[10] It is no surprise that the allocations of continental European countries are very similar, since these countries' currencies were highly correlated from 1990 through 1998, and, from January 1, 1999, they share the same currency. Thus, differences arise mainly from differences in inflation rates.

[11] This is calculated as the annualized CEWG when hedging is allowed as compared to when it is not allowed. In the base case (small market), the investor is allowed to invest in all assets, for example, the risk-free asset, all stock indices, and the FOF index, but hedging is not allowed. With hedging (large market), the investor has the same opportunity set as before but can also hedge the currency risk by borrowing in foreign currencies.

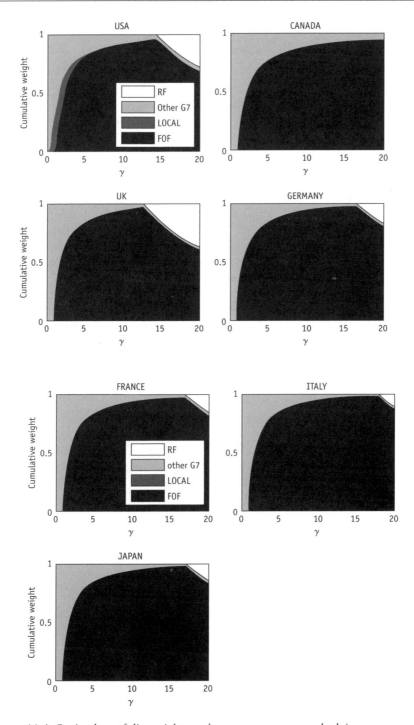

Figure 11.4 Optimal portfolio weights under currency exposure hedging

Table 11.2 Certainty-equivalent wealth gain increases from allowing
currency exposure hedging

	US	UK	JAP	ITA	GER	FRA	CAN
$\gamma = 1$	0.0020	0.0043	0.0052	0.0055	0.0053	0.0054	0.0014
$\gamma = 5$	0.0005	0.0111	0.0296	0.0223	0.0203	0.0194	0.0024
$\gamma = 10$	0.0002	0.0144	0.0324	0.0307	0.0266	0.0269	0.0051
$\gamma = 20$	0.0000	0.0078	0.0211	0.0216	0.0173	0.0181	0.0089

as having access to international equity markets. For investors in most G7 countries, the utility increase from adding funds of hedge funds becomes smaller, although still economically significant, when international equities are already included in the opportunity set. In addition, our results show that the utility increase from the inclusion of hedge fund exposure differs between investors across the G7 countries, even when they have access to each other's equity markets. The rationale for this is that international equities as well as hedge fund exposure contain currency exposure limiting investors' possibilities to take full advantage of potential diversification benefits. Our results suggest that the impact of currency exposure on optimal allocation and expected utilities substantially differs between investors in different countries. Specifically, our evidence suggests that currency exposure hedging can facilitate considerably higher expected utilities for Japanese and European investors, while the effect for U.S. investors is small.

References

Ackermann, C., McEnally, R., and Ravenscraft, D. (1999). The Performance of Hedge Funds: Risk, Return, and Incentives. *Journal of Finance*, 54(3):833–874.

DeMiguel, V., Garlappi, L., and Uppal R. (2005). How Inefficient Is the 1/N Asset-Allocation Strategy? Working Paper, London Business School.

French, K. and Poterba, J. (1991). Investor Diversification and International Equity Markets. *American Economic Review*, 81(2):222–226.

Friend, I. and Blume, M. (1975). The Demand for Risky Assets. *American Economic Review*, 65(5):900–922.

Fung, W. and Hsieh, D. A. (2000). Performance Characteristics of Hedge Funds and Commodity Funds: Natural vs. Spurious Biases. *Journal of Financial and Quantitative Analysis*, 35(3):291–307.

Grauer, R. R. and Hakansson, N. H. (1987). Gains from International Diversification: 1968–1985 Returns on Portfolios of Stocks and Bonds. *Journal of Finance*, 42(3):721–739.

Grauer, R. R. and Hakansson, N. H. (2001). Applying Portfolio Change and Conditional Performance Measures: The Case of Industry Rotation via the

Dynamic Investment Model. *Review of Quantitative Finance and Accounting*, 17(3):237–265.

Hagelin, N. and Pramborg, B. (2004). Evaluating Gains from Diversifying into Hedge Funds Using Dynamic Investment Strategies. In *Intelligent Hedge Fund Investing* (Schachter, B., ed.). Risk Books, London.

Hagelin, N., Pramborg, B., and Stenberg F. (2005). Hedge Fund Allocation Under Higher Moments and Illiquidity. In: *Hedge Funds: Insights in Performance Measurement, Risk Analysis, and Portfolio Allocation* (Gregoriou, G. N., Hübner, G., Papageorgiou, N., and Rouah, F., eds.). John Wiley & Sons, Hoboken, NJ.

Hakansson, N. H. and Ziemba, W. T. (1995). Capital Growth Theory. In: *Handbooks in Operations Research and Management Science: Finance.* (Jarrow, R., Maksmovic, V., and Ziemba, W. T., eds.). Elsevier Science, Amsterdam.

Hentschel, L. and Long, J. B., Jr. (2004). Numeraire Portfolio Measures of the Size and Source of Gains from International Diversification. Working Paper, University of Rochester, NY.

Jorion, P. (1985). International Portfolio Diversification with Estimation Risk. *Journal of Business*, 58(3):259–278.

Liang, B. (2000). Hedge Funds: The Living and the Dead. *Journal of Financial and Quantitative Analysis*, 35(3):309–326.

Martellini, L. and Ziemann, V. (2005). The Benefits of Hedge Funds in Asset Liability Management. Working Paper, Edhec Risk and Asset Management Research, Nice, France.

Sharma, M. (2004). AIRAP—Alternative Views on Alternative Investments. In: *Intelligent Hedge Fund Investing* (Schachter, B., ed.). Risk Books, London.

12 Tactical asset allocation for hedge fund indices at one- to six-month horizons

Laurent Favre

Abstract

The launch of more hedge fund investable indices will increase the number of funds of funds trying to forecast them or to arbitrage between the different index providers. The weekly or monthly liquidity of hedge fund investable indices allows a fund of funds to select the correct strategy at the correct time. We propose to see whether such a fund of funds is able to make alpha. We use a tactical asset allocation model based on economic factors, and we forecast the next one- to six-month returns for several hedge fund indices, hedge fund investable indices, and hedge funds. We obtain outperformances between 1% and 2% before transaction costs.

Light gains make a heavy purse.

— *George Chapman (1559–1634)*

12.1 Introduction

The year 2005 saw the emergence of investable hedge fund indices, the ability (or inability) of funds of funds to select the best hedge fund managers (Amenc and Vaissie, 2005), and declining hedge fund index returns (in the financial media and from the 2003, 2004, and 2005 realized returns). Table 12.1 shows the indices' annualized returns for the years 2000–2005 for three hedge fund index providers.

A fund of funds (FOF) has three options for hedge fund investing: (1) invest in liquid and illiquid hedge funds, after analyzing the hedge fund universe and expecting to outperform an FOF index, (2) invest in investable indices and use tactical allocation between strategies to outperform a FOF index, and (3) invest in liquid hedge funds with weekly to monthly liquidity. Only the second and third options can use tactical allocation, because they invest in liquid underlying hedge funds.[1]

---

[1] A fund of funds can invest in illiquid hedge funds to form the core of a portfolio and then add a tactical overlay using either liquid hedge funds or investable indices.

Table 12.1 Historical annualized hedge fund index returns,
noninvestable indices

	CSFB Tremont Hedge Fund Index[1]	HFR Fund of Funds Index	EDHEC Fund of Funds Index
2000	4.8%	4.1%	7.8%
2001	4.4%	2.8%	3.5%
2002	3.0%	1.0%	1.3%
2003	15.5%	11.6%	11.5%
2004	9.6%	6.9%	7.1%
2005	7.6%	7.5%	6.8%

[1] We used the global index, because CSFB Tremont does not have a fund of funds index.
Source: HFR, Tremont, EDHEC, data as of October 2005.

Table 12.2 Hedge fund index providers

	Start date[1]	Investable
Altvest	1993	No
Barclay Group	1997	No
CISDM	1990	No
CSFB Tremont	1994	Yes
EACM 100	1990	No
EDHEC	1997	Yes
EurekaHedge	2000	No
FTSE	1999	Yes
HFR	1990	Yes
Hedgefund.net	1979	No
Hennessee Group	1987	No
HedgeFund Intelligence	1998	No
MAR	1998	No
MSCI Lyxor	2003	Yes
S&P	1998	Yes
SIX Harcourt HFXS	2001	No
Van Hedge	1988	Yes

[1] Some indices have a backfilled start date.
Sources: Karavas and Siokos (2003), Vaissie (2003).

Table 12.2 shows the different index providers[2] and whether they offer investable indices and Table 12.3 exhibits the assets under management of the main providers of investable indices.

There are positive arguments for using investable indices:

• The liquidity is weekly or monthly.
• The capacity is high.

[2] There are other hedge fund index providers, such as LJH, Bernheim, Blue X, Feri, and MondoHedge. For details, see Vaissie (2003).

- The burden of due diligence is outsourced to the index provider.
- The transparency of positions and return computation is high.
- The index provider does the reporting.
- New funds of funds can be set up relatively quickly.

But there are a number of negative arguments against using investable indices as well:

- They provide lower return expectations than noninvestable hedge fund indices.[3]
- It is not possible to fully capture the liquidity premium.
- There are restrictions on the number of investable indices.
- Investable indices do not fully span the hedge fund universe.[4]
- Index provider fees can be burdensome.

However, assets under management in investable indices have grown rapidly in 2005. So the pros must be gaining ground against the cons.

The growing appetite for investable indices is attributable to three main things: (1) three large long-only players (S&P, FTSE, MSCI) entered the race in 2005, and they allied themselves with well-established fund of funds companies; (2) there is a growing need for indices in hedge funds; and (3) demand is growing for liquid hedge fund strategies. Table 12.3 gives the assets under management for the hedge fund investable index providers.

This chapter aims to determine whether a tactical allocation applied to hedge fund investable indices or to liquid hedge fund managers can outperform a fund of hedge funds index. To our knowledge, Amenc, El Bied, and Martellini (2002) published the first paper showing predictability using a one-month tactical asset allocation with hedge fund indices. The authors used economic factors to find a relationship between macro factors and hedge fund indices. They obtained a 2.7% per annum outperformance above the hedge fund noninvestable indices.

But several other articles have explored similar themes. For example, Gupta, Cerrahoglu, and Daglioglu (2003) presented a one-month lagged economic multifactor regression model with a nonlinear equity market factor. They obtained an alpha between 0.49% and 1.64% per annum using hedge fund noninvestable indices. Von Wyss and Ammann (2003) computed the adjusted R^2 between some economic factors and the future one-month hedge fund index return. They found low adjusted R^2 (between 11% and 26%). They did not present a tactical model with hedge fund indices.

Dash and Kajiji (2003), in a complex neural network model, were able to accurately forecast the one-month-ahead hedge fund noninvestable index return. They did not present the R^2 or alpha of their model. Padilla and Zebad's (2004)

---

[3] However, to our knowledge, no research has proven that investable index returns have statistically significantly lower returns than noninvestable index returns. Nevertheless, a rational investor should expect lower returns due to (1) the high liquidity of investable indices, which hinders hedge fund managers from capturing the liquidity premium from the alternative betas, and (2) the selection bias of the index provider, whose purpose is not to select the best future hedge fund performers.

[4] All hedge fund managers are not represented in the hedge fund investable indices.

Table 12.3 Hedge fund investable indices (assets under management, billions USD)

	Hedge fund industry	MSCI Hedge Invest. Index	CSFB Tremont	S&P Sphinx Investable	HFRX Investable	Dow Jones Hedge	Van Hedge Index	EDHEC Invest. Index	FTSE Hedge Index
1999	380								
2000	390								
2001	430								
2002	530								
2003	610	n.a	n.a	n.a	n.a	n.a	n.a	n.a	n.a
2004	750	2.1	1.2	2.5	2.2	1.5	0.1	n.a.	n.a
2005	1,000	3.0	3.5	n.a.	2.7	n.a.	n.a.	n.a.	n.a

n.a. means either the provider wishes not to publish its data or no data was available. Note that both the investable indices and their underlying hedge fund managers are candidates for tactical allocation. Both are also more liquid than average hedge fund managers.

Source: Author, Freeman & Co. (Nov. 04). Partial list as of Oct. 05.

thick modeling approach used several logit regressions between economic factors and the DJ Euro Stoxx 50 Future Index. The average of the best logit regressions served as the final model. They also used a reverse-ordered cusum method in their regressions to give fewer weights to extreme events in the returns. Padilla and Zebad obtained an annualized alpha of 9.5% over the DJ Euro Stoxx 50 Future Index for the period 2000–2003 after transaction costs, with a lower annualized standard deviation than the index.

Capocci, Corhay, and Hübner (2003) and Capocci (2005), using a ranking deciles technique, claimed there is limited persistence in hedge fund decile returns. Schneeweis, Kazemi, and Martin (2002) proposed a summary table where the contemporary exposure of each hedge fund index to economic factors and changes in economic factors are computed. They did not address whether the economic factors can be used to extract outperformance, however.

Zairi and Sideri (2004), using economic factors and straddle option payoffs on economic factors, obtained a high-adjusted R^2 when forecasting the next month's hedge fund index returns. They did not try to create a portfolio or compute alphas. Pillonel and Solanet (2004)[5] used a 60-month rolling window and presented different forecasting regression models using economic factors. They derived expected returns for each hedge fund in the CSFB Tremont indices and constructed optimal tactical portfolios that should outperform an equally weighted hedge fund index benchmark. They obtained information ratios between 1.5 and 4.0 (annualized alphas between 1.5% and 3%) for a model that uses statistically significant economic factors and a constraint on the maximum allocation to each hedge fund index.

All of this research provides evidence of a relationship between economic factors and hedge fund index returns. Hedge funds are capturing trading inefficiencies and alternative beta premiums[6] that are due, for example, to illiquidity (for example, the long-term rate is higher than the short-term rate), credit risk (low-grade bonds deliver higher returns than high-grade bonds), or volatility (sell volatility strategies in expectation that there will be no sudden increase in volatility).

Assuming we can establish the same relationship, we should be able to implement a tactical asset allocation. However, there are three issues to keep in mind. The first is that we must be able to construct a model that statistically links each hedge fund index to the relevant economic factors (for example, long-term interest rate minus short-term interest rate, low-grade bond minus high-grade bond, VIX index, small-cap equity index, government bond index, three-month T-bill, commodity index, value index). In this chapter, we use a stepwise regression to select the relevant economic factors.

The second is the importance of using a statistical technique to diminish the noise in the data, especially from extreme data points. Here, we integrate a

---

[5] This is one of the key articles on tactical asset allocation with hedge fund indices.
[6] Alternative betas are the sensitivities between economic factors and hedge fund indices.

moving average to diminish the effect of sudden extreme events in the time series.[7]

The third is to have an exhaustive list of economic factors and economic factor transformations (for example, moving average, lagged, change in value of the economic factors, nonlinear). We use lagged economic factors, lagged economic factor moving averages, lagged changes in economic factor values, and quadratic economic factors.

12.2   The model

Our model is based on information ratio maximization using a stepwise regression, with moving average economic factors and indices and lags between the hedge fund indices and the economic factors. Here is the model:

$$\underset{w_p}{\text{Max}} \frac{w_p R_{p,t+1} - w_{BM} R_{BM,t+1}}{\sqrt{\sum_{t=1}^{T}(w_p R_{p,t} - w_{BM} R_{BM,t})^2}}$$

$$s.c.$$

$$\sum_{i=1}^{N} w_{i,p} = 1$$

$$w_{i,p} \geq 0$$

$$\sum_{i=1}^{N} w_{i,BM} = 1$$

$$w_{i,p,\min} \leq w_{i,p} \leq w_{i,\max}$$

$$w_{i,p,\min} = w_{i,BM} - d$$

$$w_{i,p,\max} = w_{i,BM} + d$$

$$\text{TE}_{\min} < \sqrt{\frac{1}{T-1}\sum_{t=1}^{T}(w_p R_{p,t} - w_{BM} R_{BM,t})^2} < \text{TE}_{\max}$$

where

T = rolling window length

I = hedge fund index

N = number of hedge fund indices in the portfolio

d = maximum positive and negative deviation from the benchmark

w_p = vector of portfolio weights

---

[7] The time series implies the economic factors and hedge fund indices. We acknowledge that more robust regression techniques, such as the reverse-ordered cusum method, are available to diminish the effects of the extreme returns (see Padilla and Zebad (2004), who obtained an annual alpha of 9.5%). We will examine this technique in future research.

w_{BM} = vector of benchmark weights

$w_{i,p,\min}$ = minimum weight in the portfolio for index i

$w_{i,p,\max}$ = maximum weight in the portfolio for index i

$R_{p,t}$ = monthly return vector at time t

$R_{p,t+1}$ = expected monthly return vector at time $t+1$

$TE_{\min}$ = minimum portfolio tracking error

$TE_{\max}$ = maximum portfolio tracking error

The regression β and index expected returns $R_{i,t+1}$ are defined as follows:

$$R_{i,t} = \beta_0 + \sum_{u=1}^{U} \beta_u F_{u,t-1} + \varepsilon_{i,t}$$

$$R_{i,t+1} = \beta_0 + \sum_{u=1}^{U} \beta_u F_{u,t}$$

where U is the number of available economic factors and $F_{u,t}$ is the vector of economic factor values at time t. To perform the regression between the hedge fund indices and the economic factors, we add a moving average to the hedge fund indices and the economic factors that lowers the extreme returns effect:

$$R_{i,t-1} = \frac{\sum_{j=1}^{K} R_{i,t-j}}{K}$$

$$F_{u,t-1} = \frac{\sum_{j=1}^{K} F_{u,t-j}}{K}$$

where K is the length of the moving average. We use a stepwise regression. Consequently, the betas to economic factors are as follows:

$$\beta_i = \begin{vmatrix} \beta_i, \dfrac{\beta_i}{\left(\sum_{t=1}^{T} \beta_i F_t - \beta_i \bar{F} \right)} \geq t \\[30pt] 0, \dfrac{\beta_i}{\left(\sum_{t=1}^{T} \beta_i F_t - \beta_i \bar{F} \right)} < t \end{vmatrix}$$

where t is the critical t-statistic value and F_t is the value of the economic factor u at time t.

Table 12.4 Tactical asset allocation characteristics

	HFR noninvestable indices	HFR investable indices	Hedge funds[1]
Time window	01.90–09.05	01.03–09.05	01.95–09.05
Rolling window	12 months	12 months	12 months
Forecast horizon	6 months	1 month	3 months
Economic factors moving average	6 months	1 month	3 months
Number of assets	9	8	20
Economic factors moving average	6 months	3 months	3 months
Tracking error	2% < TE < 4%	1% < TE < 4%	2% < TE < 4%

[1] We use the hedge funds with the 20 longest track records on the Lyxor platform.

The information ratio maximization allows us to deviate from the benchmark and control for risks. The tracking error constraint diminishes the impact of extreme index or economic factor returns in the regressions.

The rolling window of 12 months, which is much shorter than in the other studies we mentioned earlier, allows us to work with younger indices, such as the HFRX hedge fund investable indices. The rolling window is the period during which the regression is performed and the betas are computed.

We use HFR noninvestable indices, HFR investable indices with daily liquidity, and, finally, the hedge funds with weekly to monthly liquidity available on the Lyxor© managed account platform. We apply the following models.

We use a three-month instead of one-month forecasting horizon for the model applied to hedge funds. We chose three months because, although the hedge funds have weekly or monthly liquidity, notice periods may lengthen the time to close a position.

The economic factors we chose for the regressions are: the change in credit spread (the change in absolute value between Moody's BAA and AAA rates), the change in term spread (the 10-year U.S. T-bill minus the 3-month U.S. T-bill change from the previous month, in absolute value), inflation (the U.S. consumer price index), the JPM Global Bond Index return, a liquidity index based on the St. Louis Monetary[8] Index, the MSCI World Index squared monthly returns, the Russell 2000 Index squared monthly returns, the term spread (the 10-year U.S. T-bill minus the 3-month U.S. T-bill), and the VIX index change (the S&P 500 implied volatility index change, in absolute value).

[8] For more information, see this link and website: http://research.stlouisfed.org/fred2/series/AMBNS/downloaddata/AMBNS.xls

Table 12.5 Benchmark, minimum, and maximum weights

	Minimum weight	Benchmark	Maximum weight	Average portfolio weight, HFR noninvestable	Average portfolio weight, HFRX investable
Barclays CTA	0%	10%	30%	4%	n.a.
HFR Convertible Arbitrage	0%	10%	30%	13%	1%
HFR Distressed	0%	10%	30%	11%	21%
HFR Equity Hedge	0%	20%	40%	18%	10%
HFR Equity Market-Neutral	0%	0%	30%	n.a.	6%
HFR Event-Driven	0%	10%	30%	18%	18%
HFR Fixed-Income Arbitrage	0%	10%	30%	7%	n.a.
HFR Macro	0%	10%	30%	16%	17%
HFR Merger Arbitrage	0%	0%	0%	n.a.	14%
HFR Relative Value	0%	20%	30%	13%	13%

12.3 The results

We tested the model out of sample with rolling windows of 12 months. Each window was characterized by a realized alpha and realized tracking error, which were recorded to generate statistics. For the sake of brevity, we present only the portfolio, the benchmark, the active annualized returns, the portfolio and benchmark Sharpe ratio, and the information ratio[9] of the active allocation.

12.3.1 Tactical asset allocation with noninvestable indices

We applied the model to the HFR noninvestable indices using a six-month rebalancing.[10] The benchmark weights are shown in the third column of Table 12.5.[11]
    The tactical asset allocation between the hedge fund noninvestable indices achieved the performance presented in Table 12.6.

---

[9] An information ratio higher than 0.5 shows abilities; an information ratio higher than 1.0 shows clear superiorities. The information ratio is the annualized alpha divided by the annualized tracking error.

[10] We use a six-month horizon because it is often difficult to decrease/increase exposure to a hedge fund strategy because the underlying hedge funds often have monthly to quarterly redemptions and 30- to 90-day notice periods. Over 15 years, the portfolio has been rebalanced only 31 times. The aim of each rebalancing is to invest in the best indices according to the model's expected return forecasts.

[11] In the three proposed models, the benchmark weights are rebalanced to their original weights each month. The portfolio is rebalanced to its optimal weights each month.

Table 12.6 Tactical asset allocation with HFR noninvestable indices, January 1990 to August 2005, rebalancing every six months, before transaction costs

	Benchmark	Portfolio	Active portfolio
Historical annualized return	12.04%	14.45%	2.21%
Historical annualized volatility	4.12%	5.46%	2.26%
Monthly skewness	−0.45	−0.48	−0.24
Sharpe ratio (R_f =4%)	1.95	1.92	—
Information ratio	—	—	0.98

Index and economic factor moving averages are six months. Twelve-month rolling window for the stepwise regression. t-statistics are significant at 60% for the stepwise regressions (t-statistic = 0.25).

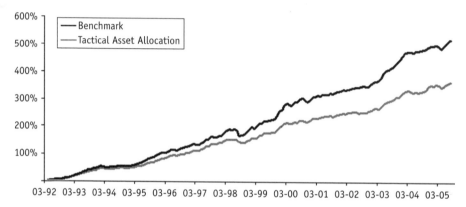

Figure 12.1 Benchmark versus tactical asset allocation cumulative returns for HFR noninvestable indices, January 1990 to August 2005, rebalancing every six months, before transaction costs

The outperformance is 2.21% per annum. This is the additional return above the benchmark when the portfolio is rebalanced each month to its fixed weights. The information ratio of the active portfolio is 0.98. The portfolio has a higher volatility of 5.46% (bad), a lower skewness of −0.48 (bad), and a lower monthly maximum loss due to the smaller portfolio diversification. This is compensated for by a higher annualized portfolio return of 14.45%. Figure 12.1 presents the portfolio and the benchmark historical cumulative returns.

12.3.2   Tactical asset allocation with investable indices

Next, we apply the model to the HFR investable indices[12] using a one-month rebalancing. Each month, the model proposed in Section 12.2 is applied and an

---

[12] These indices have daily liquidity, the assets are weighted, and the underlying hedge funds are open for investment.

Table 12.7 Tactical asset allocation with HFR investable indices, April 2003 to August 2005, rebalancing every month, before transaction costs

	Benchmark	Portfolio	Active portfolio
Historical annualized return	2.56%	3.83%	1.24%
Historical annualized volatility	2.21%	2.48%	0.82%
Monthly skewness	0.8	0.8	0.8
Sharpe ratio (R_f =4%)	−0.65	−0.07	—
Information ratio	—	—	1.52

Twelve-month rolling window for the stepwise regression and t-statistics are significant at 60% only for the stepwise regressions (t-statistic = 0.25).

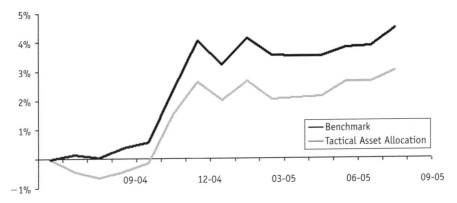

Figure 12.2 Benchmark versus tactical asset allocation cumulative returns for HFRX investable indices, January 2003 to January 2005, rebalancing every month, before transaction costs

optimization is performed to find the new monthly portfolio weights. The portfolio is held without change for one month only.

In Table 12.7 we see that the model outperforms the benchmark by 1.24% per annum before transaction costs. The portfolio has a higher volatility and higher realized returns than the benchmark from Table 12.5. The cumulative performance of the portfolio versus the benchmark is shown in Figure 12.2.

12.3.3 Tactical asset allocation with investable hedge funds

We now apply the model to the hedge funds available on the Lyxor© platform, which have weekly or monthly liquidity. We select the hedge funds with the 20 longest track records from the 144 managed accounts available in September 2005. The common first data point among these 20 accounts is January 1995. The benchmark is composed of 5% in each managed account. The minimum portfolio weight can be 0%, and the maximum can be 15%. The portfolio weights

Table 12.8 Tactical asset allocation with 20 Lyxor© managed accounts, January 1995 to August 2005, rebalancing every three months, before transaction costs

	Benchmark	Portfolio	Active portfolio
Historical annualized return	10.89%	12.31%	1.30%
Historical annualized volatility	4.81%	5.75%	2.93%
Monthly skewness	−0.42	−0.24	−0.23
Sharpe ratio ($R_f = 4\%$)	1.43	1.44	—
Information ratio	—	—	0.44

Twelve-month rolling window for the stepwise regression and t-statistics are significant at 60% only for the stepwise regressions (t-statistic = 0.25).

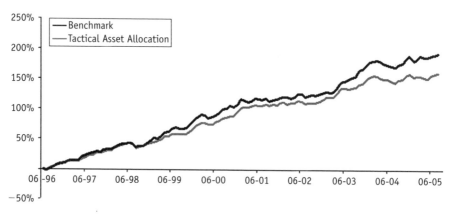

Figure 12.3 Benchmark versus tactical asset allocation for 20 hedge funds, January 1995 to August 2005, rebalancing every three months, before transaction costs

are the same, since it will be three months until a new portfolio optimization is performed. Table 12.8 gives the results of applying this model to the 20 accounts (see Figure 12.3).

Readers should be disappointed at these results.[13] Before transaction costs, using a tactical asset allocation model based on economic factors and highly liquid hedge funds, the model is generating a low annual information ratio of 0.44. This poor result is attributable to three things.

- The model does not include the correct economic factors or does not correct for extreme hedge fund returns (for example, model misspecification) (the latter comment should be tested in future research).
- There are poor links between economic factors and hedge fund returns. Only the hedge fund aggregation (for example, the hedge fund indices) is sensitive to economic factors.[14]

---

[13] We were as well.

[14] We believe that hedge fund classifications can be considered as alternative models.

- The small sample 20 hedge funds is not representative of the hedge fund market. This is certainly correct.[15]

It is possible to improve the information ratio, and consequently the alphas, by adding an additional economic factor, a three-month index moving average in the regression.[16]

12.4 Conclusion

We presented a tactical asset allocation for noninvestable hedge fund indices, investable hedge fund indices, and liquid hedge funds. We forecast the expected returns of the hedge fund indices or the hedge funds for the next one to six months and found it is possible to outperform an equally weighted benchmark before transaction costs as follows.

- Using noninvestable indices (portfolio rebalancing every six months), we obtained a 2.21% annual gain.
- Using investable indices (portfolio rebalancing every month), we obtained a 1.24% annual gain.
- Using highly liquid (weekly or monthly redemption) hedge funds (portfolio rebalancing every three months), we obtained a 1.30% annual gain.

The results show lower outperformance and lower information ratios than Amenc, El Bied, and Martellini (2002) and Pillonel and Solanet (2004). First, our model does not account for lagged moving average indices.[17] Second, two of our three models forecast the next three or six months, which is more difficult than forecasting the next one month. Consequently, we think higher performance in terms of alpha and information ratio can be obtained as follows:

- Using a combination of economic factors and moving average index returns when forecasting index returns
- Using a ranking methodology with at least moving average hedge fund returns as ranking criteria[18] when forecasting hedge fund returns

References

Amenc, N., El Bied, S., and Martellini, L. (2002). Evidence of Predictability in Hedge Fund Returns. *Financial Analysts Journal*, 59(5):32–46.

---

[15] We apply the tactical asset allocation model with a six-month horizon to illiquid hedge funds that are different than the liquid managed accounts, and we find an information ratio higher than 1.0.

[16] Pillonel and Solanet (2004) show that this is the most powerful technique, with an information ratio of between 2.6 and 3.0 at a one-month forecasting horizon.

[17] This is in fact a trend-following model, with the past three months used to forecast the next one month.

[18] See, for example, Capocci (2005) for application of this technique to arbitrage strategies.

Amenc, N. and Vaissie, M. (2005). Determinants of Funds of Hedge Funds Performance. Working Paper, Edhec-Risk, Nice, France.

Capocci, D. (2005). Neutrality of Market Neutral Funds. Working Paper, Edhec-Risk, Nice, France.

Capocci, D., Corhay, A., and Hübner, G. (2003). Hedge Fund Performance and Persistence in Bull and Bear Markets. Working Paper, University of Liege, Belgium.

Dash, G. and Kajiji, N. (2003). Forecasting Hedge Fund Index Returns by Level and Classification: Comparative Analysis of Neural Network Topologies. Working Paper, University of Rhode Island, Kingston, RI.

Gupta, B., Cerrahoglu, B., and Daglioglu, A. (2003). Hedge Fund Strategy Performance: Using Conditional Approaches. Working Paper, CISDM.

Karavas, V. and Siokos, S. (2003). The Hedge Fund Indices Universe. In: *Hedge Funds: Strategies, Risk Assessment and Returns* (Gregoriou, G. N., Karavas, V. N., and Rouah, F., eds.). Beard Books, Baltimore, MD.

Padilla, J. and Zebad, M. (2004). Tactical Asset Allocation on Market Neutral Hedge Funds. Working Paper, University of Lausanne, Lausanne, Switzerland.

Pillonel, P. and Solanet, L. (2004). Predictability in Hedge Fund Index Returns and Its Application in Fund of Hedge Funds' Style Allocation. Working Paper, University of Lausanne, Lausanne, Switzerland.

Schneeweis, T., Kazemi, H., and Martin, G. (2002). Understanding Hedge Fund Performance. *Journal of Alternative Investments*, 5(3):9–22.

Vaissie, M. (2003). A Detailed Analysis of the Construction Methods and Management Principles of Hedge Fund Indices. Working Paper, Edhec-Risk, Lille, France.

Von Wyss, H. and Ammann, H. (2003). Hedge Fund Performance and Predictability. Working Paper, University of St. Gallen, Lille, France.

Zairi, L. and Sideri, N. (2004). Hedge Fund Performance Evaluation: Macrofactor Model versus Option-Based Model Applied to Market Neutral and Long/Short Index Strategies. Working Paper, University of Lausanne, Lausanne, Switzerland.

13 Single-strategy funds of hedge funds: How many funds?

Ryan J. Davies, Harry M. Kat, and Sa Lu

Abstract

We provide a simple method to predict how the higher-order return moments of a single-strategy fund of hedge funds will vary as one or more funds are added to or removed from the portfolio. Our model-free approach uses average comoments obtained from the universe of available funds to develop a functional relationship between portfolio return distributions and the number of funds in the portfolio.

13.1 Introduction

Managers of funds of hedge funds face an important decision: How many funds to include in their portfolio. The manager must trade off possible diversification benefits with the costs of selecting and monitoring more funds. The answer is not straightforward. Hedge funds have complex higher-order return interactions, and historical return data is often nonexistent for new, investable funds. On top of this, funds of funds have to deal with stringent minimum investment requirements, typically ranging between US$250,000 and $1 million. These minimum investment requirements pose significant barriers for diversification, particularly for smaller funds of funds.

In this chapter, we present a simple method to predict how the fund of funds return distribution will change as more funds are added to or removed from the fund portfolio. More specifically, we extend the decomposition methodology employed by Elton and Gruber (1977) and Conine and Tamarkin (1981) to consider a framework for third and fourth moments and use this methodology to show how the impact of diversification depends on each of the moments' constituent comoments.

Our focus is on single-strategy funds of funds. These are funds that invest in a portfolio of hedge funds that follow the same investment strategy. While our analysis can also be extended to more complex multistrategy funds of funds, it works best in the context of funds that invest in assets with similar return characteristics.[1] The next section describes the decomposition technique.

13.2 Decomposition

Our approach follows a minimum-information perspective. In other words, we assume the investor has no more information than the individual hedge funds' strategy classification and historical returns. Although many funds of hedge funds employ analysts that study hedge fund managers' strategies, risk management procedures, and other details, it is far from obvious that this effort adds much value when it comes to portfolio selection. Most hedge fund strategies and procedures are just too complex for superficial analysis to be able to provide satisfactory insight into the comovements of the returns of the funds in question.

Our analysis assumes all funds are equally weighted in the portfolio. This is optimal if investors have no information about the comoments of future individual hedge fund returns.[2] The total number of hedge funds within a strategy class is denoted as N, and the number of hedge funds in the actual fund of funds portfolio is denoted as n.

The variance of a portfolio of n individual hedge funds can be expressed as

$$\sigma^2(n) = n^{-2}\left(\sum_{i=1}^{n} \text{var}(i) + \sum_{j=1}^{n}\sum_{i=1,i\neq j}^{n}\text{cov}(i,j)\right) \tag{13.1}$$

where $\text{var}(i)$ is the variance of the returns of fund i and $\text{cov}(i,j)$ is the covariance of the returns of funds i and j. To see how this might change as n varies, we first calculate the average variance and average covariance for the *total population* of funds ($N \gg n$) within a particular strategy class:

$$\overline{\text{var}}(i) = \frac{1}{N}\sum_{i=1}^{N}\text{var}(i) \qquad \overline{\text{cov}}(i,j) = \frac{1}{N(N-1)}\sum_{i=1}^{N}\sum_{j=1,i\neq j}^{N}\text{cov}(i,j)$$

where the overbar indicates averages over the total population of funds and the notation $\overline{\text{cov}}(i,j)$ implicitly assumes i and j are different funds. Then an asymptotic approximation of the variance of a portfolio containing n individual hedge funds is

$$E[\sigma^2(n)] \approx n^{-1}\left[\overline{\text{var}}(i) + (n-1)\overline{\text{cov}}(i,j)\right]$$

[1] To the extent that higher return moments matter for mutual funds, our decomposition method can also be useful in the context of determining the diversification benefits of investing in multiple mutual funds with the same investment objective. Thus, our research complements the empirical study of Louton and Saraoglu (2005) on the impact on standard deviation of holding multiple mutual funds with the same objective.

[2] In the case that future comoments can be forecast, equal investment is an upper limit on the risk that investors bear (Johnson and Shannon, 1974).

Under the condition that $\text{plim}_{n\to\infty}E[\sigma(n)] = (E[\sigma^2(n)])^{1/2}$, the expected standard deviation of a portfolio containing n individual hedge funds can be approximated by

$$E[\sigma(n)] \approx n^{-1/2}\,[\overline{\text{var}(i)} + (n-1)\overline{\text{cov}(i,j)}]^{1/2} \qquad (13.2)$$

This result was first derived by Elton and Gruber (1977). We now extend the analysis to the third and fourth return moments.

To begin, we will denote the third return moment of a given fund i as

$$M_3(i,i,i) = E[(R_i - E(R_i))^3]$$

and the third return comoments as

$$M_3(i,i,j) = E[(R_i - E(R_i))^2(R_j - E(R_j))]$$

and

$$M_3(i,j,k) = E[(R_i - E(R_i))(R_j - E(R_j))(R_k - E(R_k))]$$

where i, j, and k are different funds. Then the third central moment of a portfolio with n funds can be expressed as

$$E(R_p[n] - E(R_p[n]))^3 = n^{-3}E\left(\sum_{i=1}^{n}(R_i - E(R_i))\right)^3$$

$$= \frac{1}{n^3}\sum_{i=1}^{n}M_3(i,i,i) + \frac{3}{n^3}\sum_{i=1}^{n}\sum_{j=1,\neq i}^{n}M_3(i,i,j)$$

$$+ \frac{1}{n^3}\sum_{i=1}^{n}\sum_{j=1,\neq i}^{n}\sum_{k=1,\neq\{i,j\}}^{n}M_3(i,j,k) \qquad (13.3)$$

It is important to recognize at this stage that equation (13.3) would be effectively impossible to use under normal circumstances. An investor with a portfolio of 10 funds would need to solve for 820 comoments!! Worse yet, these comoments typically would need to be estimated for newly created investable funds that have little or no return history. And the comoments would need to be reestimated each time a new fund was added to or subtracted from the portfolio.

To avoid these problems, we use the same logic as we did for variance and approximate the third central moment using a function of the average comoments for the total population of available funds within the strategy class:

$$E(R_p[n] - E(R_p[n]))^3$$
$$\approx n^{-2}[\overline{M}_3(i,i,i) + 3(n-1)\overline{M}_3(i,i,j) + (n-1)(n-2)\overline{M}_3(i,j,k)] \qquad (13.4)$$

where the *population* averages of these (co-)moments across all funds are obtained as:

$$\overline{M}_3(i,i,i) = \frac{1}{N} \sum_{i=1}^{N} M_3(i,i,i)$$

$$\overline{M}_3(i,i,j) = \frac{1}{N(N-1)} \sum_{i=1}^{N} \sum_{j=1,\neq i}^{N} M_3(i,i,j)$$

$$\overline{M}_3(i,j,k) = \frac{1}{N(N-1)(N-2)} \sum_{i=1}^{N} \sum_{j=1,\neq i}^{N} \sum_{k=1,\neq\{i,j\}}^{N} M_3(i,j,k)$$

Thus, the investor would need to calculate three comoment averages only once and then could predict how the portfolio's third return moment would vary as the number of funds in the portfolio changes. These population-based comoment averages could be based on historical data and/or investor expectations. Also, these averages will be more stable and can be estimated more accurately than individual comoments.

Table 13.1 provides the average comoments for the variance and third central moment decompositions. These results are for illustrative purposes only and are based on the net-of-fees returns reported in the TASS Database from June 1994 to May 2001. Further details about the database, strategy definitions, and adjustments to reported returns can be found in Davies, Kat, and Lu (2005a, 2005b).

To illustrate how our decomposition equation for skewness can be used, suppose a fund of hedge funds manager has a portfolio of 10 merger arbitrage funds and would like to know how much the skewness of his portfolio will fall if another fund is added. Based on historical data, the manager observes that $\overline{M}_3(i, i, i) = 12.96$, $\overline{M}_3(i, i, j) = -4.20$, and $\overline{M}_3(i, j, k) = -4.14$. Using our

Table 13.1 Average comoments for the variance and third central moment decompositions

	$\overline{\mathrm{var}}(i)$	$\overline{\mathrm{cov}}(i,j)$	$\overline{M}_3(i,i,i)$	$\overline{M}_3(i,i,j)$	$\overline{M}_3(i,j,k)$
Convertible arbitrage	23.89	3.74	−202.52	−32.94	−6.04
Dedicated short bias	73.87	38.27	150.87	218.96	206.88
Distressed securities	12.64	3.34	−105.15	−36.56	−18.98
Equity market neutral	11.55	0.68	4.71	−3.85	−0.57
Global macro	34.54	5.85	96.75	31.97	13.05
Long/short equity	48.22	9.92	1.15	−11.18	−9.85
Merger arbitrage	6.18	1.22	12.96	−4.20	−4.14
Emerging markets	108.99	47.55	−618.55	−554.21	−446.45

These results are based on fund returns reported in the TASS database (June 1994 to May 2001). Fund returns are net of fees, unsmoothed, and survivorship-bias free.

decomposition in equation (13.4), we predict that:

$$E(R_p[10] - E(R_p[10]))^3$$
$$= [12.96 + 3(9)(-4.20) + (9)(8)(-4.14)]/100 = -3.9852$$
$$E(R_p[11] - E(R_p[11]))^3$$
$$= [12.96 + 3(10)(-4.20) + (10)(9)(-4.14)]/121 = -4.0136$$

Thus, the manager would predict that an additional fund would cause the third moment to fall from -3.9852 to -4.0136. Thus, adding an additional fund would cause the portfolio return to become more negatively skewed (a bad thing). The fund manager must balance this deterioration against the potential benefits in terms of reduced standard deviation and a lower fourth moment. Finding the correct cutoff point is very important — too much diversification may cause the portfolio returns to become more negatively skewed but may not add much in terms of risk reduction.

An important feature of the decomposition expression (4) is that the terms have different orders with respect to n: specifically, $O(n^{-2})$, $O(n^{-1})$, and $O(1)$. Thus, as the number of funds becomes sufficiently large, the first two terms become relatively less important, and the third central moment depends only on the average third comoment between three different funds selected from the total population. Notice that this $\overline{M}_3(i, j, k)$ term is negative for six out of the eight hedge fund strategies. This implies that highly diversified funds of funds in these strategies will typically maintain a return distribution with negative skewness.

The importance of the final third comoment term is analogous to the well-known property of portfolio variance captured in equation (13.2) — as the portfolio size increases, the idiosyncratic risk in the variance terms is reduced by diversification but the systematic risk in the covariance terms remains.

Using a similar approach, we can also extend our analysis to the fourth return moment. The fourth return moment of a given fund i is given by $M_4(i, i, i, i) = E[(R_i - E(R_i))^4]$, and the comoments are:

$$M_4(i, i, j, j) = E[(R_i - E(R_i))^2 (R_j - E(R_j))^2]$$
$$M_4(i, i, i, j) = E[(R_i - E(R_i))^3 (R_j - E(R_j))]$$
$$M_4(i, i, j, k) = E[(R_i - E(R_i))^2 (R_j - E(R_j))(R_k - E(R_k))]$$
$$M_4(i, j, k, l) = E[(R_i - E(R_i))(R_j - E(R_j))(R_k - E(R_k))(R_l - E(R_l))]$$

Thus, the fourth central moment of a portfolio with n funds is

$$E(R_p - E(R_p))^4 = n^{-4} E\left(\sum_{i=1}^{n}(R_i - E(R_i))\right)^4$$

$$= n^{-4}\sum_{i=1}^{n}\left| \begin{array}{l} M_4(i,i,i,i) + \sum_{j=1,\neq i}^{n}(4M_4(i,i,i,j) + 3M_4(i,i,j,j)) \\ +6\sum_{j=1,\neq i}^{n}\sum_{k=1,\neq\{i,j\}}^{n} M_4(i,i,j,k) + \sum_{j=1,\neq i}^{n}\sum_{k=1,\neq i,j}^{n}\sum_{l=1,\neq\{i,j,k\}}^{n} M_4(i,j,k,l) \end{array} \right|.$$

Substituting for the comoment averages based on the total available population of funds, we obtain the approximation

$$E(R_p - E(R_p))^4 \approx n^{-3}[\overline{M}_4(i,i,i,i) + 4(n-1)\overline{M}_4(i,i,i,j) + 3(n-1)\overline{M}_4(i,i,j,j)$$
$$+ 6(n-1)(n-2)\overline{M}_4(i,i,j,k) + (n-1)(n-2)(n-3)\overline{M}_4(i,j,k,l)]$$

$$(13.5)$$

where the *population* averages of these (co-)moments across all funds are obtained as:

$$\overline{M}_4(i,i,i,i) = \frac{1}{N}\sum_{i=1}^{N} M_4(i,i,i,i)$$

$$\overline{M}_4(i,i,i,j) = \frac{1}{N(N-1)}\sum_{i=1}^{N}\sum_{j=1,\neq i}^{N} M_4(i,i,i,j)$$

$$\overline{M}_4(i,i,j,j) = \frac{1}{N(N-1)}\sum_{i=1}^{N}\sum_{j=1,\neq i}^{N} M_4(i,i,j,j)$$

$$\overline{M}_4(i,i,j,k) = \frac{1}{N(N-1)(N-2)}\sum_{i=1}^{N}\sum_{j=1,\neq i}^{N}\sum_{k=1,\neq\{i,j\}}^{N} M_4(i,i,j,k)$$

$$\overline{M}_4(i,j,k,l) = \frac{1}{N(N-1)(N-2)(N-3)}$$
$$\sum_{i=1}^{N}\sum_{j=1,\neq i}^{N}\sum_{k=1,\neq\{i,j\}}^{N}\sum_{l=1,\neq\{i,j,k\}}^{N} M_4(i,j,k,l)$$

Again, note that as the number of funds in the portfolio grows sufficiently large, the expected fourth moment depends only on the fourth comoment between four different funds (i.e., $\overline{M}_4(i,j,k,l)$). Table 13.2 provides the corresponding illustrative average fourth-order comoments for different hedge fund strategies. As with the third moment decomposition, substantial differences exist in comoments across strategies. Thus, the optimal number of funds should also differ according to the fund of funds' strategy.

Table 13.2 Average comoments for fourth central moment decompositions

	$\overline{M}_4(i,i,i,i)$	$\overline{M}_4(i,i,j,k)$	$\overline{M}_4(i,j,k,l)$	$\overline{M}_4(i,i,i,j)$	$\overline{M}_4(i,i,j,j)$
Convertible arbitrage	13,421	337	65	1,990	1,969
Dedicated short bias	92,834	14,449	8,332	33,994	26,143
Distressed securities	7,172	442	228	1,428	871
Equity market neutral	2,039	8	4	33	206
Global macro	13,000	448	133	1,785	2,178
Long/short equity	34,628	1,323	458	3,879	4,892
Merger arbitrage	878	42	29	64	72
Emerging markets	135,978	29,320	20,151	53,362	45,024

These results are based on fund returns reported in the TASS database (June 1994 to May 2001). Fund returns are net of fees, unsmoothed, and survivorship-bias free.

Until now, we have expressed our decompositions in equations (13.4) and (13.5) in terms of third and fourth moments rather than in terms of skewness and kurtosis. Brulhart and Klein (2005) provide a strong argument in favor of using the return moments rather than skewness/kurtosis for investment decisions. Unlike the relative measures, these moments allow the investor to see what is driving higher variance separately from what is causing changes in the shape of the return distribution.

That said, many investors prefer to use *relative* skewness and kurtosis, particularly in the context of statistical testing of their models.[3] To obtain these, we must make these additional *strong* assumptions:

$$\text{plim}_{n \to \infty} E\left(\frac{(R_p - E(R_p))^3}{\sigma_p^3} \right) = \frac{E(R_p - E(R_p))^3}{[E(\sigma_p^2)]^{\frac{3}{2}}}$$

$$\text{plim}_{n \to \infty} E\left(\frac{(R_p - E(R_p))^4}{\sigma_p^4} \right) = \frac{E(R_p - E(R_p))^4}{[E(\sigma_p^2)]^2}$$

In effect, these assumptions imply that the portfolio (sample) size is sufficiently large that idiosyncratic risks are diversified away. If this is not true (it will not be for "small" samples), then the skewness/kurtosis decomposition will be inaccurate because of so-called Jensen's inequality issues. Using these asymptotic results, we obtain the approximate expected *relative* skewness of a portfolio with n funds as

$$E[\text{skew}(n)] \approx \frac{\overline{M}_3(i,i,i) + 3(n-1)\overline{M}_3(i,i,j) + (n-1)(n-2)\overline{M}_3(i,j,k)}{n^{1/2}[\overline{\text{var}}(i) + (n-1)\overline{\text{cov}}(i,j)]^{3/2}} \tag{13.6}$$

and approximate expected *relative* kurtosis of a portfolio with n funds as

$$E[\text{kurt}(n)] \approx n^{-1}[\overline{\text{var}}(i) + (n-1)\overline{\text{cov}}(i,j)]^{-2}$$

$$\begin{bmatrix} \overline{M}_4(i,i,i,i) + 4(n-1)\overline{M}_4(i,i,i,j) \\ + 3(n-1)\overline{M}_4(i,i,j,j) + 6(n-1)(n-2)\overline{M}_4(i,i,j,k) \\ + (n-1)(n-2)(n-3)\overline{M}_4(i,j,k,l) \end{bmatrix} \tag{13.7}$$

These two decompositions assume that the ratio of two expected values equals the expected value of the ratio, which of course need not be true. Because of this, unless there is a reason to do so, we recommend using equations (13.4) and (13.5) rather than equations (13.6) and (13.7).

Finally, in unreported results, we use a bootstrap confidence interval approach to examine how well our decomposition estimates perform. As one might expect,

---

[3] The third and fourth central moments are scale sensitive and are not amenable to significance testing (Beedles, 1979).

in general our asymptotic approximations provide very poor predictions of return moments for funds of funds with fewer than 10 funds. But for sample sizes over 10, the decomposition appears to work reasonably well: Our predicted values typically lie within the 95% range of possible outcomes obtained from repeatedly selecting a portfolio of n random funds and calculating its portfolio return moments. Of course, as with all investments, past return performance is not necessarily indicative of future results! Our companion working paper, Davies, Kat, and Lu (2005a), provides additional details.

13.3   Conclusion

In this chapter, we decompose each of the four portfolio moments into a function of portfolio size, thereby separating the effect of diversification on the distribution moments into specific components. These parsimonious, model-free decomposition equations can easily be incorporated into a portfolio optimization process, such as that proposed in Davies, Kat, and Lu (2005b). Finally, we highlight that the return comoments, rather than individual hedge fund moments, matter most in portfolio diversification.

References

Brulhart, T. and Klein, P. (2005). Are Extreme Hedge Fund Returns Problematic? Working Paper, Simon Fraser University, Burnaby, British Columbia, Canada.

Beedles, W. L. (1979). On the Asymmetry of Market Returns. *Journal of Financial and Quantitative Analysis*, 10(3):231–283.

Conine Jr., T. E. and Tamarkin, M. J. (1981). On Diversification Given Asymmetry in Returns. *Journal of Finance*, 36(5):1143–1155.

Davies, R. J., Kat, H. M., and Lu, S. (2005a). Single-Strategy Funds of Hedge Funds. Working Paper, Babson College, Babson Park, MA.

Davies, R. J., Kat, H. M., and Lu, S. (2005b). Funds of Hedge Funds Portfolio Selection: A Multiple-Objective Approach. Working Paper, Babson College, Babson Park, MA.

Elton, E. J. and Gruber, M. J. (1977). Risk Reduction and Portfolio Size: An Analytical Solution. *Journal of Business*, 50(4):415–437.

Johnson, K. H. and Shannon, D. S. (1974). A Note on Diversification and the Reduction of Dispersion. *Journal of Financial Economics*, 1:365–372.

Louton, D. and Saraoglu, H. (2005). Performance Implications of Holding Multiple Mutual Funds with the Same Investment Objective. *Journal of Investing*, forthcoming.

Part Three
Construction and Statistical
Properties of Funds of Hedge Funds

14 Distributional characteristics of funds of hedge funds returns

Elaine Hutson, Margaret Lynch, and Max Stevenson

Abstract

We examine the return distributions of 332 funds of hedge funds (Fofs) and associated indexes. Almost all exhibit excess kurtosis. Over half are significantly skewed (according to the standard skewness statistic), and these are split 50/50 positive and negative. We argue, however, that the skewness statistic can lead to erroneous inferences regarding the nature of the return distribution, because the test statistic is based on the normal distribution. Using a series of tests that make minimal assumptions about the shape of the underlying distribution, we find very little skewness in the returns of the FOFs. We then fit distributions to the FOF return series and find that the majority of the funds have a logistic distribution, confirming their excess kurtosis relative to the normal. In the final part of our analysis, we compare the ranking of the funds' performance using Sharpe ratios to their ranking based on metrics that use alternate measures of dispersion — specifically, interquartile range and median absolute deviation. We show that the comparative performance of the FOFs is very sensitive to the metric used.

14.1 Introduction

It is now well established that the returns reported by hedge funds are not normally distributed. Hedge fund returns show strong excess kurtosis, and using the skewness statistic it appears that many hedge funds and hedge fund indexes have negatively skewed return distributions. Previous researchers investigating the distributional characteristics of asset returns have usually relied on parametric tests of asymmetry, and this is no different in hedge fund research. Prior studies of hedge fund performance that have included an analysis of asymmetry (Brooks and Kat, 2001; Kat and Lu, 2002; Lamm, 2003) use the skewness statistic and generally find that hedge funds and hedge fund indexes are either not significantly skewed or negatively skewed.

Most of the early studies of hedge fund and FOFs performance used assessment techniques such as the Sharpe ratio or Jensen's alpha (Agarwal and Naik, 2001; Amin and Kat, 2003; Fung and Hsieh, 1999; Lo, 2001). The key assumptions of these performance measures are that returns are normally distributed and that investors focus only on the expected return and the standard deviation of returns. With strong evidence of nonnormality, the mean and standard deviation are not sufficient to describe the return distribution, and higher moments need to be considered. Brooks and Kat (2001) show that although hedge funds offer high mean returns and low standard deviations, the returns also exhibit third and fourth moment attributes (skewness and kurtosis) that are precisely the opposite of those that investors desire. They find that high Sharpe ratios tend to go together with negative skewness and high kurtosis, and this suggests that the relatively high means and low standard deviations offered by hedge funds and FOFs are very much a partial picture of return outcomes.

The issue of hedge fund return asymmetry is of prime importance given the phenomenal growth in hedge funds and FOFs since the mid-1980s. Many wholesale and increasingly retail investors consider hedge funds as a new and important addition to the asset class universe. In this chapter we examine the distributional characteristics, and in particular the asymmetry, of 332 FOFs and associated indexes. We argue that FOF data should be used in preference to hedge fund index data to examine asymmetry, because FOFs do not suffer from the data-conditioning biases that are well understood to affect hedge fund returns data (Fung and Hsieh, 2002).

We use three approaches to testing for nonnormality. First, we test for the symmetry of returns using a formal binomial distribution test. We examine the numbers of returns either side of the mean. If the distribution is symmetric, then the numbers of positive and negative excess returns (relative to the mean) will follow a binomial distribution with parameters n and p, where $p = 0.5$. We also conduct this test on segments of the distribution based on standard deviations either side of the mean. Second, we conduct a distribution-fitting exercise. If the FOF return distributions are not normal, then what distributional form do they take? Third, we calculate the standard Sharpe and two variations on the Sharpe ratio that use alternative measures of dispersion — the interquartile range and the median absolute deviation. Do the Sharpe rankings for our sample FOFs change when more robust measures of risk are used in the performance metric?

In our binomial tests, we find little evidence of significant asymmetry in FOF returns. While it is generally assumed that hedge fund skewness is due to observations in the left tail of the return distribution (because the nature of many hedge fund strategies means that occasional large negative returns would be a feature of the expected payoff),[1] when we do find evidence of asymmetry using this approach, it is close to the mean rather than in the tails. We also show that for FOFs, the skewness statistic can lead to incorrect inferences about the nature of return distributions.

The main shortcomings of the binomial approach are that the test may not be sufficiently sensitive (especially when testing for asymmetry in distribution intervals far from the mean, where the number of observations is small) and that it

---

[1] Fung and Hsieh (1999), for example, argue that many hedge fund strategies set up an insurance-like payoff, with the hedge fund being the insurer.

does not take into account the values of extreme observations. In our distribution-fitting exercise, we find that only 7 of the 332 funds are normal and that another 74 are approximately normal. Only about a quarter of the FOFs in our sample can therefore be considered normally distributed. Lastly, our Sharpe ratio analysis shows that the ranking of many of the FOFs changes dramatically when standard deviation is substituted for more robust measures of risk. This confirms that nonnormality of returns is an issue in FOF returns and therefore that standard performance measures are potentially misleading.

The remainder of the chapter is as follows. In Section 14.2 we review the evidence on hedge fund and FOF performance, including the most recent research on nonnormality issues. In Section 14.3 we describe the binomial, distribution-fitting, and Sharpe ratio approaches techniques that we use to test for normality. Section 14.4 presents the data and discusses the summary performance statistics for the sample, and Section 14.5 presents the results. In the final section we summarize the paper and conclude.

14.2   Hedge funds: background

The massive growth in hedge funds in the last few years has been matched by burgeoning academic evidence on their performance. Most research on hedge fund performance has found that hedge funds exhibit superior performance on a risk-adjusted basis relative to standard asset classes such as equity and bonds (Ackerman, McEnally, and Ravenscraft, 1999; Asness, Krail, and Liew, 2001; S. J. Brown, Goetzmann, and Ibbotson, 1999). On the face of it, hedge funds in general earn excellent returns relative to the risk they bear. However, research on hedge fund performance is hampered by several well-understood shortcomings. The main obstacle to gaining reliable insights into hedge fund performance is that the data suffer from several conditioning biases. Most of these biases result from the fact hedge funds are largely unregulated and thus (unlike mutual funds) are not required to report performance. Hedge funds report voluntarily to several commercial hedge fund data providers, such as CSFB/Tremont, Hedge Fund Research (HFR), Managed Account Reports (now Zurich Capital Markets), MSCI, and Van Hedge Fund Advisors. While most of these providers claim to control for survivorship bias by retaining the data on defunct and withdrawn funds in their databases and in their various performance indexes, there are several related biases that are more difficult to correct for. Liquidation bias occurs when underperforming funds withdraw from reporting in the runup to their liquidation. Assuming liquidation follows very poor or possibly catastrophically poor performance (à la LTCM) the effect of this bias is clearly to overestimate hedge fund returns and underestimate their risk. Termination bias usually refers to funds that disappear through mergers and reorganizations, and it could lead to either the underestimation or the overestimation of hedge fund returns. Self-selection (or simply selection) bias is caused by funds that cease reporting voluntarily, because, for example, they have reached capacity and no longer need the publicity associated with reporting performance (Fung and Hsieh, 2002). This bias typically includes funds that choose not to report at all, and it leads to the underestimation of hedge fund returns. With the best will in the world on the part of the data providers, these biases are difficult to eliminate, at least until regulation requires hedge funds to report performance publicly. They are often grouped under the heading of survivorship bias, and the findings generally are that the biases leading to underestimation of risk and return dominate those that might cause its overestimation. Survivorship bias has been estimated by various studies to be in the range 1.4–3.4% annually (Amin and Kat, 2002a; S. J. Brown, Goetzmann, and Ibbotson, 1999; Fung and Hsieh, 1997, 2000; Liang, 2001).

More recently, a second major shortcoming of hedge fund data has come to light. Many hedge funds hold assets for which regular arm's-length market prices are not available, such as securities traded in illiquid markets or over-the-counter products such as swaps. At the end of each month, when net asset values are calculated by hedge funds, the values of these assets must sometimes be estimated. Kao (2002) argues that such "marking to market" and "marking to model" estimates of net asset value are questionable and "most likely contribute(s) to hedge funds' low return volatilities and low correlations with other asset classes." Asness, Krail, and Liew (2001) argue that hedge funds have an incentive to "smooth" the return series and find that when returns are adjusted for stale prices, many of the return and diversification benefits of hedge fund investing disappear.

Most of the early studies of hedge fund performance used assessment techniques such as the Sharpe ratio and Jensen's alpha, which assume that returns are normally distributed. However, nonnormality is being increasingly recognized as a feature of hedge fund return distributions (Agarwal and Naik, 2001; Amin and Kat, 2003; Fung and Hsieh, 1999; Lo, 2001). More recently there have been several studies specifically examining the distributional properties of hedge fund returns.

Before discussing some of these studies, it must be remembered that there is an important difference between average skewness for individual funds and skewness figures for indexes or portfolios of hedge funds, including FOFs. This is because skewness changes in ways that are incompletely understood when portfolios are formed. In an analysis of optimal portfolios of hedge funds, Amin and Kat (2002b) find that as the number of funds increases, standard deviation falls but median skewness becomes more negative. Kat and Lu (2002) find that among individual hedge funds, funds in most strategy categories are associated with negative skewness, and all have excess kurtosis. Similar to Amin and Kat (2000b), when within-strategy portfolios are formed, standard deviation falls but skewness decreases. They conclude that "it appears that when things go bad for one fund, they tend to go bad for other funds in the same sector as well."

Research using hedge fund indexes has found evidence of nonnormality, with the findings very strong on excess kurtosis and, generally speaking, negative skewness. Brooks and Kat (2001) find significant skewness across a range of hedge fund strategies in 48 hedge fund indexes. Interestingly, of six aggregate hedge fund indexes from different data providers, only two show significant asymmetry, and these are left-skewed (including the HFR index that we use). They also find statistically significant negative skewness (across all of the data providers) for the convertible arbitrage, risk arbitrage, distressed, and emerging markets strategies, while equity market neutral, long-short equity, and macro strategies are generally not significantly skewed. Lamm (2003) finds that for the HFR composite hedge fund index from 1995 to 2002, skewness is −0.46 (which is not significant).

14.2.1 Funds of hedge funds

During the past few years the growth in FOFs has been phenomenal. The number of FOFs increased from 550 in 2001 to approximately 780 in mid-2003, and they now comprise almost one-third of the $650 billion invested in hedge funds (*The Economist*, September 18, 2003). At the same time, FOFs are becoming available to a greater range of potential investors. While most regulation around the world restricts direct investment in hedge funds to institutions and high-net-worth individuals, recent changes to regulations in various jurisdictions have opened investment in FOFs to retail investors.[2] Indeed, one of the claimed benefits of FOFs is that moderately wealthy investors are able to participate in hedge fund investment. The assumption among regulators appears to be that being portfolios, FOFs must be less risky than individual hedge funds. While by definition holding a portfolio of hedge funds must be less risky than holding only one or two hedge funds, their risk and return characteristics are not well understood.

Relative to hedge fund managers, FOF managers require a different set of skills. Like active mutual fund managers, FOF managers must attempt to pick winners. The challenge of trying to choose between 15 and 30 hedge funds from among a hedge fund universe of over 6,000 must be immense, even relative to the challenge facing active mutual fund managers. FOF managers offer other benefits for their services vis-à-vis investing directly in hedge funds. As well as diversification, FOFs managers claim ongoing monitoring of hedge funds, access to good funds that are closed to new investors, lower minimum investments, and more flexible redemption policies. For these services, FOF managers charge a management fee and usually a cut of performance.[3]

The existing evidence on FOF performance is that they tend to underperform hedge fund indexes by small but significant amounts. Most studies of FOF

---

[2] In the United States, registered FOFs are permitted to offer minimum investments as small as $25,000. In the U.K., FOFs are listed on the London Stock Exchange, and many specifically target the retail market. FOFs are available to the retail public in Finland, France, Germany, Ireland, Italy, Luxembourg, Netherlands, Sweden, and Switzerland; and in most of these countries there is no stipulated minimum investment amount (PricewaterhouseCoopers, 2003).

[3] The most visible FOFs fees are management fees, which are usually set at 1% of the total of assets under management, and performance fees, which are usually set at 10% of return. This is on top of standard hedge fund fees of typically 2% of assets under management and 20% of return (Jaffer, 2003).

performance have concluded that the "double fee structure" inherent in FOFs (that is, the FOFs as well as the underlying hedge funds charge fees) offsets any diversification benefit. S. J. Brown, Goetzmann, and Liang (2002), for example, find that FOFs offered consistently lower average returns and Sharpe ratios than hedge funds over the period 1990–1999. Amin and Kat (2003), who examined the performance of 11 FOFs as well as other categories of hedge funds, commented that "it is worrisome to see FOFs perform so badly."

The findings on skewness in FOFs are not as consistent, but in general it appears to be less negative than that of hedge fund indexes, using parametric statistics. S. J. Brown, Goetzmann, and Liang (2002) find that FOF returns are more left-skewed (a mean of −0.307) relative to individual FOFs (−0.126). However, using the same data but extended to May 2001, Kat and Lu (2002) find that the mean skewness of the FOFs in their sample is considerably less (−0.16). Gupta, Cerrahoglu, and Daglioglu (2003) report a similar skewness statistic of −0.17 for a constructed portfolio of 657 FOFs. Lastly, out of five hedge fund indexes from different data providers, Brooks and Kat (2001) find that only one of the FOFs is negatively skewed, while for the others the skewness statistics are not significant.

One explanation that is seldom advanced for the apparent underperformance of FOFs is that their reported returns, in contrast to hedge fund indexes, do not suffer to the same extent from the biases discussed earlier. Because FOFs are essentially clients of hedge funds, FOF returns reflect the full range of hedge fund performance, from the poor performers who eventually liquidate to the best out-performers. Survivorship, liquidation, and backfilling biases should be absent from the track record of an individual FOF (Fung and Hsieh, 2002). Self-selection bias should also be less in evidence because FOFs would not suffer from the same sorts of capacity constraints that might lead hedge funds to close to new investors and withdraw from supplying data to information providers. As for the survivorship bias of the FOFs themselves, because the rate of attrition is much lower than for hedge funds, survivorship bias is also lower. Fung and Hsieh (2000) estimated survivorship bias for FOFs at 1.4% annually, and Amin and Kat (2002a) estimated it at only 0.63% over the period 1994–2001, compared to 1.89% for hedge funds. In addition, FOFs report more accurately than other categories of hedge funds, so the stale-pricing bias is less in evidence in FOFs relative to hedge funds (Liang, 2003). For all these reasons, FOF data are more reliable than hedge fund data. They are less likely to understate risk-adjusted performance, and so the apparent underperformance reported in studies such as Amin and Kat (2003) is probably not explained simply by the double fee structure inherent in FOFs.

14.3   Testing for normality

Peiró (1999, 2002) points out that researchers studying asymmetry in asset prices may in the past have concluded that returns are asymmetric when the parent distribution is symmetric but not normal. For several world stock market indexes, Peiró (1999) found, contrary to prior studies, no strong evidence of asymmetry. Like prior studies of stock markets, studies examining nonnormality and asymmetry issues in hedge funds have also made conclusions based on the sample skewness statistic:

$$\hat{\alpha} = \frac{\sum_{t=1}^{T}(R_t - \bar{R})^3 / T}{\hat{\sigma}^3} \qquad (14.1)$$

where T is the sample size, R_t is the return at time t, $\bar{R}$ is the sample mean, and $\hat{\sigma}$ is the sample standard deviation. If the distribution is normal, then the asymptotic distribution of $\hat{\alpha}$ is

$$\hat{\alpha} \rightarrow N(0.6/\sqrt{T}) \qquad (14.2)$$

The asymptotic distribution of this statistic is tied to the assumption of normality in the time series being analyzed, and its behavior can be very different under alternative distributions in the series. For example, its characteristic behavior can be very different in the case of nonnormality, and it is not safe to conclude the symmetry or asymmetry of returns to financial assets on the basis of results obtained using this statistic.

Peiró's work has recently received confirmation by Kim and White (2004), who suggest that the effect of outliers is greatly amplified in the skewness calculation because each observation's distance from the mean is raised to the third power. Following a series of simulations demonstrating that the conventional measure of skewness is extremely biased in the presence of single or small groups of outliers, they go on to examine daily returns on the S&P 500 over the 20-year period from January 1982 to June 2001. The skewness statistic for the series is -2.39, indicative of extreme left-skewness. When the large negative return associated with the stock market crash of 1987 is removed, the statistic falls to -0.26, still negatively skewed but small compared with -2.39. Three alternative measures of asymmetry produce very small positive skewness figures. They conclude that "this clearly shows that the single observation must be very influential in the calculation of (the standard skewness statistic), . . . which is consistent with what we find in our simulations."

14.3.1 Binomial tests

We posit that FOF returns are symmetric if two conditions hold: (a) if the probability of obtaining a positive excess return equals the probability of obtaining a negative excess return, after zero excess returns have been excluded, and (b) if the distribution of negative excess returns in absolute values is equal to the distribution of positive excess returns. The binomial test is used to compare intervals on either side of the excess return distribution in order to address the following question. Is there asymmetric behavior occurring in the tails, as is often assumed, or is there asymmetry closer to the mean? We calculate the probability of obtaining a negative versus a positive excess return within ½, ½–1, 1–1½, and 1½–2 standard deviations of the mean, and in the tails between 2 and 3, 3 and 4, and 4 and 5 standard deviations either side of the mean.

The null distribution is the binomial distribution with parameters $p = p^*(0.5)$ and n = number of observations. Because the values of n are large, the normal approximation is used:

$$x_q = np + z_q \sqrt{np(1 - p)} \tag{14.3}$$

where x_q is the qth quantile of a standard normal random variable.

The hypothesis takes the form of a two-tailed test: H_0: $p = ½$ and H_1: $p \neq ½$. The rejection region of desired size α corresponds to the two tails of the null distribution of T. We use equation (14.3) to approximate the $\alpha/2$ quantile t_1 and the $(1 - \alpha_2)$ quantile t_2 of a binomial random variable with parameters $p^* = 0.5$ and n = number of observations. The parameter t_1 is a number such that

$$P(Y \le t_1) = \alpha_1 \tag{14.4}$$

and t_2 is a number such that

$$P(Y \le t_2) = 1 - \alpha_2 \tag{14.5}$$

The p-value is found using

$$P(Y \le t_\gamma) \approx \frac{P(Z \le t_\gamma - np^* + 0.5)}{\sqrt{np^* (1 + p^*)}} \tag{14.6}$$

where t_γ represents the choice of test statistic; see Conover (1999) and B. W. Brown and Hollander (1977) for a discussion.

14.3.2 Distribution fitting

Best Fit 4.5[4] is a program that analyzes a set of data, and out of 18 univariate distributions it identifies those that are potential candidates for the underlying data-generating process. For a given distribution, Best Fit looks for the parameters of

[4] Best Fit is part of a suite of programs that comprise the package Decision Tools and is distributed by the Palisade Corporation.

the function that optimize the goodness of fit (a measurement of the probability that the input data was produced by the given distribution) and goes through the following steps when finding the best fit for input data.

- For input sample data, parameters are estimated using maximum-likelihood estimators. For density and cumulative data, the method of least squares is used to minimize the distance between the input curve points and the theoretical function.
- Fitted distributions are then ranked using the Anderson–Darling and Kolmogorov–Smirnov statistics.

The Kolmogorov–Smirnov statistic is defined as

$$D_n = \sup[|F_n(x) - \hat{F}(x)|] \tag{14.7}$$

where n = total number of data points
$\hat{F}(x)$ = fitted cumulative distribution function
$F_n(x) = \dfrac{N_x}{n}$
N_x = number of values of the variable X that is less than x

A weakness of the Kolmogorov–Smirnov statistic is that it focuses on the middle of the distribution and does not detect tail discrepancies very well.

The Anderson–Darling statistic is defined as

$$A_n^2 = n \int_{-\infty}^{+\infty} [F_n(x) - \hat{F}(x)]^2 \, \Psi(x)\hat{f}(x)dx \tag{14.8}$$

where n = total number of data points
$\Psi^2 = \dfrac{1}{\hat{F}(x)[1 - \hat{F}(x)]}$
$\hat{f}(x)$ = hypothesized density function
$\hat{F}(x)$ = hypothesized cumulative distribution function
$F_n(x) = \dfrac{N_x}{n}$
N_x = number of X_i less than x

Unlike the Kolmogorov–Smirnov statistic, the Anderson–Darling statistic highlights differences between the tails of the fitted distribution and input data.

14.3.3 Sharpe ratios

The Sharpe index measures a risky asset's excess return, $(\bar{r}_i - r_f)$, per unit of risk as measured by its standard deviation. Sharpe described this index as a reward-to-variability index and suggested its use as an indicator of past performance of portfolios in general and of mutual funds in particular. It is defined as follows:

$$\text{Sharpe index} = \frac{\bar{r}_i - r_f}{\sigma_i} \tag{14.9}$$

where $\bar{r}_i$ = mean annual rate of return on security i
 r_f = mean risk-free rate of interest for the period
 σ_i = standard deviation of the return series for FOF i

In this study, we use three alternative versions of the Sharpe index. In each we use the median in lieu of the mean of the return distribution, because the median is a better measure of central tendency in skewed distributions. Being unaffected by extreme values, it is a more robust measure of central tendency. We also use the median instead of the mean risk-free rate.

Our first alternative Sharpe ratio (denoted SharpeMED) replaces the mean of asset i with its median:

$$\text{SharpeMED} = \frac{\tilde{r}_i - \tilde{r}_f}{\sigma_i} \tag{14.10}$$

where $\tilde{r}_i$ = median annual rate of return on FOF i
 $\tilde{r}_f$ = median risk-free rate for the period
 σ_i = standard deviation of the return series for FOF i

In our second and third alternative Sharpe ratios, we use two robust estimates of dispersion in lieu of the standard deviation of returns. With the presence of negative or positive skew, the mean becomes biased and is no longer an appropriate measure of central tendency. If the mean is biased, so too is the standard deviation, which is a function of the mean. In our second alternative Sharpe ratio we use the interquartile range (IQR) as the measure for dispersion. It is obtained by subtracting the first from the third quartile:

$$\text{IQR} = Q_3 - Q_1 \tag{14.11}$$

where Q_1 equals the $[(n + 1)/4]$th ordered observation, and Q_3 equals the $[3(n + 1)/4]$th ordered observation. The interquartile range measures the spread in the middle half of the data, and it is not influenced by extreme values. This is also a disadvantage of the interquartile range as a measure of the dispersion of asset returns; because it measures the variability of observations near the center of the distribution, it does not take into account extreme realizations of returns. The median absolute deviation (MAD) overcomes this problem with a broader measure of dispersion:

$$\text{MAD} = \frac{\sum \left| X_i - \tilde{X} \right|}{n} \tag{14.12}$$

where $\tilde{X}$ is the median return of X and n is the number of observations. Unlike the standard deviation, the absolute deviation from the median $\left| X_i - \tilde{X} \right|$ is not squared, and therefore it does not inflate extreme values.

The adjusted Sharpe index using the IQR, referred to here as SharpeIQR, is calculated as follows:

$$\text{SharpeIQR} = \frac{\tilde{r}_i - \tilde{r}_f}{\text{IQR}_i} \tag{14.13}$$

where $\tilde{r}_i$ is the median annual rate of return on FOF i, $\tilde{r}_f$ is the median risk-free rate for the period, and IQR is the interquartile range of the return series for FOF i.

The adjusted Sharpe index using the median absolute deviation as the measure for dispersion, referred to here as SharpeMAD, is calculated as follows:

$$\text{SharpeMAD} = \frac{\tilde{r}_i - \tilde{r}_f}{\text{MAD}} \tag{14.14}$$

where $\tilde{r}_i$ is the median annual rate of return on FOF i, $\tilde{r}_f$ is the median risk free rate for the period, and MAD is the median absolute deviation of the return series for FOF i.

The funds in our sample are ranked first using the standard Sharpe measure and then reranked using the three alternative Sharpe ratios. The funds are then separated into deciles, and the distance in deciles between the standard Sharpe and alternative Sharpe indexes is calculated. If the FOFs are normally distributed, then the rankings using each of these different Sharpe measures would be the same. If the rankings change substantially, not only will we have further evidence of nonnormality, but it will also show that the standard Sharpe ratio can give a misleading picture of FOF performance.

14.4 Data and summary performance information

The data for this study were obtained from Hedge Fund Research, Inc. (HFR), which is the main provider of FOF information. It includes return data on 525 hedge funds for the period from January 1988 to May 2003. Returns are monthly

Table 14.1 FOF age profiles

Age	Count	Cumulative count	Proportion of sample (%)	Cumulative proportion (%)
<6 months	26		5.0	
6–12 months	32	58	6.1	11.1
12–18 months	61	119	11.6	22.7
18–24 months	38	157	7.2	29.9
24–30 months	36	193	6.9	36.8
30–36 months	26	219	5.0	41.8
3–4 years	60	279	11.4	53.2
4–5 years	50	329	9.5	62.7
5–7 years	64	393	12.2	74.9
7–10 years	76	469	14.5	89.4
>10 years	56	525	10.6	100.0
Total	525			

and represent the change in net asset value during the month relative to net asset value at the beginning of the month. All returns are in U.S. dollars and are net of all fees and expenses. HFR data includes both domestic (U.S.) and offshore funds; in order to avoid survivorship bias in returns, it also includes defunct funds.[5]

The age profile of these funds is summarized in Table 14.1, which confirms the massive growth in FOF formation in recent years. The mean (median) fund age is 57 (45) months, and over half (53%) are less than 4 years old, with only 10% being more than 10 years old. While the data for the individual FOFs begins in January 1988, because the hedge fund indexes are available only from January 1990, we eliminate observations before January 1990. Due to data limitations, we also remove funds that have been in existence for less than 2½ years, leaving a data set of 332 FOFs. The attrition rate for the sample is low. Of the 525 funds in the data set, 14 had ceased reporting by March 2003.[6] Of these, 10 had more than 30 return observations and so were retained, leaving more than 70% of the defunct funds in the sample, which is more than the 63% of the full sample that had greater than 30 observations.

HFR produces an equally weighted composite FOF index comprising funds of various ages and asset sizes. It also produces four equally weighted subindexes: conservative, diversified, market defensive, and strategic. An FOF is classified as

[5] According to Ackerman, McEnally, and Ravenscraft (1999), HFR began keeping data on funds that stop reporting in December 1992. However, this should not affect our findings unduly because between January 1990 (the start of our data period) and December 1992, FOFs were rare. Approximately 10% of FOFs in the database started before December 1992.

[6] Some funds had missing observations for April and May 2003. We assume that these funds were simply late reporting their asset values rather than had ceased reporting.

Table 14.2 Descriptive statistics for indexes

	Average annual return	Annual standard deviation	Monthly Sharpe ratio	Jensen's $\hat{a}$	Skewness	Kurtosis	JB-statistic
S&P 500	10.88	15.25	0.12	—	−0.43*	3.37*	5.69 (.06)
Hedge fund	13.94	7.22	0.38	0.61*	−0.62*	5.50*	49.62 (.00)
FOF composite	9.93	5.86	0.27	0.37*	−0.27	6.79*	94.22 (.00)
Conservative	8.78	3.36	0.37	0.31*	−0.54*	6.45*	83.98 (.00)
Diversified	9.19	6.30	0.22	0.30*	−0.10	6.69*	87.63 (.00)
Market defensive	10.30	6.08	0.28	0.50*	0.16	4.26*	10.42 (.01)
Strategic index	13.19	9.51	0.26	0.57*	−0.38*	6.06*	63.37 (.00)

This table shows the average annualized return, the annualized standard deviation, Sharpe ratio, Jensen's alpha, and skewness and kurtosis statistics for the various fund and market indexes (these kurtosis statistics have been standardized such that the kurtosis of the normal distribution is zero). An asterisk denotes significant difference from zero at the 5% level. The last column reports the Jarque–Bera statistic and, in parentheses, the p-value for the test that the returns distribution is normal against the alternate hypothesis that it is nonnormal.

conservative if its constituent funds conduct market-neutral (low-volatility) strategies. Diversified funds invest in hedge funds with a variety of strategies and are designed for minimal loss in down markets and superior returns in up markets. Market-defensive FOFs invest in short-biased hedge funds and are constructed to be negatively correlated with the returns on standard asset classes. Lastly, strategic funds invest in hedge funds with opportunistic strategies such as emerging markets and are expected to perform well in up markets and underperform in down markets. Seventy-four funds in our sample are classified as conservative, 153 are diversified, 34 are market defensive, and 71 are strategic.

Table 14.2 presents descriptive statistics for the indexes and for the S&P 500 for the period January 1990 to May 2003. Consistent with prior studies of hedge fund performance, the hedge fund index appears to generate higher returns (13.9% versus 10.9%) and lower volatility (a standard deviation of 7.22% compared with 15.25%) than the S&P 500 over the same period. All of the FOF indexes show lower annual average returns than the hedge fund index, but these lower returns are offset by lower standard deviations for all of the subindexes except for the strategic index (which is to be expected given that strategic FOFs specialize in hedge funds with aggressive strategies). Also consistent with its construction, the conservative index has both the lowest return and the lowest standard deviation of all the FOF indexes. It appears that the funds' diversification benefits are outweighed by the double fee structure inherent in FOFs.

Relative to the hedge fund index, lower average annual returns do not seem to be compensated for by substantial reductions in standard deviation. This is

Table 14.3 Summary statistics and basic performance measures for individual FOFs

	Annualized average return	Annualized standard deviation	Skewness	Kurtosis	Sharpe ratio	Jensen's $\hat{a}$
Full sample	9.48	7.76	−0.12 (53%)	7.03 (100%)	0.27	0.45 (56%)
Substrategies						
Conservative ($n = 74$)	8.47	3.50	−0.96 (58%)	9.64 (100%)	0.44	0.38 (81%)
Diversified ($n = 153$)	10.11	7.15	0.11 (56%)	6.68 (99%)	0.26	0.51 (59%)
Market defensive ($n = 34$)	12.18	9.06	0.17 (47%)	6.52 (100%)	0.31	0.70 (68%)
Strategic ($n = 71$)	8.05	12.88	0.11 (46%)	5.32 (100%)	0.09	0.28 (20%)

This table shows the mean values for the sample's average annualized return, annualized standard deviation, skewness and kurtosis, monthly Sharpe ratio, and Jensen's alpha. In parentheses under the values for skewness, kurtosis, and alpha is the proportion of the sample or subsample where the parameter is significantly different from zero (or, in the case of kurtosis, significantly more than 3) at the 5% level.

confirmed by the Sharpe ratios and Jensen's alphas. All of the indexes have monthly Sharpe ratios that are much higher than that of the S&P index of 0.12; but apart from the conservative index, which has a comparable Sharpe ratio, the FOF indexes have Sharpe ratios that are between 26% and 42% lower than for the hedge fund index. The alphas for all of the indexes are positive and significant, although the hedge fund index has a higher alpha (0.61) than any of the others, with the strategic (0.57) and market defensive (0.50) not far behind. Interestingly, the alpha for the FOF composite index is about 60% the size of the alpha for the hedge fund index, and the comparable proportion for the Sharpe ratio is 70%.

Table 14.3 presents the summary statistics and performance measures for the 332 FOFs. The table presents the mean for the average and standard deviation of returns, mean values for skewness and kurtosis, and monthly Sharpe ratio and Jensen's alpha for the full sample and then for the four substrategies. For the full sample the summary statistics are as would be expected. Fifty-six percent of the sample recorded significant alphas, and these were all positive. Six percent of FOFs' alphas are negative, and the majority fall between 0 and 1. In 96 cases (29%) the fund alpha is greater than that of the hedge fund index, and 199 (60%) exceed the alpha for the FOF index.

Of the 332 FOFs in our sample, 74 are classified as conservative, 153 are diversified, 34 are market defensive, and 71 are strategic. The lower part of

Table 14.3 presents the summary statistics for the four substrategy categories. The average returns and standard deviations for the conservative, diversified and market defensive substrategies are comparable to the statistics for the equivalent indexes. For the strategic substrategy, however, the average return is much lower than the strategic subindex and the standard deviation much higher. Among the other performance parameters, the Sharpe ratios and alphas are higher and the betas lower than for the equivalent indexes for the conservative, diversified and market defensive substrategies. However, the mean Sharpe ratio and alpha for the strategic FOFs are lower than for the index. This is difficult to explain. They are not overrepresented in the newer funds that have been removed from the sample (they represent 21 percent of the deleted young funds), nor are these young strategic funds particularly good performers (the average annual return for these 37 funds is 5.68 percent, which is even lower than that for the included strategic funds of 8.05 percent). They are also not overrepresented in the defunct funds (of which they comprise 20 percent).

14.4.1 Distribution issues

The last column of Table 14.2 reports the results of the Jarque–Bera test for normality. For all of the FOF indexes, the null hypothesis of normality is rejected at the 1% level, whereas for the S&P 500 normality is rejected only at the 10% level. In all cases the index return distributions show significant excess kurtosis, but the findings for skewness are not as consistent. Interestingly, while the hedge fund index is significantly left-skewed, the FOFs composite is negatively skewed but not significantly so. This is consistent with Brooks and Kat (2001), who found that all but one of the FOF indexes in their sample were not significantly skewed. The conservative and strategic subindexes are significantly negatively skewed, but there is no significant skewness for the market-defensive and diversified subindexes. While investing in FOFs on the face of it looks like an inferior risk–return tradeoff relative to the hedge fund index, the skewness statistics give some indication that this may be offset by a distribution of returns with fewer small or negative values. Figures 14.1 and 14.2 present histograms for all of the indexes (including the S&P 500) and substrategy indexes, respectively.

For the individual FOFs, more than two-thirds (229/332 cases, or 69%) have nonnormal return distributions according to the Jarque–Bera statistic (at the 5% level of significance or better). This is a smaller proportion than reported for hedge funds by Amin and Kat (2003), who found that 86% of their sample of 77 hedge funds had significantly nonnormal return distributions.[7] Table 14.4 shows the mean and median skewness and kurtosis for the full sample. The sample overall appears to show excess kurtosis rather than skewness. The mean (median) kurtosis is rather high at 7.03 (5.19), but the skewness is small

---

[7] Amin and Kat (2003) state that their sample is highly skewed but do not report skewness statistics.

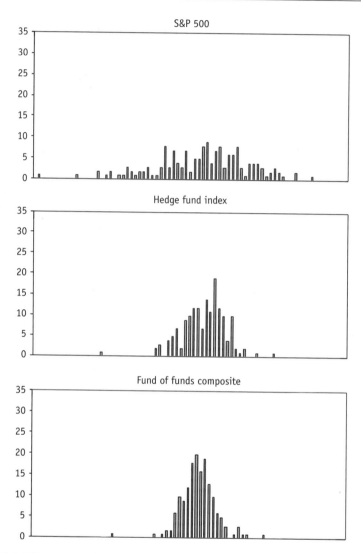

Figure 14.1 Histograms of returns on the S&P 500, hedge fund index, and FOF composite index, January 1990 to May 2003

at an average (median) of −0.12 (0.01). This is very close to the mean skewness statistic of −0.16 calculated for FOFs by Kat and Lu (2002) using the TASS database.

Almost all of the FOFs (331/332) have return distributions with significant excess kurtosis. Skewness, however, is not only rarer, but equally positive and negative. In only half of the sample (177, or 53%) does the skewness statistic show significant asymmetry. In contrast with the apparent negative skewness of

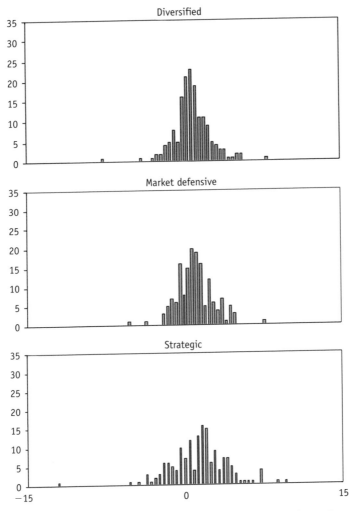

Figure 14.2 Histograms of the returns for the FOF substrategy indexes, January 1990 to May 2003

hedge fund returns, these significantly skewed FOFs exhibit both positive and negative skewness in almost equal measure. Ninety-one (51%) are negatively skewed and 86 (49%) are positively skewed. For the individual funds, between 46 and 58% of significantly skewed cases are negatively skewed. Of these significantly skewed cases (not reported in the table), the conservative FOFs appear to be the most negatively skewed (36 out of 43, or 84%). However, as we will see in the next section, the case of the conservative FOFs illustrates very well the danger of making strong inferences about the shape of the underlying distribution simply from the skewness statistic.

Table 14.4 Distribution characteristics of indexes: binomial test of intervals

		±½σ	½σ–1σ	1σ–1½σ	1½σ–2σ	>2σ
S&P 500	negative	22	26	10	8	5
	positive	39	25	16	7	3
	p-value	0.04*	1	0.33	1	—
Hedge fund	negative	28	23	12	7	3
	positive	40	28	14	4	1
	p-value	0.18	0.58	0.85	0.55	—
FOF composite	negative	39	23	13	5	2
	positive	36	24	9	3	6
	p-value	0.82	1	0.52	0.72	—
Conservative	negative	36	16	11	6	5
	positive	40	32	9	1	5
	p-value	0.73	0.03*	0.82	0.13	1
Diversified	negative	44	22	12	4	3
	positive	36	20	9	6	5
	p-value	0.83	0.88	0.66	0.75	—
Market defensive	negative	38	25	14	6	2
	positive	33	19	13	7	4
	p-value	0.63	0.45	1	1	—
Strategic index	negative	31	22	15	4	3
	positive	41	25	11	3	6
	p-value	0.29	0.77	0.56	1	—

This table gives the proportion of the sample between the mean and ½, ½–1, 1–1½, and 1½–2, and beyond 2 standard deviations either side of the mean. For each index, the negative and positive counts and, in brackets, the proportions of the sample in that category and the p-value for the test that the distributions of the absolute value of the excess returns are equal. An asterisk denotes significance at the 5% level.

14.5   Results

14.5.1   Binomial tests

Table 14.4 presents the results for the binomial tests of the S&P 500, the hedge fund index, the FOFs index, and the four substrategy indexes. There are two significant findings in the table. For the S&P 500, there are significantly more positive excess returns than negative excess returns within half a standard deviation of the mean. The only other significant finding is for the conservative FOF index. Between ½ and 1 standard deviation either side of the mean, positive excess returns significantly outnumber negative excess returns. Also of interest are the positives outnumbering the negatives close to the mean (by about 25%) for the hedge fund index and the FOFs strategic index, although these differences are not significant using the binomial test.

As can be seen on the right-hand side of the table, there is a relatively low frequency of observations in the tails. At between 4 and 5 standard deviations from

Table 14.5 Distribution characteristics of FOFs: significant cases of asymmetry using the binomial test

		Conservative	Diversified	Market defensive	Strategic	Total
Panel A: Cases of significant asymmetry anywhere in the distribution						
	Count	13	33	7	13	66
		(18%)	(22%)	(21%)	(18%)	(20%)
	Negative	1	26	7	11	45
		(1%)	(17%)	(21%)	(15%)	(14%)
	Positive	12	7	0	2	21
		(16%)	(5%)	(0%)	(3%)	(6%)
Panel B: Asymmetry in different intervals either side of the mean						
$\pm\frac{1}{2}\sigma$	Count	3	18	4	8	33
	Negative	1	16	4	6	27
	Positive	2	2	0	2	6
$\frac{1}{2}\sigma$–1σ	Count	7	12	3	4	26
	Negative	0	8	3	4	15
	Positive	7	4	0	0	11
1σ–$1\frac{1}{2}\sigma$	Count	3	3	0	1	7
	Negative	0	2	0	1	3
	Positive	3	1	0	0	4

The cells in this table show the count of cases where significant asymmetry was found using the binomial test. Panel A summarizes the cases where asymmetry was found anywhere in the distribution, and in parentheses underneath the count is the proportion of cases in each listed substrategy found to be significant. Panel B separates the significant cases into locational categories: $\frac{1}{2}$ standard deviation, $\frac{1}{2}$–1 standard deviation, and 1–1$\frac{1}{2}$ standard deviations either side of the mean. No significant asymmetry was found further out toward the tails than 1$\frac{1}{2}$ standard deviations from the mean. Four cases appear twice; 1 each of strategic, conservative, and diversified were found significant in both the $\frac{1}{2}$–1σ and the 1–1$\frac{1}{2}\sigma$ regions, and 1 diversified case was found significant in both the $\pm\frac{1}{2}\sigma$ and 1–1$\frac{1}{2}\sigma$ regions.

the mean there is no more than one observation for each index, and the situation is similar for between 3 and 4 standard deviations. Interestingly, while those between 4 and 5 standard deviations away from the mean are all negative, observations between 3 and 4 standard deviations are both negative and positive. There is more activity at between 2 and 3 standard deviations from the mean, but here the positives outnumber the negatives. It is clear that if asymmetry in hedge fund portfolio returns is found, it is likely to be due to asymmetry in the intervals close to the mean. In addition, for the indexes when there is substantial asymmetry close to the mean, it is more likely to be positive rather than negative.

Table 14.5 summarizes the findings on the binomial tests for the 332 FOFs. Panel A summarizes the cases in which significant asymmetry was found in any interval of the distribution, and Panel B separates these results into three regions within the distribution: ½, ½–1, and 1–1½ standard deviations either side of the mean. No results are presented for further out in the distributions because we found very little significant asymmetry in the tails. As can be seen in the first row of Panel A, between 18% and 22% of the FOFs in each substrategy are significantly asymmetric. However, there are vast differences between the substrategies when the asymmetrical cases are separated into negative and positive asymmetries. For the diversified, market-defensive and strategic substrategies, most of the asymmetry is negative; this is particularly so for the diversified substrategy, where all cases of significant skewness are negative. Of particular interest is the conservative substrategy: 16% of these FOFs have significantly positive asymmetry. This positive asymmetry advantage was not picked up in the standard summary statistics.

In fact, Table 14.3 shows that the mean skewness value for the conservative FOFs was −0.96 and that 58% of conservative FOFs demonstrated significant skewness. Most of these are negatively skewed, so over 50% of the sample ended up being significantly negatively skewed according to the standard skewness statistic. However, our binomial testing finds only one conservative case of significant negative asymmetry. Figure 14.3, which presents a histogram of the skewness statistics for the conservative FOFs, clearly shows there is no error here. There is heavy skewness to the right, close to the mean. The figure demonstrates that mean skewness figures can give a very misleading picture of the skewness of a particular sample.

Delineation of the asymmetry by distribution interval in Table 14.5 (Panel B) gives further insight into the distributional characteristics of the FOFs. Most of the asymmetry occurs within one standard deviation of the mean, and the vast majority of this asymmetry is negative. This bunching of negative observations just below the mean in approximately 12% of FOFs is consistent with the argument

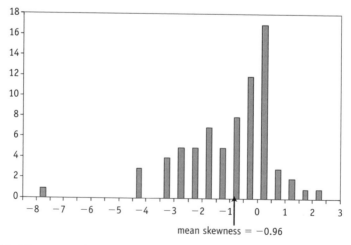

Figure 14.3 Histogram of skewness statistics for conservative FOFs ($n = 74$)

that the double fee structure of FOFs reduces month-to-month returns. But this is a very small proportion of the sample; it must be remembered that most FOFs show no significant asymmetry either way.

14.5.2 Distribution fitting

Table 14.6 presents the findings on the distribution-fitting process. It is clear that the majority of the FOFs are not normally distributed. Using the Anderson–Darling criterion, the normal distribution is chosen as the best fit for only 7 of the 332 funds. The logistic distribution is the best fit for 156 funds, and the log logistic distribution is the best distribution for a further 127 funds. Using the Kolmogorov–Smirnov criterion, the normal distribution is again the best fit for only 7 of the funds, the logistic and the log logistic distributions continue their dominance, with each being the best distribution for 181 and 102 FOFs, respectively. Using both criteria the normal distribution ranks 5th most common, with a median rank of 4.

The normal distribution was the distribution of best fit for only 7 out of 332, or 2% of the sample FOFs. This is considerably different from the result obtained using the Jarque–Bera test for normality, which rejected normality for 69% of the funds, leaving over 30% apparently normal. If we expand our classification of normality to include those funds for which the normal distribution was chosen as the first or the second best fit, then almost 25% can be classified as normal. Given that the mean and median rank for the normal distribution is 5 and 4, respectively, it is clear that if an FOF is not classified as normal, it is likely to be far from normal.

Table 14.6 Distribution fitting

	Anderson–Darling		Kolmogorov–Smirnov	
	1st choice	2nd choice	1st choice	2nd choice
Logistic	156	107	181	85
Log logistic	127	18	102	44
Triang	2	2	3	1
Normal	7	74	7	74
Beta general	6	51	4	48
Weibull	10	28	14	32
LogNorm2	5	12	2	5
Pearson5	5	18	0	15
Student	8	5	6	4
InvGauss	2	5	2	8
Erf	1	1	1	3
Extreme value	1	9	2	6
Erlang	—	—	3	4
ChiSq	—	—	1	0
Gamma	—	—	2	1

Table 14.7 Sharpe ratios: absolute change in deciles

		Versus standard Sharpe			Versus SharpeMED	
	Change in decile	Count	Proportion (%)	Change in decile	Count	Proportion (%)
SharpeIQR	0	107	32.42	0	109	33.03
	1	129	39.09	1	124	37.58
	2	55	16.67	2	53	16.06
	3	28	8.48	3	33	10.00
	4	8	2.42	4	8	2.42
	5	3	0.91	5	3	0.91
SharpeMAD	0	103	31.21	0	105	31.82
	1	129	39.09	1	122	36.97
	2	64	19.39	2	65	19.70
	3	25	7.58	3	28	8.48
	4	7	2.12	4	8	2.42
	5	2	0.61	5	2	0.61

14.5.3 Sharpe calculations

The standard deviation, interquartile range, and median absolute deviation are not directly comparable. The standard deviation measures the dispersion of approximately 34% of observations either side of the mean, while the inter-quartile range measures the dispersion of 25% either side of the median. For a normally distributed variable, the mean equals the median, so the standard deviation and the interquartile range measure dispersion simply in different proportions. A similar argument can be extended for the standard deviation and the median absolute deviation.[8] To get around this problem of comparability, we first rank the performance of our sample FOFs using the standard Sharpe and SharpeMED and then rerank them using SharpeIQR and SharpeMAD. Under the normal distribution, the standard Sharpe ratio and the adjusted versions should all be equal. A change in rankings between the unadjusted and adjusted Sharpes would contribute further evidence on the nonnormality of FOF returns.

Our findings using the Sharpe ratios are summarized in Tables 14.7 and 14.8.[9] In Table 14.7 we have separated the standard Sharpe and SharpeMED ratios into deciles, and for each of the other two measures — SharpeIQR and SharpeMAD — we have reranked them into new deciles. The table shows how many FOFs changed deciles in absolute terms, beginning with no change (zero) and then a change of 1, 2, 3, 4, and 5 deciles. The findings are similar for the SharpeIQR and

---

[8] No empirical studies have been completed to analyze the proportion of data measured by the MAD on either side of the median.

[9] The full results for all 330 FOFs are available from the authors on request.

Table 14.8 Sharpe ratios: absolute change in ranks

	Change in rank	Versus standard Sharpe		Versus SharpeMED	
		Count	Proportion (%)	Count	Proportion (%)
SharpeIQR	0	4	1.21	4	1.21
	1–10	67	20.30	68	20.61
	11–20	54	16.36	54	16.36
	21–30	48	14.55	48	14.55
	31–40	29	8.79	31	9.39
	41–50	29	8.79	27	8.18
	51–60	26	7.88	18	5.45
	61–70	19	5.76	23	6.97
	71–80	12	3.64	17	5.15
	81–90	15	4.55	8	2.42
	91–100	6	1.82	9	2.73
	101–110	7	2.12	6	1.82
	111–120	5	1.52	6	1.82
	121–130	3	0.91	5	1.52
	131–140	1	0.30	1	0.30
	141–150	3	0.91	3	0.91
	150+	2	0.61	2	0.61
SharpeMED	0	3	0.91	6	1.82
	1–10	67	20.30	64	19.39
	11–20	59	17.88	61	18.48
	21–30	43	13.03	45	13.64
	31–40	40	12.12	29	8.79
	41–50	26	7.88	30	9.09
	51–60	22	6.67	24	7.27
	61–70	27	8.18	27	8.18
	71–80	10	3.03	6	1.82
	81–90	10	3.03	13	3.94
	91–100	7	2.12	6	1.82
	101–110	5	1.52	5	1.52
	111–120	3	0.91	6	1.82
	121–130	2	0.61	2	0.61
	131–140	2	0.61	2	0.61
	141–150	2	0.61	2	0.61
	150+	2	0.61	2	0.61

SharpeMAD measures, and there is also little difference between the change in rankings when measured against the standard Sharpe and the SharpeMED ratios. Around one-third of the sample FOFs do not move out of their original decile when using the alternative Sharpe measures. The most common outcome is a move one decile above or below the Sharpe/SharpeMED decile — just under 40% of the sample. The remaining 25–30% of FOFs move between 2 and 5 deciles away from their original position ranked by Sharpe/SharpeMED.

With such a large sample — there are 33 funds in each decile — zero absolute change in decile does not necessarily mean that the ranks do not change; it simply means that the change in rank is less than or equal to 32. To obtain a finer picture, Table 14.8 summarizes our findings on absolute change in ranks. Again, there is very little difference between the changes in rank using the various Sharpe ratio alternatives. Just under 40% of the funds have alternative Sharpe rankings within 20 ranks of the standard Sharpe; a substantial proportion of funds, therefore, are reasonably robust to alternative performance measures. Almost one-third of the funds, however, have alternative Sharpe rankings more than 50 ranks away from their standard Sharpe rank.

14.6 Conclusion

Using data for 332 FOFs for the period from January 1990 to May 2003, we examine the return distribution of 332 funds of hedge funds. Over half the sample is significantly skewed according to the skewness statistic, and these significantly skewed cases are split 50/50 positive and negative. Almost all exhibit excess kurtosis. Using the binomial test of asymmetry in various intervals of the distribution, we find no evidence of significant asymmetry in the FOFs composite index or in the indexes for the substrategies diversified, market defensive, and strategic. However, we find evidence of positive asymmetry in the interval ½–1 standard deviation either side of the mean for the conservative index.

For the individual FOFs, we find evidence of asymmetry using the binomial test in about 20% of cases. Most of this asymmetry occurs within half a standard deviation of the mean, and in most cases the asymmetry is negative. In fitting distributions to our FOF data, we find that FOF returns are normally distributed in only about one-quarter of cases. We also find, using two "alternative" Sharpe ratios with interquartile range and median absolute deviation in the denominator, that in many cases performance metrics are very sensitive to the measure of dispersion. It is clear that in many cases the use of standard performance measures such as the Sharpe ratio can be extremely misleading.

References

Ackermann, C., McEnally, R., and Ravenscraft, D. (1999). The Performance of Hedge Funds: Risk, Return, and Incentives. *Journal of Finance*, 54(3): 833–874.

Agarwal, V. and Naik, N. (2001). Multi-Period Performance Persistence Analysis of Hedge Funds. *Journal of Financial and Quantitative Analysis*, 35(3):309–326.

Amin, G. S. and Kat, H. M. (2002a). Welcome to the Dark Side: Hedge Fund Attrition and Survivorship Bias over the Period 1994–2001. ISMA Discussion Paper 2002–02, University of Reading, U.K.

Amin, G. S. and Kat, H. M. (2002b). Portfolios of Hedge Funds. ISMA Discussion Papers in Finance 2002–07, University of Reading, U.K.

Amin, G. S. and Kat, H. M. (2003). Hedge Fund Performance 1990–2000: Do the "Money Machines" Really Add Value? *Journal of Financial and Quantitative Analysis*, 38(2):251–274.

Asness, C., Krail, R., and Liew, J. (2001). Do Hedge Funds Hedge? *Journal of Portfolio Management*, 28(1):6–19.

Brooks, C. and Kat, H. M. (2001). The Statistical Properties of Hedge Fund Index Returns and Their Implications for Investors. ISMA Discussion Papers in Finance 2001–09, University of Reading, U.K.

Brown, B. W. and Hollander, M. (1977). *Statistics: A Biomedical Introduction*. John Wiley & Sons, New York.

Brown, S. J., Goetzmann, W. N., and Ibbotson, R. G. (1999). Offshore Hedge Funds: Survival and Performance, 1989–95. *Journal of Business*, 72(1): 91–117.

Brown, S. J., Goetzmann, W. N., and Liang, B. (2002). Fees on Fees in Funds of Funds. Working Paper, Yale University, New Haven, CT.

Conover, W. J. (1999). *Practical Nonparametric Statistics*, 3rd edition. John Wiley & Sons, New York.

Fung, W. and Hsieh, D. A. (1997). Survivorship Bias and Investment Style in the Returns of CTAs. *Journal of Portfolio Management*, 24(1):30–41.

Fung, W. and Hsieh, D. A. (1999). A Primer on Hedge Funds. *Journal of Empirical Finance*, 6(3):309–331.

Fung, W. and Hsieh, D. A. (2000). Performance Characteristics of Hedge Funds and Commodity Funds: Natural vs. Spurious Biases. *Journal of Financial and Quantitative Analysis*, 35(3):291–307.

Fung, W. and Hsieh, D. A. (2002). Hedge Fund Benchmarks: Information Content and Biases. *Financial Analysts Journal*, 58(1):22–34.

Gupta, B., Cerrahoglu, B., and Daglioglu, A. (2003). Evaluating Hedge Fund Performance: Traditional Versus Conditional Approaches. *Journal of Alternative Investments*, 6(3):7–24.

Jaffer, S. (2003). *Funds of Hedge Funds: For Professional Investors and Money Managers*. Euromoney Books, London, U.K.

Kao, D. (2002). Battle for Alphas: Hedge Funds Versus Long-Only Portfolios. *Financial Analysts Journal*, 58(2):16–36.

Kat, H. M. and Lu, S. (2002). An Excursion into the Statistical Properties of Hedge Funds. ISMA Discussion Paper 2002–12, University of Reading, U.K.

Kim, T. H. and White, H. (2004). On More Robust Estimation of Skewness and Kurtosis. *Finance Research Letters*, 1(1):56–73.

Lamm, R. M. (2003). Asymmetric Returns and Optimal Hedge Fund Portfolios. *Journal of Alternative Investments*, 6(2):9–21.

Liang, B. (2001). Hedge Fund Performance: 1990–1999. *Financial Analysts Journal*, 57(1):11–18.

Liang, B. (2003). The Accuracy of Hedge Fund Returns. *Journal of Portfolio Management*, 29(3):111–122.

Lo, A. W. (2001). Risk Management for Hedge Funds: Introduction and Overview. *Financial Analysts Journal*, 57(6):16–33.

Peiró, A. (1999). Skewness in Financial Returns. *Journal of Banking and Finance*, 23(6):847–862.

Peiró, A. (2002). Skewness in Individual Stocks at Different Investment Horizons. *Quantitative Finance*, 2:139–146.

PricewaterhouseCoopers. (2003). *The Regulation and Distribution of Hedge Funds in Europe: Changes and Challenges*. Author, London.

15 Funds of funds and the diversification effect

Maher Kooli

Abstract

We examine whether investors can improve their investment opportunities through the addition of a fund of funds portfolio to different sets of benchmark portfolios. Using data from 1994–2004, we find that funds of funds, as an asset class, improve the mean-variance frontier of sets of benchmark portfolios sorted by firm size and book-to-market ratio. However, we find that the improvement comes mainly from a leftward shift of the global minimum-variance portfolio rather than the tangency portfolio.

15.1 Introduction

Funds of funds (FOFs hereafter) are an increasingly popular avenue for hedge fund investment. For those who do not meet the definition of accredited investor, investing in FOFs is presently the only way to gain access to absolute-return strategies. Indeed, FOFs let investors with as little as $10,000 participate in a diversified mix of hedge funds, while traditional hedge funds require a minimum investment of $250,000. FOFs can offer the most attractive risk-adjusted rates of return, with low to zero correlation, to most traditional portfolios. However, the diversification across manager styles comes at the cost of a multiplication of the fees paid by the investor (Brown, Goetzmann, and Liang, 2004).

Whether the addition of FOFs, as an asset class, can significantly expand the mean-variance efficient frontier relative to traditional assets and provide substantial diversification benefits for investors or fund managers is an important and intriguing question.

Our objectives here are threefold. First, we examine whether an FOF portfolio significantly enlarges an investor's investment opportunities relative to different sets of benchmark portfolios. We rely on mean-variance spanning tests to answer this question. To the best of our knowledge, this is the first study that uses these tests in the FOF context. Throughout the chapter, we consider that a set of asset returns provides diversification benefits relative to a set of benchmark returns if adding these returns to the benchmark leads to a significant leftward shift in the mean–standard deviation frontier. As noted by Bekaert and Urias (1996), even if the analysis is based on historical returns, the benefits we find could have little bearing on future performance. Our general conclusion is that, when we consider benchmark portfolios sorted by firm size and book-to-market ratio, investing in FOFs does bring diversification benefits for mean-variance investors.

Second, to further investigate the sources of rejection of the spanning hypothesis, we implement a step-down procedure as suggested by Kan and Zhou (2001). We find that the tangency and the global minimum-variance portfolios can be improved by the inclusion of an FOFs portfolio. However, the evidence is stronger in favor of the enhancement of the global minimum-variance portfolio. Third, as a robustness test, we examine the added value of the FOFs portfolio in terms of the Sharpe ratio and Jensen's alpha, using mean-variance spanning tests. We find that adding an FOFs portfolio to a set of benchmark portfolios (U.S. stocks only) provides an extra return for a unit increase in standard deviation. However, this conclusion is less evident when we consider an internationally diversified portfolio as a benchmark.

The rest of the chapter is organized as follows. Section 15.2 presents previous work on mean-variance spanning and sets out the methods used to evaluate mean-variance spanning. Section 15.3 describes the data for FOFs and benchmark portfolios. Section 15.4 discusses the empirical results, and Section 15.5 concludes the chapter.

15.2   Mean-variance spanning tests

A mean-variance spanning test was first introduced by Huberman and Kandel (1987). This method tests whether adding a set of new assets allows investors to improve the minimum-variance frontier derived from a given set of benchmark assets. Mean-variance spanning tests (MVSTs hereafter) have been previously applied in a variety of research topics in finance (for example, Bekaert and Urias, 1996; Errunza, Hogan, and Hung, 1999; Petrella, 2005; DeRoon, Nijman, and Werker, 2001; Chen, Ho, and Lu, 2004; Aitken, Harris, McInish, and Segara, 2005; Chen, Ho, and Wu, 2004). We extend the literature by using MVSTs in the context of FOFs. To the best of our knowledge, this is the first study that uses these tests in the FOF context.

These tests enable us to analyze the effect on the mean-variance frontier of adding new assets to a set of benchmark assets. For example, we can say that spanning occurs when the mean-variance frontier of the set of benchmark portfolios and that of the benchmark portfolios plus an FOFs portfolio coincide. In this case, investors do not benefit from adding a hedge fund to their current portfolio.

In finite samples, the question of whether an observed shift is statistically significant can be tested using regression-based tests of mean-variance spanning.

15.2.1   Asymptotic and finite-sample test statistics

In this section, we briefly describe the statistical tests used to examine whether adding an FOFs portfolio can significantly improve the investment opportunities relative to a set of benchmark assets. For convenience, we follow the notation and treatment in Kan and Zhou (2001).

We denote by K the set of benchmark portfolios (for example, without-private-equity portfolio) with return R_{1t} and by N the set of test assets (the FOFs portfolio) with return R_{2t}. We estimate the following model using ordinary least squares:

$$R_{2t} = \alpha + \beta R_{1t} + \xi_t, \qquad t = 1, 2, \ldots, T,$$

$$(R = XB + E \text{ in matrix notation}) \tag{15.1}$$

Following Huberman and Kandel (1987), the null hypothesis of "spanning" is

$$H_0: \alpha = 0_N, \qquad \delta = 1_N - \beta 1_K = 0_N, \tag{15.2}$$

where 0_N is defined as the zero vector of N elements. We then denote by λ_1 and λ_2 the two eigenvalues of the matrix $\hat{H}\hat{G}^{-1}$ (see the appendix to this chapter for the definition of $\hat{H}$ and $\hat{G}$). The distribution of the asymptotic Wald test statistic of the null hypothesis is

$$W = T(\lambda_1 + \lambda_2) \sim \chi^2_{2N} \tag{15.3}$$

In this case, if we fail to reject the null hypothesis, then the benchmark assets span the mean-variance frontier of the benchmark plus an FOFs portfolio; that is, investors are not able to enlarge their investment opportunities by adding an FOFs portfolio. On the other hand, if the null hypothesis is rejected, adding an FOFs portfolio does improve the investment opportunities.

The corresponding asymptotic likelihood ratio and Lagrange multiplier tests are:

$$LR = T \sum_{i=1}^{2} \ln(1 + \lambda_i) \sim \chi^2_{2N} \tag{15.4}$$

$$LM = T \sum_{i=1}^{2} \frac{\lambda_i}{1 + \lambda_i} \sim \chi^2_{2N} \tag{15.5}$$

Because the Wald test is not the uniformly most powerful test, we also use the likelihood ratio and Lagrange multiplier tests for mean-variance spanning. The exact finite-sample distribution of the likelihood ratio test under the null hypothesis, as in Huberman and Kandel (1987), is:

$$\left(\frac{1}{U^{1/2}} - 1 \right) \left(\frac{T - K - N}{N} \right) \sim F_{2N, 2(T-K-N)} \qquad \text{for } N \geq 2 \tag{15.6}$$

$$\left(\frac{1}{U^{1/2}} - 1\right)\left(\frac{T - K - 1}{2}\right) \sim F_{2, 2(T-K-1)} \qquad \text{for } N = 1 \qquad (15.7)$$

where $U = |\hat{G}|/|\hat{H} + \hat{G}|$

In general, the test for mean-variance spanning can be divided into two parts: (1) the spanning of the global minimum-variance portfolio and (2) the spanning of the tangency portfolio. Therefore, we can rewrite the Wald test as

$$W = T\left(\frac{(\hat{\sigma}_{R_1})^2}{(\hat{\sigma}_R)^2} - 1\right) + T\left(\frac{1 + \hat{\theta}_R(R_1^{\text{GMV}})^2}{1 + \hat{\theta}_{R_1}(R_1^{\text{GMV}})^2} - 1\right) \qquad (15.8)$$

where R is the return of the benchmark assets plus the hedge fund portfolio; $\hat{\sigma}_{R_1}^2$ and $\hat{\sigma}_R^2$ are the global minimum-variance of the benchmark assets and that of the benchmark assets plus an FOFs portfolio, respectively; $\hat{\theta}_{R_1}(R_1^{\text{GMV}})$ is the slope of the asymptote of the mean-variance frontier for the benchmark assets; and $\hat{\theta}_R(R_1^{\text{GMV}})$ is the slope of the tangency line of the mean-variance frontier for the benchmark portfolios plus an FOFs portfolio.

The first term measures the change of the global minimum-variance portfolios due to the addition of an FOFs portfolio. The second term measures whether there is an improvement of the squared tangency slope after adding an FOFs portfolio to the set of benchmark portfolios. Kan and Zhou (2001) suggest a step-down procedure, which requires us first to test $\alpha = 0_N$ and then to test $\delta = 1_N - \beta 1_K = 0_N$, conditional on $\alpha = 0_N$.

The step-down asymptotic Wald tests can be written as:

$$W_1 = T(\lambda_i) \sim \chi_N^2 \qquad (15.9)$$

$$W_2 = T(\lambda_i) \sim \chi_N^2 \qquad (15.10)$$

If the rejection is due to the first test, we conclude that it is because the two tangency portfolios are very different. If the rejection is due to the second test, we conclude that it is because the two global minimum-variance portfolios are very different.

15.2.2 Spanning tests under nonnormality

The tests described in Section 15.2.1 assume that returns are normally distributed and that the error term in equation (15.1) is homoskedastic. However, FOF returns are generally not normally distributed. In this case, we relax the normality assumption and use a GMM Wald test to adjust for return nonnormality:

$$W_a = T \times \text{vec}(\hat{\Theta}')'[(A_T \otimes I_N)S_T(A_T' \otimes I_N)]^{-1} \text{vec}(\hat{\Theta}') \sim \chi_{2N}^2 \qquad (15.11)$$

where the moment condition is $E[g_t] = E(X \otimes E) = 0'_{N(1+K)}$ (15.12)

$$S_T = E[g'_t \, g_t]$$ (15.13)

$$A_T = \begin{bmatrix} 1 + \hat{a}_1 & -\hat{\mu}_1 \hat{V}_{11}^{-1} \\ \hat{b}_1 & -1'_K \hat{V}_{11}^{-1} \end{bmatrix}$$ (15.14)

15.2.3   Mean-variance intersection tests

A mean-variance intersection test is equivalent to a test for mean-variance spanning for a specific value of the zero-beta rate. Huberman and Kandel (1987) show that the null hypothesis of mean-variance intersection is

$$H_0: \alpha = R^0(1_N - \beta 1_K)$$ (15.15)

where R^0 is the zero-beta of return associated with the mean-variance efficient portfolio at the intersection point. DeRoon and Nijman (2001) show that the Wald test for mean-variance intersection is

$$W^{\text{intersection}} = T\left(\frac{1 + \hat{\theta}_R(R^0)^2}{1 + \hat{\theta}_{R_1}(R^0)^2} - 1 \right)$$ (15.16)

where $\hat{\theta}_{R_1}(R^0)$ is the Sharpe ratio of the benchmark assets and $\hat{\theta}_R(R^0)$ is the Sharpe ratio of benchmark plus test assets. DeRoon and Nijman (2001) show that the Wald test intersection statistic can easily be interpreted as the percentage increase in Sharpe ratios scaled by the sample size. Hence, the intersection hypothesis is equivalent to the hypothesis that the Jensen performance measure is zero. If there is intersection, then there is no possible improvement in the Sharpe measure to be achieved by including the additional N assets in the investor's portfolio K.

For the spanning test, the Wald test statistic can be rewritten as

$$W = T\left(\frac{1 + \hat{\theta}_R(R^0)^2}{1 + \hat{\theta}_{R_1}(R^0)^2} - 1 \right) + T\left(\frac{(\hat{\sigma}_{R_1})^2}{(\hat{\sigma}_R)^2} - 1 \right)$$ (15.17)

where $\hat{\theta}_{R_1}(R^0)$ is the Sharpe ratio of the benchmark assets and $\hat{\theta}_R(R^0)$ is the Sharpe ratio of benchmark plus test assets. $\hat{\sigma}_{R_1}^2$ and $\hat{\sigma}_R^2$ are the global minimum-variance of the benchmark assets and that of the benchmark assets plus a PE portfolio, respectively. The equation shows that the spanning test statistic consists of two parts. The first is similar to the intersection statistic test and is determined by a change in Sharpe ratios; the second is determined by the change in the global minimum-variance of the portfolios.

To sum up, there is intersection even if there is only one value for which mean-variance investors cannot improve their mean-variance efficient portfolio by including $R_{2,t+1}$ in their investment set. In other words, the mean-variance frontier of $R_{1,t+1}$ intersects $R_{1,t+1} + R_{2,t+1}$. Furthermore, there is spanning if there are no mean-variance investors that can improve their mean-variance efficient portfolio by including $R_{2,t+1}$ in their investment set. In other words, the mean-variance frontier of $R_{1,t+1}$ spans $R_{1,t+1}$ $R_{2,t+1}$.

15.3   Data description

To represent the funds of funds universe, we choose to use TASS fund of funds index (TASS FOF hereafter), published by TASS Research, a research unit of Tremont Data. We use two benchmark sets. First, we take five size and five book-to-market portfolios to form 25 value-weighted size and book-to-market portfolios of NYSE, AMEX, and Nasdaq stocks. The 25 benchmark portfolios are obtained from French's Website.[1] Panel A of Table 15.1 presents the summary statistics of the 25 size/book-to-market portfolios. These portfolios show a mean return range from 0.55% to 1.88% and a range of standard deviation from 4.37% to 9.79%. Second, we enlarge our benchmark set by including international asset classes, bonds, and commodities. Thus, our second benchmark includes: Standard & Poor's 500 for U.S. large-capitalization stocks, Standard & Poor's SmallCap 600 for U.S. small-capitalization stocks, Morgan Stanley Capital International (MSCI) EAFE for Europe, Australia and Far East stocks, Morgan Stanley Capital International (MSCI) EM for emerging markets stocks, Goldman Sachs Commodity Index (GSCI) for commodities, Lehman Brothers Aggregate Index for fixed income, and Payden & Rygel (P&R) 90-day T-Bill for short-term investments. Panel B of Table 15.1 presents the summary statistics of the second benchmark assets.

15.4   Empirical results

15.4.1   Full sample results

To examine if an FOFs portfolio allows investors to improve the minimum-variance frontier derived from a given set of benchmark assets, we perform a battery of spanning tests. As highlighted previously, the spanning hypothesis is

---

[1] French, Kenneth R. (2005). *Data Library* (http://mba.tuck.dartmouth.edu/pages/faculty/ ken.french/data_library.html).

Table 15.1 Summary statistics of benchmark portfolios (1994 to 2004)

Panel A

Book-to-market	Size				
	Smallest	2	3	4	Largest
Lowest	0.55	0.82	0.74	1.06	1.02
	(9.79)	(8.31)	(7.67)	(6.86)	(4.86)
2	1.53	1.03	1.07	1.17	1.15
	(7.99)	(5.81)	(5.17)	(4.73)	(4.50)
3	1.62	1.30	1.16	1.32	1.11
	(5.78)	(4.74)	(4.51)	(4.61)	(4.48)
4	1.88	1.37	1.15	1.32	1.06
	(5.14)	(4.92)	(4.58)	(4.45)	(4.37)
Highest	1.77	1.40	1.52	1.13	0.79
	(5.24)	(5.39)	(4.98)	(4.85)	(5.02)

Panel B

	S&P 500	S&P SmallCap 600	MSCI EAFE	MSCI EM	Lehman Brothers Aggregate Index	P&R U.S. 90-day T-Bill	GSCI
Mean return	0.97%	1.12%	0.59%	0.42%	0.55%	0.33%	0.86%
Standard deviation	4.40%	5.26%	4.29%	6.69%	1.15%	0.16%	5.67%

Panel A presents the mean monthly percentage returns and monthly percentage standard deviations (in parentheses) of the 25 size/book-to-market portfolios. Panel B presents the mean monthly returns and monthly standard deviations of the second benchmark (B2) assets. B2 includes: Standard & Poor's 500 for U.S. large-capitalization stocks, Standard & Poor's SmallCap 600 for U.S. small-capitalization stocks, Morgan Stanley Capital International (MSCI) EAFE for Europe, Australia, and Far East stocks, Morgan Stanley Capital International (MSCI) EM for emergent markets stocks, Lehman Brothers Aggregate Index for fixed income, Payden & Rygel (P&R) 90-day T-Bill for short-term investments, and Goldman Sachs Commodity Index GSCI for commodities.

rejected when the benchmark assets are not able to mimic the mean-variance characteristics of the FOFs portfolio. In other words, the FOFs portfolio is an autonomous asset class relative to the benchmark assets.

Panel A of Table 15.2 reports the MVST results for the period 1994–2004. Based on LM, LR, and W tests, we reject the null hypothesis that the 25 size/book-to-market portfolios as benchmark portfolios (B1 hereafter) can span the FOFs portfolio at the 1% confidence level. We also confirm these results using the GMM Wald (Wa) test, allowing for heteroskedasticity. Therefore, we suggest that investing in FOFs does bring diversification benefits for mean-variance investors. More interestingly, when we enlarge our investment opportunities by including fixed

Table 15.2 Mean-variance spanning tests of fund of hedge funds portfolio (1994–2004)

	Regression-based mean-variance spanning tests			GMM Wald test
	Panel A: Benchmark (B1)			
	LM	LR	W	Wa
TASS FOF Index	107.46	222.10	578.12	462.79
	(<0.000)	(<0.000)	(<0.000)	(<0.000)
	Panel B: Benchmark (B2)			
TASS FOF Index	7.073	7.269	7.473	4.821
	(0.029)	(0.026)	(0.023)	(0.089)

TASS FOF Index for TASS Fund of Funds Index. Benchmark (B1) includes 25 size/book-to-market portfolios that are constructed by all of the firms trading on the NYSE, AMEX, or Nasdaq. Benchmark (B2) includes: Standard & Poor's 500 for U.S. large-capitalization stocks, Standard & Poor's SmallCap 600 for U.S. small-capitalization stocks, Morgan Stanley Capital International (MSCI) EAFE for Europe, Australia, and Far East stocks, Morgan Stanley Capital International (MSCI) EM for emergent markets stocks, Goldman Sachs Commodity Index GSCI for commodities, Lehman Brothers Aggregate Index for fixed income, and Payden & Rygel (P&R) 90-day T-Bill for short-term investments. LM, LR, and W represent the asymptotic Lagrange multiplier, likelihood ratio, and Wald tests, respectively. Wa is the GMM Wald test, allowing for heteroskedasticity. The p-values are in parentheses.

income, international assets, and commodities (B2 hereafter), we confirm the value added of the FOFs portfolio.

To further investigate the sources of rejection of the spanning hypothesis, we implement a step-down procedure as suggested by Kan and Zhou (2001). These authors divide the spanning test into two. The first test is related to the tangency portfolio and refers to the restriction on the intercepts of the regression $(\alpha = 0_N)$; the second is related to the global minimum-variance portfolio and refers to the constraint on the estimated coefficients $(\delta = 1_N - \beta 1_K = 0_N)$. As sustained by Petrella (2005), this division is important for investors with a low risk aversion, for they will benefit more from the improvement of the tangency portfolio's characteristics.

Table 15.3 reports results of the step-down procedure. We find that, when we use B1, the null hypothesis related to the tangency portfolio is not rejected, while we reject the null hypothesis of the global minimum-variance portfolio at the 1% confidence level. Thus, investing in an FOFs portfolio improves the global minimum-variance portfolio but not the tangency portfolio. We also confirm this result using B2. Investors who already hold a diversified portfolio with international assets, bonds, and commodities do improve their investment opportunities by adding an FOFs portfolio.

Table 15.3 Mean-variance intersection and spanning tests of a fund of
hedge funds portfolio (1994–2004)

| | Step-down tests | | | |
| | Benchmark (B1) | | Benchmark (B2) | |
	W_1	W_2	W_1	W_2
TASS FOF Index	1.138	462.795	0.004	4.821
	(0.566)	(<0.000)	(0.997)	(0.089)

TASS FOF Index for TASS Fund of Funds Index. Benchmark (B1) includes 25 size/book-to-market portfolios that are constructed by all of the firms trading on the NYSE, AMEX, or Nasdaq. Benchmark (B2) includes: Standard & Poor's 500 for U.S. large-capitalization stocks, Standard & Poor's SmallCap 600 for U.S. small-capitalization stocks, Morgan Stanley Capital International (MSCI) EAFE for Europe, Australia, and Far East stocks, Morgan Stanley Capital International (MSCI) EM for emergent markets stocks, Goldman Sachs Commodity Index GSCI for commodities, Lehman Brothers Aggregate Index for fixed income, and Payden & Rygel (P&R) 90-day T-Bill for short-term investments. The first test (W_1) is a Wald test of $H_0: \alpha = 0_N$, and the second test (W_2) is a Wald test of $H_0: \delta = 1_N - \beta 1_K = 0_N$, conditional on $\alpha = 0_N$. The p-values are in parentheses.

15.4.2 Mean-variance spanning tests in terms of performance measures

The purpose of this section is to examine the added value of FOFs in terms of the Sharpe ratio and Jensen's alpha, using MVSTs. Bekaert and Urias (1996) point out that the change in the Sharpe ratio of the tangency portfolio measures the economic importance of the shift in the efficient frontier. Because the Sharpe ratio of the tangency portfolio gives the largest mean return per unit of standard deviation, a difference between the Sharpe ratios computed for the benchmark assets (K) and the $K + N$ (new assets) indicates that investors can enhance their returns per unit of risk by investing in the additional N assets.

Further, in addition to using the change in the maximum Sharpe ratio, we use Jensen's alpha as a measure of portfolio efficiency. To do so, we conduct mean-variance intersection tests that are, as previously shown, equivalent to Jensen's alpha measure of portfolio performance.

Table 15.4 reports the results for the mean-spanning tests (using the Sharpe ratio) and the mean-variance intersection tests (equivalent to Jensen's alpha) for the FOFs portfolio. Our general observation is that, when we consider B1 as the benchmark portfolio, we reject the mean-variance intersection hypothesis. In other words, there is a significant abnormal performance on FOF portfolio relative to a set of 25 size/book-to-market portfolios as benchmarks. However, we fail to reject the mean-variance intersection hypothesis for the FOFs portfolio when we consider B2 as a benchmark portfolio.

Table 15.4 Mean-variance intersection tests and mean-variance spanning tests
(in terms of Sharpe ratios) of a fund of hedge funds portfolio (1994–2004)

	Benchmark (B1)		Benchmark (B2)	
	Intersection hypothesis	Spanning hypothesis	Intersection hypothesis	Spanning hypothesis
	$W^{Intersection}$	$W^{Spanning}$	$W^{Intersection}$	$W^{Spanning}$
TASS FOF Index	65.978	257.908	0.070	3.729
	(<0.000)	(<0.000)	(0.791)	(0.053)

TASS FOF Index for TASS Fund of Funds Index. Benchmark (B1) includes 25 size/book-to-market portfolios that are constructed by all of the firms trading on the NYSE, AMEX, or Nasdaq. Benchmark (B2) includes: Standard & Poor's 500 for U.S. large-capitalization stocks, Standard & Poor's SmallCap 600 for U.S. small-capitalization stocks, Morgan Stanley Capital International (MSCI) EAFE for Europe, Australia, and Far East stocks, Morgan Stanley Capital International (MSCI) EM for emergent markets stocks, Goldman Sachs Commodity Index GSCI for commodities, Lehman Brothers Aggregate Index for fixed income, and Payden & Rygel (P&R) 90-day T-Bill for short-term investments. W represents the asymptotic Wald test. The p-values are in parentheses.

Our general conclusion is that including an FOFs portfolio in a set of benchmark portfolios (U.S. stocks only) provides an extra return for a unit increase in standard deviation. However, this conclusion is less evident when we consider a diversified benchmark.

15.5 Conclusion

We examined whether investors can improve their investment opportunities by adding a fund of funds portfolio to different sets of benchmark portfolios. We applied a battery of mean-variance spanning tests using data from 1994–2004. To the best of our knowledge, our study is the first to use these tests in the FOF context.

When we consider benchmark portfolios sorted by firm size and book-to-market ratio, we find that FOFs, as an asset class, improve the mean-variance frontier set. However, the improvement comes mainly from a leftward shift of the global minimum-variance portfolio rather than the tangency portfolio. These results are especially important to low-risk investors who are looking for alternative assets to enlarge the minimum-variance frontier. Additionally, we find that investors who already hold a diversified portfolio with international assets, bonds, and commodities do improve their investment opportunities by adding an FOFs portfolio.

Further, to investigate the economic importance of the shift in the efficient frontier that results from adding FOFs, we conducted further tests: mean-variance spanning tests using Sharpe ratios and mean-variance intersection tests that are equivalent to the Jensen's alpha measure of portfolio performance. Our general conclusion is that including FOFs portfolios in a set of benchmark portfolios (U.S. stocks only) provides an extra return for a unit increase in standard deviation. However, this conclusion is less evident when we consider an internationally diversified portfolio as a benchmark.

As noted by several academics, research in FOFs is still in its early days. FOFs pose new challenges for financial theory, and much remains to be done to better understand the importance of FOFs to asset allocation.

References

Aitken, M., Harris, F., McInish, T., and Segara, R. (2005). Are Warrants Redundant? Spanning Tests and Price Discovery. Working Paper, University of New South Wales.

Bekaert, G. and Urias, M. (1996). Diversification Integration and Emerging Market Closed-End Funds. *Journal of Finance*, 51(3):835–869.

Brown, S. J., Goetzmann. W. N., and Liang. B. (2004). Fees on Fees in Funds of Funds. Working Paper, Yale ICF No. 02–33, New Haven, CT.

Chen, H., Ho, K., and Lu, C. (2004). An Asset Allocation Perspective of Real Estate: The Case of Real Estate Investment Trusts. Working Paper, Yuan Ze University, China.

Chen, H., Ho, K., and Wu, C. (2004). Initial Public Offerings: An Asset Allocation Perspective. Working Paper, Yuan Ze University, China.

DeRoon, F. A. and Nijman, T. E. (2001). Testing for Mean-Variance Spanning: A Survey. *Journal of Empirical Finance*, 8(2):111–155.

DeRoon, F. A., Nijman, T. E., and Werker, B. (2001). Testing for Mean-Variance Spanning with Short Sales Constraints and Transaction Costs: The Case of Emerging Markets. *Journal of Finance*, 56(2):721–742.

Errunza, V., Hogan, K., and Hung, M.-W. (1999). Can the Gains from International Diversification Be Achieved Without Trading Abroad? *Journal of Finance*, 54(6):2075–2107.

French, K.R. (2005). Data Library (http://mba.tuck.dartmouth.edu/pages/faculty/ken.french/data_library.html).

Huberman, G. and Kandel, S. (1987). Mean-Variance Spanning. *Journal of Finance*, 42(4):873–888.

Kan, R. and Zhou, G. (2001). Test of Mean-Variance Spanning. Working Paper, University of Toronto, Toronto, Canada.

Petrella, G. (2005). Are Euro Area Small Cap Stocks an Asset Class? Evidence from Mean-Variance Spanning Tests. *European Financial Management*, 11(2):229–253.

Appendix: Asymptotic and finite-sample test statistics for mean-variance spanning tests

Following Huberman and Kandel (1987), the null hypothesis of "spanning" is:

$$H_0: \alpha = 0_N, \qquad \delta = 1_N - \beta 1_K = 0_N.$$

We can write the null hypothesis as $\hat{\Theta} = [\alpha \ \delta] = 0_{2 \times N} = AB - C$, where

$$A = \begin{bmatrix} 1 & 0'_K \\ 0 & -1'_K \end{bmatrix} \qquad \text{and} \qquad C = \begin{bmatrix} 0'_K \\ -1'_K \end{bmatrix}$$

The distribution of the null hypothesis is $\text{vec}(\hat{\Theta}) \sim N(\text{vec}(\Theta'), A(X'X)^{-1}A' \otimes \Sigma)$. By defining

$$\hat{G} = TA(X'X)^{-1} A' = \begin{bmatrix} 1 + \hat{\mu}'_{1'} \hat{V}_{11}^{-1} \hat{\mu}_{1'} & \hat{\mu}'_{1'} \hat{V}_{11}^{-1} 1_K \\ \hat{\mu}'_{1'} \hat{V}_{11}^{-1} 1_K & 1'_k \hat{V}_{11}^{-1} 1_K \end{bmatrix}$$

and

$$\hat{H} = \hat{\Theta} \hat{\Sigma}^{-1} \hat{\Theta} = \begin{bmatrix} \hat{\alpha}' \hat{\Sigma}^{-1} \hat{\alpha} & \hat{\alpha}' \hat{\Sigma}^{-1} \hat{\delta} \\ \hat{\alpha}' \hat{\Sigma}^{-1} \hat{\delta} & \hat{\delta}' \hat{\Sigma}^{-1} \hat{\delta} \end{bmatrix}$$

we then denote the two eigenvalues of the matrix, $\hat{H}\hat{G}^{-1}$, by λ_1 and λ_2.

16 Higher-moment performance characteristics of funds of funds

Zsolt Berenyi

Abstract

The performance measurement of funds of funds in the presence of skewness and kurtosis is still not widely discussed in the literature. This chapter suggests performance measurement for FOFs based on higher moments such as skewness and kurtosis using the so-called efficiency gain/loss methodology. The questions we investigate are: (1) Do FOFs create value compared to higher-moment optimized option portfolios? (2) Is it possible to alter the return distribution of FOFs in order to enhance performance?

16.1 Introduction

Funds of funds are investment vehicles with the purpose of holding shares in other, competing investment funds while at the same time charging a predefined amount for their services. The expected benefits of fund of funds investing comprise several aspects, such as access to funds not accessible elsewhere (for example, hedge funds closed to new investments), professional oversight on fund activities, better implementation of the investor's strategy, and diversification benefits.

FOFs are widely used for hedge fund investing. Certainly, the use of funds of funds is not limited to hedge funds only but can be extended to include practically any form of investment. Consequently, the FOF approach has its relevance, especially in case of investment forms with a degree of lack of transparency, informational disadvantages, or access limitations for the investing public.

When investing in FOFs, though, the benefits often come at the cost of undesirable side effects: negative skewness and double fee structure. First, diversification reduces return volatility, but, as evidence shows, it may also have unwanted effects, such as increasing negative skewness or kurtosis. Second, charging double fees (for example, fees on investments where a fee has already been charged) can lead to both underperformance compared to the underlying funds as well as distorted investment strategies. By distorted investment strategies we mean that FOF managers may take excessive risks for high absolute returns; high returns in turn could absorb the fees charged (Brown, Goetzmann, and Liang, 2004).

The definition of excessive risk is, though investors often look at conventional performance measures like the Sharpe Ratio only, not restricted to variance. We may use the term *excessive risk* as a risk profile that is undesirable for investors (for example, large negative skewness or high kurtosis).

Including not only the variance but also the higher moments of the return distribution in the performance analysis, especially for alternative investments, has been proposed by a number of scholars (Amin and Kat, 2003; Berényi, 2003). Funds of funds, however, have still rarely been investigated from this aspect. Here we aim to investigate the performance of funds of funds, with special focus on the higher-moment performance characteristics. Here are the questions being asked:

- Do FOFs create value when comparing their return distribution to higher-moment optimized option portfolios?
- Is it possible to alter the FOF return distribution in order to enhance the observed performance artificially? That is, is a kind of gambling in the case of FOFs possible or even probable? And if so, what are possible ways to utilize it?

We do not, however, offer a method that decides how funds of funds should be constructed, for example, how much capital should be invested in one fund or another.

16.2 Performance assessment basics

16.2.1 Higher-moment performance assessment: an overview

Conventional risk–value performance measures — such as the Sharpe ratio — are, as evidence shows, not exactly suitable for performance evaluation purposes when facing return nonnormality. From this background, a series of research endeavors has been carried out with the aim of providing a more robust performance measurement technique. One of these has been the inclusion of the higher moments of the return distribution in the performance evaluation.

Currently, there are three basic approaches for accounting for higher moments in the performance assessment: (1) using a multimoment CAPM, in which asset returns will be calculated based on comoment terms; (2) calculating a kind of variance-equivalent risk measure, in which the higher moments are compressed into a one-dimensional risk value; and (3) replicating the return distribution with an optioned benchmark portfolio by matching their higher moments (or distribution pins) in order to calculate efficiency.

A common feature of the first two methods is that they rely on certain assumptions regarding the process generating the marginal rates of substitution between (for example, the prices of) higher moments. The third method, however, is largely parameter free and preference free. In this chapter, we restrict our higher-moment analysis to the third method only.

16.2.2 The efficiency gain/loss concept

The so-called efficiency gain/loss concept estimates performance as the return differential between the FOF and its risk-adjusted benchmark asset. That is, the efficiency gain/loss measure is simply the difference between the expected return of the asset under investigation and that of its synthetic benchmark asset, created by using options or dynamic strategies (Amin and Kat, 2003; Berényi, 2003).

The expected return on the benchmark asset is the maximum return that one may achieve on the optioned market while holding the risk exposure constant (for example, the same variance, skewness, and kurtosis for the end-of-period return distribution). The return on the benchmark asset can certainly be interpreted as the alternative, minimum return to be achieved when holding the same risk exposure; that is, at least this expected return should be delivered by any investment portfolio. Note that throughout this chapter, risk exposure will denote the higher moments of the return distribution, restricted to the variance, skewness, and kurtosis.

16.2.3 Constructing benchmark assets

The benchmark assets are constructed for each FOF individually by using an efficient underlying (for example, Standard & Poor's 500 index) combined with options. To be more specific, benchmark portfolios are generated via nonlinear optimization, combining the underlying asset, options, and the risk-free asset, to achieve maximum expected return for a given higher-moment return characteristic. The nonlinear optimization algorithm for constructing individual benchmark assets can be formulated as follows: For any fund of funds l, construct a benchmark asset L with return r_L from the assets i, maximizing the expected return,

$$\text{Maximize } E(r_L) = \sum_i x_i E(r_i) \tag{16.1}$$

subject to

$$
\begin{aligned}
\sigma_L^2 &= \sigma_0^2 \text{ for the target variance} \\
s_L^3 &= s_0^3 \text{ (target skewness)} \\
k_L^3 &= k_0^3 \text{ (target kurtosis)} \\
\sum_i x_i &= 1 \text{ as budget constraint}
\end{aligned}
\tag{16.2}
$$

where $E(r_i)$ is the expected return on asset i; x_i is the investment in asset i (for example, the underlying asset, the risk-free asset, as well as the options), σ_L, s_L, k_L are, respectively, the standard deviation, skewness, and kurtosis for the benchmark asset L, and σ_l, s_l, k_l are respective moments for the asset l. Then, the efficiency gain/loss (in case it is negative) for the FOF l, α_l, can be defined as

$$\alpha_\ell = E(r_\ell) - E(r_L) \tag{16.3}$$

The greater α_l, the greater the efficiency of the given FOF compared to the benchmark asset (which is available without any special knowledge). A negative α_l indicates inferior performance; that is, holding the risk exposure constant, a comparable investment in the form of an optioned portfolio offers a higher expected return than the FOF under investigation.

16.3   Data and methodology

16.3.1   Data for the analysis

As FOF data we used monthly fund of funds returns from January 1998 to November 2004, obtained from the TASS database. The chosen data set contains 175 funds of funds (surviving funds only), all denominated in USD. It would certainly be possible to extend the analysis to any other currencies as well. This is left to later research.

From the monthly returns, we generated semi-ex-ante annual returns by bootstrapping, drawing 12 samples from the set of monthly data, repeating the procedure 1,000 times. This methodology is in the vein of work published by Ederington (1995).

In order to compare the FOFs with other assets as well, we decided to define a reference data set, containing monthly data for about 200 equity market neutral and long/short equity hedge funds. The data of monthly returns has also been obtained from the TASS database for the same period as for funds of funds. Again, we restricted our analysis to surviving funds only.

For the underlying asset, we used monthly returns of the Standard & Poor's 500 index, for which option prices are also readily available. For the risk-free rate, we used USD Libor rates. During the following analysis, we used returns net of the corresponding risk-free rates.

16.3.2   Return distribution of the benchmark asset

Historical return distribution

The most straightforward analysis uses historical data for calculating the performance measures. By means of Monte Carlo simulation on historical returns, we can determine option prices, and it is possible to calculate semi-ex-ante performance for each fund.

It may, on the other hand, happen that the underlying index distribution exhibits irregularities for a particular period, even in the case of highly liquid, efficient assets. Such irregularities include large negative historical returns over the time period investigated.

Since the benchmark asset is used to evaluate different asset classes, large negative historical returns may have adverse effects on the performance evaluation itself. For example, a comparison of the Sharpe ratios would be — more or less — senseless. Furthermore, calculating the effects of options on any asset would also be difficult because these could have magnified effects on the particular asset (for example, increasing the expected return without having an adverse effect on the variance and higher moments, because of the underlying's negative expected returns).

Calculating the underlying distribution from option prices

Given the foregoing background, we opted for calculating the forward-looking underlying distribution on the basis of observed option prices. For the calculation, we used a single-log-normal distribution (SLN) setting. That is, we assumed that the underlying index follows a log-normal distribution for the holding period (which is set to be one year).

We believe that using a single-log-normal distribution framework is reasonable for the S&P index. For other, unsettled markets it may be beneficial to use a double-log-normal setting, for example, combining two log-normal distributions in order to determine the underlying distribution that fits the option prices best (Melick and Thomas, 1997; Gemmil and Saflekos, 2000). This is especially true for periods of high negative skewness, high kurtosis, or multimodal distribution (election effects, etc.).

For the SLN distribution, we performed a nonlinear optimization in order to calculate the parameter of the SLN that delivers the best fit to the observed option prices. During the optimization process, we minimize the squared error between observed and calculated option prices. The probabilities for the SLN distribution have been calculated using the values obtained from the historical simulation. By doing so, the combined effects of options on the underlying as well as other assets can be computed more easily.

Note that the obtained SLN distribution also shows an expected return slightly below the risk-free rate. This also may have an undesirable effect on the returns of the synthetic benchmarks; however, it is expected to be smaller in magnitude than in the historical return case.

16.4   Performance characteristics of funds of funds

16.4.1   Basic performance attributes

One of the first questions is: What are, if any, the underlying characteristics of FOFs? Put differently, are FOF returns significantly different from that of the underlying funds in terms of skewness and kurtosis?

Funds of funds will certainly have an averaging effect with respect to the asset holdings (usually 5–15 funds). In addition, they invest in assets where a definite fee structure has already been laid down. Past research, and common sense as well, would suggest that (1) because of the double fee structure, the return shape of FOFs may be different from that of underlying funds, and

(2) an increasing number of funds in a given FOF decreases volatility (because of diversification effects), but it may change skewness and kurtosis unfavorably.

To evaluate the magnitude of these effects, we first investigate the higher-moment statistics of both funds of funds and hedge funds. Next, we have a look at the Sharpe ratio. Finally, the efficiency gain/loss for FOFs is analyzed, again with a plain comparison of the results to the reference set of hedge funds.

16.4.2   Higher statistical moments

For the higher central moments of the FOF distributions, we can assert that for the funds of funds sample, historical variance and kurtosis are in most cases below those of the underlying asset (for the variance only 8.5% of the FOFs, for the kurtosis only 9.7% of the funds have a higher value than the S&P 500).

On the other hand, a huge majority (about 87%) of the funds of funds have a lower skewness than the underlying. In one-third of the cases, the skewness is negative. Lower or negative skewness means, given the laid-down skewness preferences (for example, Scott and Horvath, 1980), a deterioration in the attractiveness of the particular fund.

When comparing these findings with the reference data set (equity-market-neutral as well as long-short equity hedge funds), however, we can encounter significant differences. For the hedge funds investigated, we perceived in roughly two-thirds of the cases higher variance; the ratio of hedge funds with lower skewness as well as higher kurtosis than the market portfolio was also roughly two-thirds, respectively. Put differently, hedge funds clearly tend to have higher risk exposure in terms of variance, skewness, and/or kurtosis than funds of funds do.

16.4.3   Sharpe ratio

For the historical underlying returns, the majority of the funds of funds indeed, show superior performance compared to that of the S&P 500. On the other hand, when we use the SLN distribution, it can be asserted that roughly 47% of the funds have higher Sharpe ratios than the underlying index. That is, the SLN setting as underlying seems to be more efficient, and it underpins the use of the forward-looking, option-based methodology.

16.4.4   Efficiency gain/loss

In this section, we look to find out whether funds of funds are an efficient form of investment. In other words, we aim at estimating whether the FOFs under investigation have created value. Value will simply be treated as the efficiency gain, which is the difference in expected returns for a particular fund of funds and its individual benchmark asset.

Thus, as the next step, we calculated the efficiency gain for the FOF sample with nonlinear optimization. Note that the setting of constraints is crucial for the nonlinear calculation. We limited the share of the individual options within the portfolio to a weight between −0.1 and 0.4.

The overview of the optimization results can be found in Figure 16.1. Note that all of the following figures contain the data (efficiency gain/loss as well as the Sharpe ratio differences, etc.) sorted by their magnitude for an easier understanding and interpretation. It can be seen that all FOFs have a large, significant negative performance (efficiency loss). Again, negative values for the efficiency gain/loss measure indicate that the given risk level (variance-skewness-kurtosis) can be achieved by using options more efficiently, for example, by getting a higher expected return. Consequently, negative performance indicates that at the time of the investigation, optioned portfolios show uniformly very high efficiency when compared to the FOF Monte Carlo returns.

Next, we also computed the efficiency gain/loss ratio for the reference set of hedge funds. The results of this step can be seen in Figure 16.2. It can be observed that hedge funds show a slightly higher efficiency according to the efficiency gain/loss measure. However, the pattern and magnitudes of the efficiency gain/loss are very similar to that of funds of funds. Note that similar magnitudes of

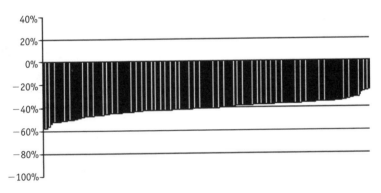

Figure 16.1 Efficiency gain/loss for the FOF sample

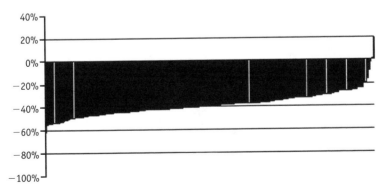

Figure 16.2 Efficiency gain/loss for the hedge fund sample

benchmark returns indicate — because of the definition of the efficiency gain/loss measure — similar risk exposure, since, on the optioned market, positions with identical expected returns can be substituted for each other.

This finding confirms the piece of evidence that funds of funds do not seem to take excessive risk, neither compared to the underlying asset nor compared to the hedge fund reference set. Consequently, we can conclude that although FOF returns may indeed be influenced by the double fee structure, it seems in effect not very substantial compared to other factors.

16.5 Enhancing FOF performance

16.5.1 Ex-ante optimization: portfolio setup

Let us assume that a fund manager could add optionlike returns to his fund of funds, for example, by using some dynamic strategies. Thus, the question being asked is whether the performance of FOFs could be, theoretically, enhanced. To resolve this, we analyzed the performance of funds of funds in the presence of leverage in the form of options. The effects of options on funds of funds can be determined by estimating the portfolio efficiency for the combined portfolios, given a set of options (calls, puts) and strategies (long, short).

The normal way of calculating the effect of options on the funds would be to compute all comoment terms from historical data. We believe, however, that this not only is time consuming but may also have some undesirable effects: Although the higher moments of return distributions are believed to be more stable than expected returns, comovement terms do not necessarily follow this pattern. That is, using comoment terms for an ex-ante optimization requires both stability and prediction precision, together with a high computing capacity.

Because of this, the ex-ante optimization was made using a simple, but not overly simplistic, approach. In this approach, using the SLN distribution and the historical returns for the FOFs, return pairs of underlying and FOFs are simply kept together in the Monte Carlo simulation (that is, the Monte Carlo loops for underlying, and FOF historical returns are not independent of each other).

On this basis, for each FOF option/strategy option combination, we run a separate optimization, calculating individual benchmark returns. This is certainly a simplifying methodology and thus may neglect some aspects, but we believe it is useful for demonstration purposes.

16.6 Results

Based on the methodology laid down previously, for each FOF we constructed 24 different optioned portfolios with varying option parts (which call or put option, since here we use only one option at a time), strategy (long or short), and option share in the portfolio (from -0.05 to 0.05).

For each optioned portfolio, we calculated the Sharpe ratio (see Figure 16.3) as well as the efficiency gain/loss measure (see Figure 16.4). Figures 16.3 and 16.4 show the maximum performance achievable for the particular FOF (given the direction and strategy for portfolio composition), sorted by their magnitude.

Our results can be summarized as follows: It is obvious that adding a long call/put to the underlying FOF does not increase the Sharpe ratio. On the other hand, selling options, especially out-of-the money ones, does indeed increase the Sharpe performance.

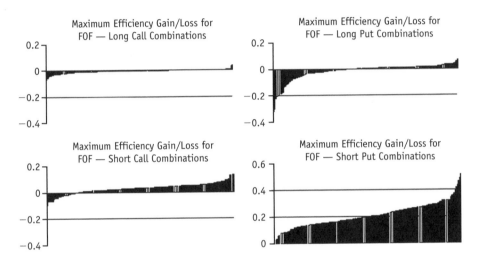

Figure 16.3 Sharpe ratios of the optioned portfolios

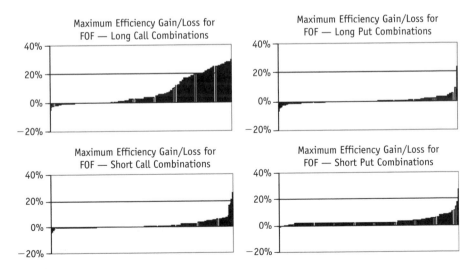

Figure 16.4 Efficiency gain/loss for the funds of funds

This result for funds of funds is actually not surprising. As has been pointed out by a number of scholars, the Sharpe ratio can be enhanced by shorting deep-out-of-the-money options for traditional investments (Dert and Oldenkamp, 2000). Our observation is very much in line with their observations; thus, for funds of funds, the same is true as for conventional portfolios or hedge funds.

For the efficiency gain/loss measure, the results are slightly different, as Figure 16.4 shows. First, FOFs combined with single call as well as put options still exhibit very modest efficiency according to the efficiency gain/loss measure. In several cases, however, an increase in the efficiency is also recognizable.

It can be observed that long call strategies will have a significant positive effect on the FOF performance in terms of the efficiency gain/loss measure. We believe this is plausible because long options have a high positive skewness. Interestingly, the inclusion of long put options did not significantly enhance performance, but neither did it decrease it.

On the other hand, shorting options does not seem to have a considerable positive effect on the fund efficiency. Moreover, since the foregoing figures show the maximum performance measure achievable, one can clearly consider including short options in the portfolio as counterproductive.

Summing up, it can be seen that altering performance is possible, even when investing a relatively small amount of money (2–5%) into optionlike strategies. Moreover, if shifting the Sharpe ratio is possible, then it is also possible to use options in order to manipulate the Sharpe ratio.

In fact, our results emphasize the utility of multimoment performance measures. The efficiency gain/loss measure proved to be robust to option-shorting strategies, or, put differently, shorting options will not further enhance performance. The multimoment measure can be modified only by investing in long calls — this is a rather plausible way of enhancing performance, given the observed skewness preferences.

16.7 Conclusion

We investigated the performance characteristics of funds of funds, with special focus on higher moments. Our findings can be summarized as follows. First, we found that in spite of theoretical consideration, funds of funds do not seem to take excessive risks. Based on our findings, they are, when looking through the glass of the multimoment efficiency measure, not much different from ordinary hedge funds. That is, hedge funds and funds of funds exhibit similar risk levels. Moreover, the absolute risk in terms of statistical returns tends to be higher for hedge funds than for funds of funds.

Second, we also found that the current set of funds of funds do not — in much the same way as the reference set of hedge funds does — show high performance when analyzed with the efficiency gain/loss measure. However, using another underlying, the results would be different.

Third, we observed that the Sharpe ratio may indeed be subject to manipulation, in that fund managers could increase their Sharpe ratios, for example, by selling OTM call options.

Fourth, we learned that portfolio efficiency can, theoretically, be enhanced using long calls (or equivalent dynamic strategies) if such a strategy is present. Furthermore, we also found that multimoment performance measures are more difficult to manipulate with short option strategies.

References

Amin, G. and Kat, H. (2003). Hedge Fund Performance 1990–2000: Do the Money Machines Really Add Value? *Journal of Financial and Quantitative Analysis*, 38(22):251–274.

Berényi, Z. (2003). *Risk and Performance Evaluation with Skewness and Kurtosis for Conventional and Alternative Investments*. Peter Lang, Frankfurt, Germany.

Brown, S. J., Goetzmann, W. N., and Liang, B. (2004). Fees on Fees in Funds of Funds. *Journal of Investment Management*, 2(4):43–48.

Dert, C. and Oldenkamp, B. (2000). Optimal Guaranteed Return Portfolios and the Casino Effect. *Operations Research*, 48(5):768–775.

Ederington, L. H. (1995). Mean-Variance as an Approximation to Expected Utility Maximization: Semi Ex-Ante Results. In: *Advances in Financial Economics* (Mark Hirschey and M. Wayne Marr, eds.). JAI Press, London.

Gemmil, G. and Saflekos, A. (2000). How Useful Are Implied Distributions? Evidence from Stock Index Options. *Journal of Derivatives*, 7(3):83–98.

Melick, W. R. and Thomas, C. P. (1997). Recovering an Asset's Implied PDF from Option Prices: An Application to Crude Oil During the Gulf Crisis. *Journal of Financial and Quantitative Analysis*, 32(1):91–115.

Scott, R. C. and Horvath, P. A. (1980). On the Direction of Preference for Moments of Higher Order Than Variance. *Journal of Finance*, 35(4): 915–919.

17 The market risk of funds of hedge funds: a conditional approach

Florent Pochon and Jérôme Teïletche

Abstract

We propose a Bayesian approach based on mixtures of normal distributions as an alternative to the usual approaches to hedge fund market risk. This framework is more relevant from both theoretical and empirical points of view since it tackles several unique features of risk management for hedge funds. First, it provides a conditional measure of risk by explicitly modeling a portfolio's profit and loss according to the state of the financial markets, mirrored by core assets (S&P stock market index, credit spreads). Second, by doing so it also deals with the nonlinearities between hedge fund returns and standard asset returns. These two points give this approach a clear advantage over the standard unconditional value-at-risk (VaR) measure of risk. Third, this approach circumvents the issue of small sample size in hedge fund data. Since we first separately identify the regimes on core assets (hectic and normal), we use longer-term historical data than the hedge fund industry and achieve greater precision in the estimation of parameters. Fourth, from an operational point of view, the framework is parsimonious. We apply the technique to major FOF indices and to a panel of single FOFs.

17.1 Introduction

With the great development of the hedge fund industry since the mid-1990s and, as a corollary, the increasing share of institutional portfolios dedicated to alternative investments, risk management for hedge funds has been a growing concern for the investment community. In addition to transparency, liquidity, credit, and operational risks, which are key aspects of risk management for alternative assets, some risk management is specific to hedge funds. On the one hand, because hedge funds are characterized by partial exposure to the markets on which they intervene, their risk as evaluated via the standard deviation and related measures (VaR, etc.) is lower than that of a simple buy-and-hold position on the underlying assets. On the other hand, the view of hedge funds as a distinct asset class providing absolute performances (delivering mostly alphas instead of betas) has been substantially revised. Although characterized by partial exposures to standard assets, several periods of disappointing returns have proven that hedge fund returns remain globally linked to the absolute returns, momentum, and/or volatility patterns of these assets. Several recent episodes, such as the collapse of Long-Term Capital Management (LTCM), have shown more dramatically that low variance does not mean low risk. Apart from the operational risk dimension, these incidents reveal the unique nature of hedge fund risk. In particular, hedge funds present nonlinear exposures to standard assets (Argawal and Naik, 2004; Fung and Hsieh, 1997, 1999, 2001, 2002b, 2004; Mitchell and Pulvino, 2001). These nonlinear exposures partly account for the non-Gaussian (asymmetrical and leptokurtic) nature of the distributions of hedge fund returns that is characteristic of assets with a significantly extreme loss risk (Brooks and Kat, 2002).

These features render the traditional mean-variance risk management tools ill adapted, including VaR, which is the generic measure of risk for institutional investors. As stressed by Lo (2001), one of the most severe limitations of VaR when it comes to analyzing hedge fund risk is that it provides an unconditional measure of risk. It is thus unable to capture the dependence of hedge returns on standard asset performances and more importantly its nonlinear character. One way to incorporate the latter is to use a factor model and either to introduce threshold effects or to reproduce payoffs of options on major underlying assets. It is, however, difficult to project such models and predict the probabilities of extreme events. An alternative approach is to assume that the returns on hedge funds follow a regime-switching model. While fitting Markovian models to hedge fund returns is difficult because of limited track records, a mixture of normal distribution models offers an appealing solution because this type of model is able to reproduce the non-Gaussian characteristics of empirical distributions of financial assets (Zangari, 1996). Relying on Kim and Finger's (2000) Bayesian methodology, Pochon and Teïletche (2005) find that these models are well adapted to hedge fund strategies.

While many studies have already documented the nonlinear character of returns with traditional assets for the case of hedge fund strategies, studies dedicated to the market risk of funds of hedge funds (FOFs) are scarcer. This is all the more surprising because FOFs have been the most attractive vehicles for new investors in hedge funds seeking to immunize their portfolios against downside risk. The assets under management of FOFs have grown sixfold since 1999 and reached more than US$550 billion in early 2005 according to data from the Barclay Trading Group, as compared to US$1,140 billion for the hedge fund strategies industry. In addition, market risk remains the key risk FOF investors have to support since other risk management parameters (selection, monitoring, and rebalancing) are delegated to FOF managers against the payment of a fee. One area of the literature focuses on this double fee structure of FOFs (FOF managers charge fees on top of those of individual funds they invest in) and shows that it penalizes the risk-adjusted performances of FOFs as compared to hedge funds (Amin and Kat, 2002; Brown, Goetzmann, and Ibbotson, 1999; Brown, Goetzmann, and Liang, 2003). The other major area analyzes the FOF performances, with an aim of estimating the alpha component (Liew and French, 2005). While estimations for alphas vary, recent studies point out that, similarly to hedge fund strategies, FOFs have to be considered through conditional approaches (Gregoriou, 2004; Kazemi and Schneeweis, 2003).

This chapter intends to investigate whether, despite diversification across strategies, a multiregime risk structure applies to FOF return distributions. We follow Pochon and Teïletche (2005) and propose an application of a Bayesian conditional multivariate model to FOF data. We first estimate a mixture of two normal distributions for core assets meant to act like a catalyst for the peripheral assets defined as the FOFs. One regime is interpreted as the quiet regime (characterized by low volatility) and the other as the hectic regime (characterized by higher volatility). We study the behavior of funds of funds returns in each regime and test whether their distributions (mean, variance, correlation with the core assets) significantly change between regimes. For the core asset, we chose the S&P 500 equity index and the Baa/Treasuries yield spread, which are key systematic factors that drive hedge fund returns (Fung and Hsieh, 1999, 2004). The peripheral assets are funds of hedge funds indices and a panel of individual FOFs. Our results are in line with those obtained on hedge fund strategies by Pochon and Teïletche (2005). We find that despite diversification, most FOF return distributions exhibit a multiregime risk structure, which corresponds in most cases to lower mean returns and higher volatility in hectic periods. Results are less clear-cut with regard to the correlation with standard assets, since changes in the correlation structure essentially seem to reflect a selection bias implied by the Bayesian conditional approach.

We believe that this framework is relevant to hedge fund investments from both the theoretical and empirical points of view since it tackles the several unique aspects of risk management for hedge funds mentioned earlier. First, it provides a conditional measure of risk by explicitly modeling a portfolio's profit and loss according to the state of the financial markets, mirrored by the core assets. Second, by doing so it also deals with the nonlinearities between hedge fund returns and standard asset returns. These two points are clear advantages over the standard unconditional value-at-risk (VaR). Third, this approach circumvents the issue of small sample size in hedge fund data, which also constitutes a limitation to VaR calculation. Since we first separately identify the regimes on core assets (hectic and normal), we use longer-term historical data than the hedge fund industry to identify regimes and thus achieve greater precision in the estimation of parameters. Fourth, from an operational point of view, the framework is parsimonious. Last, FOF returns are presumably more accurate measures of hedge fund returns since their track records avert numerous biases contained in individual funds or hedge fund indices of vendor databases (Fung and Hsieh, 2002a). FOF data do not suffer from either survivorship bias (since dead funds are included in FOF performance) or selection bias and instant-history bias.

This chapter is organized as follows. In Section 17.2 we estimate the mixture of distributions for the core assets. In Section 17.3 we analyze the implications for distribution of returns of FOFs. Section 17.4 presents an application of the methodology to stress testing. Section 17.5 is the conclusion.

17.2 Estimation of the regimes for the core assets

We first estimate a mixture of Gaussian distributions for the core asset returns, each distribution being interpreted as regimes. We follow Kim and Finger (2000) and Pochon and Teïletche (2005) and concentrate on a mixture of two normal distributions, which offers a satisfactory arbitrage between parsimony and adjustment quality.

With t as the period of the core asset and s_t, $s_t = 1$, 2, let x_t be a random latent variable that stands for the regime that prevails in period t. The unconditional density of x_t is given by

$$f(x_t; \theta) = \omega \times \Phi(x_t|s_t = 1; \theta) + (1 - \omega) \times \Phi(x_t|s_t = 2; \theta) \qquad (17.1)$$

where $\Phi(.)$ is the density of the normal distribution, $\Phi(x_t|s_t = i; \theta) \equiv \Phi(x_t; \mu_i, \sigma_i^2)$ stands for the normal distribution associated with regime i (with mean μ_i and variance σ_i^2), $\theta = \{\mu_i, \sigma_i^2, \mu_2, \sigma_2^2, \omega\}$ stands for the vector of parameters to be estimated, and ω is the mixture parameter, interpreted as the unconditional probability of being in regime 1 (hence $1 - \omega$ is the probability of being in regime 2). We use the *EM* algorithm to estimate the mixture (Hamilton, 1994, pp. 688–689). Table 17.1 reports the results obtained for the two core assets over a long period (January 1925 to April 2005).

Table 17.1 Estimation of mixtures of normal distributions for core assets

	Core asset	
	S&P 500	Baa/Aaa spread
Single normal		
Mean	0.005	−0.063
Standard deviation	0.045	20.527
Log-likelihood	1744.0	−4280.3
Akaïke information criterion	−3.357	8.891
Schwarz information criterion	−3.333	8.916
Hannan–Quinn information criterion	−3.348	8.900
Mixture of normal distributions		
Mean for "quiet regime"	0.010	−1.123
Standard deviation for "quiet regime"	0.029	8.479
Mean for "hectic regime"	−0.032	3.581
Standard deviation for "hectic regime"	0.095	40.046
Probability of the "quiet regime"	0.881	0.775
Log-likelihood	1902.1	−3995.7
Akaïke information criterion	−3.668	8.294
Schwarz information criterion	−3.659	8.304
Hannan–Quinn information criterion	−3.664	8.298

The table reports the maximum-likelihood estimates of the parameters of a single normal distribution and of a mixture of two normal distributions for both core assets (S&P and Baa/Treasuries yield spread) over the period January 1925 to April 2005.

A natural interpretation of this mixture is that it is a mixture of a hectic regime and a quiet regime. The hectic regime is characterized by a higher variance, a lower mean in the case of S&P returns and a higher mean in the case of the Baa spread, and in both cases by a low unconditional probability of occurrence (lower than 25% in both cases). Table 17.1 also reports goodness-of-fit tests. Using standard likelihood ratio tests, the null hypothesis is very easily rejected, meaning that the mixture leads to far better modeling of core asset returns than the single normal distribution. Because likelihood ratio tests do not satisfy standard regularity conditions in the case of mixtures of distributions, we report further information criteria: They unanimously confirm the superiority of the mixture over the simple distribution.

From this estimation, we deduce ex-post-conditional probabilities of being at a given date either in the normal regime or in the hectic one. Formally:

$$\Pr\{s_t = 1 | x_t; \theta\} = \omega \times \frac{f(x_t | s_t = 1; \theta)}{f(x_t; \theta)} \tag{17.1a}$$

$$\Pr\{s_t = 2 | x_t; \theta\} = (1 - \omega) \times \frac{f(x_t | s_t = 2; \theta)}{f(x_t; \theta)} \tag{17.1b}$$

Figure 17.1 represents the results of equations (17.1a) and (17.1b) for the hectic regime for the two core assets. While the two core assets unsurprisingly present common sensitivity to periods of major economic and financial shocks (the Great Depression, the oil shock, the technology bubble), they also show specific stress periods. This confirms the interest in using both assets as core assets in the following stage.

17.3 Implications for hedge fund returns modeling

17.3.1 Methodology and data

We use the ex-post-conditional probabilities of being in either regime according to the core asset to estimate the different moments of the distribution of peripheral assets conditionally on the regime observed for the core asset (Hamilton, 1994; Kim and Finger, 2000). If we denote as $\mu_{y,s_t=i}$ the mean of returns on asset y when the core asset is in regime i, a natural estimator is the following:

$$\mu_{y,s_t=i} = \frac{\displaystyle\sum_{t=1}^{T} \Pr\{s_t = i | x_t; \theta\} \times y_t}{\displaystyle\sum_{t=1}^{T} \Pr\{s_t = i | x_t; \theta\}} \tag{17.2a}$$

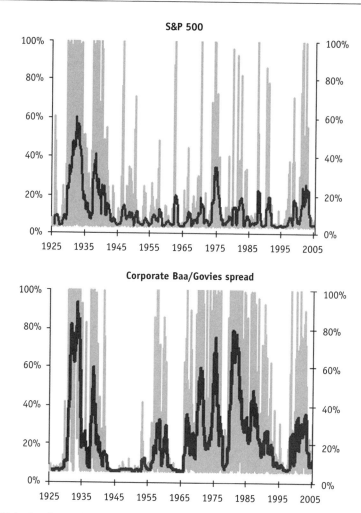

Figure 17.1 Conditional probability of the hectic regime for the core assets (1-year moving average is dark line)

The conditional mean is therefore built as a weighted mean of observations of returns on asset y, with weights calculated as the conditional probabilities of being in either regime according to the core asset. We apply the same method to deduce conditional variance and correlation, denoted respectively as $\sigma^2_{y,s_t=i}$ and $\rho_{xy,s_t=i}$:

$$\sigma^2_{y,s_t=i} = \frac{\displaystyle\sum_{t=1}^{T} \Pr\{s_t = i \mid x_t; \theta\} \times (y_t - \mu_{y,s_t=i})^2}{\displaystyle\sum_{t=1}^{T} \Pr\{s_t = i \mid x_t; \theta\}} \qquad (17.2b)$$

$$\rho_{xy,s_t=i} = \frac{\sum_{t=1}^{T} \Pr\{s_t = i \mid x_t; \theta\} \times (y_t - \mu_{y,s_t=i}) \times (x_t - \mu_{x,s_t=i})}{\sigma_{y,s_t=i}^2 \times \sigma_{x,s_t=i}^2 \times \sum_{t=1}^{T} \Pr\{s_t = i \mid x_t; \theta\}} \qquad (17.2c)$$

where $\mu_{x,s_t=i}$ and $\sigma_{x,s_t=i}^2$ stand respectively for the mean and the variance of x in regime i.

Once the conditional moments are obtained, we test the significance of changes in correlation levels between the two regimes. This issue is crucial in terms of both risk management and asset allocation. In particular, if distributions differ significantly across regimes, an allocation based on unconditional distributions will probably be suboptimal and will result in exposure to losses, especially in stress periods. We follow Kim and Finger (2000) and use Monte Carlo simulation tests. For the mean and the standard deviation, the null hypothesis of the simulation states that x and y are distributed according to a simple multivariate normal distribution and not according to a mixture. For correlation, we run two types of simulations. The first one assumes that returns are derived from a mixture of two normal bivariate distributions, with a different mean and variance but with an equal correlation in the two distributions. The second relies on the same hypothesis but is modified to take into account the potential selection bias that exists when we calculate the statistics by conditioning them on the regime of the core asset (Boyer, Gibson, and Loretan, 1999). The approach here described (in equations 17.2a, 17.2b, and 17.2c) is indeed a "smoothed" form of sample-splitting between low- and high-volatility regimes. We follow Pochon and Teïletche (2005) and split the sample of simulated returns by classifying them according to absolute value. We alternatively compare the correlation in the quiet regime with the correlation obtained for the (x, y) pairings corresponding to the $(1 - \omega)T$ *lowest* absolute observations of x and the correlation of crisis with the correlation obtained for the (x, y) pairings corresponding to the ωT *highest* absolute observations of x. While this way of proceeding is somewhat more extreme, it allows us to gain information about the importance of the selection bias in the analysis of the correlation.

We use two types of data for peripheral assets. We first use FOF indices. Given the competitive nature of the hedge fund industry, indices are key references for managers, because they represent natural benchmarks they seek to outperform. We use indices from the Hedge Fund Research (HFR), from the Center of International Securities and Derivatives Markets (CISDM), and from the Investor Force. HFR provides a composite index and four subindices: (i) the Conservative Index, which contains funds focused primarily on neutral strategies, such as Equity Market Neutral and Fixed Income Arbitrage; (ii) the Diversified Index, which retains funds that are invested in a variety of strategies among multiple managers; (iii) the Market Defensive Index, which represents funds engaged in short-selling strategies, with a view to outperforming in a down-market environment; and

(iv) the Strategic Index, which contains funds more involved in long-bias strategies (Equity, Emerging, Sector). CISDM provides one aggregate index and two subindices (Diversified and Niche). Both HFR and CISDM indices starts from January 1990. Finally, we use the ALTVEST Funds of Funds index from Investor Force, which begins in January 1993. HFR and ALTVEST indices are equal-weighted indices, while CISDM indices are calculated as median returns of the respective strategies. For all indices, our sample terminates in April 2005.

We also use a panel of individual FOFs as alternative peripheral assets. First, although FOF mortality is low (Gregoriou, 2003), FOF indices may reintroduce some measurement problems, such as survivorship and selection biases, albeit to a lower magnitude than single funds. Second, Fung and Hsieh (2002a) point out that exposure to traditional assets can be substantially different for hedge fund indices and typical individual funds. We use the HedgeFund.net-PerTrac database, which includes monthly returns for 1,416 funds of hedge funds as of January 1985 (on July 21, 2005). Because many funds offer short track records, we only consider funds with at least 100 months of performance history, or approximately 8 years. We are left with 182 funds (10 classified in Pertrac as market neutral, 135 as multistrategy, and 37 as single strategy), with an average of 110 monthly observations; virtually all funds are still alive. All returns are net of fees.

17.3.2 Analysis of the mean and variance

Table 17.2 shows the conditional means and standard deviations of hedge fund monthly returns for the various strategies in the case of FOF indices (Panel A) and that of individual FOFs (Panel B). In order to save space, we report only summary statistics for estimations related to individual FOFs and, for each test, the number of times the null hypothesis is rejected. Since fund classification is self-declaratory and can thus be misleading, we do not split our sample accordingly and work on the whole sample of funds. The p-values stand for the probability of wrongly rejecting the null hypothesis of equality in means or standard deviations with its unconditional value. We consider the change as significant if the p-value is lower than 10%.

As expected, the state of the equity market significantly influences the FOF returns. All the indices deliver lower mean returns when the hectic regime prevails in the stock market, with the exception the HFR Defensive Index, which logically performs better in stress periods, due to its short-selling exposures. Apart from this index, the average difference between the unconditional mean and the hectic regime's mean is 0.71% per month, ranging from 0.36% for the CISDM Niche Index to 1.33% for the HFR Strategic Index, which confirms its stronger beta exposure. On the other hand, all the p-values are higher than 10% in the case of the quiet regime, meaning that the conditional means are not significantly different from their unconditional values. Results are broadly similar for individual FOFs. The mean returns associated with the normal regime are not statistically different from their unconditional ones, with no exception. In the hectic regime,

Table 17.2 Estimations and significance tests for a mixture of two normal distributions conditionally on the S&P 500

Panel A: FOF indices

	Mean					Standard deviation				
	Unconditional	Normal regime	p-value	Hectic regime	p-value	Unconditional	Normal regime	p-value	Hectic regime	p-value
HFRI FOF Composite	0.79	0.86	0.54	0.10	0.00	1.62	1.53	0.34	2.14	0.00
HFRI FOF Conservative	0.69	0.73	0.58	0.31	0.00	0.94	0.89	0.31	1.26	0.00
HFRI FOF Diversified	0.74	0.81	0.52	0.01	0.00	1.73	1.65	0.40	2.22	0.00
HFRI FOF Market	0.77	0.77	0.98	0.80	0.87	1.72	1.67	0.58	2.13	0.00
Defensive										
HFRI FOF Strategic	1.06	1.19	0.48	−0.27	0.00	2.60	2.45	0.29	3.45	0.00
CISDM FOF Composite	0.74	0.81	0.49	0.11	0.00	1.23	1.14	0.17	1.75	0.00
CISDM FOF Diversified	0.77	0.83	0.47	0.10	0.00	1.32	1.23	0.20	1.82	0.00
CISDM FOF Niche	0.78	0.82	0.72	0.43	0.00	1.36	1.27	0.21	1.98	0.00
ALTVEST FOF	1.25	1.34	0.66	0.37	0.00	2.31	2.22	0.53	2.83	0.00

Panel B: Individual FOFs

	Mean			Standard deviation		
	Unconditional	Normal regime vs. unconditional (difference)	Hectic regime vs. unconditional (difference)	Unconditional	Normal regime vs. unconditional (ratio)	Hectic regime vs. unconditional (ratio)
All funds: 182						
Mean	0.878	0.069	−0.613	2.258	0.946	1.250
Median	0.862	0.066	−0.598	1.842	0.963	1.201

(*continued*)

Table 17.2 (continued)

Panel B: Individual FOFs

	Mean			Standard deviation		
	Unconditional	Normal regime vs. unconditional (difference)	Hectic regime vs. unconditional (difference)	Unconditional	Normal regime vs. unconditional (ratio)	Hectic regime vs. unconditional (ratio)
Max	1.906	0.481	2.711	9.478	1.028	2.110
Min	−0.084	−0.332	−4.772	0.527	0.790	0.622
# p-value < 0.1	—	0	161	—	32	134
%	—	0%	88%	—	18%	74%
Number of funds with higher mean in hectic periods: 17						
Mean	1.002	−0.109	0.992	3.060	0.973	1.098
Median	1.002	−0.063	0.613	2.937	0.992	1.044
# p-value < 0.1	—	0	11	—	1	10
%	—	0%	65%	—	6%	59%
Number of funds with lower mean in hectic periods: 165						
Mean	0.865	0.087	−0.779	2.175	0.943	1.265
Median	0.849	0.074	−0.668	1.774	0.960	1.226
# p-value < 0.1	—	0	150	—	0	124
%	—	0%	91%	—	0%	75%

Number of funds with lower volatility in hectic periods: 41					
Mean	0.924	0.042	−0.379	2.684	1.001	0.912
Median	0.903	0.047	−0.436	2.038	1.000	0.926
# p-value < 0.1	—	0	28	—	0	14
%	—	0%	68%	—	0%	34%

Number of funds with higher volatility in hectic periods: 141					
Mean	0.864	0.077	−0.682	2.134	0.930	1.348
Median	0.850	0.074	−0.668	1.836	0.942	1.291
# p-value < 0.1	—	0	133	—	32	120
%	—	0%	94%	—	23%	85%

Returns are expressed in percent per month. p-Values are obtained from 5,000 simulations, with the null hypothesis stipulating that the returns are distributed according to a simple normal distribution and refer to two-sided tests. For Panel B, the number of funds showing significant p-values is reported for each stipulated case in addition to the corresponding percentage of the stipulated sample.

88% of the funds exhibit significant changes in mean returns, with an overwhelming majority of funds (82% or 150 out of 182 funds) showing weaker significant mean returns and a minority of short-selling-oriented funds showing higher mean returns (6%, for example, 11 out of 182).

Results are similar for standard deviations. For all the indices (including the HFR Defensive Index) and a vast majority of individual funds (82%), the volatility in the quiet regime is not statistically different from the unconditional volatility estimate. On the contrary, all indices and 66% of the FOFs (120 out of 182) display a significant higher volatility in the hectic regime (8% display a significant lower volatility). Finally, we observe that on average, the increase in standard deviation is slightly more pronounced for indices (with a 35% increase) than for individual funds (25%). All in all, these results justify the hypothesis of a mixture of distributions conditional on the equity market versus that of a single unconditional distribution. For most cases, this reflects both an upsurge in volatility and a decrease in mean returns during hectic periods.

Table 17.3 presents the equivalent results when the Baa/Treasuries spread is used as the core asset. Results are close to those observed with the S&P 500, though slightly less pronounced. With no exceptions, normal mean regime returns again do not prove statistically different from their unconditional estimates. For all the indices but the HFR Defensive and for about 66% of funds, the hectic period is characterized by a significant fall in mean returns as compared to unconditional mean estimates. In these cases, however, the decrease in return is less dramatic than in the case of the S&P 500: For indices, the average decrease in mean returns amounts to 0.32% per month (versus 0.71% for the S&P), whereas for individual funds it amounts to 0.44% (versus 0.78% for the S&P). As far as volatility is concerned, only the HFR indices display significant higher volatilities in hectic periods, whereas CISDM and ALTVEST indices do not. For individual funds, about 50% of them experience a significant increase in volatility in hectic times; in most cases this effect is coupled with a decrease in mean returns. Similarly to the mean effect, the adverse impact on variance in hectic times is substantially lower than in the case of the S&P since, for the funds concerned, the average increase in volatility amounts to only 16% (versus 35% for the S&P).

Modeling FOF returns with a mixture of two normal distributions thus appears particularly relevant. For both FOF indices and most individual FOFs, return distributions are significantly altered in equity and credit hectic periods, with in most cases a decrease in mean and an increase in volatility. These shifts in distributions are substantially more pronounced in the case of the equity markets than in the case of the credit market. Although these results are in line with those obtained by Pochon and Teïletche (2005) on the HFR and CSFB/T hedge fund strategy indices, two interesting differences appear. First, for FOFs the unconditional variance seems a fairly good estimate of the quiet-regime variance, whereas hedge fund strategy indices exhibit both a significant decrease and an increase in volatility across equity regimes. This presumably reflects the greater diversification of funds as well as their goal to minimize variance. Second, most FOFs

Table 17.3 Estimations and significance tests for a mixture of two normal distributions conditionally on the Baa/Treasury spread

Panel A: FOF indices

	Mean					Standard deviation				
	Unconditional	Normal regime	p-value	Hectic regime	p-value	Unconditional	Normal regime	p-value	Hectic regime	p-value
HFRI FOF Composite	0.79	0.87	0.54	0.43	0.00	1.62	1.55	0.46	1.83	0.01
HFRI FOF Conservative	0.69	0.73	0.59	0.52	0.01	0.94	0.90	0.37	1.10	0.00
HFRI FOF Diversified	0.74	0.83	0.50	0.33	0.00	1.73	1.65	0.36	2.00	0.00
HFRI FOF Market Defensive	0.77	0.82	0.72	0.59	0.13	1.72	1.67	0.63	1.90	0.06
HFRI FOF Strategic	1.06	1.17	0.56	0.53	0.00	2.60	2.52	0.57	2.86	0.05
CISDM FOF Composite	0.74	0.81	0.46	0.42	0.00	1.23	1.22	0.90	1.20	0.74
CISDM FOF Diversified	0.77	0.83	0.52	0.48	0.00	1.32	1.28	0.66	1.40	0.21
CISDM FOF Niche	0.78	0.85	0.54	0.50	0.00	1.36	1.36	0.98	1.32	0.60
ALTVEST FOF	1.25	1.31	0.73	0.91	0.08	2.31	2.26	0.78	2.43	0.32

Panel B: Individual FOFs

	Mean			Standard deviation		
	Unconditional	Normal regime vs. unconditional (difference)	Hectic regime vs. unconditional (difference)	Unconditional	Normal regime vs. unconditional (ratio)	Hectic regime vs. unconditional (ratio)
All funds: 182						
Mean	0.878	0.078	−0.352	2.258	0.958	1.107
Median	0.862	0.067	−0.299	1.842	0.966	1.105
Max	1.906	0.525	1.270	9.478	1.058	1.696
Min	−0.084	−0.297	−2.501	0.527	0.691	0.668

(continued)

Table 17.3 (*continued*)

Panel B: Individual FOFs

	Mean			Standard deviation		
	Unconditional	Normal regime vs. unconditional (difference)	Hectic regime vs. unconditional (difference)	Unconditional	Normal regime vs. unconditional (ratio)	Hectic regime vs. unconditional (ratio)
# p-value < 0.1	—	0	128	—	15	104
%	—	0%	70%	—	8%	57%
Number of funds with higher mean in hectic periods: 20						
Mean	1.085	−0.081	0.354	2.993	0.952	1.152
Median	1.003	−0.040	0.177	3.150	0.960	1.144
# p-value < 0.1	—	0	7	—	3	12
%	—	0%	35%	—	15%	60%
Number of funds with lower mean in hectic periods: 162						
Mean	0.852	0.098	−0.439	2.167	0.959	1.102
Median	0.835	0.077	−0.345	1.781	0.967	1.104
# p-value < 0.1	—	0	121	—	12	92
%	—	0%	75%	—	7%	57%
Number of funds with lower volatility in hectic periods: 40						
Mean	0.913	0.061	−0.278	2.100	1.006	0.926
Median	0.828	0.054	−0.260	1.730	1.002	0.953
# p-value < 0.1	—	0	24	—	0	10
%	—	0%	60%	—	0%	25%
Number of funds with higher volatility in hectic periods: 142						
Mean	0.868	0.083	−0.372	2.302	0.945	1.158
Median	0.869	0.071	−0.314	1.951	0.955	1.138
# p-value < 0.1	—	0	104	—	15	94
%	—	0%	73%	—	11%	66%

Compare with Table 17.2.

mean returns seem more sensitive to equity markets than hedge fund strategies mean returns. The latter effect could stem from the diversification process. An explanation is given by Fung and Hsieh, who state that by "diversifying among hedge funds, an investor may be exchanging idiosyncratic hedge fund risk for systematic exposure" (Fung and Hsieh, 2002a). A more basic explanation is the predominance of equity-oriented funds within the hedge fund industry (the long/short equity strategy only represents more than 30% of the universe). If on average managers hold market-strategic portfolios, they will naturally be biased toward equity exposures.

17.3.3 Analysis of the correlation

We finally focus on the correlation coefficient using equation (17.2c). From a risk management point of view, the risk of correlation breakdowns is fundamental. Basically, if the correlation becomes higher (in absolute value) during hectic periods, the portfolio will be more exposed than initially expected and the diversification effect will tend to disappear when it is most needed. For hedge funds this issue is all the more important because they are often sold as powerful diversifying assets to immunize portfolios against downside risk. Moreover, investors should logically expect this diversifying effect to be even more pronounced in the case of FOFs that are diversified portfolios of funds.

Tables 17.4 and 17.5 show the results obtained in the cases of FOF indices (Panel A) and individual FOFs (Panel B) when the core asset is the S&P and the Baa/Treasuries spread. Note that we show two p-values, because we have carried out two simulations; both impose the null hypothesis, according to which the population is drawn from a mixture of two normal bivariate distributions with different parameters, with the exception of the correlation, but the second one takes into account the potential selection bias implied by our conditional approach.

We begin with the first type of p-values (p-values 1). As expected in the hectic regime, in most cases (for example, for nondefensive or short-selling funds) the correlation becomes more positive in the case of the S&P and more negative in the case of the BBB spread. According to the first type of simulations (p-value 1), five FOF indices see their correlations with the S&P significantly altered during equity hectic periods (the HFR Strategic, the HFR Conservative, the CISDM Niche, and the ALTVEST indices, for which the positive correlation increases, and the HFR Market Defensive Index, for which the correlation turns negative). On the contrary, the correlation surprisingly changes for the vast majority of indices in the case of the credit spread. For FOFs, results are more homogeneous: In both cases (S&P and BBB spreads), roughly 60% of the funds see their correlation altered in hectic periods.

These results are, however, largely challenged by the second type of simulations (p-value 2), since no indices and virtually no FOFs display significant p-values. We have mentioned previously that this type of simulation is probably extreme, since we have not conditioned as explicitly but in a rather smoothed manner.

Table 17.4 Conditional correlations with the S&P 500

Panel A: FOF Indices

	Unconditional correlation	Normal regime			Hectic regime		
		Conditional correlation	p-value 1	p-value 2	Conditional correlation	p-value 1	p-value 2
HFRI FOF Composite	0.39	0.37	0.73	0.55	0.45	0.31	0.29
HFRI FOF Conservative	0.44	0.39	0.44	0.75	0.57	0.01	0.45
HFRI FOF Diversified	0.38	0.37	0.88	0.45	0.41	0.59	0.26
HFRI FOF Market Defensive	0.01	0.07	0.44	0.47	−0.15	0.03	0.50
HFRI FOF Strategic	0.42	0.36	0.40	0.84	0.54	0.02	0.46
CISDM FOF Composite	0.49	0.46	0.58	0.53	0.56	0.16	0.23
CISDM FOF Diversified	0.49	0.45	0.59	0.54	0.57	0.11	0.25
CISDM FOF Niche	0.42	0.34	0.24	0.91	0.62	0.00	0.73
ALTVEST FOF	0.48	0.41	0.41	0.83	0.70	0.00	0.86

Panel B: Individual FOFs

	Unconditional correlation	Conditional correlation	
		Normal regime	Hectic regime
All funds: 182			
Mean	0.330	0.300	0.408
Median	0.362	0.323	0.503
Max	0.636	0.582	0.757
Min	−0.561	−0.470	−0.784
# p-value 1 < 0.1	—	8	111
%	—	4%	61%

# p-value 2 < 0.1	—	4	0
%	—	2%	0%
Number of funds with positive unconditional correlation: 170			
Mean	0.363	0.323	0.467
Median	0.374	0.334	0.515
# p-value 1 < 0.1	—	4	100
%	—	2%	59%
# p-value 2 < 0.1	—	1	0
%	—	1%	0%
Number of funds with negative unconditional correlation: 12			
Mean	-0.149	-0.027	-0.426
Median	-0.108	0.011	-0.432
# p-value 1 < 0.1	—	4	11
%	—	33%	92%
# p-value 2 < 0.1	—	3	0
%	—	25%	0%
Number of funds with two distinct correlation regimes according to p-value 1: 8			
Mean	0.167	0.203	0.098
Median	0.194	0.187	0.128
# p-value 1 < 0.1	—	8	8
%	—	100%	100%
# p-value 2 < 0.1	—	4	0
%	—	50%	0%

Returns are expressed in percent per month. p-Value 1 stands for the p-value obtained from 5,000 simulations when the null hypothesis stipulates that the returns are drawn from a mixture of two normal bivariate distributions with different parameters between the regimes, with the exception of the correlation. p-Value 2 stands for the p-value obtained in the simulations where the distribution is the same but where we split the sample of the simulated data according to the absolute value of the return, to take into account the sampling bias. Both p-values refer to two-sided tests. For Panel B, the number of funds showing significant p-values is reported for each stipulated case in addition to the corresponding percentage of the stipulated sample.

Table 17.5 Conditional correlations with the Baa/Treasuries spread

Panel A: FOF indices

	Unconditional correlation	Normal regime			Hectic regime		
		Conditional correlation	p-value 1	p-value 2	Conditional correlation	p-value 1	p-value 2
HFRI FOF Composite	−0.24	−0.09	0.04	0.33	−0.49	0.00	0.55
HFRI FOF Conservative	−0.23	−0.08	0.04	0.33	−0.48	0.00	0.61
HFRI FOF Diversified	−0.25	−0.10	0.03	0.32	−0.51	0.00	0.59
HFRI FOF Market Defensive	−0.03	0.05	0.27	0.37	−0.15	0.09	0.58
HFRI FOF Strategic	−0.19	−0.06	0.09	0.40	−0.41	0.00	0.61
CISDM FOF Composite	−0.17	−0.05	0.12	0.42	−0.39	0.00	0.57
CISDM FOF Diversified	−0.20	−0.08	0.13	0.54	−0.40	0.00	0.73
CISDM FOF Niche	−0.06	0.02	0.30	0.47	−0.17	0.14	0.74
ALVEST FOF	−0.15	−0.09	0.51	0.89	−0.26	0.14	1.00

Panel B: Individual FOFs

	Unconditional correlation	Conditional correlation	
		Normal regime	Hectic regime
All funds: 182			
Mean	−0.165	−0.081	−0.286
Median	−0.180	−0.099	−0.320
Max	0.285	0.220	0.401
Min	−0.415	−0.338	−0.702
# p-value 1 < 0.1	—	31	106
%	—	17%	58%

# p-value 2 < 0.1	—	1	0
%	—	1%	0%
Number of funds with positive unconditional correlation: 23			
Mean	0.111	0.097	0.142
Median	0.112	0.101	0.164
# p-value 1 < 0.1	—	1	6
%	—	4%	26%
# p-value 2 < 0.1	—	0	0
%	—	0%	0%
Number of funds with negative unconditional correlation: 159			
Mean	−0.204	−0.107	−0.348
Median	−0.199	−0.108	−0.357
# p-value 1 < 0.1	—	30	100
%	—	19%	63%
# p-value 2 < 0.1	—	1	0
%	—	1%	0%
Number of funds with two distinct correlation regimes according to p-value 1: 30			
Mean	−0.245	−0.077	−0.457
Median	−0.237	−0.070	−0.472
# p-value 1 < 0.1	—	30	30
%	—	100%	100%
# p-value 2 < 0.1	—	1	0
%	—	3%	0%

Compare with Table 17.4.

As in Pochon and Teïletche (2005), however, these results show ultimately that the apparent change in correlation levels could partly result from a selection bias similar to the one identified by Boyer, Loretan, and Gibson (1999).

17.4   An application to stress testing

We present an application of our results to stress testing. To save space, we only present examples related to the S&P for the FOF indices. We calculate expected returns for hedge fund strategies conditionally on a given shock for the S&P. The shock, denoted by z_t, is expressed as a standardized return in excess of the average. To measure the impact of this shock, we use the standard formula of conditional expectation in a Gaussian linear problem, that is,

$$E(y_t|x_t) = \mu_y + \rho\sigma_y z_t \tag{17.3a}$$

In equation (17.3a), the parameters are not linked to a particular regime, and we restrict its use to the unconditional case reported later for comparison. In contrast, our results show that distribution parameters (mean, standard deviation, and, with less confidence, correlation) are altered during hectic regimes. We thus modify equation (17.3a) accordingly:

$$E(y_t|x_t) = \sum_{i=1}^{2} \Pr\{s_t = i|x_t; \theta\} \times (\mu_{y,s_t=i} + \rho\sigma_{y,s_t=i} z_t) \tag{17.3b}$$

$$E(y_t|x_t) = \sum_{i=1}^{2} \Pr\{s_t = i|x_t; \theta\} \times (\mu_{y,s_t=i} + \rho_{xy,s_t=i}\sigma_{y,s_t=i} z_t) \tag{17.3c}$$

The difference between equation (17.3b) and equation (17.3c) is that the former assumes the correlation remains unchanged in both regimes, while in the latter we relax this assumption. We use both hypotheses because our results in Section 17.3.3 regarding the significance of correlation change are not clear-cut. Table 17.6 shows the results of the application of the preceding formula to three alternative stress scenarios for the S&P shock (expressed as units of standard deviation): $z_t = -10, -5, -2$. Using historical figures from the period 1925–2005 (see Table 17.1), these four shocks correspond to S&P monthly returns of the S&P: -45.2%, -22.4%, and -8.6%. Note that the corresponding conditional probabilities of the S&P, being in a hectic regime, are 100%, 100%, and 88%.

Results are unambiguous. Expected losses are substantially larger when the mixture approach is used, as opposed to a standard unconditional approach. This is all the more true as we allow the correlation to differ across regimes. All in all, the results make clear that the regime approach is not only statistically relevant

Table 17.6 Stress and other scenarios on the S&P 500 and implications for FOF returns

	Parameter values								
	Unconditional			Mixture of Distributions (unchanged correlation) Shock z			Mixture of Distributions (modified correlation)		
	-10	-5	-2	-10	-5	-2	-10	-5	-2
HFRI FOF Composite	-5.575	-2.392	-0.482	-8.329	-4.115	-1.438	-9.588	-4.744	-1.650
HFRI FOF Conservative	-3.440	-1.375	-0.136	-5.242	-2.467	-0.713	-6.953	-3.323	-1.004
HFRI FOF Diversified	-5.880	-2.571	-0.585	-8.480	-4.235	-1.540	-9.120	-4.555	-1.648
HFRI FOF Market Defensive	0.524	0.650	0.725	0.488	0.643	0.734	3.901	2.349	1.314
HFRI FOF Strategic	-9.743	-4.343	-1.103	-14.609	-7.440	-2.864	-19.004	-9.637	-3.606
CISDM FOF Composite	-5.276	-2.266	-0.460	-8.464	-4.175	-1.447	-9.721	-4.804	-1.659
CISDM FOF Diversified	-5.665	-2.450	-0.520	-8.772	-4.337	-1.520	-10.241	-5.072	-1.769
CISDM FOF Niche	-4.891	-2.053	-0.350	-7.836	-3.704	-1.107	-11.871	-5.721	-1.795
ALVEST FOF	-9.720	-4.236	-0.947	-13.099	-6.365	-2.140	-19.588	-9.610	-3.251

Returns are expressed in percent per month. The table reports the application of equations (17.3a) to (17.3c) for various shocks (expressed in terms of standard deviations). Equation (17.3a) is based on unconditional (for example, one single normal distribution) parameter values. Equation (17.3b) assumes that hedge fund returns are drawn from a mixture of two normal distributions, each posting the same correlation with the S&P returns. Equation (17.3c) relaxes this last assumption.

but also truly valuable in terms of risk management, since relying on a simple unconditional analysis may strongly underestimate losses in stress periods.

17.5   Conclusion

Studies dedicated to the market risk of funds of hedge funds are scarce. We proposed a simple Bayesian approach based on mixtures of normal distributions as an alternative approach to hedge fund market risk, and we applied it to FOF returns. Recently applied with success to hedge fund strategies (Pochon and Teïletche, 2005), this model also appears well-adapted to funds of funds returns. Our results indeed show that despite being diversified portfolios of hedge funds, most funds of funds exhibit not only dependence toward standard assets (in our case, equity and corporate credit markets) but also regime-switching behaviors. For FOF indices as well as for a majority of the individual funds of funds we studied, this feature corresponds to significantly lower mean returns and a higher volatility in hectic times. These shifts are more pronounced in the case of equity hectic periods, with the average increase in volatility approximately two times larger than in the case of credit hectic periods. As compared to hedge fund strategies, however, the multiregime risk structure of FOF returns is more concentrated on the mean returns and more dependent on the equity markets. This result may stem from the predominance of equity-oriented funds and thus from the larger average exposure of FOFs to equity markets. In contrast, conditional correlations do not seem significantly altered in hectic periods when the selection bias (implied by our conditional modeling) is properly addressed in significance tests. All in all, our results show that funds of funds display nonlinear exposures to standard assets. In other words, diversification does not provide full protection against downside risks. In the end, our results highlight that using unconditional models such as traditional VaR could be dangerously misleading for gauging market risk, even in the case of diversified funds of hedge funds. Conditional approaches, such as mixtures of distributions, are powerful alternatives and should thus be adopted for stress testing.

References

Agarwal, V. and Naik, N. (2004). Risk and Portfolio Decisions Involving Hedge Funds. *Review of Financial Studies*, 17(1):63–98.

Amin, G. S. and Kat, H. M. (2002). Welcome to the Dark Side: Hedge Fund Attrition and Survivorship Bias over the Period 1994–2001. ISMA Discussion Paper 2002–02, University of Reading, U.K.

Boyer, B., Gibson, M., and Loretan, M. (1999). Pitfalls in Tests for Changes in Correlations. *International Finance Discussion Papers*, No. 597, Board of Governors of the Federal Reserve System.

Brooks, C. and Kat, H. M. (2002). The Statistical Properties of Hedge Fund Index Returns and Their Implications for Investors. *Journal of Alternative Investments*, 5(2):26–44.

Brown, S. J., Goetzmann, W. N., and Ibbotson, R. G. (1999). Offshore Hedge Funds: Survival and Performance, 1989–95. *Journal of Business*, 72(1):91–117.

Brown, S. J., Goetzmann, W. N., and Liang, B. (2003). Fees on Fees in Funds of Fund. NBER Working Paper No. 9464, Cambridge, MA.

Gregoriou, G. N. (2003). The Mortality of Funds of Hedge Funds. *Journal of Wealth Management*, 6(1):42–53.

Gregoriou, G. N. (2004). Are Managers of Funds of Hedge Funds Good Market Timers? *Journal of Wealth Management*, 7(3):61–76.

Fung, W. and Hsieh, D. (1997). Empirical Characteristics of Dynamic Trading Strategies: The Case of Hedge Funds. *Review of Financial Studies*, 10(2):275–302.

Fung, W. and Hsieh, D. (1999). A Primer on Hedge Funds. *Journal of Empirical Finance*, 6(3):309–331.

Fung, W. and Hsieh, D. (2001). The Risk in Hedge Fund Strategies: Theory and Evidence from Trend Followers. *Review of Financial Studies*, 14(2):313–341.

Fung, W. and Hsieh, D. (2002a). Hedge Fund Benchmarks: Information Content and Biases. *Financial Analysts Journal*, 58(1):22–34.

Fung, W. and Hsieh, D. (2002b). Asset-Based Style Factors for Hedge Funds. *Financial Analysts Journal*, 58(5):16–27.

Fung, W. and Hsieh, D. (2004). Hedge Fund Benchmarks: A Risk-Based Approach. *Financial Analysts Journal*, 60(5):65–80.

Hamilton, J. (1994). *Time Series Analysis*, Princeton University Press, Princeton, NJ.

Kazemi, H. and Schneeweis, T. (2003). Conditional Performance of Hedge Funds. Working Paper, University of Massachusetts, Amherst, MA.

Kim, J. and Finger, C. (2000). A Stress Test to Incorporate Correlation Breakdown. *Journal of Risk*, 2(3):6–19.

Liew, J. and French, C. (2005). Quantitative Topics in Hedge Fund Investing. *Journal of Portfolio Management*, 31(4):21–32.

Lo, A. (2001). Risk Management for Hedge Funds: Introduction and Overview. *Financial Analysts Journal*, 57(6):16–33.

Mitchell, M. and Pulvino, T. (2001). Characteristics of Risk in Risk Arbitrage. *Journal of Finance*, 56(6):2135–2175.

Pochon, F. and Teïletche, J. (2005). A Conditional Approach to Hedge Fund Risk. IXIS CIB Special Study 2005–5, Paris, France.

Zangari, P. (1996). An Improved Methodology for Measuring VaR. *RiskMetrics Monitor*, Second Quarter:7–25.

18 Revisiting the Fama and French model: an application to funds of funds using nonlinear methods

Eric Dubé, Clément Gignac, and François-Eric Racicot

Abstract

We examine the monthly returns of funds of funds and of hedge funds for statistical differences between two periods, 1997 to date and 2001 to date. In doing so we seek to determine whether the tech crash has affected the management of funds of funds and hedge funds. We also test for nonlinearity in series of hedge fund returns. The results of such an inquiry could have a nonnegligible influence on the construction of funds of funds. Our inquiry uses various simple asset pricing models. The results show a presence of nonlinearity that in some cases significantly affects estimates of alphas.

18.1 Introduction

Funds of funds have gained in popularity over recent years. This trend is related to the very rapid growth of hedge funds, both in number and in assets under management. Seco (2005) estimates that more than 10,000 active hedge funds now manage more than US$1 trillion in assets. By all indications their popularity will continue to grow in coming years. Liang (1999) and Ackerman, McEnally, and Ravenscraft (1999) showed that hedge funds tend to outperform conventional funds. It is thus no surprise that more and more fund managers are using hedge funds to create funds of funds. The use of hedge funds in a portfolio has also been shown to reduce its volatility (Kat, 2005). There are counterarguments, however. Some researchers have shown that combining hedge funds leads to an increase in the third and fourth moments, skewness and kurtosis, of the distribution of their returns (Amin and Kat, 2003). Also, the unconventional structure of hedge funds leaves portfolio managers with few indicators to aid in selecting them for a fund of funds (FOF). In addition to the four moments of the distribution, there is the alpha. Although debate about this indicator has been widespread, a number of studies tend to show that Jensen's alpha is very useful in capturing abnormal return of hedge funds (Agarwal and Naik, 2004;

Capocci and Hübner, 2004). As has also been demonstrated by Racicot (2003), Racicot and Théoret (2004), and Coën, Desfleurs, Hübner, and Racicot (2005), the alpha estimate can vary widely with the econometric method and type of model used. In this chapter we first investigate whether monthly returns since 2001 for a range of hedge fund management strategies show statistically significant changes from those for a reference period, 1997 to date. Second, we investigate for significant variation in alpha estimates derived according to four different models: Lhabitant's (2004) simple market model, Fama and French's (1993) three-factor model, and two models based on the three-factor model with modifications to capture nonlinear factors.

18.2 Methodology

Since our purpose is to assess the possible effect of nonlinearity on the alpha, we began by choosing different asset pricing models to check for nonlinearity in monthly returns of funds of funds and hedge funds.

We first used the classic simple market model (Lhabitant, 2004). Assuming the dependent variables are measured without error and that pricing errors are homoscedastic and normally distributed, the following market model is estimated with ordinary least squares (OLS):

$$r_t = \alpha + \beta_1 \text{Mkt}_t + \varepsilon_t \qquad\qquad (18.1)$$

where r_t is return in excess of the 13-week U.S. T-bill rate and Mkt_t is the excess return over the 13-week U.S. T-bill rate of the market index proposed by Fama and French (1993).

Our second model is the three-factor asset pricing model of Fama and French (1993):

$$r_t = \alpha + \beta_1 \text{Mkt}_t + \beta_2 \text{SMB}_t + \beta_3 \text{HML}_t + \varepsilon_t \qquad\qquad (18.2)$$

where SMB_t (small minus big) is the factor mimicking size (market equity) and HML_t (high minus low) is the factor mimicking the book-to-market effect. Factors are extracted from French's Website (http://mba.tuck.dartmouth.edu/pages/faculty/ken.french/data_library.html).

We next wanted to test for nonlinearity in the series of returns. This idea is supported by Christie and Huang (1994), who do not think the relationship between returns and market determinants is linear. To this end we modified Fama and French's three-factor model. First we included the square and the cube of the Mkt variable. Given the specification of an OLS, this amounts to considering the effect of cross-skewness and cross-kurtosis:

$$r_t = \alpha + \beta_1 \text{Mkt}_t + \beta_2 \text{Mkt}_t^2 + \beta_3 \text{Mkt}_t^3 + \beta_4 \text{SMB}_t + \beta_5 \text{HML}_t + \varepsilon_t \quad (18.3)$$

For our fourth model we added two other factors to equation (18.3), the squares of SMB and HML:

$$r_t = \alpha + \beta_1 \text{Mkt}_t + \beta_2 \text{Mkt}_t^2 + \beta_3 \text{Mkt}_t^3 + \beta_4 \text{SMB}_t$$
$$+ \beta_5 \text{SMB}_t^2 + \beta_6 \text{HML}_t + \beta_7 \text{HML}_t^2 + \varepsilon_t$$

(18.4)

If our premise is correct, equation (18.4) should increase the precision of the alpha estimate by distributing the nonlinearity among its parameters. In this manner and by testing for nonlinearity in monthly returns, we will be able to measure their change between the period from 1997 to date and the period from 2001 to date.

18.3 Data

The data is from Hedge Fund Research, Inc., and it consists of monthly returns for the following strategies:

Funds of funds (184 funds since 1997, 445 since 2001)
Convertible arbitrage (24 funds since 1997, 49 since 2001)
Distressed securities (20 since 1997, 35 since 2001)
Emerging markets (45 since 1997, 101 since 2001)
Equity hedge (120 since 1997, 326 since 2001)
Equity market neutral (24 since 1997, 61 since 2001)
Equity nonhedge (51 since 1997, 76 since 2001)
Event-driven (31 since 1997, 61 since 2001)
Fixed income (36 since 1997, 87 since 2001)
Foreign exchange (13 since 1997, 23 since 2001)
Macro (24 since 1997, 56 since 2001)
Market timing (7 since 1997, 18 since 2001)
Merger arbitrage (11 since 1997, 27 since 2001)
Relative value arbitrage (18 since 1997, 27 since 2001)
Sector (36 since 1997, 87 since 2001).

In all, stylized facts were observed and regressions were carried out on 644 funds for 1997 to date and 1497 funds for 2001 to date. The data was compiled separately for the two periods. The number of funds in each strategy group is given in parentheses in the preceding list. To avoid duplication, we eliminated funds that correlated more than 99% with another fund. To eliminate survivor bias, we kept in our database and in each of the strategy groups the funds that disappeared during the periods studied. Definitions of each strategy can be found at http://www.hedgefundresearch.com/index.php?fuse=indices-str.

18.4 Results

Table 18.1 presents a comparative study of the moments of distribution of monthly returns of funds of funds and each hedge fund management strategy

Table 18.1 Empirical facts about the monthly returns

	Average		Standard deviation		Skewness		Kurtosis	
	1997	2001	1997	2001	1997	2001	1997	2001
FOF *	0.766	0.505 (0.873)	2.314	1.328 (0.928)	−0.229	−0.236 (0.416)	8.266	3.893 (0.867)
CA	0.715	0.602 (0.875)	1.579	1.466 (0.500)	−0.544	0.076 (0.875)	5.523	4.372 (0.833)
DS	0.690	1.231 (0.150)	2.844	2.578 (0.550)	−0.206	0.106 (0.750)	7.284	5.865 (0.800)
EM	1.280	1.571 (0.454)	8.078	4.627 (0.954)	−0.472	0.125 (0.568)	9.920	4.514 (0.886)
EH	1.106	0.658 (0.841)	5.556	3.929 (0.933)	0.399	0.048 (0.283)	5.718	4.243 (0.758)
EMN	0.585	0.423 (0.875)	2.490	2.061 (0.875)	0.031	0.020 (0.625)	4.101	4.435 (0.500)
ENH	1.280	0.889 (0.765)	6.549	5.236 (0.824)	0.080	−0.118 (0.510)	4.985	3.644 (0.824)
ED	0.826	0.783 (0.710)	3.703	2.886 (0.839)	−0.700	−0.243 (0.677)	8.050	5.179 (0.742)
FI	0.705	0.787 (0.676)	2.599	2.086 (0.676)	−1.448	0.146 (0.706)	14.447	5.769 (0.706)
FX	0.714	0.643 (0.923)	3.315	2.900 (0.692)	0.996	0.741 (0.308)	6.599	5.709 (0.769)
MC	0.811	0.890 (0.682)	4.071	3.752 (0.773)	0.385	0.098 (0.409)	6.658	4.211 (0.682)
MT	1.073	0.528 (0.857)	4.046	3.262 (0.714)	0.729	−0.103 (0.286)	4.998	4.058 (0.571)
MA	0.595	0.310 (1.000)	1.543	1.238 (0.818)	−0.443	−0.620 (0.636)	6.709	7.453 (0.636)
RVA	0.879	0.644 (0.875)	1.845	1.763 (1.000)	−0.824	0.035 (0.625)	10.891	5.988 (0.688)
SC	0.993	0.710 (0.686)	6.442	4.982 (0.886)	0.051	−0.082 (0.400)	6.583	4.341 (0.629)
Mean	0.875	0.762	3.904	3.055	−0.141	0.016	7.319	4.984

*The numbers in parentheses indicate the following facts: percentage of funds that have an average return that is weaker in 2001 than in 1997, a standard deviation that is weaker in 2001 than in 1997, a reduction in the symmetry of the distribution and a flattening of the distribution tails; e.g., (0.886) = 88.6%. FOF = funds of funds, CA = convertible arbitrage, DS = distressed securities, EM = emerging market, EH = equity hedge, EMN = equity market neutral, ENH = equity non-hedge, ED = event-driven, FI = fixed income, FX = foreign exchange, MC = macro, MT = market timing, MA = merger arbitrage, RVA = relative value arbitrage, SC = sector.

over the two periods under study, 1997 to date (reference period) and 2001 to date (current period). The data outside parentheses in Table 18.1 shows average return, standard deviation, skewness, and kurtosis for each strategy in each period. The numbers in parentheses are, for each of these four parameters, the proportions of the funds appearing in both periods that have absolute values lower in the current period than in the reference period. On the basis of Table 18.1 we make the following general observations about the current period: Average monthly return is lower, standard deviation is lower, and distribution of returns is more symmetrical (less skewed) and thinner-tailed (kurtosis closer to that of a normal distribution). This implies that, statistically, the hedge fund market is less risky today than in the past. We note that the improvement in management did not come at the expense of return. The Sharpe ratio rose from 0.224 for the reference period to 0.249 for the current period, indicating a small improvement in the risk-adjusted return. Among funds of funds, 87.3% had a lower monthly return in the current period; their average monthly return fell to 0.505% from 0.766%. Standard deviation was lower for 92.8% of the funds of funds in the current period, with the average declining to 1.328 from 2.314. In the higher moments, the funds of funds showed similar leftward skews in the two periods: -0.229 in the reference period and -0.236 in the current period. Their kurtosis declined impressively. The data for the funds of funds suggests fairly thick tails in the base period and much thinner tails in the current period, in which kurtosis is close to that of a normal distribution — an average 3.893. Among the 14 hedge fund strategies, as Table 18.1 shows, only the nonhedge strategy is flatter-tailed than the funds of funds in the current period. As Kat (2005) explains, the improvement in kurtosis visible in the table might be due in part to the addition of options to hedge fund strategies. However, adding options often means introducing nonlinearity.

We next consider the regression results obtained for each of the four equations set out earlier. Table 18.2 shows the results for the first equation, the simple market model. Average adjusted R^2 for all strategies is 0.171 for the reference period and 0.175 for the current period, well below the results obtained by Coën, Desfleurs, Hübner and Racicot (2005) in regressions on indexes. One possible explanation of the divergence is that hedge fund indexes are generally better at diluting outliers from normal trends. In our analysis we give as much weight to funds that have gone bankrupt as to those that are doing well. As Table 18.2 also indicates, abnormal return seems higher for the current period, with a monthly alpha of 0.58% compared to 0.45% in the reference period. Although there were some changes in the significance of the coefficients (the merger arbitrage strategy no longer seems to generate abnormal returns), we can conclude that there is no major difference between the two periods in this regard. Net market return seems to influence monthly return in most strategies.

Table 18.3 shows the results for equation (18.2), the three-factor model. Adjusted R^2 is higher than for the simple market model, averaging 0.238 and 0.219, respectively, for the periods under review. On average the hedge fund managers appear to be generating less abnormal return since 2001. The same

Table 18.2 Results for equation (18.1)

	R^2 adjusted		Alpha		Mkt	
	1997	2001	1997	2001	1997	2001
FOF* **	0.226	0.172	0.366	0.324	0.209	0.092
			(2.561)	(2.367)	(5.521)	(3.420)
CA	0.043	0.016	0.383	0.419	0.063	0.039
			(2.740)	(3.092)	(1.914)	(1.063)
DS	0.092	0.114	0.573	1.049	0.158	0.146
			(2.565)	(3.941)	(3.090)	(2.533)
EM	0.245	0.224	0.608	1.390	0.806	0.456
			(1.091)	(2.934)	(5.756)	(3.971)
EH	0.284	0.261	0.581	0.487	0.488	0.388
			(1.579)	(1.615)	(6.649)	(4.512)
EMN	0.148	0.125	0.226	0.242	0.122	(0.019)
			(1.553)	(2.114)	(4.505)	(2.987)
ENH	0.408	0.472	0.631	0.711	0.761	0.726
			(1.463)	(1.636)	(9.156)	(7.808)
ED	0.245	0.268	0.354	0.602	0.368	0.321
			(2.456)	(2.346)	(5.792)	(4.630)
FI	0.124	0.125	0.331	0.604	0.149	0.110
			(2.752)	(4.122)	(3.250)	(2.629)
FX	(0.006)	(0.003)	0.412	0.461	(0.003)	(0.034)
			(1.358)	(1.231)	(0.538)	(0.813)
MC	0.099	0.110	0.439	0.708	0.154	0.078
			(1.471)	(1.647)	(3.107)	(2.516)
MT	0.293	0.281	0.558	0.346	0.462	0.401
			(1.832)	(2.442)	(6.577)	(4.707)
MA	0.152	0.125	0.237	0.128	0.117	0.108
			(2.313)	(1.198)	(4.255)	(2.823)
RVA	0.045	0.056	0.554	0.462	0.047	0.057
			(3.585)	(2.630)	(1.927)	(1.659)
SC	0.229	0.281	0.420	0.535	0.585	0.569
			(1.395)	(1.679)	(5.517)	(4.727)
Mean	0.171	0.175	0.451	0.582	0.305	0.239
			(2.011)	(2.331)	(4.431)	(3.384)

*Regression coefficients.
**t-statistic.

is true of funds of funds, where the current-period alpha is not significant at a 90% confidence level, compared to a reference-period alpha significant at 95% confidence. The market factors SMB and HML do not seem, on average, to have affected monthly return significantly in the current period, but they have done so with a 95% confidence level in the reference period. For mean SMB, the t-statistic is 2.170, for mean HML 1.964. This is a generalization, however.

The 76 funds of the nonhedge equity strategy, for example, were on average affected by SMB in the current period. These results thus discredit, at least in part, the simple market model for some strategies. Its bias in these cases makes it unreliable for optimal portfolio allocation.

Table 18.4 presents the results for equation (18.3), the three-factor model with nonlinearity in the Mkt variable. R^2 adjusted for the two periods is larger than that for equations (18.1) and (18.2). For the hedge fund strategies as a whole, it can be said with 95% confidence that abnormal return no longer seems to be a significant factor in monthly return. Neither do the FOFs appear to generate abnormal return for the current period, though they do for the reference period. Although the t-statistics (level of confidence 95%) show that on average the variables Mkt^2 and Mkt^3 do not affect monthly average return, they do so for some strategies. For example, the convertible arbitrage strategy shows nonlinearity in Mkt^2 for both current and reference periods. The FOFs, with respective t-statistics of 0.712 and 1.364 for 1997 and 1.037 and 1.105 for 2001, do not appear to follow a nonlinear specification in Mkt^2 and Mkt^3.

Table 18.5 presents the results for equation (18.4), which provides for non-linearity in Mkt, SMB, and HML. The R^2 adjusted is higher still, 0.283 for 1997 and 0.271 for 2001. With this specification, we note that FOFs generate abnormal return with a 90% degree of confidence. If we exclude the convertible arbitrage strategy, which shows signs of nonlinearity in Mkt^2 for the current period, we can say that on average, none of the investment strategies shows nonlinearity in either the current or the reference period. For the reference period the average t-statistic for all hedge strategies is 0.981 for Mkt^2, 1.415 for Mkt^3, 0.948 for SMB^2, and 1.161 for HML^2. For the current period the average t-statistic is 1.009 for Mkt^2, 1.057 for Mkt^3, 1.132 SMB^2, and 1.181 for HML^2. The story is the same for the FOFs.

At first glance these results appear inconclusive. They clearly demonstrate that many variables posited to capture nonlinearity were not significant. The same applies to SMB and HML in Eqs. (18.2), (18.3), and (18.4). It should be kept in mind, however, that these are results from 8,564 distinct regressions, grouped into big-picture averages. But a manager creating an FOF looks at funds individually, not as a group. To take this reality into account, we created a series of tables that provide results based more on an analysis of individual types of funds.

Table 18.6 shows the proportion of funds in each strategy category whose regressors (excluding nonlinearity) are significant with 95% confidence. For the simple market model, equation (18.1), we note that there are more funds with abnormal return for the current period, 45.4%, than for the reference period, 40.4%. For FOFs the proportions for the two periods are practically identical. For the three-factor model, Table 18.6 indicates that 30.8% of funds generated some alpha since 2001, compared to 38.7% since 1997. It also indicates that in the current period, SMB was significant with 95% confidence for 25.2% of funds and HML was significant for 18.8%. This result highlights an

Table 18.3 Results for equation (18.2)

	R² adjusted		Alpha		Mkt		SMB		HML	
	1997	2001	1997	2001	1997	2001	1997	2001	1997	2001
FOF* **	0.323	0.225	0.351 (2.629)	0.200 (1.568)	0.168 (4.961)	0.067 (2.793)	0.131 (2.877)	0.079 (1.683)	0.055 (2.030)	0.037 (1.205)
CA	0.093	0.099	0.341 (2.541)	0.180 (2.026)	0.052 (1.699)	0.002 (0.863)	0.094 (2.135)	0.086 (1.257)	0.028 (1.385)	0.136 (1.836)
DS	0.179	0.166	0.510 (2.310)	0.836 (2.922)	0.135 (2.833)	0.105 (1.847)	0.152 (2.760)	0.119 (1.459)	0.026 (2.165)	0.076 (1.383)
EM	0.274	0.265	0.472 (1.000)	1.008 (2.144)	0.758 (5.175)	0.380 (3.236)	0.330 (1.980)	0.229 (1.524)	0.056 (0.935)	0.120 (1.074)
EH	0.399	0.331	0.506 (1.553)	0.149 (1.198)	0.427 (6.354)	0.320 (3.951)	0.278 (2.995)	0.207 (1.826)	0.027 (2.771)	0.102 (1.557)
EMN	0.233	0.182	0.260 (1.793)	0.299 (2.083)	0.117 (4.794)	0.013 (2.856)	0.037 (1.978)	0.011 (1.161)	0.045 (2.770)	0.065 (1.632)
ENH	0.519	0.540	0.491 (1.295)	0.282 (1.129)	0.701 (9.507)	0.633 (7.114)	0.364 (3.597)	0.353 (2.531)	0.039 (2.999)	0.020 (1.370)
ED	0.330	0.326	0.210 (2.346)	0.225 (1.559)	0.343 (5.636)	0.251 (3.809)	0.280 (3.145)	0.182 (1.622)	0.107 (2.081)	0.164 (1.425)

FI	0.148	0.151	0.285 (2.615)	0.456 (3.496)	0.136 (3.287)	0.083 (2.299)	0.102 (1.764)	0.067 (1.114)	0.026 (1.168)	0.070 (1.224)
FX	(0.001)	(0.012)	0.413 (1.358)	0.412 (1.160)	0.009 (0.538)	0.048 (0.776)	0.031 (1.054)	0.067 (0.887)	0.020 (0.971)	(0.023) (0.573)
MC	0.130	0.122	0.426 (1.484)	0.555 (1.304)	0.121 (2.855)	0.045 (2.311)	0.103 (1.285)	0.123 (1.187)	0.046 (1.056)	0.015 (0.829)
MT	0.404	0.306	0.585 (2.159)	0.230 (2.015)	0.372 (5.686)	0.367 (4.178)	0.186 (2.296)	0.163 (1.492)	0.189 (2.829)	(0.059) (0.775)
MA	0.161	0.147	0.226 (2.220)	0.053 (0.974)	0.116 (3.966)	0.091 (2.222)	0.020 (0.935)	0.067 (1.324)	0.010 (1.450)	0.000 (0.804)
RVA	0.083	0.100	0.533 (3.441)	0.303 (1.929)	0.043 (1.742)	0.026 (1.390)	0.043 (1.906)	0.084 (1.091)	0.014 (1.295)	0.061 (1.300)
SC	0.374	0.344	0.296 (1.381)	0.189 (1.353)	0.520 (5.607)	0.496 (4.056)	0.353 (2.815)	0.266 (1.921)	0.013 (3.548)	0.037 (1.354)
Mean	0.238	0.219	0.394 (2.008)	0.358 (1.791)	0.268 (4.382)	0.187 (2.913)	0.158 (2.170)	0.140 (1.472)	0.002 (1.964)	0.046 (1.223)

* Regression coefficients.

** t-statistic.

Table 18.4 Results for equation (18.3)

	R^2 adjusted		Alpha		Mkt		Mkt^2		Mkt^3		SMB		HML	
	1997	2001	1997	2001	1997	2001	1997	2001	1997	2001	1997	2001	1997	2001
FOF*	0.357	0.238	0.422	0.272	0.122	0.114	-0.001	-0.004	0.001	-0.001	0.126	0.068	-0.056	0.037
**			(2.227)	(1.544)	(2.682)	(1.940)	(0.712)	(1.037)	(1.364)	(1.105)	(2.832)	(1.413)	(2.068)	(1.228)
CA	0.156	0.178	0.167	-0.115	-0.026	-0.060	0.011	0.153	0.001	0.001	0.098	0.109	0.027	0.128
			(1.275)	(1.612)	(1.199)	(1.047)	(2.081)	(2.312)	(2.658)	(1.140)	(2.338)	(1.656)	(1.425)	(1.787)
DS	0.242	0.177	0.829	0.984	0.051	0.058	-0.010	-0.006	0.001	0.001	0.136	0.121	0.023	0.087
			(2.962)	(2.812)	(1.258)	(0.896)	(1.205)	(0.847)	(1.072)	(0.787)	(2.573)	(1.408)	(2.194)	(1.433)
EM	0.334	0.270	0.711	1.258	0.481	0.293	0.002	-0.011	0.004	0.001	0.312	0.235	0.050	0.134
			(1.014)	(1.948)	(2.428)	(1.477)	(0.794)	(0.805)	(2.197)	(0.932)	(1.982)	(1.523)	(0.956)	(1.126)
EH	0.412	0.343	0.386	0.211	0.437	0.422	0.005	-0.004	0.000	-0.002	0.283	0.186	-0.026	0.099
			(1.069)	(1.176)	(4.045)	(2.304)	(0.811)	(0.866)	(1.164)	(1.053)	(3.059)	(1.665)	(2.781)	(1.582)
EMN	0.250	0.195	0.133	0.262	0.065	-0.007	0.008	0.002	0.001	0.000	-0.034	0.011	-0.045	-0.066
			(1.108)	(1.763)	(3.194)	(1.542)	(1.122)	(0.934)	(1.464)	(1.023)	(1.931)	(1.220)	(2.794)	(1.647)
ENH	0.525	0.552	0.415	0.424	0.683	0.813	0.004	-0.008	0.000	0.003	0.366	0.314	0.039	0.015
			(0.819)	(1.000)	(5.868)	(3.851)	(0.784)	(0.909)	(1.150)	(1.039)	(3.603)	(2.260)	(3.016)	(1.410)
ED	0.380	0.339	0.583	0.436	0.302	0.331	-0.014	-0.012	0.000	-0.002	0.263	0.159	0.103	0.168
			(2.471)	(1.596)	(2.725)	(2.422)	(1.014)	(1.089)	(1.478)	(1.116)	(3.046)	(1.421)	(2.108)	(1.452)

FI	0.179	0.160	0.392	0.477	0.116	0.014	−0.004	60.897	0.000	0.001	0.097	0.078	0.025	0.074
			(2.349)	(2.906)	(2.322)	(1.370)	(0.943)	(0.859)	(1.341)	(0.925)	(1.674)	(1.103)	(1.205)	(1.259)
FX	−0.010	−0.010	0.477	0.380	−0.008	−0.082	−0.002	0.002	0.000	0.001	−0.034	0.074	0.019	−0.022
			(0.967)	(0.907)	(0.334)	(0.697)	(0.631)	(0.900)	(0.504)	(0.671)	(1.058)	(0.937)	(0.973)	(0.552)
MC	0.155	0.126	0.341	0.538	0.107	0.095	0.004	0.000	0.000	−0.001	0.106	0.115	−0.046	0.012
			(1.040)	(1.042)	(2.233)	(1.182)	(0.774)	(0.793)	(1.208)	(0.848)	(1.320)	(1.126)	(1.068)	(0.834)
MT	0.420	0.338	0.333	0.139	0.478	0.628	0.006	0.000	−0.001	−0.004	0.200	0.119	−0.186	−0.075
			(1.218)	(1.393)	(4.910)	(3.337)	(0.856)	(0.828)	(1.175)	(1.516)	(2.479)	(1.240)	(2.837)	(0.890)
MA	0.205	0.169	0.381	0.213	0.069	0.146	−0.004	−0.009	0.001	−0.001	0.013	0.050	0.008	0.003
			(2.461)	(1.334)	(1.455)	(1.603)	(0.774)	(1.465)	(1.135)	(0.981)	(0.833)	(1.079)	(1.210)	(0.796)
RVA	0.132	0.123	0.600	0.318	0.009	0.028	−0.001	−0.001	0.000	0.000	0.039	0.083	0.014	0.061
			(2.697)	(1.659)	(0.996)	(1.093)	(0.912)	(1.134)	(1.899)	(0.967)	(1.902)	(1.114)	(1.338)	(1.279)
SC	0.389	0.350	0.419	0.276	0.476	0.585	−0.003	−0.006	0.001	−0.002	0.347	0.247	0.012	0.036
			(1.163)	(1.234)	(3.170)	(2.132)	(0.660)	(0.619)	(1.031)	(1.020)	(2.785)	(1.856)	(3.569)	(1.376)
Mean	0.269	0.236	0.440	0.414	0.231	0.233	0.000	4.357	0.001	0.001	0.157	0.136	0.001	0.047
			(1.615)	(1.599)	(2.581)	(1.782)	(0.954)	(1.026)	(1.391)	(1.001)	(2.185)	(1.401)	(1.962)	(1.245)

*Regression coefficients.

**t-statistic.

Table 18.5 Results for equation (18.4)

	R^2 adjusted		Alpha		Mkt		Mkt^2		Mkt^3
	1997	2001	1997	2001	1997	2001	1997	2001	1997
FOF* **	0.369	0.291	0.425 (2.079)	0.361 (1.932)	0.126 (2.774)	0.112 (2.025)	−0.002 (0.759)	−0.003 (0.963)	0.001 (1.333)
CA	0.178	0.206	0.087 (0.882)	0.038 (1.434)	−0.027 (1.239)	−0.071 (1.160)	0.010 (1.970)	0.014 (2.101)	0.001 (2.662)
DS	0.246	0.236	0.830 (2.809)	1.062 (3.015)	0.048 (1.294)	0.057 (0.904)	−0.009 (1.227)	−0.005 (0.822)	0.001 (1.003)
EM	0.332	0.280	0.446 (0.824)	1.205 (1.788)	0.464 (2.400)	0.304 (1.511)	0.004 (0.826)	−0.007 (0.782)	0.004 (2.260)
EH	0.426	0.387	0.393 (1.141)	0.296 (1.203)	0.442 (4.113)	0.423 (2.398)	0.003 (0.814)	−0.003 (0.882)	0.000 (1.200)
EMN	0.260	0.274	0.239 (1.375)	0.354 (1.815)	0.072 (3.131)	−0.009 (1.614)	0.007 (1.109)	0.002 (1.027)	0.001 (1.350)
ENH	0.538	0.586	0.436 (0.967)	0.475 (1.058)	0.683 (5.896)	0.816 (4.086)	0.005 (0.827)	−0.004 (0.877)	0.000 (1.185)
ED	0.397	0.392	0.648 (2.420)	0.578 (2.012)	0.308 (2.860)	0.327 (2.499)	−0.015 (1.128)	−0.011 (1.069)	0.000 (1.405)
FI	0.198	0.191	0.443 (2.376)	0.552 (2.754)	0.120 (2.415)	0.012 (1.394)	−0.004 (1.028)	0.001 (0.841)	0.000 (1.421)
FX	−0.02	−0.01	0.471 (1.062)	0.473 (0.952)	−0.009 (0.312)	−0.087 (0.698)	−0.002 (0.652)	0.001 (0.899)	0.000 (0.536)
MC	0.163	0.125	0.398 (1.149)	0.430 (0.829)	0.112 (2.223)	0.103 (1.190)	0.003 (0.757)	0.001 (0.810)	0.000 (1.202)
MT	0.433	0.352	0.376 (1.235)	0.167 (1.456)	0.490 (5.026)	0.628 (3.394)	0.003 (0.794)	0.001 (0.859)	−0.001 (1.306)
MA	0.231	0.221	0.392 (2.356)	0.348 (1.881)	0.074 (1.514)	0.142 (1.594)	−0.006 (1.018)	−0.008 (1.421)	0.000 (1.037)
RVA	0.165	0.169	0.495 (2.148)	0.373 (1.748)	0.006 (1.035)	0.023 (1.121)	−0.002 (0.933)	−0.002 (1.087)	0.001 (1.960)
SC	0.404	0.383	0.356 (1.098)	0.306 (1.303)	0.480 (3.237)	0.584 (2.188)	−0.006 (0.651)	−0.006 (0.655)	0.000 (1.056)
Mean	0.282	0.271	0.429 (1.560)	0.475 (1.661)	0.233 (2.621)	0.232 (1.839)	−0.001 (0.981)	−0.002 (1.009)	0.001 (1.415)

*Regression coefficients.
**t-statistic.

(continued)

important finding: Although the average t-statistics presented in Table 18.3 show a general nonsignificance of SMB and HML, they affect the monthly return of some funds.

This confirms that in several cases the simple market model is biased. Table 18.7 presents the same information as Table 18.6 for the two models with non-linearity, equations (18.3) and (18.4). As it shows, the alphas for the current period are significant for 27.0% (equation 18.3) and 30.3% (equation 18.4) of funds in all strategies combined. This contradicts the general results showing no abnormal return with these two models. SMB and HML are significant factors

Table 18.5 Results for equation (18.4) (*continued*)

2001	SMB		SMB^2		HML		HML^2	
	1997	2001	1997	2001	1997	2001	1997	2001
−0.001	0.113	0.110	−0.005	−0.012	−0.054	0.083	0.005	−0.005
(1.262)	(2.426)	(2.129)	(1.007)	(1.428)	(2.069)	(1.420)	(1.432)	(1.099)
0.001	0.078	0.131	0.000	−0.016	0.036	0.019	0.004	0.017
(1.216)	(1.750)	(1.785)	(0.625)	(1.199)	(1.619)	(0.613)	(1.235)	(1.505)
0.000	0.146	0.162	0.004	−0.012	0.023	0.139	−0.003	−0.007
(0.835)	(2.620)	(1.999)	(0.899)	(1.554)	(1.993)	(1.529)	(0.785)	(1.057)
0.001	0.292	0.273	0.019	0.001	0.071	0.335	−0.002	−0.029
(0.920)	(1.795)	(1.515)	(0.765)	(0.623)	(0.998)	(1.310)	(0.602)	(1.115)
−0.002	0.265	0.231	−0.007	−0.012	−0.024	0.168	0.006	−0.009
(1.164)	(2.710)	(1.798)	(1.191)	(0.985)	(2.756)	(1.603)	(1.368)	(1.432)
0.000	−0.026	0.054	−0.008	−0.013	−0.053	−0.025	0.001	−0.005
(1.121)	(1.766)	(1.479)	(1.180)	(1.338)	(2.882)	(1.513)	(0.983)	(1.585)
−0.003	0.373	0.387	0.000	−0.013	0.037	0.221	−0.001	−0.028
(1.151)	(3.434)	(2.490)	(1.090)	(1.022)	(2.937)	(1.781)	(1.122)	(1.574)
−0.002	0.257	0.209	−0.008	−0.018	0.100	0.175	0.004	0.001
(1.226)	(2.858)	(2.114)	(1.167)	(1.529)	(1.987)	(1.432)	(1.337)	(1.221)
0.001	0.096	0.111	−0.005	−0.010	0.022	0.099	0.002	−0.003
(0.955)	(1.578)	(1.320)	(1.092)	(1.139)	(1.292)	(1.093)	(1.144)	(1.089)
0.001	−0.032	0.096	0.001	−0.011	0.012	−0.057	−0.001	0.006
(0.644)	(1.197)	(1.029)	(0.636)	(0.659)	(0.914)	(0.884)	(0.365)	(0.935)
−0.001	0.104	0.106	−0.006	0.010	−0.049	0.101	0.003	−0.014
(0.844)	(1.113)	(1.064)	(0.708)	(0.795)	(1.092)	(0.894)	(0.817)	(0.815)
−0.004	0.170	0.136	−0.014	−0.004	−0.183	−0.048	0.011	−0.003
(1.567)	(1.983)	(1.222)	(0.997)	(1.139)	(2.781)	(0.847)	(1.614)	(0.760)
−0.001	0.001	0.107	−0.005	−0.018	0.010	0.040	0.004	−0.003
(1.061)	(0.602)	(1.852)	(1.122)	(1.763)	(1.218)	(0.830)	(1.995)	(0.762)
0.000	0.019	0.079	0.003	−0.005	0.024	−0.022	0.003	0.013
(1.035)	(1.554)	(1.285)	(0.894)	(1.187)	(1.541)	(1.113)	(1.249)	(1.272)
−0.002	0.309	0.257	−0.007	−0.004	0.022	0.034	0.010	0.001
(1.061)	(2.407)	(1.731)	(0.906)	(0.914)	(3.432)	(1.482)	(1.635)	(1.416)
−0.001	0.146	0.167	−0.003	−0.009	0.003	0.084	0.003	−0.005
(1.057)	(1.955)	(1.620)	(0.948)	(1.132)	(1.960)	(1.209)	(1.161)	(1.181)

in more than 19% of funds for the models for equations (18.3) and (18.4). Among FOFs, abnormal return is significant for 29.6% of cases with the equation (18.3) model and 45.8% of cases with the equation (18.4) model.

Table 18.8 shows, for each strategy, the proportion of funds showing nonlinearity (at a 95% confidence level). For the current period, 13.1% of the funds show Mkt^2 nonlinearity and 12.6% show Mkt^3 nonlinearity. Mkt^2 nonlinearity is more common for 2001 to date, and Mkt^3 nonlinearity is more common for 1997 to date. For the current period, 19.3% of the funds show SMB^2 nonlinearity and 18.4% show HML^2 nonlinearity. SMB^2 nonlinearity is more

Table 18.6 Alpha, SMB, and HML

| | Equation (18.1) | | Equation (18.2) | | | | | |
| | 1997 | 2001 | 1997 | | | 2001 | | |
	Alpha	Alpha	Alpha	SMB	HML	Alpha	SMB	HML
FOF*	0.559	0.552	0.543	0.684	0.385	0.301	0.301	0.200
CA	0.791	0.591	0.708	0.541	0.208	0.204	0.142	0.408
DS	0.550	0.857	0.500	0.550	0.550	0.628	0.228	0.142
EM	0.156	0.683	0.156	0.511	0.089	0.445	0.287	0.118
EH	0.300	0.349	0.316	0.683	0.600	0.187	0.377	0.322
EMN	0.125	0.213	0.125	0.458	0.541	0.213	0.196	0.344
ENH	0.352	0.355	0.196	0.725	0.607	0.171	0.578	0.263
ED	0.612	0.507	0.612	0.774	0.483	0.285	0.301	0.238
FI	0.416	0.712	0.333	0.250	0.138	0.597	0.183	0.172
FX	0.230	0.304	0.230	0.153	0.000	0.268	0.043	0.000
MC	0.208	0.375	0.208	0.250	0.208	0.267	0.107	0.017
MT	0.428	0.277	0.571	0.428	0.714	0.277	0.333	0.055
MA	0.545	0.259	0.545	0.090	0.181	0.111	0.222	0.037
RVA	0.722	0.533	0.666	0.444	0.333	0.400	0.133	0.288
SC	0.222	0.344	0.250	0.638	0.805	0.252	0.402	0.229
Mean	0.404	0.454	0.387	0.464	0.390	0.308	0.252	0.188

*Proportion of funds in each strategy category whose regressors are significant with 95% confidence, e.g., (0.886) = 88.6%.

common for 2001 to date, and HML^2 nonlinearity shows up in about the same proportion of funds in the two periods. This result is important because it shows the existence of nonlinear effects on monthly hedge fund returns, which were not evident from the t-statistics of Tables 18.3 and 18.4.

Furthermore, the addition of nonlinear parameters has a direct effect on R^2 adjusted. This effect is shown in Table 18.9, listing average R^2 adjusted for each hedge fund strategy. The numbers in parentheses indicate the proportion of funds whose R^2 adjusted was higher with the addition of nonlinearity than in the three-factor model. For equation (18.3), R^2 adjusted was higher for 54.5% of all funds in the current period and for 69.4% of all funds in the reference period. For equation (18.4), the respective proportions are 73.3% and 76.9%. The foreign exchange strategy seems to stand alone, in that none of the equations seem capable of explaining any significant part of the monthly returns of this type of fund. This may be related to the extreme speculation found in currency markets.

Having confirmed that nonlinearity exists in the series of monthly hedge fund returns and that R^2 adjusted rises significantly when it is included, we investigate its potential effect on the alpha. Tables 18.10 and 18.11 present the average difference in alphas relative to the three-factor model for the funds whose

Table 18.7 Alpha, SMB, and HML

| | Equation (18.3) | | | | | | Equation (18.4) | | | | | |
| | 1997 | | | 2001 | | | 1997 | | | 2001 | | |
	Alpha	SMB	HML	Alpha	SMB	HML	Alpha	SMB	HML	Alpha	SMB	HML
FOF*	0.532	0.706	0.407	0.296	0.200	0.206	0.456	0.548	0.440	0.458	0.507	0.242
CA	0.250	0.500	0.250	0.122	0.387	0.326	0.125	0.375	0.375	0.102	0.387	0.040
DS	0.800	0.550	0.550	0.742	0.228	0.200	0.650	0.550	0.500	0.742	0.571	0.342
EM	0.111	0.489	0.089	0.455	0.297	0.118	0.089	0.467	0.044	0.366	0.257	0.158
EH	0.158	0.733	0.600	0.159	0.337	0.325	0.141	0.658	0.600	0.205	0.361	0.337
EMN	0.083	0.416	0.625	0.213	0.196	0.327	0.167	0.291	0.583	0.213	0.262	0.295
ENH	0.078	0.745	0.607	0.118	0.473	0.289	0.156	0.705	0.607	0.157	0.500	0.407
ED	0.548	0.774	0.548	0.269	0.222	0.238	0.580	0.677	0.419	0.507	0.539	0.253
FI	0.388	0.194	0.138	0.517	0.195	0.229	0.361	0.222	0.138	0.551	0.264	0.137
FX	0.153	0.230	0.000	0.086	0.043	0.000	0.076	0.153	0.076	0.086	0.087	0.130
MC	0.083	0.208	0.208	0.142	0.107	0.017	0.208	0.250	0.208	0.089	0.178	0.071
MT	0.285	0.428	0.714	0.111	0.278	0.055	0.142	0.428	0.714	0.056	0.166	0.000
MA	0.636	0.090	0.181	0.222	0.148	0.037	0.545	0.000	0.181	0.444	0.481	0.074
RVA	0.555	0.444	0.388	0.355	0.155	0.288	0.444	0.388	0.388	0.466	0.200	0.177
SC	0.138	0.611	0.805	0.275	0.402	0.264	0.166	0.500	0.777	0.264	0.356	0.252
Mean	0.305	0.458	0.407	0.270	0.248	0.194	0.275	0.405	0.401	0.303	0.329	0.191

*Proportion of funds in each strategy category whose regressors are significant with 95% confidence, e.g., (0.886) = 88.6%.

Table 18.8 Proportion of funds showing nonlinearity

	Equation (18.3)				Equation (18.4)			
	1997		2001		1997		2001	
	Mkt^2	Mkt^3	Mkt^2	Mkt^3	SMB^2	HML^2	SMB^2	HML^2
FOF*	0.048	0.228	0.123	0.168	0.086	0.239	0.265	0.146
CA	0.541	0.750	0.673	0.102	0.000	0.166	0.224	0.326
DS	0.250	0.050	0.028	0.057	0.300	0.100	0.285	0.174
EM	0.000	0.467	0.059	0.069	0.022	0.044	0.059	0.154
EH	0.075	0.150	0.086	0.162	0.175	0.225	0.098	0.261
EMN	0.125	0.291	0.147	0.098	0.208	0.000	0.245	0.364
ENH	0.059	0.156	0.092	0.118	0.156	0.117	0.131	0.342
ED	0.129	0.290	0.079	0.158	0.190	0.258	0.412	0.190
FI	0.111	0.138	0.091	0.126	0.138	0.222	0.229	0.149
FX	0.000	0.000	0.130	0.000	0.071	0.000	0.000	0.086
MC	0.040	0.291	0.089	0.071	0.000	0.080	0.089	0.070
MT	0.000	0.142	0.000	0.333	0.142	0.286	0.166	0.055
MA	0.000	0.272	0.185	0.111	0.090	0.727	0.407	0.037
RVA	0.055	0.333	0.155	0.133	0.055	0.222	0.177	0.200
SC	0.027	0.166	0.029	0.183	0.027	0.222	0.103	0.206
Mean	0.097	0.248	0.131	0.126	0.111	0.194	0.193	0.184

*At a 95% confidence level.

nonlinear regressors are significant at a 95% confidence level. For example, the 0.414 in the FOF line in Table 18.10, which presents results for the model of equation (18.3), indicates that when Mkt^2 and the alpha are significant, and when the equation (18.3) alpha is greater than the alpha of the three-factor model, the average abnormal monthly return is 0.414 percentage points greater. The number 7 underneath the 0.414 is the number of funds meeting the condition that alpha and nonlinear variable both be significant. Tables 18.10 and 18.11 show many more funds with nonlinearity for 2001 to date than for 1997 to date, which is to be expected since the hedge fund market has been expanding rapidly. Table 18.10 shows that for the period since 2001, the funds with significant Mkt^2 and Mkt^3 contributions whose alphas are greater than for the three-factor model have an average alpha 0.870 percentage points higher in the case of Mkt^2-significant funds and 0.292 percentage points higher in the case of Mkt^3-significant funds. When the alpha is smaller, it averages 0.590 percentage points smaller for Mkt^2-significant funds and 0.247 percentage points smaller for Mkt^3-significant funds.

Table 18.11 shows the analogous results for the cases of SMB^2 and HML^2 significance. We note that many more funds show SMB^2 and HML^2 nonlinearity than Mkt^2 and Mkt^3 nonlinearity.

Table 18.9 R^2 adjusted for each equation

	Equation (18.1)		Equation (18.2)		Equation (18.3)		Equation (18.4)	
	1997	2001	1997	2001	1997	2001	1997	2001
FOF* **	0.226	0.172	0.323	0.225	0.357 (0.630)	0.238 (0.489)	0.369 (0.766)	0.291 (0.746)
CA	0.043	0.016	0.093	0.099	0.156 (1.000)	0.178 (0.898)	0.178 (1.000)	0.206 (0.918)
DS	0.092	0.114	0.179	0.166	0.241 (0.800)	0.176 (0.514)	0.246 (0.800)	0.236 (0.828)
EM	0.244	0.223	0.273	0.265	0.333 (0.822)	0.269 (0.485)	0.332 (0.778)	0.280 (0.485)
EH	0.283	0.260	0.399	0.331	0.411 (0.600)	0.343 (0.530)	0.430 (0.741)	0.387 (0.736)
EMN	0.148	0.125	0.232	0.181	0.250 (0.708)	0.195 (0.475)	0.259 (0.833)	0.274 (0.836)
ENH	0.408	0.472	0.519	0.540	0.525 (0.431)	0.552 (0.592)	0.538 (0.588)	0.585 (0.763)
ED	0.244	0.268	0.330	0.325	0.380 (0.741)	0.338 (0.571)	0.397 (0.838)	0.391 (0.857)
FI	0.123	0.125	0.148	0.151	0.179 (0.500)	0.159 (0.460)	0.197 (0.638)	0.190 (0.712)
FX	0.000	0.000	0.000	0.000	0.000 —	0.000 —	0.000 —	0.000 —
MC	0.098	0.110	0.130	0.122	0.155 (0.625)	0.126 (0.464)	0.162 (0.667)	0.125 (0.357)
MT	0.292	0.280	0.403	0.305	0.420 (0.714)	0.337 (0.611)	0.433 (0.857)	0.351 (0.777)
MA	0.151	0.125	0.16	0.146	0.204 (0.901)	0.168 (0.703)	0.231 (0.818)	0.220 (0.851)
RVA	0.451	0.051	0.083	0.099	0.132 (0.722)	0.122 (0.454)	0.165 (0.833)	0.168 (0.681)
SC	0.228	0.280	0.374	0.343	0.388 (0.527)	0.345 (0.390)	0.404 (0.722)	0.383 (0.712)
Mean	0.200	0.175	0.237	0.220	0.270 (0.694)	0.236 (0.545)	0.284 (0.769)	0.271 (0.733)

*Average R^2 adjusted for each hedge fund strategy.
**The numbers in parentheses indicate the proportion of funds whose R^2 adjusted was higher with the addition of nonlinearity than in the three-factor model, e.g., (0.886) = 88.6%.

Table 18.10 Alpha impact*

| | When alpha is higher than for the 3-factor model | | | | When alpha is lower than for the 3-factor model | | | |
| | 1997 | | 2001 | | 1997 | | 2001 | |
	Mkt²	Mkt³	Mkt²	Mkt³	Mkt²	Mkt³	Mkt²	Mkt³
FOF**	0.414	0.130	0.265	0.144	−0.368	−0.108	−0.456	−0.085
***	*7*	*33*	*52*	*67*	*2*	*9*	*2*	*8*
CA	0.000	0.000	0.000	0.000	−0.264	−0.230	−0.342	−0.182
					13	*18*	*33*	*5*
DS	0.537	0.089	0.283	0.132	0.000	0.000	0.000	0.000
	5	*1*	*1*	*2*				
EM	0.000	0.377	0.760	0.368	0.000	−0.339	−1.358	−0.201
		13	*5*	*5*		*8*	*1*	*2*
EH	0.800	0.512	0.689	0.241	−1.046	−0.305	−0.920	−0.305
	3	*4*	*21*	*30*	*6*	*13*	*7*	*22*
EMN	0.000	0.000	0.372	0.279	−0.502	−0.229	−0.291	−0.246
			4	*2*	*3*	*7*	*5*	*4*
ENH	3.647	0.000	1.786	0.198	−0.799	−0.574	−0.494	−0.254
	1		*6*	*4*	*2*	*8*	*1*	*5*
ED	1.696	1.005	1.255	0.231	0.000	−0.060	0.000	−0.073
	4	*7*	*5*	*9*		*2*		*1*
FI	0.448	0.187	0.456	0.305	−0.461	−0.016	−0.355	−0.256
	3	*4*	*2*	*5*	*1*	*1*	*6*	*5*
FX	0.000	0.000	0.739	0.000	0.000	0.000	−0.414	0.000
			1				*2*	
MC	0.517	0.290	0.541	0.607	0.000	0.180	−0.843	−0.456
	1	*4*	*4*	*1*		*3*	*1*	*3*
MT	0.000	0.112	0.000	0.264	0.000	0.000	0.000	−0.314
		1		*2*				*4*
MA	0.000	0.184	0.238	0.253	0.000	0.000	0.000	0.000
		3	*5*	*3*				
RVA	0.000	0.054	0.654	0.380	−0.171	−0.060	−0.291	−0.091
		2	*2*	*4*	*1*	*4*	*5*	*2*
SC	3.236	0.507	2.669	0.252	0.000	0.000	0.000	−0.341
	1	*6*	*2*	*9*				*7*
Mean	1.554	0.332	0.870	0.292	−0.541	−0.181	−0.590	−0.247
Number of funds	18	45	58	76	26	64	61	60

*Average difference in alphas relative to the three-factor model for the funds whose nonlinear regressors are significant at a 95% confidence level.

**Percentage points.

***Number of funds meeting the condition that alpha and nonlinear variable both be significant.

Table 18.11 Alpha impact*

	When alpha is higher than for the 3-factor model				When alpha is lower than for the 3-factor model			
	1997		2001		1997		2001	
	SMB^2	HML^2	SMB^2	HML^2	SMB^2	HML^2	SMB^2	HML^2
FOF**	0.176	0.161	0.251	0.204	−0.176	−0.149	0.000	−0.198
***	*12*	*28*	*118*	*59*	*4*	*16*		*5*
CA	0.000	0.000	0.152	0.206	0.000	−0.338	−0.083	−0.157
			6	*5*	*4*		*5*	*11*
DS	0.670	0.000	0.475	0.738	−0.020	0.000	−0.243	−0.103
	1		*9*	*4*	*2*		*1*	*2*
EM	0.000	0.200	0.720	0.248	−2.183	−2.183	−0.837	−0.517
		1	*3*	*7*	*1*	*1*	*3*	*4*
EH	0.422	0.362	0.698	0.368	−0.778	−0.475	−0.838	−0.370
	13	*10*	*26*	*51*	*8*	*17*	*6*	*34*
EMN	0.164	0.000	0.349	0.312	−0.004	0.000	−0.218	−0.216
	4		*11*	*12*	*1*		*4*	*9*
ENH	1.356	2.058	0.988	0.493	−0.720	−1.139	−0.919	−0.279
	4	*2*	*9*	*17*	*4*	*4*	*1*	*9*
ED	0.338	0.226	0.372	0.954	0.000	−0.673	−0.352	−0.427
	6	*7*	*25*	*10*		*1*	*1*	*2*
FI	0.296	0.377	0.627	0.519	0.000	−0.005	−0.258	−0.248
	5	*7*	*13*	*7*		*1*	*7*	*6*
FX	0.000	0.000	0.000	0.103	−0.989	0.000	0.000	−0.338
				1	*1*			*1*
MC	0.000	0.000	1.412	0.000	0.000	−1.612	0.000	−0.811
			1			*2*		*1*
MT	0.204	0.000	0.173	0.000	0.000	−0.254	−0.461	−0.468
	1		*1*			*2*	*2*	*1*
MA	0.254	0.184	0.306	0.987	0.000	−0.001	0.000	0.000
	1	*7*	*11*	*1*	*1*			
RVA	0.000	0.000	0.433	0.333	−0.366	−0.154	−0.515	−0.254
			5	*4*	*1*	*4*	*3*	*5*
SC	0.000	0.784	0.460	0.407	−1.093	−0.634	−0.979	−0.405
		2	*6*	*10*	*1*	*6*	*3*	*8*
Mean	0.463	0.599	0.551	0.472	−0.769	−0.679	−0.518	−0.353
Number of funds	35	36	126	129	19	43	36	93

*Average difference in alphas relative to the three-factor model for the funds whose nonlinear regressors are significant at a 95% confidence level.

**Percentage points.

***Number of funds meeting the condition that alpha and nonlinear variable both be significant.

18.5   Conclusion

Although this book's primary subject is funds of funds, we cannot discuss these properly without a detailed study of the statistical and empirical characteristics of hedge funds. As we have noted, the characteristics of hedge fund monthly returns can vary greatly over time. Examination of two observation periods, 1997 to date and 2001 to date, brings out significant changes in their averages, standard deviations, and kurtosis. We also see that some regressors have been highly significant for some management strategies over the longer period but not statistically significant since 2001. We can also see that most of the series of monthly returns showed nonlinear relationships. The data tends, in part and for certain funds, to discredit the simple market model and the three-factor model of Fama and French (1993). In some cases, use of these models induces bad specification because the omission of variables biases the results obtained. This could lead fund managers to choose the wrong hedge funds in constituting a fund of funds. In addition, managers could be under the impression they have reduced risk when they have in fact increased it. We also note that funds of funds appear to be generating smaller alphas today than in the past. The use of nonlinear techniques could help managers better estimate the alpha and thus make choices that would result more often in abnormal returns. As we have indicated, alpha estimates can vary a great deal depending on the model used to calculate them. While the models are far from perfect, they tend more and more to confirm the presence of nonlinearity in the market. That said, the results obtained only confirm that managers of funds of funds should watch for new estimating models and consider shifts in the trend of monthly returns when selecting hedge funds for a fund of funds.

References

Ackermann, C., McEnally, R., and Ravenscraft, D. (1999). The Performance of Hedge Funds: Risk, Return, and Incentives. *Journal of Finance*, 54(3):833–874.

Agarwal, V. and Naik, K. (2004). Risks and Portfolio Decisions Involving Hedge Funds. *Review of Financial Studies*, 17(1):63–98.

Amin, G. S. and Kat, H. M. (2003). Stocks, Bonds, and Hedge Funds: No Free Lunch! *Journal of Portfolio Management*, 29(4):113–120.

Capoci, D. and Hübner, G. (2004). An Analysis of Hedge Fund Performance. *Journal of Empirical Finance*, 11(1):55–89.

Christie, W. G. and Huang, R. D. (1994). The Changing Function Relation between Stock Returns and Dividend Yields. *Journal of Empirical Finance*, 1(2):161–191.

Coën, A., Desfleurs, A., Hübner, G., and Racicot, F. E. (2005). The Performance of Hedge Funds in the Presence of Errors in the Variables. In: *Hedge Funds: Insights in Performance Measurement, Risk Analysis, and*

Portfolio Allocation (Gregoriou, G. N., Hübner, G., Papageorgiou, N., and Rouah, F., eds.). John Wiley & Sons, Hoboken, NJ.

Fama, E. F. and French, K. R. (1993). Common Risk Factors in the Returns on Stocks and Bonds. *Journal of Financial Economics*, 33(1):3–56.

Kat, H. M. (2005). Integrating Hedge Funds into the Traditional Portfolio in Hedge Funds. In: *Insights in Performance Measurement, Risk Analysis, and Portfolio Allocation* (Gregoriou, G. N., Hubner, G., Papageorgiou, N., and Rouah, F., eds.). John Wiley & Sons, Hoboken, NJ.

Lhabitant, F. S. (2004). *Hedge Funds: Quantitative Insights*. John Wiley & Sons, London.

Liang, B. (1999). On the Performance of Hedge Funds. *Financial Analysts Journal*, 55(4):72–85.

Racicot, F. E. (2003). *Trois Essais sur l'Analyse des Données Économiques et Financières*. Chapter 3, Ph.D. dissertation, Université du Québec à Montréal (UQAM).

Racicot, F. E. and Théoret, R. (2004). *Le Calcul Numérique en Finance Empirique et Quantitative*. Chapter 15, Presses de l'Université du Québec.

Seco, L. A. (2005). Hedge Funds: Truths and Myths. Working Paper, University of Toronto, Toronto, ON.

19 Investor's choice: an investor-driven, forward-looking optimization approach to fund of hedge funds construction

Clemens H. Glaffig

Abstract

A method is proposed to optimize portfolios of hedge funds, taking investor preferences as the starting point to define an objective function that will be flexible enough to include general investor preferences. In particular, we can include path- and market-dependent objectives. We also develop a method to produce a forward-looking data set on which the optimization can be based. Our method is also particularly apt for a case when a portfolio of hedge funds is used as an overlay. We compare this approach to classical optimizations on empirical data to highlight the effects of the additional degrees of freedom we have included.

19.1 Introduction

Portfolio construction and optimization has attracted a vast amount of research over the last several decades, and it is now embedded into a well-developed mathematical framework. The classical portfolio optimization approach is concerned with a universe of standard assets and how to combine them into a portfolio that maximizes investor utility under general constraints relative to some perception of risk. Most frequently, the result is a type of mean-variance optimization. The typical form of utility functions and the definitions of risk, however, need to conform to demands of general acceptance and ease of solvability. Little room remains for individual investor preferences and risk perceptions.

With the evolution of financial markets, however, standard assets are being supplemented by various alternative assets. Hedge funds in particular differ in content and behavior from classical assets and funds. There is currently considerable interest among practitioners in the problem of portfolio construction and optimization based on these new assets and trading styles. With hedge funds as the portfolio constituents, any deficiencies of the classical approaches become even more pronounced.

In this chapter, we deviate from the traditional approach by making investors' own preferences the starting point of our optimization. Our setup of objective function and constraints is fully flexible to reflect path- and market-dependent preferences. Specifically, we let the investors decide what constitutes risk, because not all forms of risk are equally undesirable. Often, perceived risk is a function of current wealth (or accumulated profit) and of the state of other markets. The price we pay for this flexibility is that a simple analytical solution to our optimization problem is typically not derivable. We will solve the optimization by using a heuristic search method, in this case a genetic search.

The issue in simply extending methods of classical portfolio optimization to hedge fund portfolios is twofold. On the one hand, for portfolios of classical assets, assumptions of market behavior translate easily into the corresponding behavior of the assets to be included in the portfolio; this is not the case for alternative assets and hedge funds. Under a future return scenario for major markets, hedge fund returns are not at all clear.

In order to draw conclusions about the behavior of hedge funds from specifications of major market behavior, it is necessary to better understand the fund's strategies. In other words, we need to understand the fund's mapping from a specific market situation into trading action. As a consequence, obtaining reliable forward-looking data turns out to be very difficult. So producing a forward-looking data set on which the optimization can be performed is much more problematic than it is for classic portfolio optimization.

On the other hand, however, alternative assets and trading strategies depend in a nonlinear and asymmetric way on underlying markets, so the classical mean-variance approach for portfolio optimization is inadequate. Risk is not properly reflected within this framework. Progress has been made by considering utility functions that depend on other measures of risk, such as VAR, CVAR, and downside risk (Morton, Popova, and Popova, 2004; De Souza and Gokcan, 2004), or, because many hedge funds exhibit considerable skew and kurtosis, by using a four-factor, mean-variance skew-kurtosis utility function (Davies, Kat, and Lu, 2004).

However, as we have noted, it is much more important with alternative assets to allow for objective functions and definitions of risk that reflect investors' own risk preferences. For most investors, risk perception varies with market developments and with the performance of their other assets. None of the standard approaches reflects the necessary path and market dependence.

With regard to the data set underlying our optimization, we use a mixture of forward-looking and historical data and formulate a market view on patterns of general market behavior for the future (or a weighted partition of views). We then return to the historical data set and select those periods of time "closest" to that pattern. The difference is that, in the pure forward-looking approach, which is based on a regression against style factors or strategy-learning algorithms, one has complete freedom with regard to the specification of future market developments. The fund behavior in this situation comes as an approximation/optimization from the past and hence can only be approximately correct.

In our approach, the data is a close approximation of our modeled/assumed scenario (as we search for past periods with market developments close to our specification), but the behavior is precise. In spirit, our view is forward-looking by ensuring that the "mapping" problem (mapping market behavior into hedge fund behavior) is circumvented by having history solve it for us. We split the optimization into two parts: (1) the data set and (2) the methodology.

19.2   Data set: defining market patterns

The data set underlying the optimization is of crucial importance for the results. As is well known from classical mean-variance optimization, slightly different data sets underlying the optimization can produce vastly different portfolio decompositions. In the case of alternative assets and hedge funds, one of the following four approaches for data sets underlying the optimization has typically been used.

19.2.1   Historical data

Much of the fund of hedge funds optimization is performed on the basis of historical data. The advantage is that data for the behavior of hedge funds is objectively available, so all the risk parameters and statistics can easily be computed. However, if history does not more or less precisely repeat itself, the optimization becomes useless for construction purposes. For example, stop loss or limit behavior may not become obvious for the underlying data set, but it may dominate the fund's behavior subsequently. Or trends may have fed the performance in the past, but subsequent sideways market movements may steer the investment managers toward more risk.

19.2.2   Simulations

If we know the return distribution of a fund, we can perform a simulation. However, historically fitted return distributions are a statistical summary of past behavior, an interpolated historical frequency count of returns. Given that hedge fund returns are highly nonstationary, this approach suffers from similar defects to those of historical data because future return distributions may look completely different. In addition, while it certainly makes sense to allow for heavy-tailed distributions, they should be truncated to reflect stop losses, which are hardwired into the risk procedures of many hedge funds. This fact is often ignored in simulations.

19.2.3   Future projections

We could use future projections of hedge fund returns conditioned on market behavior in conjunction with a Black–Litterman type of approach. Here, the future behavior of the primary markets influencing a given hedge fund is weighted according to its plausibility to the investor. The success of this approach depends on the way market behavior can be related to hedge fund behavior (the mapping problem), for example, the degree to which one is able to extract the dynamics of the fund and the strategies employed by the fund.

19.2.4 Partitioning of history

The partitioning-of-history approach tries to combine the advantages of historical data and future projections. It forms a collection of likely market developments, each attached to the investor's probability of occurrence. It then goes through history selecting periods of time that fit the individual market patterns and performs the optimization on the data set.

For our optimization we use the partitioning-of-history method, which classifies historical data into predefined market patterns. We choose the pattern or weighted average of patterns that we (or the investor) deem most likely for the future period. The chosen patterns can include scenarios that may be problematic for the other assets the investor is holding. In that context, this method will be valuable if the portfolio being constructed is to be used as an overlay to an existing, classical portfolio.

To illustrate this method, we need to define market patterns. The more formal approach we take to describe a pattern is justified because a market pattern such as an uptrend can be defined in a variety of ways into a set of conditions on market prices over a specific time period. This again can lead to very different data sets for the same targeted pattern and hence to very different optimal portfolios. We therefore define a pattern class, a set of time intervals over which the market behavior is close to the desired pattern.

A pattern could be defined by specifying a market M and a pattern period T and then defining a set of rules that market M must fulfill starting from some initial time t and ending at $t + T$. The set of rules could be expressed via a product of indicator functions, expressing the fulfillment of the rules. For example, a continuous upward pattern could be defined by the product of indicator functions

$$1_{\{M(t) \le M(t+1)\}} \cdot 1_{\{M(t+1) \le M(t+2)\}} \cdots 1_{\{M(t+T-1) \le M(t+T)\}} \tag{19.1}$$

More generally, we define a pattern by first specifying the number d of different markets, which will be part of the definition (for example, if we use the S&P 500 index, the 10-year U.S. Treasury rate, and the USD-EUR exchange rates, it would be $d = 3$). The length of the pattern, T, is chosen to correspond to the period in the future on which we construct the portfolio. We denote t as a time scale that is coarse, such as a weekly or monthly time scale, where s denotes smaller time scales, such as daily or more frequent.

Patterns are defined by describing the behavior of certain statistics on a coarse scale and aggregating information from small scales; for example, a weekly maximum of a market is typically aggregated by taking the maximum overall tics of that market during a week. Here, t denotes one week and s indicates a specific tic within a week.

We define a set of m statistics/functionals that we apply to the individual markets to enter the pattern definition:

$$
\begin{aligned}
&X_k(i,t) = F_k(M_i(s); s \in (t-1,t]) \in \Re, \\
&\qquad \text{with } i \in \{1,2,\dots,d\}, k \in \{1,2,\dots,m\}
\end{aligned} \tag{19.2}
$$

Each $X_k(i, t)$ aggregates and maps the information of market M_i for time interval $(t-1, t]$ into a real number. Functions F_k determine the statistics of the markets to be used. Common examples include $X_k(i, t) := \max(M_i(s), s \in (t-1, t])$ or $X_k(i, t) := \min(M_i(s), s \in (t-1, t])$, the maximum or minimum of the ith market during the time interval $(t-1, t]$.

A T-period market M_i pattern starting at time t_0 is defined by a map from $\Re^{mT} \to \{0,1\}$:

$$
\begin{aligned}
&PM_i(t_0,T):(X_1(i,t), X_2(i,t),\dots, \\
&\quad X_m(i,t), t \in \{t_0+1, t_0+2, \dots, t_0+T\}) \to \{0,1\}
\end{aligned} \tag{19.3}
$$

Definition: *A time interval* $[t_0, t_0+T]$ *will have T-period pattern* PM_i *if for* PM_i: $\Re^{mT} \to \{0,1\}$.

$$
PM_i(t_0, T) = 1 \tag{19.4}
$$

A general T-period pattern P starting at time t_0 for markets M_1 to M_d will be defined as follows.

Definition: *A time interval* $[t_0, t_0+T]$ *will have d-market, T-period pattern* P *if for* P: $\Re^{dmT} \to \{0,1\}$.

$$
P(t_0, T) := \Pi_i\, PM_i(t_0, T) = 1 \tag{19.5}
$$

The definition of P represents the rules that combine the functionals and statistics as defined by X_k into a temporal pattern.

Example

Let $d = 1$, $m = 3$. For $t \in \{t_0+1, t_0+2, \dots, t_0+T\}$,

$$
\begin{aligned}
X_1(1,t) &= F_1(M_1(s), s \in (t-1,t]) := M_1(t) \\
X_2(1,t) &= F_2(M_1(s), s \in (t-1,t]) := \max(M_1(s), s \in (t-1,t]) \\
X_3(1,t) &= F_3(M_1(s), s \in (t-1,t]) := \min(M_1(s), s \in (t-1,t])
\end{aligned} \tag{19.6}
$$

If we then let P be given by the indicator function,

$$P(t_0, T) = PM_1(t_0, T) = \Pi_k 1\{X_k(t_0 + 1) \leq X_k(t_0 + 2) \leq \ldots X_k(t_0 + T)\}, \tag{19.7}$$

we have defined a pattern by which the successive closing levels, the successive highs, and the successive lows of the market M_1 are each increasing over the time interval $[t_0, t_0 + T]$, which would be a definition of a solid upward trend of market M_1.

For practical purposes, it is also useful to define pattern classes as time periods, which may not have a predefined pattern but are close. The use of pattern classes ensures that the set of time periods classified is not too small. It also serves the stability of solutions for our optimization method, because slightly different pattern definitions may lead to very different optimal portfolios.

We note that with each d-market pattern P, we can associate the d maps PM_i defining P, and to each of these maps we associate a subset $\wp_i \subset \Re^{mT}$ by

$$\wp_i(t_0, T) = PM_i(t_0, T)^{-1}(\{1\}) \tag{19.8}$$

We then define

$$\begin{aligned}Z_i(t) &= \{F_1(M_i(s)), F_2(M_i(s)), \ldots, F_m(M_i(s)); s \in (t-1, t)\} \in \Re^m \\ &= (X_1(i, t), \ldots, X_m(i, t)) \end{aligned} \tag{19.9}$$

and

$$Z_i(t_0, T) = (Z_i(t_0 + 1), Z_i(t_0 + 2), \ldots, Z_i(t_0 + T)) \in \Re^{mT} \tag{19.10}$$

We define pattern class P as those periods for which market behavior, as encoded by $(Z_1(t_0 T), \ldots, Z_d(t_0 T))$, is close to the (dmT)-dimensional set $(\wp_1(t_0, T), \wp_2(t_0, T), \ldots, \wp_d(t_0, T)) \subset \Re^{dmT}$.

Definition: *The time period $[t_0, t_0 + T]$ is said to belong to ε-pattern class P if*

$$\sum_i \|\wp_i(t_0, T) - Z_i(t_0, T)\| \leq \varepsilon \tag{19.11}$$

where $\|\bullet\|$ corresponds to the Euclidian distance in $\Re^{mT}$.

The set of all time periods belonging to ε-pattern class P will be denoted by $[P] \varepsilon$. Note that:

- A time period can belong to more than one pattern class.
- If history must be partitioned into a family of pattern classes, we can easily use a kernel-based classification instead of the preceding definition.

19.3 Methodology: investor-driven objectives and the optimization algorithm

The methodology used for most traditional optimizations is largely influenced by the desire to solve problems analytically. The mathematical theory of constrained optimization is well developed and can accommodate the more obvious constraints, such as integer constraints, for investment sizes as well as nonlinear objective functions. But adding more customized preferences will require numerical procedures or search algorithms.

Our approach is driven by translating all the preferences of a specific investor into a quantitative framework without any restriction on the functional form of these preferences. As the perception of risk is not unique, we will not limit ourselves to a predefined and dogmatic definition of risk via volatility, semivolatility, VAR, CVAR, or downside risk. We allow the investor to choose what he or she perceives as "risk" by essentially allowing him or her to decide which scenarios to avoid.

We will reflect strict boundary conditions via constraints on the optimization. We also build preferences into the objective function, penalizing scenarios to be avoided and rewarding desired scenarios. Specifically, we allow scenarios that depend on the return history of the portfolio, on the market environment, or on any other form of path dependence. Restrictions like the minimum number of portfolio members, leverage conditions, and maximum fund allocation can easily be accommodated and will be reflected in the constraints.

We consider portfolios

$$\text{Port}(\omega, t) = \sum w_i F_i(t) \tag{19.12}$$

where the $F_i(t)$ are the funds to be considered for inclusion valued at time t and $\omega = (w_1, w_2, \ldots, w_N)$ is the vector of weights, constant throughout the specific future investment period for the individual funds within the portfolio.

19.3.1 Objective function: the sum of all fears

The investor preferences will be reflected in the objective functions via rewards and penalties. The objective function to be maximized is

$$\text{Obj}(\omega, t) = \sum_i \alpha_i 1_{\{S_i\}}(\omega, t) \tag{19.13}$$

where $1_{\{S_i\}}$ is the indicator function for S_i, which denotes the ith situation rewarded ($\alpha_i \geq 0$) or penalized ($\alpha_i \leq 0$). S_i may be time-, path-, and market-dependent. Given that any continuous function can be approximated by step functions, this form is more general than any of the classic utility functions.

For the following three examples, we assume the investment period is from t_0 to $t_0 + T$ and between R_{i-1} and R_i.

Example 1

If S_i = {the portfolio return over the target period $[t_0, t_0 + T]$ is between R_{i1} and R_i}, with α_i, for example, equal to a concave function of R_{i-1} or constant, then:

$$\alpha_i 1_{\{Si\}}(\omega, t) = \begin{cases} \alpha_i & \text{if } (\text{Port}(\omega, t_0 + T) - \text{Port}(\omega, t_0))/ \\ & \text{Port}(\omega, t_0) \in [R_{i-1}, R_i] \text{ and } t = t_0 + T \\ 0 & \text{otherwise} \end{cases} \quad (19.14)$$

Example 2

S_i = {negative tail comovement with market M over period $[t - 1, t] \subset [t_0, t_0 + T]$}, characterized by:

$$\alpha_i 1_{\{Si\}}(\omega, t) = \alpha_i 1_{\{R(t) \leq -x\}} 1_{\{|RM(t)| \geq y\}} \quad (19.15)$$

where $1_{\{R(t) \leq -x\}}$ denotes the indicator function for event $R(t) \leq -x$ and $R(t)$ is the portfolio return over period $[t - 1, t]$. $1_{\{|RM(t)| \geq y\}}$ denotes the indicator function for the event $|RM(t)| \geq y$, where $|RM(t)|$ is the absolute value of the return of market M over the period $[t - 1, t]$, x and y to be specified, so that

$$\alpha_i 1_{\{Si\}}(\omega, t) = \begin{cases} \alpha_i & \text{if } R(t) \leq -x \text{ and } |RM(t)| \geq y \\ 0 & \text{otherwise} \end{cases} \quad (19.16)$$

Example 3

S_i = {the portfolio return over period $[t - 1, t] \subset [t_0, t_0 + T]$ is between R_{i-1} and R_i, and the accumulated portfolio return over period $[t_0, t]$ is larger than x}.

$$\alpha_i 1_{\{Si\}}(\omega, t) = \begin{cases} \alpha_i(x) & \text{if } (\text{Port}(\omega, t) - \text{Port}(\omega, t - 1))/ \\ & \text{Port}(\omega, t - 1) \in [R_{i-1}, R_i] \text{ and } (\text{Port}(\omega, t) \\ 0 & - \text{Port}(\omega, t_0))/\text{Port}(\omega, t_0) \geq x \\ & \text{otherwise} \end{cases} \quad (19.17)$$

19.3.2 Constraints — the aggregation of hard exclusions

The constraints will summarize the scenarios we exclude. We list only a few examples, which typically include:

- Nonnegativity of weights, for example, $w_i \geq 0$
- Fully invested portfolio or no leverage, for example, $\Sigma w_i = 1$ or $\Sigma w_i \leq 1$
- The maximum share of individual funds, for example, $\max(w_i) \leq A$
- The minimum number of funds in which the portfolio is invested
- Any hard stop loss that is potentially contingent on other markets
- Minimum investment sizes

19.3.3 Path to optimization

The optimization proceeds as follows. Let $[t_1, t_n]$ denote the time period for which we have reliable historical data for all the funds we want to consider. Let T denote the period into the future for which the portfolio is to be constructed and over which the portfolio weights will not be changed. We first define a T-period pattern P for the market development in the future, according to our earlier definitions, by specifying a set of defining markets M_i and statistics F_k (we restrict ourselves to a single pattern; optimizations over a weighted average of patterns works analogously).

Within $[t_1, t_n]$, we consider all connected T-period time intervals, from which we select those in pattern class $[P]$ ε for prespecified ε. We allow different periods to overlap by a prespecified maximum number of time intervals. The members of this set of connected T-period time intervals will be close to the originally defined pattern P, and they will serve as the data set on which our optimization is based.

The optimal portfolio is found by maximizing the sum of the objective functions over all T-period intervals belonging to pattern class $[P]$ with respect to weight vector ω:

$$\text{Max}(O(\omega)) := \text{Max}_\omega \left(\sum_{[t, t+T] \in [P]} \sum_{u \in \{t+1, t+2, \ldots, t+T\}} \text{Obj}(\omega, u) \right) \quad (19.18)$$

where the inner sum runs over all time steps u within a given T period, the outer sum runs over all T periods in pattern class $[P]$, and the constraints C are satisfied.

We use a genetic search algorithm to solve the problem. We recommend that readers uninterested in the specifics of this algorithm skip the next subsection and move on to Section 19.4, the empirical analysis section.

19.3.4 Search algorithm

In our genetic search algorithm, each portfolio $\text{Port}(\omega)$ is represented by its weight vector ω. The algorithm produces an initial population G of portfolios, each represented by its weight vector. All the portfolios within the population will compete against each other and must fulfill the constraints.

Let F_i denote the ith fund of the pool of admissible funds, and let $\omega(n, j)$ denote the weight vector representing the nth portfolio of the jth population, $\omega(n, j) \in \Re^N$ with

$$\omega(n, j) = (w(1, n, j), w(2, n, j), \ldots, w(N, n, j)) \tag{19.19}$$

where $w(i, n, j)$ is the weight of the ith fund, F_i.

The first population of portfolios is generated with random $w(k, n, l) \ \forall \ k, n$. After the objective function of all portfolios corresponding to the $\omega(n, 1)$ of the first population is evaluated, we choose the two with the highest objective functions in order to generate the next population (ties are broken by random choice). In the literature, a number of alternative selections are discussed, for example, tournament selection. The next generation is generated from the top two portfolios (the parents) by using the following genetic operators.

Crossover: We randomly select a coordinate k. Then we generate a portfolio of the new generation by taking the first k portfolio weights from the first top portfolio and the remaining $N - k$ from the second top portfolio. A second new portfolio is generated the same way by interchanging the two top portfolios and applying the same procedure.
Mutation: We randomly change a portfolio weight with a predefined probability. The two top portfolios of a given generation will always be members of the next generations. Genetic operators are applied to the parents of a given population, until the number of the new population is $G - 2$. The new population then consists of the $G - 2$ new portfolios and the old parents. This procedure is repeated until a termination condition is fulfilled or after a fixed number of generations. The portfolio in the last population with the highest objective function is termed the *optimal portfolio*.

Note a number of refinements to the genetic operators that are useful: The algorithm should find a good balance between local search, for example, local optimization, and exploration, for example, exploring other regions of weight space to avoid being trapped with local maxima. Both previously mentioned operators can also be split into fine and broad search sections by restricting crossover to interchanging. For more details, see Banzhaf, Nordin, Keller, and Francone (1998) or Weicker (2002).

19.4   Empirical analysis: exhibiting the new degrees of freedom

This section compares results for different classical approaches to the foregoing approach. The emphasis here is not to determine superiority but to illustrate the flexibility of the different approaches and how changes in optimization parameters influence the resulting optimal portfolio.

For all approaches, we let the obtained optimal portfolio run over a forward-looking period; for example, we analyze out-of-sample performance. For our universe of hedge funds, we use a set of CSFB/Tremont hedge fund indices, which represent the following trading styles:

- Global macro
- Convertible arbitrage
- Equity market-neutral
- Distressed
- Event-driven
- Fixed-income arbitrage
- Dedicated short
- Long/short equity
- Managed futures
- Emerging markets
- Risk arbitrage

Clearly, this universe of assets is not an optimal base from which to set up a realistic portfolio. However, for our analysis this is essentially unimportant. We want to emphasize the workings of our method and demonstrate the effects of its individual degrees of freedom. We use monthly data, even though most hedge funds nowadays provide daily performance data.

We construct our portfolio based on information before December 31, 2004. Our investment horizon is six months, for example, a portfolio left unchanged from January 1, 2005 to June 30, 2005. Over that six-month horizon, the various individual indices we consider as our funds have performed as shown in Table 19.1.

We run three different classical optimizations, characterized by their respective objective functions.

$$\text{CL1: } R/(\alpha\text{Vol}) \tag{19.20}$$

where R is the portfolio return over the period, $\text{Vol} = \Sigma|R_i|$, R_i is the return of the portfolio in the ith month of the period, and α is a parameter.

$$\text{CL2: } R/(\beta\text{Semivol}) \tag{19.21}$$

where R is the return of the portfolio over the period, $\text{Semivol} = -\Sigma\min(R_i, 0)$, R_i is the ith monthly return of the portfolio in the period, and β is a parameter.

$$\text{CL3: } R/(\gamma\text{MaxDD}) \tag{19.22}$$

where R is the portfolio return over the period, MaxDD is the maximum drawdown of the portfolio during the period, and γ is a parameter.

We run all these optimizations under the same set of constraints:

- Nonnegativity of weights, that is, $w_i \geq 0$
- No leverage, that is, $\Sigma w_i \leq 1$

Table 19.1 Performance of various indices*

	Global macro	Convertible arbitrage	Equity market-neutral	Distressed	Event-driven	Fixed-income arbitrage	Dedicated short arbitrage	Long/short equity	Managed futures	Emerging markets	Risk arbitrage
Return (%)	2.97	-6.34	1.45	4.09	3.60	-1.12	13.42	0.86	-0.91	5.62	1.02
Max Mthly DD (%)	-0.25	-3.13	-0.34	-0.06	-0.64	-1.24	-5.91	-1.55	-5.39	-1.88	-0.54
Max DD (%)	-0.25	-7.42	-0.56	-0.06	-0.64	-2.39	-6.12	-2.69	-5.39	-1.88	-0.54

*Max Mthly DD denotes maximum monthly drawdown, and Max DD denotes maximum drawdown over the period.

- Maximum share of individual funds of 25%, that is, $\max(w_i) \leq 25\%$
- Minimum investment size of 1% of the total portfolio

We run the optimizations of CL1, CL2, and CL3 over the data set, which consists of the last 60 months before our starting point, that is, a purely historical data set.

The performance results over the six-month period immediately following the optimization period and the obtained weightings for the indices are shown in Table 19.2 (all numbers in percent).

In general, the specific penalty form of the classical approach — here a form of volatility, semivolatility, and drawdown — weights the historical behavior over the entire history under that very specific penalty. For example, the index for distressed funds had a large drawdown in the fall of 1998 during the Russian crisis, which resulted in a high penalty and a low weight specifically within CL3. Conversely, throughout time, the low volatility of that index led to a large weight under CL1.

Moreover, funds (or indices here) were excluded due to a bias in the data set. This may not at all reflect an investor's expectations of future market behavior. Additional preferences, such as including or excluding certain sectors, must be considered on an ad hoc basis by restricting the universe of admissible funds for the portfolio. Note that a number of pure (for example, 100% weighted) fund investments perform better than any of CL1, CL2, and CL3 on a risk-adjusted basis over the out-of-sample period. These disadvantages of the classical models would also prevail in simulation approaches.

For comparison, we run various models under the new methodology. We group them first according to which six-month market patterns we want to use to optimize the portfolio. We define three simple patterns:

Pattern A: For a given six-month period, the S&P 500 has at least four months of successively lower monthly highs and lows (a downtrend).

Pattern B: For a given six-month period, the S&P 500 has at least four months of successively higher monthly highs and lows (an uptrend).

Pattern C: For a given six-month period, the credit spread of Euro BBB Corporate Bonds has three up and three down months.

We run our optimizations on six-month time periods each of which has the specified pattern (note that in this simple analysis we do not use pattern classes). We allow overlaps of up to three months; for example, the starting month for two time periods of the same pattern must be at least three months apart. We use data from January 1, 1994, to December 31, 2004, to select the six-month time periods.

Pattern A corresponds to a downtrend in equities. The market of our horizon period, from December 31, 2004, to June 30, 2005, exhibits pattern A. Consequently, our horizon period does not have pattern B, which corresponds to an equity uptrend. Pattern C corresponds to a sideways movement in credit spreads. The horizon period also exhibits pattern C.

Table 19.2 Return, drawdown statistics, and decomposition of optimized portfolios

Return	DD	DD	GM		CA	EMN	D	ED	FIA	DS	LSE	MF	EM	RA
CL1 α = 1	1.07	−0.45	−0.64	25	13	25	10	0	0	0	0	0	0	0
CL2 β = 1	1.85	−0.78	−0.99	11	11	25	13	14	16	7	0	1	1	1
CL3 γ = 1	2.11	−1.08	−1.09	15	13	22	0	21	16	11	0	0	2	0

The remaining cash was invested at LIBOR flat.

For each pattern, we run optimizations under different objective functions.

Pattern A:
- Obj A1: The portfolio return over each six-month period in the data set, plus a penalty of 0.50% for months the portfolio return is below −4% while the S&P 500 return is larger than 3%.
- Obj A2: The portfolio return over each six-month period in the data set, plus a penalty of 0.50% for months the portfolio return is below −4% while the BBB corporate bond spread increases more than 25%.

Pattern B:
- Obj B1: The objective function is the same as in A1.

Pattern C:
- Obj C1: The objective function is the same as in A2.

The objective functions are obviously somewhat randomly chosen. But our purpose is to demonstrate the effects of using different data sets to underlie the optimization and the effects of reflecting different preferences within the objective functions.

The A1 objective function balances pattern A. The pattern of an equity downtrend strongly favors a negative correlation to equity markets, but the penalty term of the objective function limits the correlation between negative portfolio return tails and positive equity return tails.

The A2 objective function limits the correlation between negative portfolio return tails and the tails of credit spread widening, and it thus retains its corporate bond–friendly bias even during an equity downturn. While downturns in equity markets generally correspond to widening spreads, this is not necessarily true for soft downturns. In this sense, the A2 objective function favors soft equity downturns (downturns via the defined pattern, filtering out the soft downturns via the objective function). All of these optimizations will be run under the same set of constraints as before.

Table 19.3 gives the performance results over the six-month period January 1, 2005 to June 30, 2005, as well as the obtained weightings for the indices (all numbers in percent).

We make the following observations.

- Patterns matter. The right pattern versus the wrong pattern, A versus B, results in a clearly superior performance for A1 and A2 (although drawdown was not part of our objective in this example). It also confirms that the chosen portfolio reflects the pattern. A1, assuming an equity downtrend, weights the dedicated short at the

Table 19.3 Return, drawdown statistics, and decomposition of optimized portfolios over the period January 1, 2005 to June 30, 2005

	Return	DD	DD	GM	CA	EMN	D	ED	FIA	DS	LSE	MF	EM	RA
A1	4.27	−0.85	−0.85	25	0	0	2	0	0	25	0	25	0	0
A2	3.48	−1.49	−1.49	25	14	2	0	1	0	25	0	11	0	0
B1	2.72	−0.25	−0.25	25	0	0	25	2	0	0	15	0	7	1
C1	2.15	−0.26	−0.26	25	5	1	25	3	0	0	6	0	1	0

maximum allowed (25%), while B1 weights it at its allowed minimum (0%). The classical approaches have weights somewhere in between because of drawdown reduction effects and the fact that the data set (the 60 months preceding December 31, 2004) displays extended periods of equity upturns and downturns.

- The long/short equity index has a 0% weight for downtrend patterns A1 and A2 due to its long bias. This is a part of the uptrend pattern in B1, but it plays no part in classical approaches due to bias in the data set (more severe equity downturns overall).
- The distressed index carries full weight under B1 and C1, for their data sets exclude the problematic periods of that index and make use of their consistently good performance outside market downturns.
- Managed futures are included for A1 and A2, because they do relatively well in equity downtrends. That relative advantage diminishes, however, if more equity uptrends enter the data set.
- The added penalty in the objective function A1 results in the omission of some of the indices with high negative tail correlations. Changing the objective function from A1 to A2 to reflect a corporate bond–friendly bias results in consideration of the convertible arbitrage index, which contains a corporate credit feature.

These are only a few observations about some variations in the full flexibility of our new approach. However, it is clear that our approach greatly increases the number of degrees of freedom as compared to classical approaches. Different assumptions about future market developments translate directly into different portfolio decompositions, while the use of pattern classes ensures that similar future pattern definitions produce similar or the same optimal portfolios. Changes in the objective function that allow us to consider individual investor preferences are reflected in the optimal portfolio.

19.5 Conclusion

Our methodology for constructing a portfolio of hedge funds starts from investor preferences and aversions and defines a fully flexible objective function and set of constraints. We have thus addressed some of the deficiencies of previous approaches, in which individual preferences and risk perceptions are subordinated to general definitions of objectives and risk. This flexibility allows investors to base risk/return objectives on path- and market-dependent measures and to express preferences about markets or trading styles to be included in the optimization, rather than having them arbitrarily imposed ex ante. Thus the translation of investor preferences into portfolio weights is inherent within the optimization. This feature is what gives our approach a clear edge over classical approaches.

Moreover, we have combined a forward-looking approach with historical information on conditional hedge fund behavior to produce a data set underlying the optimization. Investors can thus base their optimizations on a pattern of future market development for which reliable data on hedge fund behavior exists, without the problematic use of historical data (pure or in simulations via historically derived distributions) or of the unreliable projections of conditional future hedge fund behavior.

However, the price of this flexibility is the need for more elaborate search algorithms to solve the optimization problem. We used a genetic search here for its ease of implementation and its effectiveness in expressing constraints, but any other successful search algorithm will also do (Schlottmann and Seese, 2004). The disadvantage of our data set is that we can only use past or close-to-past patterns. Reliable methods for predicting conditional hedge fund behavior would not suffer from this restriction. But practitioners must decide which method is preferable to produce the data set underlying the optimization: using patterns that are close to past patterns and thus yielding more reliable data, or using the full flexibility to define a future pattern with potentially unreliable predictions about future hedge fund behavior.

Acknowledgments

The author thanks Dan Beghegeanu and Axel Gengenbach for useful comments and suggestions.

References

Banzhaf, W., Nordin, P., Keller, R., and Francone, F. (1998). *Genetic Programming: An Introduction*. Morgan Kaufmann, San Francisco.

Davies, R., Kat, H., and Lu, S. (2004). Funds of Hedge Funds Portfolio Selection: A Multiple-Objective Approach. Working Paper, Case Business School, London.

De Souza, C. and Gokcan, S. (2004). Allocation Methodologies and Customizing Hedge Fund Multi-Manager Multi-Strategy Products. *Journal of Alternative Investments*, 6(4):7–21.

Morton, D., Popova, E., and Popova, I. (2004). Efficient Hedge Fund Construction Under Downside Risk Measures. Working Paper, University of Texas, Austin.

Schlottmann, F. and Seese, D. (2004). Modern Heuristics for Finance Problems. In: *Handbook of Computational and Numerical Methods in Finance* (Rachev, S., ed.). Birkhäuser, Boston.

Weicker, K. (2002). *Evolutionäre Algorithmen*. Teubner, Stuttgart, Germany.

Part Four
Monitoring Risk, Overview of Funds of Funds, Due Diligence, and Special Classes of Funds of Funds

20 Moments analysis in risk and performance monitoring of funds of hedge funds

David K. C. Lee, Kok Fai Phoon,
and Choon Yuan Wong

Abstract

We introduce a practical approach to monitoring the risk and performance of funds of hedge funds from the viewpoints of U.S. and global equity investors. We focus on the impacts when we include funds of hedge funds into investors' portfolios and examine whether the inclusion helps to insulate the overall portfolio when the market is down, to capture the upside, and to reduce portfolio volatility under different market conditions. An advantage of this approach is that it alleviates the problems that can arise if hedge fund returns are skewed and leptokurtic and nonlinearly related to market returns. Our results also show that very few of the funds provide downside protection, upside capture, and reduced volatility on the downside. We conjecture that there is an implicit trade-off between funds of hedge funds returns and our risk measures, which is an interesting question for future research.

20.1   Introduction

In 1990, the entire hedge fund industry was estimated at about US$20 billion. By the end of 2004, there were close to 7,000 hedge funds worldwide, managing more than US$830 billion. Additionally, about US$200–300 billion was estimated to be in privately managed accounts. Ineichen (2002) estimated that funds of hedge funds manage around 20–25% of this amount. While high-net-worth individuals remain the main source of capital, hedge funds are becoming more popular among institutional and retail investors. In particular, funds of hedge funds and other hedge fund–linked products are increasingly being marketed to the retail market.

In this chapter, we introduce a practical approach to analyzing the risk and performance of hedge funds from the viewpoints of U.S. and global equity investors. For the empirical work, we focus on the impact when we include funds of hedge funds in investors' portfolios and examine whether the inclusion helps to insulate the overall portfolio when the market is down. We also analyze the impacts when the market is up and how the volatility of fund of hedge funds returns differ during up and down market conditions. An advantage of this approach is that it alleviates the problems that can arise if hedge fund returns are skewed, leptokurtic, and nonlinearly related to the market returns. Section 20.2 reviews related works that focus on funds of hedge funds. The analytical methodology is described in Section 20.3. Data description and results are provided in Section 20.4. We analyze the trade-off in returns between funds that meet our selection criteria and those that do not in Section 20.5. Section 20.6 concludes the chapter.

20.2   Funds of hedge funds

Hedge funds, including funds of funds, are characterized by their wide dispersion of returns. Ineichen (2002) reiterated the importance of evaluating individual fund of hedge funds managers because he found that dispersion of returns has increased on the downside more recently. Several papers have attempted to answer the question: Why funds of hedge funds? While describing the results of a survey on industry practices in the European funds of hedge funds industry, Amenc, Giraud, Martellini, and Vaissie (2004) noted that one question asked by investors is whether the value added justifies the extra layer of fees charged by these managers. In particular, they found that current institutionalization of the industry reflects a profound modification in investors' requirements that impact on several dimensions of the industry. These include the need of the industry to adapt tools and methods to support the specific risks hedge funds are exposed to and the need to improve due-diligence processes to meet investors' requirements.

Gregoriou (2004) and Gregoriou, Hübner, Papageorgiou, and Rouah (2005) focus on the skills of funds of hedge funds managers. Gregoriou (2004) found that these managers do not possess above-average market-timing skills and are hence not expected to add value in this dimension. Gregoriou, Hübner, Papageorgiou, and Rouah (2005) found that a simple hedge fund strategy can dominate the best fund of hedge funds in terms of alpha, Sharpe ratio, and information ratio. These findings show that investors need to carefully consider their decision to invest in such opportunities and to carefully examine the benefits provided by funds of hedge funds.

Kat (2004) found that returns of funds of hedge funds are possibly skewed and leptokurtic. He noted that investors may wish to use funds of hedge funds in risk reduction or yield enhancement. In such cases, it is important to know how to hedge against the negative skewness that can be expected when hedge funds are added to their portfolio.

We propose a practical approach to filter funds of hedge funds based on past returns. The approach takes into account the fact that even funds of hedge funds returns are possibly skewed and leptokurtic and nonlinearly related to market returns. Investors who use this approach are assumed to have sophisticated preferences — for example, they like downside protection while looking for yield enhancement.

20.3   Investing in funds of hedge funds: a practical approach

The main motivation for our approach is the findings that hedge funds, including funds of hedge funds, exhibit nonnormal returns and that these returns are also nonlinearly related to market returns. In particular, the correlation between hedge fund returns and market returns differs under different market conditions.

Traditional asset allocation optimizes the use of equities, bonds, real estate, and private equity to invest in a portfolio that maximizes returns and minimizes portfolio risk. Thus, hedge funds become a natural candidate for enhancing returns in an investment portfolio. Moreover, in a bear market, many investment managers find it uninteresting merely to beat the market index, which may have negative returns. They generally prefer to go short or avoid long positions to have positive returns. Investing in appropriately chosen hedge funds can provide the possibility of obtaining positive absolute returns.

It is also generally believed that hedge funds have returns that are usually uncorrelated with the traditional asset classes. In fact, hedge funds may even have a lower risk profile. For example, Morgan Stanley Dean Witter (2000, p. 1) reported that hedge funds "exhibit a low correlation with traditional asset classes, suggesting that hedge funds should play an important role in strategic asset allocation."

20.3.1   Mean, variance, skewness, and kurtosis

Due to the type of strategies employed by hedge fund managers, evidence is strong that hedge fund returns and hedge fund indices returns are not normally distributed. Typically, hedge fund investments are based on absolute-return strategies. They are expected to deliver performance regardless of market conditions. To do so, hedge fund managers use two main approaches to achieve absolute-return targets: (a) directional (or market timing) and (b) nondirectional approaches.

The directional approach dynamically bets on the expected directions of the markets. Funds will invest long or short-sell securities to capture gains from their advance and decline. In contrast, the nondirectional approach attempts to extract value from a set of embedded arbitrage opportunities within and across securities. The nondirectional approach typically exploits structural anomalies in the financial market.

Mean-variance analysis is appropriate when returns are normally distributed or investors' preferences are quadratic. The reliability of mean-variance analysis therefore depends on the degree of nonnormality of the returns data and the nature of the (nonquadratic) utility function. While the utility function may not be a serious problem, the nonnormal distribution of returns presents an issue.

According to Fung and Hsieh (1999), "when returns are not normally distributed (as it is the case for hedge funds), the first two moments (for example, mean and standard deviation) are not sufficient to give an accurate probability." Fung and Hsieh found that hedge fund returns are leptokurtic, or fat-tailed. One likely explanation is that net returns include spreads that are distributed with fat tails.

Many hedge fund indices exhibit relatively low skewness and high kurtosis, especially in the case of funds investing in convertible arbitrage, risk arbitrage, and distressed securities. Brooks and Kat (2001) found that hedge fund index returns are not normally distributed. They argued that while hedge funds may offer relatively high means and low variances, such funds give investors third- and fourth-moment attributes that are exactly the opposite of those that are desirable. Investors obtained a better mean and a lower variance in return for more negative skewness and higher kurtosis.

In sum, the dynamic trading strategies of hedge funds render traditional mean-variance measures meaningless. While some hedge funds may have low standard deviations, this does not mean they are relatively riskless. In fact, they harbor skewness and kurtosis, which makes them risky.

20.3.2   *Correlation of returns*

Fung and Hsieh (1997) examined the returns of hedge funds and commodity trading advisers. They found that hedge fund managers and commodity trading advisers generate returns that have low correlations to the returns of mutual funds and standard asset classes. This is the benefit often cited by portfolio managers in their choice of hedge funds as an alternative investment. Having an additional asset with a low or negative correlation permits the diversification of risk in a means-variance environment. However, complications arise in the case of hedge funds, where correlation-based diversification may not be valid.

Fung and Hsieh (1997) stated, "Risk management in the presence of dynamic trading strategies is also more complex." Hedge fund managers have a great deal of freedom to generate returns that are uncorrelated with those of other asset classes. But this freedom comes at a price. Dynamic trading strategies predispose hedge funds to extreme or tail events. Thus, correlations may come at a cost. They cautioned that "periodically the portfolio can become overly concentrated in a small number of markets" and market exposures converge. This would lead to an "implosion" due to diversification.

Lavino (2000) argued that many hedge funds are not consistently and continuously negatively or poorly correlated with other asset classes over time. Hedge funds also may not have meaningful standard deviations. In fact, many hedge funds have distributions with fat tails, and so normality assumptions on the distribution of hedge fund returns are generally incorrect. This means it is inappropriate to use correlation as a gauge to execute portfolio diversification.

Lo (2001) reinforced this view. He explained that many investors participate in hedge funds to diversify their returns, because hedge fund returns seem uncorrelated with market indexes such as the S&P 500. However, uncorrelated events can become synchronized in a crisis, with correlation changing from 0 to 1 overnight. These situations are examples of the phase-locking behavior encountered in physical and natural science.

Given the statistical characteristics of hedge fund returns, risk and performance measurement of hedge funds are problematic, giving rise to problems in choosing hedge funds and understanding the impact when hedge funds are included in a portfolio of assets. Given the significantly higher moments and nonlinear relation between hedge fund and market index returns, one possible approach is to employ nonlinear estimation methods. One major problem to the use of such nonlinear approaches is the choice of bandwidth (see Hardle (1991) for a discussion) so that estimates can be carried out assuming linearity over each bandwidth. In our case, we will use a more practical approach that can help in interpretation of the results and ease the use of the findings by practitioners. We begin by defining how an investor may select a hedge fund manager. When adding a hedge fund asset to a portfolio of indexed equities, we ask the following questions.

1. How would including hedge funds in a portfolio insulate it when the market is down, and how well is the upside captured when the market is up?
2. How would including hedge funds in a portfolio impact the volatility of a portfolio when the market (index) is up or down?

Investors can rank hedge funds based on these returns and risk criteria in their selection of funds. Based on the returns and risk preferences as well as on the securities in their portfolio, they may select funds that help insulate their returns when markets are hit by extreme and volatile events while providing capture of the market on the upside.

Mathematically, we can reformulate these questions in terms of the first moments between index returns and fund returns and the cross-moments between index returns and fund volatility. In the first-moments analysis, investors desire hedge fund returns to be positive when the market is down. We will call this situation *downside protection*. Furthermore, it is also desirable that hedge fund returns be positively correlated with the market when the market is up. We will call this situation *upside capture*. Koh, Lee, and Phoon (2004) termed the joint outcome *returns-enhancing diversification*. In this chapter, the funds that provide downside protection and upside capture satisfy the first-moments criteria.

	Market up	Market down
Fund up	Positive (desired)	Negative (desired)
Fund down	Negative	Positive

For the cross-moments analysis, we examine the volatility of the hedge funds in relation to the returns of the market indices. Investors would prefer the following outcomes.

	Market up	Market down
Fund volatility up	Positive (desired)	Negative
Fund volatility down	Negative	Positive (desired)

Explicitly, if cross-moments are mainly positive for the hedge funds, it means that when the market is down, the volatility of the fund returns is also low, and vice versa. When the market is up, increased volatility of the hedge funds' returns is better tolerated, while reduced volatility is desired when markets are down, for investors are unlikely to tolerate the increased likelihood of sharp losses in the hedge funds returns during such times. Funds that reduce volatility when the market is down and vice versa when the market is up satisfy the cross-moments criteria.

20.4 Data description, empirical analysis, and results

For our analysis, we included only funds that have a global mandate and that have a complete 10 years of data (January 1995 to December 2004). As a result, we analyzed 77 funds of hedge funds (including CTA/managed futures managers) that managed out of North America, Europe, and Asia. The breakdown is shown in Table 20.1.

Table 20.2 presents a breakdown of the strategies employed by 77 hedge funds that had been in existence from January 1995 to December 2004. CTA/Managed futures funds of hedge funds are the dominant group in our sample.

Traditional U.S.-based fund managers and investors may use the S&P 500 as the equity benchmark. If they are investing internationally, diversification benefits can be measured relative to a global benchmark constructed by Morgan Stanley, such as the MSCI World data. The MSCI World is used to examine the benefits of global investing and as a second benchmark for the global fund of hedge funds. Our sample period is January 1995 to December 2004. For our analysis, we used returns of 77 individual funds of hedge funds over the same sample period. The analysis was restricted to individual funds with complete returns history over the sample period.

Table 20.3 provides summary statistics for skewness and kurtosis as well as test statistics of linearity with market returns for individual hedge funds. It shows that many funds of hedge funds returns are skewed, leptokurtic, and nonnormal and are not linearly related to the market index returns. Further, though for several funds where the linear relation with the S&P 500 cannot be rejected, we reject a linear relation with the MSCI World.

To examine the use of our selection criteria, the market index returns were ranked according to monthly performance. The highest positive index returns

Table 20.1 Geographical distribution of fund of
hedge funds managers

Region	Number
North America	53
Europe	19
North America and Europe	2
Asia	2
Europe and Asia	1

Source: Eurekahedge.

Table 20.2 Strategy classification of funds of hedge fund
managers

Strategy classification	Distribution (%)
CTA	40
Multistrategy	35
Long/short equities	21
Macro	6
Arbitrage	6
Distressed debt	1
Relative value	1

Source: Eurekahedge.

months was ranked first, followed by the second highest. The hedge fund returns are then matched in that same order. The ranked sample was then divided into four parts: the first quartile is the up market, the second and third are stable markets, and the last is the down market. Effectively, we have preselected the estimation bandwidth by defining the selection objective of investors.

We present the first-moments and cross-moments results for each fund of hedge funds with the S&P 500 in Table 20.4. Based on our criteria, we desire a fund that has a negative first moment and a positive cross-moment in down markets (4th quartile), to provide protection or reduce the likelihood of large losses on the downside, and a fund that has a positive first moment and a positive cross-moment in up markets (1st quartile), for capturing or increasing the likelihood of capturing the upside.

In Table 20.5, we segregated the individual funds of hedge funds according to investment strategy. A count of the number of funds that showed the desired correlation profile for the type of investment strategy is provided. When the index was down, 33 or 43% of the funds exhibited the desired first-moments outcome, while only 11 or 15% of the funds exhibited the desired cross-moments outcome. For upside capture, only 22% of the firm exhibited a positive first moment when the market was up, although 60% of the funds exhibited positive

Table 20.3 Skewness, kurtosis, and normality of funds of hedge funds returns and test of linearity between hedge fund returns and S&P 500 & MSCI World returns

Fund of hedge funds	Skewness[1]	Kurtosis	Jarque–Bera test of normality[2]	Linearity test with S&P[3]	Linearity test with MSCI
HF01	0.269 (0.236)	0.429 (0.354)	0.353 (0.308)	0.359 (0.699)	0.597 (0.552)
HF02	0.812 (0.000)	1.052 (0.023)	18.58 (0.000)	3.409 (0.036)	2.016 (0.138)
HF03	0.094 (0.679)	0.457 (0.324)	1.210 (0.546)	0.841 (0.434)	0.435 (0.648)
HF04	0.915 (0.000)	2.221 (0.000)	41.06 (0.000)	0.124 (0.292)	0.890 (0.413)
HF05	0.068 (0.765)	0.088 (0.849)	0.130 (0.937)	3.028 (0.052)	0.770 (0.466)
HF06	0.926 (0.000)	1.214 (0.009)	24.31(0.000)	0.097 (0.907)	0.107 (0.899)
HF07	0.040 (0.859)	0.436 (0.346)	0.972 (0.615)	1.994 (0.141)	0.586 (0.558)
HF08	0.141 (0.535)	1.148 (0.013)	6.933 (0.031)	2.212 (0.114)	1.421 (0.246)
HF09	0.370 (0.104)	0.438 (0.344)	3.660 (0.160)	4.019 (0.021)	3.532 (0.032)
HF10	0.319 (0.161)	0.737 (0.111)	4.709 (0.095)	1.234 (0.295)	0.061 (0.941)
HF11	0.312 (0.093)	0.784 (0.090)	5.942 (0.051)	1.037 (0.358)	0.046 (0.955)
HF12	0.141 (0.534)	2.088 (0.000)	22.02 (0.000)	1.191 (0.308)	0.032 (0.968)
HF13	0.777 (0.000)	0.952 (0.040)	16.48 (0.000)	0.451 (0.638)	0.549 (0.579)
HF14	0.365 (0.109)	0.160 (0.730)	2.765 (0.251)	1.010 (0.367)	0.786 (0.458)
HF15	−0.537 (0.018)	0.769 (0.096)	8.645 (0.013)	0.178 (0.837)	0.219 (0.804)
HF16	−0.846 (0.000)	6.420 (0.000)	218.6 (0.000)	8.671 (0.000)	4.984 (0.008)
HF17	−0.110 (0.628)	4.158 (0.000)	85.95 (0.000)	2.901 (0.059)	1.224 (0.298)
HF18	1.136 (0.000)	2.288 (0.000)	51.52 (0.000)	3.169 (0.046)	4.076 (0.019)
HF19	2.615 (0.000)	15.04 (0.000)	1257 (0.000)	1.668 (0.193)	4.268 (0.016)
HF20	−1.180 (0.000)	3.515 (0.000)	88.87 (0.000)	1.781 (0.173)	1.097 (0.337)
HF21	−0.809 (0.000)	2.422 (0.000)	42.05 (0.000)	3.595 (0.031)	2.179 (0.118)
HF22	1.151 (0.000)	2.210 (0.000)	50.49 (0.000)	0.236 (0.790)	0.402 (0.670)
HF23	−0.149 (0.513)	0.802 (0.083)	3.627 (0.163)	0.019 (0.982)	0.272 (0.762)
HF24	0.598 (0.009)	2.001 (0.000)	27.10 (0.000)	11.79 (0.000)	10.29 (0.000)
HF25	−0.039 (0.862)	−0.393 (0.395)	0.798 (0.671)	0.114 (0.893)	0.612 (0.544)

HF26	0.140 (0.538)	−0.206 (0.655)	0.607 (0.741)	1.627 (0.201)	0.888 (0.414)
HF27	1.314 (0.000)	4.090 (0.000)	117.2 (0.000)	1.774 (0.174)	1.190 (0.308)
HF28	0.227 (0.319)	0.480 (0.299)	2.164 (0.339)	0.263 (0.770)	0.184 (0.832)
HF29	0.107 (0.637)	0.470 (0.310)	1.323 (0.516)	0.182 (0.834)	0.037 (0.964)
HF30	1.847 (0.000)	9.879 (0.000)	551.6 (0.000)	1.543 (0.218)	0.604 (0.548)
HF31	−1.556 (0.000)	6.548 (0.000)	260.6 (0.000)	11.87 (0.000)	14.52 (0.000)
HF32	−0.221 (0.330)	2.826 (0.000)	40.57 (0.000)	3.002 (0.054)	2.776 (0.066)
HF33	−1.233 (0.000)	6.990 (0.000)	272.4 (0.000)	0.082 (0.921)	0.316 (0.730)
HF34	0.163 (0.474)	0.670 (0.147)	2.754 (0.252)	2.814 (0.064)	2.116 (0.125)
HF35	−0.262 (0.248)	−0.339 (0.464)	1.937 (0.380)	2.898 (0.059)	1.454 (0.238)
HF36	−0.218 (0.337)	−0.303 (0.513)	1.399 (0.497)	2.677 (0.073)	1.172 (0.313)
HF37	0.097 (0.670)	0.058 (0.890)	0.203 (0.903)	2.411 (0.095)	1.116 (0.331)
HF38	−3.140 (0.000)	15.82 (0.000)	1450 (0.000)	2.337 (0.101)	0.762 (0.469)
HF39	0.551 (0.015)	1.878 (0.000)	23.71 (0.000)	2.489 (0.087)	0.525 (0.593)
HF40	0.064 (0.776)	1.155 (0.012)	6.748 (0.034)	1.720 (0.184)	1.457 (0.237)
HF41	−0.273 (0.229)	1.498 (0.001)	12.71 (0.002)	2.581 (0.080)	1.093 (0.339)
HF42	−1.465 (0.000)	11.27 (0.000)	678.2 (0.000)	8.096 (0.000)	9.412 (0.000)
HF43	0.684 (0.003)	3.324 (0.000)	64.61 (0.000)	2.336 (0.101)	1.417 (0.247)
HF44	−3.813 (0.000)	21.75 (0.000)	2655 (0.000)	4.545 (0.013)	2.366 (0.098)
HF45	−0.178 (0.432)	1.065 (0.021)	6.307 (0.043)	0.094 (0.910)	0.354 (0.703)
HF46	1.109 (0.000)	4.886 (0.000)	144.0 (0.000)	0.420 (0.658)	0.778 (0.462)
HF47	0.633 (0.005)	4.477 (0.000)	108.2 (0.000)	4.514 (0.013)	4.624 (0.012)
HF48	0.041 (0.856)	−0.087 (0.850)	0.072 (0.965)	6.924 (0.001)	5.564 (0.005)
HF49	4.562 (0.000)	30.15 (0.000)	4919 (0.000)	1.576 (0.211)	1.222 (0.299)
HF50	−1.209 (0.000)	3.007 (0.000)	73.81 (0.000)	1.309 (0.274)	0.962 (0.385)
HF51	0.192 (0.398)	1.922 (0.000)	19.04 (0.000)	2.313 (0.104)	1.430 (0.244)
HF52	0.378 (0.096)	0.753 (0.104)	5.652 (0.059)	5.292 (0.006)	4.029 (0.020)
HF53	−0.128 (0.573)	1.643 (0.000)	13.70 (0.000)	1.689 (0.189)	2.791 (0.065)
HF54	−0.583 (0.010)	3.556 (0.000)	69.42 (0.000)	5.911 (0.004)	6.321 (0.002)
HF55	0.516 (0.023)	0.540 (0.243)	6.724 (0.035)	2.231 (0.112)	0.898 (0.410)

(continued)

Table 20.3 (*continued*)

Fund of hedge funds	Skewness[1]	Kurtosis	Jarque–Bera test of normality[2]	Linearity test with S&P[3]	Linearity test with MSCI
HF56	0.914 (0.000)	2.221 (0.000)	41.06 (0.000)	1.244 (0.292)	0.893 (0.412)
HF57	0.358 (0.116)	0.069 (0.882)	2.561 (0.278)	2.690 (0.072)	3.150 (0.047)
HF58	−0.846 (0.000)	6.420 (0.000)	218.6 (0.000)	8.671 (0.000)	4.885 (0.009)
HF59	0.490 (0.031)	2.044 (0.000)	25.47 (0.000)	0.489 (0.614)	0.722 (0.488)
HF60	0.028 (0.901)	2.105 (0.000)	21.99 (0.000)	0.313 (0.732)	0.626 (0.537)
HF61	−0.917 (0.000)	2.563 (0.000)	49.23 (0.000)	2.210 (0.114)	2.441 (0.092)
HF62	1.426 (0.000)	4.827 (0.000)	155.9 (0.000)	17.17 (0.000)	15.06 (0.000)
HF63	−0.159 (0.484)	1.864 (0.000)	17.72 (0.000)	2.855 (0.062)	2.102 (0.127)
HF64	0.303 (0.182)	0.251 (0.588)	2.136 (0.344)	7.601 (0.001)	7.820 (0.001)
HF65	1.798 (0.000)	7.412 (0.000)	336.5 (0.000)	1.780 (0.173)	0.966 (0.384)
HF66	−1.556 (0.000)	6.548 (0.000)	260.6 (0.000)	11.88 (0.000)	14.52 (0.000)
HF67	0.601 (0.008)	−0.053 (0.908)	7.169 (0.028)	14.11 (0.000)	12.64 (0.000)
HF68	0.661 (0.004)	0.568 (0.220)	10.274 (0.006)	1.369 (0.258)	0.888 (0.414)
HF69	−0.221 (0.330)	2.826 (0.000)	40.57 (0.000)	3.002 (0.054)	2.776 (0.066)
HF70	0.720 (0.002)	1.792 (0.000)	26.19 (0.000)	3.893 (0.023)	3.173 (0.046)
HF71	0.041 (0.856)	−0.087 (0.850)	0.072 (0.965)	6.924 (0.001)	5.564 (0.005)
HF72	0.234 (0.303)	−0.219 (0.635)	1.329 (0.515)	6.436 (0.002)	6.890 (0.001)
HF73	−0.165 (0.469)	0.636 (0.169)	2.544 (0.280)	2.326 (0.102)	3.148 (0.047)
HF74	0.384 (0.092)	0.525 (0.256)	4.286 (0.117)	7.448 (0.001)	7.440 (0.001)
HF75	0.025 (0.914)	0.237 (0.608)	0.291 (0.864)	0.537 (0.586)	0.403 (0.669)
HF76	0.777 (0.000)	0.952 (0.040)	16.48 (0.000)	0.451 (0.638)	0.562 (0.572)
HF77	0.136 (0.549)	0.996 (0.031)	5.289 (0.071)	4.097 (0.019)	2.820 (0.064)

Shaded cells (at 10% level of significance).
[1] Level of significance in parentheses.
[2] Jacque–Bera is a test for normality based on the skewness and kurtosis measures combined (see Jacque and Bera, 1987).
[3] Estimated using a cubic equation as in Tsay (1989). Statistic is distributed $F(2, 115)$.

Table 20.4 First moments and cross-moments of funds of hedge funds with S&P 500

Fund of hedge funds — region in which fund is based	Investment strategy	First moment (1st quartile)	First moment (4th quartile)	Cross-moment (1st quartile)	Cross-moment (4th quartile)
HF01 — N. America	CTA/managed futures	−0.112	−0.321	0.089	−0.135
HF02 — N. America	CTA/managed futures	−0.216	−0.581	0.311	−0.390
HF03 — N. America	Multistrategy	−0.059	−0.475	0.009	−0.347
HF04 — N. America	CTA/managed futures	0.125	−0.127	0.150	−0.184
HF05 — N. America	Long/short equities	−0.056	0.665	−0.035	−0.567
HF06 — N. America	CTA/managed futures	0.043	0.013	0.201	−0.068
HF07 — N. America	Multistrategy	−0.263	0.110	−0.307	−0.056
HF08 — N. America	Multistrategy	−0.118	−0.513	0.085	−0.380
HF09 — N. America	CTA/managed futures	−0.283	−0.571	0.382	−0.519
HF10 — N. America	Long/short equities	−0.168	−0.513	0.053	−0.508
HF11 — N. America	Long/short equities	−0.189	−0.520	0.074	−0.522
HF12 — N. America	Relative value	−0.166	0.667	−0.176	−0.508
HF13 — N. America	CTA/managed futures	−0.007	0.145	0.239	0.201
HF14 — N. America	CTA/managed futures	0.013	0.485	0.104	−0.526
HF15 — N. America	Long/short equities	0.388	0.525	0.231	−0.627
HF16 — N. America	Macro	−0.069	0.722	0.005	−0.612
HF17 — N. America	Multistrategy	−0.266	0.340	−0.022	−0.316
HF18 — N. America	Distressed debt	0.158	0.176	0.247	−0.409
HF19 — N. America	Multistrategy	−0.044	0.143	−0.243	0.196
HF20 — N. America	Multistrategy	−0.158	0.339	0.017	−0.417
HF21 — N. America	Multistrategy	−0.090	0.368	0.094	−0.586
HF22 — N. America	CTA/managed futures	−0.238	0.012	−0.033	−0.123
HF23 — N. America	Long/short equities	−0.218	−0.353	−0.004	−0.226
HF24 — N. America	CTA/managed futures	−0.441	−0.582	0.178	−0.601
HF25 — N. America	Multistrategy	−0.007	0.254	0.122	0.044

(continued)

Table 20.4 (continued)

Fund of hedge funds — region in which fund is based	Investment strategy	First moment (1st quartile)	First moment (4th quartile)	Cross-moment (1st quartile)	Cross-moment (4th quartile)
HF26 — N. America	CTA/managed futures	−0.159	−0.129	0.115	−0.005
HF27 — N. America	CTA/managed futures	−0.334	−0.533	0.346	−0.275
HF28 — N. America	Multistrategy	0.035	0.103	0.074	0.006
HF29 — N. America	CTA/managed futures	−0.115	−0.136	−0.018	−0.019
HF30 — N. America	Long/short equities	−0.157	0.432	0.207	0.110
HF31 — N. America	Arbitrage	−0.026	0.582	−0.272	−0.557
HF32 — N. America	Long/short equities	−0.157	0.390	0.217	−0.476
HF33 — N. A. and Europe	Multistrategy	−0.219	0.232	0.204	0.252
HF34 — N. A. and Europe	Arbitrage	0.023	0.022	−0.046	0.125
HF35 — N. America	CTA/managed futures	−0.428	0.020	−0.007	−0.022
HF36 — N. America	CTA/managed futures	−0.402	0.028	−0.044	−0.010
HF37 — N. America	Long/short equities	−0.006	0.665	0.056	−0.552
HF38 — N. America	Multistrategy	−0.324	0.079	0.301	0.027
HF39 — N. America	Long/short equities	−0.058	0.562	−0.044	−0.061
HF40 — N. America	CTA/managed futures	−0.231	−0.398	0.027	−0.416
HF41 — N. America	CTA/managed futures	0.246	−0.055	0.216	0.056
HF42 — N. America	Multistrategy	0.063	0.517	0.033	−0.571
HF43 — N. America	Multistrategy	0.189	0.231	0.418	−0.121
HF44 — N. America	Multistrategy	−0.270	0.496	0.222	−0.371
HF45 — N. America	Long/short equities	−0.217	−0.311	−0.033	−0.180
HF46 — N. America	CTA/managed futures	−0.093	−0.271	−0.030	−0.164
HF47 — N. America	Arbitrage	0.076	0.658	0.007	−0.413
HF48 — N. America	CTA/managed futures	−0.328	−0.500	−0.056	−0.639
HF49 — N. America	CTA/managed futures	−0.224	−0.213	−0.121	−0.088
HF50 — N. America	Arbitrage	−0.125	0.260	0.304	−0.007

HF51 — N. America	Multistrategy	-0.113	0.551	-0.056	-0.001
HF52 — N. America	Macro	-0.155	-0.707	0.144	-0.748
HF53 — N. America	Long/short equities	0.048	0.520	0.124	-0.555
HF54 — N. America	Long/short equities	0.087	0.770	0.085	-0.659
HF55 — N. America	Macro	-0.320	-0.036	-0.116	0.238
HF56 — Europe	CTA/managed futures	0.125	-0.127	0.150	-0.184
HF57 — Europe	CTA/managed futures	-0.465	-0.402	-0.183	-0.330
HF58 — Europe	Macro	-0.069	0.722	0.005	-0.612
HF59 — Europe	Long/short equities	0.235	-0.040	-0.176	-0.120
HF60 — Europe	Long/short equities	0.286	-0.019	-0.222	-0.094
HF61 — Europe	Macro	-0.178	0.375	-0.132	-0.524
HF62 — Europe	Multistrategy	-0.139	-0.561	-0.023	-0.592
HF63 — Europe	CTA/managed futures	-0.240	-0.473	0.254	-0.473
HF64 — Europe	CTA/managed futures	-0.197	-0.575	0.053	-0.576
HF65 — Europe	Multistrategy	0.049	-0.196	0.107	-0.021
HF66 — Europe	Arbitrage	-0.026	0.582	-0.272	-0.557
HF67 — Europe	CTA/managed futures	-0.358	-0.759	0.112	-0.836
HF68 — Europe	CTA/managed futures	-0.163	-0.465	0.091	-0.348
HF69 — Europe	Long/short equities	0.157	0.390	0.217	-0.476
HF70 — Europe and Asia	Long/short equities	-0.262	-0.183	0.323	-0.045
HF71 — Europe	CTA/managed futures	-0.328	-0.500	-0.056	-0.639
HF72 — Europe	CTA/managed futures	-0.388	-0.592	0.150	-0.662
HF73 — Europe	CTA/managed futures	0.244	-0.292	0.422	-0.350
HF74 — Europe	CTA/managed futures	-0.275	-0.715	0.155	-0.612
HF75 — Europe	CTA/managed futures	-0.234	0.144	-0.056	-0.096
HF76 — Asia	CTA/managed futures	-0.007	0.145	0.239	0.201
HF77 — Asia	CTA/managed futures	-0.195	-0.661	-0.199	-0.638

Shaded cell indicates that result met the desired criterion.

Table 20.5 Number of funds meeting moments criteria with S&P 500

Investment strategy	Number of funds	Funds with first moment (1st quartile) > 0	Funds with first moment (4th quartile) < 0	Funds with cross-moment > 0 (1st quartile)	Funds with cross-moment > 0 (4th quartile)
CTA/managed futures	31	6	22	21	3
Multistrategy	27	5	5	12	5
Long/short equities	16	5	6	8	1
Macro	5	0	0	3	1
Arbitrage	5	1	0	2	1
Distressed debt	1	0	0	1	0
Relative value	1	0	0	0	0
Total	77	17	33	46	11

Investment strategy	Number of funds	Both first-moments criteria	Both cross-moments criteria
CTA/managed futures	31	4	3
Multistrategy	27	1	4
Long/short equities	16	2	1
Macro	5	0	0
Arbitrage	5	0	0
Distressed debt	1	0	0
Relative value	1	0	0
Total	77	7	8

	Number of funds	Percent
Meet zero criterion	14	18
Meet one criterion	25	33
Meet two criteria	32	42
Meet three criteria	5	6
Meet all criteria	1	1
Total	77	100%

cross-moments. Our results showed that for U.S. investors holding the S&P 500, few funds of hedge funds can provide both downside protection and upside capture; more importantly, fund returns tend to be more volatile when the market is down. We also present the results for funds that met both first-moments and both cross-moments criteria. Only seven funds exhibited returns-enhancing diversification, and eight funds met the cross-moments criteria.

Tables 20.6 and 20.7 present the first moments and cross-moments of each fund of hedge funds with MSCI World and the number of funds meeting the various criteria. Because a different market index is used (one that is a proxy for global investing), the results for funds meeting the moments criteria did differ from the case when the S&P 500 was used. We obtained more instances of funds meeting the various criteria when MSCI World is used as compared with the case using the S&P 500, perhaps reflecting the global mandate of the funds. Two funds met all four moments criteria, and we also found that funds that provided the desired first- and cross-moments criteria do differ when MSCI World is used rather than the S&P 500 index. In particular, an arbitrage fund provided the desired first-moments criteria and another macro and distressed debt fund provided the desired cross-moments criteria using MSCI World instead of the S&P 500 Index. From these findings, it is clear that the choice of indices used can impact the results obtained.

20.5 Analysis of trade-off

Based on our selection criteria, we found that individual funds of hedge funds met from zero to all four criteria ex-post. A useful analysis would be to check if any trade-offs exist. The basic tenet of finance is the existence of a trade-off between expected returns and risk. Hence, we conjecture that funds that performed best in meeting all criteria would provide a lower return on average than one that met none of them. Similarly, we would expect the ranking of returns to be inverse to the number of criteria met. On the other hand, perverse results may be explained by the relative skills of manager, incorrect assumptions about the investors, inappropriate choice of the market indices used, and possibly regulatory, tax, and other reasons.

The average returns of the funds meeting a different number of criteria were computed. A simple difference rank correlation test was used to analyze the trade-off. Results are presented in Table 20.8. We initially expect that funds that meet all four criteria would have a lower average return than those that meet three criteria and that those that meet three criteria will have a lower average return than two, and so on. The finding is mixed and is found to be more consistent with our conjecture for the S&P 500 than for MSCI World. Although not statistically significant, the very few funds that meet all four of our criteria provided returns that are lower than those meeting none of our criteria.

We next examined funds that satisfied concurrently both first-moments criteria and those that met both cross-moments criteria. The results in Table 20.9

Table 20.6 First moments and cross-moments of funds of hedge funds with MSCI World

Fund of hedge funds — region in which fund is based	Investment strategy	First moment (1st quartile)	First moment (4th quartile)	Cross-moment (1st quartile)	Cross-moment (4th quartile)
HF01 — N. America	CTA/managed futures	−0.282	−0.381	0.223	−0.059
HF02 — N. America	CTA/managed futures	−0.259	−0.604	0.186	−0.415
HF03 — N. America	Multistrategy	−0.224	−0.561	0.180	−0.566
HF04 — N. America	CTA/managed futures	0.051	−0.374	0.118	−0.068
HF05 — N. America	Long/short equities	−0.068	0.659	0.026	−0.723
HF06 — N. America	CTA/managed futures	0.122	−0.140	0.175	−0.054
HF07 — N. America	Multistrategy	−0.049	0.110	0.064	−0.043
HF08 — N. America	Multistrategy	−0.308	−0.614	0.198	−0.683
HF09 — N. America	CTA/managed futures	−0.304	−0.614	0.242	−0.503
HF10 — N. America	Long/short equities	−0.405	−0.607	0.370	−0.610
HF11 — N. America	Long/short equities	−0.400	−0.622	0.363	−0.633
HF12 — N. America	Relative value	−0.018	0.583	−0.047	−0.624
HF13 — N. America	CTA/managed futures	−0.188	0.095	0.281	−0.105
HF14 — N. America	CTA/managed futures	0.060	0.601	0.023	−0.501
HF15 — N. America	Long/short equities	0.168	0.644	0.129	−0.713
HF16 — N. America	Macro	0.241	0.695	0.379	−0.625
HF17 — N. America	Multistrategy	0.030	0.286	0.366	−0.377
HF18 — N. America	Distressed debt	0.385	0.296	0.489	0.070
HF19 — N. America	Multistrategy	0.168	−0.084	0.171	0.074
HF20 — N. America	Multistrategy	−0.125	0.416	0.095	−0.370
HF21 — N. America	Multistrategy	0.023	0.496	0.263	−0.599
HF22 — N. America	CTA/managed futures	−0.130	−0.084	−0.113	−0.173
HF23 — N. America	Long/short equities	−0.464	−0.300	0.093	−0.252
HF24 — N. America	CTA/managed futures	−0.054	−0.496	0.124	−0.597
HF25 — N. America	Multistrategy	0.119	0.172	0.004	0.043
HF26 — N. America	CTA/managed futures	−0.056	−0.041	0.075	0.027

HF27 — N. America	CTA/managed futures	−0.436	−0.550	0.093	−0.340
HF28 — N. America	Multistrategy	−0.211	0.167	−0.251	−0.086
HF29 — N. America	CTA/managed futures	−0.211	−0.116	−0.131	−0.012
HF30 — N. America	Long/short equities	0.279	0.447	0.353	−0.307
HF31 — N. America	Arbitrage	−0.113	0.639	−0.177	−0.544
HF32 — N. America	Long/short equities	0.186	0.396	0.228	−0.538
HF33 — N. A. and Europe	Multistrategy	−0.183	0.042	0.195	0.028
HF34 — N. A. and Europe	Arbitrage	0.043	−0.094	−0.128	0.014
HF35 — N. America	CTA/managed futures	−0.281	0.076	0.175	0.085
HF36 — N. America	CTA/managed futures	−0.271	0.044	0.139	−0.003
HF37 — N. America	Long/short equities	−0.087	0.658	0.012	−0.695
HF38 — N. America	Multistrategy	−0.278	0.202	0.339	0.134
HF39 — N. America	Long/short equities	0.174	0.683	0.285	−0.721
HF40 — N. America	CTA/managed futures	−0.339	−0.244	−0.045	−0.277
HF41 — N. America	CTA/managed futures	0.089	−0.056	0.194	0.075
HF42 — N. America	Multistrategy	−0.018	0.531	0.062	−0.540
HF43 — N. America	Multistrategy	−0.010	0.191	0.405	−0.105
HF44 — N. America	Multistrategy	−0.287	0.479	0.269	−0.392
HF45 — N. America	Long/short equities	−0.448	−0.282	0.078	−0.229
HF46 — N. America	CTA/managed futures	−0.240	−0.282	0.069	−0.026
HF47 — N. America	Arbitrage	−0.052	0.622	−0.082	−0.427
HF48 — N. America	CTA/managed futures	−0.317	−0.437	−0.108	−0.682
HF49 — N. America	CTA/managed futures	−0.115	−0.243	−0.261	−0.216
HF50 — N. America	Arbitrage	−0.162	0.285	0.296	−0.126
HF51 — N. America	Multistrategy	−0.024	0.570	0.079	0.116
HF52 — N. America	Macro	−0.172	−0.709	0.185	−0.716
HF53 — N. America	Long/short equities	−0.266	0.491	−0.222	−0.529
HF54 — N. America	Long/short equities	0.362	0.824	0.396	−0.684
HF55 — N. America	Macro	−0.042	−0.190	0.074	0.145

(continued)

Table 20.6 (continued)

Fund of hedge funds — region in which fund is based	Investment strategy	First moment (1st quartile)	First moment (4th quartile)	Cross-moment (1st quartile)	Cross-moment (4th quartile)
HF56 — Europe	CTA/managed futures	0.051	-0.374	0.118	-0.068
HF57 — Europe	CTA/managed futures	-0.268	-0.472	-0.153	-0.530
HF58 — Europe	Macro	0.241	0.695	0.379	-0.625
HF59 — Europe	Long/short equities	-0.156	0.111	-0.092	-0.037
HF60 — Europe	Long/short equities	-0.091	0.117	-0.299	-0.042
HF61 — Europe	Macro	-0.037	0.423	-0.038	-0.543
HF62 — Europe	Multistrategy	-0.108	-0.469	-0.057	-0.572
HF63 — Europe	CTA/managed futures	-0.307	-0.485	0.058	-0.490
HF64 — Europe	CTA/managed futures	-0.137	-0.613	0.121	-0.566
HF65 — Europe	Multistrategy	0.100	-0.254	0.136	-0.047
HF66 — Europe	Arbitrage	-0.113	0.639	-0.177	-0.544
HF67 — Europe	CTA/managed futures	-0.271	-0.693	0.098	-0.838
HF68 — Europe	CTA/managed futures	-0.214	-0.403	0.120	-0.357
HF69 — Europe	Long/short equities	0.186	0.396	0.228	-0.538
HF70 — Europe	Long/short equities	-0.085	-0.130	0.227	0.091
HF71 — Europe	CTA/managed futures	-0.317	-0.437	-0.108	-0.682
HF72 — Europe	CTA/managed futures	-0.255	-0.539	-0.041	-0.666
HF73 — Europe	CTA/managed futures	0.095	-0.179	0.061	-0.315
HF74 — Europe	CTA/managed futures	-0.455	-0.667	-0.098	-0.517
HF75 — Europe	CTA/managed futures	0.064	0.169	-0.201	-0.297
HF76 — Asia	CTA/managed futures	-0.188	0.095	0.281	-0.105
HF77 — Asia	CTA/managed futures	-0.272	-0.525	-0.090	-0.580

Shaded cell indicates that result met the desired criterion.

Table 20.7 Number of funds meeting moments criteria with MSCI World

Investment strategy	Number of funds	Funds with first moment (1st quartile) > 0	Funds with first moment (4th quartile) < 0	Funds with cross-moment > 0 (1st quartile)	Funds with cross-moment > 0 (4th quartile)
CTA/managed futures	31	6	24	20	3
Multistrategy	27	5	5	15	5
Long/short equities	16	6	5	13	1
Macro	5	2	1	4	1
Arbitrage	5	1	1	1	1
Distressed debt	1	1	0	1	1
Relative value	1	0	0	0	0
Total	77	21	36	54	12

Investment strategy	Number of funds	Both first-moments criteria	Both cross-moments criteria
CTA/managed futures	31	3	3
Multistrategy	27	2	5
Long/short equities	16	0	1
Macro	5	0	1
Arbitrage	5	1	0
Distressed debt	1	0	1
Relative value	1	0	0
Total	77	6	10

	Number of funds	Percent
Meet zero criterion	10	13
Meet one criterion	23	30
Meet two criteria	34	44
Meet three criteria	8	10
Meet all criteria	2	3
Total	78	100%

Table 20.8 Analysis of funds meeting zero to all criteria

Panel 1: Mean and variance of portfolio of hedge funds

	Met zero criterion	Met one criterion	Met two criteria	Met three criteria	Met all criteria
S&P 500					
Mean return (% per month)	1.116	1.041	1.084	1.211	0.827
Standard deviation	0.356	0.345	0.604	0.565	N.A.
MSCI World					
Mean return (% per month)	1.062	1.083	1.096	1.143	0.925
Standard deviation	0.292	0.390	0.608	0.379	0.138

Panel 2a: Results of test of difference in mean returns (S&P 500)

	Met zero criterion	Met one criterion	Met two criteria	Met three criteria	Met all criteria
Expected	One < None*	Two < None	Three < None	Four < None	Two < One
Result	One < None	Two < None	Three > None	Four < None	Two > One
t-value	0.638	0.222	−0.349	N.A.	−0.340
Expected	Three < One	Four < One	Three < Two	Four < Two	Four < Three
Result	Three > One	Four < One	Three > Two	Four > Two	Four > Three
t-value	−1.395	N.A.	−0.460	N.A.	N.A.

Panel 2b: Results of test of difference in mean returns (MSCI World)

	Met zero criterion	Met one criterion	Met two criteria	Met three criteria	Met all criteria
Expected	One < None*	Two < None	Three < None	Four < None	Two < One
Result	One > None	Two > None	Three > None	Four < None	Two > One
t-value	−0.172	−0.152	−0.502	0.392	−0.099
Expected	Three < One	Four < One	Three < Two	Four < Two	Four < Three
Result	Three > One	Four < One	Three > Two	Four > Two	Four > Three
t-value	−0.386	1.244	−0.280	1.198	1.319

* < means that the average return of funds that does not satisfy any criterion to be greater than the average returns of funds that satisfy one criterion and so forth. Shaded results are where finding is not as expected.

Table 20.9 Analysis of funds meeting both first-moments and both cross-moments criteria

	Met both first-moments criteria	Met both cross-moments criteria	Did not meet both first- or both cross-moments criteria
S&P 500			
Mean return (% per month)	1.159	1.077	1.068
Standard deviation	0.497	0.478	0.470
MSCI World			
Mean return (% per month)	0.987	0.991	1.099
Standard deviation	0.281	0.389	0.499

show that funds that met these criteria provided lower returns on average as compared with those that do not meet either criteria when the MSCI World is used. The results were, however, not statistically significant.

20.6 Conclusion

We introduced a practical approach in analyzing the risk and performance of funds of hedge funds from the viewpoints of U.S. and global equity investors. We focused on the impact when we include global funds of hedge funds in their portfolio and examined whether the inclusion helps to insulate the overall portfolio when the market is down, to capture the upside, and to reduce the impact of market volatility during extreme events. An advantage of this approach is that it alleviates the problems that can arise if hedge fund returns are skewed and leptokurtic and nonlinearly related to the market returns. Our approach also allows for a meaningful economic interpretation of the results.

Based on a sample of 77 global funds of hedge funds from the EurekaHedge database, we found that while all funds provide diversification, in the sense that they are not perfectly correlated with market index returns, only 33% or 42% of the funds are negatively correlated with the S&P 500 index returns in a down market (defined as the lowest return quartile of the S&P 500). Our results also show that very few funds met both our first-moments and cross-moments criteria. Recent work by Brenner, Ou, and Zhang (2004) showed that an option on a straddle can be used to hedge volatility risk. This finding is likely to shed light on our finding on moment neutrality for hedge funds. A put option (or dynamic trading) provides downside protection, trading off against upside capture. If volatility risk is to be hedged, it requires a further premium on an option on a straddle. We conjecture that the trade-off relation between our performance and risk measures provides an interesting question for future research.

Lastly, our proposed methodology can be applied to other classes of hedge funds and even other types of assets when investors exhibit our specified preferences and where returns exhibit differing relations to held portfolios in up and down markets.

References

Amenc, N., Giraud, J. C., Martellini, L., and Vaissie, M. (2004). Taking a Close Look at the European Fund of Hedge Funds Industry: Comparing and Contrasting Industry Practices and Academic Recommendations. *Journal of Alternative Investments*, 7(3):59–69.

Brenner, M., Ou, E. Y., and Zhang, J. E. (2004). Hedging Volatility Risk. Working Paper, New York University, New York.

Brooks, C. and Kat, H. M. (2001). The Statistical Properties of Hedge Fund Index Returns and Their Implications for Investors. Working Paper, ISMA Centre, Reading, U.K.

Fung, W. and Hsieh, D. A. (1997). Empirical Characteristics of Dynamic Trading Strategies: The Case of Hedge Funds. *Review of Financial Studies*, 10(2):275–302.

Fung, W. and Hsieh D.A. (1999). Is Mean-Variance: Analysis Applicable to Hedge Funds? *Economic Letters*, 62:53–58.

Fung, W. and Hsieh, D. (2001). The Risk in Hedge Fund Strategies: Theory and Evidence from Trend Followers. *Review of Financial Studies*, 14(2):313–341.

Gregoriou, G. N. (2004). Are Managers of Funds of Hedge Funds Good Market Timers? *Journal of Wealth Management*, 7(2):61–75.

Gregoriou, G. N., Hübner, G., Papageorgiou, N., and Rouah, F. (2005). Dominating Funds of Funds with Simple Hedge Fund Strategies. Working Paper, State University of New York, Plattsburgh, NY; McGill University, Montreal, Canada; HEC, Montreal, Canada; University of Maastricht, The Netherlands.

Hardle, W. (1991). *Smoothing Techniques, with Implementations*. Springer, New York.

Ineichen, A. M. (2002). Fund of Hedge Funds: Industry Overview. *Journal of Wealth Management*, 4(4):47–62.

Jacque, C. M. and Bera, A. K. (1987). A Test for Normality of Observations and Regression Residual. *International Statistical Review*, 55:163–173.

Kat, H. M. (2004). In Search of the Optimal Fund of Hedge Funds. *Journal of Wealth Management*, 6(4):43–51.

Koh, F., Lee, D., and Phoon, K. F. (2004). CTA Strategies for Returns-Enhancing Diversification. In: *Commodity Trading Advisors — Risk, Performance Analysis and Selection* (Gregoriou, G. N., Karavas, V. N., Lhabitant, F. S., and Rouah, F., eds.). John Wiley & Sons, Hoboken, NJ.

Lavino, S. (2000). *The Hedge Fund Handbook*. McGraw-Hill, New York.

Lo, A. W. (2001). Risk Management for Hedge Funds: Introduction and Overview. *Financial Analyst Journal*, 57(6):16–33.

Morgan Stanley Dean Witter. (2000). *Why Hedge Funds Make Sense*. New York.

Tsay, R. S. (1989). Testing and Modeling Threshold Autoregressive Processes. *Journal of the American Statistical Association*, 84(405):231–240.

21 An overview of funds of hedge funds

Jean Brunel

Abstract

With substantial cash flows into the fund of funds business and questions as to their tax status, it is reasonable to ask whether it still makes sense to consider investing in funds of funds, particularly because the knowledge of the so-called hedge fund industry is growing and because it is becoming fashionable to argue that one can build one's own hedge fund portfolio. We therefore look at funds of funds, with three principal areas of focus. First, we argue there is a need for funds of funds for a number of wealthy, though not ultra-wealthy, individuals, for whom the alternative involving creating a portfolio of individual funds is not realistic. We then consider the three potential conceptual approaches to constructing a successful portfolio of hedge funds or of funds of funds and, coming back to our first point, suggest that only one of these approaches would be available to all but the largest investors. Finally, we look at the so-called fund of funds universe and point to important problems for the indices being used to track it, although significant improvements have been made in the recent past.

21.1 Introduction

With the debate so often focusing on the costs associated with hedge fund investments, this question can be fairly asked: What about funds of funds, where an additional layer of fee applies? This is further compounded, as explained in Gordon (2005), if one begins to question the tax status of hedge funds, because the trader status that provides for the fees to be deductible from taxable returns is argued to be all the harder to maintain in a vehicle that invests only in other funds.

In this chapter, we look at funds of funds, with three principal areas of focus. First, we consider and discuss a commonsense observation that points to the need for funds of funds for a number of wealthy, though not ultra-wealthy, individuals, for whom the alternative involving creating a portfolio of individual funds is not realistic. We then consider the three potential conceptual approaches to constructing a successful portfolio of hedge funds or of funds of funds and, coming back to our first point, suggest that only one of these approaches would be available to all but the largest investors. Finally, we look at the so-called fund of funds universe and point to important problems for the indices being used to track it, although significant improvements have been made in the recent past.

21.2   Creating a portfolio of hedge funds

Though it is a fact that the role of hedge funds has drastically expanded as a valid investment alternative across the full spectrum of investors, it is no less clear that the amount committed to so-called hedge funds[1] is often still limited in terms of total dollar exposure per individual investor.

Consider a simple series of basic facts. Lhabitant and De Piante Vicin (2004), for instance, suggest that a portfolio would need to have between 15 and 20 different hedge funds to achieve appropriate diversification. And though this number may be lower than certain other practitioners would recommend, it is still significant, particularly when one starts considering that most such funds would have minimum investment levels of at least $1 million, when not $3–5 million or higher. Thus, imagine an investor who seeks to create a well-diversified exposure to hedge funds and who does not even follow the diversification rule suggested in Brunel (2004), that the exposure to hedge funds be incorporated into the overall portfolio risk exposures rather than segregated as a distinct asset class. Imagine that our investor will only select funds with a $1 million minimum and that his or her portfolio will not have more than 25% allocated to hedge funds–type strategies. Our investor would need to have an absolute minimum of $60 million before he or she could consider using individual funds, failing which he or she would have to accept a higher-than-desirable manager concentration risk.

Note, however, that this line of reasoning does not mandate that our investor only invest in funds of funds, the logical alternative. Indeed, with funds of funds often providing diversification, which Lhabitant and De Piante Vicin (2004) might consider excessive based on a strict statistical analysis, it might make a great deal of sense for him or her to construct a portfolio with a fund of funds core and a few individual satellites.

The need to use funds of funds for investors with less than $100–250 million goes beyond the notion of diversification. However, to address this issue, it is best to ask oneself how the ongoing management of a hedge fund portfolio might work.

21.3   Ongoing portfolio management

Though it is surely not the world's easiest task to identify an appropriate benchmark to assess the performance of a portfolio of hedge fund, it is probably not in doubt that any investor constructing such a portfolio is, mentally at least, seeking to outperform something! Conceptually, there are at least three possible approaches to achieve that goal.

---

[1] We return to this point in the last section of this paper, but the main insight here is derived from Brunel (2004), who points to the fact that it is probably little short of misleading to suggest that hedge funds constitute a single asset class. Indeed, they are much more instructively divided into at least two clusters, one offering fixed-income-like risk and the other equity-like risk.

The first goal is the analog of the traditional portfolio management objective described as superior security selection. Here, the security is the underlying manager, and superior security selection is achieved by seeking best-of-breed managers. Some measure of portfolio diversification might be achieved within the same analogy by equating hedge fund strategy with industry or geographical zones in the traditional portfolio management world. In short, therefore, the focus is primarily on identifying the best managers and secondarily on managing a notional tracking error relative to the universe by controlling for excessive strategy concentration. Note that this approach might require a larger number of individual hedge fund holdings, because Lhabitant and De Piante Vicin (2004) do not control for individual strategy risk when estimating that a portfolio of 15–20 hedge funds will achieve optimal diversification.[2]

This is no different than the often-quoted statistics according to which a portfolio comprising 21 randomly selected individual U.S. equities has achieved optimal tracking error reduction. In reality, most large-capitalization equity managers would commonly consider that they should own 35–45 stocks to achieve an acceptable diversification, precisely because they do not necessarily accept any exposure to certain stocks or sectors that would provide the diversification or because, in selected industries where specific stock risk is seen as particularly high, these managers will use a basket approach to security selection.

A second approach to superior hedge fund portfolio management focuses on identifying important macro-trends, call them strategy selectors or rotators; only after they have made those important strategy selections do they focus on individual manager selection. A well-known fund of funds based in Europe specifically seeks to achieve superior returns with a portfolio that may include as many as 120 individual managers. There, the fund of funds manager believes that the key to success is to seek those strategies that are most timely and to seek a large manager sample to achieve optimal diversification within that strategy, effectively to minimize individual manager risk. Having thus accepted to lose some of that manager-specific alpha, this fund of funds manager then applies leverage to the overall portfolio.

This approach is no different, conceptually, from the traditional, long-only equity portfolio manager who seeks to outperform by making significant factor

---

[2] Note that Lhabitant and De Piante Vicin astutely observe that diversification within individual strategies does not always produce lower risk. Indeed, they note that in strategies with a limited number of trades and significantly negatively skewed return expectations for each trade, manager diversification may actually increase rather than decrease risk. The example of merger — or risk — arbitrage comes to mind. The typical payoff pattern for such a trade involves a high probability of earning a modest return and a low probability of a potentially significant loss. This is a function of the fact that most announced mergers come to fruition, thus allowing the typical buyer of the target and simultaneous short seller of the acquirer to make a profit, scaled by the initial discount, the time it takes for the merger to be completed, and the leverage applied to the trade. Occasionally, however, an anticipated merger is cancelled, with a resulting, potentially significant, loss to the typical trade. Therefore, a diversified portfolio of merger arbitrage trades effectively maximizes the risk that the portfolio will hold that unsuccessful merger, with the "diversified" portfolio probably showing more negative a skew than most of the underlying individual managers.

bets, factor being defined here as the so-called Barra common factors or industry or geographical area focus. Size (such as large or small capitalization), style (such as value or growth), balance sheet characteristics (such as interest sensitivity or leverage), business characteristics (exposure to foreign sales or labor intensity), and a few other features total to 13 common factors that can be viewed as significant contributor to tracking error risk. Industry or geographical factors would certainly be more numerous, but these may be easier to understand as contributors to portfolio diversification or concentration. In the hedge fund world, the analog of these factors would be each of the individual strategies applied by each manager. The point of such portfolios, be they focused on individual equities, fixed-income instruments, or hedge fund strategies, is that they will often require a higher level of portfolio turnover as individual risk drivers move into or out of perceived attractiveness.

In these first two approaches, a common feature is that the fund of funds or hedge fund portfolio manager will be driving portfolio changes, reflecting changes in his or her perception of the relative attractiveness of his or her main decision axis. Thus, the best-of-breed selector will be prepared to fire a manager currently in the portfolio if he or she finds a better alternative or if that manager disappoints. Similarly, the strategy rotator will expect to hire or fire individual managers as his or her perception of the relative attractiveness of an individual strategy shifts. Though intuitively it seems reasonable and it is empirically accurate to assume that best-of-breed selectors will typically have lower portfolio turnover than a strategy rotator, this author does not, unfortunately, know of any hard-and-fast statistic that would validate this insight.

The third approach to managing a portfolio of hedge funds is to concentrate on a limited number of multistrategy managers, with or without any additional effort to select individual strategies or best-of-breed managers at the periphery. Interestingly, this approach would arguably be the oldest one in the book, with early funds of funds being little more than access vehicles to a few highly successful multistrategy managers. The concept here is that it is possible for a solid hedge fund management shop to attract top traders (the analog to our earlier best of breed) and to gain unusual insights into the relative attractiveness of individual strategies as a result of the fact that the house itself has a perfect position to identify opportunities by having this highly diversified team of traders who have an incentive to return capital when they cannot identify attractive trades within their areas of specialty. The traditional, long-only analog to this approach is much harder to describe, for it would have to be a portfolio that selects conglomerates across the world.

Though that approach was, as already noted, quite popular in the early days of the industry, the natural trend toward increased specialization and the no-less-natural ego often associated with superior hedge fund management skills are militating away from it. Further, it is also clear that the substantial increase in the size of the overall industry has transformed many of these multistrategy shops into virtual behemoths, where strategies that can successfully deploy only a few hundred million dollars or less eventually are frowned on, because their potential to contribute to the overall bottom line of the firm is viewed as overly inconsequential. Finally, for many of these firms, the growth in overall capital deployed has made the initial partners exceedingly wealthy and can lead them to lose some of the hunger that drives people to excel.[3] It is, however, important to note before moving on that a few topflight multistrategy firms still exist and that their key to success often involves a combination of the passion of the partners for their jobs and unique competitive advantages.

21.4   Returning to the problem of the individual investor

By now, the reader will probably have realized that the challenge faced by individual investors seeking to build their own portfolio of hedge funds is particularly daunting if one is philosophically inclined toward either of the first two of the foregoing portfolio construction approaches. Funds of funds indeed have compelling competitive advantages when it comes to selecting managers if their selection criteria align with either of the first two approaches, particularly with respect to strategy rotation.

Consider the challenge faced by the individual who seeks to construct a portfolio that only seeks exposure to the timeliest strategies. In that design, the investor will need to fire managers who are doing well within their own areas but whose strategies are perceived not to be as timely as others. What kind of public image or reputation will that investor gain within the relatively tight-knit hedge fund community? Fair-weather friend? Hot capital? In either case, and in any variant on either theme, the investor will likely soon find himself or herself unable to gain the access needed to the best managers in many strategies, because they will not want someone to invest in their fund only to liquidate when they stop liking the strategy. Contrast this to the situation experienced by a fund of funds using the same philosophical portfolio construction principle but that benefits from positive investor cash flows. That fund of funds will not necessarily need to fire managers active in less attractive strategies, for they may simply reduce their relative exposures by failing to allocate new funds or by reducing their overall allocation to these managers, without firing them entirely. A cynic would also add that many single-strategy managers are less likely to reject a

---

[3] It is worth noting here an interesting practice by a fund of funds manager who specializes in the emerging manager sphere. An important element in that manager's selection process is to identify the overlap, or lack thereof, between the return expectations of the given strategy, the asset level sought by the manager, and the individual's self-compensation targets. For instance, a strategy that can only accept a limited amount of assets will require any manager who seeks to earn significant compensation to accept substantial risk, so that the carried interest inherent in the typical fee structure will provide that income. The question can then reasonably be asked whether the return level sought by that manager is consistent with the risk profile of the eventual fund of funds investor. Conversely, a manager seeking a level of compensation that can easily be met simply by earning the asset-based management fee may imply that the manager will not be taking sufficient risk.

possible hot-money flow from a fund of funds that is both successful and large than from an individual whose investment is equal to the fund's minimum.

The best-of-breed manager approach presents less of a daunting challenge to the individual investor than the one based on strategy rotation, because it does not necessarily require similar portfolio turnover if one makes a critical assumption. Best-of-breed-manager–focused funds of funds may have a high level of portfolio turnover, but this is often due to the fact that these funds of funds both have the resources needed to evaluate a large sample of individual managers and can access these managers, be they seasoned or relatively new. Thus, from this wider sample, the odds are higher that new, better managers will be identified who might require the fund of funds to replace one of their existing managers. Recognizing that individual investors will often have neither the resources nor the access needed to keep refining their best-of-breed stable, the need for ongoing portfolio turnover may be lessened.

Note that individual investors who believe in the multistrategy manager selection approach often, in effect, do not need funds of funds. Indeed, assuming — and this can be a challenging and crucial assumption — that they can access a few multistrategy managers, they can build and maintain a highly successful stable, where each investment can effectively be in excess of each manager's minimum and where reasonable diversification can be said to have been achieved. It is, however, true that multistrategy managers often find it harder to provide the exposure that an investor might want in the equity long/short universe, because many of the multistrategy firms tend to be concentrated on market-neutral or macro-strategies and only have a peripheral exposure to the semidirectional equity long/short world.

21.5 Tracking funds of funds

Just as the notion that the hedge fund world is in fact one single homogeneous universe that can thus be defined as a single asset class and be used within balanced portfolios as one subportfolio, the notion that it is possible to track funds of funds with a single index may well prove dangerously misleading. Table 21.1 presents the results of a simple analysis, which we will refine as we proceed toward a possible solution.

This analysis involved identifying a number of leading and successful funds of funds,[4] clustering them into three different volatility groups and computing both for each such group and for the whole of that universe the first four statistical moments of their actual return distributions. We then compared these statistics with the same computations applied to the HFRI fund of funds index. Having found little if any statistical difference between the hybrid and the

---

[4] The universe we used comprised the following managers. Though limited by the need to remain practical, we believe that this universe is sufficiently diverse to be somewhat representative.

Table 21.1 Statistical moment comparisons of the HFRI Fund of Funds Index and selected individual funds of funds, January 1998 to September 2005

	Low-volatility	Long/short and hybrid	Strategy-weighted average	Overall average	HFRI fund of funds
Average monthly return	0.75%	0.96%	0.86%	0.92%	0.54%
Monthly return volatility	0.76%	1.95%	1.28%	1.49%	1.76%
Monthly return skewness	−1.18	0.53	−0.01	0.03	−0.28
Monthly return kurtosis	3.73	6.15	5.82	5.21	5.74

long/short-only group, we then proceeded to combine them for the sake of simplicity.

Table 21.1 compares these statistics and suggests three important initial observations.

- The HFRI fund of funds index does not seem representative of what we call the low-volatility universe. That universe has two important characteristics, which seem conceptually consistent with the strategies comprising that universe. The first is that it has a volatility closer to that of a traditional investment-grade fixed-income instrument than to equities. The second is that it has a visible negative skewness, which can be attributed to the call option pattern that many managers attempt to replicate within a universe that, at times, has a finite and relatively limited number of potential trades. Note that the fund of funds index does not share either of these characteristics. The risk profile of that universe is significantly higher — effectively exceeding the volatility typically observed within the large-capitalization domestic equity world. Further, the index has a considerably lower negative skewness, which is consistent with more of a semidirectional long/short equity approach. Clearly, one should not pay too much attention to the return differentials between the index and our universe: It can be explained by the selection bias inherent in the composition of our sample, for the author will naturally tend to follow funds that are expected to produce superior returns. Similarly, the higher kurtosis found in the broader index may also reflect the higher likelihood of finding outliers in a broader universe, although, intuitively, one might also have argued that the broader diversification found in the larger universe might reduce that statistic.
- Neither of our limited individual funds of funds averages seem to mesh perfectly with the broader index, but there is a closer match than with respect to the low-volatility

Low-volatility funds of funds: Arden Institutional Advisers, Collins Low Volatility Fund, Ivy Rosewood Fund, Lighthouse Diversified Fund, Lighthouse Low-Volatility Fund, Morgan Stanley Diversified Fund, Pine Grove Partners, Silver Creek Low-Volatility Fund, and TAG Partners.
Hybrid-volatility funds of funds: Genesee Capital Diversified Fund, Genesee Eagle Fund, Grosvenor Diversified Fund, Meridian Diversified Fund, and Meridian Performance Partners.
Long/short funds of funds: Helios Opportunity Fund, Mezzacappa Partners, Grosvenor U.S. Equity Hedge, Veritable Vittoria, Veritable Pleiades, Ivy Rising Star Fund, Ivy Seedling Fund, Collins Alpha Fund, Collins Long/Short Fund, Longchamp Equity Long/Short, and Longchamp Emerging Markets Fund.

Table 21.2 Statistical moment comparisons of HFRI specialized fund of funds indexes and selected individual funds of funds, January 1998 to September 2005

	Averages		Specialized HFRI funds of funds indexes			
	Low-volatility	Hybrid and long/short	Conservative	Diversified	Strategic	Market defensive
Average monthly return	0.75%	0.96%	0.50%	0.54%	0.56%	0.56%
Monthly return volatility	0.76%	1.95%	1.00%	1.93%	2.75%	1.53%
Monthly return skewness	−1.18	0.53	−0.40	−0.06	−0.47	−0.33
Monthly return kurtosis	3.73	6.15	4.83	5.29	5.60	2.12

Table 21.3 Statistical moment comparisons of selected individual low-volatility funds of funds and synthetic index, January 1998 to September 2005

	Low-volatility	Synthetic absolute return
Average monthly return	0.75%	0.71%
Monthly return volatility	0.76%	0.94%
Monthly return skewness	−1.18	−1.49
Monthly return kurtosis	3.73	6.62

universe. The overall average is an unweighted combination of all the individual funds of funds in the universe specified for this analysis. The strategy-weighted average is an unweighted combination of the low-volatility and the long/short and hybrid volatility subindexes in the universe specified for this analysis. This confirms the educated guess that the funds of funds universe covered in the HFRI index both comprises all underlying strategies and may well be weighted more in favor of long/short-type strategies.

- Finally, the HFRI Fund of Funds Index is not a good proxy to judge purely long/short and hybrid funds of funds, for reasons that are the exact opposite of those explaining why it is not a good index to track low-volatility funds of funds.

Aware of the limitations of this index, HFRI introduced four funds of funds subindexes to reflect the different underlying strategies followed by different funds of funds. Table 21.2 compares these to the universe of actual individual funds of funds we selected. This table does suggest that some specialization in the formulation of the composition of subuniverses will help make the resulting subindexes more relevant, but our analysis fails to find the current subindexes representative of the universe we cover.

Though these published indexes may thus suffer a number of significant and potentially debilitating deficiencies, there may well be alternatives. Table 21.3 presents one such alternative when it comes to low-volatility funds. It illustrates that a composite index derived from the underlying strategies likely to be employed by these fund of funds managers, and thus based on the specific strategic subuniverses from which these fund of funds managers are likely to select the funds in which they invest, can be significantly more relevant than one that aggregates actual funds of funds. Note that the index was created in late 1999, and its strategic weights have not been changed since its creation.[5]

---

[5] This index is a linear combination of nine individual strategies, as represented by the strategy indices of the HFR Database: convertible arbitrage, distressed securities, equity hedge, equity market neutral, event driven, merger arbitrage, relative value arbitrage, short selling, and statistical arbitrage. It was originally designed with three goals in mind. First, it had to bear some resemblance to the kinds of portfolios that absolute-return funds of funds would typically construct. Second, it had to be sufficiently simple to avoid any risk of being viewed as a data-mining exercise. Third, it had to produce as low a correlation to the equity market as feasible. Thus, though one could have achieved a more fitted result by optimizing strategy weights across these strategies, we opted for the simplest solution and have been using this index to assess the performance of absolute-return funds of funds for the last four or five years. Specific strategic weights are available on request.

Table 21.4 Statistical moment comparisons of selected individual long/short or hybrid funds of funds and synthetic benchmark index, January 1998 to September 2005

	Hybrid and long/short	Synthetic long/short or hybrid
Average monthly return	0.96%	0.81%
Monthly return volatility	1.95%	1.88%
Monthly return skewness	0.53	0.58
Monthly return kurtosis	6.15	2.58

Thus, one can probably suggest that its representativeness might be more a function of the philosophy underpinning its formulation than a result of backward-looking data mining. Note that we again find a considerably higher kurtosis in the synthetic index, which would suggest that there is more weight to the outlier effect than to the power of diversification within a larger sample. By contrast, the very modest return advantage found in the actual funds of funds probably suggests that the synthetic index is hard to beat, because it bears only one fee rather than those of the fund of funds manager as well.

A similar conceptual approach can be used to construct a benchmark for the long/short and hybrid funds of funds. Here, the idea simply is to ask what it is that a fund of funds manager in that category does and to replicate that process using strategy subindexes. Table 21.4 shows a comparison of the statistical moments of the return series derived from our hybrid and long/short universe and of a synthetic proxy, reflecting a 60/40 weighting of the HFRI Equity Hedge and Equity Market Neutral indexes. The logic behind that construction was that these relative weights seemed best to fit the typical 30–35% net market exposure targeted by these individual long/short fund of funds managers, given a net zero market exposure targeted by the equity market-neutral universe and the 50% net exposure statistically evident in the equity hedge universe.

Note that the synthetic index seems to shadow the risk profile of the actual fund of funds sample. As found in the case of Table 21.3, the index imposes a high hurdle, probably for the same reasons. By contrast, the kurtosis of the sample is this time substantially higher than that of the broader index, suggesting that more analysis should be conducted as to the phenomenon; selection bias might be the answer, but the fact that it would be playing a role that sometimes raises kurtosis and at other times lowers it deserves a more detailed review and explanation.[6] The very close skewness statistics are interesting, as is the fact that skewness is not negative. This probably reflects the much more balanced equilibrium

---

[6] More careful inspection of the individual data indeed shows that 9 of the 17 funds in the sample have a kurtosis higher than 7 and that 13 out of 17 have a kurtosis higher than that of the synthetic index.

that exists between winning and losing bets in a universe where there is a virtually limitless number of potential trades and no real capacity limit.[7]

21.6 Conclusion

Though it is probable that the anticipated increase in the admissibility of hedge fund strategies within a whole range of balance portfolios might work to limit the market share currently enjoyed by funds of funds, one would seem hard pressed to argue that this segment of the industry will not continue to grow assets significantly.

Funds of funds indeed benefit from at least two important characteristics, which many investors will find hard to replicate. First, they have the resources — and need them to justify their existence — to conduct detailed and continuing manager research, with the implication that they should have an edge when it comes to identifying superior managers. Though it may be tempting to argue that many investment consultants and other professionals in an advisory capacity should also have the same resources, a cynic would observe that compensation scales and the potential for carried interest profits that exist within the fund of funds universe could well remain quite hard to match in an advisory universe lacking the ability to charge either asset-based or performance fees.

Funds of funds also have an important advantage over many individual investors in that their size and familiarity with the industry can provide them with privileged access to new as well as the best-of-breed established managers. Note, however, that this is not an advantage relative to the advisory community, because the combined assets of their client base would provide the justification for many of these individual managers to pay attention. In fact, an argument can be made that advisory professionals have an edge there, because they are often perceived as more stable money than funds of funds.

The major disadvantages of funds of funds are no less significant and fall under two principal headings. The first relates to the explicit second layer of fees. In a world where the perception exists that hedge fund returns are more likely to be lower than higher in the future, it is tempting to try and save on fees, because these become a higher proportion of total return. This argument is particularly potent when made based on after-tax returns.

The second disadvantage also relates to taxes and to the risk identified in Gordon (2005). Indeed, should funds of funds lose their income tax characterization as traders, their management and incentive fees would lose their deductibility from the point of view of the eventual investors. This could break the back of that segment of the industry, because it would make the unattractiveness of the second layer of fees virtually unquestionable.

---

[7] Note, however, that it would be reasonable to posit that limitations might creep up as the size of the long/short universe expands. These limitations might most likely come from the short side because there may well be limits to the willingness of investors to lend securities.

Table 21.5 Toward a simpler presentation of strategic and tactical portfolio breakdown

Risk category	Market risk		Manager risk		Total
	Strategy description	Share	Strategy description	Share	
Fixed-income-type risk: volatility < 7%	Traditional bonds, both taxable and tax-exempt	15%	Arbitrage strategies	10%	50%
	Extended bond markets[1]	5%	Other relative value market-neutral strategies	10%	
	Other traditional fixed-income	5%	Other nontraditional strategies	5%	
Equity-type risk: volatility > 7%	Long-only diversified domestic stocks, both large and small capitalization	15%	Long/short or concentrated equity strategies	10%	50%
	Long-only diversified nondomestic stocks, both large and small capitalization	10%	Other nontraditional equity strategies	5%	
	Real assets	5%	Private equity	5%	
Total		55%		45%	100%

[1]These may include nondomestic bonds, hedged; high-yield domestic bonds; less liquid fixed-income strategies.

Looking ahead, though, a reasonable observer would probably guess that the role of funds of funds will become less prevalent, though still very important, at least for wealthy individuals in at least two areas. The incremental blowup risk associated with emerging managers makes it all but prohibitive for an individual investor to commit to a new manager unless the portfolio is already quite well diversified among both strategies and seasoned managers and the individual has some special connection to that new manager. Second, a solid case can be made that with the role of strategy selection being more important in the low-volatility segment, a fund of funds will often find it easier to execute these changes than an individual. This could preserve a special role for funds of funds in that area. Secondarily, funds of funds can provide a useful implementation vehicle when an investor wants to make a particular factor bet and does not have the time, resources, skills, or access needed to select the best-of-breed manager within that segment.

By contrast, an equally reasonable case can be made that large funds of funds focusing on the long/short universe will continue to find growth more difficult, at least in relative terms. Indeed, experience does confirm that there is substantial overlap among the lists of managers of many of the larger funds of funds, and this simply reflects that funds of funds will often try to construct a core exposure to a few of the largest participants in the industry. Size here is viewed as a potential indicator of forward-looking stability and overall respectability.

More important, the portfolio design suggested in Brunel (2006) would make it potentially harder for there to be a large place for long/short funds of funds. Brunel (2006) suggests that wealth managers should look at client portfolios in a simplified manner, with the portfolio broken down as illustrated in Table 21.5. In that context, while the absolute-return segment of the industry is relatively amorphous and thus potentially effectively served by low-volatility funds of funds, the case is different in the long/short universe. Indeed, as the framework invites the investor to identity whether he or she is seeking to over- or underweigh market or manager risks and may be making that decision in a regional geographical context, it typically leads the investor to consider a more detailed set of desired characteristics for the long/short managers he or she seeks.

Finally, it is important to note that one should become considerably more serious in the formulation of whatever benchmark one wishes to use to assess the performance of so-called hedge fund strategies. Indeed, with the universe defined in increasingly detailed fashion, it behooves the investor to attempt to achieve a closer match between the detailed definition of the strategy sought and the formulation of the benchmark against which it is being measured.

References

Brunel, J. L. P. (2004). Revisiting the Role of Hedge Funds in Diversified Portfolios. *Journal of Wealth Management*, 7(3):35–48.

Brunel, J. L. P. (2006). *Integrated Wealth Management: The New Direction for Portfolio Managers, 2nd edition.* Institutional Investor Books, London.

Gordon, R. N. (2005). Is Your Hedge Fund a Trader or an Investor? *Journal of Wealth Management,* 2(1):54–57.

Lhabitant, F. S. and De Piante Vicin, M. L. (2004). Finding the Sweet Spot of Hedge Fund Diversification. Working Paper, EDHEC Risk and Asset Management Research Center, Nice, France.

22 Institutional investment due diligence on funds of hedge funds

John E. Dunn III

Abstract

With institutional investors progressively entering the hedge fund arena, often with initial allocations through funds of hedge funds, the role of a well-thought-out professional due-diligence review on the funds of funds level is of growing importance. Due-diligence methodologies, which work very well on single-manager hedge funds, are often entirely inappropriate when applied to funds of hedge funds. Moreover, due to the breadth and heterogeneity within the fund of funds industry itself, with funds of funds differing in their construction methodology, their underlying hedge fund managers, their profiled and targeted client bases, as well as their historical evolution, choosing an appropriate fund of funds for one investor's purposes may be entirely inappropriate for another type of institutional investor. We review some of the due-diligence processes that are often applied by larger investors to the selection of fund of funds, and we provide insight into a reasonably specific fund of funds due-diligence methodology that can be adopted for the specific needs of different types and categories of institutional investors.

22.1 Introduction

With funds of hedge funds currently supplying a large majority of hedge fund exposure to global institutional investors, the need for a well-defined fund of hedge funds due-diligence process by which institutional investors can measure and compare competing offers is becoming paramount to many of these institutions. Yet, as practitioners will tell you, it is significantly more difficult to conduct due diligence on a fund of hedge funds manager than on a single manager, and as a result there is no universally accepted or generally agreed-on standard of due-diligence practice that an institutional investor can employ for its analysis and allocations to funds of hedge funds managers. With a progressive adoption of hedge fund exposure by the institutional investment community and with most institutions getting their start through investing in hedge funds of funds as a gatekeeper to underlying single-manager hedge funds, this chapter evaluates and highlights some of the important characteristics that an institutional fiduciary responsible investor often adopts in screening, analyzing, and conducting due diligence on funds of hedge funds.

22.2 The gap: fiduciary responsible investing vs. private client products[1]

A core concern and essential starting point to introducing a workable hedge fund of funds due-diligence process for fiduciary responsible institutional clients is that there is a large gap between the investment understandings, desires, and concerns of the average institutional investor and those of the average hedge fund of funds. The hedge fund of funds industry is in fact extremely heterogeneous, with different funds of hedge funds evolving differently, for historical reasons of client composition, fund sponsor, location, and age and as a result of investment emphasis.[2] But historically the majority of existing funds of hedge funds evolved over the decade of the 1990s, with a very strong emphasis on a private-banking, high-net-worth, family-office-investor client base — logically, of course, because this client base has traditionally been the major (and is still the major) investor base for the hedge fund industry. Correspondingly, hedge funds of funds focusing on an institutional client base are, generally speaking, a much smaller part of the funds of funds universe but represent a rapidly growing specialist niche in the industry and, of course, should capture the lion's share of assets under management (AUM) growth going forward.[3] As such, the great majority of funds of hedge funds, particularly the older, larger, and more established funds of hedge

---

[1] The term *fiduciary responsible institutional investor* is used throughout this chapter in general terms to refer to institutional investors with public investment responsibility. It is not to imply that private banks or other fund of hedge funds sponsors are not fiduciary responsible investors, but rather that the investment analytical processes of institutional investors are more concerned with fiduciary responsibility or have a higher level of fiduciary accountability and as a result different investment constraints than private banking–style investors. This is not to enter the debate among some participants in the hedge fund consultant arena who argue that it is in their best interest for institutional investors to hire directly single hedge funds and build their own hedge fund portfolios and that it is imprudent for institutional investors to obtain hedge fund exposure through funds of hedge funds. "The Employment Retirement Income Security Act (ERISA) and Uniform Prudent Investor Act (UPIA) have adopted the prudent investor doctrine and created principles which have led many to conclude that it is imprudent, and not in the best interest of the beneficiaries, to depart from the traditional portfolio investment process of direct investing with the use of a consultant," Charles Gradante, Managing Principal of Hennessee Group, LLC., Web-based document, http://www.hennessee.com. This discussion is too complicated to be addressed in this chapter.

[2] Although the historical evolution of the funds of hedge funds industry is interesting, it is outside the scope of this chapter.

[3] Historically speaking, the original roots of the funds of hedge funds industry was private banking oriented, and most of the earlier funds of hedge funds evolved out of the private banking industry's desire to have hedge fund product accessible to their high-net-worth clients. A good estimate is that there is close to U.S.$850 billion in hedge fund assets held by private banking/ultra-high-net-worth individual (UHNWI)/family office–type investors and probably $200 billion in institutional hands. Of this total, U.S. institutions account for about $100 billion — on their way to $300 billion by 2008, estimated by investment-management consultants Casey, Quirk & Associates LLC. Christopher Merlini of Swiss Capital Group comments as follows: "Historically, the core investor base for funds of hedge funds has been high-net-worth individuals, who, even today, are estimated to account for over 70% of this base" (Merlini and Koppel, 2004).

funds, still have this private client investment tilt built into their mentality as well as into their marketing and due-diligence materials, their modus operandi, and their perception of what investors think of them. A corollary to this private banking client tilt is a different level of fiduciary concern of the investment process and controls than is commonly acceptable to the majority of larger global fiduciary responsible institutional investors, hence the gap between the majority of the fund of hedge funds industry and the institutional investment community.

On the other side of the gap stand the investment fiduciary concerns of public investors. These investors have in general a higher level of fiduciary concern than the majority of private banking–style hedge fund of funds sponsors, being largely controlled by investment committees, having significant internal and sometimes external controls on their investment choices, and having a more targeted type of investment appetite than the hedge funds of funds private banking–style traditional client base. It never ceases to amaze me that funds of hedge funds often spend enormous amounts of energy (and money) marketing to the institutional sector when their company, their fund, and their product offerings clearly do not have institutional flavor, processes, controls, and transparency, which fiduciary responsible investors demand. There is in fact an enormous gap between the majority of the hedge fund of funds industry and the fiduciary responsible institutional investment community, both in investment perception and operational expectations.[4] And although institutional investors screen, consider, and conduct due diligence on a wide variety and large number of funds of hedge funds, only a small percentage of the funds of hedge funds community actually receives significant institutional allocations. Only the most clever and forward-looking among the fund of hedge funds community (still a relatively small percentage) have till now built out an investment process that appeals to public fiduciary responsible institutional investors, and this small niche fund of funds group has a very good chance of developing into larger institutional service providers.

22.3   Exploring institutional fiduciary responsibility

Although there are wide differences among the investment analysis processes used by fiduciary responsible institutional investors, it is instructive to illustrate a simple model of a typical fiduciary responsible investor and the processes and constraints that apply to hiring a fund of hedge funds. This fiduciary-level investment governing process, as is well known, is common to a wide variety of institutional investors and impacts directly the investment culture of that organization as well

---

[4] The parallel is to the biblical parable of the rich man and Lazarus, the rich man being the hedge fund industry and Lazarus being the institutional investment community. "And besides all this, between us and you there is a great gulf fixed, so that they would pass from hence to you cannot, neither can they pass to us, that would come from thence." The point is that bridge building is needed, and a better understanding of the due-diligence expectations and processes of larger institutional investors is needed for funds of hedge funds wishing to tap this marketplace.

as the choices of instruments and managers that fit into its asset allocation plan. In sum, a typical fiduciary responsible institutional investor would have the following characteristics.

- The institutional investment board or investment committee determines the broad investment objectives of the institution as well as a policy benchmark portfolio. Asset-class selections are done at this level.
- The board oversees the portfolio manager and his or her team, which have the responsibility for implementation.
- The investment team has two goals, meeting or exceeding the policy benchmark and keeping their tracking error relative to the policy benchmark within a committee-defined risk budget. This process is adopted for alternative investments.
- The smart investment officer desirous of increasing allocations to alternatives gets his or her board involved as much as possible with newer asset classes, such as private equity and hedge funds, in order for the board to become more familiar and hence more comfortable with these investments.
- Boards are made up of working professionals who are not specialists in financial markets. For example, investment trustees of the Fireman's Pension Fund are firefighters, and trustees of a state teachers' retirement plan can be elementary school teachers. As such, boards often misunderstand the prudent-man rule to maintain that traditional asset management is safer than alternative investment management.
- Once the decision to allocate to hedge funds of funds has been made, there is, generally speaking, still a significant level of fear and trepidation on the board, "in case something goes wrong with these new types of investments."
- The board monitors the performance of the investment officer and offers real-world checks and balances (and often significant constraints) on the ability of the investment officer to run the portfolio.

One of the keys governing the foregoing process is the level of comfort, which is directly related to familiarity with the investment instruments and markets and funds of funds operations. Hence significant in my experience is the fact the more the hedge fund of funds' organization, marketing documents, sales presentations, and due-diligence documentation and the fund of hedge fund's cultural posture resemble those of a large, traditional institutional investor, the greater the chance of receiving an allocation from this type of investor. No one has ever gotten fired, at least to my knowledge, for buying IBM.

22.4 Exploring fiduciary responsibility: what IBM has that the average hedge fund of funds needs to incorporate

For the average fund of hedge funds to appeal to the average fiduciary responsible institutional investor, a variety of emphases must be present in the fund of funds' investment and operational culture. Conveniently, we can break these down into two main themes that govern fiduciary responsible investing: (1) a significantly stronger reliance on process and controls, in both the operational and the investment arenas, than is common in the private banking/HNWI/family office investment arena, and (2) a higher reliance on the quantitative aspects of investment management, which include, in particular, a quantifiable risk management function as well as some measurable system of performance and style drift benchmarking. For a fund of hedge funds to receive significant allocations from fiduciary responsible institutional investors, these points need to be addressed in their entirety and at a level of transparency by means of which institutional investment managers and their investment boards will be able to illustrate to outside observers that their fiduciary responsibilities have been discharged.

22.4.1 Analyzing investment process and controls as well as underlying hedge fund portfolios

Although the fund of hedge funds task of selecting hedge fund managers and combining and monitoring hedge fund exposures appears a conceptually simple process, it can be fraught with many difficulties. In practice, running a good fund of hedge funds entails all manner of implementation problems, ranging from the operational difficulties of running a small business, to a consistent skill in identifying capable managers, to successful tactical portfolio strategy allocations, to creating and running a successful risk management process. Furthermore, evaluating a fund of hedge funds, including manager selection, portfolio construction, risk management, and ongoing monitoring among hedge fund managers, is significantly more difficult than evaluating a traditional single-asset manager or single-strategy hedge fund. This second level of complexity of analyzing a manager who analyzes hedge fund managers means that on the practical level the due-diligence process through which fiduciary responsible institutional investors evaluate funds of hedge funds will almost always be focused on the fund of funds level of investment control and operational process rather than (typically for a traditional single- or hedge fund manager) on the fund's underlying portfolio and securities selection process. Even provided the institutional investor demands and gets underlying position transparency for each of the fund of hedge funds' underlying managers, the complexities involved in understanding and portfolio modeling a total impact of this selection of securities on the institutions portfolio usually mean that the due-diligence process is heavily tilted toward an analysis of the investment process and operational controls of the fund of hedge funds itself.

Successful investment control, however, entails a high degree of specialist investment analytical knowledge, particularly as applied to the hedge fund industry. Essential to a fiduciary responsible investor analysis in selecting a fund of hedge funds is the hedge fund knowledge base that a fund of hedge funds has to illustrate to its potential institutional buyers. First, the fund has to have an up-to-date knowledge of all hedge fund strategies as well as all instruments used by hedge funds. This fundamental understanding of the hedge fund–related capital markets by the fund's analysts is sometimes easily assumed, but it needs to be illustrated. Common in this industry is for analysts to come from the proprietary desk or from the investment buy side. But, ideally, funds of hedge funds analysts hired by funds of hedge funds should come off the proprietary trading desks or come from hedge funds themselves. A second point, equally relevant, is that there needs to be a large diversity in the individual skill set in a fund of funds, just as wide and complete as the investment markets in which hedge fund trading ideas operate. It almost goes without saying that a fund of funds sponsor without a world-class analytical team versed in the latest financial instruments and current market anomalies will not have much chance of competing going forward.[5]

Another key related to investment control is what I like to call the *hedge fund information loop*.[6] Although there has been a drastic improvement in recent years in the data vendors and service providers surrounding the hedge fund industry, in general the industry is still fairly opaque and closed to outsiders. But a fund of hedge funds can best differentiate itself by having capable, experienced people with proven track records in spotting hedge fund investment talent in all of the major financial centers globally. Particularly considering the amount of money flowing into the industry in the recent past and still yet to be allocated from the institutional sector, any edge in knowing what is going on in the industry, knowing who is going where, and who is setting up what will certainly aid in the task of identifying top-quartile investment skill and talent.

A third point concerning the investment process relates to the systems a fund of hedge funds manager has put in place to select, monitor, and manage single-manager hedge funds. It is not enough for a fund of hedge funds manager to show to a potential institutional investor that he or she has a well-thought-out and identifiable due-diligence process in place for each single manager in his or her universe. This process must also be documentable and updated on a regular basis and communicated to investors in a manner that demonstrates fiduciary prudence. In other words, in much the same way that a fund of hedge funds has to document that a single hedge fund manager in its portfolio has a well-thought-out and disciplined investment process, it also has to demonstrate to its institutional clientele that its own investment process and methodology in choosing underlying managers is consistently disciplined. Such an investment process review has to reveal the discipline inherent in the investment manager's process and delve deeply into the underlying manager's portfolio analytics, a topic in itself too lengthy and complicated to outline well in this chapter. Suffice it to say that the more disciplined and documented an investment manager's approach to analyzing its underlying managers, the easier it is to explain allocations to and receive them from fiduciary responsible investors.

A corollary to this idea of investment process discipline deals with the level of sophistication of a fund of hedge funds client interface. A sophisticated client interface has implications for both the quantitative and qualitative databases

---

[5] Alexander Ineichen (2002) puts it this way: "A fund of hedge funds manager not understanding capital markets, financial instruments, leverage, and risk is probably similar to a doctor not familiar with human anatomy."

[6] Alexander Ineichen first used this term, but it is a perfect way of explaining the idea. See footnote 5.

a fund of hedge funds keeps on its underlying managers as well as the managers it follows, as well as a qualitatively documented process of explaining and documenting to investors why it chose and how it monitors any particular manager. This entails a rather more sophisticated client interface and investor relations communication than the average fund of hedge funds has yet to adopt.

With any discussion of investment process discipline and the depth of portfolio analytics, the question of investment strategy innovation and trading on new ideas has to be addressed, that is, how fund of hedge funds managers who have hired fantastic managers have to deal with style drift in portfolios for their institutional clientele. In order for style drift to be measurable on the single-manager level, the fund of hedge funds manager must show sufficient knowledge and ongoing familiarity with the underlying portfolios of his or her single managers. Merely having full position transparency does not mean that the hedge fund of funds necessarily has a clue to what is going on at the portfolio level. Of course it is assumed that in any institutional mandate the underlying hedge fund portfolio will be looked at carefully at least once quarterly and that the manager will be monitored on a regular basis by means of phone calls, visits, perhaps daily position-level transparency in some cases, perhaps by returns-based analysis if the fund is liquid enough. This is all to be negotiated in putting together a fund of funds mandate. The level of transparency is not of significant importance here but, rather, the fact that a fund of funds manager can prove that his or her underlying managers are doing exactly what they were hired to do.[7] Investment style drift has significantly higher implications on the level of fiduciary investing, because any modification to the investment style of one of the underlying managers can have dramatic and overriding consequences on the institutional portfolio, a risk that fiduciary responsible investors seek to avoid at all costs.

22.4.2 Operational concerns: ongoing manager monitoring, risk management, and expertise in analyzing small businesses

High levels of underlying position transparency are rarely able to help investors avoid blowup risk. Interestingly, experience has shown that most of the hedge fund blowups originated from investment processes and managers that were initially sound and that would have passed even the strictest due-diligences processes. Trouble came, in the majority of cases, when a manager got into trouble and then tried to cover it up or correct the problem. Blowup risk in itself is fairly nebulous, and quantitative due-diligence processes will not help much at all; here we need to deal with integrity and trust and knowing what is happening all the time with underlying managers. This is not to repeat the story of the investment manager who had an intriguing strategy dealing with S&P

---

[7] There are two facets to transparency: (1) style drift, as discussed earlier, and (2) a positional-level transparency to investors at the funds of funds level. Fiduciary responsible investors cannot really consider investing in a fund of hedge funds without underlying manager-level transparency.

futures arbitrage and then started buying Thailand stocks just before blowup.[8] In fund of hedge funds investment, essentially the main protection we have against blowup risk on the single-manager level comes only from the level of trust and integrity between the underlying hedge fund and the fund of funds. But this level of trust can be fostered by having very close and frequent working relationships (monitoring) between the underlying funds and the fund of hedge funds. Hence, those funds of funds that can demonstrate that they have built very close relationships of trust with and even a level of intimate knowledge of their underlying managers have the best shot at avoiding fund disasters and even a better chance at receiving increasing institutional AUM allocations.[9]

With any discussion of underlying hedge fund portfolio monitoring and style drift, the importance that institutional investors place on style purity should be underlined. Institutional investors have as a key component of their mandate a necessity for performance evaluation and the ensuing problems of benchmarking. It is clear that traditional performance evaluation approaches do not work very well for hedge funds. But this does negate a fiduciary investor's necessity to have some type of performance benchmark, however imperfect, in order to assess, follow, and evaluate their hedge fund of funds exposure. On the single-manager hedge fund level, style evaluation and therefore performance evaluation can be conducted with at least some degree of accuracy through a variety of quantitative methods,[10] together with comparing the funds against a variety of style indices. But because funds of hedge funds are combinations of various style exposures, each with differing weightings and degrees of style purity, leverage, and tracking error, each created with different historical precedents, style benchmarking and performance evaluation of funds of hedge funds is significantly more difficult.[11] This is true on both the underlying hedge fund level as well as the funds of hedge funds level. Of course, the fear of blowup risk makes investors want to make sure that the fund of hedge funds is controlling its single managers, that the fixed-income arbitrage manager is not dealing Thailand taxi stocks. But, on a more general level, institutional investors hire a fund of hedge funds itself because

---

[8] Those of you less familiar with some of the stories of hedge fund blowups might want to read some of the writings of Victor Niederhoffer, a hedge fund manager/author who wrote several good books on his experience (Niederhoffer, 2000; Niederhoffer and Kenner, 2003).

[9] Headline risk is the single largest fear among institutional portfolio managers and investment committee members. This is not to say that it will not happen to even the best of all funds of funds. Michael Romanek (2004) of Fortis Prime Fund Solutions quotes a representative of a multibillion-dollar fund of hedge funds who adds a level of practical pessimism to this theme: "Over the next five to ten years, do I think that our firm will be holding a fund that turns out to be a debacle? Absolutely. I just hope that when it happens it is done in such a new and innovative way that we can merely shrug and say, 'No one could have seen that one coming.'"

[10] Ronald Surz (2005) has proposed an intriguing Monte Carlo/portfolio simulation process for hedge fund peer group analysis, which appears to work with some success in some hedge fund strategies.

[11] In a typical Swiss understatement, Alexander Ineichen (2004) wrote, "The fund of hedge funds industry is probably as heterogeneous as the hedge fund industry."

that fund will have a specific investment impact on their portfolio in a style-measurable way. But because the fund of hedge funds industry is so heterogeneous, the traditional benchmarking of funds of hedge funds with their current performance of their fund against, for example, the HFRI Fund of Fund Index is about as accurate as comparing a raisin to a basket of fruit (rather than apples and oranges). But at the very least, a fund of hedge funds can add to the level of institutional comfort by providing a peer group analysis of whom it sees as its own competitor base, with all the resulting bias of having the sell side choose a peer group from which it ought to be compared.[12] But by making a stab at trying to illustrate its risk-adjusted performance edge as compared to a peer group of fund of funds managers likely to offer a similar set of investment style exposure sought by the institutional investors, the fund of hedge funds is at least giving a starting point by which fiduciary responsible investors will be able to address their performance measurement concerns. However, benchmarking against a generic fund of funds database is not enough, and it certainly will not be so in the future.

Investment process discipline as well as the issue of style drift are also demonstrated in the risk management approach taken by a fund of hedge funds. There are a variety of risk management approaches one might take on the funds of hedge funds level, ranging from underlying portfolio analytics, position consolidation, and returns-based analysis, all with competing and interesting differences and implications. But whatever variation of a risk management system is chosen, it has to be robust enough to illustrate to the institutional investor that a fund of hedge funds not only takes a qualitative approach to risk management but also harnesses all the techniques of modern risk management (a heavily quantitative science). Risk management, and by implication due diligence, is not primarily a quantifiable process. But there has to be a balance. Clearly a good amount of accumulated capital markets wisdom[13] is the key driver in fund of hedge funds risk management, but robust quantitative portfolio analytics and risk management systems can certainly add significant insight into portfolio risk. If an institutional investor can be convinced that a fund of hedge funds has instituted a world-class portfolio analytics and risk management system, he or she will, generally speaking, understand by implication that the manager will have chosen underlying managers who also have a very strong risk management system and risk-aversion mentality in place.

Risk management and risk oversight are probably the best place to start with in any discussion of a fund of hedge funds' approach to operational controls. Although the mass of AUM in the hedge fund arena is important, it should not be forgotten that the industry is still pretty much in its infancy and that the great majority of investable hedge funds in today's universe are still small

---

[12] "The sell side knows how to deal with these problems: Use the peer group that makes them look best" (Surz, 2005, p. 79).

[13] See several recent interesting comments on the risk management process applicable to the hedge funds world: Rahl and Lucas (2005) and Greenberg and Silverstein (2005).

entrepreneurial businesses, with all the operational risks and dangers such small businesses entail. If a fund of hedge funds manager can illustrate to an institutional investor that he or she has a well-defined and careful methodology for reviewing the operational risks inherent in smaller startup companies,[14] by inference investors are led to believe, correctly so, that the fund of hedge funds manager himself or herself probably has a well-defined, operationally excellent business organization. Successful, well-run entrepreneurial funds of hedge funds will, by implication, have an edge in choosing successfully run, operationally world-class underlying hedge funds. This is often why institutional investors get the private equity team involved in their due-diligence review of funds of hedge funds, because private equity analysis has a very strong focus on operational capabilities and business risk.

In summary, it has become clear that the level of complexity in conducting fiduciary responsible due diligence on funds of hedge funds is high, such that a generalized universal due-diligence process will be hard to implement for most institutional investors. Yet in general terms, fiduciary responsible institutional investors are very much concerned with the forms and process of investment management control, and the fund of hedge funds that can illustrate its expertise in these areas has the best chance of growing up to be a giant.

There are a few characteristics common to funds of hedge funds that have been successful in raising assets under management from institutional clients. Although what follows is not comprehensive, it reveals the general thread.

Most institutional investors, when they complete their due-diligence studies and make final allocations to funds of hedge funds, almost always end up choosing funds of hedge funds in the bottom percentiles of the fund of hedge funds universe. In fact, there seems to be an observable inverse relationship between the level of fiduciary institutional investment concern and hedge fund of funds performance. Part of the rationale for this inverse relationship has to do with the level of risk and targeted volatility levels that higher-performing funds of hedge funds are comfortable with, but this does not explain all the differences. Seemingly paradoxical, many of these higher-quartile-performing funds of hedge funds have the experience, quality, informational loop, integrity, and alignment of interest to be of significant interest to institutional investors, but they fail in their quest to attract large institutional interest mainly because they cannot communicate their investment processes and document their operational controls at the fiduciary level.

The era of the generic one-size-fits-all fund of hedge funds portfolio is probably soon over, at least for the more fiduciary responsible institutional investors. Rather, these more sophisticated investors are much more concerned with allocating to a specialist fund of hedge funds, which can fit different parts of an institutional asset allocation plan. In this case, a low-volatility fund of hedge funds will be a replacement for bond exposure, a fund of asset-backed hedge funds might be a replacement for credit exposure with a natural interest rate

---

[14] Almost a private equity function.

hedge,[15] a fund of CTAs might be a replacement for market directionality, and a fund of equity long/short funds might be a good replacement for small-cap equity exposure. In essence, the core satellite approach of adding a few nondiversified hedge fund of funds components to an overall institutional portfolio is losing popularity to the idea that a carefully constructed specialist fund of hedge funds exposure can more significantly replace traditional market exposure in an institutional portfolio.

The era of the fund of hedge funds, however, is not over. As the years pass, institutional investors will progressively see funds of hedge funds as a good way of obtaining targeted hedge fund exposure, but with a bent. In the future, there will be more and more funds of hedge funds opening managed account platforms, through which institutional investors can pick and choose between a fund of hedge funds holdings or platform members and build and structure targeted investment exposure. Funds of funds will no longer sell hedge fund exposure, but instead sell targeted components of structured alternative risk exposures that fit an institutional investor's asset allocation plan. This evolution will not be overnight, but it can already be seen among some of the more successful institutional players, who are specializing quite rapidly.

22.5   Conclusion

The fund of funds business is alive and well, but it is evolving rapidly, both in client base and in specialization. Funds of hedge funds that emerge as industry leaders going forward, however, will almost surely have a strong institutional emphasis. Currently, however, the majority of the funds of hedge funds community has no quality institutional investment management process in place. Such a transition to service an institutional fiduciary responsible investor base for the majority of the funds of hedge funds industry will be difficult if not impossible. There is no quick fix to go up the institutional quality ladder; for the majority of the hedge funds of funds industry, this transition entails a substantial investment in human capital, in risk management systems, and in product-structuring expertise and a significant improvement in a manager-monitoring process. Those that fail to make the necessary investment or lack the vision and decisiveness will fall by the wayside of mediocrity and will probably become consolidation

---

[15] The great majority of asset-backed securities are issued with floating rates and hence are low duration and naturally hedged to interest rate risk. This type of investment can be extremely complimentary to an institutional investor with a longer duration fixed bond portfolio for which some hedge is sought. CTA funds can replace small-cap market directional funds to some extent, as they have similar correlation characteristics in some markets. The era of the specialist strategy fund of fund is on the way, as institutional investors progressively see the opportunity of buying hedge fund of fund specialized strategies to meet specific asset allocation targets for nonmarket correlated risk exposures, but whom want the safety and diversification of buying more than one or two managers in a particular hedge fund strategy.

candidates of the larger, more flexible houses going forward. On the other hand, those who succeed in making the institutional transition will have the chance to evolve into larger, globally based world-class hedge fund investment houses as hedge fund investment becomes progressively more and more mainstream among institutional investors.

References

Greenberg, N. R. and Silverstein, S. (2005). Emphasizing the Practical Components of Risk. *AIMA Journal*, September.

Ineichen, A. M. (2002). Do Fund of Hedge Funds Managers Add Value? *AIMA Newsletter*, February.

Ineichen, A. (2004). The Case for Funds of Funds. *Funds of Hedge Funds*, Euromoney, London.

Merlini, C. and Koppel, P. (2004). *Market Characteristics, Funds of Hedge Funds*. Euromoney publications, London.

Niederhoffer, V. (2000). *The Education of a Speculator*. John Wiley & Sons, New York.

Niederhoffer, V. and Kenner, L. (2003). *Practical Speculation*. John Wiley & Sons, New York.

Rahl, L. and Lucas, B. (2005). Risk Management: An Evolution from "Gut" to "Quant" to "Wisdom." *AIMA Journal*, September.

Romanek, M. (2004). Due Diligence, Not Always a Quantifiable Process. *AIMA Journal*, June.

Surz, R. J. (2005). Testing the Hypothesis "Hedge Fund Performance Is Good." *Journal of Wealth Management*, Spring.

23 Synthetic collateralized debt obligations (CDO) squares and the continuing evolution of funds of funds

Paul U. Ali

Abstract

Funds of funds, whether they invest in hedge funds or other funds, all share a common characteristic: The investor in the fund of funds receives variable or equity-based returns, primarily in the form of capital appreciation on the investment. Recently, a new class of pooled investment funds has emerged that replicate the structural features of funds of funds but deliver debt-based, rather than equity-based, returns. These products are known variously as *CDO (collateralized debt obligations) squares* and *structured finance CDOs*. The cash contributions of investors are pooled by the fund manager and invested in an actively managed portfolio of, typically, asset-backed securities and synthetic securities. In contrast to conventional funds of funds, the investors do not normally participate in the capital appreciation of the portfolio but, instead, receive predetermined principal and interest payments. We examine the legal structure of these new "fund of funds" products and the key legal issues confronting investors.

23.1 Introduction

Funds of funds, whether they invest in mutual funds, hedge funds, or other pooled investment vehicles, all share a common characteristic: The investor in the fund of funds receives variable or equity-based returns, primarily in the form of changes to the capital value of the interests held in the fund of funds. Recently, a new class of pooled investment vehicles has emerged that replicate the structural features of funds of funds but deliver debt-based, rather than equity-based, returns. These products are also known variously as *synthetic CDO (collateralized debt obligations) squares* and *structured finance CDOs*.

These synthetic CDO squares, in common with conventional funds of funds, are attractive to investors because they offer exposure to diversified portfolios and also enable investors to participate indirectly in securitization transactions where the securities are illiquid or otherwise in short supply. This chapter examines the legal structure of synthetic CDO squares and the key legal risk confronting investors.

23.2 Development of synthetic CDO squares

Synthetic CDO squares represent the latest step in the evolution of the global credit derivatives market and are indicative of the ongoing convergence of that market and the market for mutual funds, hedge funds, and other pooled investment vehicles. The earliest synthetic CDO transactions involved the issuance of debt securities to investors, with principal and interest payments on the securities being serviced out of the cash flow generated by a credit derivative referencing a static portfolio of, typically, corporate debt obligations (Ali and de Vries Robbé, 2003).

These early transactions were predicated on an unchanging credit derivative and a stable reference portfolio. Accordingly, the original credit derivative around which the transaction was based remained in place for the duration of the transaction and there was no trading of obligations in and out of the portfolio. A major drawback for investors was that, in the absence of a liquid market for the securities issued in the securitization transaction, they could be locked into exposure to reference obligations of deteriorating creditworthiness, with there being no possibility for defensive action to be taken in respect of the portfolio (Ali and de Vries Robbé, 2005).

This structural drawback was placed in sharp relief with the collapses of Enron, WorldCom, and Parmalat, which led investors to suffer significant losses in many synthetic CDO transactions. As a result, synthetic CDO transactions that are purely passive are now rare. Instead, synthetic CDO transactions now incorporate lightly managed structures enabling the replenishment of portfolio constituents (where the reference obligations have been depleted due to scheduled amortization, prepayments, or payment defaults) and the substitution of fresh reference obligations for the original portfolio constituents (where the latter no longer meet portfolio eligibility criteria) (de Vries Robbé and Ali, 2005).

However, these lightly managed structures, while addressing the drawback of original synthetic CDO structures, are essentially reactive in nature. Changes to the underlying portfolio occur only in response to adverse changes to the portfolio constituents. That has led to the creation of a new class of synthetic CDO structures where the reference portfolio is actively managed (de Vries Robbé and Ali, 2005). These new structures permit not only proactive changes to the portfolio (where portfolio constituents are replaced, as a defensive measure, in anticipation of an adverse change occurring) but also, like actively managed mutual funds and hedge funds, the trading of obligations in and out of the portfolio. In this manner, investors in the structure can take the benefit of mispricings in those obligations and changes in market conditions.

The synthetic CDO square is a natural progression from these actively managed structures (Watterson, 2005). The synthetic CDO square, like funds of hedge funds and funds of mutual funds, intermediates between the investors and other pooled investment vehicles, with the investors receiving their returns from indirect exposure to the underlying vehicles.

23.3 Structure of synthetic CDO squares

23.3.1 Synthetic CDOs squares: the fund of funds level

In a synthetic CDO square, the investors, in common with mutual funds and hedge funds, receive market-tradable interests or securities in exchange for cash contributions. These cash contributions are pooled and invested in other pooled investment vehicles (de Vries Robbé, 2005; de Vries Robbé and Ali, 2005; Das, 2005; Nomura Securities, 2005). However, there are three key structural aspects of synthetic CDO squares that distinguish them from conventional funds of funds.

• The securities received by the investors are debt securities; that is, they have a scheduled maturity date and pay out predetermined amounts of capital and income (in the form of principal and interest). In contrast, investors in mutual funds and hedge funds receive equity securities or other equity interests (such as a limited partnership interest in the case of many hedge funds) (Ali, Stapledon, and Gold, 2003).
• The investors obtain exposure to debt securities issued in other securitization transactions. Admittedly, many hedge funds and, to a lesser extent, some mutual funds are also major investors in securitization transactions (Fitch Ratings, 2005c). It is, nonetheless, rare to find the fixed-income portfolios of hedge funds and mutual funds comprising exclusively the securities issued in securitization transactions or otherwise obtaining exposure only to such securities.
• Exposure to the debt securities is created, not by acquiring the physical securities, but by trading credit derivatives that reference those debt securities.

The debt securities in a synthetic CDO square are issued by a special-purpose vehicle (SPV) (usually a corporation or trust), whose business purposes are limited to entering into credit derivatives and the issue of debt securities serviced by those credit derivatives (de Vries Robbé and Ali, 2005). The SPV is, in common with the issuing vehicles in other securitization transactions, established as an orphan entity, meaning that its assets and liabilities do not have to be recognized on the balance sheet of any other entity and that it is bankruptcy-remote from other entities.

23.3.2 Synthetic CDO squares: the portfolio level

The proceeds from the issuance of the debt securities to the investors are used by the SPV to support its credit derivatives–trading activity (again, in the same manner that a hedge fund or pooled commodity fund that participates in the over-the-counter derivatives markets will be required to collateralize its derivatives obligations). That support may take the form of cash deposits, cash substitutes (namely, highly rated, highly liquid debt securities, such as U.S. treasuries) or repos (de Vries Robbé and Ali, 2005).

The securities are serviced out of the fees paid to the SPV from its entry into credit derivatives and the cash flows derived from the SPV's investment of the issuance proceeds in cash deposits or other collateral arrangements.

The extent of the trading discretion given to the SPV varies from transaction to transaction. The SPV may be empowered, in the same manner as the SPVs in lightly managed synthetic CDOs, to assume credit risk in respect of the debt securities issued in other securitization transactions, with the variation of the portfolio constituents limited to replenishment and substitution. Alternatively, the SPV may have the power to manage the portfolio actively, by acquiring and disposing of credit risk through the entry into and the early closing out of credit derivatives (in the same manner as a hedge fund or pooled commodity fund derives its investment returns from trading derivatives, options, and futures contracts).

23.3.3 Credit derivatives

The credit derivatives that lie at the center of synthetic CDO squares and other synthetic CDOs are, in common with all other derivatives, risk-shifting instruments. In the particular case of a credit derivative, the risk that is transferred is the risk that the obligor, in relation to the loan or bond referenced by the credit derivative, will default in the performance of its obligations or become insolvent (de Vries Robbé and Ali, 2005).

The most common type of credit derivative and the one invariably used in synthetic CDO squares is a credit derivative known as a *credit default swap* (de Vries Robbé and Ali, 2005). A credit default swap involves one party (called the *protection seller*, according to market convention) agreeing to assume the credit risk in respect of one or more reference obligations, in exchange for the payment to it of a fee from the other party to the swap (called the *protection buyer*). These reference obligations usually represent the obligations of corporations with an investment-grade credit rating in respect of loans undertaken by them or debt securities issued by them. In synthetic CDO squares, the reference obligations are dominated by the debt securities issued in residential-mortgage-backed securitizations and CDOs (cash CDOs as well as other synthetic CDOs) (Fitch Ratings, 2005b).

The protection seller agrees to pay a settlement amount to the protection buyer if a *credit event* occurs in relation to the reference obligations. The principal credit events found in the credit default swaps employed in synthetic CDO squares and other synthetic CDOs are the bankruptcy of the underlying obligor and its failure to make payments when due in respect of the reference obligations (de Vries Robbé and Ali, 2005).

The credit default swaps entered into by the SPV in a synthetic CDO square may relate only to the debt securities issued in a single synthetic CDO, in which case the swap will terminate and the protection seller will be obligated to pay a settlement amount to the protection buyer on the first occurrence of a credit event in relation to the reference obligations. Alternatively, the credit default swap may relate to the debt securities issued in two or more synthetic CDOs. Credit default swaps that cover the reference obligations of multiple obligors are called *portfolio credit default swaps* (Fitch Ratings, 2005a). Depending on how the portfolio credit default swap has been structured, the obligation of the protection seller to pay the settlement amount may arise on the occurrence of the first credit event with respect to any of the reference obligations (called a *first-to-default credit default swap*) or on the second or a later credit event. The majority of portfolio credit default swaps are structured as first-to-default swaps (de Vries Robbé and Ali, 2005).

The portfolio in a synthetic CDO square commonly comprises between 3 and 20 portfolio credit default swaps, which, in total, deliver exposure to the reference obligations of 60–80 securitizations and 50–150 corporate entities (Fitch Ratings, 2004a, 2004b).

The credit default swaps used in a synthetic CDO square (and other synthetic CDOs) typically provide for cash settlement (de Vries Robbé and Ali, 2005). If no credit event (or, in the case of a portfolio swap, a nontriggering credit event) occurs during the term of the swap, the protection seller will continue to receive a fee from the protection buyer until the swap expires. If, however, a credit event occurs that triggers the termination of the swap, the protection seller will become obligated to pay a settlement amount to the protection buyer (and the protection buyer's obligation to pay a fee to the protection seller will come to an end). This settlement amount is a cash amount, calculated by reference to the loss in the value of the reference obligations (de Vries Robbé and Ali, 2005).

Less commonly, the credit default swap will provide for physical settlement. In that case, the settlement amount will comprise the cash amount necessary to purchase the reference obligations (or other obligations of the relevant entity that meet previously agreed-on criteria) for their full face value.

23.4 Recharacterization risk

The major — and persistent — legal risk for participants in synthetic CDO squares (a risk shared by participants in other synthetic CDOs) concerns the proper characterization of the credit derivatives entered into by the SPV. It is possible that a regulator or court could construe the role of the protection seller under a credit default swap as being legally equivalent to that of an insurer. This carries with it a number of adverse consequences for the parties: The protection seller and its officers may face criminal liability for carrying on an insurance business without the requisite regulatory authority; the credit default swap may be rendered unenforceable as a result; and the protection buyer will be subject to a duty of utmost good faith, preventing it from exploiting information that it possesses about the reference obligations (de Vries Robbé and Ali, 2005).

Credit default swaps superficially resemble insurance contracts. In both cases, one party agrees, in exchange for the payment to it of fees by its counterparty, to make a payment to the latter on the occurrence of an event, in respect of which there is uncertainty as to whether or when that event will occur. The legal consensus among market participants is that, notwithstanding this similarity, credit default swaps are not contracts of insurance.

That position may be summarized in the following terms. A payment obligation triggered by the occurrence of an uncertain event is a necessary but not sufficient condition for contracts of insurance. What differentiates contracts of insurance from other arrangements is the requirement that the payment be by way of indemnity or compensation for a loss incurred by the insured party as a consequence of the occurrence of the insured-against event. It is possible that the payment by the protection seller of a settlement amount under a credit default swap that is linked to a decline in value of a particular reference obligation may operate to compensate the protection buyer for suffering that decline in value (alternatively, for physically settled swaps, the purchase of the reference obligations or other eligible obligations by the protection seller for their face value may have the effect of making the protection buyer whole in relation to the reference obligations). It is, however, not necessary, in the case of credit default swaps, for the protection buyer to hold the reference obligations and thus be exposed to the bankruptcy or failure to pay of the underlying obligor. The obligation of the protection seller to pay the settlement amount to the protection buyer is therefore not conditional on the protection buyer's actually suffering a loss in relation to the reference obligations. Consequently, it cannot be said that the payment to the protection buyer of the settlement amount is by way of indemnity or compensation for such a loss.

Although there is considerable merit in the preceding argument, the continuing absence of statutory protection from the laws regulating the carrying of an insurance business in the major credit derivatives markets means there is a residual risk that a regulator or court could take the contrary view. That is, in fact, what happened in the United States in late 2003, when the Property and Casualty Insurance Committee of the National Association of Insurance Commissioners opined that weather derivatives, which are structurally equivalent to credit derivatives, should be regulated as insurance contracts (weather derivatives provide for the payment of a settlement amount on the occurrence of a particular climatic condition, such as the average daily temperature in a stipulated city falling below or rising above a specific threshold) (National Association of Insurance Commissioners, 2003).

The committee resiled from that position following intense lobbying by the major financial markets associations, including the International Swaps and Derivatives Association (International Swaps and Derivatives Association, 2004). Nonetheless, this event serves to demonstrate the fragile legal basis of credit derivatives in general and synthetic CDO squares in particular (Ali and de Vries Robbé, 2005). In this context, the declaration by the New York Insurance Department that credit default swaps are not insurance contracts (because the settlement amount must be paid regardless of whether the protection buyer has suffered a loss) is to be welcomed (New York Insurance Department, 2000).

A second, though markedly less significant, risk for the participants in synthetic CDO squares and other synthetic CDOs relates to the potential application of antigambling laws to the underlying credit derivatives. As noted earlier, there is no requirement for the protection buyer to hold the reference obligations that are the subject of the credit default swap. Accordingly, the only interest of the protection buyer in the credit default swap is whether it will lose the fees paid by it (if a credit event does not occur during the term of the swap) or win the settlement amount (if a credit event occurs). The absence of a pecuniary interest beyond the amounts that may be won or lost entails the risk that the credit default swap could be recharacterized as a gaming or wagering contract (de Vries Robbé and Ali, 2005). The consequences are similar to those that flow from the characterization of a credit default swap as an insurance contract: The parties may be subject to criminal penalties and the contract will be rendered unenforceable. This risk, in contrast to the risk of recharacterization as an insurance contract, has, however, been mitigated by statutory and judicial intervention in the major credit derivatives markets. There are statutory safe harbors for credit and other derivatives from the antigambling laws in those jurisdictions; moreover, the courts there have opined that arrangements entered into for a commercial purpose are not gaming or wagering contracts, even if they may otherwise possess the attributes of a gaming or wagering contract.

23.5 Conclusion

This chapter has examined the synthetic CDO square, one of the latest innovations in the rapidly growing global market for credit derivatives. This product possesses the structural features of a fund of funds and is further evidence of the ongoing convergence in the financial markets. The synthetic CDO square, like other funds of funds, provides investors with intermediated exposure to a diversified portfolio of instruments and also enables investors to benefit from securitization transactions whose securities may be illiquid or otherwise unobtainable.

Despite the expanding transaction volumes and almost relentless innovation in the global credit derivatives market, there are legal risks that require comprehensive resolution. Chief among these risks is recharacterization risk, which is the risk that the credit derivatives that are central to synthetic CDO squares and other synthetic CDOs could be construed by a regulator or court as an insurance contract. The prevailing legal consensus is that credit default swaps, the most common type of credit derivative, are not insurance contracts. Nonetheless, in the absence of a statutory safe harbor, the risk of regulatory or judicial recharacterization remains.

References

Ali, P. U., Stapledon G., and Gold, M. (2003). *Corporate Governance and Investment Fiduciaries*. Thomson Legal & Regulatory, Sydney, Australia.

Ali, P. U. and de Vries Robbé, J. J. (2003). *Synthetic, Insurance and Hedge Fund Securitisations*. Thomson, Sydney, Australia.

Ali, P. U. and de Vries Robbé, J. J. (2005). New Frontiers in Credit Derivatives. *Journal of Banking Regulation*, 6(1):175–182.

Das, S. (2005). *Credit Derivatives: CDOs and Structured Credit Products*. John Wiley & Sons, Singapore.

de Vries Robbé, J. J. (2005). Synthetic Squares, or the Securitisation of Russian Dolls. In: *Securitisation of Derivatives and Alternative Asset Classes* (de Vries Robbé, J. J. and Ali, P. U., eds.). Kluwer Law International, the Hague.

de Vries Robbé, J. J. and Ali, P. U. (2005). *Opportunities in Credit Derivatives and Synthetic Securitisation*. Thomson Financial, London.

Fitch Ratings. (2004a). Synthetic Structured Finance CDOs. *Credit Products Special Report*, 17(February):1–14.

Fitch Ratings. (2004b). Analysis of Synthetic CDOs of CDOs. *Global CDO Criteria Report*, 13(September):1–14.

Fitch Ratings. (2005a). Considerations for Funded Portfolio Credit Derivatives (Synthetic CDOs). *Credit Products/Global Special Report*, 8 (June):1–17.

Fitch Ratings. (2005b). Structures, Supply and Spreads: Challenges Facing Cash Arbitrage CDOs of European Structured Finance. *CDOs Special Report*, 13(June):1–26.

Fitch Ratings. (2005c). Hedge Funds: An Emerging Force in the Global Credit Markets. *Credit Policy Special Report*, 18(July):1–7.

International Swaps and Derivatives Association. (2004). Member Update. 24 March.

National Association of Insurance Commissioners. (2003). Weather Financial Instruments (Temperature): Insurance or Capital Markets Products? Property and Casualty Insurance Committee Draft White Paper, 9 September.

New York Insurance Department. (2000). Letter. 16 June.

Nomura Securities. (2005). CDOs-Squared Demystified. *Fixed Income Research*, 4(February):1–16.

Watterson, P. N. (2005). The Evolution of the CDO Squared. *Journal of Structured Finance*, 11(1):6–12.

24 Natural resources funds of funds: active management, risk management, and due diligence

Rian Akey, Hilary Till, and Aleks Kins

Abstract

We discuss three features of natural resources fund of funds investing. We first review the evidence that active commodity-trading managers are well positioned to identify alpha opportunities within the natural resources markets. The implication of this evidence is that a specialist natural resources fund of funds investment could potentially add value over an investor's core exposure in commodity indexes. Second, we review the types of risk management analyses that fund of funds investors should expect of their commodity managers. And finally, using numerous real-world examples, we discuss how a fund of funds investor should carry out sensible analyses of a commodity manager's business operations.

24.1 Introduction

This chapter comprehensively covers the new field of natural resources fund of funds investing. We first explain why the demand for such an investment has emerged, and then we discuss the opportunities that an actively managed natural resources fund of funds can potentially exploit. Next we examine the types of risk management analyses that fund of funds investors should expect of their commodity managers. And last, and perhaps most important, we provide a from-the-trenches view of the crucial due-diligence steps that a fund of funds investor should follow before investing in this emerging investment field.

24.2 Emerging demand for natural resources investments

The history of inflation-adjusted commodity prices has largely been one of secular decline, with a great deal of cyclicality around this trend. Until very recently, commodity investments could not rely on a commodity boom for profitability and instead had to take into account the largely mean-reverting nature of commodity prices.

Over the long sweep of history, though, there have been exceptions. During the late nineteenth century's industrialization in the United States and during the post–World War II recovery of Europe and Japan, spot commodity prices did boom. If we are witnessing an equivalent large-scale industrialization of developing Asia, as discussed in Heap (2005), then new types of commodity investment strategies will need to be developed in order to take advantage of this opportunity.

There are two ways to take advantage of natural resources investment opportunities. First, investors may elect to invest in a commodity index product. In doing so, the investors will earn the inherent return of the asset class, will be able to do so cheaply, but will not be provided with any downside-risk protection. It will be the responsibility of investors either to time their investments in commodity indices or to create a properly balanced overall portfolio so as to avoid downside risk.

Second, investors can choose to invest with active natural resources managers. As noted in Till and Eagleeye (2005), an institution can obtain its core commodity exposure through a commodity index investment and then include active commodity managers for further value added. This is analogous to the evolving nature of institutional equity management, whereby active management is being unbundled from passive index investments. A number of institutions are now getting core equity exposure through equity index funds, exchange-traded funds, and/or futures and then investing in long/short equity hedge funds for further value added.

Now, when deciding whether to invest with either commodity trading firms or natural resources hedge fund firms, investors must decide if they are comfortable with the boutique nature of these firms. A hedge fund may only have one or two key decision makers, for example. This does not give a lot of comfort to institutional investors, who require a deep investment team, who in turn would be expected to carry out a disciplined and repeatable investment process that does not rely on any one individual for its continued success, as discussed in Till (2004).

In contrast, funds of funds provide the type of structure that gives comfort to institutional investors. One possible organizational model is for institutions to use funds of funds to diversify away the idiosyncratic, operational risk of an individual hedge fund or commodity-trading firm.

In the next section, we show how a diversified investment in active commodity and natural resource managers can potentially provide an investor with a very attractive set of returns with acceptable risk. Such an investment can be accessed through a specialist natural resources fund of funds. The succeeding sections discuss the unique risk management and due-diligence issues that arise with such investments.

24.3 Diversified, active-management opportunities in natural resources investing

The majority of attention to recent asset flows into commodity investments has focused on allocations to commodity index–linked products. Current estimates suggest that the total assets linked to the six main commodity indexes are about

Table 24.1 The main commodity indices

Deutsche Bank Liquid Commodity Index (DBLCI)
Dow Jones–AIG Commodity Index (DJ-AIG)
Goldman Sachs Commodity Index (GSCI)
Reuters/Jeffries Commodities Research Bureau Index (RJ-CRB)
Rogers International Commodities Index (RICI)
Standard and Poor's Commodities Index (SPCI)

Table 24.2 Risk and return characteristics of commodity indexes, 1994–2004

Index	Compound annual return	Annualized standard deviation	Sharpe ratio	Worst drawdown
DBLCI	15.70%	19.74%	0.60	−46.11%
DJ-AIG	9.16%	12.76%	0.41	−36.20%
GSCI	8.75%	19.55%	0.25	−48.25%
RJ-CRB	12.84%	13.61%	0.66	−37.04%
RICI	13.95%	14.93%	0.67	−36.94%
SPCI	11.44%	16.48%	0.46	37.57%

$70 billion, up from less than $10 billion just five years ago. For a list of the six main commodity indices, see Table 24.1.

Given that most of the attention to these asset flows has focused on passive, long-only exposure, an investor making an initial foray into commodities may conclude that the only decision to make is determining which commodity index is best. We find that while commodity-index investing does provide scalable opportunities for investing, the natural resources universe is sufficiently rich in opportunities that an investor should also consider active investments in this asset class, which would add further value over an indexed investment.

Tables 24.2 and 24.3 verify that commodity indexes have historically produced equity-like returns with little correlation to traditional asset classes (or traditional alternative asset classes, such as hedge funds and managed futures), confirming the case for including commodities in a broadly diversified portfolio.

Commodity markets, particularly those where the underlying commodity is difficult or expensive to store, are vulnerable to short-term booms and busts, regardless of long-term secular trends. Markets facing near-term disruptions create price fluctuations as one of the few mechanisms available to restore equilibrium. Prices that spike in one month have had a historical tendency to mean-revert as the crisis dissipates.

Commodity markets are far more independent of each other than the constituents of other asset classes. Consider equities, where a decision to be long on the asset class can be executed through generally correlated positions across different market capitalizations or sectors. Individual commodity markets — even sectors — are far less likely to be correlated. Fundamentals affecting corn versus aluminum versus gasoline are, largely, unique. Faber (2004) warns that even

Table 24.3 Correlational characteristics of commodity indexes, 1994–2004

Index	S&P 500	Lehman Brothers Long-Term Treasury Index	HFR Funds of Funds Index	Barclay CTA Index
DBLCI	0.02	0.03	0.21	0.15
DJ-AIG	0.1	0.05	0.23	0.26
GSCI	0.01	0.11	0.19	0.21
RJ-CRB	0.09	0.01	0.21	0.19
RICI	0.07	0	0.21	0.16
SPCI	0.02	0.1	0.13	0.28

within a long-term bullish environment for commodities, individual markets may see periodic drawdowns of 50% or more.

Extreme commodity price volatility and the heterogeneous nature of individual commodity markets can potentially create trading opportunities for those who approach the commodity markets tactically. In addition, active commodity-trading strategies can take advantage of short positions, cyclical trades, or short-term positions based on weather or other fundamental information as well as relative-value and arbitrage opportunities, such as spread trades. These are all opportunities that a commodity-index investor will be missing.

Akey (2005) shows that active management can potentially provide commodity investors with attractive returns on both an absolute and a risk-adjusted basis, without harming the diversification benefits of the asset class (see Table 24.4).

Still, even an actively managed commodities investment faces limitations in the context of a futures-only portfolio, which will be based primarily on the limited number of deeply liquid futures markets. Outside of the most liquid energies and metals markets, few commodities markets trade in enough volume to support active trading of any significant size. This makes developing a diversified active portfolio very challenging.

In addition, futures markets cannot facilitate any trading in a variety of natural resources and resource-linked markets that are without futures contracts. These additional markets are not esoteric commodities of little economic impact, but include very recognizable resources, such as water, alternative energy sources, such as uranium, and forestry products as well as resources-linked opportunities such as in shipping, infrastructure, and utilities.

While creating an active commodity portfolio that includes securities investments can expand the investor's opportunities, one concern is that adding equity investments to a commodity portfolio will detract from the diversification benefits by adding equity exposure. Published research has typically concluded that investors seeking commodity exposure should avoid accessing that exposure via equities. That is, investors who buy energy companies should expect their investment to behave more like a stock and less like a commodity. However, this research has relied on long-only passive-sector equity indexes to arrive at its conclusions.

Table 24.4 Active futures portfolio vs. commodity indexes, 1994–2004

Index or portfolio	Compound annual return	Annualized standard deviation	Sharpe ratio	Worst drawdown	Correlation to S&P 500
Active commodity traders	15.17%	7.87%	1.43	−7.02%	0.08
DBLCI	15.70%	19.74%	0.60	−46.11%	0.02
DJ-AIG	9.16%	12.76%	0.41	−36.20%	0.10
GSCI	8.75%	19.55%	0.25	−48.25%	0.01
RJ-CRB	12.84%	13.61%	0.66	−37.04%	0.09
RICI	13.95%	14.93%	0.67	−36.94%	0.07
SPCI	11.44%	16.48%	0.46	−37.57%	0.02

The commodity index universe is rapidly evolving.
Source: Updated from Akey (2005).

Table 24.5 Active futures and hedge fund portfolio vs. commodity indexes, 1994–2004

Index or portfolio	Compound annual return	Annualized standard deviation	Sharpe ratio	Worst drawdown	Correlation to S&P 500
Active commodity traders	15.17%	7.87%	1.43	−7.02%	0.08
Active commodity traders & HF	18.40%	8.60%	1.68	−16.58%	0.26
DBLCI	15.70%	19.74%	0.60	−46.11%	0.02
DJ-AIG	9.16%	12.76%	0.41	−36.20%	0.10
GSCI	8.75%	19.55%	0.25	−48.25%	0.01
RJ-CRB	12.84%	13.61%	0.66	−37.04%	0.09
RICI	13.95%	14.93%	0.67	−36.94%	0.07
SPCI	11.44%	16.48%	0.46	−37.57%	0.02

Source: Updated from Akey (2005).

Akey (2005) constructs a second portfolio that includes both active futures traders and natural-resources-sector hedge funds, concluding that adding actively managed equity exposure to the sector can expand the investor's opportunities and add incremental amounts of absolute and risk-adjusted returns without a significant degradation in diversification benefits (see Table 24.5).

We conclude this section by noting that a diversified investment in active commodity and natural resources managers can potentially provide an investor with a very attractive set of returns with acceptable risk. Further, institutional investors who use the core satellite approach to portfolio management can obtain their core commodity exposure through cost-effective index products and then use a natural resources fund of funds to provide additional returns over those of the institution's commodity-index investments.

Now that we have established the case for active natural resources investments, we turn to discussing the unique risk management and due-diligence issues that one must confront in this emerging investment category.

24.4   Risk management in natural resources futures trading

A fund of funds manager will proactively attempt to limit downside risk in three ways: (1) by constructing a portfolio of diverse investment managers; (2) by choosing to invest in those managers who have a strong risk management culture; and (3) by mitigating the business risk associated with hedge funds and commodity-trading firms. This section discusses the second point and gives examples of the types of risk analyses that fund of funds investors should expect of their managers.

As noted in Till and Gunzberg (2005), a commodity manager needs to address both idiosyncratic risks and macro-risks when designing a risk management program. Idiosyncratic risks include those unique to a specific commodity market. Examples include simulating the impact of the discovery of mad cow disease in the United States on live cattle futures positions as well as examining the impact of the freezing over of New York harbor on the price of near-month heating oil futures positions. Macro-risks include discovering those risks in the portfolio that can create inadvertent correlations among seemingly uncorrelated positions. Examples include simulating the impact of a September 11, 2001, event on a portfolio that is long economically sensitive commodities as well as examining the impact of surprisingly cold weather at the end of the winter on a portfolio of energy positions.

Table 24.6 and Figures 24.1 through 24.4 provide examples of crucial risk analyses that a commodity manager should perform.

24.4.1   Risk report by strategy

Table 24.6 provides an example risk report for a commodity portfolio. This report shows the value at risk per strategy as well as each strategy's worst-case loss during normal times and during eventful periods. *Eventful periods* are defined as those times when the financial markets have performed very poorly, as discussed in Till (2002). The report also shows the incremental risk of adding each strategy to the portfolio.

Table 24.6 Example risk report for a commodity portfolio

Strategy	Value at risk	Worst-case loss		Incremental contribution to	
		During normal times	During eventful period	Portfolio value-at-risk*	Worst-case portfolio event risk*
Deferred reverse soybean crush spread	2.78%	−1.09%	−1.42%	0.08%	−0.24%
Long deferred natural gas outright	0.66%	−0.18%	−0.39%	0.17%	0.19%
Short deferred wheat spread	0.56%	−0.80%	−0.19%	0.04%	0.02%
Long deferred gasoline outright	2.16%	−0.94%	−0.95%	0.33%	0.81%
Long deferred gasoline vs. heating oil spread	2.15%	−1.04%	−2.22%	0.93%	2.04%
Long deferred hog spread	0.90%	−1.21%	−0.65%	0.07%	−0.19%
Portfolio	3.01%	−2.05%	−2.90%		

* A positive contribution means that the strategy adds to risk, while a negative contribution means the strategy reduces risk.
Source: Till (2005).

24.4.2 Rolling value at risk

Figure 24.1 shows an ongoing analysis of the value at risk (VaR) of a portfolio during a time of intense uncertainty in the energy markets. In examining VaR, a commodity manager attempts to ensure that a portfolio's positions have not been sized so large that he or she cannot sustain the random fluctuations in profits and losses that might ensue. As the figure shows, VaR is obviously not a static number in the very dynamic energy futures markets.

24.4.3 Beta risk

Figure 24.2 provides an example of evaluating a portfolio's sensitivity to a commodity market, specifically, in this case, the gasoline market. A commodity manager may have limits on the amount of exposure to the outright direction of an individual commodity market, especially if that manager specializes in relative-value trades. The analysis in Figure 24.2 would be necessary under such a constraint.

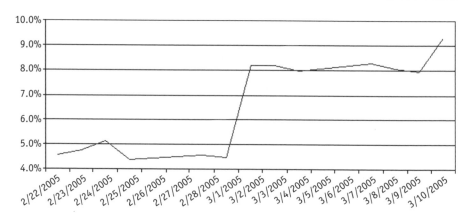

Figure 24.1 Rolling value at risk for an energy-focused portfolio, based on seven previous business days; VaR = 2 × standard deviation (From Premia Capital Management, LLC)

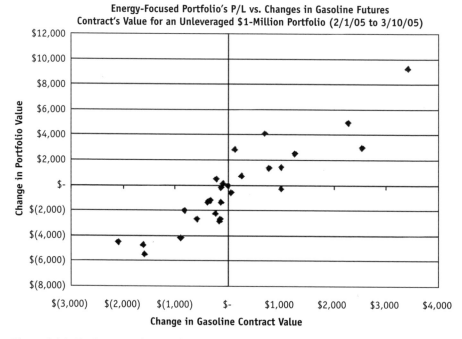

Figure 24.2 Evaluation of a portfolio's gasoline beta (or exposure) (This portfolio has a beta-weighted exposure of 2.4 gasoline contracts per $1 million in account size. From Premia Capital Management, LLC)

24.4.4 Inadvertent-concentration risk

Figure 24.3 provides an example of inadvertent-concentration risk. In order to meet the goal of creating a diversified portfolio, a commodities portfolio manager

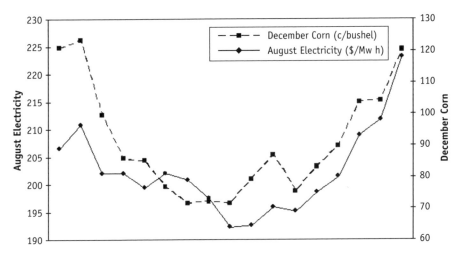

Figure 24.3 Example of inadvertent concentration risk: CBOT corn and NYMEX electricity prices during July 1999 (The August electricity prices are specifically for the futures contract on Cinergy electricity, which services portions of Ohio, Indiana, and Kentucky. This futures contract traded on the NYMEX until being delisted on 2/15/2002. CBOT is the Chicago Board of Trade; NYMEX is the New York Mercantile Exchange. From Premia Capital Management, LLC)

needs to exercise due care in ensuring that each additional trade is in fact a risk diversifier rather than a risk amplifier, as discussed in Till and Eagleeye (2005). If two trades are in fact related, then one should consider them as part of the same strategy bucket and require them to share risk capital. If each trade is instead allocated full-risk capital, then the manager may be inadvertently doubling up on risk.

If a manager had invested in corn and electricity futures contracts during July 1999, that manager would have indeed doubled up risk. During that time, the U.S. Midwest had blistering temperatures (which even led to some power outages). During that time, both corn and electricity prices responded in nearly identical fashion to weather forecasts and realizations.

This example shows that a manager must understand what the key factors are that drive a strategy's performance. If two strategies have common drivers, then it can be assumed that their respective performances will be similar.

24.4.5 Extreme-weather risk

Figure 24.4 shows an example of monitoring the potential for extremely cold weather to cause a near stock-out in storage for natural gas. When U.S. natural gas storage inventories have been drawn down to uncomfortably low levels at the end of winter, the natural gas price has historically responded by exploding. Lammey (2005) quotes a futures trader regarding the extremely cold winter of 2002–03: "I remember that season well, because we started off the winter with

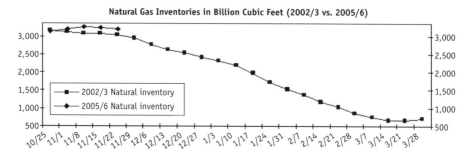

Figure 24.4 Monitoring the potential of a (near-) stock-out in natural gas (This graph specifically shows the U.S. Department of Energy's total estimated storage data for working natural gas inventories. From Premia Capital Management, LLC)

early intense cold, and ended the season late with intense cold — and many participants in the industry were seriously worried that there might not be enough gas to get us across the finish line." Figure 24.4 shows an example of monitoring the changes in natural gas inventories during the winter of 2005–06 versus what happened during the winter of 2002–03.

This section has covered the types of market-risk reports that fund of funds investors should expect their commodity managers to employ. The next section covers how a fund of funds investor should attempt to mitigate the business risk associated with commodity and natural resources investment firms, many of which are start-ups.

24.5   Due diligence in natural resources fund of funds investing

The term *due diligence* is commonly applied by many people in various fields. In fact, the term has become so widespread in business and especially in the professional investment process that it has become almost cliché. The remarkable fact is that despite the ubiquity of chatter in the investment world regarding due diligence, it remains a loosely defined and vague concept with parameters that are subject to broad interpretation. *Merriam-Webster's Collegiate Dictionary* (11th edition) defines *due diligence* as "the care that a reasonable person exercises under the circumstances to avoid harm to other persons or their property." It sounds like Webster never experienced a double-digit drawdown.

Many would-be investors utilize *due diligence* as an all-encompassing umbrella term to cover everything from the understanding of an investment's return driver to the process of recovery from an information technology disaster. Yet other investors think due diligence is nothing more than conducting background checks on the principals, while the analysis of return generation becomes a separate process.

To add to the potential confusion, not only is the interpretation of the practical meaning of the term inconsistent across various investors, but implementation of the process varies greatly as well. Some investors prefer to generate massive checklists that leave no stone unturned, while others prefer face-to-face interviews that rely on personal instinct and industry experience.

Perhaps the best way to come up with a proper understanding of due diligence is to take a step back and examine the desired outcome of a successful due-diligence process. In such an examination, an investor clearly hopes to confirm all material assertions made by an investment manager. It further becomes clear that numerous methods of uncovering information could lead to the same desired result and shows that there is certainly no single correct methodology to conduct due diligence.

The intention of this section is not to meander through the nuances of interpretation of what a thorough due-diligence process is, nor is it to outline an exhaustive A-to-Z recipe for such a process. Instead, the goal is to highlight some practical points of interest and real-world experiences that the author has encountered while interviewing hundreds of commodity-trading advisors (CTAs) and hedge funds. Where applicable, we will note the points that are of particular relevance to natural resources–trading managers. These observations can largely be classified into market risk and business risk. Because market risk is more appropriately addressed in a discussion of trading strategy and risk management, the focus of this portion of the chapter is on (1) business risk and (2) business risk mitigation in relation to natural resources–trading managers.

24.5.1   Business risk

An initial observation is that investors assess the risks and rewards of any investment opportunity by focusing heavily on the underlying market risks of a particular trading strategy while overlooking an often more easily understandable and controllable risk: *business risk*. The irony is that some measure of market risk is an inevitable component of any investment strategy, and investors are hopefully paid to assume such risks, while business risk does not pay a premium and can be largely reduced with thorough due diligence and some common sense. This observation is not meant to deemphasize the importance of vetting the degree of market risk associated with a particular trading strategy but to suggest that one of the most significant ways an investor can reduce unnecessary risk is to avoid business risk.

Business inexperience

Business risk can exist in any organization of any size, but it is generally most prevalent in newer and/or smaller firms. The start-up business risk factor is especially pertinent to the fledgling universe of natural resources managers, due to the rapid growth of investment firms in the space. While some CTAs and a few hedge funds have been in existence and operating independently for decades, the vast majority of natural resources trading firms have emerged only recently. There is currently a huge demand for experienced and skilled traders working independent of large organizations. This phenomenal demand for natural resources traders parallels what began in the early 1990s for equity and fixed-income traders on Wall Street. Until recently, natural resources traders were found primarily within sizable corporations trading internally on proprietary desks. Due to current global investor demand to diversify portfolio exposure into hard assets, many of these traders have been able to leave their former employers to engage in entrepreneurial trading ventures, including setting up their own hedge funds. While many of these individuals may posses superior experience in trading in natural resources markets, most have little, if any, practical experience managing a business. Historically, these individuals were able to focus solely on trading without worrying about the details of developing and running an entire business. The demands of growing and managing a business can substantially detract from the trader's ability to focus on the markets. The transition is certainly not impossible, but it definitely requires significant consideration when one is assessing the viability of a new firm.

Loss of information edge

In addition to a potential lack of experience in running a business, one factor that may further impede the success of a newly launched natural resources–trading firm is the loss of information flow. Such a potential problem mirrors what many foreign exchange traders face when leaving large banks. Many traders in sizable organizations benefit from extensive information flow, and many of these traders do not even realize the degree of their dependence on such information. Once removed from the deep information channels, many formerly successful traders may become incapable of trading profitably. In some cases, such a scenario is readily apparent as a trader is never able to replicate the performance that he or she generated while employed at a large firm. In other instances, the deteriorating effects of reduced information flow are more difficult to detect. In these scenarios, it appears at first that a trader is unaffected by his or her new situation and is able to perform as well as he or she had historically. After a period of time (in some cases even years), the trader's performance dissipates dramatically. This phenomenon is often caused by the fact that when an individual leaves an institution, he or she may be able to maintain several key relationships with former colleagues, clients, or counterparties who are still in a position to provide valuable information flow for some while. As time passes, however, this information flow can and often does dwindle, for various reasons, such as colleagues leaving their positions, or the independent trader is unable to reciprocate with valuable information, thereby leaving these traders unable to perform as they had historically. In order to avoid such a situation, flow traders either need to find new return drivers or become large enough so they can obtain similar information themselves before their relationships expire.

Unverifiable track record

An additional problem that exists with many natural resources traders, which is also a result of leaving the employment of a large institution, is that many of these traders are unable either to demonstrate or to calculate the track record generated while trading for their previous employer. For example, some traders are limited by nondisclosure agreements from displaying their trading performance to anyone external to the firm. In addition, some proprietary traders are given trading lines without knowing their underlying funding. As such, calculating a rate of return becomes impossible because the numerator is known without knowing the denominator. For example, a trader who makes a $1,000 average daily profit on a $1 million account size is far more profitable than a trader who makes the same dollar amount on a $2 million account. Many proprietary traders are only able to express their profits in dollars. As such, a profitable proprietary trader may have false confidence in his or her capabilities to be successful as an asset manager.

Fraud

Another form of business risk is fraud. Fraud is perhaps the most damaging risk to the industry and the most difficult for the investor to withstand because it is intentional and generally receives enormous media attention after the deceit is exposed. The vast majority of traders are not frauds, but it would be naive to think that there are currently no hedge funds that are practicing deception. It seems that the best protection against fraud is a thorough background check and a heavy dose of common sense.

With regard to the background check, there are several financial industry service providers who will verify that a person is who he or she says he or she is and that the manager has not misled his or her clients about educational credentials, bankruptcies, past criminal charges, or other important personal details. This information generally exists in the public realm; with the Internet and enough perseverance, investors can frequently perform this work themselves, but it is often more cost and time efficient to utilize a service. Additionally, for registered CTAs, one can access a database managed by the National Futures Association (http://www.nfa.futures.org) to check whether a trader has had any history of violations with the NFA. The aforementioned steps are necessary in any responsible due-diligence effort, but no amount of work in this area can guarantee against fraud. A clean background check does not unequivocally indicate that an individual is not a fraud, for a criminal with a clean record is simply one who has not yet been caught.

Perhaps the most important way to avoid fraud is to use common sense. This assertion is easier stated than accomplished. The clues in this process or the pieces of the puzzle are found in the mundane details of a trader's story. The moral of the story is that if the details do not add up logically, avoid the investment at all costs.

Each detail that does not act to confirm the material assertions a trader makes to an investor or potential investor in the due-diligence process is commonly considered a red flag. Red flags can be found in any part of a trader's story. The following examples are just a few of endless scenarios to demonstrate that what is missing in a trader's story can be potentially even more important than what is found in a background check.

Missing performance

A game occasionally played by trading firms (generally with systematic trading programs) is that they may have a fund or many funds with established track records that have become lackluster in performance over time. As interest in their firm from the investment community tapers off, they almost magically present an audited track record with tremendous performance, just in the nick of time to spark interest in their business and to generate new investment. What appears to be legitimate, due to the audit, may not really be as forthcoming when the entire scheme is uncovered. In this scenario, the trader may have had many track records funded with his or her own money and might only be showing the most successful trading program while hiding many losing track records. In light of this cherry-picking scenario, an investor should inquire about any missing performance by asking the trader to confirm and verify that only one track record existed. Verification can be made by requesting that the trader make all of his personal brokerage accounts and personal tax records available to the auditors to confirm the sole existence of the track record in question.

Missing assets

There are many reasons to determine whether a trader has personal assets invested in his or her trading strategy, but the following example is perhaps the most extreme one this author has experienced. On one occasion, a trader presented himself as being a former senior executive at a major hedge fund. Such a position should have generated substantial personal wealth for the trader. Despite the fact that the trader made a very convincing argument to fund a start-up trading operation and had a tremendous pedigree within the industry, it was not logical that he was unable to at least partially fund the start-up from his personal wealth. The trader had intricate explanations as to why his personal assets were unavailable, but it seemed illogical or suspicious that such an experienced individual needed seed investors. Several years later it surfaced that this trader had found not only seed investors but also hundreds of millions in additional investor capital that he later lost in high-risk trades in which losses were concealed. It turned out that the manager had lost all of his own money with an insatiable appetite for taking risk in the markets and had subsequently done the same with countless investors in one fund after another.

Unnecessarily complicated corporate structure

This example seems obvious after the Enron collapse, but periodically traders present unnecessarily complicated corporate structures without valid explanations of the existence of multiple firms. In many cases such structures are designed to disguise true ownership or to mask conflicts of interest.

24.5.2   Business risk mitigation

The best way for a due-diligence analyst to mitigate business risk is to become "hands on" with the infrastructure of the candidate investment firm. Such an assertion might sound absurd, but that is precisely what an investor is able to accomplish by investing through a managed account. Most established financial market hedge funds resist offering managed accounts, but that is not the case for the majority of CTAs and many natural resources hedge funds as well, due to the start-up nature of many of these firms.

In a managed account scenario, the risk of fraud is virtually eliminated because no money is transferred to the trader. Only a "trading line" via a limited power of attorney to trade the account is provided to the trader, and, as such, assets remain at the brokerage firm and out of control of the trader. Further, with a managed account an investor is able to reduce dependence on the infrastructure of the trading firm. The investor is able to verify the profit-and-loss and cash-to-margin levels of the account without relying on calculations made by an unfamiliar back office managed by the trader or outsourced to a third party. While a managed account offers complete transparency into an investment, it is not a perfect solution because it potentially creates administrative difficulties for both the trading manager as well as the investor and does not have limited liability for the investor.

A fund investment is more convenient for both the trader and the investor to administer, but it puts 100% of the control of the transparency of the investment in the hands of the trader. In this scenario, most investors accept what information the trader disseminates to them at face value. If the trading manager is unwilling to give the investor direct transparency, the next best source of verification is to confirm what the trader states with as many third-party service providers as possible including, but not limited to, the prime broker, auditor, administrator, legal counsel, and custodian of the fund. Do note that the trader is a client of the service provider and that service providers often are reluctant to disseminate information on paying customers. Despite the business relationship between the trading firm and the service providers, an investor can use any and all statements made by service providers to corroborate what the trader has stated.

In either a fund or a managed account investment, an investor must determine that a trader has an adequate internal infrastructure. As mentioned earlier, many natural resources traders have little experience in managing businesses. As such, in order to maintain focus on the markets, a trader must either hire an experienced team of professionals or outsource operational responsibilities or some combination of the two options. A red flag in this area certainly occurs when all operational responsibilities fall on one or a few internal individuals. In such cases, these firms are generally unable to sustain any sort of growth efficiently or responsibly.

24.5.3 Due-diligence in natural resources fund of funds investing

We conclude this section by noting that when confirming all material assertions made by an investment manager, one must remember that logic and persistence are certainly an investor's most valuable weapons. There is no Holy Grail or sure-fire method to uncover all of the risks in an investment opportunity. The best prac-tice is to request proof for each and every major assertion a trader puts forward to potential or existing investors. If, for example, a trader states that they have con-ducted research to validate the use of value at risk, request to see that work on the spot. If a pattern develops that demonstrates that a trader cannot back up his or her claims, the best way to avoid trouble is obvious: *Avoid that trader.*

24.6 Conclusion

In this chapter we discussed how an investor could go about investing in the com-modity markets, especially if that investor believes that we are in the midst of a historic industrial revolution in developing Asia, which could provide numer-ous opportunities in the natural resources markets.

An investor can cheaply obtain long-term exposure in the commodity markets through an indexed investment. And then for further value-added, that investor could choose to invest in a specialist natural resources fund of funds, which may be able to take advantage of opportunities that an indexed investment could miss.

An investor may decide to invest through a fund of funds for his or her active commodities allocation because this type of structure would typically be suffi-ciently diversified to limit the idiosyncratic, operational risk of an individual commodity manager.

A fund of funds manager in turn will attempt to limit the market risk of his or her overall portfolio by investing in diverse investment strategies and by choosing managers with a strong risk management culture.

Finally, an experienced fund of funds manager will employ a number of common-sense tools to mitigate the risk of investing in commodity firms that are frequently start-ups in this emerging investment field.

Acknowledgments

Hilary Till would like to note that the risk management ideas in this chapter were jointly developed with Joseph Eagleeye, Co-founder of Premia Capital Management, LLC, http://www.premiacap.com. She would also like to thank Galina Kalcheva for assistance in risk management research.

References

Akey, R. (2005). Commodities: A Case for Active Management. *Journal of Alternative Investments*, 8(20):8–30.

Faber, M. (2004). Booming Commodity Prices. *The Gloom, Boom, & Doom Report*. April 22.

Heap, A. (2005). China — The Engine of a Commodities Super Cycle. Citigroup Global Equity Research, March 31.

Lammey, A. (2005). Choppy Winter Forecasts Suggest Healthy End to Drawdown. *Natural Gas Week*, December 5:2–3.

Till, H. (2002). Risk Management Lessons in Leveraged Futures Trading. *Commodities Now*, 6(3):84–87.

Till, H. (2004). On the Role of Hedge Funds in Institutional Portfolios. *Journal of Alternative Investments*, 6(4):77–89.

Till, H. (2005). Risk Management in Commodity Futures Trading. Presentation at GAIM June 2005 Conference, Lausanne, Switzerland.

Till, H. and Eagleeye, J. (2005). Commodities — Active Strategies for Enhanced Return. In: *The Handbook of Inflation Hedging Investments* (Greer, R., ed.). McGraw-Hill, New York; *Journal of Wealth Management*, 8(2):42–61.

Till, H. and Gunzberg, J. (2005). Absolute Returns in Commodity (Natural Resource) Futures Investments. In: *Hedge Fund Investment Management* (Nelken, I., ed.). Elsevier, London.

25 Identifying and monitoring risk in a fund of hedge funds portfolio

Meredith Jones

Abstract

Funds of hedge funds are often viewed as an entry-level investment vehicle for investors making their first foray into hedge funds. With more than 2,600 funds of hedge funds available to investors and more opening every day, it's clear that fund of hedge funds investing has become one of the most popular ways to invest in hedge funds. A large part of funds of hedge funds' popularity rests with their less risky profile, whether real or perceived. However, it remains important for investors and fund of funds managers to be able to identify and monitor the risks in their fund portfolios. We address specific fund of hedge funds risk considerations, including transparency, liquidity, diversification, and factor and impact analysis.

25.1 Introduction

Although early indications show that capital inflows to funds of hedge funds (FOFs) slowed in 2005 and that the inflows of assets that did occur benefited primarily the largest FOFs (Peltz, 2005a), funds of hedge funds continue to offer investors a less complicated and often less costly way to access a diversified hedge fund portfolio. Indeed, funds of hedge funds allow investors to make a single investment without having to engage in a lengthy (and costly) data-collection, screening, due-diligence, and ongoing monitoring process on a large number of funds. However, FOFs have their own unique risk factors, including diversification and overdiversification, liquidity, transparency, and factor and impact analysis, which require specific due diligence and risk monitoring.

In fact, a lingering misperception in the marketplace is the "rose is a rose" theory of FOF investing. It is important to remember that funds of hedge funds, although often called a hedge fund strategy, do not technically represent a specific investment style. A fund of hedge funds is, rather, a vehicle or a means by which to make hedge fund investments, but it is not an investment strategy in and of itself. A fund of funds can be focused on a single strategy or invest in multiple strategies. An FOF can be market neutral, conservative, or aggressive and can exhibit a number of different return, reward, and risk profiles. Because of the

Table 25.1 Performance of multistrategy funds of funds

					Calendar year						
	2005 YTD*	2004	2003	2002	2001	2000	1999	1998	1997	1996	1995
Funds in universe	740	934	772	591	438	348	276	212	169	130	94
Mean	4.78%	6.72%	12.07%	3.19%	6.87%	12.73%	24.69%	4.63%	17.75%	17.54%	13.29%
Median	3.63%	6.41%	10.33%	2.45%	6.91%	12.52%	19.55%	3.81%	17.06%	16.14%	12.84%
Standard deviation	19.30%	4.23%	10.09%	7.29%	7.78%	13.15%	19.03%	17.69%	7.51%	8.67%	10.40%
Maximum	305.43%	27.42%	105.15%	51.16%	59.68%	85.87%	106.43%	163.79%	47.89%	88.01%	64.85%
Minimum	-15.12%	-16.71%	-30.13%	-17.30%	-33.73%	-32.20%	-49.93%	-76.37%	-3.23%	-2.23%	-23.03%
5th percentile	9.61%	14.20%	26.19%	17.81%	19.93%	32.65%	58.07%	27.50%	31.01%	32.22%	28.83%
10th percentile	7.99%	11.77%	21.18%	10.53%	15.15%	23.97%	47.79%	18.67%	26.36%	24.43%	23.55%
20th percentile	6.07%	9.71%	14.65%	6.69%	10.32%	18.68%	34.98%	12.57%	22.43%	20.56%	18.47%
25th percentile	5.55%	8.82%	13.54%	5.71%	9.44%	16.93%	32.51%	11.22%	21.56%	19.50%	16.84%
30th percentile	5.14%	8.25%	12.60%	4.82%	8.84%	16.21%	28.65%	9.43%	20.24%	18.93%	15.63%
40th percentile	4.24%	7.28%	11.43%	3.54%	7.74%	14.27%	22.74%	6.26%	18.05%	17.14%	14.27%
50th percentile	3.63%	6.41%	10.33%	2.45%	6.91%	12.52%	19.55%	3.81%	17.06%	16.14%	12.84%
60th percentile	2.96%	5.39%	9.28%	1.57%	5.67%	10.15%	17.35%	1.39%	15.46%	15.16%	11.14%
70th percentile	2.22%	4.77%	8.02%	0.21%	4.32%	8.00%	15.00%	-1.12%	14.24%	14.19%	10.44%
75th percentile	1.74%	4.39%	7.54%	-0.43%	3.53%	6.98%	13.96%	-3.02%	13.63%	13.11%	8.77%
80th percentile	1.22%	3.95%	6.74%	-1.19%	2.27%	5.78%	12.66%	-4.90%	12.04%	12.83%	8.07%
90th percentile	-0.74%	2.32%	4.99%	-4.40%	-1.08%	0.00%	9.46%	-8.72%	10.02%	11.18%	1.65%
95th percentile	-2.72%	0.78%	3.70%	-7.00%	-4.50%	-6.57%	3.97%	-14.35%	8.56%	9.07%	-2.49%

*Year to date 2005 includes those funds that have reported through October 2005. Copyright 2005, Strategic Financial Solutions, LLC. All rights reserved.

vast variation of investment profiles among FOFs, it is imperative that investors develop their investment mandate beyond the simple statement "I want to invest in a fund of hedge funds." Table 25.1 shows the wide range of returns that are offered by multistrategy funds of hedge funds. Note that in many years, there are as many as 50–100+ percentage points separating the minimum and maximum returns for the FOFs in the sample. Therefore, it is incumbent on the investor to carefully select an FOF that closely matches his or her specific risk–reward mandate; to fail to do so is to risk disappointment in the FOF's results.

25.2   Diversification and overdiversification

One of the primary reasons that family offices, endowments, pensions, foundations, and high-net-worth individuals choose to invest in hedge funds through an FOF vehicle is for the diversification that FOFs often provide. However, just because one makes an investment in an FOF does not guarantee that the FOF is adequately diversified; nor does it mean that one cannot invest in a portfolio that is, in fact, overdiversified. On one hand, investors certainly want to protect themselves from a catastrophic hedge fund blowup and normal hedge fund volatility within their hedge fund portfolio — if it turns out the FOF has invested in Long Term Capital Management, Bayou, Manhattan, or Maricopa, it is important to ensure that the overall portfolio can withstand writing down an underlying investment to zero and that everyone lives to invest another day. On the other hand, there is growing proof that you can overdiversify a portfolio, thus compromising returns and diluting alpha.

It is undeniable, however, that one of the primary reasons to make an investment into an FOF is for painless diversification into a portfolio of hedge funds. That is, FOF investors want to achieve a diversified hedge fund portfolio that does not require an extensive time commitment for data collection, manager screening and selection, due diligence, and ongoing monitoring on multiple, single-manager hedge funds nor a significant monetary investment in staff or outside consultants to complete that work. The question of how many funds it takes to achieve that diversification has been the subject of debate for years, but it is possible to draw some conclusions by simulating a number of portfolios.

For our purposes, three portfolios were constructed, one with five underlying hedge fund investments, one with 12, and one with 20. Each portfolio has been simulated from October 2002 to September 2005 and contains the same fund that experiences a catastrophic event in September 2005, which caused our simulated FOF manager to write the investment down 100%. The risk–reward tables and a VAMI graph for each portfolio have been provided in Tables 25.2–25.4 and Figures 25.1–25.3. One can clearly see that the simulated hedge fund blowup has a much more pronounced effect on the portfolio that contains five funds. The monthly drawdown in September 2005 is much greater for the five-fund portfolio than either the 12- or 20-fund portfolio; as a result, the compound

Table 25.2 Risk table for simulated five-fund portfolio

	Annualized
Compound rate of return	3.45%
Standard deviation	12.61%
Semi deviation	22.45%
Gain deviation	3.03%
Loss deviation	25.62%
Down deviation (2.00%)	11.70%
Down deviation (0%)	11.59%
Sharpe (2.00%)	0.18
Sortino (2.00%)	0.12
Sortino (0%)	0.29

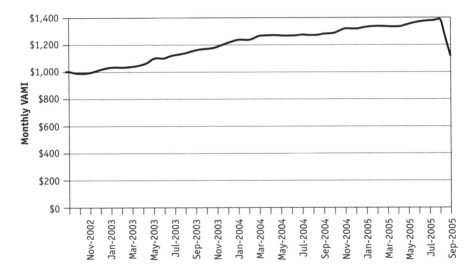

Figure 25.1 VAMI graph of simulated five-fund portfolio

rate of return for the portfolio is lower and the standard deviation higher for the five-fund portfolio.

You can also see the clear advantage that the larger portfolios offer in terms of loss prevention by examining Monte Carlo simulations (Tables 25.5–25.7). Looking at 1,000 simulations and normal distribution methods for the three-year period ending September 2005, the five-fund portfolio has the potential to deliver a 49.3% maximum drawdown, while the 12-fund portfolio predicts a maximum drawdown of less than half that amount, at 21.6%. The 20-fund portfolio exhibited the lowest probability for devastating downside volatility, with only a 14.7% maximum drawdown predicted.

Table 25.3 Risk table for simulated 12-fund portfolio

	Annualized
Compound rate of return	10.24%
Standard deviation	7.88%
Semi deviation	9.45%
Gain deviation	4.25%
Loss deviation	6.55%
Down deviation (2.00%)	5.06%
Down deviation (0%)	4.83%
Sharpe (2.00%)	1.03
Sortino (2.00%)	1.54
Sortino (0%)	2.03

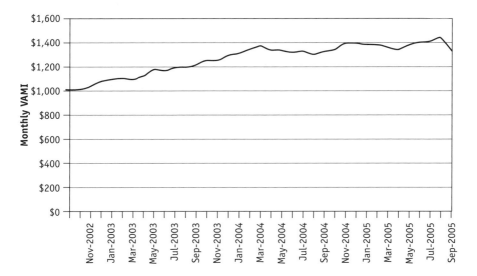

Figure 25.2 VAMI graph of simulated 12-fund portfolio

It is important to note in these simulations that, although the potential for drawdown was minimized as the number of funds in the portfolio grew, so too was the potential for profit. In the simulations, the five-fund portfolio exhibited the greatest potential for profit, with a maximum potential compound annual return of 31.9%, while the 20-fund portfolio displayed the lowest maximum potential compound annual return of 20.9%. Unfortunately, this means that more underlying funds are not always better.

While the capital-preservation capabilities of a portfolio with more funds are certainly unquestionable, most investors are not investing simply to lose the least money — they are also interested in turning a profit. Amin and Kat examined

Table 25.4 Risk table for simulated 20-fund portfolio

	Annualized
Compound rate of return	10.24%
Standard deviation	5.77%
Semi deviation	6.35%
Gain deviation	3.62%
Loss deviation	3.07%
Down deviation (2.00%)	3.09%
Down deviation (0%)	2.83%
Sharpe (2.00%)	1.38
Sortino (2.00%)	2.53
Sortino (0%)	3.46

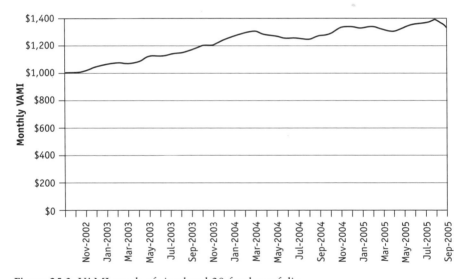

Figure 25.3 VAMI graph of simulated 20-fund portfolio

the issue of hedge fund diversification in a 2002 paper, only to discover that, based on 500 randomly generated portfolios ranging from 1 to 20 funds, "increasing the number of hedge funds in a portfolio can lead not only to lower standard deviation but also, and less welcome, to lower skewness and higher correlation with equity" (Amin and Kat, 2002).

While the Amin and Kat (2002) study used portfolios that were randomly generated, random selection is seldom the way in which investors and FOF managers select their underlying portfolio funds. To examine the issue of over-diversification further, five portfolios were constructed using the funds from the HedgeFund.net database with the highest Sharpe ratios for the period January

Table 25.5 Monte Carlo simulation of five-fund portfolio

	Annualized return	Annualized standard deviation	Annualized Sharpe (RF)	Maximum drawdown
Number of simulations	1,000	1,000	1,000	1,000
Mean	3.26%	12.57%	0.144	17.67%
Median	2.80%	12.53%	0.125	16.23%
Standard deviation	7.35%	1.48%	0.576	7.51%
Maximum	31.93%	17.60%	2.185	49.34%
Minimum	−19.15%	6.97%	−2.131	4.23%

Table 25.6 Monte Carlo simulation of 12-fund portfolio

	Annualized return	Annualized standard deviation	Annualized Sharpe (RF)	Maximum drawdown
Number of simulations	1,000	1,000	1,000	1,000
Mean	10.30%	7.80%	1.050	6.79%
Median	10.15%	7.75%	1.012	6.25%
Standard deviation	5.26%	0.96%	0.647	3.01%
Maximum	31.64%	11.31%	4.017	21.61%
Minimum	−4.59%	5.02%	−0.846	1.14%

Table 25.7 Monte Carlo simulation of 20-fund portfolio

	Annualized return	Annualized standard deviation	Annualized Sharpe (RF)	Maximum drawdown
Number of simulations	1,000	1,000	1,000	1,000
Mean	10.16%	5.73%	1.390	4.12%
Median	10.14%	5.71%	1.370	3.77%
Standard deviation	3.60%	0.68%	0.616	1.83%
Maximum	20.90%	8.05%	3.285	14.71%
Minimum	−1.63%	3.55%	−0.521	0.77%

1998 to December 1999, which may be a more accurate proxy for manager selection than a random method. Portfolios were then constructed using the top 5, 10, 20, 50, and 75 single-manager funds (based solely on Sharpe ratios) for that time and simulated forward for the period January 2000 to September 2005. While results, measured by Sharpe ratio, compound annual return, and standard deviation, improved when moving from the portfolio of five funds to the portfolio of 10 funds, they diminished when going from a portfolio of 10 managers to those with 20, 50, and 75 underlying funds (see Table 25.8). Based on this information, it is important that an FOF manager ensure that his or her portfolio offers maximum capital preservation and return generation, guarding against overdiversification, and that potential FOF investors examine that the

Table 25.8 Effect of overdiversification on simulated portfolios

	Annualized Sharpe ratio	Annualized compound return	Annualized standard deviation
5-manager portfolio	2.58	6.35%	0.50%
10-manager portfolio	3.19	9.59%	1.35%
20-manager portfolio	2.66	9.45%	1.57%
50-manager portfolio	1.22	9.48%	3.48%
75-manager portfolio	0.99	8.91%	3.77%

FOF he or she chooses has adequate diversification that minimizes volatility while still maximizing returns.

25.3 Liquidity

Another important issue to examine before making an FOF investment or constructing an FOF portfolio is the liquidity of the underlying funds. Funds of hedge funds commonly invest directly into hedge fund limited-partnership vehicles, meaning that the FOF is subject to the same redemption policies as any other investor in the underlying fund, including any lockups, notice periods, and early-redemption penalties. A liquidity mismatch, where the FOF offers more generous liquidity than the underlying hedge funds that comprise the FOF, can, in a worst-case scenario, result in the suspension of redemptions for an FOF. Unfortunately, a suspension of redemptions often sets in motion a death spiral for a fund; once investors are notified of the liquidity problem, other investors rush to redeem, not wanting to be the last out the door. The FOF must then redeem from underlying funds before they might ideally wish to, incurring redemption penalties and selling at market lows, which can further compromise the FOF returns.

It is vitally important, then, for investors to investigate and consider any potential liquidity issues before making an FOF investment and for FOF managers to bear the liquidity of their underlying funds in mind while constructing their FOF portfolio. To further examine the issue, funds from the TASS database were compared to determine what the average number of redemption days, lockup, and notice periods were for each strategy. Funds with daily redemption periods were excluded from the average, since a small number of funds with daily redemption periods had a disproportionate effect on the average. In Table 25.9, it is clear that while the redemption policies of the average fund of hedge funds seem to be fairly conservative, they are not as restrictive as many of their potential underlying hedge fund managers. Some funds of hedge funds bypass this problem by negotiating with the underlying funds for better liquidity terms, investing in separately managed accounts (which often offer greatly improved liquidity to the FOF manager, even daily in many cases) or by securing a line of

Table 25.9 Average liquidity parameters for hedge fund strategies

	Average redemption days per year	Average redemption notice (days)	Average length of lockup (months)
Event driven	5.7	55.6	6.4
Long/short equity	8.9	34.5	4.3
Equity market neutral	13.1	26.6	1.9
Convertible arbitrage	8.5	42.7	4.0
Fixed-income arbitrage	10.1	41.1	2.7
Dedicated short bias	10.1	23.6	3.3
Emerging markets	12.0	36.0	3.0
Managed futures	13.4	12.8	0.8
Global macro	13.2	24.1	2.9
Fund of funds	9.3	46.4	2.8
Average of all strategies	10.4	34.3	3.2

credit to provide for normal redemptions in between liquidity events in the underlying funds. However, it is a due-diligence consideration that should not be overlooked.

25.4 Transparency

It is no secret that different fund of hedge funds managers provide assorted levels of transparency to their end investors. An investor may ultimately receive more or less information on the portfolio than he or she would ideally desire. Therefore, it is important to understand the degree of control one surrenders and the FOF's business practices before investing in a fund of hedge funds.

The most basic level of transparency for an FOF investor is to know the identity of the portfolio funds in which the FOF is invested. While many FOFs will provide the identity of the underlying funds, some do not do so until after an investment has been made. Still others never provide information on underlying managers, preferring instead to substitute strategy breakdowns or other information to protect their FOF's competitive advantage. The audits of the FOF may provide information on the underlying investment managers since, per the American Institute of Certified Public Accountants (AICPA), all positions, including those in a fund of hedge funds according to many accounting firms, that comprise more than 5% of a portfolio should be disclosed in the audits to receive a clean audit opinion. It is up to the FOF manager to decide what level of information he or she intends to provide, and when, and up to the FOF investor to determine whether this is an acceptable level of disclosure.

The next level of transparency revolves around the staff that is involved in manager selection and monitoring and the due-diligence process that the FOF employs. Those employees of the FOF that have decision-making authority for investments, redemptions, and portfolio rebalancing should be disclosed and their work and educational backgrounds investigated. The investor must, in turn, determine if this level of staffing is adequate for the job at hand, bearing in mind that staffing levels can vary widely, even at large FOF shops. For example, in the 2005 Fund of Funds Compensation Survey completed by Infovest21, which surveyed approximately 100 FOF managers with more than $500 million under management, the average FOF had 49 employees. Approximately 12% had fewer than 10 employees and the largest percentage, 46%, had between 11 and 29 employees (Peltz, 2005b).

In addition, the process of manager screening, selection, and ongoing monitoring should be disclosed at the potential investor's request. For example, if the FOF gets position-level data from each underlying manager, what is the frequency of that data and what does the FOF do with it if they see something in it they do not like? Do they have overlays they can put into place? Are there side letters that allow for increased liquidity? How does the FOF manager source underlying hedge funds? How many funds do they investigate, and how much time do they spend with a fund prior to making an investment? This level of information can make an investor comfortable with a fund, even without an in-depth review of each underlying fund manager.

The highest level of transparency on an FOF is to obtain full due-diligence information and ongoing risk analysis, as well as NAV verification, on the underlying funds. In a letter to the Securities Industry Association in 2003, the National Association of Securities Dealers (NASD) addressed this issue, which had been broached in its Notice to Members 03-07 regarding the sale of hedge funds and funds of hedge funds by broker-dealers. In it the NASD indicated that

> NtM 03-07 was not intended to suggest, in the case of a fund of hedge funds, that such due diligence [investigating the background of the hedge fund manager, reviewing the offering memorandum, reviewing the subscription agreements, examining references, and examining the relative performance of the fund] must be performed at each of the underlying funds in a fund of hedge funds. . . . When a member's due diligence on a fund of hedge funds establishes a sufficient basis to evaluate the merits and risks of the investment, then generally, for regulatory purposes, no further due diligence into the underlying funds would be required
>
> (NASD/Goldsholle, 2003).

While this is generally a sound practice, and while most investors choose funds of hedge funds specifically so they do not have to investigate an entire portfolio of single-manager funds, there does still need to be a certain level of transparency available to the FOF investor. And each investor will determine what degree of transparency brings him or her comfort — some investors may be satisfied by simply knowing the process or by viewing the FOF due-diligence and ongoing monitoring materials on a single manager, others may want and need the full boat.

Finally, it is important that the FOF investor be provided enough transparency into the FOF and the underlying managers to ensure that they are avoiding some key conflicts of interest, many of which were spelled out by the SEC in November 2005 remarks made before the Funds of Funds Forum. They noted eight areas of an investment advisory business that could have potentially high risk for conflict of interest (SEC/Gohlke, 2005):

- Allocations of investment opportunities among clients
- Fund manager's relationships with managers of one or more of the underlying hedge funds
- Manager's affiliate's banking and investment banking relationships with issuers of securities held in underlying hedge funds
- Advisers to underlying hedge funds purchasing for those funds interests in instruments underwritten or distributed by a fund manager or its affiliates
- Proprietary trading by the manager or personal trading by its staff
- Side letter agreements with certain investors in a managed fund
- Valuations of interests in underlying funds held by a fund of hedge funds
- Calculation of fund of hedge funds' performance numbers, especially when performance that is below a high-water mark is the only factor preventing an adviser from getting an incentive allocation

In addition, they noted the following sound practices for FOF valuation and net asset value (NAV) calculation (SEC/Gohlke, 2005):

- Fund of funds will only invest in underlying funds that give portfolio transparency.
- Fund of funds will only invest in underlying funds whose financial statements are audited by an accounting firm active in the hedge fund industry.
- Fund of funds will only invest in underlying funds that use an independent administrator to value holdings and calculate NAV.
- Fair value procedures are to be adopted by and can only be changed with approval of the fund's governing body or entity.
- Fair value procedures provide guidance on when they are to be used.
- NAVs reported by underlying funds are compared to summary information contained in audited financial statements and tax-reporting forms provided by underlying funds, and discrepancies are followed up and resolved.
- Monthly performance and change in NAV of each underlying fund is analyzed in the context of expectations of what performance of the underlying fund should be in light of each fund's objectives and sector investments and market returns in those sectors during the month. All outlier conditions are investigated and resolved.
- Differences between NAVs of underlying funds used to calculate fund of funds NAV and realized NAVs used to price interests in underlying funds which are redeemed are analyzed to determine if, over time, patterns of over- or undervaluation are evident.
- Regular testing is conducted of differences between fair values used in place of actual NAVs for underlying funds and subsequent NAVs reported by underlying funds to determine if, over time, patterns of over- or undervaluation are evident which may require changes in fund of funds fair value procedures.
- Over longer periods of time, actual returns in market sectors in which underlying funds are invested are compared to changes in NAV reported by such underlying funds

and to the reported performance of the fund of funds to look for discrepancies that may be indicative of valuation issues by either underlying funds or the fund of funds.

The most important things to remember are that the level and methods of due diligence and NAV verification vary from FOF to FOF and that a fund of hedge funds manager may do more or less due diligence or ongoing monitoring than an investor would, assuming they had similar resources. In general, an investor cannot pressure a fund of funds manager into investing in or withdrawing from a particular underlying fund, nor do they have access to verify their own NAVs. Therefore, it is vitally important for a manager to be comfortable with the manager-selection and -monitoring process as well as the NAV calculation process prior to making an investment into the FOF.

25.5 Factor and impact analysis

A final fund of hedge funds (or portfolio) specific component to the due-diligence and ongoing-monitoring process comes in the form of factor and impact analysis. Factor analysis allows FOF managers to better see and make adjustments to their portfolios due to changing fund profiles, such as increasing or decreasing alpha, beta, and correlations. Impact analysis allows FOFs managers to see exactly how additions to and redemptions from their FOF portfolio will impact their risk–reward profile.

Let's again build a simulated portfolio with five funds. In an attempt to build a diversified portfolio, the fictitious FOF manager has selected funds with low, no, or negative correlations with one another or to the FOF benchmark, in this case the S&P 500, as shown in Table 25.10. The FOF manager may run this correlation table monthly and not necessarily notice any trends that begin to develop in the fund until it is too late. For example, in the factor analysis in Figure 25.4, the funds in the simulated FOF portfolio have been compared to their benchmark. Notice how, at certain points in time, the rolling correlation of the underlying funds to the S&P 500 spikes dramatically. To see this trend on a correlation table, the FOF manager would have to be able to construct and interpret massive

Table 25.10 Correlation table for a five-fund FOF portfolio, January 1997 to March 2000

	Fund 1	Fund 2	Fund 3	Fund 4	Fund 5	S&P 500
Fund 1	1.000					
Fund 2	0.353	1.000				
Fund 3	−0.061	0.283	1.000			
Fund 4	−0.390	−0.110	0.000	1.000		
Fund 5	0.201	0.157	0.037	0.254	1.000	
S&P 500	−0.154	−0.084	0.148	0.068	0.342	1.000

spreadsheets, by which time a market dislocation could already have significantly impacted his fund. In addition, it is important to look at the rolling factors for each of the funds in the portfolio. Notice in Figure 25.4 how the rolling correlation of Fund 3 in the simulated portfolio changes relative to the other funds in the

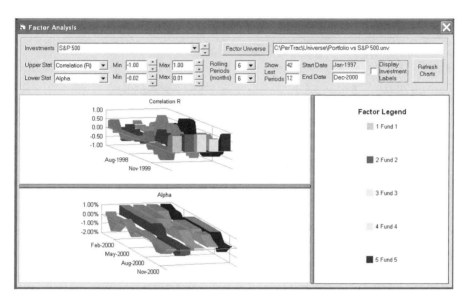

Figure 25.4 Factor analysis: correlation of the simulated portfolio to the S&P 500

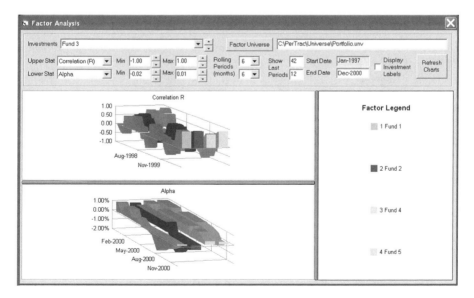

Figure 25.5 Factor analysis: correlation of the Fund 3 to the simulated portfolio

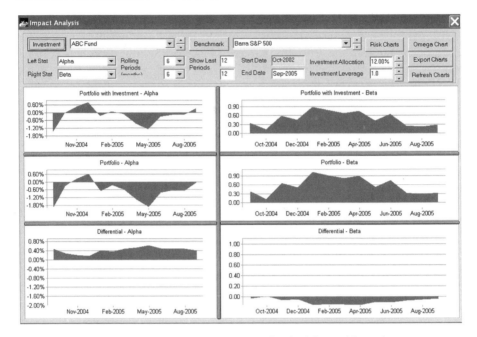

Figure 25.6 Impact analysis for adding stronger fund: alpha and beta charts

portfolio over time. Although the fund may have entered the portfolio with low to no correlations, over time that profile has changed dramatically.

Factor analysis can be run on a number of different statistics, including alpha, beta, correlation, R-squared, t-statistic, and others, but it is important that the FOF closely watch the rolling factors for changes that might negatively impact the portfolio and not just look at snapshots in time. By the time the snapshot develops, it may be too late to avoid losses.

Another aspect of factor analysis is impact analysis, which affects both FOF managers and investors. Impact analysis provides investors, both at the fund level and the FOF management level, with the ability to see exactly what impact a particular addition or redemption would have had on a portfolio. How would have adding a distressed debt or emerging markets hedge fund have impacted an existing portfolio of primarily long/short equity, convertible arbitrage, event-driven, and equity market-neutral investments? How would have removing a currency trader affected the volatility in the portfolio? Impact analysis allows managers to play out such "what-if" scenarios, and the results they send to their investors allow the investors to gain a better understanding of how the FOF manager is running the portfolio.

In Figure 25.6 and Table 25.11, one can see how a weaker portfolio may be positively impacted by adding a stronger fund. A set of "before and after" charts quickly reveals the impact the new investment would have on the port-folio relative to a chosen benchmark in terms of correlation, beta, alpha, etc.

Table 25.11 Impact analysis for adding a stronger fund: risk table

	Portfolio with investment	Current portfolio	Difference
Compound rate of return	6.14%	2.09%	4.05%
Standard deviation	12.28%	13.74%	−1.46%
Gain deviation	8.34%	7.68%	0.66%
Down deviation (2.00%)	7.29%	8.92%	−1.63%
Down deviation (0%)	6.95%	8.56%	−1.61%
Sharpe (2.00%)	0.38	0.07	0.31

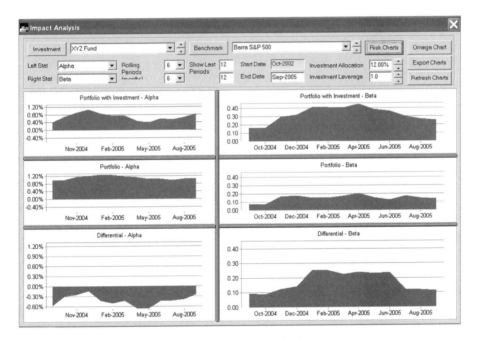

Figure 25.7 Impact analysis for adding weaker fund: alpha and beta charts

For the FOF manager, this may provide confirmation that a good choice of additional investment has been made. For the FOF investor, it can increase the level of confidence in the FOF.

However, on the opposite side of the coin, Figure 25.7 and Table 25.12 show how a strong portfolio may be affected by adding a weaker investment. This may deter the FOF manager from making the investment in the first place. However, if an investment is made, it would lead the investor to a set of ongoing due-diligence questions to understand exactly why the investment was made. Perhaps it is due to the FOF manager's long-term market outlook, or, on the other hand, perhaps it is due simply to poor judgment or miscalculation on

Table 25.12 Impact analysis for adding stronger fund: risk table

	Portfolio with investment	Current portfolio	Difference
Compound rate of return	15.58%	17.49%	−1.91%
Standard deviation	3.35%	1.66%	1.69%
Gain deviation	2.85%	1.66%	1.19%
Down deviation (2.00%)	0.82%	0.00%	0.82%
Down deviation (0%)	0.65%	0.00%	0.65%
Sharpe (2.00%)	3.78	8.61	−4.83

the part of the FOF manager. Or, in a worst-case scenario, perhaps the FOF manager has worked a side deal with the new fund, resulting in a conflict of interest. In any case, having this kind of information at your disposal can greatly enhance your ongoing monitoring of your FOF.

25.6 Conclusion

Funds of hedge funds present investors with a good entry point into the hedge fund arena, offering diversification and manager selection expertise for one low minimum investment. However, FOFs are not without their own set of special due-diligence and ongoing monitoring considerations, and investors would be wise to check out issues such as diversification, overdiversification, liquidity, transparency, and factor and impact analysis prior to and during their investment.

References

Amin, G. and Kat, H. (2002). Portfolios of Hedge Funds. Working Paper, University of Reading, Reading, U.K.

NASD/Goldsholle, G. (2003). Response to Michael D. Udoff Letter Dated August 6, 2003.

Peltz, L. (2005a). Fund of Funds' Redemptions Balanced by Earlier Inflows but Next Few Months Are Critical. *Infovest21 News Provider Service.*

Peltz, L. (2005b). Fourth Annual Executive Compensation Survey of Funds of Funds. *Infovest21 News Provider Service.*

SEC/Gohlke, G. (2005). Remarks before the Fund of Funds Forum, November 14, 2005, New York.

26 The wizardry of analytics for funds of funds

Mary Fjelstad and Leola Ross

Abstract

Ironically, the very diversification that funds of hedge funds provide limits their ability to define, measure, and report risks. In this chapter we help investors evaluate the complex problem of managing and reporting hedge fund risks.

What would you do with a brain if you had one?
Dorothy Gale to the Scarecrow, The Wizard of Oz, *MGM Studios, 1939*

26.1 Introduction: If only I had good risk analytics

For many investors, funds of hedge funds serve as important intermediaries that research managers, create instant diversification, smooth liquidity across managers, and report back to investors the exposures encountered of the underlying funds (Stemme and Slattery, 2002; Hennessee and Gradante, 2002). The most difficult of these four tasks is reporting to investors their exposures. In this chapter we explore the difficulty faced by funds of hedge funds (FOFs) in obtaining and reporting accurate information regarding fund level exposures, the relative importance of accurate information, and we help investors evaluate their FOF's practices and accuracy in providing such information.

So why do investors want or even need accurate exposure information? The need for accurate exposure information is most critical to large institutional investors, such as pension funds, endowments, and foundations. Institutional investors have a fiduciary obligation to carefully allocate their assets to achieve particular return targets that fulfill obligations to pensioners, charities, universities, scholarship recipients, etc. To meet this need for very accurate information, a large industry of analytics providers has evolved to report exposures and attribute returns for institutional investors in a very timely fashion (Golub and Tillman, 2000). Traditional (long-only benchmarked) active managers provide position-level information to custodians, to investors directly, or to third-party analytics providers. To neutralize an unattractive exposure, institutional investors may fire a manager, hire a diversifying manager, or simply create an offsetting "completion portfolio." Whether such jostling of managers and exposures truly protects investors from risks is uncertain. We explore the difference between exposure management and risk management.

Institutional investors need to take a step back to keep their perspective when considering an initial investment in hedge funds. The lure of low-volatility hedge fund returns has attracted many assets since the extreme volatility of 2000 and 2001 in equities. Even though investors thought they had properly measured and monitored risks during the technology boom and bust at the turn of the millenium, many realized that measuring and monitoring exposures did not protect them from risk. Nevertheless, old habits die hard, and institutional investors felt like they'd been transported to Oz when they found out their favorite FOFs could not produce the comprehensive and timely exposure reports that gave them such comfort in other asset classes — albeit, possibly false comfort.

Why is it so difficult for FOFs to cough up their exposures? Well, hedge funds are different (Lo, 2001). Hedge funds are not restrained by asset class, region, or style per se. While many hedge fund managers remain within particular comfort zones, others are more opportunistic and evolve with the markets. Indeed, the better FOFs will constantly seek out new, innovative managers and trim old, outdated managers. Moreover, the better FOFs will research a multiplicity of styles and regions to diversify the risks each individual manager takes. Unfortunately, as the FOF increases diversification to reduce exposure to a specific manager risk at the fund of funds level, the ability to define, measure, and report those risks becomes increasingly difficult. Fortunately, risk measurement (or risk analytics) is only a small component of risk management, so a poor risk report is not necessarily an indicator of high risk. Indeed, ex-post analytics are a poor substitute for good fund construction. Ultimately, the investor needs to know that the FOF is constructing a well-diversified portfolio with a thorough due-diligence process.

In the sections that follow, we first discuss the difficulties faced by anyone seeking to evaluate the exposures encountered by a collection of hedge funds. Next we define risk management for hedge fund portfolios and indeed for all portfolios. While we highlight the problems associated with too heavy a reliance on analytics, we include a review of the types of risk analysis available for funds of hedge funds as well as their advantages and shortcomings. In our final section we provide some advice for navigating the "yellow brick road" of hedge fund analytics.

26.2 You're not in Kansas anymore

The role of analytics is to help the investor understand the nature and level of diversification in his or her portfolio and to measure and monitor intentional or unintentional bets. Therefore, analytics provide an ex-post descriptor of how a portfolio looks. When a portfolio is highly liquid and easily described, the analytics tool can play a useful role in risk management; however, when portfolios do not meet these criteria, as hedge funds do not, the ability of an analytics product to contribute to risk management is compromised.

Hedge fund analytics might give us a sense of what risk exposures used to be. Fortunately, such information is useful in corroborating an FOF's previous understanding of what exposures were and providing additional information about an underlying manager. Certainly, such information is valuable in building a portfolio over a long period of time, for evaluating the skill of research analysts and portfolio managers, and for communicating with managers. Therefore analytics are quite useful for risk monitoring, which involves understanding the past and the present. Risk management is a forward-looking concept. For hedge fund risk management, analytics are generally too little, too late.

Regardless of the role of analytics, many FOFs seek to dazzle clients and prospects with tales of the latest, greatest risk analytics. Investors in FOFs are in the best possible position to evaluate such claims when armed with an understanding of the many obstacles to using analytics to monitor the risks and exposures in their funds. Let's consider some of those obstacles.

26.2.1 Holdings transparency

The most accurate picture of exposures requires both position-level holdings and the ability to get information from those holdings. Many hedge fund managers are unwilling to give access to holdings on a regular and timely basis. Many fear that their competitive advantage would be eroded or disappear should others learn what they are doing. For example, managers that play in thinly traded markets or specialize in shorting securities resist transparency. Thinly traded markets may be profitable but may accommodate only a few market makers — adding more will erode the profits of players already there. Managers may also be very discrete about their shorts. When building a short position, the manager wants the price to stay high. Revealing positions before they have a desired portfolio weight may drive the price down as others clamor to copy.

Other managers are loathe to disclose holdings simply because of inconvenience or skepticism regarding the benefit thereof. If a manager tracks highly complex securities, the effort required to truly educate the investor about the holdings may be significant and far outweigh the benefit to the investor.

The investor may choose to restrict his or her choice set only to those managers willing to provide such information, but such a decision may be counterproductive. Good managers are far and few between, and the investor may lose return by rejecting the nontransparent manager.

26.2.2 Delays

Even when managers agree to holdings transparency, they often insist that reporting be lagged, sometimes as much as 60 days. Transparency delayed is transparency denied. Modeling the risks and exposures with so long a delay is of little value, especially given the rapid change that can occur in hedge fund strategies and exposures.

26.2.3 Complex strategies and securities

Hedge funds can employ derivatives, complex and exotic strategies, or strategies with nonnormal return distributions. For example, every analytics tool will read a merger arbitrage position as a set of factors long and a set of factors short. However, the promise of that position lies not in the exposures to those securities per se, but rather in the exposure to the merger deal. To accommodate convertible arbitrage, the tool must incorporate expert understanding not only of the credit quality of the long bonds and factor exposures of the short equities, but also of the gamma and delta exposures of the combined position.[1] And the list goes on: Distressed securities risks relate to the probability of a firm's recovery rather than merely very low credit, and high-yield bonds are more like equity than bonds, though analytics are likely to evaluate interest rate and credit but not equity factors.

Hedge funds often combine complex strategies with equally complex and exotic securities: options, exotic asset-backed securities, convertible bonds, credit default swaps, collateralized debt obligations, etc. Valid descriptions and pricing of these positions are often unavailable. Analyzing these strategies and securities is a formidable task, perhaps too much for any one analytics provider.

26.2.4 Diversification

The well-managed and constructed FOF is diversified across all markets, strategies, securities, and even managers. While essential for good hedge fund investing, such diversification presents exceptional difficulties for an analytics program in terms of data coverage and risk modeling.

When investors choose to ease into the hedge fund space, they often feel like they are in Oz.[2] Because hedge fund managers rarely provide holdings lists without a delay, investors can only evaluate what their managers did quite some time ago. Even if an investor knows the same day what the hedge fund manager holds in the portfolio, most funds have a liquidation period of at least three months, and the investor has little power to bail out. The combination of these factors gives analytics a very small role in FOF risk management. While the FOF may boast the best analytics in the business, these analytics are a minor player in risk management. Fortunately, the FOF has other tools at its disposal.

26.3 Click your heels and say, "There's nothing like diversification"

Ultimately, hedge fund risk management is about fund selection and construction as well as diversification (Ross, 2003). While no investor can ever fully understand or even fully verify a manager's investment process, due diligence is critical for hedge fund investing. Whether the investor takes the time to learn

---

[1] Delta is the ratio comparing the change in the price of the underlying asset to the corresponding change in the price of a derivative. Gamma is the rate of change for delta with respect to the underlying asset's price. See http://www.investopedia.com/dictionary/ for other definitions.
[2] For some detailed discussion on risk management as it relates to many species of hedge funds, see Parker (2005).

about hedge fund investing and conduct the due diligence her- or himself, hires a consultant, or invests through an FOF is a function of budget, asset size, educational and professional background, and preferences. To complicate the due-diligence process, tight capacity constraints and the flood of money into this area mean there is no rest for the weary. Delaying investigation of a good manager may cost the investor the opportunity to place money with her or him. Gaining capacity with a skillful, honest manager is, therefore, full of trade-offs: Move quickly, but research thoroughly. The bottom line is that skill in evaluating managers is fundamental to good risk management.

The other side of the risk management equation is diversification. Just as the equity manager must diversify benchmark relative risk by owning a diverse selection of stocks, the FOF should place money with a diverse group of managers. Diversification of hedge fund managers begins with investment style, but it does not end there. Certainly, hedge fund land offers a variety of styles with differing risk characteristics and risk exposures; and the well-diversified investor will seek a balance of styles and substyles.

Markets, styles, and strategies are not the only factors that need to be diversified for hedge funds. The well-known debacle of 1998, closely aligned with the business practices of Long-Term Capital Management, demonstrated clearly the firm-specific risks of hedge fund investing (Lowenstein, 2000). Success in the hedge fund area does not come by following convention. Managers attracted to hedge fund investing are often too out of the ordinary for standard large-firm bureaucracy and find a happier situation on their own. These small boutique firms are more willing and able to take on risky positions, maneuver illiquid markets, and jump on opportunity than firms with layers of management. The cost of all these benefits is a higher risk of firm failure. The good news is that this failure risk is generally uncorrelated; indeed, the niche nature of small-firm investing may reduce the risk of contagion recently observed among large firms. Therefore, diversifying failure risk requires a deep list of hedge fund managers with very different approaches.

Diversification among firms is, therefore, superior to style and strategy diversification within a firm. Such intrafirm diversification, generally called *multistrategy* investing, has gained popularity among hedge fund investors. In particular, investors may prefer a multistrategy hedge fund to an FOF to avoid the FOF's fees. The multistrategy approach may diversify style risk to some extent but not manager-specific business or governance risk. The investor who opts for the lower fees of a multistrategy fund over an FOF is well advised to acknowledge the higher level of firm-specific risk being assumed by doing so.

Pulling all these ideas together, we have the following.

1. Solid risk management means conducting thorough research and due diligence on firms that may have highly complex strategies, unconventional management, and unproven business acumen.
2. The FOF must research these managers quickly to avoid losing access to managers with the best performance potential but limited capacity.
3. We must find quite a lot of them to diversify strategy and business risk.

As already noted, such a task is likely too much for a small or inexperienced investor. All but the wealthiest individuals and the largest of institutional investors will rely on consultants or funds of hedge funds to do the work for them.

Suppose the properly resourced institutional investor, the FOF, or the very wealthy and wise investor constructs a well-diversified collection of hedge funds with good credentials. Will such diversification prevent loss or individual hedge fund failure? The short answer is no. Diversification means that a manager failure should not bring down the whole fund. It does not mean that no individual fund will fail. Most hedge fund investors will experience disappointment at some point; however, by doing one's homework and by spreading risk across many funds, the disappointment should not be catastrophic.

26.4 We're off to see the wizard

By relying on the Wizard to solve their problems, Dorothy and her friends exposed themselves to more danger than they otherwise would have. Similarly, while hedge fund analytics may reveal some truths about an FOF, relying on those analytics too much is very dangerous.

26.4.1 Complacency

Putting in place a risk analytics system or program for an FOF is no substitute for ongoing qualitative evaluation and due diligence of underlying managers. FOFs need to be careful not to rely too much on risk analytics that have been implemented and are being maintained usually at great cost. No one system or set of risk models will cover all managers, strategies, and FOFs completely and accurately. Looking at the numbers is no substitute for continuing and maintaining personal interaction and oversight of the managers.

26.4.2 Partial coverage

Somewhere between 100% and 0% position-level transparency, the true relevance of good analytics goes away. Where that point lies is a matter of judgment. What good does it do to evaluate 70% of a portfolio and have no clue about the rest? There is a danger that the fine print in the footnote reporting the coverage and relevance statistics for the risk numbers is overlooked. Having useful information about part of the portfolio may be pretty useless.

26.4.3 Delayed risk exposure numbers

Even in the best of worlds, where managers report holdings in a timely manner, there will be a lag between the holdings date and the date of the risk reports. All risk numbers, unless they are real time, are ex post.

26.4.4 Delayed security coverage/risk modeling

Certain areas of the market, most notably fixed income, on a seemingly continuous basis, create new securities and new forms of existing securities, which available risk models and databases do not cover or handle. In a sense, all risk analytics vendors are playing catch-up in the very dynamic and innovative fixed-income area. New securities and new markets offer significant opportunities to make and to lose money. Good fixed-income hedge fund managers will be active players here. By the time your analytics system is able to capture the impact of these securities on your risk exposures, something new and different will emerge.

26.4.5 Better analytics/lower alpha, higher risk?

Making risk analytics and transparency over alpha potential may necessitate that your FOHF invest in managers and styles that do not have the best alpha or risk diversification potential in the hedge fund world. Very wealthy or very large institutional investors have another option, namely, setting up separate accounts with managers rather than investing in a fund. This arrangement has the potential to expand the set of the available styles and managers while retaining for the owner the right to demand complete and speedy transparency. The hedge fund manager may not utilize his or her best strategies in the separate account, however, again sacrificing alpha.

26.5 The man behind the curtain

Dorothy and her friends had the tools to get what they wanted all along, but it took the Wizard and the knowledge of his limitations to help them understand that they did. Similarly, even though measuring and monitoring the risks of an FOF is problematic, analytics are still necessary for evaluating what was in the portfolio and how the underlying funds interacted in the past. A key ingredient of the value proposition of investing in FOFs is that the FOF organization shoulder the responsibility for managing and monitoring the operational and investment risks of the FOF. The FOF needs to implement a program for measuring the risks of the investments to the best extent possible while always recognizing the limitations of those risk numbers and communicating them clearly to investors.

What are the available tools? Hedge fund analytics come in many forms, from the most basic — manager-supplied risk reports — to the most elaborate — in-house installation enterprisewide risk management systems.

26.5.1 Approaches to analytics

Manager-supplied risk reports

Most hedge fund managers will provide information regarding the exposures and risks associated with their portfolios. Most managers author monthly commentaries and reports to educate their investors on their portfolios. The level of detail on exposures and risks vary widely across managers, however, and managers will use their own methods and models to estimate these exposures. These monthly risk reports, as well as the models and reported risks may change from time to time. Such changes make it difficult to track exposures through time for any given manager, to compare exposures across managers, and especially to aggregate risk exposures across managers and styles. These reports may be valuable in that the manager may have the best understanding of risks and positions, in which case on the manager level these are the best risk numbers, but the FOF needs to go beyond these reports for time series analysis, comparative risk analysis, and aggregation.

Standardized manager-supplied risk reports

FOFs can often work with their managers to tailor the information received in these monthly reports or in a separate report. Designing a risk-reporting template for a given style, with defined reporting requirements and specifications of the algorithms to be used to calculate each exposure, allows consistent tracking over time of exposures for a given manager and more accurate comparisons across managers. Some static risk exposures (%NAV in a given quality rating, for example) may be aggregated across managers to the style and even the fund levels. More sophisticated measures of risk that take into account cross-correlations of risk exposures cannot be aggregated. Some managers will cooperate and provide these numbers as requested. Some will not.

Returns-based risk analysis

Returns-based risk analysis allows inclusion of all managers in risk estimations, at least all managers that have a return history. Originally, these models were designed for the long-only side, producing a static mix of market indexes or variables that best explains the return pattern of a given manager. The original models also constrained all exposures to be positive (no short positions). More recent models have relaxed the long-only constraint and built in a dynamic aspect to better meet the needs and better model the characteristics of hedge funds. Returns-based risk analysis is ex-post only and has no reliability for prediction of future risks or even accurate measurement of current risk. New dynamic models can be plagued by delays in picking up changes in exposures. Nevertheless, these newer models offer a method to validate past risk exposures (as reported by managers or measured by a holdings-based risk analytics system) for managers, for styles, and for the FOF as a whole. These tools may foster communication between managers and clients and confirm the value added from portfolio construction. Returns-based risk exposures calculated for non-transparent managers can be added to most holdings-based risk systems to arrive at an estimate of the risks of the total fund.

Holdings-based risk analysis

A variety of systems and services are available to model the risks and estimate the exposures of portfolios based on holdings. The applicability of these systems to the hedge fund space is severely compromised by the low level of coverage many FOFs will receive from their managers. As discussed earlier, many managers will not provide holdings-level data for their portfolios and even if they do, on a delayed basis. Therefore, any holdings-based package will only be able to evaluate a limited portion of any FOF. Moreover, even when returns are provided, many styles, such as merger arbitrage and distressed securities, may not be included in the analytics package. To improve the relevance of their systems, most holdings-based services combine both exposure-based and returns-based analysis to give the FOF a more complete portfolio-level analysis.

We offer general descriptions of the different types shortly, but we caution that the reality of hedge fund manager holdings is that they are chock-full of atypical securities, private, customized deals, hedges that are difficult to decompose, and identifiable positions that are very difficult to model. Hedge funds can be distinguished, compared, and evaluated along a number of different dimensions. Here we focus on two of these dimensions: types of risk factor models (fundamental vs. statistical) and type of installation (in-house vs. service bureau).

Fundamental models: These models identify exposures to fundamental firm, market, and economic variables as the sources of risk. Exposures to these variables are customarily estimated on the security level; estimated risk is derived from each security's exposure to each variable, the risk of each variable, and the correlations among the variables. Aggregated risk estimates on the portfolio, style, and fund levels are built up from the security level. Fundamental models differ widely on the number of variables used, methods of estimating exposures to the variables, method of aggregation, distributional assumptions, how much history is used, time-weighting, etc. Current products using fundamental variables range from single-factor models (for example, the only variable is the historical volatility of the security price) to complex multifactor models. At least one test of three of these models suggests that the multifactor approach performs better than the single-security-price-factor approach (Penfold, 2004), but multifactor models must deal with the complication of cross-correlations among variables.

Statistical models: The most widely used statistical model is principal component analysis (PCA), where the variance/covariance matrix of historical security prices or returns is decomposed statistically into factors that are completely independent (orthogonal). This has the clear advantage of eliminating the problem of correlations among variables. The disadvantage is that the statistical factors are not necessarily intuitive. It may be possible to identify market or economic variables that a given principal component factor resembles, but the relationship is not always clear. Managers do not construct portfolios or make investments based on principal components. Statistical models may be useful at the total-fund-aggregate-risk level, but identifying which bets or which market/economic variables are the sources of risk is not straightforward.

Total enterprise or fundwide risk systems

Systems and services targeting risk modeling of all managers, styles, markets, and asset classes are available through in-house installation or service bureau structures.

In-house: The most elaborate analytics, or combination of analytics, offer in-house, user-controlled products that handle most security types and provide factor exposures, profiling, and risk forecasting through a rich variety of summary statistics and reports. These products may even have the ability to accommodate unidentified securities by means of descriptive characteristic information and nontransparent manager risk analytics via manager-provided-factor or returns-based methods. Such analytics or analytics systems will be very expensive, both in dollars spent and resources used. The level of resource commitment to a comprehensive in-house system is significant and possibly overwhelming for all but the largest FOFs.

Service Bureaus: An alternative is the enterprise or fundwide risk models sold through a service bureau structure. Here the vendor or service provider receives the holdings, scrubs the data, runs the risk analysis, and creates the reports, normally posting them on a secure Website. This requires very little involvement on the part of the FOF organization beyond paying the fee and setting up the relationships between the vendor and the managers. By outsourcing the data collection and cleaning, the FOF drastically reduces the resources required to obtain analytics. If the FOF does not have transparency rights to the holdings underlying the analysis, the FOF is completely reliant on the service bureau that the assets are all priced reasonably and that all holdings are in fact modeled. The FOF substitutes reliance on the manager reports with reliance on the service bureau reports. A final caveat is that the reporting capabilities of these service bureau vendors may not be as rich or fully detailed or as accurate as an in-house or stand-alone specialized system.

All holdings-based systems differ dramatically from each other along a variety of dimensions, so careful due diligence based on the FOF needs will be required before making a final choice between in-house, service bureau, and a non-holdings-based system altogether. The investor, in turn, must evaluate the FOF's decision-making process.

Stand-alone asset class/market-specialized analytic systems

Products and services are available to model the risks of different markets and asset classes. Most of these have been developed for the long-only investment manager or trader. The value for FOF risk analysis depends on (1) the desired level of detail on each portfolio (these will give a lot of detail); (2) how many asset classes/markets to which the FOF is exposed (this can get expensive with a system for each style/market, and for some styles there is no stand-alone system available); and (3) the level of aggregation needed. These stand-alone systems will normally aggregate only up to the style/asset class level, not the FOF.

26.5.2   Three favorite risk measures

The hedge fund industry has relied historically heavily on value at risk (VaR), scenario analysis, and stress testing.

Value at Risk

VaR measures are intended to evaluate tail risk or extreme but unlikely loss over some time under normal market conditions assuming some distribution of outcomes. Usually, the time frame is over the next few days, and the extreme improbable loss refers to a two- or three-standard-deviation event. The reliance on VaR in the alternative investment space is a direct result of the difficulties noted earlier with respect to modeling exotic securities and options. Rather than attempting to produce factor exposures for securities that do not lend themselves to well-known factors, analytics designed for alternatives simply express how much value might be lost at any given time.

VaR may be calculated using any number of distributional assumptions including historical return distributions (that ignore what has not yet happened), normal distributions, and Monte Carlo simulations. Many analytics packages will allow the user to select from among several assumptions. Different calculation methods for VaR also exist (see Jorion, 1996) but criticisms of the mathematical properties of VaR (Artzner et al., 1997, 1999; Mausser and Rosen, 1999; McKay and Keefer, 1996) have led to a lengthy literature on alternatives to VaR including conditional value at risk (see Embrechts, 1999; Pflung, 2000; Uryasev, 2000). Therefore, the FOF is well advised to consider VaR sensitivity to formula, distributional assumption, and engine and only one of many risk measurement techniques. As well, the ability to compare VaRs across managers is compromised by the lack of industry standard. VaR numbers are most likely to be internally consistent for small portions of a portfolio (such as an individual manager's fund) when the underlying holdings are used directly, but they will generally be inconsistent across sections of the portfolio, across managers, and across aggregation levels (such as the case where some managers give holdings, some give exposures, and still others provide only returns).

Scenario analysis

Scenario analysis exhibits the behavior of a fund or combination of funds in various market or economic "states" (Ross, 2002). An example of an economic state affecting a fixed-income arbitrage portfolio might be the widening of low credit bond spreads (vs. Treasury bonds). By evaluating how different portfolios react to the spread widening, the FOF may ascertain the consistency of a manager over time or even a manager's success in hedging against a negative outcome.

Most analytics packages will provide scenario analysis. Scenario analysis works best when long histories of economic states are available, when evaluating only those economic variables that are truly relevant to the portfolio, and when the portfolio being analyzed is consistent over time. The greatest difficulty lies in the determination of what is truly relevant. First, what was relevant to a manager, style, or FOF in the past may not be mutually inclusive of what will be relevant going forward. Ultimately, consistency over time is a rarity, though for the short-term future the past may be useful in many cases. Second, knowing even what *was* relevant can be a challenge. A well-developed qualitative understanding of a manager's investment process is the best tool, but even the well-informed manager research analyst may be surprised from time to time.

Stress testing

A common criticism of economic and financial models is that the accuracy of their output depends on the validity of model assumptions. In particular, assumptions are made about the distribution of risks or returns, the interaction or correlations of risks, prepayment sensitivities, the joint probability of default, and/or a variety of other factors. Whether these assumptions are sensible or heroic, all models are susceptible to the weakness that the assumed relationships and behavior are either wrong or variable.

Ideally the user can shock the underlying assumption of the model(s) for estimating risk. Shocks to volatility levels, exposure estimations, distributions, and correlations help estimate the amount of "model risk" embedded in the risk estimations. Unfortunately, unless the investor builds a proprietary model, this type of stress testing is difficult to do. Most vendors do not allow access to the underlying inputs or model parameters.

Many systems have the functionality of stress testing through user-defined shock scenarios. Users should exercise caution when creating their own scenarios, however. This functionality does allow the user to see the impact of changing the behavior of certain market or economic variables and to estimate the resulting impact on portfolio risk. Tests such as these are informative but do not change many of the assumptions in the model and in the underlying data. Moreover, figuring out reasonable and rational changes to all the factors of a multifactor model is a formidable task, which can sometimes number in the hundreds (a good fundamental risk model for global fixed-income portfolios may have well over 400 variables across currencies, interest rate environments, and credit markets). Changing a few key variables while holding the others constant may result in irrational, perhaps impossible, relationships among market variables.

Another stress-testing strategy is to recreate known market conditions during past stress or crisis conditions. Running a portfolio or fund through the market crisis of August 1998 is a good test of liquidity and credit risks as well as assumed correlations. Other crises that can give information about the portfolio risk under extreme conditions are the bursting of the tech bubble in early 2000, the equity market crash in October 1987, and the period of steadily rising interest rates in 1994. While it is undoubtedly true that the next crisis, when it comes, will be different from what has gone before, these exercises do produce information about the exposure of the portfolio to certain risks that are difficult to capture in any other way, such as liquidity, the flight to quality, and changing correlations. This is a valuable supplementary method to VaR in the estimation and understanding of tail risk.

26.5.3 The Right tool and the right risk measures?

No perfect solution exists for the FOF. Each one must evaluate the landscape independently and choose a method for reporting exposure and expectations to clients based on the construction of the fund, the needs of its clients, and the desired level of financial and resource commitment. In choosing an FOF, the investor also should acknowledge that imposing too much on the FOF will likely lead to a frustrating partnership. In delaying a foray into hedge fund land, the investor risks losing capacity with a good FOF. That said, hedge funds are not for every investor.

26.6　Follow the yellow brick road

FOF risk management is a combination of manager selection and due diligence, fund construction, diversification, and to some extent analytics. In choosing analytics products, the FOFs will weigh many factors. Likewise, in evaluating an FOF, the investor will want to know the process the FOF followed in choosing.

Manager and style coverage: All risk systems are not created equal. Systems and models differ in terms of coverage and model accuracy. The best model for one FOF may not be the best for another. Which funds are in the FOF, which asset classes, which styles, what types of strategies and securities are important determinants of which risk analytics system or model works best for any given FOF.

Respect for limitations: Good manager research involves getting to know the strengths and weaknesses of an investment organization, what works well and what doesn't. Selecting and implementing a risk analytics system or program that will be used effectively by an FOF requires an honest assessment of the strengths and weaknesses of the FOF organization and staff. If the best risk system available requires an in-house installation projected to take years and massive IT resources and an FOF does not have strengths in that area, then a better solution may be outsourcing with a service bureau. Though perhaps not as comprehensive or cutting edge as the in-house system, this will be easily and speedily implemented and integrated into the manager research, fund construction, and risk monitoring process. The FOF staff may then focus on strengths that lie elsewhere, perhaps in fund construction and/or manager selection.

26.6.1 Identify/prioritize needs and requirements

1. *Reporting level:* What risks/styles/managers are most concerning? Is the overriding need to get aggregated risks numbers on the total fund level, for the portfolio manager(s), or for marketing to clients and internal management? Is the greatest concern style risks or individual manager investment exposures?

2. *What numbers you need to see:* Is VaR enough for strict risk measurement only, or should the system help foster a better understanding of the major positions and strategies managers employed to generate alpha?

3. *Speed vs. accuracy:* How soon do you need to see the numbers? Are you willing to wait longer if that gives better and more accurate exposure information?

The answers to these questions influence the choice between risk systems and models, between, for example, an enterprisewide system structure that encompasses all asset classes and markets and focuses on the FOF level and different systems for different styles, offering presumably more accurate risk and strategy analysis on the style and manager levels but no fundwide aggregation.

Learn about the models and the markets

While no model is perfect, some models are better than others. This is true even in equity space, where data and pricing are normally readily available public information (Penfold, 2004). Criteria for judging the relative merits of models and systems vary market by market, style by style. Testing actual predictive power and accuracy at the aggregate fund level risk of loss, especially for risk of tail loss, is problematic, but the building blocks — the component parts — of models can be evaluated and compared. Model structure, granularity (how many factors), relevance (are they the important factors), proxy variables (are they good proxies for the underlying risk variables), measurement of exposures, etc., differ widely and allow differentiation of value and accuracy among models.[3]

Diversify your risk model exposures

Multiple methods of evaluating risk, when put together, give a better picture than any one distinct and separate view. Investing in multiple risk-reporting processes and systems leads to better understanding and measurement of risks across managers and styles. An FOF needs a risk analytics toolkit, not just one system. This toolkit would include holdings-based, returns-based, manager-provided risk analytics and exposures and a reporting system that integrates these various measures of risk into reports that are easily accessible and interpreted by manager research analysts, portfolio managers, and senior investment professionals.

Find other users for corroboration

Checking references is a standard step in the selection of an analytics vendor. Truth in advertising, service level, honesty, reliability, and responsiveness are

---

[3] For a very nice comparison of various buy-side systems (Rahl, 2001), go to http://www.cmra.com/ html/buy-side_risk_management_syste.html and click on the "Buy-Side Risk Systems Comparison Matrix" at the bottom of the page. While this survey was conducted in December 2001, it gives the reader a good sense of what different systems will offer.

issues we all know to ask about. A crucial concern, however, is whether the model/system is used and validated by market participants. This is especially important for markets, strategies, and styles that are illiquid and complex. There is no independent benchmark or quality control test available for the numbers that come out of the model for those parts of the funds. The best way to ensure quality numbers is to find a system that is constantly vetted by expert users and a vendor that speedily updates and corrects data and models in response to the needs of the expert user, making the corrected versions available to all users.

26.7 Conclusion: You're never going back to Kansas

For Dorothy, Oz was a dream . . . or was it really a parallel universe? Investors are unlikely to wake up one day to find that hedge funds were just a dream. FOFs are a mechanism for investing in the parallel universe of hedge fund styles and strategies. Investors must understand that hedge funds are complex and that the depth of understanding to be had is limited by that complexity. A healthy respect for the multiplicity and murkiness of hedge fund risk should induce the FOF to use a comprehensive risk management plan combining skillful manager research, due diligence of business and operational risks, broad diversification, and the use of risk analytics with a healthy awareness of its limitations and advantages.

References

Artzner, P., Delbaen, F., Eber, J. M., and Heath, D. (1997). Thinking Coherently. *RISK*, 10(11):68–71.

Artzner, P., Delbaen, F., Eber, J. M., and Heath, D. (1999). Coherent Measures of Risk. *Mathematical Finance*, 9(3):203–228.

Embrechts, P. (1999). Extreme Value Theory as a Risk Management Tool. *North American Actuarial Journal*, 3(2):30–41.

Golub, B. W. and Tillman, L. M. (2000). *Risk Management: Approaches for Fixed-Income Markets*. John Wiley & Sons, New York.

Hennessee, E. L. and Gradante, C. J. (2002). Direct Investing in Hedge Funds versus Fund of Funds Hedge Funds Products. In: *Hedge Fund Strategies: A Global Outlook*. (Bruce, B., ed.). Institutional Investor, New York.

Jorion, P. (1996). *Value at Risk: A New Benchmark for Measuring Derivatives Risk*. Irwin Professional Publications, Baldwinsville, NY.

Lo, Andrew W. (2001). Risk Management for Hedge Funds: Introduction and Overview. Working Paper, Massachusetts Institute of Technology, Sloan School of Management, Cambridge, MA. Available at SSRN: http://ssrn.com/abstract=283308.

Lowenstein, R. (2000). *When Genius Failed: The Rise and Fall of Long-Term Capital Management*. Random House, New York.

Mausser, H. and Rosen, D. (1999). Beyond VaR: From Measuring Risk to Managing Risk. *ALGO Research Quarterly*, 1(2):5–20.

McKay, R. and Keefer, T. E. (1996). VaR Is a Dangerous Technique. *Corporate Finance: Searching for Systems Integration Supplement*, September:30.

Parker, V. R. (2005). *Managing Hedge Fund Risk: Strategies and Insights from Investors, Counterparties, Hedge Fund and Regulators*, 2nd edition. Risk Books, London.

Penfold, R. (2004). How Well Do Three Risk Models Forecast Risk? Russell Research Commentary, Tacoma, WA.

Pflug, G. C. (2000). Some Remarks on the Value-at-Risk and the Conditional Value-at-Risk. In: *Probabilistic Constrained Optimization: Methodology and Applications* (S. Uryasev, S., ed.). Kluwer Academic, Norwell, MA.

Rahl, L. (2001). *Buy-Side Risk Systems Comparison Matrix* (http://www.cmra.com/html/buy-side_risk_management_syste.html).

Ross, Leola B. (2002). Risk Exposure and Hedge Funds. Russell Research Commentary, Tacoma, WA.

Ross, Leola B. (2003). Hedge Fund Diversification: How Much Is Enough and Where Does One Start? Russell Practice Note #52, Tacoma, WA.

Stemme, K. and Slattery, P. (2002). Hedge Fund Investments: Do It Yourself or Hire a Contractor? In: *Hedge Fund Strategies: A Global Outlook* (Bruce, B., ed.). Institutional Investor, New York.

Uryasev, S. (2000). Conditional Value-at-Risk: Optimization Algorithms and Applications. *Financial Engineering News*, 14:1–5.

27 Quantitative hedge fund selection for funds of funds

Stephan Joehri and Markus Leippold

Abstract

Selecting the best hedge funds is of paramount importance for funds of funds. We present several quantitative measures to rank hedge funds. The funds of funds are then simulated by applying these ranking measures to past hedge fund data and investing accordingly. We perform three different types of analyses. First, we create several setups for rebalancing periods and implementation lags to distinguish between different fund of funds types. We show how the choice of parameter affects performance. Second, we apply the ranking techniques during different market states (flat market, bull market, and bear market) to see how different indicators perform under different market conditions. Third, we analyze the usability of the ranking measures for the different hedge fund strategies. Some quantitative measures allow the simulated funds of funds to strongly outperform the HFR benchmarks. The results show that some ranking measures are appropriate to construct a fund of funds with low volatility, while others can be used to construct a fund of funds with high returns.

27.1 Introduction

Funds of funds usually justify their existence and fees because of their exceptional ability to select the best hedge funds. This chapter presents and tests several indicators that can be used in fund of funds construction. These indicators include performance-based measures as well as risk-adjusted measures. We use these indicators to rank the available hedge funds, and we select those hedge funds with the highest ranking for the fund of funds construction.

In a simulation based on historical data, we analyze the out-of-sample performance of these portfolios. Our study relates to the recent literature on the persistence of hedge fund performance. While most studies are unable to provide empirical evidence on the persistence of hedge fund returns beyond a six-month horizon (Agarwal and Naik, 2000; Barès, Gibson, and Gyger, 2003), some studies find some stability of the hedge funds' risk profile (Kat and Menexe, 2003; Mozes and Herzberg, 2003). If an indicator related to the risk profile exhibits some degree of persistence, then it can serve as a valuable guide for the construction of a hedge fund portfolio.

Our study tries to provide some empirical evidence on whether some indicators are more suitable than others for hedge fund selection. For this purpose, we perform three different types of analyses. First, we create several setups for rebalancing periods and implementation lags to distinguish between three different fund of funds types. We show how the choice of parameter affects performance. Second, we apply the ranking techniques during different market states (flat market, bull market, and bear market) to see how different indicators perform under different market conditions. Third, we analyze the usability of the ranking measures for different hedge fund investment styles.

We find that some quantitative measures indeed allow the simulated funds of funds to strongly outperform the HFR benchmarks. Furthermore, the results show that some ranking measures are appropriate to construct a fund of funds with low volatility, while others can be used to construct a fund of funds with high returns.

The chapter is organized as follows: In Section 27.2, we briefly introduce the indicators that we use for hedge fund selection and we present the simulation framework. Section 27.3 describes the data used for the simulation. Section 27.4 reports the empirical results of our out-of-sample simulations, and Section 27.5 concludes the chapter.

27.2 Indicators for hedge fund selection

27.2.1 The model

We develop a simulation framework to test each indicator's ability to select the best hedge funds. The framework consists of sequential out-of-sample tests. In the simulation, a certain amount of data (in-sample period) is chosen to calculate the indicator values. After the last data point of this in-sample period, the simulated fund of funds buys the hedge funds with the best indicator values. This investment is then held for a certain amount of time (out-of-sample period).

The next in-sample period has the same length as the previous one but is shifted into the future to align the out-of-sample periods successively. We again calculate the indicator values for the new in-sample period and invest accordingly during the successive out-of-sample period. This means that the in-sample period and the corresponding out-of-sample period never overlap, which guarantees that the simulation, at the time of investment, never knows the future return of the hedge funds. In practical terms, the out-of-sample period also corresponds to the rebalancing period of the fund of funds. The performance of the simulated fund of funds is finally calculated based on the returns of the selected hedge funds during the out-of-sample periods. For simplicity, we assume that the investment is equally weighted among all hedge funds.

The simulation has other parameters besides the length of the in-sample and out-of-sample periods. Investments do not close immediately; we impose a certain lag. This accounts for the notice and redemption periods that many hedge funds have. In addition, the number of hedge funds to be invested in is defined as a percentage of the total number of available hedge funds in the database at that time. Since the amount of reporting of hedge funds is increasing over time, the number of hedge funds in our simulated portfolio also increases. This setup makes sense because, as the assets under management of the fund of funds increases, portfolio managers tend to invest in more hedge funds. Furthermore, we assume that the percentage of exceptional hedge fund managers and not their absolute number is constant.

Our model does not take into account transaction costs. However, to get an idea on the approximate transaction costs, we present the turnover generated by the portfolio adjustment for different fund of funds constructions.

27.2.2 Individual indicators

The following describes the indicators we use to select the best hedge funds.

Historical return (HR)

As a purely return-based indicator for hedge fund performance, we use the annualized geometric mean of the fund returns during the in-sample period.

Sharpe ratio (SR)

The Sharpe ratio sets the fund's excess return in relation to the risk taken to achieve the return. Since we choose the hedge funds on a relative basis, for example, the hedge funds with the highest Sharpe ratios, the level of the risk-free rate in the Sharpe ratio is not important.[1]

Sortino ratio (SoR)

The Sortino ratio is the excess return divided by the downside volatility $\sigma_{(-)}$. In our simulation, some hedge funds may not have enough negative returns to calculate a meaningful downside deviation, because the in-sample period consists of a small sample of data points. These hedge funds are then assigned a value equal to the highest Sortino ratio found and are ranked according to their individual historical return.

Modified value at risk (MVaR)

Modified value at risk (see, for example, Favre and Galeano, 2002) is a deviation from the value at risk that has been enhanced by skewness and kurtosis. A standard measure like VaR does not capture the fat tails in the distribution of

---

[1] Some hedge funds may generate negative Sharpe ratios. In such a case, the indicator is hard to interpret. However, for our fund of funds construction, we are only concerned with the top-ranked hedge funds (see Section 27.4.1). For these hedge funds the Sharpe ratios are positive. The same holds true for the subsequent indicators, for which negative values might become problematic for a consistent ranking.

hedge fund returns. Neither does the Sharpe ratio. In contrast, the MVaR measure tries to overcome these deficiencies by incorporating the higher moments of the return distribution. More precisely, MVaR is defined as

$$
\text{MVaR}_\alpha = \mu + \left(z_c + \frac{1}{6}(z_c^2 - 1)S + \frac{1}{24}(z_c^3 - 3z_c)K \right.
$$
$$
\left. - \frac{1}{36}(2z_c^3 - 5z_c)S^2 \right) \sigma
$$

where z_c is the critical value at the requested α percentile for a normal distribution and μ, σ, S, and K are, respectively, the mean, standard deviation, skewness, and kurtosis of the return distribution.

Alpha

Alpha is a widely used return-based performance measure in the hedge fund industry. To obtain the alpha, we have to divide hedge fund returns into two parts: one generated by the general market movements and one generated by the manager's skill. In a one-factor model, we obtain the alpha by first estimating the sensitivity of the hedge funds using an OLS regression. Then the alpha is the missing return needed to complement the total hedge fund return. More precisely, for a time period ranging from 1 to N, we calculate the alpha as

$$
\alpha = \mu - \beta * \mu_b \qquad \text{with} \qquad \beta = \frac{\displaystyle\sum_{i=1}^{N} r_i * b_i}{\displaystyle\sum_{i=1}^{N} b_i^2}
$$

where r_i and b_i are, respectively, the hedge fund return and benchmark return at time i, μ is the average hedge fund return, and μ_b is the average benchmark return. A high alpha implies that the hedge fund is able to outperform the market. Using such a model, we assume that hedge fund returns are linearly related to benchmark returns. Of course, this is a strong assumption.

Information ratio (IR)

The information ratio is based on the same idea as the Sharpe ratio. We define it as the alpha divided by the standard deviation unexplained by the market:

$$
\text{IR} = \frac{\alpha}{\sigma_{\text{unexpl}}} = \frac{\mu - \beta * \mu_b}{\sqrt{\dfrac{1}{N}\displaystyle\sum_{i=1}^{N}(r_i - (\beta * b_i + \alpha))^2}}
$$

X ratio (XR)

As a further criterion, we propose combining the ideas of the Sortino ratio with those of the information ratio. As with the concept of the Sortino ratio, this new criterion uses only the downside deviation for the risk adjustment, and, like the information ratio, it uses the alpha in the numerator. This leads to

$$X = \frac{\alpha}{\sigma_{(-)}}$$

The effect of having hedge funds with few negative returns is treated the same way as in the case of the Sortino ratio.

Average drawdown (AD)

Drawdown measures periods of consecutive negative returns. The drawdown DD_i at time i is defined as the difference between the highest cumulative return level ever achieved (the so-called high-water mark), HWM_i, and the current cumulative return level, cr_i:

$$DD_i = \frac{cr_i - HWM_i}{HWM_i}$$

In order to extract more information from the funds' track records, we calculate a weighted average of the drawdown over the last N months:

$$AD = \sum_{i=0}^{N-1} (DD_{N-i} * 0.9^i)$$

Therefore, one of the major advantages of this risk measure is that it preserves the order and the autocorrelation of the returns in the time series. Drawdown is also of special interest when assessing hedge funds, because hedge fund managers are often paid according to their performance above the high-water mark. This type of incentive may lead to an increased risk profile once the hedge fund is strongly below this threshold, because the manager desires to improve his or her performance. For more about drawdown and hedge funds, see López de Prado and Peijan (2004). Note that among the best hedge funds, several may have an AD of 0%. Therefore, based on AD only, we may not obtain a unique ranking of the best hedge funds.

Calmar ratio (CR)

The Calmar ratio is another risk-adjusted performance measure. A hedge fund with a high drawdown is likely to engage in more risky trades to improve performance.

The Calmar ratio accounts for such behavior by relating the mean return to the maximum drawdown as the relevant measure of risk:

$$CR = \frac{\mu}{DD_N}$$

Combined indicator (CI)

The indicators so far presented can be combined into a new indicator. For simplicity, we propose a linear and equally weighted combination of all indicators. To obtain such a combined indicator, we first have to map the range of indicator values to the interval [0, 1] at each ranking time point. The combined indicator is then the equally weighted sum of these scaled values.

27.3   Data

Our data comes from the Lipper TASS database. We use monthly return series from January 1994 to September 2005. The starting point is defined as the date when Lipper TASS began to leave defunct hedge funds in their TASS database, therefore reducing survivorship bias. For more discussion about the advantages and disadvantages of various data sources, see Liang (2000) and Brown, Goetzmann, and Ibbotson (1999).

27.3.1   Strategy indices data

We use the HFR indices as proxies for the different hedge fund strategies: Convertible Arbitrage, Fixed-Income Arbitrage, Equity Market-Neutral, Event-Driven, Equity Hedge, Macro, Short Seller, and Emerging Markets. As benchmarks, we use the two HFR indices HFR Fund Weighted Composite and HFR Fund of Funds. The first two years, 1994 and 1995, are neglected because they are used to calculate the indicator values during the first in-sample period.

27.3.2   Hedge fund data

We apply the following criteria to the hedge funds in the TASS database in order to further narrow the pool of hedge funds:

- Monthly reporting
- At least 12 months of data
- No missing data for more than five months in total
- No almost-identical funds (the correlation between the funds and the difference in their returns must be larger than a certain threshold).

These filter criteria reduce the pool of funds from 3,916 to 3,130. Our aim in this procedure is to retrieve different hedge funds from the database so that we do not invest several times in almost-identical funds (for example, class funds).

27.3.3   Adjusting for autocorrelation

Hedge funds often price their securities at a lag. One of the main reasons is that many hedge funds hold illiquid securities or securities that are difficult to price, especially when they are traded over the counter. The lack of tradability may leave hedge funds with a lot of flexibility for their month-end reporting, leading to some degree of artificial autocorrelation in the return series. The evaluation of the risk-adjusted performance of an asset for which the return series is autocorrelated is liable to be strongly biased. In their analysis, Okunev and White (2002) show that only the first-order autocorrelation coefficients are systematically significant in the case of alternative investments. Therefore, as in Amenc, Malaise, Martinelli, and Vaissié (2004), we suggest correcting the first-order autocorrelation only, using the Geltner (1991) method. To do so, we assume that the return observed at time t is equal to a linear combination of the real return recorded at t and the return observed at $t - 1$. Geltner (1991) suggests using

$$r_t = \frac{r_t^0 - (1 - a)r_{t-1}^0}{a}$$

where r_t^0 is the return observed at time t and r_{t-1}^0 is the return observed at time $t - 1$. The parameter a is set between 0 and 1. If no smoothing is present in the returns, then a equals 1. Because the value of a cannot be statistically estimated, its value is based on a judgment concerning the degree of smoothing present in the time series. However, when we assume that returns are generated by an AR(1) model, then it holds that

$$r_t = \frac{r_t^0}{1 - a} - \frac{ar_{t-1}^0}{1 - a}$$

and we can estimate a parameter a from a simple OLS regression. In the following, we will use this specification to calculate the performance indicators on which we base our hedge fund selection. However, to calculate the performance of the resulting strategies and benchmarks, we use the observed returns.

27.4   Empirical results

Table 27.1 summarizes the performance of the two benchmarks from January 1996 to September 2005. For the Sharpe ratio, we use a fixed risk-free rate of 4% per annum. The numbers show that the HFR Fund-Weighted Composite provides an 11.47% annual return, versus the HFR Fund of Funds with a 8.23%

Table 27.1 Descriptive statistics for the two benchmarks HFR Fund-Weighted Composite and HFR Fund of Funds for the full out-of-sample period January 1996 to September 2005

Benchmark	Historical annualized return	Historical annualized volatility	Monthly skewness	Monthly excess kurtosis	Sharpe ratio	Maximum drawdown	Negative monthly returns
HFR Fund-Weighted Composite	11.47%	7.50%	−0.47	2.75	0.99	−11.42%	29%
HFR Fund of Funds	8.23%	6.06%	−0.25	4.38	0.70	−13.08%	32%

For the Sharpe ratio, we use a fixed risk-free rate of 4% per annum. We also provide the maximum drawdown for the full data period and the percentage of negative monthly returns versus the total number of returns.

annual return. Accordingly, the Fund of Funds Index exhibits less volatility. This leads to a Sharpe ratio of 0.99 for the HFR Fund-Weighted Composite and 0.70 for the HFR Fund of Funds. The skewness is slightly negative for both, while the excess kurtosis is positive. The HFR Fund-Weighted Composite exhibits a maximum drawdown of −11.42% (during August 1998), and the HFR Fund of Funds has a maximum drawdown of −13.08% (during October 1998). For the two benchmarks, 29% and 32% of the monthly returns were negative returns.

In order to make a fair comparison with the HFR Fund of Funds Index, administration and incentive fees should be subtracted from the simulated results.

27.4.1 Different types of investors

We perform our analysis by assuming three different types of investors. They differ in their rebalancing frequency, in the length of the in-sample period they use for calculating the hedge funds' indicator values, and in the number of hedge funds they invest.

The first investor type might correspond to a large pension or endowment fund constructing a fund of funds for its own portfolio. It has considerable assets under management and therefore invests in the 10% best funds of the TASS database. This corresponds to about 50 hedge funds in 1996 and about 270 in 2005. With this large number of hedge funds, we also account partially for closed funds. For such an investor, a large number of hedge funds is also justified since the investor favors a certain amount of diversification as he or she looks for stable performance with low volatility. Because the pension fund has a long investment horizon, we set the in-sample period at two years. Rebalancing is done every year to select the best hedge funds over the long run. We assume that, on average, it takes six months to close a hedge fund position for this type of investor. This implies that after the signal to close the position, the hedge fund will still remain in the fund of funds (and contribute to its performance) for the next 6 months.

Table 27.2 Parameter values for the three investor types

Investor type	Top hedge fund percentage	In-sample period	Out-of-sample period	Sell lag
Pension fund	10%	24 months	12 months	6 months
Family office	2.5%	12 months	6 months	3 months
Tactical investor	1%	12 months	1 month	0 months

The second type of investor might be a family office investing in hedge funds. It has a smaller amount to allocate to alternative investments, so it picks only the 2.5% best hedge funds. This corresponds to 12 hedge funds in 1996 and about 65 in 2005. This type of investor wants to react faster to changes in hedge fund rankings, so we set the in-sample period to one year. We assume that rebalancing is done every six months. The sell lag is three months.

We call the last type of investor a tactical investor. This investor has access to hedge funds with high liquidity. The framework allows the tactical investor to buy and sell hedge funds as frequently as every month and to sell immediately after the performance is announced. This type of investor can completely rebalance the portfolio at the end of each month. Furthermore, we assume that the tactical investor selects only the 1% best hedge funds into his or her portfolio.

Table 27.2 summarizes the parameterization of the three investor types.

With the parameters defined in the table, we can now evaluate the performance of the three investor types, if they select their hedge funds according to the different indicators discussed in Section 27.2. Table 27.3 reports the results. The first column shows the ranking indicators used to select the best hedge funds. The following columns depict the statistical description of the resulting time series using one particular indicator. For the simulation, we use the full data period from January 1996 to September 2005. The risk-free rate for the Sharpe ratio and the Sortino ratio is set to 4% per annum. For the alpha, information ratio, and X ratio criteria, we used the HFR Fund-Weighted Composite Index as benchmark.

Starting with the pension fund (Table 27.3, Panel A), we find a difference between the absolute return criteria (the historical annualized return and alpha) and the risk-adjusted criteria/ratios. The historical return criterion produces an annual performance of 14.74%. For the alpha criterion, the corresponding return is 14.17%. However, this comes at a cost of increased volatility, maximum drawdown, and number of negative returns. The volatility is more than 12% for the historical return criterion and over 7% for the alpha criterion, leaving Sharpe ratios of 0.88 and 1.45, respectively.

The risk-adjusted criteria perform more moderately (between 9.65% and 12.59% annual returns). However, they lower the volatility significantly in comparison to the benchmarks (between 1.90% and 4.18%), which results in very desirable Sharpe ratios above 2 for all risk-adjusted indicators. In addition, for all those ranking indicators, the maximum drawdown and the number of negative returns are lower as well.

Table 27.3 Fund of funds performance for the different investor types when different indicators are used for hedge fund selection

Ranking indicator	Historical annualized return	Historical annualized volatility	Monthly skewness	Monthly excess kurtosis	Sharpe ratio	Alpha vs. HFR Fund-Weighted Composite	Alpha vs. HFR Fund of Funds	Maximum drawdown	Negative monthly returns
Panel A: Pension fund									
Return-based criteria									
HR	14.74%	12.23%	-0.52	2.85	0.88	-0.15%	-0.03%	-21.93%	35%
Alpha	14.17%	7.02%	0.12	1.54	1.45	0.65%	0.61%	-6.83%	27%
Risk-adjusted criteria									
SR	12.59%	4.18%	0.57	4.54	2.05	0.47%	0.52%	-3.89%	17%
SoR	12.04%	3.75%	0.40	3.45	2.14	0.48%	0.52%	-3.16%	13%
MVaR	9.65%	2.00%	-0.68	1.75	2.82	0.51%	0.52%	-3.01%	9%
IR	9.73%	1.90%	-1.25	5.22	3.02	0.51%	0.53%	-2.93%	7%
XR	11.01%	2.51%	-0.47	2.14	2.79	0.55%	0.57%	-3.54%	9%
AD	10.24%	1.96%	-0.94	2.69	3.19	0.54%	0.56%	-2.87%	7%
CR	10.94%	3.05%	0.65	5.50	2.27	0.48%	0.51%	-3.50%	12%
CI	11.95%	3.81%	0.27	3.47	2.08	0.60%	0.68%	-4.24%	17%
Panel B: Family office									
Return-based criteria									
HR	20.09%	16.08%	-0.23	1.08	1.00	0.02%	0.11%	-39.87%	28%
Alpha	22.54%	8.69%	0.68	1.09	2.13	1.25%	1.20%	-8.58%	21%

SR	15.34%	3.02%	0.57	4.40	3.76	0.81%	0.84%	-2.20%	9%
SoR	16.01%	6.57%	-0.41	4.69	1.83	0.55%	0.61%	-7.24%	18%
MVaR	11.07%	1.61%	-0.66	0.69	4.41	0.68%	0.69%	-0.89%	5%
IR	9.50%	1.42%	-0.46	1.47	3.89	0.57%	0.58%	-1.48%	3%
XR	15.95%	4.91%	-0.90	4.14	2.43	0.68%	0.72%	-5.93%	12%
AD	11.24%	2.28%	-1.73	8.62	3.17	0.64%	0.65%	-3.99%	9%
CR	13.51%	2.34%	-0.30	0.77	4.07	0.75%	0.78%	-1.95%	7%
CI	12.92%	1.92%	0.34	0.93	4.66	0.85%	0.89%	-0.33%	6%

Panel C: Tactical investor

Return-based criteria

HR	36.84%	22.56%	0.72	2.36	1.46	0.96%	1.02%	-26.93%	31%
Alpha	36.12%	15.28%	-0.02	0.71	2.10	2.22%	2.12%	-11.80%	26%

Risk-adjusted criteria

SR	16.76%	3.74%	4.62	39.34	3.41	0.92%	0.96%	-1.43%	4%
SoR	22.99%	11.25%	0.56	4.44	1.69	0.76%	0.77%	-13.13%	18%
MVaR	14.91%	4.05%	3.03	23.63	2.69	0.81%	0.82%	-2.98%	7%
IR	8.66%	1.09%	-0.37	2.64	4.29	0.55%	0.57%	-0.54%	2%
XR	22.92%	7.82%	0.16	4.17	2.42	1.03%	1.04%	-6.01%	13%
AD	11.01%	2.46%	-2.24	12.10	2.84	0.65%	0.65%	-3.58%	9%
CR	16.02%	4.99%	-1.61	6.18	2.41	0.85%	0.86%	-5.62%	7%
CI	13.44%	1.93%	0.12	1.76	4.90	0.88%	0.94%	-0.86%	3%

The highest Sharpe ratio of 3.19 is achieved by the average drawdown criterion. This criterion also leads to the smallest number of negative monthly returns (7%). Its annualized return is comparable to the HFR Fund-Weighted Composite, but it has a much lower volatility (1.96% compared to 7.50%; see Table 27.1). From the risk-adjusted indicators, the highest returns are generated by the Sharpe ratio and the Sortino ratio, but they also have the highest volatility and a substantial number of negative monthly returns. Not surprisingly, the largest number of negative returns is observed for the Sharpe ratio, since it is only a symmetrical measure for risk.

When we examine the results for the family office investor type, we see that the historical return and the alpha criteria produce high absolute returns of more than 20%, but again with high volatilities. Nevertheless, for the alpha criterion, the Sharpe ratio still lies above 2. However, for this investor, we have other criteria that bring more favorable risk and return trade-offs: The Sortino ratio gives a 16.01% annual return with 6.57% volatility, average drawdown gives an 11.24% annual return with 2.28% volatility, and the Calmar ratio provides a 13.51% return with 2.34% volatility. The highest Sharpe ratio of 4.41 is achieved by ranking the hedge funds using the MVaR criterion, because this leads to an extremely small volatility of 1.61%. Furthermore, the MVaR and the information ratio generate a time series with 5% or less negative returns during the full out-of-sample period.

For the tactical investor, we observe that, on the one side, we have indicators like historical return, alpha, and the Sortino ratio[2] that create an annual performance of between 22.99% (Sortino ratio) and 36.84% (historical return) combined with two-digit volatility. On the other side, we have the Sharpe ratio, MVaR, the information ratio, and average drawdown, which construct funds of funds with good performance (8.66–22.92% annual returns) and low volatility (between 1% and 5%). Note that the Sharpe ratio criterion leads to strongly skewed returns with high kurtosis. The highest Sharpe ratio is achieved by the information ratio (4.29). This selection criterion also leads to a time series with only 2% negative monthly returns from 1996 through 2005.

Finally, comparing the combined index for all three investors, we first note for the pension fund that the combined index provides some disappointing results. The Sharpe ratio is the second lowest among all risk-adjusted criteria, but it still lies substantially above the Sharpe ratio of the return-based criteria. The same holds true for the other risk statistics. Obviously, for the pension fund investor, there is no diversification effect arising from using a portfolio of indicators that would lead to a better fund of funds performance. However, this picture changes when looking at both the family office investor and the tactical investor. In both cases, the combined index generates the largest Sharpe ratios; at the same time, the downside risk measures are kept very low. For the family office investor, the combined index even delivers the smallest maximum drawdown; for the tactical

---

[2] The performance of the Sortino ratio may come as a surprise. However, we suspect that the Sortino ratio performs poorly due to the problems involved with calculating the downside deviation.

investor, the maximal drawdown and the negative monthly returns are close to the numbers generated by the information ratio.

When we cross-compare the risk/return profiles of the three investor types, we see that the pension fund, with its longer in-sample period of two years and six-month sell lag, generally has the lowest absolute returns, with similar volatility and maximum drawdown as the family office investor.

The tactical investor outperforms both of the other two investor types in terms of absolute return. No investor type consistently generates the highest Sharpe ratio. All three outperform the HFR Fund-Weighted Composite Index and the Fund of Funds Index in terms of Sharpe ratios for all selection criteria, except for the situation in which the pension fund uses the historical return for fund of funds construction.

In general, the historical return criteria are very sensitive to the length of the in-sample and out-of-sample periods and to the percentage of selected hedge funds. However, as we noted earlier, the simulation does not account for transaction costs. To get an idea of the trading activity of the selection criteria, we calculate the turnover for each simulation (turnover being the number of hedge funds that enter a portfolio at a certain rebalancing time, divided by the total number of hedge funds in the portfolio).

The turnover for the pension fund is about 50% per rebalancing period (12 months), calculated as the average value over all rebalancing time points and over all selection criteria. The family office investor has an average turnover of about 55% per rebalancing period (six months). The tactical investor has a turnover of about 25% (one month). Figure 27.1 presents bar charts of the annualized turnovers for the different investors.

For all investor types, we observe that the ranking based on return-based indicators generates a large turnover. The same holds true for the Sortino ratio and the X ratio. The reason lies in the fact that we use the historical return for the ranking of funds whenever we are unable to calculate a reasonable downside deviation. In contrast, some of the risk-adjusted indicators have only a small turnover and, therefore, are likely to generate lower transaction costs. This is especially true for the average drawdown and the information ratio, the two indicators that also produce high Sharpe ratios and other favorable statistics for all investor types (see Table 27.3). We conclude that trading hedge funds more frequently may generate higher returns, but at higher risk and at a much higher turnover, leading to substantial transaction costs. However, depending on the indicators used, these costs can vary substantially. In particular, purely return-based indicators are more likely to generate substantial transaction costs.

We close this section with a remark on the length of the in-sample period we use. For the historical return criterion, we also execute the simulations for a shorter in-sample period, as suggested by Barès, Gibson, and Gyger (2003) and Agarwal and Naik (2000). In order to better use the return momentum that seems present in hedge fund monthly returns, we set the in-sample period to four months. Thereby, we consider only the last four returns to select the best-performing hedge funds. This leads to an increased expected return and slightly increased

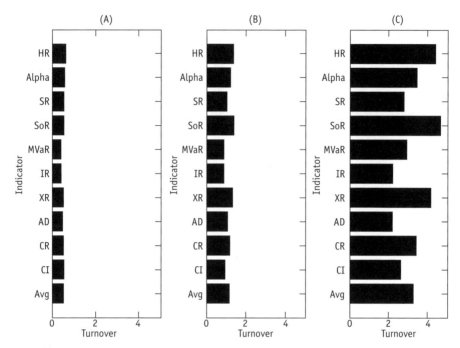

Figure 27.1 Turnover of different investor types: The three panels show the turnover of the different investor types. Panel (A) corresponds to the pension fund investor, Panel (B) to the family office investor, and Panel (C) to the tactical investor. The turnover is expressed as annualized portfolio rebalancing in percentage of the actual portfolio value.

volatility. The Sharpe ratio is then 1.33 for the pension fund investor, 1.52 for the family office investor, and 1.64 for the tactical investor. These results support the statement that there is more return persistence in the short run.

27.4.2 Different market states

To analyze returns under differing market conditions, we use the simulation parameter values for the family office investor type: a 12-month in-sample period, 6-month out-of-sample data, a 3-month sell lag, and 2.5% of the best hedge funds in the portfolio.

The results in the previous section suggest that some criteria increase the performance of the fund of funds compared to the benchmarks, for example, the HFR Fund-Weighted Composite and the HFR Fund of Funds indices. Others seem more appropriate for lowering volatility in the fund of funds. In this section, we investigate whether this behavior depends on the market condition. We define three time periods representing different market states with respect to the HFR Fund-Weighted Composite Index.

Table 27.4 Performance of the two benchmarks under the three different market conditions

Benchmark and time period	Historical annualized return	Historical annualized volatility	Monthly skewness	Monthly excess kurtosis	Sharpe ratio	Maximum drawdown	Negative monthly returns
HFR FWC, flat mkt	1.55%	5.95%	−0.13	−0.87	−0.41	5.71%	42%
HFR FOF, flat mkt	1.90%	2.85%	−0.25	−0.21	−0.74	2.52%	42%
HFR FWC, bull mkt	11.04%	4.30%	−0.51	−0.75	1.64	2.36%	25%
HFR FOF, bull mkt	8.00%	3.46%	−0.32	−0.69	1.15	2.09%	25%
HFR FWC, bear mkt	−18.50%	12.64%	−1.41	0.51	−1.78	11.42%	67%
HFR FOF, bear mkt	−24.45%	9.32%	−1.39	0.46	−3.05	13.08%	100%

The two benchmarks — HFR Fund-Weighted Composite and HFR Fund of Funds — are listed in the first column, together with the three market states — flat, bull, and bear. The risk-free rate is again set to a 4% annual return to calculate the Sharpe ratio.

The first time period, January 2000 to December 2002, represents a flat market, with no significant up or down movements. The second, October 2002 to September 2005, is used as the proxy for a bull market. Both time periods are three years long, from which the first year will be used for the first in-sample period, leaving two years for investments. The overlapping period from October 2002 to December 2002 will be used for both periods.

The third time period is May 1997 to October 1998. It consists of one in-sample period from May 1997 to April 1998 and the following six months as an out-of-sample period. These six months are during the period when the two benchmarks have the largest drawdown during January 1990 to September 2005. This setup is especially challenging because the hedge funds are evaluated during an up-market period (May 1997 to April 1998), but the investment takes place during a bear market (May 1998 to October 1998).

Table 27.4 shows the statistical description of the return of the two benchmarks during the three periods (without the first in-sample period). As expected, the bear market produces the worst return and the highest volatility (a −18.50% annual return for the HFR Fund-Weighted Composite and a −24.45% annual return for the HFR Fund of Funds). During the flat market, the two indices generate annual returns of 1.55% and 1.9%, respectively. During the bull market, they generate annual returns of 11.04% and 8%, respectively.

The results for the constructed fund of funds during the three market states are presented in Table 27.5. Table 27.3, Panel B, can be used for comparison with the performance of the family office investor during the full data period.

Table 27.5 Performance of family office investor type during different market periods

Ranking indicator	Historical annualized return	Historical annualized volatility	Monthly skewness	Monthly excess kurtosis	Sharpe ratio	Alpha vs. HFR Fund-Weighted Composite	Alpha vs. HFR Fund of Funds	Maximum drawdown	Negative monthly returns
Panel A: Performance during flat market period, January 2000–December 2002									
Return-based criteria									
HR	21.09%	8.81%	−0.02	−0.38	1.94	1.54%	1.31%	−6.29%	17%
Alpha	23.75%	7.77%	0.05	0.46	2.54	1.80%	1.63%	−4.96%	13%
Risk-adjusted criteria									
SR	14.34%	2.41%	−0.30	0.20	4.30	1.10%	1.02%	−0.46%	13%
SoR	11.84%	2.05%	−0.69	−0.25	3.82	0.93%	0.87%	−0.37%	8%
MVaR	9.48%	1.63%	−0.61	−0.19	3.37	0.75%	0.71%	−0.39%	8%
IR	8.81%	1.15%	0.52	0.15	4.17	0.69%	0.65%	0.00%	0%
XR	11.83%	2.08%	−0.81	−0.28	3.76	0.93%	0.87%	−0.43%	8%
AD	9.45%	1.62%	−0.66	1.04	3.36	0.74%	0.69%	−0.54%	8%
CR	10.94%	2.07%	−0.64	1.33	3.36	0.85%	0.79%	−0.81%	8%
CI	11.45%	1.73%	−0.24	0.16	4.30	0.91%	0.88%	−0.21%	8%
Panel B: Performance during bull market period, October 2002–September 2005									
Return-based criteria									
HR	28.24%	10.58%	−0.77	−0.16	2.29	0.09%	0.29%	−8.88%	21%
Alpha	23.18%	6.33%	−0.96	0.77	3.03	0.43%	0.57%	−4.15%	17%

SR	16.17%	3.59%	−0.70	−0.07	3.39	0.42%	0.51%	−1.05%	8%
SoR	19.19%	6.38%	−0.48	0.64	2.38	0.25%	0.39%	−4.49%	13%
MVaR	10.58%	1.89%	−0.60	0.65	3.49	0.34%	0.39%	−0.56%	8%
IR	6.56%	0.94%	−0.66	0.19	2.73	0.26%	0.28%	−0.17%	4%
XR	18.78%	4.11%	−0.35	0.32	3.60	0.49%	0.59%	−1.51%	8%
AD	10.34%	2.33%	−0.57	0.50	2.73	0.29%	0.35%	−0.84%	13%
CR	11.67%	3.17%	−0.53	0.80	2.42	0.28%	0.35%	−1.47%	8%
CI	11.05%	2.16%	−0.60	0.10	3.26	0.44%	0.54%	−0.65%	8%

Panel C: Performance during bear market period, May 1998–October 1998

Return-based criteria

HR	−34.81%	19.24%	−1.36	0.36	−2.02	−0.79%	0.47%	−19.77%	67%
Alpha	6.43%	9.05%	−0.72	−0.40	0.27	0.10%	0.48%	−4.49%	33%

Risk-adjusted criteria

SR	−1.86%	5.34%	−1.00	−0.31	−1.10	−0.15%	0.19%	−3.81%	50%
SoR	−11.94%	14.49%	−1.41	0.62	−1.10	0.68%	1.01%	−9.91%	50%
MVaR	2.15%	2.81%	−0.53	−0.77	−0.66	0.14%	0.26%	−1.33%	33%
IR	1.90%	2.98%	−0.54	−0.59	−0.71	0.10%	0.24%	−1.45%	33%
XR	−6.50%	11.13%	−1.33	0.50	−0.94	0.72%	0.87%	−7.01%	50%
AD	−3.57%	5.24%	−0.97	−0.43	−1.44	−0.23%	0.13%	−4.09%	50%
CR	−1.27%	4.15%	−0.36	−1.54	−1.27	0.11%	0.39%	−3.24%	50%
CI	0.52%	5.06%	−1.38	0.47	−0.69	−0.04%	0.08%	−2.77%	17%

Panels A through C show the performance of the different indicators as applied by the family office investor type during different time periods. Each time period represents one particular market state. The first column shows the ranking indicators used to select the best hedge funds. The following columns depict the statistical description of the resulting time series using one particular indicator. The risk-free rate for the Sharpe ratio and the Sortino ratio is set to 4% per annum. For the alpha, information ratio, and X ratio criteria, we used the HFR Fund-Weighted Composite Index as benchmark.

The family office investor performs better during the flat market period from 2000 to 2002 (see Table 27.5, Panel A) as compared to the full market period. Based on the lower volatility, the Sharpe ratio gets larger for most indicators. In the resulting fund of funds track record, the maximum Sharpe ratio is 4.30. This Sharpe ratio is generated if the fund of funds construction is based on either the Sharpe ratio itself or the combined index. However, the first construction would have 13% negative monthly returns, whereas the latter construction produces only 8% negative monthly returns. The information ratio, with an impressive Sharpe ratio of 4.17, generates no drawdown at all and has no negative return in its track record. Both return-based indicators, the historical return and the alpha, produce disappointing Sharpe ratios (relative to the risk-adjusted criteria), and they also have large maximum negative returns (-6.29% and -4.96%, respectively, compared to maximum negative returns below -1% for all risk-adjusted indicators). As a consequence, the number of negative monthly returns is also high. For the flat market, these foregoing results are remarkable because the two benchmarks both have negative Sharpe ratios, and all strategies based on the different criteria have positive Sharpe ratios of 1.94 and more.

During the following bull market period (see Table 27.5, Panel B), the ranking indicators were generally able to increase the historical annualized return of the resulting fund of funds. But this again came at the cost of higher volatility, leading to a decrease in the Sharpe ratios as compared to the flat-market results. In this market period, the X ratio did the best job for choosing the hedge funds that produced the highest Sharpe ratio for the fund of funds.

Table 27.5, Panel C, depicts the results of the simulation during the bear market in 1998. During this time period, the return-based criterion alpha beats all the risk-adjusted selection criteria. Alpha-selected hedge funds would have generated a positive annual return of 6.43% with a volatility of 9.05%. As a result, this is the only fund of funds that has a positive Sharpe ratio. All other criteria were affected by the poor market conditions and suffered severe losses, with historical return and the Sortino ratio returning the worst, -34.81% and -11.94%, respectively. However, the performance of the combined index appears promising. The historical return is slightly positive, the maximum drawdown is at a moderate -2.77%, and there are 17% of monthly negative returns. Obviously, combining the different indicators seems to be advisable in such a market situation. We note that we did only some naive weighting of the indicators. We conjecture that we could obtain better results if we based the weighting scheme on some optimization routine.

To conclude this subsection, we note that the results during a bull market and a flat market do not change very much. However, they change a lot during a bear market, with only one criterion able to generate a positive Sharpe ratio. Therefore, for a sensible fund of funds construction, negative market periods should be of particular concern.

27.4.3 Different hedge fund investment styles

Finally, we want to determine how the hedge fund selection criteria perform on the different hedge fund investment styles. We perform the simulation separately on the subset of funds in the database that belong to the same strategy. As benchmarks for alpha, the information ratio, and the Sortino ratio, we use each hedge fund strategy's corresponding HFR index. For example, for the hedge funds classified Global Macro, we use the HFR Macro Index.

For the simulation, we take the 10% best hedge funds to construct the fund of funds because we are now operating with a smaller set of candidates. The in-sample period is again one year, the out-of-sample period is six months, the sell lag is three months, and we use the full available data period.

For the sake of simplicity, we display only the Sharpe ratio for each hedge fund strategy and each hedge fund selection criterion. In order to compare the fund of funds with the HFR strategy indices, Table 27.6 gives their Sharpe ratios.

The results for the fund of funds strategies are reported in Table 27.7. Again, we observe that the purely return-based indicators fail to do a good job. Their Sharpe ratios mostly fall short of the Sharpe ratios obtained by the risk-adjusted indicators. For the fixed-income arbitrage, the Sharpe ratio becomes even negative. Only for the short bias funds do the return-based measures seem comparable to the other indicators.

Table 27.7 reports Sharpe ratios for different hedge fund styles and selection criteria. The simulation parameters are 12-months in-sample period, 6 months out-of-sample period, 3 months sell lag and 10% of the best hedge funds are taken for the fund of funds. The risk-free rate is set as 4% per annum for the Sharpe ratio and Sortino ratio calculations. The data used in the simulation spans from January 1996 to September 2005.

Table 27.6 Sharpe ratios for the HFR strategy indices, January 1996 through September 2005, with a risk-free rate of 4%/annum

Benchmark	Convertible arbitrage	Equity hedge	Event-driven	Macro	Emerging markets	Fixed-income arbitrage	Equity market-neutral	Short bias
HFR Strategy Index	1.58	1.08	1.37	0.85	0.53	1.26	1.20	−0.11

Table 27.7 Sharpe ratios for different hedge fund styles and selection criteria

Ranking indicator	Convertible arbitrage	Equity hedge	Event-driven	Macro	Emerging markets	Fixed-income arbitrage	Equity market-neutral	Short bias
Return- based criteria								
HR	0.93	1.11	0.69	0.92	0.44	−0.04	1.11	0.83
Alpha	0.90	1.96	1.57	1.19	0.90	−0.19	0.91	0.82
Risk-adjusted criteria								
SR	1.73	2.25	2.30	1.67	1.48	1.87	1.44	1.06
SoR	2.00	2.67	1.53	1.32	1.35	0.86	1.52	0.73
MVaR	1.18	1.92	1.67	0.54	1.03	1.28	1.53	0.62
IR	2.28	3.12	2.67	2.01	2.94	1.93	2.10	1.02
XR	2.01	2.99	1.66	2.12	1.28	0.73	1.54	0.81
AD	1.02	2.00	1.81	0.63	0.99	1.14	1.64	0.53
CR	1.24	2.66	2.13	2.28	2.01	2.36	1.81	1.05
CI	1.99	2.83	1.93	2.52	1.58	2.13	1.77	1.01

The first column names the hedge-fund selection criterion that has been used for the simulation. The following columns give the Sharpe ratios for the simulated fund of funds strategies that are constructed from hedge funds assigned to a certain investment style. The styles are given in the first row. Again we observe that the purely return-based indicators fail to do a good job. Their Sharpe ratios mostly fall short of the Sharpe ratios obtained by the risk-adjusted indicators. For the Fixed Income Arbitrage, the Sharpe ratio becomes even negative. Only for the Short Bias funds, the return-based measures seem to be comparable to the other indicators.

Looking at the risk-adjusted criteria, we see that the information ratio performs particularly well. For the convertible arbitrage, the equity hedge, the event-driven, the emerging markets, and the equity market-neutral, the information ratio achieves the highest Sharpe ratio of all. Only for the macro, the fixed-income arbitrage, and the short bias, is the information ratio outperformed by the combined indicator (macro) and the Calmar ratio (fixed-income arbitrage, short bias). Finally, we note that the Sharpe ratio, Sortino ratio, information ratio, X ratio, Calmar ratio, and combined indicator are ranking rules that produce funds of funds whose style-specific Sharpe ratios are larger than those of the corresponding HFR indices.

27.5 Conclusion

We test several return-based and risk-adjusted hedge fund selection criteria under different market conditions and investor behaviors. Most of them generate fund of funds track records with Sharpe ratios above 1 and more desirable risk properties than the benchmarks. From the results, we can distinguish between criteria appropriate for generating higher absolute returns and criteria capable of generating a lower-risk profile than the benchmark. This suggests that it is possible, with the appropriate measures, to construct funds of funds with superior statistical properties than the benchmarks. It turns out that basing the fund selection on risk-adjusted criteria not only leads to more favorable results in terms of portfolio statistics, but also decreases the portfolio turnover compared to purely return-based criteria. The lower turnover is at least partially due to the higher persistence of risk-adjusted measures. Overall, from the risk-adjusted measures, the information ratio and the average drawdown provide some very favorable results. Only in a bear market are they somewhat disappointing, and fund of funds selection becomes a very delicate task.

There are several ways to improve the selection process. We could perform an additional return smoothing before calculating the indicator values or an indicator value smoothing in order to avoid extreme values. However, one should keep in mind that the hedge funds with the currently best indicator values are not always the best choices. Hedge funds that appear mediocre today may be high performers in the future. Also, we could improve on the weighting of the different rankings in order to come up with an optimized combination of indicators. These points are left as suggestions for further research.

Acknowledgments

The authors would like to thank Laurent Favre from AlternativeSoft, Inc., for his thoughtful and valuable comments. They also thank Lipper-Tremont for providing the TASS database for this chapter. Markus Leippold acknowledges the financial support of the Swiss National Science Foundation (NCCR FINRISK) and the University Research Priority Program "Finance and Financial Markets" at the University of Zurich.

References

Agarwal, V. and Naik, N. (2000). Multi-Period Performance Persistence Analysis of Hedge Funds. *Journal of Financial and Quantitative Analysis*, 35(3): 327–342.

Amenc, N., Malaise, P., Martinelli, L., and Vaissié, M. (2004). Fund of Hedge Fund Reporting. EDHEC Working Paper, Lille, France.

Barès, P.-A., Gibson, R., and Gyger, S. (2003). Performance in the Hedge Fund Industry: An Analysis of Short- and Long-Term Persistence. *Journal of Alternative Investments*, 6(3):25–41.

Brown, S., Goetzmann, W., and Ibbotson, R. (1999). Offshore Hedge Funds: Survival and Performance, 1989–95. *Journal of Business*, 72(1):91–117.

Favre, L. and Galeano, J.-A. (2002). Mean-Modified Value-at-Risk Optimization with Hedge Funds. *Journal of Alternative Investments*, 5(2):16–28.

Geltner, D. (1991). Smoothing in Appraisal-Based Returns. *Journal of Real Estate Finance and Economics*, 4(3):327–345.

Kat, H. and Menexe, F. (2003). Persistence in Hedge Fund Performance: The True Value of Track Record. *Journal of Alternative Investments*, 5(4):66–72.

Liang, B. (2000). Hedge Funds: The Living and the Dead. *Journal of Financial and Quantitative Analysis*, 35(3):309–326.

López de Prado, M. M. and Peijan, A. (2004). Measuring the Loss Potential of Hedge Fund Strategies. *Journal of Alternative Investments*, 7(1):7–31.

Mozes, H. A. and Herzberg, M. (2003). The Persistence of Hedge Fund Risk: Evidence and Implications for Investors. *Journal of Alternative Investments*, 6(2):22–42.

Okunev, J. and White, D. (2002). Smooth Returns and Hedge Fund Risk Factors. Working Paper, University of Otago, New Zealand.

Index

A

Absolute return criteria. *See* Historical return criteria

Accuracy, speed v., 430

Active futures portfolio, commodity indexes v., 387

AD (average drawdown), 437, 442–446

AICPA (American Institute of Certified Public Accountants), 409

Alpha indicator, 436, 437, 441–446, 450, 451

Alphas. *See also* Jensen's alpha; Lower alpha/higher risk, analytics relating to estimates of, 6, 23, 264
FOF portfolios, exposure of, 65–69, 103, 104, 105, 113, 114, 128
of hedge funds, 3, 4, 287, 288, 293, 298, 300, 301, 302, 304–305, 306
hypotheses about, 60
performance relating to, 27, 31, 36–38, 45, 46, 103, 104, 113, 119–131
rank of, 3, 4, 17, 20–22, 111, 114–115, 128
value of, 3, 4, 68
variations in, 288

Alternative asset classes. *See also* Traditional assets, FOFs and
correlation coefficient matrix relating to, 85, 265
co-skewness coefficient matrix relating to, 86, 91
CTAs, 79–96
hedge funds, 79–96
REITs, 79–96

Alternative investment strategies, 3, 4, 80, 263

Alternative risk, 60–61, 77

ALTVEST, 270, 274

American Institute of Certified Public Accountants. *See* AICPA

Analytics
of hedge funds, 418–419, 422
in-house, 426
lower alpha/higher risk relating to, 423
risk management, as part of, 429
for risk monitoring, 419
service bureaus, 426

Analytics, approaches to
holdings-based risk analysis, 425
manager-supplied risk reports, 423–424
returns-based risk analysis, 424
scenario analysis, 427–428

stand-alone asset class/market-specialized analytic system, 426
standardized manager-supplied risk reports, 424
stress testing, 428–429
total enterprise or fundwise risk systems, 426
VaR, 427

Analytics tool, 419–420

Ancient history, modern history v., 102–103

Anderson-Darling statistic, 221, 233

Anti-gambling laws, 381

Arbitrage-based option pricing theory, 47, 68, 80, 102

Asset allocation, optimal, 79–96
data relating to, 81–84
impact on, 269
measurement of, 145–166
methodology of, 84–87
statistics about, 82–84

Asset returns, lagged equity return, correlation with, 116–117

Asset-based style factors, 111–113

Assets. *See also* Alternative asset classes; Exotic asset-backed securities; Traditional assets, FOFs and; specific Core assets headings
benchmark, 253–256
missing, 396
peripheral, 265, 269, 270

AUM (assets under management), 62–63, 77, 364, 370, 371

Autocorrelation
adjusting for, 439
hedge fund indices, of returns of, 146, 152, 153–156

Average drawdown. *See* AD

B

Baa/Treasuries, 265, 266, 267–268, 274, 275–276, 277, 280–281

Balance sheet characteristics, 352

Barclay Trading Group database, 28, 29, 81, 264

Barra common factors, 352

Base case factor model, 4, 7, 9, 10, 22

Bayesian approach, 163, 263, 265, 284

Benchmark assets
construction of, 253–254
return on, 253, 254–255, 256